ANGLO-NORMAN STUDIES XV

Proceedings of the XV Battle Conference
and of the
XI Colloquio Medievale of
the Officina di Studi Medievali

1992

The present volume includes papers given at the Battle Conference held
jointly with the Officina di Studi Medievali in Palermo and Carini, and
has a general theme 'The Norman Age'. There is a special slant towards
the Mediterranean world; subjects treated include the policies of the
Norman rulers, their military and naval organisation and coinage,
chronicle sources and aspects of Church history in their principalities,
and the relations of the Normans with Byzantium, the Fatimid rulers
and the crusading states. Other papers treat more generally of art,
literature and language in the Norman period.

ANGLO-NORMAN STUDIES

XV

PROCEEDINGS OF THE XV BATTLE CONFERENCE
and of the
XI COLLOQUIO MEDIEVALE OF
THE OFFICINA DI STUDI MEDIEVALI

1992

Edited by Marjorie Chibnall

THE BOYDELL PRESS

First published 1993 by The Boydell Press, Woodbridge

The Boydell Press is an imprint of Boydell & Brewer Ltd
PO Box 9, Woodbridge, Suffolk IP12 3DF, UK
and of Boydell & Brewer Inc.
PO Box 41026, Rochester, NY 14604, USA

ISBN 0 85115 336 4

ISSN 0954-9927
Anglo-Norman Studies
(Formerly ISSN 0261-9857: Proceedings of the Battle Conference
on Anglo-Norman Studies)

British Library Cataloguing-in-Publication Data
A catalogue record for this series is available
from the British Library

Library of Congress Catalog Card Number: 89-646512

706979
P

This publication is printed on acid-free paper

Printed in Great Britain by
St Edmundsbury Press Ltd, Bury St Edmunds, Suffolk

CONTENTS

LIST OF ILLUSTRATIONS   vi

EDITOR'S PREFACE   ix

ABBREVIATIONS   x

Ideological Representation of Military Combat in Anglo-Norman Art   1
J.J.G. Alexander

A Norman-Italian Adventurer in the East: Richard of Salerno 1097–1112   25
George Beech

Norman Naval Activity in the Mediterranean c.1060–c.1108   41
Matthew Bennett

Mimo Giullaresco e Satira del Villano nel *De Clericis et Rustico*   59
Armando Bisanti

Simon Magus in South Italy   77
H.E.J. Cowdrey

Nobiltà e Parentela nell'Italia Normanna   91
Vincenzo D'Alessandro

The Marriage of Henry VI and Constance of Sicily: Prelude and
Consequences   99
Walter Fröhlich

The Coinages of Norman Apulia and Sicily in their International Setting   117
Philip Grierson

The Norman Kings of Sicily and the Fatimid Caliphate   133
Jeremy Johns

The *Oratio de Utensilibus ad domum regendum pertinentibus* by Adam
of Balsham   161
Patrizia Lendinara

The Genesis and Context of the Chronicle of Falco of Benevento   177
G.A. Loud

The Sword on the Stone: Some Resonances of a Medieval Symbol
of Power (The Tomb of King John in Worcester Cathedral)   199
Jane Martindale

The Normans through their languages   243
Lucio Melazzo

The Knight, his Arms and Armour, c.1150–1250   251
Ian Peirce

The Uses of the Franks in Eleventh-Century Byzantium   275
Jonathan Shepard

A New Aspect of the Porphyry Tombs of Roger II, First King of Sicily,
in Cefalù   307
Livia Varga

ILLUSTRATIONS

Ideological Representation of Military Combat

Figures
1   Hildesheim, Basilica St Godehard, St Albans Psalter, p. 72. Initial 'B'   2
2   Detail of Fig. 1. Knights fighting the *sanctum terrenum bellum*   3
3   London, BL, MS Cotton Titus D XVI, f.4. Superbia attacking   3
    Humilitas
4   Avranches, Bibl. mun., MS 50, f.1. St Michael fighting the Devil   6
5   Avranches, Bibl. mun., MS 76, f.Av. St Michael, St Augustine and   7
    King David
6   Avranches, Bibl. mun., MS 76, f.1. Initial 'B'   10
7   Brinsop, Herefordshire. St George fighting the Dragon   10
8   Evreux, Bibl. mun., MS 131, f.1. Initial 'B' with David fighting   11
    Goliath
9   Paris, BN, MS lat. 12032, f.1. The Siege of Jerusalem   12
10 Dijon, Bibl. mun., MS 14, f.13v. The Tower of King David   13
11 Monreale. Cloister capital with fighting knights   16
12 S. Georges-de-Boscherville, transept. Relief sculpture with fighting   16
    knights
13 Dijon, Bibl. mun., MS 2, f.380v. Initial 'E' with Judas Maccabeus   17
    and fighting knights
14 Paris, BN, MS lat. 12048, f.229v. Initial 'D' with knight   17
15 Hildesheim, St Albans Psalter, p. 231. Evil knights slaughter the   20
    faithful
16 Le Mans, Bibl. mun., MS 263, f.10v. Pliny the Younger offering his   21
    book to the Emperor Vespasian
17 London, BL, MS Add. 49622, f.146. Detail of border with knight   22
    fighting a snail

A Norman-Italian Adventurer in the East

Map
    Places in Europe and the Near East associated with the career of   26
    Richard of Salerno

Norman Naval Activity in the Mediterranean

Map
    Norman naval activity in the Mediterranean c.1060–c.1108   46

The Coinages of Norman Apulia and Sicily

Plates 129

I   Figures 1–8   130
II   Figures 9–20   131
III Figures 21–31   132

The Norman Kings of Sicily and the Fatimid Caliphate

Figures

1   Palermo, the Zisa: ground plan   141
    (after Chirco)
2   Ashir. Algeria, Zirid palace: ground plan   142
    (after Golvin)
3   Palermo, Palazzo Reale: ground plan   143
    (after Valenti)
4   Qualᶜa Bani Hammad, Algeria: reconstruction section, plan   144
    (after Marcais)
5   Inscription No. 1   148
    (Palermo, Galleria regionale della Sicilia, Palazzo Abatellis)
6   Inscription No. 2   148
    (Palermo, Galleria regionale della Sicilia, Palazzo Abatellis)
7   Palermo, Capella Palatina ceiling, painted panel   154
    (photo R. Hillenbrand)
8   Al-Mahdiyya, Tunisia: carved marble relief   155
    (after Marçais)

The Sword on the Stone

Plates

 1 Effigy of King John (detail), Worcester cathedral   201
 2 Effigy of King John, Worcester cathedral   207
 3 Effigy of King Louis VII, formerly Barbeau   212
 4 Effigy of Rudolf of Swabia, cathedral of Merseberg   216
 5 Effigy of King Richard I, Fontevraud   218
 6 Engraving of King John's corpse   220
 7 Engraving of corpse of Emperor Frederick II, Palermo cathedral   222
 8 Tomb of Bishop Peter of Poitiers   224
 9 Funerary plaque of Count Geoffrey 'Le Bel', formerly in Le Mans   226
    cathedral
10 Seal of King Richard I   228
11 Seal of King John   229
12 Seal of King Louis VII as *Rex Francorum* and *Dux Aquitanorum*   231
13 Effigy of William Marshall, Temple church, London   238

The Knight, his Arms and Armour c.1150–1250

Plates

1	Joshua initial from the Winchester Bible	252
2	Leaf related to the Winchester Bible	253
3	Fresco depicting the death of Becket: Santi Giovanni e Paolo, Spoleto	255
4	Illustration from the Eneid of Heinrich von Veldeke	257
5	A portion of the equestrian frieze, c.1200, Claverley, Shropshire	259
6	Early illustration of a face-guard, early twelfth century (Madrid, Archaeological Museum)	262
7	Face-guard fashioned in one piece, c.1155 (Santa Maria la Real, Sanguesa, Navarre)	263
8	Conical helmet bearing a broad-based nasal and decoration	264
9	Conical helmet of spangenhelm construction	265
10	Sword of c.1200–1250, with original leather grip (Burrell Collection, Glasgow)	269
11	The Santa Casilda Sword (Reproduced by permission of the Board of Trustees of the Royal Armouries)	269
12	A mounted knight from the cloister of Monreale	271
13	A knight from the former chapel of the Templars at Cressac	271
14	Mounted knights, St Georges-de-Boscherville	273
15	Knights from Rebolledo de la Torre, c.1186	273

A New Aspect of the Porphyry Tombs of Roger II

Figure

1	Ground plan of the cathedral of Cefalù, from Krönig	308

EDITOR'S PREFACE

The fifteenth Battle Conference was a special occasion; it was held jointly with the eleventh Colloquio Medievale of the Officina di Studi Medievali in Carini and Palermo. Like the tenth conference in Caen, it was longer than usual and more papers were read: it was a particular pleasure to add Italian to French and English as one of the regular languages of the Conference. We are deeply grateful to our colleagues in Sicily for their generous help in the complicated organisation of the conference; in particular we thank Professor Patrizia Lendinara of the University of Palermo and Professor Cataldo Roccaro, Director of the Officina di Studi Medievali, whose unstinting help over two years made the event possible. The University of Palermo kindly allowed the opening session to be held in the magnificent Palazzo Steri. Residence was in the peaceful Franciscan Centro Kolbe at Carini, and we owe a special debt to Padre Paolo Fiasconaro, whose skill in organising everything, including coaches that arrived on time to take us on our visits, was exceeded only by the kindness of his welcome, which extended to meeting late-comers at midnight at the airport in person. Our excursions included visits to the Palazzo dei Normanni and other buildings in Palermo, to the cathedrals of Monreale and Cefalù, and to the Benedictine abbey of S. Martino delle Scale, where we were welcomed by the abbot and taken to hear the Gregorian chant of the monks as they sang Latin Vespers. Behind the scenes, during the long period of preliminary organisation, we were more than ever grateful to Mrs Gillian Murton, who also saw us safely through the hazards of the conference.

This year the conference had a theme: 'The Norman Age'. Special emphasis was given to the Normans in the Mediterranean world, but a number of papers dealt more generally with aspects of art, literature and language in the culture of the period. Sixteen of the papers read are published in the present volume; the two or three that were not quite ready in time to go to press will be included, we hope, in next year's volume of *Anglo-Norman Studies*. Dr Richard Barber and his skilled and ever helpful staff have excelled themselves in bringing an exceptionally complicated volume to completion.

Photographs in Professor J.J.G. Alexander's paper are published by courtesy of the Conway Library, Courtauld Institute of Art (nos. 3–8, 11–12, 17), the Bibliothèque nationale, Paris (nos. 9, 14, 16), the Bibliothèque municipale, Dijon (nos. 10, 13), and the Warburg Institute, University of London (nos. 1, 2, 15); and in Dr Jane Martindale's paper by courtesy of the Conway Library, Courtauld Institute of Art (nos. 1, 2, 5), the British Library, London (no. 7), The School of AHM, UEA (nos. 4, 9, 12) and the Bodleian Library, Oxford (nos. 3, 8). Thanks are due to the Society of Antiquaries, London, for the material on which plates 6, 10, 11 and 13 in Dr Martindale's paper are based. In Ian Peirce's article, Plate 1 is reproduced by permission of the Dean and Chapter of Winchester, Plate 2 by permission of the Pierpont Morgan Library, New York, Plate 4 by permission of the Deutsche Staatsbibliothek, Berlin and Plate 11 by permission of the Board of Trustees of the Royal Armouries.

Clare Hall, Cambridge
Marjorie Chibnall

ABBREVIATIONS

AHP	*Archivum Historiae Pontificiae*
Al. Tel.	Alexander of Telese, *Gesta Rogerii Regis Siciliae*, Del Re, i
Amatus	*Storia de' Normanni di Amato di Montecassino*, ed. V. de Bartholomeis (Font. stor. Italia, xiii, Rome 1935)
Antiqs Journ.	*The Antiquaries Journal* (Society of Antiquaries of London)
Arch. Journ.	*Archaeological Journal* (Royal Archaeological Institute)
Arch. Soc. Nap.	*Archivio Storico per le provincie napoletane*
Arch. Soc. Rom.	*Archivio della [R.] Società romana di storia patria*
ASC	*Anglo-Saxon Chronicle*, ed. D. Whitelock *et al.*, London 1969
Battle Chronicle	*The Chronicle of Battle Abbey*, ed. Eleanor Searle, Oxford Medieval Texts, 1980
BIHR	*Bulletin of the Institute of Historical Research*
BL	British Library
BN	Bibliothèque Nationale
Bull. Ist. stor. ital.	*Bullettino dell'Istituto storico italiano e Archivio Muratoriano*
Cal. Docs France	*Calendar of Documents preserved in France* . . . i, 918–1206, ed. J. H. Round, HMSO, 1899
Carmen	*The Carmen de Hastingae Proelio of Guy bishop of Amiens*, ed. Catherine Morton and Hope Muntz, Oxford Medieval Texts, 1972
Del Re	G. Del Re, *Cronisti e scrittori sincroni napoletani editi e inediti*, 2 vols, Naples 1845–68
De gestis pontificum	William of Malmesbury, *De gestis pontificum Anglorum*, ed. N. E. S. A. Hamilton, RS 1870
De gestis regum	William of Malmesbury, *De gestis regum Anglorum*, ed. W. Stubbs, RS 1887
Domesday Book	*Domesday Book, seu liber censualis* . . ., i, ii, ed. A. Farley 2 vols, 'Record Commission',, 1783; iii, iv, ed. H. Ellis, 1816
Dudo	*De moribus et actis primorum Normanniae Ducum auctore Dudone Sancti Quintini Decano*, ed. J. Lair, Société des Antiquaires de Normandie, 1865
Eadmer	*Historia novorum in Anglia*, ed. M. Rule, RS 1884
EHD	*English Historical Documents*, 2nd edn. i, ed. D. Whitelock, London 1979; ii, ed. D.C. Douglas, London 1981
EHR	*English Historical Review*
Falco	Falco of Benevento, *Chronicon*, Del Re, i
Fauroux	*Recueil des actes des ducs de Normandie (911–1066)*, ed. M. Fauroux, Mémoires de la Société des Antiquaires de Normandie xxxvi, 1961

Font. stor. Italia	*Fonti per la storia d'Italia*, Rome 1887–
GEC	*Complete Peerage of England, Scotland, Ireland, Great Britain and the United Kingdom*, 13 vols in 14, London 1910–59
Gesta Guillelmi	William of Poitiers, *Gesta Guillelmi . . .*, ed. R. Foreville, Paris 1952
Historia Novella	William of Malmesbury, *Historia Novella*, ed. K.R. Potter, Nelson's Medieval Texts, London 1955
HMSO	Her Majesty's Stationery Office, London
Huntingdon	Henry of Huntingdon, *Historia Anglorum*, ed. T. Arnold, RS 1879
IP	*Italia Pontifica sive Repertorium privilegiorum et litterarum*, ed. P. Kehr, 10 vols, Berlin 1906–75
Journ. BAA	*Journal of the British Archaeological Association*
Jumièges	William of Jumièges, *Gesta Normannorum Ducum*, ed. J. Marx, Société de l'histoire de Normandie, 1914
Lanfranc's Letters	*The Letters of Lanfranc Archbishop of Canterbury*, ed. H. Clover and M. Gibson, Oxford Medieval Texts, 1979
Med. Arch.	*Medieval Archaeology*
MGH SS	*Monumenta Germaniae Historica, Scriptores*
Monasticon	William Dugdale, *Monasticon Anglicanum*, ed. J. Caley, H. Ellis and B. Bandinel, 6 vols in 8, London 1817–30
ns	New Series
Orderic	Ordericus Vitalis, *Historia Ecclesiastica*, ed. M. Chibnall, Oxford Medieval Texts, 1969–80
PL	*Patrologiae cursus completus, series latina*, ed. J.P. Migne
PRO	Public Record Office
Procs BA	*Proceedings of the British Academy*
QF	*Quellen und Forschungen aus italienischen Archiven und Bibliotheken*
Regesta	*Regesta Regum Anglo-Normannorum*, i, ed. H.W.C. Davis, Oxford 1913; ii, ed. C. Johnson, H.A. Cronne, Oxford 1956; iii, ed. H.A. Cronne, R.H.C. Davis, Oxford 1968
RIS	*Rerum italicarum scriptores*, ed. L.A. Muratori, 25 vols, Milan 1723–51
RIS[2]	*Rerum italicarum scriptores: Continuatio*, 36 vols, Citta di Castello and Bologna, 1900–
RS	Rolls Series, London
ser.	series
Trans.	Transactions
TRHS	*Transactions of the Royal Historical Society*
VCH	*Victoria County History*
Vita Eadwardi	*The Life of Edward the Confessor*, ed. F. Barlow, Nelson's Medieval Texts, London 1962
Wace	Wace, *Le Roman de Rou*, ed. A.J. Holden, 3 vols, Société des anciens textes français, Paris 1970–3
Worcester	Florence of Worcester, *Chronicon ex Chronicis*, ed. B. Thorpe, English Historical Society, London 1848–9

IDEOLOGICAL REPRESENTATION OF
MILITARY COMBAT IN ANGLO-NORMAN ART

J. J. G. Alexander

The starting point of this paper is an image in a famous early twelfth-century Anglo-Norman Psalter known as the St Albans Psalter from its place of production, or the Psalter of Christina of Markyate from its owner.[1] The manuscript begins with a Calendar illustrated with Occupations of the Months and Zodiac signs, and this is followed by forty full-page miniatures. Then come an Anglo-Norman poem, the Chanson d'Alexis, illustrated with two tinted drawings, the text of Gregory the Great's defence of images in both Latin and Anglo-Norman and three tinted drawings of the story of the Journey to Emmaus. Finally on page 72 the Psalter opens with a large 'B', the initial of Psalm 1, 'Beatus vir' (Fig. 1). Each succeeding Psalm is introduced by an historiated initial and the manuscript ends with the Canticles and a final miniature of the martyrdom of St Alban.

The evidence for the ownership and date of the Psalter is contained in the Calendar and the additions to it. The obit of Roger the Hermit has been added under 12 September. He was a monk and deacon of St Albans who, after becoming a hermit became Christina's spiritual guide and protector. This has been argued by C.R. Dodwell to result in a *terminus ante* of c.1123, his death having occurred in 1121 or 1122, though the making of the Psalter has more recently been put in the decade 1120–30.[2] Christina of Markyate inherited Roger's cell and had close relations with St Albans and its abbot Geoffrey of Maine (1119–45).[3] Other obits connected with Christina were added still later and include those of her parents. She was still alive in 1155.

The image I am concerned with occurs in the top right corner of the Beatus page where two armed, mounted knights are shown riding at each other (Fig. 2). They have already pierced each other with lances which protrude from their backs spurting blood and which have symmetrically broken. However, they still continue the fight, brandishing their swords above their heads.

What function do these knights perform as an image occurring in a book made in a Benedictine abbey of monks devoted to the religious life and, even more

[1] Basilika St Godehard, Hildesheim. Otto Pächt, Charles R. Dodwell, Francis Wormald, *The St Albans Psalter (Albani Psalter)*, London 1960. Michael C. Kauffmann, *Romanesque Manuscripts 1066–1190* (Survey of Manuscripts illuminated in the British Isles, ed. J.J.G. Alexander, 3), London 1975, cat. 29. Exhibited *English Romanesque Art 1066–1200*, Arts Council, Hayward Gallery, London 5 April – 8 July 1984, catalogue edited by George Zarnecki, no. 17.
[2] Rodney M. Thompson, *Manuscripts from St Albans Abbey 1066–1235*, Cambridge 1982, xxii, 119–20 (cat. 72).
[3] Christopher J. Holdsworth, 'Christina of Markyate', *Medieval Women. Dedicated and presented to Professor Rosalind M.T. Hill* (Studies in Church History, Subsidia 1), ed. Derek Baker, Oxford 1978, 185–204.

Fig. 1.
Hildesheim, Basilica St Godehard. St Albans Psalter, p. 72. Psalm 1. Initial 'B'

Fig. 2.
Detail of Fig. 1. Knights fighting the 'sanctum terrenum bellum'

Fig. 3.
London, BL MS Cotton Titus D. XVI, folio 4.
Superbia attacking Humilitas

strangely, in a book used by and very probably specifically made for a female anchorite? Surely it is a surprising image to find in such a context? It seems that even at the time it was felt that some explanation was called for. An accompanying text of some two thousand four hundred words has been inserted, beginning in the right margin on the preceding page, page 71, and continuing in the left margin of this page. From it we deduce that the knights represent the 'Church's holy battle on earth', 'de sancto terreno bello in ecclesia'.

The metaphor of armed conflict is frequently applied to the spiritual life in both the Old and New Testaments. In his discussion of this accompanying text Otto Pächt traced the origin of the description of specifically the monastic vocation as a spiritual warfare to the Pseudo-Basilean text, *Admonitio ad filium spiritualem*.[4] From there the notion passed in the ninth century into Benedict of Aniane's *Codex Regularum*.[5] It was then taken up by Peter Damian (1007–72) in his *de spirituali certamine* and also in the *Liber qui dicitur dominus vobiscum*.[6] The latter text was certainly known at St Albans since a copy was made there in the early twelfth century.[7] It also occurs in a contemporary early twelfth-century text, the Ps. Anselm, *Similitudo militis*.[8] The idea of the monk's life as a form of warfare or struggle, was well established by this date, therefore. It coexisted, however, with a strong current of hatred and fear of the military aristocracy on the part of monastic communities, who were frequently attacked or intimidated by them. This ambivalence is also found in the accompanying text in Christina's Psalter, to which I will return later.

The aim of this paper is to compare the St Albans image of the fighting knights with other representations of conflict and struggle. In this way we shall see that the St Albans Psalter image is not a completely isolated occurrence. Though an historical actuality is, of course, a background to these representations, questions of realism in representation are not my direct concern here. I am not, therefore, concerned with attempts to match images of soldiers, knights, warfare, or weapons with historical, archaeological or literary evidence.[9] Rather, by referring in my title to ideological representation I mean to signal that my aim is to chart the ways in which images in a variety of media and contexts construct positive and negative views of the military, which can then be applied as metaphors with different meanings.

We may start with some observations on the visualization of the spiritual life as one of struggle between opposed forces of good and evil in which Good is inevitably triumphant. In early Christian art this is already established in a cycle

---

4 Pächt, 149–64.
5 *PL*, ciii, 683f.
6 *PL*, cxliv, 919f and *PL*, cxlv, 247f.
7 Oxford, Christ Church, MS 115. Thompson, 22–4, 111–12 (no. 58), pls 32–3, 56–8.
8 *PL*, clix, 702ff. Richard W. Southern, F.S. Schmitt, *Memorials of St Anselm* (Auctores Britannici Medii Aevi, 1), London 1969, 1991, 97–102.
9 That was the project, for example, of Jenny Kiff, 'Images of warfare in early eleventh-century England', *ante* vii, 1985, 177–94. See also Ian Peirce, below, pp. 251–74. The Bayeux Embroidery is constantly invoked as evidence in this way. See for example David J.A. Ross, 'L'originalité de "Turoldus": le maniement de la lance', *Cahiers de civilization médiévale* vi, 1963, 127–38. For an exemplary demonstration of how updatings in later copies of a cycle of manuscript illustrations, in this case in copies of the Utrecht Psalter, can be analysed see Martin Carver, 'Contemporary artefacts illustrated in Late Saxon manuscripts', *Archaeologia* cviii, 1986, 117–45.

of illustrations to Prudentius' poem, the *Psychomachia*, originally composed in Spain in the fourth century. The cycle survives in manuscripts from the ninth century onwards and the illustrations have been studied by Stettiner and Woodruff.[10] Both scholars concluded that the Carolingian miniatures copy an earlier cycle already attached to the poem by the fifth century.

The *Psychomachia* illustrations continued to be copied in succeeding centuries.[11] And there is an illustrated copy surviving from St Albans itself, illuminated, according tp Pächt, by a pupil of the main artist of the St Albans Psalter (Fig. 3).[12] By this time certain variations and contaminations occur in a stemma traced by Woodruff. But the main features of the narrative of the poem and of the earlier illustration to it are retained. The scenes show a series of armed conflicts between women who personify the Virtues and Vices. Almost all are on foot. Only Luxuria rides in a chariot and Superbia rides on a horse. The Virtues are all unmounted. Though they have arms, spears, swords and shields they do not, for the most part, wear armour.

Some seventy to eighty years later in the *Hortus Deliciarum*, an encyclopedic treatise put together by Herrad of Hohenbourg, and fully illustrated in a manuscript preserved formerly at Strasburg, the Virtues are fully armed in chain mail and helmets. The artist has, however, taken care to show that they are women by emphasising their long dresses trailing around their legs.[13]

The Prudentius images are a direct visualization of the conflict of Good and Evil on equal terms even though the outcome cannot be in doubt. They continue to be used commonly until the twelfth century, occurring also in other contexts, in metalwork and in monumental sculpture, as Katzenellenbogen has shown, for example at Aulnay in Western France c.1130, where they are also wearing mail and carrying shields.[14] Another example is on a capital at Clermont Ferrand.[15]

The conflict was represented in the Christian monastic context of the early Middle Ages in other ways as well. One was in the context of the Apocalypse where the text of Revelation XII.7 beginning 'And there was war in heaven: Michael and his angels fought against the Dragon' was illustrated with an image of the triumph of St Michael and the Good angels over Satan and the Fallen

[10] Richard Stettiner, *Die illustrierten Prudentius-Handschriften*, Berlin 1905. Helen Woodruff, 'The illustrated manuscripts of Prudentius', *Art Studies* vii, 1929, 3–49.

[11] For later illustrated Prudentius *Psychomachia* manuscripts see Gernot T. Wieland, 'The Anglo-Saxon manuscripts of Prudentius' "Psychomachia" ', *Anglo-Saxon England* xvi, 1987, 213–31. Joanne Norman, *Metamorphosis of an allegory: the iconography of the Psychomachia in medieval art* (American University Studies, series IX, vol. 29), New York 1988.

[12] London, BL, MS Cotton Titus D. XVI. Stettiner, ills. 193–6. Pächt, 166, 168, pl. 151f. Kauffmann, cat. 30, ills 69–71. Thompson, cat. 19. *English Romanesque Art*, no. 16.

[13] The manuscript was burnt in the Franco-Prussian War of 1870, so we depend on nineteenth-century copies. Rosalie Green, *et al.*, *Herrad of Hohenbourg Hortus Deliciarum*, London 1979, 190–6, pls 110–19. Adolf Katzenellenbogen, *Allegories of the Virtues and Vices in Mediaeval Art from Early Christian times to the thirteenth century*, London 1939, repr. Nendeln 1977, 10–11, figs 8a, b.

[14] Katzenellenbogen, 17, pl. VIII.

[15] Arthur K. Porter, *Romanesque Sculpture of the Pilgrimage Roads*, Boston 1923, ills. 1180–2. Norman, figs 1–3. At Châlons-sur-Marne column figures in the Cloister of c.1170–80 include both armed knights and female mailed Virtues triumphing over Vices. Sylvia and Léon Pressouyre, *Le Cloître de Notre-Dame-en-Vaux à Châlons-sur-Marne. Guide du Visiteur*, Nancy 1981, 96–7, pls 52–3

Fig. 4.
Avranches, Bibliothèque municipale, MS 50, folio 1. St Michael fighting the Devil

INCIPIT.TRACTATUS
PSALMORVM
AUGVSTINI EPI

Fig. 5.
Avranches, Bibliothèque municipale, MS 76, folio Av. St Michael, St Augustine and King David

angels. The surviving ninth-century illuminated manuscripts are once again thought to copy in their images cycles of the fifth or sixth centuries.[16] In certain contexts St Michael was represented as a cult figure, extracted as it were from the narrative cycle, as on an ivory in Leipzig of the early ninth century.[17] Certainly by the later eleventh century, if not before, there were cult images at two great pilgrimage centres, Monte Gargano in Apulia and Mont St Michel in Normandy.[18] St Michael is shown in prefatory miniatures in two of the surviving manuscripts of Mont St Michel. The first, dating from the late tenth century, is a Cassian, *Collationes*, a text concerning the lives of the early Desert Saints which was recommended for monastic reading in the Rule of St Benedict.[19] The Archangel is shown spearing down not the dragon of the Apocalypse, but the Devil himself (Fig. 4). The emphasis here would seem to be on triumph over Evil personified, appropriately in view of the spiritual struggles narrated in the text. The second manuscript is a copy of St Augustine on the Psalms of the mid-eleventh century.[20] Here the St Michael is juxtaposed with an author portrait of David as author of the Psalms and Augustine as author of the Commentary (Fig. 5). He spears the Apocalyptic dragon, and the image certainly functions as does the previous miniature, as a title of ownership of the book. But the image here too may refer to the conflict of Good and Evil in the context of Psalm 1: 'Blessed is the man who has not walked in the way of the Ungodly'.

The initial 'B' introducing Augustine's commentary on the recto opposite contains a figure battling in the scroll (Fig. 6).[21] Such a figure, who is often shown naked, defenceless, and sexless, is entwined in the foliage of many Romanesque initials and carved capitals. The naked, sexless figure, the opposite of an armed warrior, is found specifically in the opening 'B' initials of two English twelfth-century Psalters.[22] It also occurs in many of the later Psalm initials in the St Albans Psalter itself.[23] It also occurs in non-Christian texts, for example a copy of Lucan's *Pharsalia* from Rochester of c.1120, where such a figure is in the bowl of the letter with three mounted, armed knights shown in the stem.[24] Here perhaps one can say that the Christian life is envisioned either as resignation and powerlessness symbolised by the naked figure, or as a struggle against nature and animality as symbolised by the armed knights and a second, clothed figure in the bowl, who is entwined in the scroll with the animals and birds.

The St Michael in the *Augustine* from Mont St Michel is less military than that in the *Cassian*, having no helmet, and in his frontal pose is more a triumphant than a fighting warrior. The more active *Cassian* image can be compared in this

[16] See Peter K. Klein in *Trierer Apokalypse. Kommentarband* (Codices selecti, xlviii*), Graz 1975, 112 (Stemma).

[17] Adolph Goldschmidt, *Die Elfenbeinskulpturen aus der Zeit des karolingischen und sächsischen Kaiser*, 1, Berlin 1914, 12–13, Taf. 11a.

[18] Jonathan J.G. Alexander, *Norman illumination at Mont St Michel 966–100*, Oxford 1970, 85–100.

[19] Avranches, Bibliothèque municipale, MS 50. Alexander, 85ff., pl. 17b.

[20] Avranches, Bibliothèque municipale, MS 76. Alexander, 93ff., pl. 20.

[21] Alexander, pl. 12b. See Thomas A. Heslop, 'Brief in words but heavy in the weight of its mysteries', *Art History* ix 1986, 1–11, for a valuable discussion of meaning in such initials.

[22] Biblioteca nacional, Vit. 23–8, folio 81v. Kauffmann, cat. 77, ill. 216. Another example is Oxford, Bodl. MS Auct. D. 2.4, Kauffmann, cat. 81, ill. 213.

[23] For example on page 121. Pächt, pl. 50d.

[24] Cambridge, Trinity College, MS R.3.30, folio 1. Kauffmann, cat. 24, ill. 45.

respect to that in a mid eleventh-century Anglo-Saxon Psalter.[25] There the conflict is again with the dragon not the Devil, but an active battle is taking place, the victory is not already won. There are other Anglo-Saxon examples of St Michael in sculpture, for example at Southwell, where this is the case, and in the Anglo-Saxon examples the angel commonly uses a sword not a spear.

Another significant image of Good triumphant is the so-called *Christus super aspidem*, based on the words of Psalm 91, and an image consequently occurring a number of times in Psalters. Usually the Christ figure is not armed, however. Sometimes he may hold a staff as sign of authority which may also be used to pierce one of the animals. This is seen again in the same Anglo-Saxon Psalter.[26] Rather rarely, however, Christ is shown in armour, as in the Stuttgart Psalter, made perhaps at St Denis in the early ninth century,[27] and in the silver-gilt shrine of S. Hadelin at Visé in Belgium, of c.1070.[28] This makes use of a tradition of representing '*Christus miles*' going back at least to the sixth century since it is found in a mosaic in the Archbishop's Palace in Ravenna of that date.[29]

St Michael, being winged, does not ride, and Christ too is seldom shown on horseback, perhaps surprising, but perhaps because the one scene where he is mounted, the Entry to Jerusalem, has specific contextual meanings which it was not wished to evoke in a different image. The rider triumphant over evil does occur, however in a variety of contexts. One is the series of images on the facades of twelfth-century churches in western France, for example at Parthenay-le-Vieux, which Linda Seidel and others have shown refer back to Imperial Roman equestrian monuments, the Marcus Aurelius believed in the early Middle Ages to represent Constantine.[30] Seidel links these images with the contemporary conflict with the Saracens, both in Spain and in the First Crusade.

The same historical events must explain the appearance at this period in the West of images of St George. He becomes the most frequently represented equestrian military saint in the West from this period onwards. At the taking of Antioch in 1098 the Christians saw the saints led by St George, St Demetrius and St Mercurius riding on white horses to aid them. St George is shown not as a standing figure as commonly in Byzantine art, but as a sort of mounted St Michael, for example at Ferrara c.1130 or at Brinsop, Herefordshire, carved at about the same time (Fig. 7).[31]

Turning to negative images of military figures who stand for the power of Evil,

25 BL, MS Cotton Tiberius C.VI. Alexander, pl. 18d. *English Romanesque Art*, no. 1.

26 Folio 114v. Francis Wormald, 'An English eleventh-century Psalter with pictures, British Library Cotton Tiberius C.VI', *Collected writings, 1. Studies in Medieval Art from the sixth to the twelfth centuries*, ed. Jonathan Alexander, Julian Brown, Joan Gibbs, London 1984, 123–37, ill. 152 (reprinted from *Walpole Society* xxxviii, 1962, 1–13).

27 Württembergische Landesbibliothek, Bibl. Fol. 23, folio 107v. Florentine Mütherich in *Der Stuttgarter Bilderpsalter, Bd II. Untersuchungen*, Wilhelm Hoffmann *et al.*, Stuttgart 1968, 121.

28 Hans Swarzenski, *Monuments of Romanesque Art. The Art of Church Treasures in North-Western Europe*, London 1954, fig. 226.

29 Friedrich W. Deichmann, *Frühchristliche Bauten und Mosaiken von Ravenna*, Baden-Baden 1958, Taf. 217. *Ravenna. Hauptstadt des spätantiken Abendlandes. Kommentar, I. Teil*, Wiesbaden 1969, 203.

30 Linda Seidel, *Songs of Glory. The Romanesque facades of Aquitaine*, Chicago 1981, 21, 59, 68, 70–80, fig. 8.

31 George H. Crichton, *Romanesque sculpture in Italy*, London 1954, 22–7, fig. 11. George Zarnecki, *Later English Romanesque Sculpture 1140–1210*, London 1953, 12–3, 36, 55, fig. 31.

EATVS VIR QVI

Fig. 6.
Avranches, Bibliothèque
municipale, MS 76, folio 1.
Initial 'B'

Fig. 7.
Brinsop,
Herefordshire.
St George
fighting the
Dragon

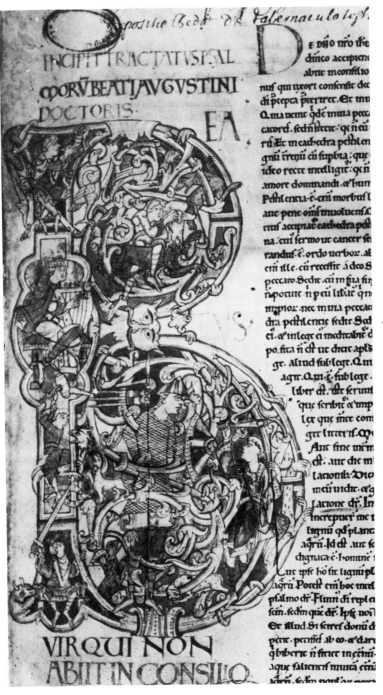

Fig. 8.
Evreux, Bibliothèque municipale, MS 131, folio 1. Initial 'B' with David fighting Goliath

Fig. 9.
Paris, BN, latin 12032, folio 1. The Siege of Jerusalem

Fig. 10.
Dijon, Bibliothèque municipale, MS 14, folio 13v. The Tower of King David

Good is now shown as on the defensive. When it triumphs, as it must, it is as it were against the odds, not from a position of strength as was the case in the images surveyed so far. Undoubtedly the commonest negative image of the soldier or fighting man as personification of Evil is that of Goliath. The fight between the boy David and the Philistine champion from the earliest examples is shown as unequal in both size and weaponry, as the biblical text, of course, stresses. From the twelfth century images are, however, updated so that the Philistine is in contemporary armour, thus providing a negative image of the contemporary fighting man. Striking images occur in two initials from Lyre and Saint Évroul in Normandy, both in copies of Augustine on the Psalms and both of the late eleventh century (Fig. 8).[32] A little later the same towering figure appears in the Bible of Stephen Harding for Cîteaux, where he breaks out of the frame to emphasise his size.[33] The same device is used later still, in the third quarter of the twelfth century, in the Winchester Bible detached leaf for 1 Kings (see below, 252, pl. 1).[34]

Within the Psalter text there are frequent mentions of the enemies of the Psalmist and they are represented in the fully illustrated manuscripts, the ninth-century Utrecht and Stuttgart Psalters, and in later copies of the Utrecht Psalter made in England in the eleventh and twelfth centuries and in the St Albans Psalter too.[35] A significant variation on the representation of Evil as active and threatening is to show the representatives of Good within a defensive structure attacked by the powerful forces without. An example is the illustration of Jeremiah XXXIX:1 in the late tenth-century Spanish Apocalypse manuscript with the commentary of Beatus now at Girona,[36] and another is in a late tenth-century Haimo on Ezekiel from S. Germain d'Auxerre in Paris, where it illustrates Ezekiel IV, 1–7, the account of the siege of Jerusalem (Fig. 9).[37] In the same Bible of Stephen Harding from Cîteaux just mentioned a miniature of King David as Psalmist shows him enclosed in crenellated walls from which defendants repulse the assailants (Fig. 10).[38] This is the *'turris David'* mentioned in the Song of

[32] Rouen, Bibliothèque municipale, MS 456 (A.19) from Saint Évroul. François Avril, *Manuscrits normands XI–XIIème siècles*, Rouen, Bibliothèque municipale, Musée des Beaux-arts 1975, no. 73. The Lyre copy is Evreux, Bibliothèque municipale, MS 131. Pächt, pl. 146a.
[33] Dijon, Bibliothèque municipale, MS 14, fol. 13. Yolanta Załuska, *L'enluminure et le scriptorium de Cîteaux au XIIe siècle*, Cîteaux 1989, 193, ill. 43. Yolanta Załuska *et al.*, *Manuscrits enluminés à Dijon*, Paris 1991, 51–2, pl. A.
[34] New York, Pierpont Morgan Library, M. 619. *English Romanesque Art*, no. 65; see below, 253, pl. 2.
[35] For the Utrecht Psalter, see Ernest T. Dewald, *The illustrations of the Utrecht Psalter*, Princeton 1932. The English copies are BL, Harley 603, early eleventh century, exhibited *The Golden Age of Anglo-Saxon Art*, British Museum, British Library, catalogue edited by Janet Backhouse, Derek H. Turner, Leslie Webster, London 1984, no. 59; Cambridge, Trinity College, MS R.17.1, mid twelfth century, *English Romanesque Art*, no. 62; and BN, MS latin 8846, late twelfth century, *English Romanesque Art*, no. 73. For the St Albans Psalter see e.g. Ps. 2, Pächt, pl. 43.
[36] Museu de la Catedral de Girona, Num. Inv. 7, folio 242. Made at Tabara in 975. *Beati in Apocalipsin Libri Duodecim: Codex Gerundensis* (facsimile), J. Camon Aznar *et al.*, Madrid 1975.
[37] BN MS latin 12302, folio 1. Produced for and possibly by Abbot Heldricus of Saint Germain d'Auxerre (989–1010). Marie-Thérèse d'Alverny, *et al.*, *Catalogue des manuscrits en écriture latine portant des indications de date, de lieu ou de copiste, iii. Bibliothèque nationale, fonds latin (nos 8001–18613)*, Paris 1974, 285. Patrica Stirnemann, 'L'illustration du commentaire d'Haymon sur Ezékiel, Paris, BN. latin 12302', *L'école carolingienne d'Auxerre de Murethach à Remi 830–908. Entretiens d'Auxerre*, eds. Dominique Iogna-Prat *et al.*, Paris 1991, 93–107.
[38] Dijon, Bibliothèque municipale, MS 14, folio 13v. Załuska, 1989, 194, ills. 52–3. Załuska, 1991, 52, pl. XVI.

Songs and identified as the citadel of Jerusalem by the Crusaders.[39] Here too warfare is presented as defence.

Within the images so far discussed textual content or specific attributes or symbols give meaning, enabling St Michael for example to be recognised. There are, however, a wide variety of images of military combat in which the meaning is not clear from inscription, context or attributes. For example on a double capital at Monreale of the late twelfth century two pairs of knights are shown in combat (Fig. 11).[40] A second example is from the doorway at St Marcello Maggiore, Capua, early twelfth century.[41] A third example is the panel from the south transept of S. Georges de Boscherville in Normandy, sometimes dated to the eleventh century, but more likely from the context I have been sketching to be of the twelfth (Fig. 12).[42]

At San Zeno, Verona, c.1130 to the right of the door on the two lowest panels a mounted rider blows a horn and pursues a stag. An accompanying inscription makes clear the identification of the scene as the hunt of the Emperor Theodoric. To the left of the door on the equivalent two panels two mounted knights are in combat, to the left while to the right two figures fight on foot, and here there is no inscription. Stiennon and Lejeune have suggested that this pair of panels illustrate episodes from the Chanson de Roland, the battle between Roland and Ferragut.[43] Another example which they link to the Roland story is a capital at Conques.[44] It is perfectly possible that the panels or the capital were intended to carry such meanings by the original patrons or artists. It is also possible that some viewers at some point in their history would have read them as images of Roland as Christian knight. But without inscriptions or other confirmatory evidence we cannot be sure.

Many more examples of such opposed knights in monumental sculpture could

---

[39] The *Turris David* from which a thousand shields hang is referred to metaphorically in *Cantica*, 4.4. Peter Damian likens the monk's cell to it. *PL*, 145, 247. For the actual citadel of Jerusalem, known as the 'Turris David', see Joshua Prawer, 'The Jerusalem the Crusaders captured: a contribution to the medieval topography of the city', *Crusade and Settlement*, ed. Peter W. Edbury, Cardiff 1985, 1–16.

[40] Roberto Salvini, *Il Chiostro di Monreale e la scultura Romanica in Sicilia*, Palermo 1962, 131 (Lato sud capitello 24). On the other side of the double capital are shown Sts Eustace and George. They, together with Sts Mercurius and Theodore, both also mounted, occur on the panels in Santa Restituta, Naples. Émile Bertaux, *L'Art dans l'Italie méridionale*, 2, Paris 1903 [reprinted 1968], 775–777, pl. XXXIV. They are dated to the second decade of the thirteenth century by Dorothy Glass, *Romanesque sculpture in Campania. Patrons, Programs and Style*, Philadelphia 1991, 146–7, 197–201, fig. 197. Mounted warrior saints in pairs also occur on the bronze doors at Monreale, Ravello and Trani. See Albert Boeckler, *Die Bronzetüren des Bonanus von Pisa und Barisanus von Trani. Die frühmittelalterlichen Bronzetüren*, 4, Berlin 1953, Taf. 124–5, 134–5, 150–1.

[41] Bertaux, 476, fig. 206. Reginald Allen Brown, *The Normans*, Woodbridge 1984, 104.

[42] Brown, 37. Maylis Baylé, 'Le décor sculpté de Saint-Georges-de-Boscherville: quelques questions de style et d'iconographie', *ante* viii, 1985, 27–45, especially 36, giving a date of c.1113, the refoundation, to c.1125. Another pair of jousting knights is on a capital of similar date at Graville-Sainte-Honorine (Seine-Maritime), as Dr L. Grant points out to me.

[43] Rita Lejeune, Jacques Stiennon, *The legend of Roland in the Middle Ages*, 2 vols, London 1971, 72–6, figs 45–9.

[44] Stiennon, Lejeune, 19–23, figs 1, 6.

Fig. 11.
Monreale, Sicily. Cloister capital with fighting knights

Fig. 12.
S. Georges-de-Boscherville, Normandy. Transept.
Relief sculpture with fighting knights

Fig. 13.
Dijon, Bibliothèque municipale, MS 2, folio 380v. Initial 'E' with
Judas Maccabeus and fighting knights

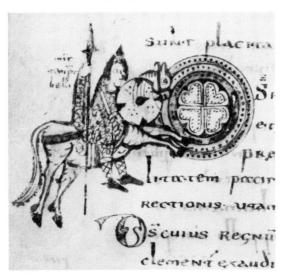

Fig. 14.
Paris, BN, latin 12048, folio 229v.
Initial 'D' with knight

undoubtedly be quoted, as also in other artistic media in the twelfth century.[45] Similar figures of knights, either singly or in pairs, occur frequently in twelfth-century manuscript illumination in the context of decorated letters. Here sometimes the text gives a clue to their meaning, as in the well-known image of a single knight in the copy from Bec of Geoffrey of Monmouth's *History of the Kings of Britain*. It has been suggested that he may represent Robert, Earl of Gloucester, to whom the prologue is addressed.[46]

In an initial 'E' in the early-twelfth-cetury Bible of S. Benigne in Dijon two knights fight in the lower part of the initial (Fig. 13).[47] The larger figure above is no doubt Judas Maccabeus, the saviour of the Jewish people, since the letter stands at the beginning of this book of the Bible. Though there is not the opportunity now to address the question of the pennon, whose importance Erdmann strongly emphasised, I would like to note its occurrence in this and a number of my other examples.[48] So far as I am aware no art historical examination of this important topic has been undertaken, in spite of Erdmann's lead.

However, in the same Bible in a 'V' for Micah there is no apparent reason to represent a mounted knight nor in the one of the Canon Tables where knights ride out of towers on each side.[49] The question, therefore, remains what meaning such mounted figures had for their original viewers. Yet another example is on the Shrine of the Three Kings at Cologne made by the Mosan goldsmith, Nicholas of Verdun, in the late twelfth century.[50] Were they there simply as suitable but generalised decoration? Or did they carry particular connotations of Good or Evil?

This returns us to the St Alban's Psalter image. It seems to me that we can very well see these images as a parallel to the crucial debates going on among contemporaries about the justification and the necessity of Holy War.[51] On the one hand there was the negative perception of violence and warfare on the part of the Church, voiced in the Peace Movement in the eleventh century and powerfully expressed at the Council of Lyons of 1031 when God's anger was invoked on 'all

---

[45] Dr Richard Eales has kindly drawn my attention to a chesspiece in the Louvre, cat. 3297, with jousting knights on one long side, the Fall of Adam and Eve on the other, and Adam delving and Eve spinning on the short sides. In this secular context this is no doubt a social comment on the orders, *bellatores* and *laboratores*, See Goldschmidt, 4, no. 180 a–d, Taf. LXIII and H. and S. Wichmann, *Chess: the story of chesspieces from ancient to modern times*, London 1964, 281.

[46] Leiden, Bibliotheek der Rijksuniversiteit, B.P.L. 20, folio 20. Swarzenski, fig. 320. Ralph H.C. Davis, *The Medieval Warhorse, Origin, Development and Redevelopment*, London 1989, 24.

[47] Dijon, Bibliothèque municipale, MS 2, folio 380v. Załuska, 1991, 133, pl. XLI.

[48] Carl Erdmann, *The Origin of the Idea of Crusade*, transl. Marshall W. Baldwin, W. Goffart, Princeton 1977 [1935].

[49] Folios 225v, 402v. Załuska, 134–5, 1991, pls XL, XLII. Another example is in an early twelfth-century copy of Gregory, *Moralia in Job*, from Rochester, BL, MS Royal 6 C. VI. On folio 79v, a knight in an initial 'P' pierces the dragon forming the bowl of the initial with his lance. Kauffmann, cat. 15, ill. 37.

[50] Swarzenski, fig. 526.

[51] There is, of course, a very considerable literature. In addition to Erdmann see Jonathan S.C. Riley-Smith, *The First Crusade and the Idea of Crusading*, London, Philadelphia, 1986. Also especially relevant in the present context Herbert E.J. Cowdrey, 'The Peace and the Truce of God in the eleventh century', *Past and Present* xlvi, 1970, 42–67 and Christopher J. Holdsworth, 'Ideas and reality: some attempts to control and defuse war in the twelfth century', *The Church and War*, ed. William J. Sheils, *Studies in Church History* xx, 1983, 59–78.

knights, upon their arms and their horses'.[52] This negative view of the knight is also represented in another image, that of the Horsemen of the Apocalypse, as it were the mounted equivalent of Goliath on foot, for example in the Apocalypse from Silos completed in 1109.[53]

On the other hand there was the opposing perception in the justification of Christian violence as Holy when in defence of the Church or directed against its enemies, heretics and Saracens. This justification of Holy War, enshrined in Anselm of Lucca's Collectio Canonum of 1083, for example, has been traced by Erdmann and by other scholars following him in relation to the Crusades.[54] A much earlier image in the Sacramentary of Gellone of the late eighth century is significant in already showing for the text of the blessing of a warrior a knight attached to the initial 'D' (Fig. 14).[55] Professor Riley-Smith in his book on the First Crusade writes of 'the ideals of the eleventh-century reformers whose chief aim had been to infuse secular life with monastic values'.[56] He argues that it was in the reformist circles of Gregory VII that the earlier idea of monastic vocation as spiritual conflict and the later idea of the Crusade as a Holy War against the disbeliever came together.

The St Albans Psalter accompanying text is significantly ambivalent. At one moment it speaks of the 'bellatores' as models: 'these men are virile and prudent in their horsemanship'. But it also refers to them as 'swollen with pride and malice', whereas we who are addressed in the text must be 'gentle in our humility'.[57] Among the historiated initials in the Psalter there are also negative images of knights as violent murderers, for example for Psalm 78 (Fig. 15).[58]

Another important ambivalence in the text should also be noted. While the 'we' who are exhorted are in the main gendered as male, the text starts by exhorting its readers as 'females armed in a manly spirit' and then refers to those who become '(female) friends of Christ and heavenly athletes'.[59] This surely confirms Christina as recipient and reader of the Psalter.

In conclusion, I think these varied and contextually unspecific images of warfare are most likely to have been seen by contemporaries as figures like themselves struggling for victory over outside Evil and inner Temptation. In Christina's Psalter the symmetricality of the combatants neither of whom triumphs (Fig. 2), unlike in the Maccabees initial (Fig. 13) suggests it is a generalised image of struggle, emphasising that the Christian must bear the inevitable wounds with patience, as indeed the texts stress.[60] I cannot agree, therefore, with

[52] Riley-Smith, 4.
[53] BL, MS Add. 11695, folio 102v. Davis, fig. 22. The horsemen wear mail, a significant alteration to the earlier iconography as seen in Madrid, Biblioteca nacional, Cod. Vit. 14–2, the *Beatus* of Fernando and Sancha, dated 1047.
[54] For reservations, however, see John T. Gilchrist, 'The Erdmann thesis and the Canon Law 1083–1141', *Crusade and Settlement*, 37–45.
[55] BN, MS latin 12048. Davis, fig. 23.
[56] Riley-Smith, 3.
[57] 'isti viriles sunt et prudentes in cursu equitationis'. 'tumentes superbia et maledictione'. 'mansuetos in humilitate'.
[58] Page 231. Pächt, 233, pl. 65a.
[59] 'in spiritu virili armatae'. 'facte sunt Christi amicae et celestes atlete'.
[60] Holdsworth, 77, puts it thus: 'The hermit in his cell, the monk in his cloister, the knight in his lord's household, all served, *militare*, they belonged to their distinct *militia* but for each the struggle could be hard and long.'

Fig. 15.
Hildesheim, Basilica St Godehard. St Albans Psalter, p. 231. Psalm 78.
Evil knights slaughter the faithful

Fig. 16.
Le Mans, Bibliothèque municipale, MS 263, folio 10v. Pliny the Younger offering
his book to the Emperor Vespasian

Fig. 17.
London, BL, MS Add. 49622, folio 146. Detail of border with knight
fighting a snail

Besson's characterisation of all these 'evenly-matched combattant' images (as he calls them) as being negative representations of social violence, even if such connotations were present to some observers.[61]

If, on the contrary, they could be thought of as representing 'Fighting the Good Fight', they reflect an ideological construction which certain forces in the Church were working to put in place. It should be emphasised how opposed this is to the pacificism of the Early Church.[62] There is at least one specific case where we can see this change happening. Orderic Vitalis tells how Gerold, chaplain of Hugh of Avranches, Earl of Chester, collected tales of the combats of Holy Knights from the Old Testament and from modern Christian stories.[63] 'He told them vivid

61 François M. Besson, ' "A armes égales": une représentation de la violence en France et en Espagne au XIIe siècle', *Gesta* xxvi/2, 1987, 113–26. Besson's supposition that these images may also refer to the Trial by Ordeal is interesting but unproven.

62 Elizabeth Siberry, *Criticism of crusading 1095–1274*, Oxford 1985. Among the subjects singled out for condemnation in cloister sculpture by St Bernard in the well-known passage in the *Apologia* are fighting soldiers. For the passage and for images of 'incoherent violence' see Conrad Rudolph, *The 'Things of Greater Importance'. Bernard of Clairvaux's 'Apologia' and the medieval attitude toward art*, Philadelphia 1990, especially ch. 3.

63 Orderic, iii, 216–7. Marjorie Chibnall, *The World of Orderic Vitalis*, Oxford 1984, 15.

stories of the conflicts of Demetrius and George, of Theodore and Sebastian and of the Theban Legion and Duke Maurice, its leader, and of Eustace, supreme commander of the army. He also told them of the holy champion, William (St William of Gellone), who after long service in war renounced the world and fought gloriously for the Lord under the monastic rule'. An apposite illustration of knights from the Old Testament would be the representations of the Maccabees already referred to (Fig. 13), or the prefatory drawing of them as combatants in the Winchester Bible.[64] The saints referred to are precisely those whose newly popular images we have been discussing, St George as already seen at Ferrara and Brinsop, St Eustace, shown with St George on the reverse of the same Monreale capital already referred to with the anonymous battling knights (Fig. 11), and St Maurice shown, for example, on a twelfth-century precious metal shrine containing his relics still preserved at St Maurice d'Agaune.[65]

These stories Gerold told to great barons, ordinary knights and noble boys. He thus gave them both a role model and a context to read the figures sculpted on doors and capitals and painted on walls and in books. In so far as those representations were read positively, therefore, as I think we are justified in concluding they were by at least some of their audience, they both constructed a function for the *bellatores* in relation to the institutions of the Church, and they served to give authority and ideological justification to the *bellatores* as a class. Thus, though still as we have seen, an image with a certain ambivalence in the St Albans Psalter context, we can see how it was possible for such an image to be placed there as exemplifying a positive model of the spiritual life. And it becomes understandable how an earlier pictorial tradition such as that of the Prudentius cycle, with which I began, was modified, so that the Virtues become in effect male armed knights, as at Aulnay, in Herrad's *Hortus*, and in the capital from Clermont Ferrand.

Just how benign an image of the knight could be is nicely shown in a manuscript very probably made at Winchester in the mid-twelfth century, a copy of Pliny's *Natural History* (Fig. 16).[66] Here the Roman author is represented as a retired soldier having hung up his shield and pennon, just as did St William of Gellone and many others after him. To present his finished work to the Emperor Vespasian, however, Pliny again dons his arms and armour. Like the famous Theodore carved on the south porch at Chartres in the early thirteenth century, he is the idealised, good soldier. If in such images dissent seems to be silenced, it lived on to reappear in the later thirteenth and fourteenth century, notably within the context of the margins of illuminated manuscripts and in opposition to the

[64] Kauffmann, cat. 83, ill. 234. Walter Oakeshott, *The Two Winchester Bibles*, Oxford 1981, pl. VI. For varying uses of the Maccabees as 'archetypal heroic warriors' see Jean Dunbabin, 'The Maccabees as exemplars in the tenth and eleventh centuries', *The Bible in the Medieval World. Essays in memory of Beryl Smalley* (Studies in Church History, Subsidia, 4), ed. Katherine Walsh, Diana Wood, Oxford 1985, 31–42.
[65] Daniel Thurre, *L'atelier roman d'orfèvrerie de l'abbaye de Saint-Maurice*, Sierre 1992, 139, 141–56, pl. VI.
[66] Le Mans, Bibliothèque municipale, MS 263, folio 10v. Swarzenski, fig. 293. *English Romanesque Art*, no. 57.

positive images of donors such as the well-known depiction of Sir Geoffrey Luttrell in his Psalter.[67] The knight's credentials of nobility and his pretensions to bravery are frequently satirised in the marginalia, as in the early fourteenth-century English Gorleston Psalter, where the knight kneels before a snail (Fig. 17)![68]

[67] BL, MS Add. 42130, folio 202v. Janet Backhouse, *The Luttrell Psalter*, London 1989, fig. 1.
[68] BL, MS Add. 49622, folio 146. Lilian M.C. Randall, *Images in the margins of Gothic manuscripts*, Berkeley 1966, 138, lists marginal representations of knights and snails. See also Lilian M.C. Randall, 'The Fieschi Psalter', *Journal of the Walters Art Gallery* xxiii, 1960, 27–48, figs 13–14. The theme of jousting continues on Psalter Beatus pages of the thirteenth and fourteenth centuries, as shown by Howard Helsinger, 'Images on the *Beatus* page of some medieval Psalters', *Art Bulletin* liii, 1971, 161–76. Helsinger argues they continue the positive significance of spiritual struggle as in the St Albans Psalter, which he illustrates, fig. 17, and discusses, page 174. I should like to thank François Avril, Neil Stratford and John Williams for help in connection with this paper.

A NORMAN-ITALIAN ADVENTURER IN THE EAST: RICHARD OF SALERNO 1097–1112

George T. Beech

The adventures, hardships, and disappointments awaiting the Europeans who went on the crusades have long been well known; indeed enough information has survived for modern authors to be able to write biographies of a very few of the most famous leaders. I would like to add to this list a smaller biographical notice of Richard of the Principate who is of interest, I would contend, not because he was a great and influential man but because the scope and variety of his experiences on the First Crusade was quite extraordinary. Richard rose to prominence in that expedition in which contemporary historians considered him one of the leading figures of second rank. But since their comments on him are widely scattered, and inconclusive when viewed in isolation, he has escaped the attention of modern historians. The purpose of this paper is to assemble the fragments and tell the story of his spectacular life and career in the East.

Richard of the Principate took his name from the principality of Salerno, a former Lombard state which had been created in 846 from a division of the former province of Benevento.[1] In the mid-eleventh century the Lombard prince of Salerno, Gisulf II, saw his rule threatened by the appearance of Norman adventurers who first entered his service, then became his allies, and finally overthrew and drove him into exile in 1077. The men to accomplish this were William, the tenth son of Tancred of Hauteville, who ruled as the first Norman count of the Principate from 1056–80, and his brother Robert Guiscard of Apulia.[2] With his wife, Maria, daughter of the neighboring Lombard prince Guy of Sorrente, whom he married c.1057, William fathered a daughter and four sons, the third of whom was Richard, the subject of the present essay. His eldest son, Robert, succeeded William of San Nicandro, as he was also known, (as well as Hauteville), as count from 1088–99, and Robert's son William followed his father from 1099–1128.

The third son and perhaps fourth child of a marriage dating from c.1057, Richard was presumably born in the 1060s and may thus have been in his late 30s at the beginning of the first crusade.[3] He would thus have been around fifty at the time of his death sometime between 1112–1114, an age which is consistent with

---

[1] F. Hirsch, M. Schipa, *La Longobardia Meridionale 570–1077. Il ducato de Benevento. Il Principato de Salerno*, ed. N. Acocella, Rome, 1968.
[2] A brief summary of the eleventh- and twelfth-century counts of the principate by L.-R. Menager is the only history to have been written on the Norman counts of Salerno. 'Les fondations monastiques de Robert Guiscard duc de Pouille et de Calabre', *QF* 39 (1959), 1–116; Excursus G.-B. Prignano, 'Les comtes du principat et les "coutumes" d'Eboli 1128', 65–82.
[3] Menager, 'Fondations Monastiques', 71.

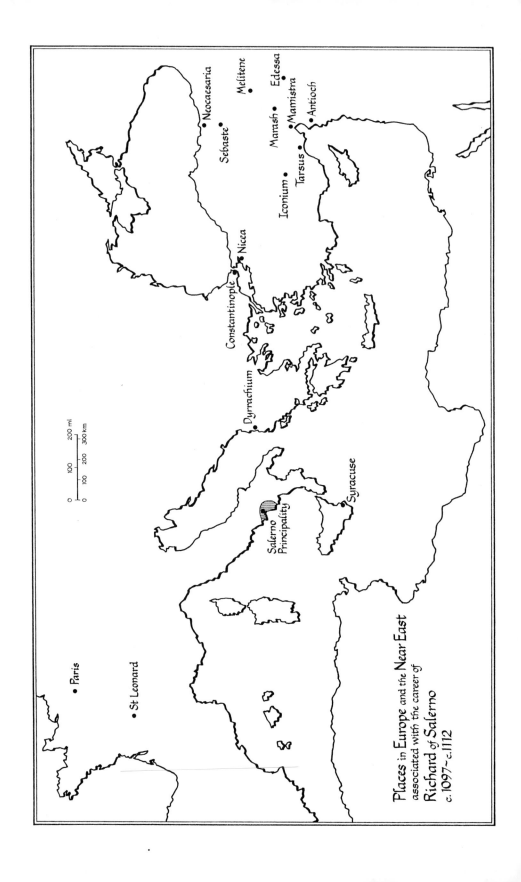

Places in Europe and the Near East
associated with the career of
Richard of Salerno
c. 1097–c. 1112

his son Roger becoming temporary ruler of Antioch on the death of Tancred, second prince of that city, in 1112. To have had a son at the age of majority in 1112 Richard must have married by 1090 at the latest when living in Salerno. Through his mother he traced his ancestry to the Lombard rulers of Sorrente, a relationship which he and his wife commemorated by naming their only known daughter, Maria, after her paternal grandmother.[4] Through his father he was grandson of Tancred of Hauteville and claimed direct descent from the most distinguished family in Norman Italy. He was thus closely related to the most famous members of the second and third generations of that lineage. As nephew of Robert Guiscard he was a cousin of Bohemond of Taranto. Due to the difficulty in determing exactly the maternal ancestry of Tancred of Antioch, it is not clear just what was Richard's relationship to him. If Tancred's mother, Emma, was a sister of Robert Guiscard, the two were cousins; if she was a daughter, then they were first cousins once removed.[5]

The almost complete lack of references to him in contemporary south Italian charters and chronicles makes it very difficult to learn much about the first thirty five years of Richard's life in the Principate in Italy before the First Crusade. Yet some inferences are possible and the darkness surrounding that earlier part of his life can be pierced if only slightly. With two older brothers alive and active, one, Robert, as their father's successor as Count of the Principate, and the second, Tancred, as Count of Syracuse in Sicily after 1091, he would have grown up knowing that he would have no hope of succeeding to ancestral lands and offices at home but would have to seek these elsewhere. There are strong suggestions that for a number of years he cast his lot with his brother Tancred in participating in the Norman conquest of Sicily under the command of their uncle, Count Roger. When writing about Richard in his account of Tancred of Antioch's life and career, Ralph of Caen says that the former left his own brother Tancred of Syracuse in order to join Bohemond on the crusade.[6] This implies that Richard was living in Syracuse in some capacity in 1097. A charter of 1104 from the priory of St Lucia of Bagnara in Sicily would seem to confirm this for Richard had returned to Syracuse at that date to approve donations made by his brother Tancred and the latter's wife to that church.[7] He must have had some kind of landed interest there for his approval to have been necessary. The Norman campaign to conquer Syracuse came to a successful conclusion in 1085. Richard's brother, Tancred, acquired that county sometime around 1091 after the death of the first Norman count, Jordan, Count Roger's natural son, doubtless as a reward

---

4 On the marriage of Maria to the Count of Edessa see R. L. Nicholson, *Joscelyn I, Prince of Edessa*, Illinois Studies in the Social Sciences xxxv, no. 4, Urbana 1954, 62.

5 F. de Saulcy, 'Tancrede', *Bibliothèque de l'Ecole des Chartes* iv (1842), 301–15; E. Jamison, 'Some Notes on the *Anonymi Gesta Francorum* with special reference to the Norman Contingent from South Italy and Sicily in the First Crusade', *Studies in French Language and Medieval Literature presented to Professor Mildred E. Pope*, Manchester 1939, 196–99; R. L. Nicholson, *Tancred: A Study of his Career and Work in their Relation to the First Crusade and the Establishment of the Latin States in Syria and Palestine*, Chicago 1938, 3–9.

6 'Is (i.e. Richard) comitis Wilhelmi filius, Wiscardi nepos, relicta fratri Tancredo Syracusa, Boamundum secutus amitalem suum . . .', *Gesta Tancredi in Expeditione Hierosolymitana*, Recueil des Historiens des Croisades, Historiens Occidentaux (hereafter cited as RHC, OCC.) III, 638.

7 'Quae omnia concedit quoque et confirmat domina Muriel uxor mea et frater meus Richardus . . .', R. Pirro, *Sicilia Sacra*, Panormita, 1733 edn, I, 619.

for his earlier contributions to that campaign.[8] Richard could well have participated in that effort as a young man in his early twenties and probably was given lands there in compensation. But he obviously did not receive a county as did his elder brother. And his joining the First Crusade in 1097 shows that, whatever the reason may have been, he did not make Sicily a career.

It could have been in the Sicilian campaign against the Muslims of Syracuse that Richard learned Arabic. The anonymous Italian author of a history of the First Crusade identifies Richard and Tancred by name as two crusaders who knew Syriac (taken by modern scholars to mean Arabic) and who could thus negotiate directly with the enemy commander at the siege of Antioch in 1098.[9] No one knows how many of the early crusaders already knew Arabic – many must have learned it later – but the care taken by this author to name these two men probably means that such bi-linguists were exceptionally rare at the outset. The Sicilian campaign would not, however, have been the only or perhaps even the best opportunity for Richard to learn Arabic. Growing up in Salerno in the 1060s to 80s would of necessity have exposed him to the intellectual life then thriving in that town. Nothing in the surviving evidence suggests that Richard was educated and literate but even if he had no formal link with it, he could hardly have been unaware of the growing fame of the medical school of Salerno or of the learned reputation of the local Archbishop Alfano (1058–85) author of a number of works biographical and medical, and translator from Greek.[10] Constantine the African, a distinguished translator of Arabic medical texts into Latin, lived briefly in Salerno at this time and it is to be presumed that a knowledge of Arabic could have been acquired there then.

The author of the chronicle of Montecassino reports that Bohemond of Taranto first heard of plans for a crusade while besieging Amalfi near Salerno in the summer of 1096.[11] Filled with enthusiasm for the new cause, he immediately began organizing his own expedition and for this called upon the aid of a number of close supporters, his 'captains' or commanders, and the first three named were Tancred, son of the Marquis (later of Antioch), Richard of the Principate, and his brother Rainulf. This is the earliest reference to Richard's ties with these two prominent leaders of the first crusade, and it reveals that an association which would decisively reshape Richard's later life and would last until his death nearly twenty years later, had already been formed. How this nobleman of Salerno came to be linked with Bohemond can scarcely be a mystery even if no records survive to document it. As first cousins from the same part of southern Italy, they would have known one another since childhood though Bohemond was perhaps ten years Richard's senior.[12] And after Robert Guiscard's death in 1085 they shared a common dilemma; neither had prospects of inheriting paternal lands at home. It is

[8] Menager, 'Fondations Monastiques', 73; F. Chalandon, *Histoire de la Domination Normande en Italie et en Sicile*, Paris 1907, I, 339–40, 347.

[9] '. . . Riccardus autem de Principatu et Tancredus qui linguam Syriacam sciebant, consulabant quotidie ammirario ut domino Boamundo redderet castrum, et ille sibi daret honorem maximum', *RHC*, OCC., III, 198.

[10] P.O. Kristeller, 'The School of Salerno. Its Development and Contribution to Learning', *Bulletin of the History of Medicine* 17, 1945, 138–94. H. Rashdall, *The Universities of Europe in the Middle Ages*, Oxford 1895, I, 75–88.

[11] *Die Chronik von Montecassino*, ed. H. Hoffmann, MGH, SS 34, 1980, 476–77.

[12] R.P. Yewdale, *Bohemond I Prince of Antioch*, Princeton 1917, 5.

conceivable that Richard participated with Bohemond under Robert Guiscard in the unsuccessful invasion of Byzantine Macedonia from 1081–85 in addition to the Sicilian campaign with his brother Tancred. More likely, however, he joined Bohemond some time between 1085–95 during which years the latter disputed control of Apulia with his brother Duke Roger.[13] The attraction of a crusade for these men, with its promise of new lands and commands in the East hardly needs commentary.

Due to Anna Comnena's curiously detailed story in her *Alexiade*, the precise date of Richard's departure for the East can be fixed as St Nicholas' day, 6 December 1096. Even though writing over forty years later, Anna somehow found and repeated a story about Richard's crossing the Adriatic, which, although found nowhere else, is so detailed and unusual as to sound authentic.[14] After Bohemond had gone on ahead Richard brought his own men over in a three masted pirate ship which he rented for 6000 gold staters. A Byzantine fleet guarding the coast, taking it for a privateer, accosted and eventually boarded it though not until after some skirmishing in which Richard was wounded in the arm by an arrow. Quick action by the Greek commander avoided a major encounter and brought the ship and Richard and his men, captives, to shore.[15] It is doubtful that they were kept prisoner for long for the author of the *Gesta Francorum* reports that Richard and his men formed part of the third crusader army on the march through Hungary and Bulgaria on the way to Constantinople.[16]

Much of the crusaders' stay in Constantinople hinged upon the emperor's demand that their leaders swear oaths of fidelity to him and their efforts to resist so doing.[17] Richard and Tancred stood out in the confused negotiations which acompanied this issue by avoiding the oath, slipping away and secretly crossing the Bosphorus into Asia Minor.[18] Neither Orderic Vitalis nor the author of the *Gesta Francorum* explain the reluctance of the two men to take the oath but in the case of Richard it is conceivable that he resented what he considered rough treatment at imperial hands when apprehended crossing the Adriatic. It is also conceivable that Alexius remembered this slight when dealing with Richard six years later at the time of the latter's imprisonment, as will become apparent below.

In June 1097 the crusading armies began their long march across Asia Minor, and on the nineteenth of that month inflicted a serious defeat on the Turks with the capture of Nicea. They followed with another major victory at the battle of Dorylaeum on 30 June, an engagement in which Richard is listed as one of the

[13] Yewdale, *Bohemond*, 25–33.

[14] On Anna's knowledge of Normans from southern Italy and their affairs see Graham Loud, 'Anna Komnena and her sources for the Normans of Southern Italy', *Church and Chronicle in the Middle Ages. Essays Presented to John Taylor*, ed. G.A. Loud and I. Wood, London 1991, 41–57.

[15] *Anna Comnena: Alexiade. Regne de l'empereur Alexis I Comnene 1081–1118*, ed. B. Leib, Paris 3 vols 1966–89, II, 215–20.

[16] *The Deeds of the Franks and the Other Pilgrims to Jerusalem*, ed. R. Hill, London 1962, 5. From this point on I make no attempt to cite all the European sources for the campaigns, battles, etc. of the First Crusade but only those in which Richard is singled out by name by the author.

[17] J. Pryor, 'The Oaths of the Leaders of the First Crusade to Emperor Alexius I Comnenus: Fealty, Hommage, Pistis, Douleia', *Parergon*, New Series 2, 1984, 111–142.

[18] *Deeds of the Franks*, 13; Orderic, V, 50–51.

crusader commanders.[19] Their march continued further south and east to Iconium and Heraclea during the months of July and August, meeting with relatively minor opposition. After it reached Heraclea in late August, the crusader army divided into two segments with the main branch continuing to Antioch via a northerly route which took it through Kayseri before descending into Marash in Armenian Cilicia. But two much smaller contingents led by Baldwin of Boulogne and Tancred of Apulia chose a shorter but also more difficult route south across the dangerous pass of the Cilician Gates through the Anti-Taurus mountains into southern Cilicia. Both men were eager to conquer towns and lands in Cilicia over which they could then establish a claim to lordship. For reasons unknown Richard left Bohemond here and followed Tancred who led a group of several hundred men. The two leaders, Baldwin and Tancred, quarreled over the control, first of Tarsus and then of Mamistra, both of which the Italian commander initially took, and their disagreements finally led to violence and loss of life and prefigured the bitter hostilities which lay ahead in future campaigns. The two principle sources for these disputes, Albert of Aachen and Ralph of Caen, present differing accounts of the troubles at Mamistra but agree in picturing Richard as playing a central role in them. According to Albert it was Richard who incited Tancred into initiating a battle outside Mamistra which turned into a disaster for the latter. An earlier argument at Tarsus set the stage. After Tancred and his men had taken that town, Baldwin appeared with his much larger force and compelled the furious but helpless Italian general to surrender it to him. Later Baldwin turned up again outside Mamistra which Tancred had just occupied. Albert of Aachen pictures Richard as goading a hesitant Tancred into action with a speech in which he questions his relative's courage. 'Ah, Tancred, you are the vilest of men if you put up with the presence of Baldwin who caused you to lose Tarsus. If you had any sense of dignity you would already have roused up your men to avenge this wrong done to you.'[20] These taunts took effect; Tancred attacked, but being greatly outnumbered was pushed back, and in the retreat into Mamistra a number of his men, including Richard were taken prisoner. No such speech is recorded by Ralph of Caen and the hostilities began in a different fashion but with Richard again a key figure. Tancred had granted Baldwin's men the right to buy provisions in Mamistra but individual bargaining soon led to quarrelling and finally fighting. Richard, at the center of it, had his horse cut out from under him by a lance after which some of Baldwin's men pounced on him. Finding him helpless they took him prisoner and this precipitated full scale fighting.[21] In both versions Baldwin and Tancred made up their differences the next morning and exchanged their prisoners. This campaign will have given Richard his first acquaintance with the province of Cilicia in which he was later to acquire his lordship at Marash.

The two crusader armies rejoined forces in the fall for a march on the city of Antioch which they invested on 21 October 1097. It was in the epic siege of this stronghold, which lasted until its capitulation on 28 June 1098, that Bohemond used the Arabic speaking Richard and Tancred to try and persuade the Turkish commander of the inner citadel to surrender without further fighting.[22] Otherwise

[19] *Deeds of the Franks*, 20.
[20] *Albert of Aachen, Historia Hierosolymitana*, RHC, OCC. IV, 349.
[21] *Gesta Tancredi*, RHC, OCC. III, 638.
[22] RHC, OCC. III, 198.

none of the crusader historians mentions Richard's role in the victory. In the succeeding months Bohemond bent all his efforts to consolidating his hold on Antioch which he established as one of the two great crusader principalities in northern Syria, and he bypassed the Jerusalem campaign of 1099. Whether Richard remained with him in Antioch or took part in the conquest of the Holy City is unknown.

The spectacular successes of the crusaders in the Holy Land in 1098 and 1099 must have led to an immediate scramble for lands and commands with too little of either to go around. In turn this must have created dilemnas for men of the second rank like Tancred and Richard who had to wonder how best to realize their own hopes for advancement. Richard's presence as Bohemond's second in command in their Cilician campaign in the early summer of 1100 shows that Richard had decided to rely on his cousin who had been his commander from the outset as the patron who would provide for him. The northern frontier of the principality of Antioch was particularly vulnerable to attacks from unreliable Armenians in Cilicia and enemy Turks further to the north. As part of his campaign to protect the Cilician frontier Bohemond, seconded by Richard, undertook in early 1100 the conquest of the town of Marash, a town vital to his interests because it lay at the intersection of several key routes leading from Anatolia in the west to one of the two manageable mountain passes across the Taurus mountains to Edessa to the east and Antioch to the south. It could well be that Bohemond had already decided to entrust this important northern outpost to his cousin and that their siege of the town in the summer of 1100 gave Richard his first exposure to it.[23]

This was not to happen, however, for all plans were brutally interrupted by their sudden and disastrous capture at the hands of Danishmend Turks at the time of the Marash siege in 1100.[24] During the course of that campaign Bohemond received an urgent appeal from Gabriel, the Armenian lord of Melitene northeast of Marash, promising to turn the town and its province over to him if he would rescue them from a Turkish army then invading from the northern Emirate of Sebaste. It was while marching to Melitene from Marash that Bohemond and Richard were caught in an ambush and their army virtually annihilated. Their captors took the two commanders in chains to Neocaesaria near the Black Sea and kept them there for the next three years.[25]

Because of the now almost legendary fame of Bohemond as a warrior among the Turks as well as among the Europeans, his falling into Turkish hands attracted a good deal of attention from historians at the time with the result that a fair bit is known not only about his capture but also his captivity and his release. But in addition to several historical accounts there also exists a substantial hagiographical literature in the form of stories of the miracles of St Leonard which attribute the liberation of Bohemond and Richard to the intervention of St Leonard de Noblat, a saint whose shrine was located near Limoges in central France, and who had begun to acquire renown as the patron saint of prisoners and captives in the course of the eleventh century. Bohemond himself was almost certainly the

[23] A.E. Dostourian, *The Chronicle of Matthew of Edessa: translated from the Original Armenian with a Commentary and Introduction*, Rutgers University Ph.D. dissertation 1972, I, 316–17.
[24] Dostourian, *Matthew of Edessa*, I, 318.
[25] *Matthew of Edessa*, 318.

source of the most detailed of the miracles which he recounted during a pilgrimage to St Leonard's shrine in 1106.[26]

This is not all. The contemporary Anglo-Norman historian Orderic Vitalis, who may have met or heard Bohemond during the latter's 1106 trip to France, but who in any case is exceptionally well informed about him, makes a quite different contribution to the captivity literature. In his *Ecclesiastical History* he tells a long and bizarre story about Melaz, the Muslim daughter of Bohemond's captor, Malik Ghazi, falling in love with her father's prisoner, playing an essential role in liberating him, and after converting to Christianity, finally marrying, not her beloved, but Roger future prince of Antioch and son of Richard of the Principate.[27] One literary historian who examined this tale saw it as the earliest known example of the penetration into the West of what later became a staple there, namely, the story of the beautiful Muslim princess who becomes enamoured of both Christianity and a crusader prince.[28]

Finally, memories of Bohemond's captivity may have worked their way into the European vernacular epics on the Crusades. It has been suggested that the author of *Les Chetifs*, a *chanson de geste* from the epic Cycle of the Crusades, based several of the episodes in that poem on stories circulating in Syria in the twelfth century of the captivity of Bohemond and Richard.[29] Taken together, these various historical, hagiographical, and literary accounts make Bohemond's one of the best documented captivities of the Middle Ages though the historian is faced with substantial problems when trying to filter out the legendary and devotional elements in them.

Bohemond's capitivity is of interest to my subject because the authors of these different versions of the story give a considerable amount of space to his fellow prisoner and relative, Richard of the Principate. Three episodes from the entire complex of stories cast an interesting light on these years of Richard's life and warrant mention here. In the first, for which Orderic is the source of information, Bohemond has temporarily turned the tables on his Turkish captors and made them his captives even though still surrounded in their stronghold in Neocaesaria. Negotiating a settlement with him, the Turks insist that certain of their countrymen still held prisoner by the crusaders in Antioch after the fall of the city in 1098, be released as counterparts for his own release. It is his fellow prisoner, Richard, along with an otherwise unidentified Sarcis of Mesopotamia, whom Bohemond designates as envoys to go to Antioch to arrange the exchange with Tancred, now temporarily his replacement as prince of that city. Richard and Sarcis carry out their mission and return fifteen days later bringing with them the released Turks, including the daughter of the former Turkish Emir of Antioch.[30] The Arab historian Ibn al-Athir independantly reports the same exchange of the daughter thus suggesting that there may be an historical basis to this part at least

[26] A. Poncelet, 'Bohemond et S. Leonard', *Analecta Bollandiana* 31, 1912, 24–44, at 30–31.

[27] Orderic, V, 359–79.

[28] F.M. Warren, 'The enamoured Moslem Princess in Orderic Vitalis and the French Epic', *Publications of the Modern Language Association* xxix, 1914, 341–58.

[29] U.T. Holmes Jr and W.M. McLeod, 'Source Problems of the *Chetifs*', *Romanic Review* 28, 1937, 102, 104–5.

[30] Orderic, V, 372–75.

of Orderic's story.[31] In any case Bohemond's reliance in this instance on Richard as his personal ambassador is consistent with the latter having served as a translator-negotiator at the siege of Antioch, and with his later service to his cousin in France.

The story of Richard's own captivity and release is another important element in the entire collection. According to Matthew of Edessa, Richard's Turkish captors sold him to the Emperor Alexius of Constantinople for a great sum of money.[32] On the surface of it this story sounds improbable; why would the Byzantine emperor have been willing to spend a large sum for a man who could not be ranked as one of the great crusader leaders like Bohemond? Yet Matthew's testimony on this point must be taken seriously for, as an Armenian monk living and writing in Edessa prior to 1136, he would have been well informed about and perhaps have known Richard who governed that city for sometime between 1104 and 1108. Moreover the first story in the St. Leonard miracle collection, a story written between 1106 and 1111, thus contemporary to the event, confirms Matthew's account and adds new details which cannot be dismissed out of hand as pious legend.[33] The author of this story tells of the emperor learning of the capture of Richard and then immediately sending legates to the pagans offering gifts, food, and money in return for their prisoner. For this man, namely Richard, was one of those Normans who, under the guise of going to fight the pagans, really aspired to take over the rule of the Greek Empire and had done great evil to it in the past.[34] The pagans accepted his offer and he then imprisoned Richard in the highest and safest tower in Constantinople. Richard, never losing faith, prayed for aid to St Leonard, the guardian of prisoners, and his prayers were answered when the saint began to appear in the emperor's dreams pleading for the captive's safety and warning against harming him. Terrified when the visions did not stop the emperor summoned Richard to his presence and denounced him for his crimes but then informed him that he would rather release him than face God's wrath. Richard then cast off his prisoner's uniform, put on clothes of imperial

[31] Ibn al-Athir, *Kamel-Altevarykh*, RHC, OCC. I, 212.

[32] A. Poncelet, 'Bohemond', 28, note 3, points out that the meaning of the passage where Matthew reports this incident may be obscure as shown by the fact that Ed. Dulaurier changed his mind in his two successive translations of it in 1858 and 1869. In the second Dulaurier rendered it with 'Danischmend le relacha par consideration pour Alexis' whereas in the earlier he had written 'Danischmend en fit don a l'empereur Alexis en retour de sommes considerables que celui-ci lui donna'. The recent translation by the American, A. Dostourian, *Matthew of Edessa*, 345–6, returns to the notion that the Turkish ruler sold Richard to the emperor and the Armenian historian, Claude Mutafian, *La Cilicie au carrefour des empires*, Paris, 2 vols, 1988, very kindly checked this passage for me and tells me that he has no doubt that this is the correct version. Thus I have followed it here.

[33] *AS*, Nov. III, 159–60. On the date of this story, Poncelet, 'Bohemond', 35, note 5; on the identity of the author, his sources of information, and the manuscript tradition see below p. 34.

[34] The author calls his subject Richard the Norman not Richard of the Principate, which might lead to doubts that he is writing about the Richard from Salerno. However, as Poncelet notes ('Bohemond', 35, note 5), the circumstances are so unusual and this agrees so closely with Matthew of Edessa's account, that it is almost inconceivable that there could have been a second Richard the Norman in such a dilemna. Since, as argued below, the author of this miracle may well have taken down almost verbatim what Richard reported to him in person, this may indicate that Richard referred to himself in this way.

magnificence, and the emperor, giving him horses, mules, weapons and money, led him peacefully back to his own people.

A good case can be made for the accuracy of the nucleus of this story, namely that Richard was transfered from Turkish to Byzantine captivity before being released in 1103. Alexius would certainly have known of him – his daughter Anna Comnena's exceptionally detailed story of Richard's capture when crossing the Adriatic in 1097 makes this quite clear – and would have had special reasons for disliking and perhaps fearing him. The unpleasant encounter on the Adriatic was one, but even more important, the emperor would have known that Richard was one crusader commander who managed to slip away across the Bosphorus and avoid taking the oath of fidelity to him early in 1097. An opportunity to punish such insubordination must not be missed, especially in the case of a man who was an Hauteville, the deadly enemies of Alexius from their attempt to overthow his government in their Macedonian campaign of 1081–85, and whom he may have taken for a man of considerable importance in the crusader chain of command. So he availed himself of the occasion to buy him from the Danischmend Turks in 1100. Why he would have released him in 1103 will remain more puzzling until the final chapter in the story of the relations between Alexius and Richard of the Principate becomes known. For the story is not yet finished and the most surprising phase is yet to come.

Another argument in favour of the historical accuracy of this episode at least in its broad outlines comes from a consideration of its authorship. Paris BN Latin MS 5347 which is the unique source of the six miracle stories about St Leonard of which this is the first, comes from St Martial of Limoges very close to St Leonard in the Limousin and dates from the twelfth century. The stories themselves contain no clue as to the identity of their author(s) but A. Poncelet, in a careful study of the second one, by far the longest and most detailed on the captivity, concluded that Bohemond himself had been the source.[35] In the course of his pilgrimage to St Leonard's shrine in 1106, made in thanksgiving for his release from captivity, Bohemond recounted the story of his troubles and an anonymous monk of St Martial converted that into the Latin story found today in MS 5347. Both internal and external evidence prove that it was written down between 1106 and 1111 and Poncelet comments that the same dates apply for the time of the composition of the first miracle story, the one under discussion here, dealing with Richard's imprisonment.

Just as Poncelet's analysis of the contents of the second miracle convinced him that Bohemond himself had been its source so it seems highly likely to me that Richard is the source of the first one about his own captivity. No other written account is known which could have been the source of this striking story about a crusader's imprisonment in Constantinople and its exclusive focus on Richard and his troubles with the emperor would suggest that it came either from some one who knew him well, or, more likely, from the Norman prince himself. From Orderic we know that Bohemond sent Richard to the shrine of St Leonard after their release from captivity in 1103 with a set of silver chains, an elegant souvenir of their captivity, to be dedicated to the saint in gratitude for bringing about their

---

[35] Poncelet, 'Bohemond', 30–31.

release.[36] Richard's visit then would have provided him with the chance to give thanksgiving for his own release and tell the story of his own harrowing imprisonment in Constantinople after the earlier one in Neocaesaria. The highly laudatory picture the author paints of Richard as the ideally brave, peerless, and faultless knight sounds indeed like the kind of self-image a powerful and self-confident nobleman of this period might have wanted to project to others. Its exclusive concentration on Richard, and complete neglect of Bohemond whom the author never even mentions, could also reflect the views of an ambitious man who for once desired to shine on his own after always previously basking in the reflected glory of his great and more famous lord. If this proposal, that Richard himself is the ultimate source of the first miracle story, is correct, then this latter affords an unexpected opportunity to hear this man speak about one dangerous episode in his life. And it strengthens the belief that he actually was held captive in Constantinople.

After long months of seclusion, fear, and inactivity, the next four years after his release in 1103 must have come as a stunning contrast to Richard and certainly they were the highlight of his career. During this time we find him travelling constantly between Europe and the Near East, performing prestigious diplomatic missions, assuming new commands, and extending the range of his contacts. He presumably delivered the aforementioned silver chains of Bohemond to St Leonard's shrine in the Limousin in late 1103 or early 1104 at which time he also made his own pilgrimage and told the story of his captivity contained in the first miracle story. During this European trip he also visited in his native Italy and called upon his brother Tancred in Syracuse where, sometime in 1104, he confirmed landed donations to the Sicilian abbey of St Lucia of Bagnara.[37] But he cannot have lingered either in France or Sicily for he was back in the East before the end of 1104, by which time he had become temporary ruler of the great crusader county of Edessa in northern Syria.

In May of that year Turkish forces from Aleppo defeated a crusader army led by Bohemond, now once again prince of Antioch, at Harran south of Edessa and captured Baldwin, count of that county, who remained in captivity until 1108. Bohemond first named his relative Tancred the interim ruler of Edessa but then, after deciding to return to Italy and France late in 1104, he appointed him as his replacement as prince of Antioch. Once he had taken over in Antioch, Tancred chose Richard to administer Edessa for him and the latter could now congratulate himself on having received his first important command in the crusader East six years after having arrived there.[38]

Richard held this office for four years until Baldwin's release in 1108 but it cannot have been an entirely satisfying one for him. During that time he incurred the undying hatred of the Edessan population for the 'evils' his administration inflicted on them. Several contemporary eastern sources stress this point, especially the anonymous Syriac chronicler who bitterly denounces him for his cruelty in the form of torture and imprisonment of local people and for his

---

[36] Orderic, V, 377.
[37] See above page 27.
[38] *Chronique de Michel le Syrien patriarche Jacobite d'Antioche (1166–99)*, ed. J.-B. Chabot, Paris 1905, I, 195.

cupidity in amassing a personal fortune during his tenure there.[39] Coins bearing his name have survived from his administration in Edessa.[40] He left such an evil reputation, writes Matthew of Edessa, that later on in 1109 when news arrived in Edessa of the death of Count Baldwin (this news proved to be false) at Turbessel, wild fears arose among the population that Richard would once again be named governor and reintroduce the abuses which had made him notorious earlier.[41] Matthew also criticizes Richard on another score. During a Turkish siege of Edessa in 1105–6, Richard, commanding the Edessan army, unwisely, says Matthew, ventured outside the city walls to attempt a frontal assault on the superior forces of the enemy and lost 450 foot soldiers to the despair of the local population.[42] But Richard cannot have viewed Edessa as the answer to his wishes since, as the Syriac chronicler puts it, 'he knew he was only a temporary guest and not the true master and heir of the county'. So, and this is a later quotation from the same writer, 'when Baldwin and Joscelin were freed, Richard gathered up everything he had accumulated and went to his own country, Marash'.[43]

To judge from the condemnations of these local historians, the population of Edessa must have been relieved when Richard left in 1105 or 1106 to return to Europe and rejoin his cousin Bohemond. Hard pressed in Antioch by both Turks and Byzantium, Bohemond had decided to try and raise new forces in Italy and France to defend his principality. In addition he was under the personal obligation of a vow made in prison to make a pilgrimage to St Leonard's in the Limousin and he arrived there in the spring of 1106.[44] It was during a triumphal tour of France at this time that he marrried the princess Constance, daughter of King Philippe I. In his history of the crusades, Guibert of Nogent reveals that Richard had arranged the marriage as Bohemond's envoy to the French king.[45] Shortly after speaking in favor of a crusade at a council in Poitiers in June 1106, Bohemond returned to Italy, quite likely accompanied by Richard, to spend the following year building a fleet and preparing for the new undertaking.

From 1107 to 1108 Richard participated in Bohemond's ambitious campaign, no longer veiled as a crusade to relieve Antioch, but now an openly avowed attempt to overthrow the emperor Alexius in Macedonia. After a promising beginning in which the Italian forces invaded and besieged Durazzo on the coast, the imperial tactics of avoiding direct military confrontation and cutting off Bohemond's sources of supply succeeded splendidly and Bohemond's great career came to a painful and humiliating end. The threat of starvation for his men forced him to accede to all major imperial demands in a peace treaty of September 1108 after which he went back to Italy. Richard's role in this campaign appears to have been an ambiguous one. Anna Comnena reports in considerable detail a curious episode in which the emperor attempted to discourage Bohemond by

---

[39] *Anonymi Auctoris Chronicon ad A. D. 1234 Pertinens* II, translated by Albert Abouna, introduction J.-M. Fiey (Corpus Scriptorum Christianorum Orientalium, vol. 354. Scriptores Syrii, T. 154, Louvain 1974), 53.

[40] J. Porteous, 'Crusader Coinage with Greek or Latin Inscriptions', *History of the Crusades*, ed. H. Hazard, Madison 1989, V 1, 354–420, at 356, 364, and 410.

[41] Dostourian, *Matthew of Edessa*, I, 363–64.

[42] Dostourian, *Matthew of Edessa*, 354.

[43] *Anonymi Auctoris Chronicon*, 53–54.

[44] Yewdale, *Bohemond*, 108–9.

[45] *Gesta Dei per Francos*, RHC, OCC. 1V, 152.

planting the suspicion that several of his chief advisors, including Richard, had secretly abandoned him and were conspiring with the imperial court against him.[46] Alexius sought to do this by sending ostensibly secret letters to the treacherous advisors thanking them for aiding his cause and then alerting Bohemond in advance of their arrival so that the latter could intercept them. Bohemond was initially frightened and baffled by the letters but after several days of uncertainty decided to ignore them, never confronted the suspects, and the affair passed.[47] However, Albert of Aachen and Orderic Vitalis report that several of Bohemond's Norman advisors had been corrupted by the emperor's blandishments and bribes and sought to persuade him to abandon the campaign.[48] The suspicion that some kind of movement of protest in fact had come to divide the Norman ranks during the campaign would seem to be confirmed by the ceremony for the formal signing of the treaty in September 1108. For among the various witnesses who signed the agreement was a small group of Normans whom Anna Comnena describes as coming from, that is representing, the imperial court. Among these figured Richard of the Principate.[49] What this means, and Anna is silent on the subject, is not immediately clear. As surprising as it seems, the description that these men came from the imperial court most likely means that they had been clandestinely negotiating with the emperor and now emerged openly as his advisors. If so the Norman ranks would have been in complete disarray at this moment. Perhaps the most satisfactory explanation for the curious stories surrounding this expedition is that some of Bohemond's leading advisors, including Richard, had grave doubts about the wisdom of prolonging what had become a disastrous venture and, unable to convert their leader to this view, had gone behind his back and treated directly with the enemy.[50]

In Richard's case, however, other considerations may have entered into his decision to join the imperial camp in this war. From the earlier discussion it will be recalled that the emperor Alexius's release of Richard from prison in 1103 seeemed inexplicable. Why would the emperor so drastically change his mind and free a hated Norman enemy after going to such pains and expense to buy him from the Turks? It should not be thought irreverent to suggest that other calculations than the fear of God and St Leonard, the explanation offered by the author of the First Miracle, entered into Alexius's decision. A solemn promise by Richard that in the future he would do his utmost to promote the interests of the Byzantine Emperor while still in the service of the Prince of Antioch might have tempted Alexius. As a close relative, subordinate, and confidant of Bohemond, Richard was, after all, ideally placed to influence the latter's policies. His presence in the imperial court at the September 1108 treaty suggests that Richard did collaborate with the emperor in the 1107–8 campaign. This does not necessar-

---

[46] See note 14 above.

[47] *Alexiade*, III, 101–4.

[48] Albert, *Hierosolymitana*, 651–52. Orderic, VI, 100–105.

[49] *Alexiade*, III, 138–39. Marquis de la Force, 'Les conseillers latins du basileus Alexis Comnene', *Byzantion* 11, 1936, 153–65.

[50] In his treatment of this campaign Yewdale, while acknowledging the testimony of western writers that some of the Normans were betraying their commander, rejects the possibility mainly on the grounds that Anna Comnena makes no reference to it. Yewdale, *Bohemond*, 120–21. But he did not notice or take into account the presence of the Norman leaders in the imperial party at the signing of the treaty.

ily prove that he did so because of an earlier secret agreement with the emperor since he could honestly have believe that Bohemond's tactics were disastrous and had to be stopped. But it does leave open the possibility that Richard betrayed his cousin and lord out of base, personal motives which had nothing to do with the Macedonian campaign. If so Bohemond's reaction upon learning of it can only be imagined.

After the peace treaty of September 1108 Bohemond sailed back to Italy a broken man and never returned to resume his rule in Antioch, dying in his homeland in 1111. Richard, on the other hand, must have gone back without delay for before the end of the year Count Baldwin, freed from his own captivity, came to reclaim his county of Edessa. It was on this occasion that the anonymous Syriac chronicler reported bitterly that Richard, having gathered together everything he had accumulated during his rule there, went to his own country, Marash. This is the first surviving indication that Richard was lord of Marash and although it dates from 1108, the wording makes clear his lordship there had already been established. Nothing in contemporary sources gives the slightest hint as to when and how he acquired Marash, but Richard's close ties to Bohemond make it most plausible that he received that lordship from his cousin in return for his loyalty and service in the earlier years of the crusade. Richard's acquisition of Marash ushers in the last phase of his career, a phase which lasted only four to six years and about which the surviving sources give very little information. Yet their very silence probably means that the exciting and adventurous times of the preceding years had now come to an end and that Richard had settled down to the more routine tasks of administering and defending his frontier lordship in Armenian Cilicia. Bohemond's departure from the scene after 1108 deprived him of the internationally famous patron in whose service he had gained entry into royal and imperial courts of both friend and foe. Not that governing Marash would have been dull and monotonous. Its geographical location as the most northerly of all the crusader lordships in the East left Marash exposed and highly vulnerable to three different Turkish emirates in the west, north, and east, and life was dangerous in that town.[51] The date and manner of Richard's death are unknown though it is quite possible that he was the unnamed lord of Marash killed by a great earthquake of 1114 which destroyed the town and wiped out its population.[52] The fact that no contemporary writer mentions his death or place of burial certainly shows that as the lord of a single crusader state in the far away north he no longer commanded the attention he had as Bohemond's personal envoy and second-in-command.[53] Still in his last years Richard must have been able to look back with satisfaction on his life and accomplishments in the East. He

[51] For a more detailed treatment of Marash and Richard's rule there see G. Beech, 'The Crusader Lordship of Marash in Armenian Cilicia 1103–49', *New Directions in Crusade Studies. Proceedings of the Third International Conference of the Society for the Study of the Crusades and the Latin East*, forthcoming.
[52] *Galterii Cancellarii Antiocheni. Bella Antiochena*, RHC, OCC., III, 83–4.
[53] Many of the members of the Hauteville family were buried in the south Italian abbey, La Trinità di Venosa. The otherwise unidentified *Riccardus comes* listed as a benefactor at the end of the abbey's martyrology may have been Richard of the Principate. *Il 'libro del capitolo' del monastero della SS Trinità de Venosa* (Cod. Cass. 334). *Una testimonianza del Mezzogiorno normanno*, ed. H. Houben, (Università degli Studi di Lecce. Dipartemento de Scienze Storiche e Sociale. Materiali e Documenti, I, Lecce 1984), 111–12, 139.

had acquired a substantial lordship of his own, though our ignorance of the family origins of the next lord of Marash makes it impossible to learn whether he had established an hereditary claim to it and passed it to his heirs. Moreover two of his children advanced to high positions in the crusader world at the time of or after his death. His son Roger, named by Tancred, became a celebrated regent of Antioch from 1112–1119 and his daughter Maria married Count Joscelin I of Edessa as the latter's second wife.[54] In these respects Richard could rest secure that part at least of his family had made the transition from the Italian Principate of Salerno to the Crusader northeast.

His contemporaries who wrote about him give only a few hints about the kind of person Richard was. Guibert of Nogent, who apparently observed him at the French royal court, says he was a handsome man; otherwise we know nothing about his appearance.[55] The descriptions of him as a brave and noble warrior may be discounted as stereotypes but his position at the head of the crusaders troops in the skirmish in Mamistra in 1097 shows that he had no reluctance to fight.[56] He seems to have been impetuous and given to brash moves which he could later have regretted. This is certainly the spirit of his taunting remarks provoking Tancred to an unwise and disastrous attack against a numerically superior foe at Mamistra.[57] Matthew of Edessa criticizes him for exactly the same kind of hotheaded bravery in leading an attack against besieging Turks when he was count and commander of the Edessan army in 1105–6.[58] This trait would seem to be at variance with his having been a successful diplomat. As a ruler we know only that Syriac and Armenian writers are unanimous in condemning him as a ruthless and cruel count of Edessa who had no scruples about extorting money from the local population for personal gain.[59] His poignant plea to St Leonard for help against his captors, both Turks and Greeks, brings out quite conventional Christian beliefs.[60]

On the other hand his knowledge of Arabic leaves open the possibility that his interest extended beyond a purely practical ability to speak the language, as one sometimes sees in military people, to a broader curiosity about the Islamic world, its people and culture. Their reliance on Richard as soldier, commander, governor, and ambassador throughout the entire First Crusade shows that Tancred and above all Bohemond had the highest confidence in him as an able, loyal, and reliable relative and servant. Yet the possibility that he betrayed the latter in 1107–8 calls for caution in confirming this judgement. But of course the same reservations also apply to any attempt to come to any coherent picture of the man as a whole: too much is unknown.

The career of Richard of the Principate in the East offers a good illustration of the ways in which the crusades could transform the life of a nobleman in late eleventh-century Europe. Of those who chose to leave the security of their homelands and expose themselves to the adventures, perils, and uncertainties of those

54 Nicholson, *Tancred*, 225; Nicholson, *Joscelin I of Edessa*, 62.
55 *Gesta Dei*, 152.
56 See above notes 19 and 20.
57 See above notes 19 and 20.
58 See above note 42.
59 See above notes 39 and 41.
60 See above page 33.

expeditions, many died and lost everything save the salvation of their souls. Richard was one of those who succeeded and, I suspect, far beyond his fondest hopes when setting out. His is a classic example of the way in which the crusade offered the possibility of a new career to a nobleman whose elder brothers obstructed his rise to power on the family lands. In his case it came relatively late in life when, after perhaps fifteen years as a mature man, he had failed to acquire distinction on his own in Italy and might well already have begun to lose hope. Not that he had to rise through merit alone. Far from that, he had the good fortune to be a Hauteville and to start out as a close relative and trusted advisor of the man who became the most celebrated leader of the crusade and thereby carried Richard with him to the highest seats of power in the crusader political hierarchy. But he would not have maintained and improved that position had he not been an able and persevering man. Then, given this advantage and his own talents, what a life Richard led when he was in his forties! As a second in command he fought in most if not all campaigns in the First Crusade, was wounded at least once, and survived four separate imprisonments following capture in battle at the hands of three different foes, Greeks (twice), Turks, and his own fellow crusaders. In the meantime his cousin Bohemond employed him on a series of missions which took Richard back and forth between Europe and the East into royal courts of both friend and foe not to mention religious shrines. Then Richard began to put down roots in northern Syria, serving as a temporary count of Edessa before finally acquiring a lordship of his own in Cilicia where he ended his career. By definition crusading meant adventure but few men who took part in those expeditions can have had the range of experiences of Richard of Salerno.

NORMAN NAVAL ACTIVITY IN THE MEDITERRANEAN
c.1060–c.1108

Matthew Bennett

The sea was crucial to the creation and expansion of the Norman states of Sicily and southern Italy. Eighty years ago, Willy Cohn produced his History of the Norman-Sicilian fleet during the reigns of Roger I and Roger II (1060–1154).[1] This is a slim book. There is a paucity of evidence with which to answer the very questions which require answers. Forty years ago, Daniel Waley wrote a short article ' "Combined Operations" in Sicily AD 1060–1078', concerned largely with amphibious landings on the island, but also the creation of the 'Norman' fleets in general.[2] He too bemoans the limited information available to the historian and draws attention to the vexed question of horse-transportation by sea. Recent work by John Pryor, has made it possible to look at the subject anew, which is why I have been emboldened to attempt it, although the evidence has been hardly, if at all, increased in volume.[3]

The sort of questions I set out to answer include the following. How did Robert and Roger d'Hauteville create their navies? Who provided the ships, in what numbers and what types. Who crewed and directed them? For how long were they obliged to serve? How was strategy conceived and how were tactics organised? How were the Normans able to defeat the established powers of

I must record my thanks to many people who helped me with this paper: Dr Graham Loud for advice on sources and bibliography and for his kindness in sending me copies of his work, both published and unpublished; Dr James Howard-Johnston for talking through the Byzantine sources, and especially Anna Comnena, with me; Dr Jonathan Shepard for further Byzantine insights; Prof. Rosalind Hill; Prof. Jonathan Riley-Smith; Prof. Donald Matthew; and at RMAS, Mr Andrew Orgill, Chief Librarian, Mr Brian Jones, Director of Studies, for allowing me the time and financial assistance to attend the conference at Palermo, and finally all my friends and colleagues of the War Discussion Group.

[1] Willy Cohn, *Die Geschichte der normannisch-sicilischen Flotte unter der Regierung Rogers I und Rogers II (1060–1154)*, Breslau 1910, 104 pp. A bare dozen pages deal with financing the fleet and obligations of service, 74–87.

[2] D.P. Waley, ' "Combined Operations" in Sicily, A.D. 1060–78', *Papers of the British School at Rome* xxii, 1954, 118–125. H. Ahrweiler, *Byzance et la Mer*, Paris 1966, 124 and Appendix IV, 442, draws attention to the refusal of Calabrians to serve in Byzantine fleets. This opposition may have been connected with the still insecurely dated revolts of the first two decades of the eleventh century, and may even have extended to the destruction of vessels. This evidence suggests on the one hand that there was a tradition of naval service for the Normans to inherit, but on the other hand that it may have been of little value.

[3] John H. Pryor, *Geography, technology, and war: Studies in the maritime history of the Mediterranean, 649–1571*, Past and Present Publications, CUP 1988. Donald Matthew, *The Norman Kingdom of Sicily*, CUP 1992, appeared too late for inclusion in this paper. Most of the evidence cited comes from the mid twelfth century, or later. See, however, the valuable insights in Ch. 9, 'The kingdom's defences and its enemies' esp. 260–62, and 'fleets' *passim*.

Muslim Sicily and Africa, of Byzantium and its ally Venice, within a few decades of taking to the sea? For there should be no illusions that the Normans (by which I mean all the 'Transalpini' recognisable as Franks to the native inhabitants of the area) came south with the sea in their blood, ready to go a-viking as their Scandinavian ancestors had a century-and-a-half earlier![4] But their leaders must have had an overall, grand strategic vision, combined perhaps with an empirical pragmatism, in order to attempt and achieve as much as they did. And it is to the vision of the Mediterranean as I believe it was conceived by medieval rulers that I now turn.

The Mediterranean sea is a fascinating point of juncture. It lies between two great land masses to north and south and it points (if that is the right word) to the east. At least that is how medieval man saw it. Looking at a modern projection with east at the top helps to show that medieval world-view is not as strange as it may first appear. For example, the Hereford *mappa mundi* has the conventional tripartite division of the world with the Mediterranean as a finger pointing to Jerusalem, its navel. Ranulph Higden's map is even more abstract; but both stress the role of the peninsulas and islands in forming stepping stones toward the east, and towards the Holy Land.[5] The Italian peninsula played a crucial role in linking both shores of the sea. This was made even more significant because it cut across a line of political and ideological fracture, a line which had run roughly through the middle of the sea for the previous two centuries.

This line had shifted north-south depending upon the strength of the Christian-Muslim power blocs. The tenth century had seen a Byzantine revival and re-covery of the islands of Crete (961) and Cyprus (965). Under Basil II the Italian Catepanate had been established and even after his death the momentum still took Byzantine forces to Sicily in 1038-41, although without final success.[6] The Muslim response was limited before the upsurge of Almoravid power in the late eleventh century and this was largely restricted to the Maghrib. For as Fatimid authority weakened and fractured it left a string of *taifur* states from Spain to Tripoli. This increased the crucial strategic importance of Sicily as the island formed the jumping-off point for expansion to Africa and the western Mediterranean. Similarly, southern Italy gave access to the Adriatic and northern

---

[4] On the 'Norman-ness' of the Franks in southern Italy see: G.A. Loud, 'The "Gens Normanno-rum" – Myth or Reality?' *ante* iv, 1982, 105–116, 204–209 and the work of Leon-Robert Ménager, notably 'Inventaire des familles normandes et franques emigrées en Italie méridionale et en Sicile (XIe et XIIe siècles)' in *Roberto il Guiscardo et il suo tempo*, Centro di studi normanno-svevi Universita' degli studi di Bari, Fonti e studi del *Corpus membranarum italicarum* (Appendix) xi, Rome 1975, 261–390; and, for additions to this, *Hommes et institutions*, Variorum, London 1981, IV, 1–17. Waley, 118, talks of 'Vikings finding their sea-legs again'; while Cohn, 2, even wonders if 'the old Viking ships still crossed the ocean waves'.
[5] P.D.A. Harvey, *Medieval maps*, British Library, London 1991, 29 (Hereford) 34 (Ranulph Higden) and Ch.3. The 'strip-map' view of the Mediterranean is made explicit by a fifteenth-century 'pocket-sized' *portolan*, (30 x 15cm) designed to be rolled around a wooden handle, made by Giovanni Battista Cavallini in 1456, displayed in the National Maritime Museum's recent 'Pirates' exhibition (Ref. NMM G230. 1/3 12/02).
[6] Arnold Toynbee, *Constantine Porphyrogenitus and his World*, London 1973, Ch.7, 'The Navy', 323–345 esp. 343ff. Pryor, *Geography*, 104–111. F. Chalandon, *Histoire de la Domination nor-mande en Italie et en Sicile*, Burt Franklin Research & Source Works Series 6 (reprint), New York 1960, 88ff. See also: John H. Pryor, 'Transportation of horses during the era of the Crusades eighth century to 1285, Part I: To c.1225', *Mariners' Mirror* 70, 1984, 9–27.

Greece, the Ionian Sea, and also potentially to the Aegean and the Levant. With the appearance of aggressive Latin Christian forces in the area – to whit the Normans – defensive weakness was to be ruthlessly exploited. Sea power was crucial to the balance of power in the region, so it was not surprising that they seized upon this tool and made it work for them.

It is important to recognise that contemporaries saw the sea not as a barrier but as a bridge between land masses. Malaterra has a flowery description of Robert Guiscard's first expedition to Dyrrachium in 1081, which: 'Per liquidum pontum classis conflatur Ydrontum' (III, 14).[7] A calm sea enables the transport of sizeable amounts of men and materiél. Not that it was as easy as all that, of course. The sea was still a doubtful passage, as I shall go on to explain. I have been greatly aided in my understanding of the physical realities of sailing in the Mediterranean by the innovative work of Dr John Pryor. His publications have brought the essential ground rules of sea travel into a new and clearer focus, and it is worth considering the lessons he draws.

The first concerns the prevailing winds and currents of the sea and their implications for naval strategy. During the sailing season – generally April to October – prevailing winds are north, north-west funnelling out of the mountain ranges on the northern shore and so favouring north-to-south and west-to-east passages. Those in the opposite directions are correspondingly more difficult. The southern coast of the Mediterranean also forms a dangerous lee shore; hard to leave and risky to approach. This gave the Christian powers a notable strategic advantage. The other factor – the current – runs anti-clockwise around the coast-line, commonly two or three knots in strength but faster in the narrows. Sailors used the current to help them travel against the wind. As a result the main sailing routes were in the northern third of the sea and usually close to the coast. Intelligent use of these climatic factors could be put to good use in naval strategy. For example, the convergence of wind and current on the western side of the Adriatic and their opposition on the eastern shore, aided Norman invasion attempts on Byzantine territories.[8]

What are the sources available for this study? Unfortunately, they are essentially narrative in nature. Now, this was not my intention when I set out. I had hoped for some documentary support to the chronicles, but this has been hard to obtain. Charters, on the whole do not concern themselves with the sea but are grounded in territorial concerns. Cohn's thin haul should have warned me, perhaps. Furthermore, I found little evidence of recent documentary or archaeological research in British libraries (although this does not mean that it is not being done, merely that it is not reaching our shores, or that it takes a long time to do so). So my sources are largely restricted to the following list. But I have attempted some *Quellenkritik* as it seems to me that it would be unwise to take what they say too much at face value.

Geoffrey Malaterra's *De rebus gestis Rogerii Calabriae et Sicilae Comitis* is essentially a celebration of the Hautevilles's success story, with an emphasis on Roger Great Count. There is more than a hint of a calculated contrast, I feel, between the older Guiscard and impetuous, fiery Roger, so that the latter

---

7 Geoffrey Malaterra, *De rebus gestis Rogerii Calabriae et Sicilae comitis et Roberti Guiscardi ducis fratris eius*, ed. E. Pontieri in RIS², V, I, n.d. Bologna, 66.
8 Pryor, *Geography*, Ch. 1, 'The sea', 12–24, also 89–90, 93–94.

represents youth to Robert's older, slower counsels. The *Gesta Roberti Wiscardi* of William of Apulia is a panegyric of the duke, dedicated to his son and successor on the mainland, Roger Borsa. Needless to say, its format as poem in classical hexameters also affects the information it presents.[9]

The third main source comes from outside the Norman ambit, in that Anna Comnena's *Alexiad* is also a panegyric, this time of her father, Alexius I. In many ways it is the most detailed account, for Guiscard and his redoubtable son Bohemond were Alexius's most dangerous opponents for over three decades between them. The Normans are portrayed by Anna as the classic barbarian stereotype: physically impressive and brave but prey to cupidity and faithlessness. She draws upon a long tradition in showing how Alexius defeats all his barbarian foes to justify his role as *basileus*. She is also attracted to the exotic and the extravagant anecdote rather than being concerned with chronological detail. This may be due to the fact that she was writing between fifty and sixty years after the events in question. For while she may have felt herself to be a player, in the form of her beloved father at least, they took place either before her birth or when she was still very young.[10]

Against this it can be said that she was well-informed. First, she could draw upon eyewitness accounts. In addition to her father's relation of the events she quotes informants from the Latin side, some of whom were undoubtedly Normans who swapped paymaster after Guiscard's death. Secondly, she had to hand the notes and text of Nicephoros Bryennios, her husband. He had written four books of history himself, and until his death in 1138/39 had been the intended author of the work in praise of Alexius. Anna, who was as devoted to him as to her father, took up the responsibility in the decade after Bryennios's death. Dr James Howard-Johnston, who has studied both authors, considers that several passages in the *Alexiad*, are, on stylistic grounds, taken directly from Bryennios. Essentially, these are the ones which make sense in military, naval and strategic terms. Anna, the denizen of the court, not the battlefield, is frequently guilty of error and confusion in these matters, when writing on her own. She may also have had access to official archives.[11]

The final major work is that of Amatus of Montecassino, or rather, as he should

---

[9] M. Mathieu, ed., *Guillaume de Pouille: La Geste de Robert Guiscard*, Istituto Siciliano di Studi Bizantini e Neoellenici, Palermo 1961 (henceforth WAp).

[10] *Alexiad*, most recent ed. P. Gauthier, *Corpus Fontium Historiae Byzantinae*, 1987; page reference will be made to the translation of E.R.A. Sewter, *The Alexiad of Anna Comnena*, Penguin Classics 1969. Recent assessments of her work include: J. Chrysostimides, 'A Byzantine Historian: Anna Comnena' in D.O. Morgan, ed., *Medieval History Writing in the Christian and Islamic World*, London 1982, 30–46; J. France, 'Anna Comnena, the Alexiad and the First Crusade' in *Reading Medieval Studies*, x, 1984, 20–38.

[11] See J. Shepard, 'When Greek meets Greek: Alexius Comnenus and Bohemond in 1097–98' in *Byzantine and Modern Greek Studies*, xii, 1988, 185–277, esp. 186 and n.4, and 195 (emphasising the role of the Italo-Norman Peter of Alifa). Two speakers at the Belfast International Byzantine Colloquia 2: 'Alexios Komnenos', reported in the *Bulletin of British Byzantine Studies*, 16, 1990, have also analysed Anna's sources. J. Howard-Johnston's unpublished paper, which is summarised on pages 62–3, stresses the important role of her husband, Nikephoros Bryennios, in providing material for the *Alexiad*. G.A. Loud's contribution has been published as: 'Anna Komnena and her Sources for the Normans of Southern Italy' in *Church and Chronicle in the Middle Ages. Essays presented to John Taylor*, edd. G.A. Loud and I.N. Wood, London 1991, 41–57.

be entitled, Aimé.[12] After all, the work only survives as a fourteenth century translation into Italianate French. Commentators seem happy that this was based upon an original Latin work, and to assume that other Latin sources drew upon it. I remain to be convinced that what we have is a pristine translation from a single source, whatever the translator's glosses may say (but that is material for another paper). For now, it must be sufficient to stress that we possess only a vernacular prose history, with all that that implies. Style has certainly affected content on occasion; there are examples of formulaic expression and anecdotes typical of the vernacular tradition which fit uneasily with Aimé's supposed Latin original.[13]

To turn to a study of the events; a brief narrative will serve to highlight the importance of ports in the Norman expansion.[14] Robert Guiscard had arrived in Italy about 1046, and was soon supporting himself as a bandit from his castle at S. Marco Argentano, in central Calabria. He came to prominence following the assassinations of Drogo d'Hauteville in 1051 and Gaimar in 1052. The Normans then united in the face of a combined papal-imperial threat. They won a signal victory at Civitate on 17 June 1053. This reinforced Guiscard's authority and saw him dictating terms (as the pope's most humble vassal) in Rome the following year. Some dim outlines of his strategy of aggrandisement may by now be discerned.

He had seized control of Otranto, Minervino and Gallipoli and by 1055, with the death of Duke Humphrey, was the most powerful man in the region. He was reinforced by the arrival of his younger brother Roger in 1057, though they quarrelled and Roger fled to the court of William of the Principate (another brother). This was typical of the relationship between the Hauteville kin, but it was these two brothers who were to carve out territorial lordships in the area, and they were to do it by deploying forces at sea as much as on land.

In August 1059, Robert Guiscard became a papal vassal at Melfi in a ceremony which recognised him as Duke of Apulia and Calabria and the future Duke of Sicily. He then took Cariati, Rossano and Gerace, and in 1060 Taranto and Brindisi (which was lost again in 1061 – see map, p. 46). These last ports were crucial to his naval ambitions. Meanwhile Reggio, still controlled by the Byzantines, was blockaded through the winter of 1059–60 although there is no mention of a fleet being involved. As soon as the town was forced to surrender Guiscard followed up with an immediate reconnaissance to Sicily. He then had to turn and deal with a rebellion in 1060, which delayed a follow-up campaign. But, in mid-February 1061, on the invitation of the Muslim ruler Ibn Timnah to intervene

[12] *Amatus.* For the most recent historiography of the western sources see: J. France, 'The occasion of the coming of the Normans to southern Italy', *Journal of Medieval History*, xvii, 1991, 185–205.

[13] Cf. G.A. Loud, 'The *Gens Normannorum* – Myth or Reality?', *ante* iv, 1982, 104–16 esp. 105, 107.

[14] The following abbreviated narrative is intended to highlight Robert and Roger d'Hauteville's strategy of capturing and using ports. This may also be followed by reference to the accompanying map. Chalandon, *Domination normande*, is still most valuable for narrative and this can be supplemented by J.J. Norwich, *The Normans in the South*, London 1967. Guiscard's difficulties in maintaining his authority as he expanded his territories are well illustrated by W.B. McQueen, 'Relations between the Normans and Byzantium 1071–1112', *Byzantion* lvi, 1986, 427–76, esp. 434–35. I do not deal with Norman expansion south or west of Sicily, for which see: David Abulafia, 'The Norman Kingdom of Africa and the Norman Expeditions to Majorca and the Muslim Mediterranean', *ante* xii, 1990, 26–49.

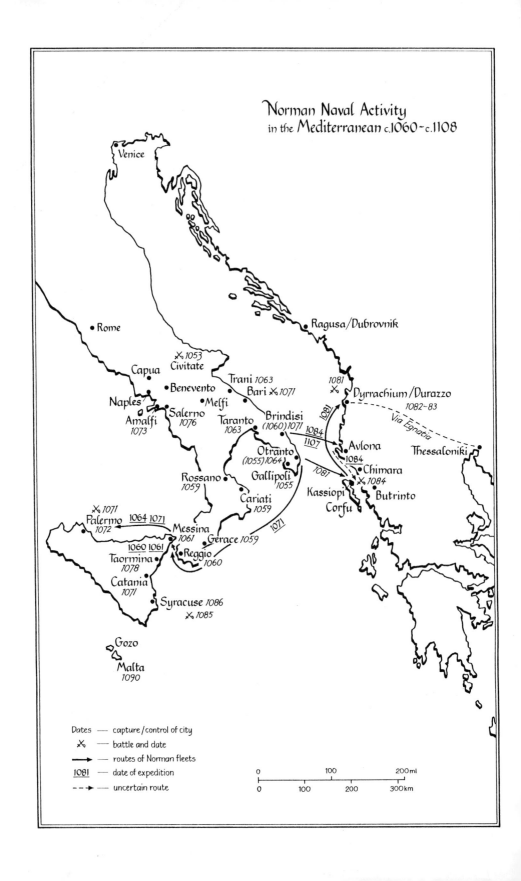

Norman Naval Activity
in the Mediterranean c.1060–c.1108

Venice

Rome

Ragusa/Dubrovnik

✗ 1053
Civitate
Capua

Trani 1063
Benevento   Bari ✗ 1071

1081
✗
Dyrrachium/Durazzo
1082–83

Naples   Melfi
Amalfi   Salerno   Taranto   Brindisi
1073   1076   1063   (1060) 1071

1084
1107

Via Egnatia

Otranto
(1055) 1064

Avlona
1084

Thessaloniki

Rossano
1059

Gallipoli
1055

1081

Chimara
✗ 1084

Cariati
1059

Kassiopi
Corfu

Butrinto

✗ 1071
Palermo   1064 1071
1072   Messina
1061
1060 1061   Gerace 1059
Taormina   Reggio
1078   1060

1071

Catania
1071

Syracuse 1086
✗ 1085

Gozo

Malta
1090

Dates ——— capture/control of city
✗ ——— battle and date
——➤ ——— routes of Norman fleets
1081 ——— date of expedition
--➤ ——— uncertain route

0   100   200 ml
0   100   200   300 km

in a dispute, Roger took the initiative. Once more this was a flying visit which was almost disastrous and ended in the Normans being chased back to Reggio after nearly becoming trapped outside Messina. Roger returned in May. This time he was successful in capturing Messina and so beginning the conquest of Sicily. In fact, this was not easily achieved. There was continual conflict between the Hautevilles and their vassals, and a Byzantine counter-attack, all of which served to delay its achievement. There was a siege of Palermo in 1064 – the city was the key to Muslim control of the island – but it was unsuccessful.

Also, Guiscard soon had his attention directed elsewhere. In early 1068, a Byzantine palace revolution provided him with new opportunities. Romanus Diogenes, the new emperor, left Italy to its own devices while he concentrated on the Turkish threat in Anatolia. Mopping up rebellious vassals Robert began a siege of Bari. The city was the centre of the surviving Byzantine administration in Italy – very well fortified and guarded by sea on three sides. It needed a naval blockade to take it after a siege lasting from 5 August 1068 to 16 April 1071, which included several naval actions. This was the turning point in the creation of an effective navy for Guiscard.

His new confidence at sea was shown by his immediate move to Sicily. By the end of July his fleet was at Reggio; then Catania was surprised, then on to Palermo (the scene of the failed siege seven years before). Again the fleet was decisive, defeating a relief force from Africa and blockading the defenders into starvation. Palermo fell in January 1072. In 1073 Amalfi placed itself under Robert Guiscard's protection, providing yet another source of ships. In summer 1076 Salerno was besieged. A six month siege was concluded by 13 December 1076 with the capture of the most important east-coast town south of Rome. Robert supported Richard of Capua in an unsuccessful siege of Naples, and at the end of 1077 attacked Benevento. The town was papal territory and this did produce the political problem of excommunication in March 1078, which was promptly followed by the revolt of Guiscard's territories.[15] After this was put down, reconcilation with the pope was achieved at Ceprano on 29 June 1080. Now Guiscard could afford to look elsewhere.

So in 1081 Robert's thoughts turned to Byzantine territories. There had been an attempted marriage alliance with Emperor Michael VII (or rather his son) since 1073. Guiscard had sent his daughter Helena to Constantinople in 1074, but Michael VII was deposed in 1078, leaving the girl languishing in a nunnery. This was used as a *casus belli* with a pseudo-Michael as the puppet claimant. In May 1081, Guiscard attacked Durazzo. The siege included several naval battles and a blockade. The city fell in February 1082, though Guiscard's involvement in Apulia and Rome until 1084 led to a recovery by the Byzantines who recaptured Durazzo and Corfu. A successful counter-attack by the Normans ended with his death on 17 July 1085. Yet that year was the most successful for the Normans at sea. It saw Roger besieging Syracuse and defeating a Muslim fleet on 25 May 1085. The conquest of the city was the end of the line for Muslim resistance (though the last places, Butera (1088) and Noto (1091), were still to fall). Roger's 1091 expedition to Malta led to that island (and Gozo) falling easily.

I want to leave the chronological survey there except for two last points.

---

[15] For Guiscard's 're-excommunication', see Norwich, 215.

During the First Crusade ships from Calabria transported the Norman contingent across to northern Greece. Finally, there was Bohemond's 1107–8 pseudo-Crusade against Alexius, which also contains valuable descriptions of naval activity.

It is worthwhile summarising at this point. The essential strategy of Robert and Roger (= the Normans) was based on a combined land and sea approach. The policy of capturing important ports after 1053 provided vessels for further expansion. Once a fleet was 'in being' – for however long – it was used to reduce places by blockade: Bari, Palermo, Salerno were taken in this way. So the fleet provided stepping-stone transport to new strategic objectives; though it should be stressed that the Normans still preferred to move by land. All the Norman sources stress the distinction between knights and sailors in sources, though they could and did move the knights' horses by sea. Sea battles were not sought initially, but the Norman fleets gradually proved superior to Muslim, Byzantine and Venetian fleets, and this in encounters perhaps even more subject to luck than land battles. The fleets suffered losses, of course, through battles, but more often through storm damage. How these losses were made good and how the captains and crews were kept motivated to serve is not clear, but of great significance in a continuing naval strategy. For the Normans could only succeed for as long as the Norman rulers could retain the trust and support of their Italian subjects: Lombard, Greek (and quite possibly Muslim) upon whom they relied for their naval forces.

What types of vessels made up the Norman fleets?[16] This is an area in which there has been some development since Waley wrote. Words used to describe ship-types are far from clearly distinguished. This is mainly because of the confusion of languages: Latin, Greek and Arabic and translations between them. Essentially the vessels fall into three main categories: war-ships (of varying sizes), supply vessels and horse transports. This last group caused Waley particular difficulty, but recent research has produced some interesting conclusions. The Norman dependence upon heavy cavalry meant that they needed such vessels if they were to deliver their battle-winning troops to the battlefield.

The usual fighting-ship was the dromon, a two-banked vessel of 25 oars a side and two or three masts, some 40m long by 5.5m wide. She could vary in size, as crew numbers indicate. The most detailed information comes from Byzantine sources, Leo VI's *Taktika* (early tenth century) and Constantine Porphyrogenitus's *De Cerimoniis* of the mid-tenth century, and there is little reason to suspect that much had changed a hundred years later. Arnold Toynbee divides the Byzantine fleets of 949 into 'first-raters' with crews of 200 to 220 men (sometimes divided into 150 marines and 50 rowers, or 200 rowers, 50 marines), the true dromon, and 'second-raters' with around 110 to 150 in the crew. These are also called *khelandia*, which is the term always used by Arab sources of Byzantine vessels. John Pryor takes the *khelandion* (or *salandria* as it became in Latin sources) to mean a horse transport, but it does not seem to have that restricted meaning in Greek sources. Also, as Waley points out, the word *uscieri* in Italy and *huissiers* in France became the common description of such vessels since they

---

[16] Cohn's analysis of ship-types is still worth reading, *Geschichte der normannisch-sicilischen Flotte*, Ch. 4, 87–97.

had a door (or ramp) in their sides which could be let down to disembark the horses.[17] I shall return to these in a moment.

When Italo-Norman vessels are distinguished from the generic *naves* or *nefs* they are usually called 'triremes'! Is this anything but a conscious archaism when all evidence suggests that fighting-ships were two-banked?[18] Malaterra mentions *germundi*, which may be a corruption of the Greek *dromon* and hence a warship, or (more likely) the Arabic *djerma*, meaning a transport.[19] William of Apulia talks of *liburni*, which meant light galleys in the later Empire.[20] This may be valid for the eleventh century too, although again there is the risk that William is archaising or classicising his language. The emphasis upon a light type of galley may be reinforced by the frequency of the designation *cattus* or cat. This appears as *gath* in Aimé. The origin may lie in the Greek word *ghalaía* or cat-fish, describing a small, swift galley. It is not unlikely that the fleets of southern Italy were made up of such smaller, lighter vessels.[21] Certainly William of Apulia describes Venetian 'triremes' as towering over the Norman fleet off Corfu in 1084, and Anna Comnena suggests as much at Durazzo in 1081.[22] This may explain why the Normans found it so difficult, at first, to achieve victories over Greek or Venetian fleets. Norman sources do not state that any attempt was made to build bigger vessels to compensate for this disparity. But by 1113, when Princess Adela set out for the Holy Land, it seems that the Sicilian fleet did include vessels of dromon status since her flagship (and one other) had a complement of 250 crew and passengers.[23]

What of the horse transports? There can be no doubt that these were used in the attacks on Muslim Sicily. When George Maniakes took 300 to 500 Norman *equites* on his expedition of 1038 it is clear that their warhorses went with them.[24] In 1061, the Hautevilles also took *chevaliers* across the Straits of Messina. According to Aimé, 270 went in the first wave, on 13 ships, that is approximately 20 per vessel (the ships than returned to bring another 166). This has led Bernard Bachrach to speculate that either there were 20 on each transport and the copyist has slipped in making the resulting 260 ten more; or that the 20 stood in the main body of the ship with one in the prow.[25] There is nothing improbable about such numbers. Pryor estimates that tenth-century Byzantine horse-transports could carry 12 animals. There is solid evidence that the late twelfth-century *taride* (an Arabic word, they were called *busses* in the West) could carry 40 horses.[26] So, as

[17] Toynbee, *Constantine Porphyrogenitus*, 331–34; Ahrweiler, *Byzance et la Mer*, 408–18; Waley, 'Combined Operations', 119–21; Pryor, *Geography*, Ch. 2, 'The ships', esp. 57–59 and figs. 19 and 20.

[18] See J.S. Morrison and J.F. Coates, *The Athenian Trireme*, CUP 1986, *passim* and also Pryor, *Geography*, 66–7, for the word 'trireme' referring to the number of men per oar rather than three banks of oars.

[19] Malaterra, 32; Waley, 120.

[20] WAp, IV, 214–15, line 200; R.H. Dolley, 'The warships of the later Roman Empire', *Journal of Roman Studies*, xxxviii, 1948, 47–53.

[21] Toynbee, *Constantine Porphyrogenitus*, 332; Amatus, 234, 277; Waley, 120.

[22] WAp, IV, 212–13, lines 161–2; Anna, IV, ii, 137–8.

[23] Chalandon, i, 362; Cohn, *Geschichte*, 16, citing Albert of Aachen in *RHC* iv, 696–97.

[24] Pryor, 'Transportation', i, 12.

[25] Amatus, 235; B.S. Bachrach, 'On the Origins of William the Conqueror's Horse Transports', *Technology and Culture* xxvi, 1985, 505–531, esp. 527, n.54.

[26] Pryor, 'Transportation' i, 18.

part of a continuum, 20 is not an unreasonable number. Unfortunately, as we have already seen, 270 is not guaranteed as an accurate total. In fact, Malaterra gives different numbers: 150 in the first wave and 300 in the second (although, as Waley points out, the totals are very similar).[27]

Can we be sure that the Normans possessed specialised craft? For the second siege of Palermo in 1071, Guiscard raised some 60 ships, of various types.[28] Waley quotes Malaterra's reference to loading horses at Otranto. This involved lessening the gradient in order to make an easier descent to the sea; which Waley interprets as constructing a ramp. No detailed description of the operation exists for this period; but when we do have one, this implies backing the ships onto the beach. For the *tarida*, the classic form of horse transport which comes into view in the twelfth century, resembled a roll-on-roll off ferry in operation. It had twin stem-posts at its flat stern, containing one or two doors which dropped down to provide a ramp (rather like a modern landing craft). Hence it was suited by a gently shelving shoreline. This does not contradict Malaterra's description.[29]

Waley is dubious that such an outpost of empire as the Catepanate should possess horse-transports, which he considered were probably kept in a pool at Constantinople.[30] An alternative hypothesis, that the ship-type was widely dispersed throughout the Mediterranean by the mid eleventh century, cannot, to my knowledge, be disproved. One feature of the *tarida* (so some sources claim) was that it could deliver an armoured and mounted man straight onto the beach and ready for action. Robert de Clari provides a vivid picture of such a disembarkation at Constantinople in 1204:

> As soon as they reached the shore, the knights came out from the transports on their horses, for the transports were made in such a way that there was a door that could be opened and a bridge thrust out by which the knights could ride out onto the land, already mounted.[31]

Is this epic exaggeration? For it is exactly what Anna Comnena says of Guiscard's 1081 fleet:

> The ships numbered 150, and the soldiers, all told, came to 30,000, each carrying 200 men with armour and horses. The expedition was equipped thus because they would probably meet the enemy in full armour and on the beaches.[32]

The numbers are obviously exaggerated (she may be confusing the numbers with those crewing a *dromon*) but this need not invalidate her description of the Normans's intention. More worrying is the fact that Anna was writing in the

[27] Waley, 'Combined Operations', 122–23.
[28] Waley, 'Combined Operations', 123, n.28.
[29] Malaterra, 51, 'Toto junio et julio mense apud Ydrontum moratus, montem, quo facilius decensus ad mare – equos navibus introducens – fieret, rescindere facit.' Waley's impression of 'inadequate port installations', 122, should be set against the fact that wharfage was unusual in the Mediterranean at this time. Even that great entrepôt, thirteenth-century Acre, used lighters to load and unload vessels. I am grateful to Prof. J. Riley-Smith for this information.
[30] Waley, 'Combined Operations', 122; see Morrison and Coates, *Trireme*, for horse transportation as a tradition from the fifth century BC.
[31] P. Lauer, ed., *Robert de Clari. La Conquête de Constantinople*, CFMA, Paris 1924, 42.
[32] *Alexiad*, I, xvi, 69.

1130s and 1140s. Was she extrapolating from the western fleets that came in the wake of the First Crusade? For example, Fulcher of Chartres's description of the Venetian expedition of 1123–24, deals unequivocably with horse transportation.[33] So the problem remains unsolved, for lack of evidence. But given that the Normans did transport horses, it seems likely that they had the vessels to hand to do it.

Let us now turn to examine campaigns in detail. The first expedition in February 1060 was a reconnaissance force reckoned at 60 knights.[34] This probably indicates one or two ship-loads intended to do no more than land for a brief attack on Messina to pillage followed by a swift retreat to their vessel(s). It seems dangerously early in the year, but perhaps this was to avoid interception by Muslim ships? This supposition is reinforced by the fact that Roger chose the same month to land in the following year with 160 knights. They landed north of Messina, near Faro, and pillaged again, but bad weather prevented re-embarkation and they were trapped on the beach for three days before they were able to escape. Aimé says that there was a pursuit during which a ship and 40 men were lost.[35]

The need to capture Messina was made apparent by these expeditions. So Roger and Robert combined to provide invasion forces at S. Maria del Faro (just north of Reggio) in May. Aimé and Malaterra differ on troop movements, as we have seen. Aimé has 270 followed by 166; Malaterra 150 crossing at night to establish the bridgehead.[36] The importance of getting horses ashore under cover of darkness, or at least in the early dawn, is reinforced by Richard I's actions on Cyprus, as reported by Ambroise.[37] Clearly this was considered a tricky operation, leaving the animals vulnerable. Having secured a position by land, some five miles south of Messina, Roger sent back for 300 more troops. Both Aimé and Malaterra then have the ships sent back so that there should be no retreat (a common theme, as we shall see later). The Muslims were completely taken by surprise, and Messina fell almost without resistence. Guiscard followed with the rest of the troops, a total of up to 2,000, decisively defeating Muslim forces in battle.[38]

It is important to note that the Muslims had responded with naval forces, according to Aimé. He describes the Emir of Palermo sending 800 men to Messina supported by twenty-four ships called *gath* (meaning the light galley, or 'cat').[39] But Roger and Robert had reconnoitred the Straits of Messina in two galleys 'subtilissime et molt velocissime' (secretly and very quickly).[40] This must have enabled them to slip past the attempted blockade. But then, as we shall see in relation to the Adriatic expeditions, it was very difficult to intercept a fleet at sea. What happened to the unsuccessful Muslim covering force is unfortunately

---

[33] Pryor, 'Transportation', 14–15.

[34] Malaterra, 29.

[35] Amatus, 234. This may imply a ship's complement of 20 sailors and 20 knights, cf. footnotes 25 and 26 above.

[36] Amatus, 235–36; Malaterra, 32.

[37] Ambroise, *The Crusade of Richard the Lionheart*, trans. M.J. Hubert and J.L. La Monte, New York 1942, 88–9, lines 1,560–577.

[38] Malaterra, 32; Amatus, 236–43.

[39] Amatus, 234–5.

[40] Amatus, 235; Cohn misreads this as 11 ships, 93.

not clear. After all, such detailed insights into the difficulties and practicalities of sea transport, as we have seen, are pretty rare. Even more regrettable is that there is nothing on how the ships were raised or equipped. Aimé, with his epic brevity, is particularly unhelpful. So, for example, William the Conqueror 'prist son navie' in 1066, Guiscard's men 'appareillerent lor navie' or 'E puis assembla une grant compagnie de navie'.[41] What must also be watched out for is the easy formula. So, after landing in May 1061, 'Et puiz, quant il fu jor, li Normant se leverent et se adomerent de lor armes, et monterent sur lor chevaux'. Waley expresses surprise that the troops did not get off the beach quickly.[42] (It could be true, of course!) On the other hand, Aimé's handling of the siege of Palermo in 1064 is much more convincing. The brothers 'assemblast autre multitude de navie pour estreindre Palerme, que né par terre né par mer avoir ajutoire' – but an African Muslim fleet broke through and the siege was lifted.[43]

This was the turning point of Norman naval achievement, recognised by contemporary commentators (though perhaps not fully exploited by historians). Bari's peninsula site has already been referred to; this gave the fleet a major role. William of Apulia states that the ships were chained together to form a complete blockade and also to support siege engines. He provides no numbers.[44] The blockade was insufficient, for at an early stage the defenders broke out and destroyed the engines, and other initial actions against the Greeks were equally unsuccessful. When Byzantius, the Greek patriarch, set out for Constantinople with a plea for relief he was pursued by four Norman vessels. He got clean away and the chasing vessels suffered a disaster – two were sunk and two damaged in the pusuit. A Byzantine relief force was then able to fight its way into the blockaded harbour. A second attempt was defeated, but apparently more from the land than the sea.[45]

Guiscard's attempted diversionary attack on Brindisi by land and sea was also a failure. A Byzantine fleet under George Mabrikas drove off the Normans.[46] Returing to Bari, Robert called up Roger with the Sicilian fleet to his aid. The united fleets produced a significant change in outcome. The next Byzantine attempt at relief was commanded by Jocelin (an old enemy of Guiscard). His ships, packed with arms and supplies, attempted to creep into Bari by night, with the help of masthead lanterns. But he was attacked and decisively defeated, prompting William of Apulia's exclamation: 'Gens Normannorum navalis nescia belli / Hactenus, ut victrix rediit, spem principis auget.' (Bk III, lines 132–33). Matthieu's translation is: 'Les Normands jusque là ignorants de la guerre navale accrurent la confiance de leur prince en revenant victorieux.' I take it to mean that the Normans, previously unsuccessful at sea, gained the victory due to Guiscard's efforts (that is, in building up the fleet). It may also be significant that the combined Norman fleet was skilful enough to risk and win a night action. This suggests supreme confidence in their ability to fight at sea.[47]

---

[41] Amatus (fleet references) 11, 232, 275.
[42] Amatus, 236; Waley, 'Combined Operations', 124 n.35. This pre-battle formula is typical of the *chansons de geste*, but need not be understood literally.
[43] Amatus, 246; Malaterra, 46.
[44] WAp, II, 160–61, lines 522–29.
[45] Amatus, 250.
[46] Chalandon, i, 188.
[47] Jocelin, lord of Molfetta had been a leading rebel against Guiscard between 1064 and 1067, see

Whatever may be the case, Robert was very pleased at the outcome and looked to future victories with the Normans. In fact, as Waley has pointed out, the fleet was made up of Calabrians, meaning largely Greek and Lombard sailors.[48] Any Normans presumably served as marines not mariners. When Bari fell in the following spring it was through subversion, as Guiscard exploited divisions within the Bariots' ranks – not through military or naval action. There had been a Norman party within the walls, but it is still a little surprising that William of Apulia stresses the Bariots' role in the next expedition against Palermo, which followed soon after the city's fall.[49]

Guiscard's fleet which went to Sicily is numbered by several sources at 50 ships or more. Aimé gives it as 40 galleys and 10 'cats', Lupus Protospatharius at 58 in total. It should be stressed that this represents a considerable naval force, over four times larger than both brothers had been able to deploy only twelve years earlier. The crews included Normans, Calabrians, Bariots and, according to William of Apulia 'captive Greeks' – a rare insight into how they were made up and one which suggests that not all the sailors were enthusiastic supporters of the Norman cause.[50]

The combined force outside Palermo is not given, but it is significant that it achieved a victory over the Muslim relief force. This came from Africa and its vessels were protected against stones and arrows by felt coverings. We are told the battle was hard but there are no actual details of the fighting. Eventually the Muslims fled for cover into the port of Palermo, seeking protection behind its chain. But the victorious Normans pursued them and broke through the chain, capturing some vessels and burning the rest. The victory made possible a closer blockade of the city. The fleet may have played an important role in the attack on the lower town (the Kalsa). After a series of assaults the final submission of Palermo took place on 10 January 1072.[51] This did not end naval activity in Sicilian waters. In 1085, Roger engaged an African fleet off Syracuse and defeated it. By this time the Normans were accustomed to victory at sea, although their toughest opponents – the Venetians – had proved very difficult to overcome.

Robert Guiscard's ambitions across the Adriatic, which extended as far as the imperial throne itself, drew him to attack Durazzo in 1081. It is impossible to be sure of the overall size of his fleet. William of Apulia assures us that he had transport ships brought over from the Dalmatian coast, and that Guiscard had 50 *liburni* under his command. Anna's 150 vessels may be exaggeration, as we have seen (although Malaterra concurs for the 1084–85 attempt). But then, if we believe Malaterra's 1,300 knights, we have around 60 horse transports already.[52] Bohemond crossed first, with an advance guard of 15 vessels, to Avlona to land a force of knights to raid and subject the coastline. The main force either left Brindisi (Anna) or Otranto (William) and sailed to Corfu to capture the island and

W.B. McQueen, 'Relations', 434. WAp, 170–71, states that Jocelin and his vessel were captured while another Byzantine ship was sunk; Amatus, 251–54, puts Jocelin's fleet at twenty strong, with nine ships falling into Norman hands.

[48] See Waley, 'Combined Operations', 121, who points out that both fleets and sailors were 'Byzantine' while the soldiers on board 'were Normans on either side'.

[49] WAp, III, 172–75; see also Matthieu's Commentary, 298, notes to lines 149–57; Amatus, 277.

[50] WAp, III, 176–77, lines 235–36.

[51] WAp, III, 176–83.

[52] WAp, IV, 210–11, 214–15; *Alexiad*, I, xvi, 69; Malaterra, 71.

from there coasted northwards, meeting Bohemond at Butrinto.[53] Here the army was divided, half going by land (the cavalry and light troops)and half by sea. We have seen that using the current to carry a fleet up from the south was a standard ploy. Unfortunately for the the Normans their fleet was badly damaged off Cape Glossa, just to the south of their goal, Durazzo, causing a great loss of supplies.[54]

The vessels straggled into position to blockade the town and the siege began on 17 June (according to Anna whose chronology is very suspect and otherwise confused with 1084/85).[55] The absence of a Byzantine fleet is striking. Hélène Ahrweiler has explained why Alexius found himself defenceless at sea. He was forced to beg aid from the Venetians, who sold their services dear, as is confirmed by the Chrysobull of 1082.[56] But the arrival of their fleet in late July or August was to transform the strategic situation and they soon proved their worth. Tactics will be examined in detail later, but suffice to say that Venetians had several battle-winning devices. One was Greek Fire, mentioned by Malaterra, though surprisingly not by Anna; another was the use of masthead towers or ship's boats from which they could bombard the Norman ships with wooden bombs spiked with nails; finally there was the 'sea harbour' in which the larger ships were linked by chains.[57] Their attack soon overwhelmed the lighter Norman craft. Whether this took three encounters or one assault which drove the Normans back into their trenches is uncertain. But William of Apulia describes the Norman fleet's cables being cut and their ships driven onto the shore. All sources agree that the Norman naval defeat had important political effects, in that it encouraged the defection of coastal and island bases away from Guiscard.[58]

It was not naval power but military superiority that saved the Normans, however. In a battle outside Durazzo on 17 October, Alexius was driven off in disorder.[59] Although the city did not fall immediately, its citizens were unable to depend upon a Byzantine rescue attempt. After a nine month siege the city fell through treachery on 21 February 1082.[60] Although the Venetians were masters of the sea they were unable to influence events on land further, and their fleet disappears from the narrative. An interesting question is what happened to the Norman fleet after its defeat in the early autumn? Guiscard is described as burning the fleet (or just its transports acording to Anna) in order to make his men fight more desperately. Is this true or just a topos?[61] How did the ships' masters feel about such a tactic? How could a fleet be rebuilt after such a blow? For Guiscard needed a fleet only two years later. He was drawn back to Italy leaving

[53] *Alexiad*, III, xii, 133.

[54] WAp, IV, 216–217; *Alexiad* III, xii, 132.

[55] Dr J. Howard-Johnston has expressed the view in conversation that Anna 'sprinkled' her description of the 1081–82 campaign with events from 1084–85. I am grateful for his advice on her often confusing chronology.

[56] Ahrweiler, *Byzance et la Mer*, 180, 181 and n.5. No text survives for 1082, but the terms have been reconstructed from Manuel I's Chrysobull of 1148.

[57] In other respects Malaterra, 73, and *Alexiad*, IV, ii, 138, are very close, save for the omission of Greek Fire from Anna's account. Only Anna describes the 'sea harbour'.

[58] WAp, IV, 220–221, lines 313–16; *Alexiad*, IV, ii, 138–39; Malaterra, 72–3.

[59] The most detailed account of the land-battle is found in the *Alexiad*, IV, vi–viii, 145–53; WAp, IV, 224–25 states that the sailors were useless in this combat and took flight, lines 373–74; Malaterra, 73–4.

[60] WAp, IV, 228–29, Commentary 324.

[61] Malaterra has all the ships burnt, 73; *Alexiad*, IV, v, 145, has the transports scuppered and

Bohemond to exploit the situation in Greece. But, despite victories in land battles, Bohemond lost the war. Durazzo was recaptured by a Greek and Venetian fleet in the summer of 1083.[62]

So in 1084 Robert launched an even bigger expedition. According to William of Apulia, a ship fleet 120 strong was gathered at Taranto in September. This must represent a considerable force drawn from all over Guiscard's territories in southern Italy, although Dalmatian vessels may also have made a significant contribution. As it was late in the year, Otranto was considered an unsafe harbour. So despite the shorter passage from this port the crossing was made from Brindisi.[63] The season seems to have affected strategy since the Normans are described as being pinned for two months on the Adriatic coast near Butrinto. Eventually the fleet moved to Corfu to engage the Byzantine and Venetian fleets.[64]

Anna and William disagree as to the initial outcome, as she describes two Venetian victories, followed by their defeat through overconfidence. William gives some very detailed information about the battle (seemingly off Butrinto). The Venetians with nine large triremes and three Greek *khelandia* are attacked by three groups of five triremes each supported by many smaller craft. Although the enemy ships are taller the determined Norman attack uses concentrated archery against the crews and iron weights to sink the ships. The Greek ships are cut out and driven off leaving the nine Venetian ships isolated. Seven are sunk and two captured.[65] Anna has a conspiracy theory for the defeat. After the initial victories a renegade Venetian – Pietro Contarini – leads the Normans to attack them off Corfu, while they are riding high in the water, so that when the Venetians form their sea harbour the movement of marines on their decks leads to them overturning with huge loss. That is to say, 13,000 drowned, in comparison with 2,500 captured according to William of Apulia.[66] But Guiscard's death ended the campaign and turned victory into defeat.

Bohemond's expedition of 1107–1108, although a generation distant, forms a useful comparison to the previous campaigns. In fact, the First Crusade is worth a mention, not for Anna's well-known anecdote about the Frankish crossbow, but for interesting insights into the Byzantine guard fleet. In 1096, Anna describes a western, three-masted vessel of 200 rowers crossing straight to Chimara, but

---

baggage burnt. Professor Rosalind Hill suggests that perhaps only the ships' boats and lighters were destroyed.

[62] Matthieu, WAp, Commentary, 330, deals with the uncertain chronology of the recapture of Durazzo. The town was in Greek hands some time in the late summer or autumn of 1083, but it seems that the citadel was retained by the Normans until Guiscard's death (17 July 1085) when the Venetians and Almafitians handed it back to Alexius.

[63] WAp, V, 242–43; *Alexiad*, VI, v, 189, reverses the order, Malaterra, 81, has the muster at Otranto. G. Loud, 'Anna Komnena', 49, rationalises these differences. In fact, the size of a harbour, the direction which it opens to the sea (in relation to prevailing winds especially) and how well it is protected by land or artificial moles, are crucial. It is worth noting that both Taranto (the mustering point) and Brindisi (the port of embarkation) had very well protected inner harbours. See: G. Schmiedt, 'I porti italiani nell'alto medioevo' in *La navigazione mediterranea nell'alto medioevo* vol. 2, Settimane di studio, xxv, Spoleto, 1978, 129–254, esp. pls xxiv (Taranto); xxvii, fig. 1 (Otranto); xxx (Brindisi). The maps and charts of these ports (and many other places mentioned in this paper) are post-medieval but still instructive.

[64] WAp, V, 244–45; *Alexiad*, VI, v, 189.

[65] WAp, V, 245–46.

[66] *Alexiad*, VI, v, 189–90.

being intercepted by the Greek fleet. This stark contrast with 1081 is explained by Alexius's reconstruction of the Byzantine navy in 1091–92 to deal with the Turkish pirate Tzachas.[67] This was to be an important factor a decade later, too. Bohemond's fleet of 1107 is only described by Anna as being very strong, with no indication as to its overall numbers. The interesting point is the Byzantine reaction. Despite initially weak leadership the Greeks manage to control the seas. One fascinating detail is the mention of a map. The first Greek commander is unable to intercept enemy movements because he cannot predict where the Normans will land. So Anna describes her father drawing up a map showing the likely landing places, which is a valuable insight into both strategic thinking and cartographical competence at the time.[68]

In the event Bohemond's fleet is too strong to be opposed. But once it has landed the Greek and Venetian fleets resume control of the sea. There is evidently a much greater confidence and better organisation than at the beginning of Alexius's reign. This time there are no sea-battles, perhaps by Alexius' deliberate choice. As in 1084–85 the Normans are blockaded on the Adriatic coast. Bohemond is forced to burn his transports, as his father had done. But unlike Guiscard he could not achieve a victory on land. In the circumstances Bohemond was forced to sue for peace. His land strategy had failed for him as it had in 1082.

I shall conclude with a brief survey of the practicalities of naval wafare as they have emerged from my research. The first point to note is the seeming superiority of attack over defence (when an attacker can be clearly identified). This appears to be the case at Bari in 1068, Durazzo in 1081 and Corfu in 1084 . This contrasts with the usual outcome on land, where those in defensive positions tend to have an advantage. Perhaps it has to do with the extra mobility possible at sea, enabling an attacker to manoeuvre against an opponent's weak spot?

Secondly, technology was apparently of great significance. The size of vessels, with the Venetians having a decided advantage, was an important factor. Taller ships were more difficult to board, the principal form of attack in a period when the the beak had replaced the classical ram.[69] Also, a height advantage made it possible to hurl heavy weights through an opponent's bottom and sink her. Greek Fire gave the Byzantino-Venetian forces an advantage in 1081. It was also employed against the Pisans in 1099, but it is not recorded as being used extensively.[70]

Ships provide bases for siege towers at Bari and Durazzo (although without noticeable success). The 'masthead bases' (or 'fighting tops') of the Venetians described in 1081 seem to have been copied by the Normans in 1084. The ability to hurl such weights seems to have been crucial in actually sinking the enemy, but

---

[67] *Alexiad*, X, viii, 315–18; Ahrweiler, 189–97, ascribes this to the construction of three great fleets under Alexius, which apparently enabled him to defeat his enemies on all sides.

[68] *Alexiad*, XIII, vii, 414–15, Isaac Contostephanus is unable to prevent supplies reaching Bohemond once he has landed.

[69] The description of the sea-battle between Greeks and Crusaders in 1096 makes specific reference to boarding at the prow, which is where the dromon's beak locked-on to an enemy vessel, *Alexiad*, X, viii, 316.

[70] Greek Fire is described as being used on land in the defence of Durazzo on several occasions, *Alexiad*, IV, iv, 142 (1081), XIII, iii, 402–4, and at sea against the Pisans, XI, x, 360–2. Only Malaterra, 73, states that Venetians used it in 1081. It may be that the Greeks did not, in fact, divulge the secret of its composition to their allies.

there does not seem to be much evidence of shipboard artillery, rather the missiles are hand-held.[71] Bowmen seem to have provided the only long-range weaponry and their archery was of great importance. Ragusan and Dalmatian archers are mentioned as the Norman fleet's most effective response to the attacking Venetians in 1081. And in 1084 a heavy barrage of arrows from the Norman vessels was instrumental in defeating the Venetians.[72]

Tactical deployment was evidently also of significance. Anna describes the 'sea harbour' of the Venetians, which involved chaining their ships together. This seems to have worked extremely well in 1081. At first, I wondered if this was to give a more stable fighting platform, minimise the risk of sinking and provide mutual support. The problem with this idea is that its effectiveness is surely limited to defensive action. It was a formation that had its place in naval tactics, but it is difficult to see how a vast, unwieldy raft of ships could be made to manoeuvre offensively. In fact, I think Anna misunderstands the formation. It was probably intended for defence, and simply as a night-time naval camp. In the morning the ships would separate and act independently. This was probably the case in 1081, anyway.[73]

In 1084 the Venetians were either caught in their night-formation, or adopted it in the face of a surprise attack. It was countered by the Normans in 1084 by using three separate groups of ships to attack it at different points, perhaps luring the Venetian marines to one area of their circular defence and then attacking in another, as was sometimes done when assaulting a walled town. (This may explain Anna's strange story of the ships being capsized because all the sailors rushed to one side – a possible outcome for a single craft but surely not for linked vessels.)[74]

Finally there is the formation of Bohemond's fleet in 1107, an impregnable square headed by twelve 'corsairs', with flanking vessels and transports in the centre. This may be an invention of Anna. She seems to have taken great delight in describing such formations on land. It is very like Alexius's invincible phalanx with which he frustrates the Pechenegs and Turks. Alternatively, it may simply represent the normal convoy formation. This could only be maintained in calm weather, which Anna stresses prevailed on 9 October 1107. Either the strength of Bohemond's fleet, or its formation, or both, persuaded the Byzantine fleet commander, Landulf, to avoid action.[75]

In conclusion, there is still much to be said about Norman fleets. They were crucial to the expansion of the new states of southern Italy and Sicily. 'Norman' pragmatism and the drive of two great leaders – Robert and Roger d'Hauteville also played a crucial part. There was a momentum of conquest about the Franks in the Mediterranean, rather like that of an invading tribe. Once this became

---

[71] It is possible that cranes or derricks were used to swing the 'bombs' over enemy decks, but the missiles described by Anna in 1081 as only a cubit long must have been easily manhandled. *Alexiad*, IV, ii, 138.

[72] WAp, IV, 220, lines 303–4; V, 245, lines 165–6.

[73] *Alexiad*, IV, ii, 138; R.H. Dolley, 'Naval Tactics in the Heyday of the Byzantine Thassalocracy', *Atti del'VIIIe Congresso di Studi Byzantini* i, Rome 1953, 324–39, sees some sort of platform decking as linking the vessels, but this would have suffered from the same immobility.

[74] This at least is a rationalisation of William of Apulia's and Anna's accounts.

[75] *Alexiad*, XII, ix, 392.

centrally directed it was all but unstoppable. And it does seem to have been controlled. Surprisingly there is no mention of Norman pirates, considering their usual propensity for free-enterprise activity! Piracy flourished in the contested seas of the late eleventh and early twelfth century. If the Franks of southern Italy and Sicily did not take up this career, as even the Turks did, it says much for the monopoly of naval skills in the native populations of Apulia, Calabria and Sicily. Fleets were a tool for the Normans, not a vocation, which may help to explain why information about their activities is relatively so limited.

Mimo Giullaresco e Satira del Villano
Nel *De Clericis et Rustico*

Armando Bisanti

La considerazione dell'ibridismo tipologico che costituisce la nota caratterizzante del *corpus* di 'commedie elegiache' latine del XII e del XIII secolo pubblicate oltre sessant'anni fa sotto la direzione di Gustave Cohen,[1] e più di recente sotto quella di Ferruccio Bertini,[2] è il dato preliminare dal quale bisogna partire per ogni indagine (globale o specifica) sul fenomeno della 'commedia elegiaca' che non voglia restare ad un livello puramente espositivo e/o descrittivo, ma che si proponga di cogliere le peculiarità di un genere fluttuante, che appunto in virtù di queste fluttuazioni è difficilmente riconducibile ad un modulo unitario. Un'*impasse* critica ed interpretativa che prende le mosse già agli albori delle indagini sul sorgere e l'affermarsi della commedia medievale, e che si riflette nelle oscillazioni definitorie e terminologiche cui essa è stata sottoposta, dal Müllenbach[3] al Manitius,[4] dal Creizenach[5] al Cloetta,[6] e di lì fino ai giorni nostri, soprattutto per merito delle ricerche del Bertini.[7] Occorreva però l'acume critico di Gustavo

---

[1] *La 'Comédie' latine en France au XIIe siècle. Textes Publiés sous la direction et avec une introduction de* Gustave Cohen, Paris 1931, 2 voll.

[2] *Commedie latine del XII e XIII secolo*, Genova 1976–1986, 5 voll. Il sesto ed ultimo volume della serie, almeno al momento in cui scrivo, non è ancora stato pubblicato.

[3] E. Müllenbach, *Comoediae elegiacae, fasc. I: Vitalis Aulularia*, Bonnae 1885. Come giustamente osserva F. Bertini ('La commedia latina del XII secolo', in *L'eredità classica nel Medioevo. Il linguaggio comico. Atti del III Convegno di studio del Centro di Studi sul teatro medioevale e rinascimentale di Viterbo*, Viterbo 1979, 64), il Müllenbach fu il primo studioso ad introdurre la fortunata, e discussa definizione di 'commedia elegiaca'.

[4] M. Manitius, *Geschichte der lateinischen Literatur des Mittelalters*, III, München 1931, 1015.

[5] W. Creizenach, *Geschichte des neueren Dramas*, Halle 1893, I, 26.

[6] W. Cloetta, *Beiträge zur Literaturgeschichte des Mittelalters und der Renassaince. I: Komödie und Tragödie im Mittelalter*, Halle 1890, 68. Cloetta in quell'occasione coniò la discutibile definizione di 'epische Komödien', discutibile appunto perché in essa 'veniva modificato l'aggettivo [elegiaca] che era incontestabile, e non il sostantivo, che suscitava invece parecchie perplessità; non si poteva mettere in discussione il fatto che i componimenti fossero in distici elegiaci, mentre era tutta da verificare la loro essenza di commedie' (Bertini, 64). La stessa definizione fu ripresa da P. Bahlmann, 'Die epischen Komödien und Tragödien des Mittelalters', *Centralblatt für Bibliothekswesen* x, 1893, 463.

[7] Oltre allo studio 'La commedia latina', del Bertini si ricordano qui i seguenti contributi: *La commedia elegiaca latina in Francia nel XII secolo. Con un saggio di traduzione dell' 'Amphitruo' di Vitale di Blois*, Genova 1973; 'Da Menandro e Plauto alla commedia latina del XII secolo', in *Filologia e forme letterarie. Studi offerti a Francesco Della Corte*, Urbino 1987, V, 319–333; 'Le "Commedie elegiache" del XIII secolo', in *Tredici secoli di elegia latina. Atti del convegno internazionale (Assisi, 22–24 aprile 1988)*, Assisi 1989, 249–263. Da questi contributi generali è possibile risalire alla consistente bibliografia specifica sul fenomeno della 'commedia elegiaca' (cfr. anche A. Bisanti, *L' 'Alda' di Guglielmo di Blois. Storia degli studi e proposte interpretative*, Palermo 1990).

Vinay per dipanare in modo metodologicamente ineccepibile i complicati fili dell'intricata matassa, in uno studio ancor oggi giustamente fondamentale, insieme punto di arrivo di una ormai consolidata tradizione esegetica e punto di partenza di tutte le successive analisi.[8] Il Vinay, esaminando con la consueta perizia il *corpus* delle 'commedie' pubblicate dal Cohen, affermò il concetto di dinamicità (anzi che di staticità) del genere letterario della commedia, che ha subìto nel tempo una continua evoluzione, per cui la 'commedia elegiaca' medievale non è altro che il logico e naturale esito cui dovevano giungere coloro che nel secolo XII si fossero riproposti il compito di far rinascere la commedia classica; e proprio questa evoluzione ha fatto sì che 'delle "commedie elegiache" del XII secolo alcune sono *fabliaux*, altre sono altra cosa, altre sono *simpliciter* commedie cui va mantenuta una posizione a sé nella storia del dramma'.[9] Un'impostazione critica, questa del Vinay, della quale non è possibile non tener conto in qualsiasi approccio allo studio della *comoedia elegiaca*, e che, nella consapevolezza che il *corpus* di questi testi costituisca un 'coacervo eterogeneo',[10] opera una sorta di conciliazione fra le opposte opinioni di chi individuava nel patrimonio elegiaco medievale soprattutto un prevalente indirizzo narrativo,[11] e chi, per converso, tendeva a ribadire la natura scenico-drammatica (oltre che la rappresentabilità) di quei testi mediolatini in vario modo afferenti al concetto di 'commedia' nell'età di mezzo.[12]

In quest'ambito, la posizione di un testo come il *De clericis et rustico*[13] assume una particolare connotazione, proprio in virtù del''atipicità' tipologica che lo caratterizza, diversificandolo da un lato da altri prodotti probabilmente (o sicuramente) 'teatrabili', quali il *Geta* e l'*Aulularia* di Vitale di Blois, il *Pamphilus* e il *Babio*,[14] e accomunandolo (ma solo in minima parte) a testi quali il *De tribus*

---

[8] G. Vinay, 'La commedia latina del secolo XII. Discussioni e interpretazioni', *Studi medievali* xviii, 1952, 209–271 (ora in Vinay, *Peccato che non leggessero Lucrezio*, Spoleto 1989, 173–241).

[9] Vinay, 271.

[10] Vinay, 243.

[11] Per esempio E. Faral, 'Le fabliau latin au Moyen Age', *Romania* L, 1950, 321–385 (su cui ora Bisanti, 'Fabliaux antico-francesi e commedie latine. Alcuni sondaggi esemplificativi', *Schede medievali* xviii, 1990, 5–22); F. J. Raby, *History of Secular Latin Poetry in the Middle Ages*, Oxford 1957[2], ii, 54; successivamente alla pubblicazione dell'articolo di Vinay, su questa linea si sono attestati D. Bianchi, 'Per la commedia latina del secolo XII', *Aevum* xxix, 1955, 171–178; P. Dronke, 'The Rise of the Medieval Fabliau: Latin and Vernacular Evidence', *Romanische Forschungen* lxxxv, 1973, 275–297; e, limitatamente all'*Alda* di Guglielmo di Blois, io stesso (*L''Alda' di Guglielmo di Blois*, 75–84).

[12] Per esempio G. Cohen, pp. V–XLV; più di recente, B. Roy, 'Arnulf of Orléans and the Latin Comedy', *Speculum* xlix, 1974, 258–266. Per una moderna discussione di tutte queste tesi, rimando senz'altro a Bertini, 'La commedia latina', 63–80.

[13] Edizioni: W. Wattenbach, in *Anzeiger für Kunde der deutschen Vorzeit* xxii, 1875, 343–344 (*editio princeps*); B. Hauréau, 'Notices sur un manuscrit de la reine Christine à la Bibliothèque du Vatican', *Notices et extraits des manuscrits de la Bibliothèque nationale et autres bibliothèques* xxix, 1880, 322–324; M. Janets, in *La 'Comédie' latine en France*, II, 245–250; E. Faral, 'Le manuscrit 511 du Hunterian Museum. Notes sur le mouvement poétique et l'histoire des études litteraires en France et en Angleterre entre les années 1150 et 1225', *Studi medievali* ix, 1936, 18–122 (in part., 29–32); B. Harbert, *A Thirteenth-Century Anthology of Rhetorical Poems*, Toronto 1975, 20–23; E. Cadoni, in *Commedie latine*, II, 370–377 (ivi, a 363–367, ampia discussione delle edizioni precedenti). All'edizione Cadoni si fa riferimento nel corso di questo saggio.

[14] Edite rispettivamente da Bertini, in *Commedie latine*, I e III; da S. Pittaluga, *ibidem*, III; da A. Dessì Fulgheri, *ibidem*, II. Sulla natura 'teatrale' di questi quattro testi pressoché tutti gli studiosi sono d'accordo.

sociis o il *De tribus puellis*.[15] Un'analisi esaustiva della breve *pièce* potrebbe, a mio avviso, mettere in evidenza tutta una serie di connotazioni di matrice non solamente letteraria, ma anche e soprattutto socio-antropologica, che illuminerebbero il testo di luce nuova, in contrasto con la tutto sommato scarsa ed episodica considerazione di cui esso è stato oggetto da parte di chi, a vario titolo, si è occupato del problema. Con i suoi soli 72 versi,[16] il *De clericis et rustico* è un testo oltremodo ricco di spunti, e che crea una difficoltà di interpretazione proprio alle origini della ricerca, in quanto si tratta di una 'commedia' difficilmente catalogabile sotto una tipologia precisamente individuabile, secondo una linea, quindi, che rimanda a tutta la composita *facies* del *corpus* comico-elegiaco, e che di lì si riflette anche sui singoli prodotti che di esso fanno parte. Una breve rassegna delle definizioni cui l'opera è stata sottoposta ('commedia', 'mimo', '*fabliau* latino'), marca evidentemente, e di primo acchito, un'oscillazione interpretativa che è assai più caratterizzante di un'apparente inconciliabilità di piani d'indagine. Ad esempio, già il Sanesi riteneva che, insieme al *Pamphilus* e al *Babio*, il *De clericis et rustico* potesse considerarsi una vera e propria commedia medievale, in quanto 'in tutti e tre i componimenti suddetti, e soprattutto nel *De clericis* e nella *Comoedia Babionis*, luoghi e tempi si succedono con grande rapidità; e dei continui e repentini passaggi i lettori non sono informati da altro che dal senso stesso delle parole'; e rilevava nel breve testo 'lo schema di un racconto che procede naturalmente di luogo in luogo e di tempo in tempo; ma non vi manca la nota caratteristica, e davvero indispensabile, di ogni composizione drammatica: ossia, la continuità del dialogo'.[17] Anche il Janets, l'editore del *De clericis et rustico* nel *corpus* del Cohen, osservava la continua vivacità del dialogo ('Nous noterons cependant l'extreme vivacité du dialogue, fait assez rare parmi toutes les pièces du recueil') e pensava, in virtù di questa caratteristica, ad una sua possibile rappresentazione ('La pièce se presente sous la forme de dialogue continu et malgré les déplacements de lieu, elle peut evidemment être jouée').[18] Per il Vinay invece non si può a ragione parlare di 'commedia' vera e propria, in quanto 'l'impegno dell'autore è stato modesto, estraneo un diretto influsso della commedia antica, breve lo sviluppo . . . Per contro un narrare e un dialogare breve e veloce come chi abbia di fronte a sé ascoltatori impazienti'.[19] Il Franceschini, che offrì una pregevole traduzione italiana dell'opera, oltre a metterne in rilievo il 'dialogo serrato e vivacissimo', osservava, forse per primo, come l'argomento apparisse 'strettamente legato alla scuola e alle dispute intorno al problema degli universali', concludendo la sua breve analisi del *De clericis et rustico* con l'affermazione che 'ci troviamo davanti ad una farsa dialogata, ad un mimo studentesco, che si fa garbata beffa di uno dei più dibattuti problemi filosofici del tempo, traendo profitto da un racconto a tutti noto e riducendolo a dialogo facilmente

---

[15] Editi rispettivamente da Cadoni, in *Commedie latine*, II, 340–349 (in tre diverse redazioni, cfr. *infra*); e da Pittaluga, *ibidem*, I.

[16] 72 versi (ossia 36 distici elegiaci) presenta l'edizione Cadoni, basata su entrambi i mss. che hanno trasmesso la breve *pièce*, lo *Hunterianus 511* (*V. 8. 14*) della Biblioteca Universitaria di Glasgow, del XIII secolo (sigla *H*) e il *Vaticanus Reginensis 344*, anch'esso del XIII secolo (sigla *R*). Le edizioni Wattenbach, Hauréau e Janets, basate soltanto su *R*, ne contano invece solo 62, in quanto i vv. 31–32, 37–38, 43–44, 51–52 e 61–62 si leggono soltanto in *H* e mancano in *R*.

[17] I. Sanesi, *La commedia*, Milano 1911, I, 8.

[18] Janets, 246–247.

[19] Vinay, 248.

rappresentabile'.[20] Il Franceschini, con la consueta perizia (ove si evinca la discutibilità della 'garbata beffa' argomento della *pièce*, laddove essa è invece ridanciana),[21] pone in tal modo le più corrette basi per un'interpretazione del *De clericis et rustico*, aprendo la strada ai successivi, necessariamente sommari approcci di Luigi Alfonsi[22] e di Ferruccio Bertini[23] (che riconducono l'opera alla dimensione 'mimica'), e alle più ampie analisi di H. Walter[24] e di Enzo Cadoni, l'ultimo editore del *De clericis et rustico*, che si mantiene generalmente vicino all'impostazione dettata dal Franceschini.[25]

Il breve testo 'sceneggia' una vicenda diffusissima nel Medioevo, sia a livello popolare sia a livello letterario, che trae probabilmente le sue scaturigini dalla tradizione orientale[26] e che trova nell'*exemplum* XIX della *Disciplina clericalis* dell'ebreo convertito Pietro Alfonsi la sua più nota attestazione.[27] Qui due borghesi ed un contadino compiono un pellegrinaggio alla Mecca, e durante il viaggio terminano tutte le provviste, cosicché non resta loro altro che una quantità di farina bastevole per fare un solo, piccolo pane. I due borghesi a questo punto si accordano per farla in barba al contadino, notoriamente ghiottone (*'Parum panis habemus et noster multum comedit socius, quapropter oportet nos habere consilium quomodo sibi partem panis auferre possimus, et quod nobiscum debet soli comedamus'*), cuociono il pane e decidono che esso sarebbe toccato a chi di loro tre avesse fatto il più straordinario sogno. Ma i due hanno fatto i conti senza l'oste, perché partono dal presupposto che il contadino sia sciocco ed incapace di inganni (un tema, questo, che ricorrerà con maggiore insistenza nel *De clericis et rustico*).[28] Mentre essi dormono, infatti, il villano divora il pane e se ne va anch'egli a dormire. Ridestatisi, i due fingono di aver sognato l'uno di essere stato condotto in Paradiso, l'altro all'inferno: il *rusticus*, dopo aver ascoltato i loro presunti 'sogni', dice di aver sognato che uno di loro veniva condotto in cielo, l'altro sotto la terra e quindi, credendo che essi non avrebbero mai più fatto ritorno, si era impossessato del pane, mangiandoselo tutto da solo (*'Nunc visum est mihi quod duo angeli unum ex vobis accipiebant et aperiebant portas coeli, ducebantque illum ante Deum; deinde alium accipiebant duo alii angeli, et aperta terra ducebant in infernum, et his visis putavi neminem iam amplius rediturum, et surrexi et panem comedi'*).

Prima di passare all'esame dei rapporti fra l'*exemplum* di Pietro Alfonsi ed il testo mediolatino che ne deriva, è opportuno osservare come questa parabola, non

---

20 E. Franceschini, in *Teatro latino medievale*, Milano 1960, 77–78.
21 Giustamente Cadoni, 360, osserva a tal proposito che 'la beffa sia più sapida che garbata, che tradisca le sue sane origini popolari, non dirozzate da un sufficiente talento letterario, sia nell'impostazione generale del racconto, sia nel gusto per la battuta finale'.
22 L. Alfonsi, *La letteratura latina medievale*, Firenze-Milano 1972, 209–210
23 Bertini, *La commedia elegiaca*, 29–31.
24 H. Walter, '*De clericis et rustico*. Ein Beitrag zum Wortschatz der mittelalterlichen Klosterschule', *Mittellateinische Jahrbuch* xiv, 1979, 259–264 (su cui cfr. Cadoni, 379–380).
25 Cadoni, 357–360.
26 G. Paris, *I racconti orientali nella letteratura francese*, trad. ital. di M. Menghini, Firenze 1895.
27 Petri Alfonsi *Disciplina clericalis* XIX (ed. A. Hilka – W. Söderhjelm, Heidelberg 1911, 29–30).
28 Petri Alfonsi *Disc. Cler.* XIX: *Haec artificiose dicebant quia simplicem rusticum ad huiusmodi fictitiam deputabant*. Il *topos* dell'astuzia del villano, ed insieme della sua contrapposizione sociologica con i due *burgenses* (*clerici* nel *De clericis et rustico*) è già stato brevemente da me analizzato (Bisanti, 'Fabliaux antico-francesi', 16–18). Per una più ampia analisi, cfr. *infra*.

diversamente da quella celeberrima delle 'tre anella',[29] si sia prestata ad una interpretazione che ne mettesse in evidenza le probabili radici ebraiche (e non solo perché essa sia stata rielaborata da un ebreo convertito). Il Paris infatti mise bene in evidenza, oltre un secolo fa, come in un libro arabo dal titolo *Nuzhetol Udeba* si legga una novella che mette in scena tre viaggiatori, un maomettano, un cristiano ed un ebreo, che in pieno deserto si trovano con un solo pane e decidono che lo mangerà chi farà il più bel sogno. Il maomettano racconta di essere andato in cielo, il cristiano di essere giunto all'inferno e l'ebreo (come il *rusticus* di Pietro Alfonsi) li gabba entrambi col medesimo procedimento di astuzia.[30] A tal proposito il Paris scriveva che 'la condotta dell'ebreo potrebbe passare per la messa in pratica della credenza alle ricompense terrestri in opposizione alla fede dei cristiani e dei musulmani nella vita eterna; però, qualunque siano state, su questo punto controverso, le idee degli antichi ebrei, coloro che vivevano dopo l'avvento del maomettanesimo, e che soli avrebbero potuto inventare questa storiella, credevano sicuramente alla vita futura, quanto i fedeli di Cristo e di Maometto. Questa novella non è stata certamente scritta col pensiero di glorificare senza riserva il personaggio che gabba gli altri'.[31] L'ebreo dunque, in questa versione della vulgata vicenda, non è un eroe 'positivo', e ciò balza agli occhi con ancor maggiore evidenza ove si consideri che in una più tarda redazione della storia, inserita nella curiosa *Historia de Jeschua Nazareno* di origine anch'essa ebraica,[32] la parte dell'ebreo (che sarà poi quella del *rusticus*) è ricoperta nientemeno che da Giuda, mentre i due compagni 'gabbati' sono Gesù Cristo e san Pietro.[33] Lo studioso che per primo ha collegato questo testo al *De clericis et rustico* è stato il Franceschini,[34] che così lo riassume: 'Gesù, accompagnato da Pietro e da Giuda, si ferma un giorno in un'osteria. L'oste non avendo che un'oca da offrire loro, Gesù la prende e dice: – Quest'oca è troppo piccola perché tre persone possano sfamarsi. Andiamo dunque a dormire, e chi farà il sogno migliore si mangerà l'oca –. Detto fatto, vanno a letto. Il mattino dopo, i tre si riuniscono e san Pietro dice: – Mi sono visto in sogno ai piedi del trono di Dio onnipotente – Gesù rispose: – Io sono il figlio di Dio onnipotente, ed ho sognato che tu eri seduto accanto a me; il mio sogno è superiore al tuo e perciò l'oca spetta a me –. Giuda disse allora: – Io, nel sogno, ho mangiato l'oca –. E Gesù cercò inutilmente l'oca, perché Giuda l'aveva davvero mangiata'.[35]

Le relazioni fra il *De clericis et rustico* e l'*exemplum* di Pietro Alfonsi (che

---

[29] Paris, 'La parabola dei tre anelli', in *I racconti orientali*, 29–55; M. Penna, *La parabola dei tre anelli e la tolleranza nel Medioevo*, Torino 1953.

[30] Paris, 51–52.

[31] Paris, 52.

[32] *Historia de Jeschua Nazareno*, ed. Hulrich, Leiden 1705, 51.

[33] Che la tradizione popolare si sia impadronita dei personaggi evangelici di Cristo e degli apostoli per farli protagonisti delle più svariate vicende è provato, fra l'altro, dalle serie aneddotiche di *Gesù e San Pietro in Friuli* e *Gesù e San Pietro in Sicilia* (in *Fiabe italiane*, raccolte e trascritte da I. Calvino, Torino 1956, 144–155 e 685–689).

[34] Franceschini, 78. Lo studioso forse non conosce l'opera del Paris, che pure fa un breve accenno all'*Historia de Jeschua Nazareno* (52), così come, per converso, il Paris non mostra di conoscere il *De clericis et rustico*, anche se nel 1884 (data in cui lo studioso tenne la sua conferenza alla Società di Studi Ebraici) erano già apparse due edizioni della *pièce*, quella di Wattenbach e quella di Hauréau.

[35] Franceschini, 78. La vicenda verrà rielaborata anche nei *Gesta Romanorum* (cap. 107, ed. Osterley, 433 ss.: cfr. Walter, 261–262) che presentano 'la forma più bella' (Paris, 53), e negli

costituisce il *terminus post quem* per la problematica, ed irrisolta datazione della *pièce*)[36] si configurano secondo una linea che tende a privilegiare in sommo grado la 'dialogicità' del testo a petto della 'narratività' dell'episodio come è presentato nella *Disciplina clericalis*. A parte il mutamento dei due borghesi di Pietro Alfonsi in due *clerici* nel testo comico-elegiaco (elemento, questo, di notevole rilievo socio-antropologico, e del quale si tornerà a parlare), la struttura del racconto tradizionale viene mantenuta dall'anonimo autore del *De clericis et rustico*, articolata secondo il seguente schema:

> A. Proposta del viaggio (vv. 1–12);
> B. Complotto dei *clerici* ai danni del *rusticus* (vv. 13–22);
> C. Patto fra i tre (vv. 23–30);
> D. Monologo del *rusticus* (vv. 31–46);
> E. Sogni fittizi dei due *clerici*:
> > 1. Del primo *clericus* (vv. 47–58);
> > 2. Del secondo *clericus* (vv. 59–70);
> F. Epilogo. Battuta finale del *rusticus* (vv. 71–72).

Lo schema riproduce pressoché fedelmente il tessuto narrativo dell'*exemplum* di Pietro Alfonsi, anch'esso marcato attraverso sei sezioni. Tutt'al più si può osservare che l'anonimo del *De clericis et rustico* ha inserito un notevole ampliamento nella prima sezione dell'opera, quella in cui i tre decidono di fare un viaggio assieme, mentre nella *Disciplina clericalis* si dice soltanto che *duo burgenses et rusticus causa orationis Mech adeunt* (ed ovviamente il particolare che i tre si dirigano alla Mecca viene soppresso dall''occidentale' autore del testo comico-elegiaco);[37] che egli ha inserito altresì, proprio nel mezzo dell'opera (dopo i primi 30 versi e prima degli ultimi 26) un lungo monologo del *rusticus* (22, 22% del totale), che riprende ed amplifica, per servire all'assunto 'villanesco' ed 'anticlericale' che informa la *pièce*, lo spunto di Pietro Alfonsi (*At rusticus, percepta eorum astutia, dormientibus sociis, traxit panem semicoctum, comedit et iterum iacuit*); e che egli, infine, ha cercato di mantenere una certa qual proporzione all'interno delle sezioni in cui può suddividersi la sua opera, tenendo presente che la prima presenta 12 versi (16,66%), la seconda 10 (13,88%), la terza 8 (11,11%), la quarta appunto 16 (22,22%) e la quinta si può suddividere in due sezioni equivalenti, di 12 versi ciascuna (per un complessivo 33,33%); a parte è da considerare la breve battuta finale del *rusticus*, che conta solo due versi (2,77%) e funge quasi da ridanciana e sapida *sphragìs* a tutta la vicenda.

A tal proposito, qui emerge una nota caratterizzante dell'autore del *De clericis et rustico*. Infatti, il racconto della *Disciplina clericalis* (ed in genere quello presente in tutte le altre versioni della vicenda, non escluso il più tardo *fabliau De*

Hecatonmiti di Giovan Battista Giraldi Cinzio, che mettono in iscena un filosofo, un astrologo e un soldato, ambientando la narrazione all'indomani del Sacco di Roma del 1527 (Paris, 53).

[36] Il *terminus ante quem* è invece costituito dalla datazione dei due mss. che hanno tramandato la 'commedia', entrambi risalenti all'inizio del XIII secolo (cfr. n.16 e Cadoni, 358–359, il quale scrive che 'la nostra commedia può dunque essere stata scritta in uno qualunque degli anni che vanno dall'inizio del XII all'inizio del XIII secolo, senza che nessun altro elemento interno o esterno valga a determinarne con maggiore precisione la data').

[37] Cadoni, 360.

deux borgois et d'un vilain)[38] si conclude con la considerazione del *rusticus* che, dicendo che non avrebbe creduto che i suoi due compagni sarebbero mai ritornati dai loro 'viaggi nell'aldilà', ha ritenuto ormai sua la focaccia, mangiandosela. Nel distico finale del *De clericis et rustico*, invece, vi è una nota aggiuntiva che, in un parodico ammiccamento al problema degli universali notoriamente dibattuto nelle scuole filosofiche fra XII e XIII secolo, fornisce non solo un'evidente spia della cultura e del *milieu* in cui l'autore deve essersi formato, ma costituisce altresì una novità che sposa lo scialbo finale della fonte ad una tematica non estranea alla temperie di altre 'commedie elegiache' (penso soprattutto al *Geta* ed all'*Aulularia* di Vitale di Blois).[39] Dice infatti il contadino: *'Hec vidi et libum, quia neuter erat rediturus, / feci individuum quod fuit ante genus'*,[40] in una presa in giro dei due *clerici* che anfibologicamente vengono ripagati con la loro stessa moneta (anche in una dimensione culturalizzata), ed insieme in un parodico ammicco a vulgati motivi filosofici, da Boezio[41] a Giovanni di Salisbury.[42] L'autore, il misterioso *Hugo Kancellarius* di cui si legge nel criptico *explicit* del codice Vaticano,[43] è quindi un uomo di cultura, capace di scherzare con ironia sul problema degli universali, dotato di una certa conoscenza dell'astronomia,[44] della mitologia,[45] ed abile nel tessere, nella sua breve opera, reminiscenze ed echi virgiliani[46] ed ovidiani.[47] Affermare però, come ha fatto il più recente editore, che il rapporto fra la narrazione di Pietro Alfonsi ed il nostro testo si configuri soltanto in merito al fatto che l'una è in prosa e l'altro in distici elegiaci,[48] risulta, a mio avviso, certamente discutibile e sostanzialmente viziato da una considerazione univoca al

---

[38] *De deux borgois et d'un vilain*, in *Fabliaux. Racconti comici medievali*, a cura di G. C. Belletti, Ivrea 1982, 58–63. Si tratta del 17º racconto del *Castoiement d'un père à son fils*, rimaneggiamento antico-francese, appunto, della *Disciplina clericalis*. Per un breve confronto fra il *fabliau* e il *De clericis et rustico*, Bisanti, 'Fabliaux antico-francesi', 17–18. E' da osservare inoltre che la vicenda narrata nella 'commedia' è stata da Faral ('La Fabliau latin', 378, n.1) accostata al racconto di *Ginnechochet et du Vilain* che Giovanni di Garlandia inserisce nella sua *Poetria nova* (ed. G. Mari, *Romanische Forschungen* xiii, 1902, 916–917). Ma l'unica nota che unisce i due differenti racconti è costituita dal motivo, peraltro topico, dell'astuzia del contadino, che riesce a farla in barba ad un diavolo.

[39] Bertini, 'Il "Geta" di Vitale di Blois e la scuola di Abelardo', *Sandalion* ii, 1979, 259–265.

[40] *De cler. et rust.*, vv. 71–72 (Cadoni, 376).

[41] Boetii *in Porph.* III (*PL* lxiv, 115): *Omne genus totum est, individuum vero pars.*

[42] Johannis Sarisb. *Metalogicus* II, 17 (ed. Webb, 93): *Platonem, in eo quod Plato est, dicunt individuum; in eo quod homo, speciem; in eo quod animal, genus, sed subalternum; in eo quod substantia, generalissimum.*

[43] Per un'ampia discussione circa le ipotesi attributive del *De cler. et rust.*, rimando a Cadoni, 354–358.

[44] I termini astronomici presenti ai vv. 49–54 (relativi al sogno fittizio del primo *clericus*, quello che dice di essere andato su nel cielo) ricorrono tutti (come ben osserva Cadoni, 375) nella *Philologia* di Marziano Capella, e soprattutto nell'VIII libro di quest' opera enciclopedica, ad eccezione di *minuta*, la cui spiegazione si legge in Firmico Materno (*Math.* II, 5).

[45] Per esempio i vv. 63–64, relativi al sogno del secondo *clericus*, sono riconducibili all'elenco dei dannati in Ov. *Met.* IV, 457–461 (Cadoni, 377).

[46] Si legga il v. 18 (*Rusticus est Corydon et magne simplicitatis*), chiaramente esemplato, per il primo emistichio, su Verg. *Ecl.* II, 56 (*Rusticus es, Corydon; nec munera curat Alexis*); o il v.37 (*Quicquid id est, coniecto dolos timeoque dolosos*), la cui struttura arieggia, anche *ad verbum*, Verg. *Aen.* II, 49 (*Quidquid id est, timeo Danaos et dona ferentes*).

[47] Oltre al catalogo dei dannati (cfr. n.45), il v.57 (*Singula quid numerem? sed singula quis numeraret?*) riecheggia, nel primo emistichio, Ov. *Amores* I, 5, 23 (*Singula quid referam? Nil non laudabile vidi*).

[48] Cadoni, 360.

contenuto, prescindendo invece dalla più notevole caratteristica innovativa operata dal poeta mediolatino, che non sta certo nell'invenzione della trama, quanto nella forma che riveste la vicenda di una sua peculiare specificità.[49]

E' infatti proprio la tipologia dialogica del testo che ne marca la dimensione di 'rappresentabilità' e di 'teatralità', non diversamente da quanto, oltre ottant'anni fa, aveva acutamente rilevato il Sanesi.[50] Il *De clericis et rustico* si configura, infatti, come un 'mimo' mediolatino[51] nel quale il gusto del dialogo, della tenzone e del 'contrasto' rivestono un valore di cui non è possibile, a mio parere, non tener conto per una retta e fattiva interpretazione dell'opera. Nella 'sceneggiatura' della novella di Pietro Alfonsi, l'autore oblitera l'assunto narrativo mutandolo in prospettiva dialogistica, con una tendenza alla *brevitas* ed alla rapidità dello scambio di battute che, com'è stato giustamente affermato, raggiunge spesso il parossismo.[52] Un'analisi statistica del *De clericis et rustico*, sotto questo punto di vista, offre risultati interessanti, ed anomali, nel contesto del fluttuante genere della 'commedia elegiaca' cui, tutto sommato e più per comodità classificatoria che per effettiva appartenenza tipologica, la breve *pièce* suole essere inserita. I vv. 1–11a presentano ben 32 battute, con una frequenza media di 3,04 battute per verso (alcuni versi contengono addirittura quattro o cinque battute). Segue un verso e mezzo (vv. 11b–12) di tipo probabilmente narrativo-didascalico (*Precedit solus, soli remanemus / Iamque referre licet quidquid utrique libet*),[53] caso peraltro isolato in tutta l'opera. La seconda sezione è articolata in 3 battute, due del primo *clericus* (vv. 13–16; 21–22) ed una del secondo (vv. 17–20). Una nuova fittissima gragnuola di botte e risposte incrociate fra i tre personaggi costituisce la parte seguente, 21 brevissime battute in soli 8 versi (vv. 23–30), con una frequenza media di 2,62 battute per verso. Dopo il lungo monologo del *rusticus* (vv. 31–46), l'ultima parte della 'commedia', quella relativa ai falsi 'sogni' ed allo scioglimento della vicenda, presenta i due racconti dei *clerici*, di 12 versi ciascuno (vv. 47–58; 59–70), siglati entrambi dall'affermazione *Ut breviter dicam, non rediturus eram* (vv. 58 e 70), e il distico di chiusura (vv. 71–72) pronunciato dallo scaltro contadino. Complessivamente, il nostro testo consta quindi di 60 battute su un totale di 70 versi e mezzo (tolto quindi il verso e mezzo di 'didascalia interna'),[54] con una percentuale di 0,851 battute per verso. Inoltre, fatta eccezione per i vv. 1–11a e 23–30, nei quali riesce difficoltosa, se non impossibile, l'assegnazione delle battute di dialogo ai vari personaggi (e soprattutto ai due *clerici*), si osservi che le altre battute 'lunghe' sono così distribuite: tre al primo *clericus*, due al *secondo*, due al *rusticus*, rispettivamente per un totale di 18,16 e 18 versi, e

---

[49] Giustamente Franceschini, 78, osserva che 'l'importanza del nostro testo non sta. . . nell'originalità, ma nella forma'.

[50] Cfr. n.17.

[51] Per un primo approccio al 'mimo' medievale: G. Tavani, s.v. *mimo*, in *Enciclopedia dello Spettacolo*, VII, Roma 1960, 603–604; F. Doglio, *Teatro in Europa. I. Dall'Impero romano all'umanesimo*, Milano 1982.

[52] Cadoni, 358–359.

[53] Non è escluso, peraltro, che la frase possa essere pronunziata da uno dei due *clerici* il quale, in caso di una rappresentazione della *pièce*, poteva assumere le funzioni di *meneur de jeu*.

[54] Sulle 'didascalie interne' cfr. G. Monaco, 'Dai tragici greci a Pirandello. Appunti sulle didascalie teatrali', *Dioniso* lvi, 1986, 111–129 (poi in *Scritti minori di Giusto Monaco*, Palermo 1992, 381–396). Sul loro uso nelle commedie elegiache, ed in particolare nell'*Alda*, cfr. Bisanti, *L' 'Alda' di Guglielmo di Blois*, 83–84.

quindi con un certo rispetto delle proporzioni fra le tre 'parti', che risultano pressoché equivalenti.

Uno schema compositivo siffatto, in cui il dialogo occupa il 97,92% del testo, se da un lato accomuna il *De clericis et rustico* al *Pamphilus* ed al *Babio*, commedie interamente dialogate, dall'altro lo diversifica da tutti gli altri prodotti del genere 'commedia elegiaca', nei quali, in diversa misura, l'elemento narrativo ricopre una sezione non irrilevante del testo (per non parlare del gusto del monologo o del frequente uso del discorso diretto 'a scopo non comunicativo, non coinvolgente').[55] Per fare un solo confronto, si consideri l'*Alda* di Guglielmo di Blois, le cui strutture dialogico-narrative sono state esaminate da me di recente: i dati emersi da quest'ultima, a tal riguardo, danno un 55,39% di versi narrativi, un 33,82% di versi 'monologici', e solo un 10,79% di versi propriamente dialogici, in una percentuale evidentemente bassissima, che fa sì che si possa, a mio parere, escludere per l'*Alda* la qualifica di 'commedia' *tout court*.[56] Tra il 10,79% dell'opera di Guglielmo di Blois ed il 97,92% del *De clericis et rustico* vi è evidentemente un abisso, ed allegare altri riscontri da opere quali il *De tribus puellis*, il *Baucis et Traso* o la *Lidia* di Arnolfo d'Orléans (nonché, anche se in misura più ridotta, dal *Geta* e dall'*Aulularia* di Vitale di Blois),[57] non farebbe altro che avvalorare questa prospettiva. Se dialogo è quindi, per usare una felice definizione data recentemente da Daniela Goldin, un 'discorso diretto in cui l'informazione data da un locutore richiede di essere proseguita e completata, confermata o negata da un secondo o più interlocutori vicini e dello stesso livello diegetico',[58] e se esso compare in misura così preponderante nel nostro testo, ne consegue che la 'teatralità', oltre che la 'rappresentabilità' di un'opera quale il *De clericis et rustico*, proprio in virtù di questa distintiva caratterizzazione, non può essere negata.[59] Ed i più recenti studi hanno rimarcato questo aspetto della *pièce* mediolatina, dalla stessa Goldin che ha scritto che essa 'è per metà una didascalia parlata, un prologo a più voci dove si descrive, amplificandolo, l'antefatto, per giungere poi al fatto principale, al racconto dei sogni eccezionali, più distintamente distribuito fra i tre personaggi',[60] a Luigi Allegri che ultimamente ha affermato che 'è certo probabile che l'origine di questa piccola *pièce*, sulla cui natura di copione teatrale più che di testo letterario non ci dovrebbero essere dubbi, sia goliardica', rilevando però anche che è 'difficile non individuare un'impronta giullaresca nella serratezza di quel dialogo iniziale tra i due studenti e il contadino, con l'accordo tra i primi per perpetrare l'inganno, e nella struttura a monologhi alternati della seconda parte in cui ciascuno racconta il sogno che dovrebbe servire a fargli vincere la focaccia in palio'.[61] Rilegare il testo alla tradizione giullaresca, più che a quella goliardica, vuol dire dunque inserirlo in

55 D. Goldin, 'Monologo, dialogo e "disputatio" nella commedia elegiaca', in AA. VV., *Il dialogo*, Palermo 1985, 72–86 (in particolare, 76).

56 Bisanti, L' '*Alda' di Guglielmo di Blois*, 77–83.

57 Per il *Baucis et Traso*, cfr. l'ed. di G. Orlandi, in *Commedie latine*, III, 270–303; per la *Lidia*, in attesa dell'edizione critica a cura dello stesso Orlandi, che dovrebbe apparire nel vol. VI di *Commedie latine*, si deve ricorrere ancora all'ed. di E. Lackenbacher (in *La 'Comédie' latine en France* I).

58 Goldin, 72.

59 Sulla necessità di una distinzione fra 'teatralità' e 'rappresentabilità', Goldin, 74.

60 Goldin, 84.

61 L. Allegri, *Teatro e spettacolo nel Medioevo*, Roma-Bari 1988, 114–115.

una dimensione di comunicazione scenica, di evidenza rappresentativa. Che nel *De clericis et rustico* 'dietro le spalle del chierico si intravvede il giullare' fu autorevolmente ed acutamente osservato dal Vinay,[62] laddove l'ambiente scolastico in cui sembra esser nata la *pièce*[63] non osta ad un'interazione con il *milieu* e con l'estrazione giullaresca, in una singolare compresenza, nel mimo, di elementi caratterizzanti l'una e l'altra sfera di influenza.[64] Il gusto del dialogo vertiginoso e rapidissimo, che prevede attori provetti, capaci di sopperire con i gesti e i movimenti all'arida nudità del testo; il gusto del contrasto e direi dell'*altercatio* che marca l'opposizione istituzionale fra i due furbi studenti da un lato e l'ancor più furbo villano dall'altro; i repentini salti di ambiente e di luogo, che solo l'abilità di consumati istrioni avrebbe saputo rendere di fronte al pubblico, agendo con forza evocativa sull'immaginazione collettiva: sono questi i tratti distintivi che mi fanno propendere per qualificare come 'mimo giullaresco' il nostro testo.[65] E la cultura dell'anonimo non stride a contrasto con la grossezza della farsa, in una continuità della tradizione istrionica antica e tardoantica,[66] laddove l'antitesi socio-antropologica fra *clerici* e *rusticus* è proprio marcata nelle reminiscenze astrologiche e mitologiche di cui i due studenti intessono i loro fittizi sogni dell'aldilà.[67]

Dire di più, su un'effettiva realizzazione scenica del *De clericis et rustico*, sarebbe certamente azzardato. Per qualificare un po' più chiaramente il testo, sotto tal punto di vista, è però opportuno correlarlo con il *De tribus sociis*, inserito da Goffredo di Vinsauf nella sua *Poetria nova* come *specimen* di arte comica.[68]

---

[62] Vinay, 218–219.

[63] Alfonsi, 210; Franceschini, 65.

[64] Osserva Allegri, 115, che si tratta di 'un giullare che . . . non necessariamente – anzi – abita un mondo separato da quello dei goliardi aggiullarati o anche degli studenti regolari'.

[65] Sul mimo medievale, in aggiunta ai titoli citati alla n.51, cfr. H. Reich, *Der mimus*, Berlin 1903; M. De Marco, 'Il mimo conviviale nell' Alto Medioevo latino', in *Spettacoli conviviali dall'antichità classica alle corti del '400*, Viterbo 1983, 149–169. Sulla tradizione giullaresca medievale vi è ovviamente una bibliografia sterminata: mi riferisco qui ai soli contributi fondamentali: L. A. Muratori, *De spectaculis et ludis publicis Medii Aevi*, in *Antiquitates Italicae Medii Aevi. Dissertatio XXIX*, Mediolani 1739 (rist. an. Bologna 1975), poi anche a cura di A. Viscardi, Modena 1962; G. Bonifacio, *Giullari e uomini di corte del '200*, Napoli 1907; Faral, *Les Jongleurs en France au Moyen Age*, Paris 1910; Faral, s.v. *giulleria*, in *Enciclopedia dello Spettacolo*, V, Roma 1958, 1352–1354; R. Menéndez Pidal, *Poesia juglaresca y origines de las literaturas románicas*, Madrid 1924; V. De Bartholomaeis, *Le origini della poesia drammatica italiana*, Bologna 1924; De Bartholomaeis, 'Giullari farfensi', *Studi medievali* n.s., i, 1928, 37–47; A. Viscardi, *Le origini*, Milano 1950², 585–605; J. Ogilvy, 'Mimi, scurrae, histriones', *Speculum* xxxviii, 1963, 603–619; P. Zumthor, 'Jonglerie et langage', *Poétique* xi, 1972, 321–336; Zumthor, *La poésie et la voix dans la civilisation médiéval*, Paris 1984; Zumthor, 'Jongleurs et discours: interprétation et création poétique au Moyen Age', *Medioevo romanzo*, n.s. i, 1986, 3–26; Zumthor, *La lettera e la voce. Sulla 'letteratura' medievale*, Bologna 1990, 73–99; Allegri, 59–121. In generale, poi, si ricorre con frutto agli Atti su *Il contributo dei giullari alla drammaturgia italiana delle origini. Convegno di studio del Centro di studi sul teatro medioevale e rinascimentale di Viterbo, 17–19 giugno 1977*, Roma 1978 (con la cronaca del convegno, a cura di G. Musca, *Quaderni medievali* iv, 1977, 243–253).

[66] E' questa, com'è noto, l'impostazione di Faral, *Les Jongleurs en France*, seguita da Viscardi, 585–588.

[67] Alfonsi, 210.

[68] Goffredo di Vinsauf, *De tribus sociis*, a cura di E. Cadoni, in *Commedie latine*, II, 340–343. Il testo corrisponde ai vv. 1888–1909 della *Poetria nova* (Faral, *Les arts poétiques du XIIe et du XIIIe siècle*, Paris 1924, 255). Ancora utile, soprattutto per l'introduzione e la traduzione francese,

Siamo qui all'origine di una 'drammaturgia comica elementare, in cui certamente il professionismo giullaresco è implicato anche quando dai temi traspare una mano colta'.[69] La vicenda narrata da Goffredo di Vinsauf in soli 22 esametri,[70] che probabilmente risale ad una precedente tradizione 'popolare', racconta di tre compari che si accordano per vivere insieme a patto che, a turno, ciascuno di loro si occupi della cucina. Ma un giorno uno di essi rompe la brocca dell'acqua e si reca al mercato per acquistarne una nuova. Cacciato via dal mercante che non si fida di lui, decide, di comune accordo con gli altri due amici, di vendicarsi di costui. Torna quindi al mercato, prende in mano due brocche per esaminarle e, al sopraggiungere di uno dei due suoi compari che gli comunica la finta morte del padre, finge dolore e sorpresa, lascia cadere le due brocche per terra mandandole in frantumi, e se ne fugge via a gambe levate, lasciando il venditore con un palmo di naso. Orbene, una situazione simile risulta perfettamente 'consona al mondo giullaresco e ai modi della sua comicità',[71] e se in essa (contrariamente a quanto avviene nel *De clericis et rustico*) la parte narrativa è preponderante rispetto al dialogo, ciò non toglie che essa non potesse essere recitata sotto forma di 'diceria' o di monologo giullaresco in cui un solo attore, col vario atteggiarsi del corpo e della voce, rivestisse tutti i ruoli della rappresentazione, fungendo da *meneur de jeu* per le parti didascalico-narrative e da interprete diretto per quelle dialogate.[72] Più difficile è invece pensare che il *De clericis et rustico* potesse essere recitato da un solo attore (anche se ciò ovviamente non può escludersi),[73] per la maggiore complessità del dialogo, soprattutto dei fittissimi scambi di battute della prima e della terza sezione della *pièce*, che forse prevedevano una maggiore articolazione e distribuzione dei ruoli. In tale direzione non si può non sottoscrivere l'affermazione di Massimo Oldoni, che ha scritto: 'Nel *De tribus sociis*, nonostante il continuo riferimento a tre compari, possiamo esser certi di essere di fronte ad un solo attore che recitando, riassume un breve intreccio, riferendo anche in discorso diretto le battute appartenenti ai due non figuranti. Mentre, nel *De clericis et rustico* è palese che siamo in presenza di un mimo dialogico, privo di ogni didascalia scenica, ma sicuramente ripartito tra più attori, impegnati in un dialogo fittissimo. E l'alternanza delle battute introduce l'ultimo e forse più fortunato momento del teatro e della teatrabilità profana mediolatina: il dialogo'.[74]

l'edizione a cura di P Maury, in *La 'Comédie' latine en France*, II, 258. Sui vari problemi che la *pièce* presenta, ed in particolare sull'ampia tradizione manoscritta, rimando a Cadoni, 305–335.
[69] Allegri, 113.
[70] Oltre alla redazione presentata da Goffredo nella sua *Poetria Nova*, del *De tribus sociis* esistono altre due versioni latine, una in 10 distici attestata nel ms. *Vaticanus Reginensis Latinus 344*, ed un' altra in 25 esametri tràdita dal ms. *Vindobonensis 312* (entrambe edite e tradotte da Cadoni, 344–349).
[71] Allegri, 114.
[72] Su tali caratteristiche della recitazione giullaresca, cfr. De Bartholomaeis, e, più succintamente, Viscardi, 591–592; Allegri, 114. Si aggiungano E. Pasquini, *La poesia popolare e giullaresca*, in *La letteratura didattica e la poesia popolare del Duecento*, Bari 1971, 115–175; E. Faccioli, in *Il teatro italiano. I. Dalle origini al Quattrocento*, Torino 1975, I, vii–xvi.
[73] Si pensi, in epoca recente, a certi esperimenti di 'giullarate' da parte di Dario Fo (in *Mistero Buffo*, ne *Le commedie di Dario Fo*, vol. V, Torino 1977, 3–171).
[74] M. Oldoni, 'Tecniche di scena e comportamenti narrativi nel teatro profano mediolatino (secc. IX–XII)', in *Il contributo dei giullari* 27–50 (in particolare, 46). Esclude invece (a mio avviso a torto) ogni possibilità di rappresentazione del *De tribus sociis* Cadoni, 306, n.6; 310, n.21; 361, n.30.

E che questa sia l'interpretazione più corretta del *De clericis et rustico*, in una considerazione della *pièce* non come 'commedia' (almeno secondo le classiche tipologie), ma in ogni caso come testo 'teatrale' caratterizzato appunto dal tono discorsivo e dialogistico, traspare con ogni evidenza dal fatto che Goffredo di Vinsauf, nel *Documentum de arte versificandi*, citi i primi due versi del 'mimo' come *specimen* di *iocosa materia*. Dopo aver seguito gli insegnamenti dell'*Ars poetica* oraziana in fatto di 'commedia', l'autore del *Documentum* constata l'obliterazione, ai suoi tempi, della commedia classica, e ritiene opportuno applicare regole drammatiche alla *iocosa materia*, cioè al racconto comico. E' opportuno rileggere il brano nella sua interezza:

> Sic ergo habemus quicquid boni Horatius docet in Poetria sua, tam de vitandis quam de faciendis, nisi quod quaedam docet de pronuntiatione et comoedia. Sed illa quae condidit de comoedia hodie penitus recesserunt ab aula et occiderunt in desuetudinem. Ad praesens igitur omittamus de comoedia. Sed illa quae ipse dicit, et nos de iocosa materia dicamus qualiter sit tractanda. Si materiam ergo iocosam habemus prae manibus, per totum corpus materiae verbis utamur levibus et communibus et ad ipsas res et personas pertinentibus de quibus loquimur. Talia namque poscit talis materia, qualia sunt inter colloquentes et non alia nec magis difficilia. Et cum perveniemus ad illum principium materiae, ubi iocus reponitur et reservatur, scilicet ad finem materiae, quanto expressius poterimus sequamur unum idioma per aliud, scilicet ut ita sedeat iocus in uno idiomate sicut in alio. Verbi gratia, ponamus in exemplum hanc materiam iocosam . . . Ecce aliud exemplum iocosae materiae.[75]

E a questo punto vengono citati i primi due versi del *De clericis et rustico*. La menzione dell'*incipit* della *pièce*, lungi dal costituire un indizio di paternità da parte di Goffredo di Vinsauf, come pure fu pensato a suo tempo,[76] è particolarmente indicativa di un tipo di teatro che ha ormai rotto i vincoli con la tradizione classica, in una dimensione tipicamente medievale. E così è nel giusto il Faral quando afferma che 'Geoffroi de Vinsauf n'a pas eu le moins du monde la pensée de légiférer pour le théâtre: il a voulu simplement montrer que le style du conte était le style familier de la conversation';[77] ma ancor più nel giusto è il Vinay, che da tutto ciò trae l'evidente conseguenza che, se Goffredo afferma che ai suoi tempi di commedie come quelle note ad Orazio non se ne scrivono più, ciò vuol dire che egli ha ben chiaro il concetto di 'commedia'.[78]

Risolto così il problema relativo alla tipologia del testo, in una individuazione del *De clericis et rustico* come 'mimo giullaresco', in cui il mondo dei *clerici* e quello dei giullari, talvolta contrapposti, si unificano e si integrano vicendevol-

---

[75] Galf. de Vino Salvo *Documentum de modo et arte dictandi et versificandi* II, 3, 163–166 (Faral, *Les arts poétiques*, 317).

[76] E' questa, fra l'altro, l'opinione dello stesso Faral ('Le fabliau latin, 376–379; 'Le manuscrit 511', 32), sulla quale però cfr. la convincente confutazione di Cadoni, 354–356.

[77] Faral, 'Le fabliau latin', 378.

[78] Vinay, 228–229; cfr. inoltre Bertini, *La commedia elegiaca*, 31; e G. Padoan, 'Il senso del teatro nei secoli senza teatro', in *Concetto, storia, miti e immagini del Medioevo*, a cura di V. Branca, Firenze 1973, 325–338.

mente,[79] resta da esaminare la *facies* socio-antropologica di cui l'anonimo autore si fa portavoce.

Com'è noto, uno dei *topoi* della letteratura medievale e poi rinascimentale, in latino ed in volgare, destinato ad amplissima diffusione letteraria e tradizionale, è la 'satira del villano'. La figura del contadino, caratterizzata da un tono di arcadica *rusticitas* e di edificante *pietas* nella poesia classica, durante l'età di mezzo, e soprattutto a partire dall'XI secolo, assume via via delle connotazioni tese a marcarne i tratti del diverso, del brutto e deforme, dell'empio, anche del diabolico.[80] La figura del villano, sentita come potenzialmente pericolosa e sovvertitrice di un ordine costituito, basato anche sulla tripartizione della società,[81] diventa progressivamente oggetto di scherno e di ludibrio (non diversamente dalla coeva ed altrettanto topica satira contro le donne), e così, come già ben rilevò il Merlini quasi un secolo or sono, una linea di satira 'negativa' si appunta contro il mondo dei contadini e degli agricoltori, una satira che trae le sue scaturigini dal disprezzo delle classi egemoniche (i chierici e i borghesi) per quelle subalterne, in un aggancio alla mentalità dell'epoca (anche riguardo alla presunzione riguardante i 'mestieri illeciti'),[82] in cui il mondo rurale viene considerato anche come una larga fetta di popolazione ribelle ed indocile, e potenzialmente pericolosa; ma insieme a questa corrente 'negativa' va facendosi strada, almeno a partire dai *Versus de Unibove* dell'XI secolo,[83] una correlativa satira 'positiva', tesa a rilevare come talvolta il rozzo villano riesca, in virtù della sua furbizia e astuzia, ad aver la meglio sui suoi oppressori e padroni, rivendicando l'autonomia e il sentimento di rivalsa della classe cui appartiene contro i suoi tradizionali oppositori (i chierici, i borghesi, i cavalieri).[84] E' una distinzione

[79] C. Casagrande-S. Vecchio, 'L'interdizione del giullare nel vocabolario clericale del XII e XIII secolo', in *Il contributo dei giullari*, 207–258; Casagrande-Vecchio, 'Clercs et jongleurs dans la société médiévale', *Annales* v, 1979, 913–928.

[80] Per il tema della satira del villano, cfr. D. Merlini, *Saggio di ricerche sulla satira contro il villano con appendice di documenti inediti*, Torino 1894; B. Wiese, 'Zur Satire auf die Bauern', in AA. VV., *Scritti di erudizione e di critica in onore di Rodolfo Renier*, Torino 1912, 469–474; M. Feo, 'Dal pius agricola al villano empio e bestiale. A proposito di una infedeltà virgiliana del Caro', *Maia* xx, 1968, 89–136 e 206–223; J. Le Goff, 'I contadini e il mondo rurale nella letteratura dell'Alto Medioero', in *Tempo della Chiesa e tempo del mercante, e altri saggi sul lavoro e la cultura nel Medioevo*, Torino 1977, 99–113; Bertini, 'Il "nuovo" nella letteratura in latino', in *L'Europa dei secoli XI e XII fra novità e tradizione: sviluppi di una cultura. Atti della Decima Settimana internazionale di studio (Mendola, 25–29 agosto 1986)*, Milano 1989, 216–238; Bertini, 'Il diavolo e il contadino', *Abstracta* xxxvi, 1989, 50–61; in generale, sulle condizioni dei contadini nel Medioevo: E. Power, 'Bodo il contadino. La vita in un possedimento di campagna ai tempi di Carlo Magno', in *Vita nel Medioevo*, Torino 1966, 11–36; E. Le Roy Ladurie, *I contadini di Linguadoca*, Bari 1989; G. Cherubini, 'Il contadino e il lavoro dei campi', in AA. VV., *L'uomo medievale*, a cura di J. Le Goff, Roma-Bari 1987, 125–154.

[81] La celebre tripartizione della società in *oratores, bellatores* e *laboratores* risale, com'è noto, ad Adalberone di Laon (*Carmen ad Robertum regem Francorum*, PL cxli, 779–782): cfr. G. Duby, *L'anno Mille*, Torino 1976, 57–59; e soprattutto J. Le Goff, 'Società tripartita, ideologia monarchica e rinnovamento economico nella cristianità dal secolo IX al XII', in *Tempo della Chiesa*, 41–51.

[82] Le Goff, 'Mestieri leciti e mestieri illeciti nell'Occidente medievale', in *Tempo della Chiesa*, 53–71.

[83] G. La Placa, 'I *versus de Unibove*, un poema dell'XI secolo tra letteratura e folklore', *Sandalion* viii–ix, 1985–1986, 285–306; Bertini, 'Il "nuovo" nella letteratura', 222–224; Bertini, 'Il diavolo e il contadino', *passim*.

[84] Bertini, 'Il diavolo e il contadino', 58–60.

particolarmente importante, su cui si è a lungo discusso,[85] anche se, alla luce delle
indagini più recenti in tal senso, occorre rilevare che essa non si configura in
modo così netto come voleva il Merlini, ma assume (soprattutto per quanto
concerne la satira 'positiva') toni più sfumati ed ambigui, in cui talvolta l'astuzia
del villano prende delle connotazioni di diabolicità.[86]

Nel *De clericis et rustico* quest'aspetto è particolarmente insistito, pur nella
brevità della *pièce*, in una storia in cui, appunto, il rozzo villano riesce a farla in
barba, proprio in virtù della sua furbizia, ai due studenti che imprudentemente si
erano accompagnati a lui nel viaggio verso un santuario. Nello schema contra-
stivo che caratterizza buona parte del testo, come si è detto, l'eco della mentalità
antivillanesca si scopre fin dalle prime battute dei *clerici*, quando uno di loro dice
al *rusticus*: '*Sed placet; ergo prei; plus pede namque potes*',[87] in una considerazione della sveltezza di passo del contadino rispetto agli studenti che è evidente
spia (come non è sfuggito al più recente editore) di una società in cui l'attività
manuale veniva vista come subordinata rispetto a quella intellettuale.[88] Ma ancor
più rilevante è la seconda sezione del mimo, nella quale i due *clerici* si accordano
per ingannare il loro compagno. Dice infatti il primo di essi:

> Rusticus ille vorax totum consumeret uno
> Morsu; sic nobis portio nulla foret.[89]

E gli fa eco il secondo:

> Rusticus est Corydon et magne simplicitatis,
> Inscius ille doli fallibilisque dolo.
> Est in eo nimiumque gule minimumque dolorum;
> Si vis ergo gulam fallere, finge dolos.[90]

E il primo ribatte:

> Quam bene dixisti! Non amplius exigo verbum.
> Conveniamus eum dissimulesque dolum.[91]

---

[85] Sull'opera del Merlini, cfr. le recensioni di A. D'Ancona (*Rassegna bibliografica della Letteratura italiana* ii, 1894, 256), di V. Rossi (*Giornale Storico della Letteratura italiana* xxiv, 1894,
432–436), di G. Paris (*Romania* xxiv, 1895, 142–145). Al saggio del Merlini e al problema della
'satira del villano' dedica pochissimo spazio V. Cian, *La satira. I. Dal Medio Evo al Pontano*,
Milano 1923, 54. Per una moderna ridiscussione delle tesi del Merlini, cfr. poi G. Dossena,
introduzione a G. C. Croce, *Bertoldo e Bertoldino* (col '*Cacasenno*' di Adriano Banchieri), Milano
1984, 5–23; e soprattutto G. C. Belletti, 'Su alcuni casi di presunta attenuazione della satira contro
il villano nei fabliaux', in *Studi filologici, letterari e storici in memoria di Guido Favati*, Padova
1977, I, 91–113; e L. Borghi Cedrini, *La cosmologia del villano secondo testi extravaganti del
Duecento francese*, Alessandria 1989.
[86] Bisanti, 'Dalla favola mediolatina al fabliau antico-francese', *Quaderni medievali* xxxi–xxxii,
1991, 59–105 (in particolare, 84–87 e 95–96).
[87] *De cler. et rust.*, v.10 (Cadoni, 370).
[88] Cadoni, 371.
[89] *De cler. et rust.*, vv.15–16 (Cadoni 372).
[90] *De cler. et rust.*, vv.17–20 (Cadoni 372).
[91] *De cler. et rust.*, vv.21–22 (Cadoni 372). A questa sezione del mimo, sulla scorta dell'*exemplum*
di Pietro Alfonsi, fa eco l'autore del fabliau *De deux borgois et d'un vilain* (vv.28–30 Belletti: 'Cist
paisanz est un mal glouton, / si nos convenroit porpenser / comment le puision enganner'):
Bisanti, 'Fabliaux antico-francesi', 18.

Il breve scambio di battute è indicativo, e contiene *in nuce* tutti i tratti distintivi di una visione 'negativa' del *rusticus*, vorace, insaziabile, capace di fare un sol boccone dell'unica focaccia rimasta, ma insieme sciocco e grezzo, incapace di inganni (ed in questo contesto si giustifica ampiamente l'uso reiterato e quasi poliptotico di termini afferenti alla sfera semantica della 'frode', come *doli fallibilisque dolo, minimumque dolorum, fallere, finge dolos, dissimulesque dolum*).[92] E' l'immagine di una classe privilegiata nei confronti di una classe subalterna, le cui attribuzioni tradizionali vengono schematizzate nel contrasto (che si rivelerà appunto fallimentare) fra l'enorme ingordigia del contadino e la sua 'semplicità', cui fa da contrapposto la presunta astuzia dei due studenti. Ma è evidente che la satira 'negativa' si trasforma ben presto in satira 'positiva' quando, rimasto solo il *rusticus*, rovescia la situazione a suo vantaggio, in un monologo che richiama spesso *ad verbum* alcune affermazioni già lette in queste battute dei *clerici*, in un capovolgimento di rapporti umani e sociali che è anche capovolgimento di mentalità. Dopo essersi accordati sul fatto che mangerà la focaccia chi avrà fatto il più bel sogno, il villano medita sulla strana situazione, in una serie di considerazioni e di giudizi sui cittadini e sui *clerici* che rappresentano lo speculare contrasto di ciò che i *clerici* avevano detto e pensato di lui. Frasi quali:

> Cum sint urbani, cum semper in urbe dolosi,
> Suspicor in sociis non michi esse doli[93]

o anche:

> Quicquid id est coniecto dolos timeoque dolosos;
> Utque reor, pacti causa fuere mali.
> Qui premunitur non fallitur et capientem
> Primo piget raro; me capere ergo bonum est[94]

o ancora:

> Et magis expediet libum libasse latendo
> Huncque dedisse dolum quam caruisse dolo[95]

oltre a rivelare l'astuzia del contadino, che si vuol mettere al sicuro, costituiscono il più preciso indice del rapporto di opposizione fra *clerici* e villani. Gli studenti hanno ritenuto stolto e incapace il loro rustico compagno, e se la dormono

---

[92] Il procedimento adottato dal poeta nei riguardi del termine *dolus* è un esempio di medievale *traductio* (o *polipteton*): Matth. Vind. *Ars* III, 13 (*Polipteton est quando multitudo casuum varietate distinguitur*, Faral 171); Galf. de Vino Salvo *Summa de coloribus rhetoricis* 4 (*Traductio est quando casus a casu traducitur*). Inoltre, occorre osservare che l'accumulo, in breve spazio, di termini afferenti alla sfera semantica dell''inganno' e della 'frode' ricorre con notevole frequenza nella letteratura mediolatina, fino a diventare una sorta di *topos*: cfr. *Baucis et Traso*, vv. 10, 19, 26, 32, 52, 79, 94, 105, 106 ecc.; Walther, *Aesopus* XXXIII, 11–12; XLIX, 11; XLIX, 14 (L. Hervieux, *Les fabulistes latins*, Paris 1894[2], II, 332, 342); il carme *De sponsa et marito absente*, v.20 (Bisanti, 'Il carme *De sponsa et marito absente* attribuibile a Gualtiero Anglico. Un episodio della fortuna della favola del fanciullo di neve nella letteratura mediolatina', *Pan* ix, 1989, 77–107); e il *Novus Avianus Astensis* (I, 5, vv.9, 11, 12, 16, 27 ecc.: l'edizione critica della raccolta, a cura di L. Zurli e A. Bisanti, è in corso di stampa).

[93] *De cler. et rust.*, vv.33–34 (Cadoni, 372).

[94] *De cler. et rust.*, vv.37–40 (Cadoni, 374).

[95] *De cler. et rust.*, vv.43–44 (Cadoni, 374).

saporitamente, pensando di poterlo facilmente gabbare facendo uso della loro cultura e della loro dialettica; ma il villico sa bene che non bisogna fidarsi di loro, di coloro che abitano in città, e prende le sue difese, ricorrendo alla sua furbizia. L'autore ha costruito anche questo monologo del *rusticus* su una ristretta griglia terminologica, in cui l'insistenza della sfera semantica dell'inganno' e della 'frode', oltre a richiamare contrastivamente le battute dei *clerici*, funge da vettore ideologico, in una utilizzazione del termine *dolus* come parola-chiave non solo di questa sezione del testo, ma di tutto il mimo. Uno schema di beffa doppia, come sarà poi sempre più spesso nella novellistica europea dal Duecento al Cinquecento,[96] in cui il beffatore diventa beffato e il beffato diventa beffatore, in una duplicità di piani la cui ampia attestazione, dalle 'commedie elegiache' ai *fabliaux* al *Decameron*, finisce per diventare un vero *topos* narrativo.

Ed è così che il protagonista della nostra storia, grazie alla sua furbizia, riesce ad avere la meglio sui suoi compagni, che sono anche i suoi tradizionali avversari. La figura di Coridone nel *De clericis et rustico*, anche se in misura minore e con meno evidenti connotazioni di 'diabolicità', si inserisce quindi nella linea che dai *Versus de Unibove* conduce al *Dialogus Salomonis et Marcholphi* e quindi al *Bertoldo* crocesco.[97] Ma egli assume qui anche i tratti di una figura nota alla tradizione folklorica europea, quella del *trickster* o 'briccone divino', proprio per la sua ambivalenza di piani fra la *rusticitas* che lo caratterizza (sintomo, per i suoi avversari, di sciocchezza e di rozzezza) e l'inganno che sapidamente riesce ad organizzare.[98] Come un Arlecchino (e non si dimentichino le originali attribuzioni demoniache della maschera dello 'zanni'),[99] egli fa valere la propria astuzia e raggiunge lo scopo, che è quello di mangiarsi da solo la focaccia, in un legame con il cibo, con la materialità, che si inserisce in quella dimensione 'carnevalesca'

---

[96] Rimando, a tal proposito, al mio volume *Tradizioni retoriche e letterarie nelle 'Facezie' di Poggio Bracciolini*, in corso di pubblicazione: ivi anche l'ampia bibliografia generale e specifica sul *topos* novellistico del beffatore beffato.

[97] Sul *Dialogus*, si rimanda a Q. Marini, 'La dissacrazione come strumento di affermazione ideologica. Una lettura del Dialogo di Salomone e Marcolfo', *Studi medievali* xxviii, 1987, 667–705; *Il Dialogo di Salomone e Marcolfo*, Roma 1991. Sul *Bertoldo* del Croce, cfr. l'importante contributo di P. Camporesi, *La maschera di Bertoldo. Giulio Cesare Croce e la letteratura carnevalesca*, Torino 1976.

[98] M. Bonafin, 'La parodia e il briccone divino. Modelli antropologici e modelli letterari del *Trubert* di Douin de Lavesne', *L'immagine riflessa* v, 1982, 237–272; L. Lazzerini, in *Audigier. Poema eroicomico antico-francese in edizione critica, con versione a fronte, introduzione e commento* di L. Lazzerini, Firenze 1985, 7–113; e L. Borghi Cedrini, 70–72.

[99] L. Zorzi, 'La maschera di Arlecchino', in AA. VV., *L'arte della maschera nella Commedia dell'Arte*, a cura di D. Sartori e B. Laneta, Firenze 1983, 74–83. Sull'origine demoniaca della figura di Arlecchino, cfr. A. Wesselofsky, 'Alichino e Aredodesa', *Giornale storico della Letteratura italiana* xi, 1888, 325–343; P. Toschi, *Le origini del Teatro italiano*, Torino 1955, 166–227; F. Nicolini, *Vita di Arlecchino*, Milano-Napoli 1958; M. Apollonio, s.v. *Arlecchino*, in *Enciclopedia dello Spettacolo*, I, Roma 1954, 904–909. Altra bibliografia in *Diavoli e mostri in scena dal Medioevo al Rinascimento. Atti del Convegno di studi del Centro di studi sul teatro medioevale e rinascimentale (Roma 30 giugno-3 luglio 1988)*, a cura di M. Chiabò e F. Doglio, Roma 1989, 405–511. Colgo l'occasione per osservare che in questo senso la figura del *rusticus* può essere parzialmente assimilata a quella del laido servo Spurio nell'*Alda* di Guglielmo di Blois, soprattutto in relazione alla scena in cui costui prepara il *pastillum* (vv. 271–288), a proposito della quale è stato appunto scritto che 'l'effetto complessivo . . . è quello di un Arlecchino che si muove in una gestualità espressiva, precisa e puntigliosa, che è lo specchio di una tensione mentale, finalizzata a soddisfare un'esigenza fisiologica' (Goldin, 'Lettura dell'*Alda* di Guglielmo di Blois', *Cultura neolatina* xl, 1980, 29; Bisanti, *L'*'Alda' di Guglielmo di Blois*, 33).

dell'universo medievale che Bachtin ha indagato con tanta ampiezza e profondità.[100]

Cortesi *vs* villani, *burgenses vs* villani, *clerici vs* villani. Il villano è l'oppositore delle classi egemoniche, pericoloso e indocile al giogo di categorie di lui più potenti, ma forse non altrettanto intelligenti. Nella novella di Pietro Alfonsi che costituisce la 'fonte' del nostro mimo, i compagni di viaggio e avversari del *rusticus* sono due borghesi (come sarà ancora nel *fabliau De deux borgois et d'un vilain*); ma l'autore del *De clericis et rustico* li ha trasformati in due studenti, come si è già avuto modo di osservare. Il mutamento è assai significativo, poiché mira a mettere a contrasto le due classi notoriamente più contrapposte, i *rustici* da un lato e i *clerici* dall'altro. I tratti di animosità degli uni verso gli altri si inseriscono in una lunga tradizione, che va dall'affermazione delle *XXIII Manières de vilains*, secondo cui i contadini 'héent clers et capelains', al *fabliau Des vilains*, secondo cui ogni villano che veda dei chierici esclama 'Esgardez de ces clercs bolastres!', al rutebeuviano *Pet au vilain*, secondo cui chierici e preti non amarono mai la gente villana ('Ce di je por la gent vilaine / c'onques n'amerent clerc ne prestre'),[101] e che arriva alla compiuta 'sistemazione' della tardoquattrocentesca *Altercatio rusticorum et clericorum*;[102] ma che si ripercuote anche a livello gnomico e paremiologico, di sentenze e proverbi mediolatini, quali '*Rustice callose, semper cleris odiose, / vis te formose consociare rose*;[103] oppure '*Clericus est letus, saliens, probus et repletus; / rusticus est vilis tegmine, pelle, pilis*';[104] o ancora '*In manibus cleri viole flos debet haberi; / si teneat violam rusticus, ure volam!*';[105] e infine, e soprattutto, '*Vivant omnes clerici, confundantur rustici!*'.[106]

Ma c'è un'ultima osservazione da fare, che può forse gettare una luce di ambiguità su tutto ciò. Il villano prende in giro i suoi avversari, li ripaga con la loro stessa moneta, ma, mentre i due *clerici* hanno sognato (o, per meglio dire, fingono di aver sognato) di essersi recati l'uno in Paradiso, l'altro all'Inferno, egli è rimasto legato alla terra, ha visto ciò che accadeva loro, ma non si è mosso (tutto questo nell'ambito della beffa). Insomma, egli è rimasto pur sempre escluso dal Paradiso e dall'Inferno, come nel *fabliau* di Rutebeuf *Le Pet au vilain*, già menzionato, in cui i diavoli si accordano 'qu'en enfer ne en paradis / ne puet

---

[100] M. Bachtim, *L'opera di Rabelais e la cultura popolare. Riso, carnevale e festa nella tradizione medievale e rinascimentale*, Torino 1979.

[101] Sul problema, si rimanda a Merlini, 33–37 (ivi anche le citazioni), e a Borghi Cedrini, 132–133. In particolare, sul *Pet au vilain* (in *Fabliaux. Racconti francesi medievali*, a cura di R. Brusegan, Torino 1980, 154–159), cfr. A. Limentani, 'I fabliaux di Rutebeuf', in AA. VV., *Prospettive sui 'fabliaux'. Contesto, sistema, realizzazioni*, Padova 1976, 83–98; e soprattutto Borghi Cedrini, 31–64 e *passim*.

[102] Analisi del testo in Merlini, 38–39.

[103] 27003 Walther (in H. Walther, *Proverbia sententiaeque Latinitatis Medii Aevi*, Göttingen 1963–1969, 6 voll.).

[104] 2853 Walther.

[105] 11824 Walther.

[106] 33925 Walther. Altri proverbi dello stesso genere sono 27009 W. (*Rustici barbati volunt esse nostri prelati*); 26519a W. (*Regula clericalis est omni tempore talis: / non laborat, non orat, non ieiunat; / sed tres quadrati sunt cum eo rustici nati: / primus laborat, secundus nutrit sibi uxorem, / tertius cum dolo intrat abyssum*). Si osservi che anche la contrapposizione fra *rustici* e *urbani* è presente in alcune espressioni proverbiali: 27038 W. (*Rusticus urbane factis se nescit habere*); 27038a W. (*Rusticus urbano confusus, turpis honesto*).

vilains entrer sanz doute',[107] e lo stesso autore afferma che non sa dire 'ou l'en puisse ame a vilain metre, / qu'ele a failli a ces deus raignes'.[108] La satira 'positiva' e quella 'negativa si confondono e si intersecano ancora una volta, e la lettura del mimo lascia un retrogusto acre e amaro di ambiguità sottile, celata fra le pieghe di una beffa ridanciana che, come credo sia emerso da questa analisi, rimanda ai modelli mentali, alle frontiere culturali e alle opposizioni classiste di una società in trasformazione, quale fu quella fra i secoli XII e XIII.

---

[107] Rutebeuf, *Le pet au vilain*, vv. 64–65.
[108] Rutebeuf, *Le pet au vilain*, vv. 68–69.

Simon Magus in South Italy

H.E.J. Cowdrey

Amongst the mosaics of the Cappella Palatina at Palermo, there are, in the southern and northern aisles, series which depict scenes from the lives of St Peter and St Paul, who are first shown separately and then as a pair. The mosaics are hard to date, but they probably belong to the third quarter of the twelfth century. Apart from the priority in time that they imply for Paul's missionary activities, the sequences of the apostles taken separately follow events recorded in the Acts of the Apostles. But when they are taken together, history dissolves into fiction. The fiction is located at Rome, and has three episodes. First, and so far historically according to Acts 28: 14–15, Paul journeyed there, having been accompanied from the Forum of Appius and Three Taverns by a party which came down from Rome to meet him; when Paul saw it, he thanked God and took courage. Un-historically, Peter is shown as leader of the party from Rome; upon meeting, the apostles embraced, watched by one of Peter's companions. A second episode, wholly fictitious, introduces Simon Magus, the father of all simoniacs who appeared in Acts at Samaria as a sometime practitioner of magic whose marvels had won him a following there; although he was baptised, Peter roundly rebuked him when he offered silver in return for the power of being himself able to confer the Holy Spirit (Acts 8: 9–24). The mosaic shows Peter and Paul in dispute with Simon Magus before the Emperor Nero. *Nero rex* sits crowned and enthroned with Simon Magus at his right hand, while Peter and Paul earnestly engage him. In the third mosaic, nemesis strikes: the caption runs that 'Here, by Peter's command and by Paul's prayer, Simon Magus falls to the ground.' Simon had caused Nero to erect a scaffold upon high ground so that he could demonstrate a miraculous power of flight. Icarus-like, he fell from the sky; he is shown plummeting down, escorted by two winged demons. The apostles have triumphed. There is no reference to their subsequent martyrdom by Nero's command, but Peter's victory is reinforced by a painting on the roof-timbers over the third mosaic, where he stands with three deacons and, in his hand, the keys of heaven.[1] The threefold sequence recurs in mosaics of Monreale cathedral which probaby date from the late 1180s.[2]

These and related fictitious scenes relating to Peter's dealings with Simon Magus have a familiar place in art history; they are exemplified over a wide area of place and time. In the east, the death of Simon Magus had a recognized place

---

[1] O. Demus, *The Mosaics of Norman Sicily*, London 1950, 46 and nn., 299, Plates 43AB (Demus indicates the extent and nature of restoration); E. Borsook, *Messages in Mosaic: the Royal Programmes of Norman Sicily (1130–1187)*, Oxford 1990, 29–31, 39–41, Fig. 4, Plates 16, 54–6.
[2] They are in the side-chapel at the south-east corner of the cathedral: Demus (as n.1), 119, 123–48, Plate 83; Borsook (as n.1), 53, 60–1, Plates 57, 76.

in the Painter's Manual which was the repository of age-long Byzantine artistic traditions.[3] In the west, the earliest known examples were the mosaics of the disputation before Nero and of Simon's fall and death in the Lady Chapel built at St Peter's in Rome under Pope John VII (705–7), and which are known from early seventeenth-century copies.[4] They were probably the inspiration of paintings including the same subjects in the north apse of the abbey of St John at Müstair, in Switzerland; origially dating from Carolingian times, they were partly repainted in the third quarter of the twelfth century according to ideas then current.[5] In the last decade of the tenth century, similar themes occur in the illuminations of a book, the Antiphonary of Prüm, north of Trier.[6] Early in the next century, the embroideries of the pluviale known as the mantle of St Kunigunde, wife of the German emperor Henry II, which is now at Bamberg, included four panels concerning Simon Magus.[7] The same theme occurs in the mosaics of St Mark's at Venice, which survive only in early seventeenth-century replacements which probably preserve the subjects, though not necessarily the inscriptions, of their twelfth-century predecessors.[8] It is within this broad context of artistic interest in the legends of Simon Magus that the mosaics of the Cappella Palatina and Monreale must be set.

This distribution of artistic representations of the legends of Simon Magus is the tip of an iceberg whose bulk is to be found in a proliferation from the earliest Christian times of literary versions which became no less widespread in the early and central middle ages. Upon this material, a large and important book urgently needs to be written; only a few, tentative comments can be offered now. By and large, two distinct, and to a surprising degree separate, lines of tradition developed about the Simon Magus of the Acts of the Apostles who, it should be remembered, was not there said to have done further evil, whether himself or through his followers; on the contrary, he answered Peter's rebuke by beseeching the apostle to pray for him to the Lord, that nothing of what Peter had said might come upon him. The line of subsequent tradition that is most familiar to historians was relatively late in developing. It was first presented in a sophisticated form by Pope Gregory the Great (590–604).[9] It built upon Simon as the mercenary figure who, when he saw Peter conferring the Holy Spirit, offered silver that he might

3   P. Hetherington, *The 'Painter's Manual' of Dionysius of Fourna: an English Translation, with Commentary, of cod. gr. 708 in the Saltykov-Schedrin State Public Library, Leningrad*, London 1974, 66. Although Dionysius wrote in 1730/4, the purpose of the Manual was to co-ordinate and regulate Byzantine artistic traditions.
4   J. Wilpert, *Die römischen Mosaiken und Malereien der kirchlichen Bauten von 4–13 Jahrhundert*, 4 vols, 2nd edn, Freiburg-im-Breisgau 1917, i.399–400, Fig. 136. Sketches by G. Grimaldi survive in Rome, Vatican Library, MSS Barb. lat. 2732, fo. 75v, and 2733, fo. 89.
5   L. Birchler, 'Zur karolingischen Architektur und Malerei in Münster-Müstair', in *Frühmittelalterliche Kunst in den Alpenländern*, Olten/Lausanne 1954, 167–252 at 221–4, Fig. 96; B. Brenk, *Die romanische Wandmalerei in der Schweiz*, Berne 1963, 28–61, esp. 44–7, Fig. 3ab, Plates 20–1, 23.
6   Paris, BN, MS lat. 9448, fo. 55v. See P. Lauer, *Les Enluminures romanes des manuscrits de la Bibliothèque nationale*, Paris 1927, 116–21; A. Goldschmidt, *German Illumination*, 2 vols, Munich/Florence 1928, Plate 68.
7   W. Messerer, *Der Bamberger Domschatz in seinem Bestande bis zum Ende der Hohenstaufen-Zeit*, Munich 1952, 15–16, 27, 57–61, Plates 49, 51. The pluviale is of Bavarian origin.
8   O. Demus, *The Mosaics of San Marco in Venice*, 2 vols in 4 parts, Chicago/London 1984, i.219–27.
9   *Homiliae XL in Evangelio*, 1.4.4, 17.3, *PL* lxxvi. 1091–2, 1145–6; *Epp*. 9.216, 219, 12.9,

receive a like gift. According to the Acts of the Apostles, Peter rebuked him: 'Your silver perish with you, because you thought you could obtain the gift of God with money!' Simon became the prototype of all who, by proffering service, money, or promises sought to traffic in sacred orders and offices. A second line of tradition largely left aside this aspect of the Simon Magus story. In it, Simon was built up as the figure who, at Samaria, said that he was himself someone great, and who while still unbaptised had induced a following to take him at his word, saying that 'This man is the power of God who is called Great.' It was by magic arts that Simon had so amazed the crowds. According to the legends, there ensued a contest, to the death on both sides, between Simon the counterfeit power of God and Peter who exercised God's true power. It was a contest partly of words and partly of wonders: Simon with his magic was opposed by Peter with the Holy Spirit of God. Its climax was the encounter before Nero as depicted in the Cappella Palatina mosaics. Its outcome, which they do not depict, was the apostles' martyrdom by Nero's command – Peter by crucifixion head-downwards, and Paul by beheading.

This luxuriant growth of legends involving Simon Magus, not as trafficker in orders and offices but as, literally, magician, is already exemplified in such Christian fathers as the Apologist Justin Martyr (c.100–c.165) and Hippolytus of Rome (c.170–c.236).[10] Simon Magus was deemed to be a founder of Gnostic heresy and the first and father of all heretics. Of the literature about him that proliferated in the post-Constantinian church, it must suffice to cite two examples which, in Latin translation, circulated widely into the central middle ages. The 'Clementine Recognitions' were so called after St Clement, the bishop of Rome whom, according to some traditions, Peter himself ordained to be his successor there. The Recognitions took their present form in the late fourth century, and survive in a Latin version by Rufinus of Aquileia (345–410). It survives in many manuscripts from Germany, Italy, France, and England, and gave wide currency to a prolonged rivalry between Peter and Simon Magus with the eastern cities of Caesarea, Tripolis, and Antioch as its locations.[11] The rivalry in its climax at Rome was the subject of a large literature on the martyrdoms there of Peter and Paul which made a major contribution to the medieval cult of the princes of the apostles and to the image of Christian Rome. It is well exemplified by the *Passio sanctorum Petri et Pauli auctore Marcello* (usually referred to as Pseudo-

---

S. Gregorii Magni Registrum epistularum, ed. D. Norberg, 2 vols, Corpus Christianorum, Series Latina CXL, CXLA, Turnhout 1982, ii. 776–9, 782–5, 980–2.

[10] Saint Justin, *Apologies*, ed. A. Wartelle, Paris 1987, 1.26, 56, pp. 131–2, 177; Hippolytus, *Refutatio omnium haeresium*, 6.20, ed. M. Marcovitch, Patristiche Texte und Studien 25, Berlin/New York 1986, 228–9.

[11] For the text of the Clementine Recognitions, see *Die Pseudoklementinen, ii: Rekognitionen in Rufins Übersetzung*, ed. B. Rehm, Die Griechischen christlichen Schriftsteller der ersten Jahrhunderte 51, Berlin 1965, 118–77; the MSS are listed at xvii–cvii; for a discussion, Rehm, 'Clemens Romanus II. (Ps. Clementinen)', *Reallexikon für Antike und Christentum* iii (1957), 197–206. Despite its age, there is invaluable material in G. Salmon, 'Clementine Literature', *A Dictionary of Christian Biography, Literature, Sects and Doctrines*, edd. W. Smith and H. Wace, 4 vols, London 1877–87, i.567–78 (summary of the Recognitions at 568–70). Salmon's articles 'Linus', 'Marcellus (11)', and 'Simon Magus', in the same *Dictionary* iii. 726–9, 813, iv. 681–8, also repay reading. Also useful are É. Amann, 'Simon le Magicien', and A. Bride, 'Simonie', *Dictionnaire de Théologie Catholique* xiv (1941), 2130–40, 2141–60; V.I.J. Flint, *The Rise of Magic in Early Medieval Europe*, Oxford 1991, esp. 19, 46, 81, 338–44.

Marcellus); it, too, gained widespread manuscript currency by the central middle ages.[12] It was presented through the eyes of one Marcellus, a legendary disciple of Peter whom Peter converted from his allegiance to Simon Magus. Opening with the apostles' preaching at Rome, it tells how Simon Magus delated Peter to Nero, how the apostles disputed with him before that emperor, how Peter successfully tamed savage hounds who were set upon him, how Simon botched an attempt at a miracle of resurrection, and how Simon's attempt to fly from a tower ended with his ignominious death. Then it describes the martyrdoms of Peter and Paul.

With increasing frequency during the tenth and eleventh centuries, the figure of Simon Magus also appears in Latin hymns, especially hymns in honour of St Peter, which were written over wide areas of Europe. Only seldom did they refer to Simon as the would-be purchaser of the gifts of the Holy Spirit; they drew mainly upon such legends of Peter and Simon Magus at Rome as are exemplified in Pseudo-Marcellus.[13]

Such, in broad summary, were the two lines of tradition about Simon Magus, the first, illustrated by Pope Gregory I, settling upon him as the would-be trafficker in sacred things, while the second, as illustrated by the Clementine Recognitions and Pseudo-Marcellus, settled upon him as the sectary, magician, and lifelong opponent of Peter. It seems evident, though it cannot be proved, that some value-judgements established by the second line also coloured the first; most obviously, from the time of Pope Gregory I trafficking in holy orders and offices was stigmatised as the 'simoniac heresy'.[14] But, for the most part, the two lines of tradition ran independently and without substantial interaction, at least until the reforming ferment of the later eleventh century. Moreover, most of the artistic evidence, like that at Palermo, indicates that even in the twelfth century any convergence was occasional rather than normal.

The main purpose of this paper is to ask whether, despite the range and complexity of the evidence for the perception of Simon Magus by the eleventh and twelfth centuries, Rome and Italy to the south of Rome may have played a special part in shaping and disseminating ideas about him.

The artistic evidence provides a little indication that they did so. The mosaics of John VII's Lady Chapel in St Peter's at Rome must have been familiar to many visitors to the city, and they have been suggested as a model for the Carolingian sequence at Müstair.[15] No such Roman inspiration can be claimed for the visual or literary imagery of Simon Magus in South Italy or Sicily. Instead, the general debt of the mosaics of the Cappella Palatina to Byzantine models has been persuasively argued.[16] Southern imagery had its own stamp, and it may have been by

---

[12] For the Greek text and Latin translation, see *Acta apostolorum apocrypha*, edd. R.A. Lipsius and M. Bonnet, 2 vols, Leipzig 1881–1903, i.118–77; the MSS are listed at lxxiv–lxxxiii.

[13] J. Szövérffy, 'The Legends of St Peter in Medieval Latin Hymns', *Traditio* x (1954), 275–322, esp. 294–311; Szövérffy, 'Der Investiturstreit und die Petrus-Hymnen des Mittelalters', *Deutsches Archiv für Erforschung des Mittelalters* xiii (1957), 228–40, esp. 235–8; Szövérffy, *A Mirror of Medieval Culture: Saint Peter Hymns of the Middle Ages*, Transactions of the Connecticut Academy of Arts and Sciences 42, New Haven/Copenhagen 1965, 97–403, esp. 272–80, 371–7.

[14] J. Leclercq, ' "*Simoniaca heresis*" ', *Studi Gregoriani* i (1947), 522–30.

[15] Birchler (as n.5).

[16] e.g. by E. Kitzinger, 'The Mosaics of the Cappella Palatina in Palermo: an Essay on the Choice and Arrangements of Subjects', *Art Bulletin* xxxix (1949), 269–92, repr. *The Art of Byzantium and the Medieval West: Selected Studies by Ernst Kitzinger*, ed. W.E. Kleinbauer, Bloomington/London 1976, 290–319.

one channel or another, widely influential. Demus detects an indebtedness to it in the mosaics of St Mark's at Venice: 'Although the Disputation with Simon and his Fall also appear in Byzantine representations,' he writes, 'the placing of the scene in Rome and the inclusion of Nero make it likely that the prototype was an Italian or Italo-Byzantine representation similar to those of the Sicilian mosaics.'[17] With reference to the Romanesque frescos at Müstair, Brenk notices that depictions in the central middle ages of Peter taming the savage dogs that Simon Magus set upon him centre upon Italy, and suggests that the frescos probably have an Italian inspiration.[18] Rome and South Italy may have been of special importance in the transmission of the legends of Simon Magus through the visual arts.

The principal evidence for south Italy's importance in the literary and propagandist use of the legends centres upon the abbey of Montecassino.[19] Concern there with the legends was both prolonged and intense, beginning with the Clementine Recognitions. While no surviving manuscript of them has Cassinese associations, the stories about Simon Magus that they contain were well known through their adaptation in a *Vita sancti Clementis* in three books which was commissioned and partly written between 876 and 882 by Bishop Gauderic of Velletri; it was dedicated to Pope John VIII (872–82). It is partially preserved in Montecassino, MS 234, where it was copied in the first half of the eleventh century.[20] Early in the twelfth century, a shorter version of Gaudentius's Vita was written by the sometime Cassinese monk and chronicler who from 1102/7 until his death in 1115 was cardinal-bishop of Ostia/Velletri, Leo Marsicanus. Known as the *De origine beati Clementis*, it was the first of a trilogy by Leo on the subject of Clement; though Simon Magus's debates with Peter were much abbreviated, Gaudentius's account of his activities was retained.[21]

If the stories of the Clementine Recognitions in this way kept alive at Montecassino the supposed dealings of the heretic with the apostle up to the latter's time at Antioch, manuscripts of Pseudo-Marcellus in the abbey's library made available the traditions of their confrontation at Rome which led to their contrasting deaths. Four Cassinese manuscripts of the eleventh century include Pseudo-Marcellus; they provided lections for St Peter's Day (29 June) which made the traditions familiar to the monastic community.[22]

Cassinese interest in the rivalry of St Peter and Simon Magus found its fullest expression in a long poem written at Montecassino c.1077/9 by its monk Amatus,

[17] Demus (as n.8), i.221.

[18] Brenk (as n.5), 49.

[19] For further discussion, see H.E.J. Cowdrey, *The Age of Abbot Desiderius: Montecassino, the Papacy, and the Normans in the Eleventh and Early Twelfth Centuries*. Oxford 1983, esp. 83–8.

[20] *Iohannis Hymmonides et Gauderici Veliterni, Leonis Ostiensis, Excerpta ex Clementinis Recognitionibus a Tyrannio Rufino Translatis*, ed. I. Orlandi, Milan/Varese 1968; the principal references to Simon Magus are at 1.7–13, 38–40, 47–57, 2.55, 73–80, pp. 12–18, 41–3, 49–60, 144–6, 159–64. For the MS, see *Codicum Casinensium manuscriptorum catalogus*, ed. M. Inguanez, 3 vols, Montecassino 1915–51, ii.45.

[21] Orlandi edited the text in parallel with that of Gaudentius; the principal references to Simon Magus are in caps 7, 21–7, 54, 81, 86, pp. 12–13, 33–5, 49–60, 92–4, 144–6, 164. Besides Gaudentius, Leo used Rufinus's translation itself. The sole MS of Leo is Prague, Archivum capituli metropolitani, MS N.XXIII (1547), fos 132r–147r.

[22] The MSS are: 104 (1022/35), 142 (C11²), 147 (C11²), 148 (1010), for which see Inguanez (as n.20), i.123–7, 226–8, 235–8. For their liturgical use, see A. Lentini, *Il poema di Amato su S. Pietro apostolo*, 2 vols, Miscellanea Cassinese 30–1, Montecassino 1958–9, ii. 278.

who was also the author of a history of the Norman conquest of South Italy. The full title of the poem in the sole surviving manuscript, now Bologna, Bibliotheca Universitaria, MS 2843, is *Liber Amati monachi Casinensis destinatus ad domnum Gregorium papam in honore beati Petri apostoli*.[23] Its four books bring together as does no other medieval source, literary or otherwise, all facets of the apostle's biblical and legendary biography. Books I and II are about the biblical Peter, and respectively follow closely, with only occasional accretions, the accounts of him in the Gospels and in the Acts of the Apostles. Books III and IV show a wide acquaintance with the legendary sources for his subsequent life and martyrdom. Book III tells the story from his time at Caesarea to his time at Antioch; it depends largely, but by no means only, upon Gauderic's *Vita sancti Clementis*. Book IV is entitled *De passione apostolorum Petri et Pauli*, and has Pseudo-Marcellus as the principal of its various sources.[24]

As a result of its layout and sources, Amatus's poem was unusual in that it brought out both lines of tradition about Simon Magus – the would-be trafficker in sacred things, and the magician and life-long opponent of the greater wonder-worker, St Peter. On the biblical evidence of Acts 8, Amatus devoted a powerful section to Peter's rebuking of Simon when he asked to purchase the Holy Spirit and to Peter's consequent expulsion of the 'plague of Simon' (*Symonis haec pestis*).[25] The poem placarded Simon as the exemplar of those who, in the eleventh century, traded in ecclesiastical offices and orders. The legendary evidence for Simon was then fully deployed to exhibit him as the lethal rival of Peter during the rest of his life, who eventually suffered the débâcle of his own magical powers at Rome, but who also brought about the martyrdom of Peter and Paul at the hands of a wicked Nero.

As constituting the poem a tract for the times, its dedication to Pope Gregory VII is important. Unfortunately, almost the whole of Amatus's dedicatory epistle to him is lost through damage to the manuscript. However, his regard for Gregory, whose abhorrence of simony as a current ecclesiastical offence he shared, led Amatus to conclude his account of Peter's rebuking of Simon at Samaria with a eulogy of Gregory's zeal against simony.[26] Elsewhere, Amatus referred with enthusiasm to Gregory's authority as pope, with undertones of his distance from everything simoniacal. In comment upon Christ's commission to Peter at Caesarea Philippi (Matt. 16: 13–19), he reflected that Peter's power had now passed freely (*gratis*) to Gregory who was thus the pattern of rightly-acquired authority.[27] In comment upon Christ's promise to Peter that his faith would not fail and that, when he had turned again, he would strengthen his brethren (Luke 22: 31–2), Amatus referred to Peter's *pura fides* and to his freedom from stains of evil (*pravorum . . . macula*). Christ's gifts to Peter had devolved upon Gregory, at whose feet kings prostrated themselves, whose laws they obeyed, and by whom they governed their kingdoms.[28] A reference here to the penance at Canossa in January 1077 of King Henry IV of Germany before Gregory is possible but not

---

[23] Lentini (as n.22), i.60. For Amatus, see Cowdrey (as n.19), xx, 25–6, 75–9, 83–5, 88.

[24] Amatus's sources are analysed by Lentini (as n.22), ii.45–98.

[25] 2.7, ed. Lentini, i.83–4.

[26] 2.7, lines 8–14, ed. Lentini, i.84.

[27] 1.6, lines 20–2, ed. Lentini, i.65.

[28] 1.18, ed. Lentini, i.72–3.

certain. Of greater moment is Amatus's identification of Gregory as currently the representative of Peter who embodied the purity and freedom of his authority. The question arises whether, since Gregory was thus identified with Peter, in the remainder of the poem the king who opposed him, Henry IV of Germany, was to be identified with the Emperor Nero who wickedly opposed the martyred Peter. Amatus did not make the identification, and the political sensitivity of Montecassino's position would have made it rash for him to do so.[29] Yet the tendency of Amatus's poem was towards such an identification, which others were soon to make.[30] Amatus's depiction of Peter's triumph in his contest with Simon Magus at least pointed in this direction and suggested a line of telling propaganda as the struggle between Gregory and Henry intensified.

In his poem, Amatus makes clear his active interest while a monk of Montecassino in the whole gamut of history and legend about Simon Magus. He combined it with ardent zeal against simony as an ecclesiastical abuse, and for Gregory VII in his determination to eradicate it. The next part of this paper will be concerned with the questions of where Amatus stands in the long history of the dissemination of the legends of Simon Magus, and of whether he provides evidence that these legends were especially disseminated in and from South Italy.

Amatus was certainly a pioneer in his extensive use of the legends for polemical purposes in connection with ecclesiastical reform. Widespread though the legends had for centuries been in art, in hymnody, and in manuscript diffusion, until the mid-1070s they were largely ignored in polemical literature and in the writings of reformers. Despite the propaganda opportunities presented by the story of Simon Magus's débâcle and death at Rome, there is, surprisingly, no trace of the legends in Cardinal Humbert's *Adversus simoniacos* (1057/8).[31] Peter Damiani referred to them only once – in a rhyming colophon at the conclusion of his *Liber gratissimus*, addressed in 1062 to Bishop Cadalus of Parma (the antipope Honorius II); Peter warned Cadalus that he was like Simon Magus in aspiring to the stars and that the jaws of hell would likewise swallow him.[32] The almost entire disregard of the legends by the early Roman reforming cardinals is the more remarkable since they cannot have been unaware of the mosaics of John VII at St Peter's.

From the mid-1070s and into the twelfth century, references to the Simon Magus legends of the kind that occur in Amatus's fourth book appeared sporadically but quite widely in polemical literature against simony. German writers of Gregorian stamp occasionally drew upon them. An early example is the Reichenau chronicler Berthold, who wrote the second recension of his chronicle during the late 1070s. When Bishop Henry of Speyer, whom Gregory had deposed and excommunicated for simony at his Lent council of 1075, on the very day of his sentence died by choking as he rose from an overladen meal-table, Berthold saw a wielding of St Peter's sword by which he had cast down the heresiarch Simon as

---

[29] This sensitivity is illustrated by the Chronicle of Montecassino, e.g. *Chronica monasterii Casinensis*, 3.18, 50, ed. H. Hoffmann, *MGH Scriptores*, xxxiv.385, 430–3.

[30] See below, p. 84.

[31] *Humberti cardinalis Libri III. adversus simoniacos*, ed. F. Thaner, *MGH Libelli de lite*, i. 95–253.

[32] *Die Briefe des Petrus Damiani*, no. 89, ed. K. Reindel, *MGH Die Briefe der deutschen Kaiserzeit* 4, ii. 531–72, at 572.

he made his would-be ascent to heaven. Falling to earth he was rent asunder into four pieces and dispatched to hell for eternal damnation. Let all simoniacs beware of a like fate![33] In 1081, another supporter of Gregory VII, Archbishop Gebhard of Salzburg, rounded on episcopal supporters of King Henry of Germany who in 1080 at the synod of Brixen had proclaimed Gregory's deposition and called for his supersession by Archbishop Guibert of Ravenna. Gebhard pressed them as to whether it was compatible with their office to assist a Christian king in his purpose 'after the example of Nero to make Peter and Paul once more suffer in their members, and again set Simon Magus against Simon Peter.'[34] Henry was thus the new Nero and Guibert the new Simon.

The legends of Simon Magus also found currency in popular songs and rhymes. In the domains of Countess Matilda of Tuscany, a lively poem *Adversus simoniacos* praised Gregory VII who was embattled with a wrathful Caesar. After referring to Simon Magus's building a tower against Peter and to his being struck by Peter's irresistable blow, the poem described the division of society into two camps,

> Quorum rex est alter Christus, alter est Leviathan;
> Ille vitae, iste mortis regnat super agmina;
> Ergo quorum quis sit victor, nemo sanus ambigit.[35]

In a poem by Alfanus, the friend of Abbot Desiderius of Montecassino who was archbishop of Salerno from 1058 to 1085, Nero was said to have avenged the death of his 'friend' Simon Magus by having St Peter crucified.[36] In 1095, a monk of Saint-Laurent at Liège composed a series of poems about the afflictions of his abbot and monastery at the hands of the Henrician bishop, Otbert. He had strong words to say about the plight of Rome in view of the Wibertine schism, which he depicted as directly the work of Nero and Simon Magus:

> Vel quis afflictę poterit mederi
> Cum Nero Romam teneat Symonque
> Papa vocetur?

With an eye to the struggle at Liège, the poet invoked Simon Magus's proud flight towards heaven and urged St Peter to renew his victory over him.[37] Another poem about simony, evidently written by an author in England, attacked the simony of Herbert of Losinga, abbot of Ramsey (1087–91) and bishop of Thetford (1091–1119). This simony is mocked and challenged in terms derived from the legends

---

[33] *Bertholdi Annales, a.1075, MGH Scriptores*, v. 278.
[34] *Gebehardi Salisburgensis archiepiscopi Epistola ad Herimannum Mettensem episcopum data*, cap. 32, ed. K. Francke, *MGH Libelli de lite*, i. 278.
[35] M. Lokrantz, *L'opera poetica di S. Pier Damiani*, Stockholm/Göteborg/Uppsala 1964, 153–5, no. D 7. It is preserved in a Polirone MS; for its date and background, see Lokrantz, 21–2, 206–8.
[36] A. Lentini and F. Avagliano, *I carmi di Alfano I, arcivescovo di Salerno*, Miscellanea Cassinese 38, Montecassino 1974, 183–4, no. 37.
[37] *Monachi cuiusdam exulis S. Laurentii De calamitatibus ecclesiae Leodiensis opusculum*, ed. H. Boehmer, *MGH Libelli de lite*, iii. 622–41, esp. 625, 627, 639, 640. For the circumstances, see G. Meyer von Knonau, *Jahrbücher des deutschen Reiches unter Heinrich IV. und Heinrich V.*, 7 vols, Leipzig 1898–1909, iv. 463–8.

of Simon Magus's flight and downfall.[38] It was, however, only with the voluminous writings of the Augustinian canon Gerhoh of Reichersberg (1093–1169)
that the castigation of simoniacs in such imagery occurs north of the Alps with
such great intensity.[39]

There is evidently no overall pattern to the use of material from the legends of
Simon Magus in the reformers' struggle against simony. Much, at least, of the
evidence is best interpreted as the local and independent use of material already
to hand in artistic and manuscript forms to promote a widely-shared objective
which became more sharply focused with the Wibertine schism. There is nothing
to suggest that even so remarkable an anti-Simoniac composition as Amatus's
poem circulated at all widely, or that it directly influenced any other writer. (For
comparison, it should, however, be remembered that even Cardinal Humbert's
Adversus simoniacos appears to have had only a small circulation and cannot be
shown to have had much influence.[40]) It is not even certain that Amatus's poem
reached Gregory VII: it is not likely that he saw the surviving manuscript which
is in Beneventan script; there are also numerous points of textual correction and
revision which would be hard to explain if this manuscript had reached Gregory.[41]
He may have seen another, earlier manuscript, perhaps not in Beneventan script,
but there is no unambiguous indication that he did so.

There is, nevertheless, some evidence, in addition to the Cassinese sources that
have already been noticed,[42] that interest in the Simon Magus legends was particularly a feature of South Italy. This is strongly suggested by Gregory VII
himself. For all his zeal against simony, he only twice referred to these legends in
his letters – once obliquely and once expressly. Whether or not he knew the
legends from Amatus, and the circumstances suggest that he did, both letters were
written in the midsummer of 1080, and in a South Italian environment. His
oblique reference was in a letter of 27 June, which he addressed to Abbot Hugh of
Cluny from Ceprano, a town in the marches between the lands of St Peter and the
principality of Capua; on 29 June, Robert Guiscard, duke of Apulia, took there an
oath of fealty to Pope Gregory VII. Abbot Desiderius of Montecassino had taken
a leading part in negotiations that led to the *rapprochement* between the pope and
the duke. In his letter to Abbot Hugh, Gregory exploded with wrath about a
report, freshly received, that a Cluniac monk named Robert, who was in the
Spanish kingdom of León-Castile, had been complicit in resisting the supersession of the Hispanic rite by the Latin:

> This Robert, having become an imitator of Simon Magus, has not feared
> with all the crafty malignity that he could muster to rise up against the
> authority of St Peter (*Symonis magi imitator factus, quanta potuit maligni-
> tatis astutia, adversus beati P. auctoritatem non timuit insurgere*), and by

---

[38] *De simoniaca haeresi carmen*, ed. H. Boehmer, *MGH Libelli de lite*, iii. 615–17; cf. William of
Malmesbury, *De gestis regum*, ii. 385–6.
[39] e.g. *Opusculum de edificio Dei* (1128/9), cap. 66, *Liber de novitatibus huius temporis* (1156),
caps 2, 4, *De investigatione Antichristi* (1160/2), 1.63, edd. E. Sackur, *MGH Libelli de lite*, iii.173,
290, 293, 378–9.
[40] R. Schieffer, *Die Entstehung des päpstlichen Investiturverbots für den deutschen König*, Schriften der MGH 28, Stuttgart 1981, 36–47.
[41] Lentini (as n.22), i. 29–39.
[42] See above, pp. 81–3.

his prompting to lead back into their former error a hundred thousand men who had begun through our own diligent labour to return to the way of truth.

Gregory's reference to Simon Magus's 'crafty malignity' and his contrast between error and truth appear to allude to Simon's confrontation with Peter at Rome rather than to his mercenary request at Samaria. There is no doubt about Gregory's reference to the Roman legends when, on 21 July, he dispatched an encyclical letter from Ceccano, a little to the west of Ceprano, about Henry IV of Germany's putting forward of Archbishop Guibert of Ravenna to be anti-pope. He addressed it to the bishops 'of the Principates, Apulia, and Calabria', that is, of all Italy to the south of the lands of St Peter and the duchy of Spoleto. Once again, he wrote to express a furious reaction: this time, on the day after he heard about Henry's synod of Brixen. The reference in his condemnation of the Wibertines to the legend of the contest at Rome between Peter and Simon Magus is loud and clear:

> As for these men who have no reasons to justify them, but are utterly reprobate through a conscience burdened with every kind of crime, we with the greater confidence reckon them to be of no account because they believe that they have risen to great heights. By the mercy of God, and by the prayers of St Peter which wonderfully cast down Simon Magus, their master, when he set out for such heights, we hope that their ruin will not be for long delayed.

Whatever may have been the source from which Gregory knew this legend, he thought that a reference to it was appropriate in a letter for general circulation in South Italy.[43]

Certainly there appears to have been fertile soil in South Italy for such legends to grow, for there is evidence to suggest an interplay of ideas between Rome and Montecassino and a utilization of the legends in the abbey's historical tradition. From 1059, Abbot Desiderius of Montecassino was also an 'external cardinal' of the Roman church in his capacity as cardinal-priest of Santa Cecilia.[44] A contemporary as cardinal-priest was Deusdedit of San Pietro in Vincoli, who demonstrated his attachment to Desiderius in 1087 when he dedicated his *Liber canonum* to him as Pope Victor III.[45] In his *Libellus contra invasores et symoniacos*, the longer and definitive version of which dated from c.1097, Deusdedit at some length presented the genesis of the Wibertine schism in terms of Archbishop Guibert of Ravenna as the new Simon Magus. As such, he was the evil genius of his Nero, King Henry IV of Germany. He had dragged Henry more deeply than ever into the simoniac heresy, in the usual sense of selling ecclesiastical offices. Seduced by the new Simon Magus, he considered himself to be exempt from

---

[43] For the letters, see *Gregorii VII Registrum*, 8.2,5, ed. E. Caspar, *MGH Epistolae selectae*, 2, Berlin 1920–3, 517–18, 521–3. For events in Italy, see Cowdrey (as n.19), 138–43; for those in Spain, H.E.J. Cowdrey, *The Cluniacs and the Gregorian Reform*, Oxford 1970, 230–9.

[44] K. Ganzer, *Die Entwicklung des auswärtigen Kardinalats im hohen Mittelalter*, Tübingen 1963, 17–23.

[45] V. Wulf von Glanvell, *Die Kanonessammlung des Kardinals Deusdedit*, Paderborn 1905, 1–5. For Deusdedit, see R. Hüls, *Kardinäle, Klerus und Kirchen Roms, 1049–1130*, Tübingen 1977, 194.

papal justice as though he were not of St Peter's flock. In 1084, the new Simon Magus enthroned Henry at Rome and crowned him emperor 'more by bribery than by force'. When Henry intruded schismatic bishops and abbots into offices from which catholics had been driven, he did so 'by the commerce of his master Simon', and still acted as Simon's Nero.

Deusdedit went on to make play of a setback for the anti-pope Clement III (Guibert of Ravenna) in 1097/8. Clement had recently established his forces at Argenta, a place strategically situated on the River Po to the north-west of Ravenna, and provided for its defence by building a high tower. The loss of this fortification prompted Deusdedit to draw an analogy with the fall of Simon Magus from his tower at Rome:

> Guibert . . as if for his own defence built a high tower at a township called Argenta and awaited simoniac angels, but flying with them he fell into the foulest of Stygian marshes. His legs were broken – that is, by God's favour to us, his goods are now as good as destroyed and reduced to nothing. No one showed him the reverence and obedience due to a pope except his Nero and his criminal accomplices, and those who sold themselves to him by permanent or temporary oaths on account of their avarice, which is the service of idols.[46]

This polemic of Deusdedit was quickly borrowed by the compiler of the middle section of the Chronicle of Montecassino. This great Chronicle is of composite authorship. It was begun by a master chronicler, Leo Marsicanus, to whom reference has already been made in connection with the Cassinese tradition of the Clementine Recognitions;[47] but his contribution effectively ends with the year 1075. From 1127, the Chronicle was the responsibility of another archivist and librarian of the abbey, the notorious forger Peter the Deacon. For the long inter-vening period, 1075 to 1127, the material in the Chronicle as it now stands raises formidable problems of sources and authorship. They are particularly acute in the critical years of the 1080s, for which a number of disparate traditions seem to have been drawn upon in an uncritical manner.[48] However, in one constituent part of the account of Abbot Desiderius's months as Pope Victor III, despite manifest chronological absurdity Deusdedit's polemical chapters about the anti-pope Clement as Simon Magus were lightly and crudely adapted to present Victor's pontificate as a triumphant struggle between him and his rival. Clement was a new Simon Magus who during the struggle shared, at least morally, the heresiarch's fate.[49]

A comparable view found expression in the allocution which the Chronicle placed upon Victor's lips at his synod of Benevento in late August 1087. Like all such speeches, it is likely to be a free composition made at a later date; it nevertheless represents a Cassinese viewpoint. In rehearsing the crimes of *Guibertus eresiarcha* against his predecessor Gregory VII, Victor was depicted as

---

[46] 2.11–12, ed. E. Sackur, *MGH Libelli de lite*, ii. 328–30. For the building and loss of Argenta, see Meyer von Knonau (as n.37), v.13–14.
[47] See above, p. 81.
[48] For the Chronicle, see Cowdrey (as n.19), xvii–xix, 101–2, 194–206, 239–44, 251–62.
[49] *Chron. Cas.* 3.70, *MGH Scriptores*, xxxiv.452–3. For a comparison of the texts, see Cowdrey (as n.19), 257–60.

saying that Guibert incited conspiracies and plots against him; perjured and simoniacal, so far as in him lay he deprived Gregory of his priestly office, stirring up against him the Roman empire, peoples, and kingdoms. Moved by the perfidy of Simon Magus whose officer (*officina*) he had become, he had used the emperor's army to invade the apostolic see and to make himself the head in the Roman church of all evil, wickedness, and perdition. Victor concluded by citing St Paul's saying that there could be no accord between Christ and Belial and nothing in common between believer and unbeliever (2 Cor. 6:15): 'every heretic is an unbeliever', he said; 'because a simoniac is a heretic, he is therefore an unbeliever.'[50] Here, again, the tone is taken from Simon Magus's legendary doings at Rome. The Montecassino Chronicle's presentation of Victor III and his vindication of the Gregorian papacy points to a continuing strand of thought at the abbey, already apparent in the poem of Amatus, that the full weight of the legends of Simon Magus should be brought to bear in support of Gregory VII and his cause. The Wibertine schism and the struggle against the anti-pope Clement III served to intensify this conviction. The interest of the South Italian abbey of Montecassino in the legends of Simon Magus was strong, and perhaps uniquely strong.

This study of the history and use of the legends of Simon Magus points to conclusions both particular and general. In particular, the legends were in process of formation from the earliest days of Christianity. Long before the eleventh century, they were highly developed and widely disseminated; they were known both through many manuscripts and in the visual arts. Their use in eleventh- and twelfth-century polemics was, nevertheless, sporadic and occasional; it appears in widely dispersed localities. Yet the evidence from and centring upon Montecassino suggests that South Italy was of especial importance in harnessing the legends to the cause of the Gregorian papacy, and that there was significant interplay with Roman circles in propagating them. Gregory himself seems to have thought them appropriate for citation in writing encyclically to the bishops of South Italy. The mosaics of the Cappella Palatina and at Monreale may, therefore, serve as late reminders of an interest in the fate of Simon Magus which was characteristically South Italian.

A general conclusion to which the use of the legends of Simon Magus points is that, energetic and universally promoted amongst eleventh- and twelfth-century reformers though the campaign against simony was, it cannot be regarded as having been well orchestrated from above, certainly not by the Gregorian papacy. Much depended upon individuals and upon localities; there was little pattern or co-ordination; themes so apparently promising as the fall and death of Simon Magus were developed surprisingly seldom. It was much the same with the reforming campaign against clerical marriage and fornication which was concurrently waged. This campaign affords an instructive comparison. The zeal in promoting it of the papacy as of other reforming circles is, of course, beyond question. Yet, as in the case of simony, the forms taken by propaganda were various and unco-ordinated. This is illustrated by the term 'nicolaitism' which was sometimes applied to clerical marriage and concubinage. Like simony, it was derived from the Bible and developed by legend. In the book of Revelation (2:6,

---

[50] *Chron. Cas.* 3.72, 453–5.

14–15), there are references to 'Nicolaitans' as a sect that the Lord, like all right-thinking Christians, abominated; its offences included fornication. St Irenaeus of Lyons (c.130–c.200) believed that the Nicolaitans, 'qui indiscrete vivunt', originated with Nicolaus, last-named of the seven initial deacons of the Christian church (Acts 6:1–6).[51] He had been a proselyte of Antioch, and the very little that is on record about him indicates that he was an entirely blameless and sincere young man. But the association of his name with that of the Nicolaitans was sufficient to condemn him. A sixth-century writer placed Nicholas second only to Simon Magus in his list of heresiarchs,[52] while in the twelfth century Gerhoh of Reichersberg, having branded Simon Magus as 'the leading trafficker', dubbed Nicholas 'the first fornicator among the clergy' (*Symonem magum, precipuum negociatorem, Nycolaum primum in clero fornicatorem*).[53]

It was Cardinal Humbert of Silva Candida, who was surprisingly silent about the legends of Simon Magus, by whom the word 'nicolaitism' found currency in the central medieval west. In his learned, fiery writings against the Greeks, he drew upon the work of the fourth-century refuter of heretics, Bishop Epiphanius of Salamis. In a letter of 1053 to the Studite monk Nicetas, Humbert's condemnation of the marriage of priests declared that 'the prince of this heresy, Nicholas, came forth from hell.'[54] It was, perhaps, under Humbert's tutelage that, in 1059, Pope Nicholas II prefaced his synodical letter that followed his Roman council in April by a reference to its decisions 'concerning the heresy of the Nicolaitans, that is, concerning married priests, deacons, and all appointed to be among the clergy.'[55] Cardinal Peter Damiani borrowed Humbert's language, and declared that 'married priests are called Nicolaitans, inheriting such a name from one Nicholas who propounded this heresy.'[56] Given the currency of this usage amongst the leading reformers at Rome, it is surprising that it occurs but rarely in papal letters, and only once in those of Gregory VII.[57] He appears to have had little use for the legends of Simon Magus, and next to none for that of the deacon Nicholas; it is not the only respect in which he was far from being a disciple of

---

[51] *Adversus haereses*, 1.26.3, edd. A. Rousseau and L. Doutreleau, 5 vols in 8 pts, Sources chrétiennes 100, 152–3, 210–11, 263–4, 293, Paris 1965–82, i.348.

[52] *Decretale de recipiendis et non recipiendis libris*, 5.9, in E. von Dobschütz, *Das Decretum Gelasianum de libris recipiendis et non recipiendis*, Texte und Untersuchungen zur Geschichte der altchristlichen Literatur 38/4, Leipzig 1912, 13. It is not now attributed to Pope Gelasius I (492–6).

[53] *Epistola ad Innocentium papam* (1131), cap. 7, *MGH Libelli de lite*, iii. 205.

[54] *Contra Nicetam*, cap. 25, *PL* cxliii.996–7.

[55] *MGH Constitutiones et acta publica imperatorum et regum*, i.548–9, no. 385; cf. D. Jasper, *Das Papstwahldekret von 1059: Überlieferung und Textgestalt*, Sigmaringen 1986, 21.

[56] *Ep.* 112, (as n.32), iii. 286, cf. *Ep.* 61, ii. 216–17.

[57] *The Epistolae vagantes of Pope Gregory VII*, ed. and trans. H.E.J. Cowdrey, Oxford 1972, no. 16, p. 44. Writing to King William I of England in late 1076, Gregory complained that Bishop Juhel of Dol, in Brittany, 'quasi simoniacum esse parum et pro nihilo deputaret, nicolaita quoque fieri festinavit.'

ADDITIONAL NOTE. Since this paper was completed, Dr Lindy Grant has kindly drawn to my attention the sculptures of the Flight and Death of Simon Magus upon two nave capitals of the cathedral of Saint-Lazare at Autun: A. Kingsley Porter, *Romanesque Sculpture of the Pilgrimage Roads*, 10 vols, Boston 1923, i.112, ii. Plates 73, 75; D. Grivot and G. Zarnecki, *Gislebertus, sculpteur d'Autun*, Paris 1960, p. 68 and Plates 35, 38. The sculptures date from between 1119 and 1132, and demonstrate the currency of the legends of Simon Magus in Burgundy at that time.

Cardinal Humbert. Indeed, the word 'nicolaitism' that Humbert sent upon its medieval travels never secured the currency of the word 'simony'.

There can be no doubt of the determination of the reform popes from Leo IX (1049–54) to extirpate the practices that both nouns signify. Yet the propaganda by which they were resisted was little orchestrated from above, least of all by the popes. The legends of Simon Magus and of the deacon Nicholas occur separately and sporadically. Until Gerhoh of Reichersberg, they seldom both appear prominently in the same publicist. And although regions where they were especially current may be suggested, like South Italy and Montecassino for the legends of Simon Magus, the evidence for the use of what might seem effective propaganda themes is less extensive than might be expected. One possible reason for this is the moral earnestness of the major reforming popes, especially Gregory VII, which was not easily distracted into fantasy. A second reason is the extent to which pressures for reform were arising widely in the church, whose leaders had to make the best of them that they could. They by no means settled the agenda; they had to do what they could to give direction, order, and refinement to demands and methods that came to them from below.

Nobiltà e parentela nell'Italia normanna

Vincenzo D'Alessandro

L'unione familiare appare come naturale strumento di consacrazione delle alleanze contratte dai primi condottieri normanni calati nel Meridione con i principi longobardi, ciascuno dei quali intendeva avvantaggiarsi della forza militare di cui quelli disponevano.[1] Cosí il *magister militum*, o duca, di Napoli, Sergio IV, dava una sorella in moglie a Rainulfo Drengot posto a presidio di Aversa contro i nemici principi di Capua.[2] Ma, quando rimaneva vedovo della sorella di Sergio, Rainulfo sposava una figlia del Patrizio di Amalfi e nipote del principe di Capua contro cui era stato insediato ad Aversa.[3]

Amato di Montecassino definiva Rainulfo Drengot 'home aorné de toutes vertus qui covenent à chevalier'.[4] Per il monaco Amato, infatti, quelle unioni congiungevano la nobiltà d'origine dei principi longobardi alla *nobilitas* della cavalleria normanna consacrata dalla *historia salutis* realizzata dai conquistatori nel Meridione contro principi indegni, contro i nemici della Chiesa, che non erano solo i musulmani di Sicilia. Allora maggiore era la celebrazione della parentela che univa gli Altavilla ai principi di Salerno, a Guaimario V in particolare. Non tanto per il matrimonio che univa il primo degli Altavilla giunto nel Meridione, Guglielmo Braccio di ferro, a una nipote del principe Guaimario V, il quale -si dice- era promotore della unione accolta con gioia dai compagni di Guglielmo,[5] e nemmeno per la più stretta unione fra la famiglia del principe e la dinastia normanna, per il matrimonio fra una figlia del principe e il nuovo capo degli Altavilla, Drogone successo allo scomparso Guglielmo (1046),[6] quanto invece per le esaltate nozze fra Sichelgaita e il Guiscardo. Su questa unione, si sa, si fondavano due progetti egemonici che dovevano naturalmente scontrarsi e vedere soccombere le ambizioni di Guaimario V di Salerno, di predominio politico oltre che territoriale nel Meridione in forza del braccio armato normanno, a fronte della superiorità militare normanna e della egemonia imposta ai 'comites' conquistatori dal Guiscardo. Cosí che quella unione segnava il principio della fine della antica nobiltà a vantaggio della nuova, la quale nasceva dallo innesto nella antica, oltre che dal diritto di conquista, dalla *utilitas* della conquista, come volevano dimostrare gli apologeti cronisti meridionali, anche in funzione della ideologia politico-religiosa di cui erano interpreti. Invece, il normanno Goffredo

---

[1] Su quei nuovi legami, P. Delogu, 'L'evoluzione politica dei Normanni fra poteri locali e potestà universali', *Atti del congr. intern. di studi sulla Sicilia normanna*, Palermo 1974, 69 ss.

[2] *Storia de' Normanni di Amato di Montecassino volgarizzata in antico francese*, ed. V. De Bartholomaeis (Font. stor. Italia, 76, Roma 1935), 53 s.

[3] Amatus, 55 s.

[4] Amatus, 53.

[5] Amatus, 93 s.

[6] Amatus, 101 s.

Malaterra rinnovava qui l'antico tentativo di pareggiare il lignaggio (presunto) degli Altavilla a quello dei 'sublimi ex origine' principi longobardi soccombenti innanzi alla *feritas* leonina, alla virtù militare degli *strenui* guerrieri nordici.[7]

Per tutti i cronisti, comunque, l'ascesa degli Altavilla segnava il punto di avvio della nuova storia del Meridione (come l'ascesa dei Carolingi aveva segnato il punto di avvio della storia d'Europa). Il recupero alla cristianità, alla Chiesa, di tutto il Meridione, era loro vanto ed era la nobiltà loro e di quanti ne avevano sostenuto l'opera. Cosí che poi non potevano mancare le pretese parentele con i fautori di quella storia, quando non anche con gli stessi Altavilla, con loro membri legittimi o naturali, magari attraverso le molte (e per molta parte a noi ignote) loro figlie. Accadrà dapprima con Ruggero conte di Andria, candidato opposto a Tancredi di Lecce nella successione al re Guglielmo II (m. 1189) quale congiunto della dinastia: 'de sanguine regio ortus'.[8] Accadrà poi con alcune famiglie della nobiltà meridionale desiderose di legare le proprie origini alla prima dinastia regia del Meridione.[9]

Intanto, per corroborare la loro visione ideologica, Amato di Montecassino e Guglielmo Apulo presentavano il matrimonio con Sichelgaita (1058) come promozione del Guiscardo alla parità di stato e di diritto, della nobiltà e del titolo. Diceva l'Apulo: 'Coniugio ducto tam magnae nobilitatis, / Augeri coepit Roberti nobile nomen, / Et gens, quae quondam servire coacta solebat, / Obsequio solvit iam debita iuris aviti'.[10] Per cui poi era il cognato Gisulfo II a trovarsi in torto

[7] Su tale tema si veda M. Oldoni, 'Mentalità ed evoluzione della storiografia normanna fra XI e XII secolo in Italia', *Ruggero il Gran Conte e l'inizio dello Stato normanno*, Roma 1977, 139 ss.; id., 'Intellettuali cassinesi di fronte ai Normanni (secoli XI–XII)', *Miscellanea di storia italiana e mediterranea per Nino Lamboglia*, Genova 1978; V. D'Alessandro, *Storiografia e politica nell'Italia normanna*, Napoli 1978, 51 ss.

[8] Come era presentato a Venezia, ove era uno degli ambasciatori del regno di Sicilia, dal compagno di ambasceria e principale cronista della pace col Barbarossa, l'arcivescovo Romualdo Salernitano: cf. Romualdi Salernitani *Chronicon*, ed. Carlo Alberto Garufi (*RIS²*, vii, parte I, Bologna 1935), 290. Sulla famiglia di Ruggero di Andria, il quale apparteneva al lignaggio normanno del de Ollia, si veda ora Errico Cuozzo, 'Ruggiero, conte d'Andria'. Ricerche sulla nozione di regalità al tramonto della monarchia normanna', *Arch. Soc. Nap.*, III serie, xx, 1981, 130 ss.

[9] Sulla attribuzione di cinque mogli, invece che tre, a Ruggero II si fonderà la 'leggenda' del legame fra gli Altavilla e i conti dei Marsi. Infatti, invece che le tre mogli indicate da Romualdo Salernitano, si riterrà erroneamente che Ruggero II sposasse Airolda figlia di Rinaldo conte dei Marsi e di Heria figlia di Roberto il Guiscardo (cf. Cesare Rivera, 'L'annessione delle terre d'Abruzzo al regno di Sicilia', *Archivio storico italiano*, VII serie, vi, 1926, 253 s. nota 2, 296). E già prima Ruggero II avrebbe sposato una Pierleoni sorella dell'antipapa Anacleto II (ma si veda Carlo Alberto Garufi, 'I diplomi purpurei della Cancelleria normanna ed Elvira prima moglie di re Ruggiero (1117?–6 febbraio 1135)', *Atti della Accademia di Scienze, Lettere ed Arti di Palermo*, III serie, vii, 1904, 15 ss.). Per l'ignoto autore della cronaca di S.Maria de Ferraria Ruggero II aveva da una sorella del conte Ugo di Molise un figlio naturale, Simone investito poi del principato di Taranto (Ignoti monachi S.Mariae de Ferraria *Chronica ab anno 781 ad annum 1228*, ed. Augusto Gaudenzi, Napoli 1888, 28, che dice Simone principe di Capua, ma cf. *La Historia o Liber de Regno Sicilie e la Epistola ad Petrum Panormitane Ecclesie thesaurarium di Ugo Falcando*, ed. Giovan Battista Siragusa (Font. stor. Italia, 22, Roma 1897), 51, e Ferdinand Chalandon, *Histoire de la domination normande en Italie et en Sicile*, Paris 1907, ii, 172).

[10] Guglielmo di Puglia, *La geste de Robert Guiscard*, ed. Marguerite Mathieu, 1st. stor. di studi bizantini e neoellenici, Palermo 1961, 156, e pure Amatus, 194 s.; Goffredo Malaterra, *De rebus gestis Rogerii Calabriae et Siciliae Comitis et Roberti Guiscardi Ducis fratris eius*, ed. Ernesto Pontieri (*RIS²*, v, parte I, Bologna 1927), 22; e Chalandon, i, 154 per la datazione. Il precedente matrimonio con la madre del primogenito Boemondo, Alberada, zia di Gerardo signore di Buonal-

quando si opponeva al Guiscardo, il quale rivendicava quella parità promossa dagli stessi principi e, per parte sua, dalla superiorità militare. Quando Gisulfo II rinfacciava al cognato di aver voluto dimenticare la parentela che li univa vedeva rinfacciarsi la stessa smemoratezza dal Guiscardo.[11] A tali referenze il monaco Amato aggiungeva la superiorità, etica, della *iustitia* che il normanno riportava laddove prevaleva l'iniquità per la indegnità di Gisulfo II, reo dei maggiori delitti di cui un principe potesse macchiarsi.[12] Amato raccontava che l'infermo arcivescovo di Salerno aveva la visione di san Matteo, il quale gli assicurava la guarigione e profetizzava il passaggio di tutto il Meridione in mano normanna: 'Questa terra, gli diceva, è stata data da Dio ai normanni. La giusta volontà di Dio ha trasferito loro questa terra per la iniquità di quelli che l'hanno tenuta e per la parentela che hanno stretta con quelli. Perché la legge di Dio e quella degli imperatori ordina che il figlio succeda al padre nella eredità'.[13]

Le ambizioni che sostenevano le parentele con i conquistatori dovevano pure provocare contrastanti reazioni in seno alla nobiltà longobarda, fra i membri di una stessa dinastia. Per cui le nozze del Guiscardo con Sichelgaita promuovevano il matrimonio di un fratello dello stesso Guiscardo, Guglielmo primo conte del Principato (1056–1080), con Maria figlia di Guido conte di Conza, lasciato all'oscuro dal nipote Gisulfo II, al quale pertanto egli contrapponeva l'ostile Guglielmo.[14]

D'altra parte, insieme ai legami con la nobiltà di sangue meridionale, i 'comites comitum' tessevano da tempo una trama di unioni familiari che dovevano rafforzare le solidarietà militari, sostenere le ambizioni personali e dei compagni della 'comitiva', e pure il più ambizioso progetto di conquista di tutte le terre meridionali; progetto che appare conseguente alla giornata di Civitate e che Roberto il Guiscardo intestava a se stesso per fondarvi l'egemonia sui 'comites' conquistatori.[15] Così, i Falluc si legavano ai Chiaromonte;[16] a loro volta i Chiaromonte si legavano agli Altavilla.[17] Riccardo Quarel, futuro principe di Capua, sposava una Altavilla.[18] Enrico di Montesantangelo sposava una figlia di Ruggero I.[19] Con gli Altavilla era imparentato Amico (I) padre di Gualtiero di Giovinazzo e di Petrone

bergo, primo promotore della fortuna del Guiscardo, era annullato 'pro consanguinitate' (Guglielmo di Puglia, 154; Amatus, 125 s., 194 s.).

[11] Amatus, 368 s.

[12] Sulla iniquità di Gisulfo II insiste Amatus, 207 ss., 219 ss., 339 ss.

[13] Amatus, 151 s.

[14] Amatus, 197, che rileva la nuova unione come iniziativa contrapposta al matrimonio Guiscardo-Sichelgaita.

[15] Sui legami familiari nel sistema delle solidarietà militari si è soffermato Ludwig Buisson, 'Formen normannischer Staatsbildung (9. bis 11. Jahrhundert)', in *Studien zum mittelalterlichen Lebenswesen* (Vorträge und Forschungen, V, 1960), 158 ss.

[16] Sul matrimonio fra Alessandro figlio di Ugo Falluc e di Rocca con Avenia figlia di Ugo (le Borgne) di Chiaromonte, Léon-Robert Ménager, 'Inventaire des familles normandes et franques emigrées en Italie méridionale et en Sicile (XI–XII siècles)', *Roberto il Guiscardo e il suo tempo*, Roma 1975, 275.

[17] Alberada Chiaromonte sposa in prime nozze Ruggero de Pomaria signore di Policoro morto fra il 1099 e il 1102, quindi sposava Riccardo Senescalco figlio di Drogone di Altavilla (Ménager, 279).

[18] Amatus, 112.

[19] Armando Petrucci, 'Note di diplomatica normanna. II. Enrico conte di Montesantangelo ed i suoi documenti', *Bullettino dell'Ist. stor. it. per il Medio Evo e Archivio Muratoriano*, 72, 1960, 136.

di Trani.[20] Ma bastino questi esempi fra quanti una indagine meno affrettata può far registrare. Del resto, è stato già notato, la nuova aristocrazia normanna del Meridione d'Italia risulta subito quasi tutta legata in parentela con gli Altavilla.[21]

Attuata la conquista, stabilito il dominio, il sistema delle alleanze strategiche e delle solidarietà fra i 'comites' perdeva l'originaria funzione e dava campo alla politica, al potenziamento della dinastia che aveva preso titolo e nome dalla terra conquistata. Così, il principe Riccardo di Capua dava una figlia in moglie a Guglielmo di Montreuil, perché, notava Amato: 'Cestui prince Richart, quant il vint à marier la fille, il mostra que noïent fu la hautesce de li antique prince né la gentillece, à comparation de ce que cestui (Guglielmo di Montreuil) faisoit. Et toute anichilloit lo avarice de li riche home. Et plus se delittoit de faire parenteze avec home que avec la vane arrogance de ceuz qui habitoient en la contrée'.[22] Tuttavia, di lí a poco (1063) Guglielmo di Montreuil si levava contro il suocero e ripudiava la moglie. Egli voleva, infatti, sposare la vedova di Adenolfo duca di Gaeta, Maria, la quale reggeva il ducato e aggregava contro l'aggressore Riccardo di Capua una lega. Guglielmo entrava nella lega contro Riccardo. Ma questi sapeva disgregarla offrendo agli avversari diretti legami familiari: a Maria di Gaeta proponeva il matrimonio col proprio figlio Giordano, a Landone conte di Traetto proponeva il matrimonio con la propria figlia Maria. Guglielmo di Montreuil tornava a conciliarsi con Riccardo di Capua ottenendone la metà della contea di Aquino.[23] Un nipote di Guglielmo di Montreuil, Guglielmo detto *Scalfonus*, entrato dapprima alla corte del re Filippo I, dal quale otteneva il cingolo militare, si metteva poi sulla strada per il Meridione, ove contava 'parentes magnae sublimitatis'. Qui il conte di Chieti Roberto I di Loritello gli assegnava trenta *castra* ed egli fondava la nuova famiglia sposando una donna longobarda di lignaggio.[24] E basti pure qui notare solo qualche esempio di una serie che è certo più lunga.

Allo stesso modo agivano, realizzati i progetti, gli Altavilla. Anzi essi attuavano una strategia di unioni e di solidarietà corrispondente alla strategia politica. A cominciare da Roberto il Guiscardo, il quale sperava di fare di una figlia una imperatrice facendola sposare a un figlio di Michele VII.[25] E già (1078) egli aveva mandato un'altra figlia in casa dei marchesi d'Este.[26] Per questo matrimonio della figlia con Ugo figlio di Azzone II d'Este egli imponeva ai conti normanni la corresponsione di doni (come uno degli *auxilia* previsti dalla tradizione normanna per il matrimonio della figlia maggiore del signore).[27] Un'altra delle sue figlie, Matilde, sposava Raimondo Berengario II conte di Barcellona.[28] Nello stesso

[20] Si veda la genealogia di Amico ricostruita da Mathieu (Gugliemo di Puglia, 301).
[21] É quanto risulta dal *Catalogus Baronum. Commentario*, a cura di Errico Cuozzo (Font. stor. Italia, 101, Roma 1984), e Errico Cuozzo, 'La nobiltà normanna nel Mezzogiorno all'epoca di Roberto il Guiscardo', *Rivista storica italiana*, xcviii, 1986, 551.
[22] Amatus, 200 s.
[23] Amatus, 258 ss.; Chalandon, i, 216 ss.
[24] Ménager, 310, che rimanda alle fonti.
[25] Amatus, 318 ss., e Vera von Falkenhausen, 'Olympias, eine normannische Prinzessin in Konstantinopel', *Bisanzio e l'Italia. Raccolta di studi in memoria di Agostino Pertusi*, Milano 1982, 56 ss.
[26] Amatus, 373 s.; Guglielmo di Puglia, 190.
[27] Guglielmo di Puglia, 190 s. Per la tradizione dello *auxilium* in terra di Normandia cf. Claude Cahen, *Le régime féodal de l'Italie normande*, Paris 1940, 77.
[28] E in seconde nozze Aimerico I visconte di Narbona (Chalandon, i, 283).

tempo il Guiscardo intrecciava legami familiari con alcune maggiori dinastie normanne presenti in Italia: come i Grandsmenil, i quali giungevano qui, alla fine del 1061, con Roberto eletto abate di s.Maria di Eufemia. Nell'estate del 1081 giungeva un nipote dell'abate Roberto, Guglielmo, il quale faceva in tempo a partecipare alla spedizione contro Durazzo del Guiscardo. E del Guiscardo diveniva genero, avendone in moglie la figlia Mabilia oltre a 15 *castra* in Calabria ove si stabiliva. Di lí a poco si ritrova fra i compagni di Boemondo alla prima crociata.[29] Roberto (I) di Montescaglioso e il fratello Goffredo di Conversano erano nipoti 'ex sorore' del Guiscardo.[30] I nuovi dominii e i nuovi lignaggi da essi fondati, di Montescaglioso e di Conversano, costituivano una componente essenziale della aristocrazia comitale normanna, in forza della dimensione delle dipendenze e pure della parentela con gli Altavilla, della cui egemonia dovevano essere tuttavia fra i più tenaci oppositori. Nel 1064 Roberto (I) di Montescaglioso e Goffredo di Conversano erano ribelli al Guiscardo, con cui si riconciliavano per tornare a ribellarsi nel 1078 e conciliarsi ancora nel 1080 (anno in cui Roberto di Montescaglioso moriva).

A sua volta Ruggero I sposava dapprima, a Mileto alla fine del 1061, la 'diu cupitam' Giuditta figlia di Guglielmo conte di Evreux e sorellastra di Roberto di Grandsmenil. Morta Giuditta (prima del 1080), sposava Eremburga di Mortain, alla quale seguiva Adelaide del Vasto (1089).[31] Inoltre, Ruggero I risulta esigente pure nel procurare distinti mariti alle figlie: a Matilde, figlia di Giuditta, unita (1080) a Raimondo IV di St Gilles conte di Tolosa; a Emma, figlia di Giuditta, sposata dapprima (1087) a Guglielmo III conte di Clermont, poi, rimasta vedova, a Raoul detto Maccabeo conte di Montescaglioso; a Muriella, sposata a Josberto o Gosberto de Lucy, cioè a un nobile di lignaggio normanno, come pare si debba ritenere; a Alice sposata a Enrico conte di Monte Sant'Angelo.[32] Ancora: nel 1095 Ruggero I sposava la figlia Costanza/Massimilla con Corrado figlio dello imperatore Enrico IV; un anno dopo dava un'altra figlia, Busilla, in moglie a Colomano re di Ungheria.[33]

Su tale linea, in corrispondenza con l'ascesa degli Altavilla e l'evoluzione politica della Italia normanna, Ruggero II sposava dapprima Elvira figlia di Alfonso VI e di Elisabetta di Castiglia (circa 1118). Rimasto vedovo di Elvira (1135), Ruggero II sposava nel 1149 Sibilla figlia di Ugo di Borgogna, la cui morte prematura (1150) lo portava alle terze nozze con Beatrice figlia del conte di Rethel, dalla quale, postuma, nasceva la futura imperatrice Costanza.[34] Il primo re di Sicilia tesseva con cura maggiore dei predecessori e ampliava la tela della

---

[29] Chalandon, i, 283, 398; Ménager, 316 ss.

[30] Chalandon, i, 181, 252 nota 3; Errico Cuozzo, 'La contea di Montescaglioso nei secoli XI–XIII', *Arch. Soc. Nap.*, ciii, 1985.

[31] Goffredo Malaterra, p. 35, per Giuditta; 93, per Eremburga; Chalandon, 197, 350 s.; Ernesto Pontieri, *La madre di re Ruggero, Adelasia del Vasto, contessa di Sicilia, regina di Gerusalemme*, cf. id., *Tra i Normanni nell'Italia meridionale*, II ed., Napoli 1964, 409 ss.

[32] Goffredo Malaterra, p. 70, per Matilde; 90, per Emma. Inoltre, Chalandon, i, 252 nota 3 per il matrimonio fra Emma e Raoul figlio di Unfredo di Montescaglioso, e 253 nota 1 per Enrico di Monte Sant'Angelo; Ménager, 312, 322 ss. per i de Lucy e la loro identificazione.

[33] Goffredo Malaterra, 101, per Costanza/Massimilla, e 103, per Busilla; Ménager, 324 s.

[34] Romualdo Salernitano, 222, 231 e nota 5; Petri Ansolini de Ebulo *De rebus Siculis carmen*, ed. Ettore Rota (*RIS*[2], xxxi, 1, Città di Castello 1904), 8; Carlo Alberto Garufi, 'I diplomi purpurei', e, per la cronologia Chalandon, ii, p. 106.

politica matrimoniale familiare. Dei figli avuti da Elvira il maggiore, Ruggero duca di Puglia (m. 1148) sposava Elisabetta figlia del conte Tebaldo di Champagne. In tale occasione Ruggero II inviava al conte un prezioso vaso che doveva passare poi nel tesoro di Saint-Denis.[35] Il futuro re Guglielmo I, unico sopravvissuto dei figli del re Ruggero, sposava (1151) Margherita figlia del re di Navarra Garcia VI Ramirez.[36] Al fedele Roberto de 'Basunvilla' dava in moglie la sorella Giuditta e la contea di Conversano confiscata nel 1132 al ribelle Tancredi con cui si chiudeva la dinastia dei primi conti normanni di Conversano.[37]

Congiunti illustri e illustri oppositori. A cominciare dal piú famoso cognato di Ruggero II, Rainulfo di Alife, anima della opposizione alla successione nel ducato di Puglia di Ruggero, col quale ora si riconciliava ora tornava a scontrarsi rifiutando una soggezione che diceva indebita non avendo egli ricevuto benefici dal cognato. Contro cui tornava a levarsi dopo averne avuto benefici e dopo avere prestato omaggio e fedeltà.[38] Nella schiera degli oppositori di lignaggio di Ruggero II si contava anche un Grandsmenil che era pure nipote del Guiscardo: Roberto figlio di Guglielmo e di Mabilia. Ruggero II gli prometteva il grande dominio al quale Roberto aspirava e per cui si agitava. Poco dopo, conclusasi l'annessione delle terre meridionali in mano a Ruggero II, l'impaziente Roberto tornava a ribellarsi. Ma ora (1130) Ruggero II lo obbligava ad esulare.[39] A Ugo di Molise conte di Boiano riconciliatosi nel 1140 Ruggero II dava in moglie una figlia naturale (Sechelgarda?) e pure il dominio che da lui prendeva nome di Molise (1142).[40]

Quando succedeva al padre Guglielmo I di Sicilia assegnava al cugino Roberto (II) di Conversano, figlio di Roberto (I) e di Giuditta, la contea di Loritello. Ma quella concessione, che ampliava di misura i dominii del conte di Conversano non valeva a soddisfarne le ambizioni politiche oltre a quelle signorili. Per cui egli era già a capo della nuova ribellione aristocratica contro i sovrani, i quali mantenevano i conti lontano dalla curia e dal governo del regno.[41]

Tanto piú la politica matrimoniale degli Altavilla diveniva affare di Stato dopo il concordato di Benevento che nel 1156 rovesciava i rapporti fra il papato e la monarchia di Sicilia legandone le sorti innanzi all'impero svevo. Quando, nel 1174, Federico Barbarossa tentava di staccare il regno di Sicilia dal papato e proponeva il matrimonio di una propria figlia col re Guglielmo II, questi 'utpote christianissimus et religiosus princeps, sciens hoc matrimonium Alexandro pape

---

[35] Chalandon, ii, 106 s.; S.Bernardo, Ep. 447, in J.-P. Migne, *Patrologia Latina*, clxxxii, 640. Infatti, gli inviati alla corte comitale di Champagne avevano pure il compito di contattare s.Bernardo e chiedergli l'invio nel regno meridionale di alcuni monaci.
[36] Romualdo Salernitano, 242. Sulla famiglia della regina Margherita cf. Chalandon, ii, 176 nota 2.
[37] Romualdo Salernitano, 221; Alessandro di Telese, *De rebus gestis Rogerii Siciliae regis*, G. Del Re, *Cronisti e scrittori sincroni napoletani*, i, Napoli 1845, 109, 116 s.; Armando Petrucci, 'Note di diplomatica normanna. I. I documenti di Roberto di "Basunvilla", II conte di Conversano e III conte di Loritello', *Bullettino dell'Ist. stor. it. per il Medio Evo e Archivio Muratoriano*', 71, 1959, 113 ss.
[38] Al. Tel., 92, 93, 133, 125 s.
[39] Romualdo Salernitano, p. 215, per il 1127; Al. Tel., 100; Chalandon, 403.
[40] Ugo Falcando, 32, e Errico Cuozzo, 'Il formarsi della feudalità normanna nel Molise', *Arch. Soc. Nap.*, III serie, xx, 1981, 105–127, in particolare 117.
[41] Ugo Falcando, 11; Romualdo Salernitano, 237 ss.; Vincenzo D'Alessandro, 'Corona e nobiltà nell'età dei due Guglielmi', *Potere, società e popolo nell'età dei due Guglielmi*, Bari 1981, 65 ss.

plurimum displicere et Romane ecclesie non modicam iacturam inferre, Deum et Alexandrum papam in hac parte reveritus, imperatoris filiam in uxorem et eius pacem recipere noluit'.[42] Invece, il 'christianissimus rex' di Sicilia acconsentiva alle nozze (celebrate nel 1177) con Giovanna figlia di Enrico II di Inghilterra proposte dal pontefice, il quale poteva pertanto comporre la nuova alleanza anglo-normanna contro l'imperatore svevo.[43]

Da strumento di dominio territoriale o di solidarietà militare a consorzio oligarchico, da consacrazione aristocratica a legittimazione di dignità o potestà, anche nell'Italia normanna, la parentela, e quindi l'idea di nobiltà, tenevano valore e funzioni commisurati agli accelerati processi di quei secoli XI e XII, nel Meridione e in Occidente, alla evoluzione politica (degli assetti e delle strutture di potere) e culturale (della mentalità e dei modelli sociali) che ne promuovevano e ne animavano la realtà.

---

[42] Romualdo Salernitano, 265 ss., e ivi nota 5 per la datazione.
[43] Romualdo Salernitano, 268 s., e Chalandon, ii, 376 ss.

THE MARRIAGE OF
HENRY VI AND CONSTANCE OF SICILY:
PRELUDE AND CONSEQUENCES

Walter Fröhlich

William the Conqueror, King Henry I and their successors created a powerful, efficient and wealthy Norman state in the north-west of Europe by invading and conquering independent territories separated by the sea and uniting them under the rule of the Anglo-Norman king. Two generations later and in a similar way Roger II, King of Sicily since 1130, created a new, formidable state by seizing different territories from different lords: from the Byzantine emperor, the Latin emperor of the West, the pope and from various Muslim lords. Roger II united these territories under the strict rule of the Norman king of Sicily, thus establishing a new power in the middle of the Mediterranean Sea.[1]

These Norman realms in the north-west and the south upset the old balance of power of the medieval *ordo* of Europe and created a new one. The translation of the *imperium Romanorum* to the *rex Francorum* and then to the *rex Teutonicorum* had shifted the centre of gravity from the Mediterranean to the area beyond the Alps. The formation of these new Norman kingdoms caused yet again a new shift of the European balance of power further to the west and the south. Peace and stability within these Norman kingdoms and in turn the balance of European power was dependent on the survival of the respective dynasties. In the north the insecurity about succession after the death of King Henry I led to nineteen years of civil war. It was overcome by the union of Matilda, daughter of Henry I and widow of emperor Henry V, with Geoffrey, count of Anjou and Touraine. A strengthened dynasty grew out of this union.

In the south the picture is different. The successors of King Roger II, the first king of Sicily, appear not to be as strong as he was. Roger's biographer, E. Caspar, writes that he, like Charlemagne, lost his best sons, Roger, Henry and Alphons, at the prime of their lives; the least able, his fourth son William, survived.[2] In view

I would like to thank J. Johns and G. Loud for their suggestions and helpful criticism during the discussion after the presentation of this paper.

[1] L. Boehm, 'Nomen gentis Normannorum, Der Aufstieg der Normannen im Spiegel der normannischen Geschichtsschreibung', in *I Normanni e la loro espansione in Europa nell'alto medioevo*, Spoleto 1969, 623–704; E. Jamison, 'The Sicilian Norman Kingdom in the Mind of Anglo-Norman Contemporaries', *Proceedings of the British Academy* 24, 1938, 3–51; D.C. Douglas, *The Norman Achievement*, London 1969; D.C. Douglas, *The Norman Fate,* London 1976; J.J. Norwich, *The Normans in the South*, London 1967; J.J. Norwich, *The Kingdom in the Sun*, London 1970; R.F. Cassady, *The Norman Achievement*, London 1986; *The Normans in Sicily and Southern Italy*, Lincei Lectures 1974, ed. C.N.L. Brooke, Oxford 1977.

[2] E. Caspar, *Roger II und die Gründung der normannisch-sicilischen Monarchie*, Innsbruck 1904, 428.

of this fact Roger II married again: Sibylla of Burgundy, his second wife, died in childbed together with her child; Beatrix of Rethel, his third wife, bore Roger a daughter, Constance, after the king's death on 24 February 1154. He was then succeeded by his weak son, William I. The new king was strongly influenced by his chancellor, Majo of Bari, who was the cause of prolonged internal strife. On William's death on 7 May 1166 his infant son William II, aged twelve, succeeded him and his mother, Margareta of Navarra, became his regent. William II's marriage with Joan Plantagenet remained childless. In this phase of the waning vigour of the Hauteville dynasty the marriage of Constance became increasingly important.

Otto of St Blasien in the Black Forest has the following entry in his chronicle for the year 1184:

> Emperor Frederick sent envoys to King William I of Sicily, Roger's son, in order to have William's sister betrothed to his son Henry. Thus he acquired as dowry after the King's death the kingdom of Sicily together with the duchy of Apulia and the principality of Capua, which had been promised to King Henry; he won back for the Roman empire these territories which had been extorted by Roger from the empire after the death of Emperor Lothair.[3]

The betrothal of Henry, son of emperor Fredrick Barbarossa, to Constance, daughter of King Roger II and aunt – not sister – of King William II of Sicily, was announced at the episcopal palace of Augsburg on 29 October 1184:

> Filio imperatoris Henrico regi Constantia filia Siculi regis Augustae in palatio episcopi 4. Kal. Novembris iuramento firmatur.[4]

Henry was born between October and December 1165 and was therefore nineteen years of age at the time of the betrothal. In 1169, at the age of four, his father had had him elected and crowned king of the Germans thus designating him to be his successor as German king and *imperator Romanorum*.

Constance was born after the death of her father King Roger II on 26 February 1154 and was therefore thirty years old when betrothed to Henry.

The age difference between bride and groom-to-be was not strange in itself. What was unusual, however, was that the prospective bride was a woman of mature age who, according to contemporary records is not known to have been married or betrothed, to have taken the veil or even to have had any love affairs. This lack of connections for Constance is even more surprising when we note that the marriage of her nephew, William II, to Joan Plantagenet, daughter of Henry II, King of the Angevin realm, remained childless, and that Constance was therefore the only remaining legitimate descendant of the Hauteville dynasty and sole heir to the kingdom of Sicily.

Modern research has shown little interest in Constance's late marriage although

---

[3] *Chronica Ottonis de Sancto Blasio, MM SS in usum scholarum*, 39; *Geschichte in Quellen (GiQ)*, ed. W. Lautemann, München 1970, II, 467.
[4] *Annales Augustini minores, MGH SS* X, 9.

several explanations were offered during the century following her death.[5] In the middle of the thirteenth century the *Breve chronicon de rebus Siculis* states that Constance had been a nun and only through dispensation was enabled to marry Henry VI:

> et ideo successit sibi (William II) regina Constancia que fuerat monialis, et de mandato Ecclesie Romane absoluta ab observantia religionis; copulata fuit matrimonialiter imperatori Henrici.[6]

This statement created the nun-legend which was celebrated by Dante in his *Divina Comedia, Paradiso*.[7] It was criticized in the sixteenth century as being not consistent with the scanty information on Constance's premarital life.[8]

Towards the end of the thirteenth century the *Anonymus Vaticanus* in his *Historia Sicula* spread the rather unpleasant story that Constance was so ugly in appearance that she had remained unmarried for so many years.[9] This slander cannot be taken seriously. Contemporary information, although by Hohenstaufen writers who might be biased, contradict the ugly picture painted by the *Anonymus Vaticanus*.[10] In fact appearance, good looks and love were of no consideration in the marriages of members of the nobilty. On the contrary, children of either sex were considerd to be title deeds for possessions and marriages were intended to unite these possessions. Thus marriage partners were chosen for politcal reasons alone. We therefore have to look for reasons of this kind for Constance's long delayed marriage.

As long as there was no danger to the survival of the Hauteville dynasty there was no need or hurry to get Constance married. When her brother King William I died on 7 May 1166 Constance was barely twelve years old. William I was succeeded by his eldest surviving son, William II who was about nine months older than Constance. During the minority of the new king his mother, the dowager queen, Margareta of Navarra, was regent for her son. During this period Sicilian politics lacked the purpose and decisiveness which would have been necessary to further alliances by a contract of marriage.[11]

In 1167 the Byzantine emperor Manuel Komnenos hoped to recreate the former unity and might of the empire with the assistance of pope Alexander III by

---

[5] A. Cartellieri, *Weltgeschichte als Machtgeschichte, V: Das Zeitalter Friedrich Barbarossas 1150–1190*, Aalen 1972, 419; and most useful now H. Wolter, 'Die Verlobung Heinrichs VI mit Konstanze von Sicilien im Jahre 1184', *Historisches Jahrbuch der Görres-Gesellschaft* 105, 1985, 30–51 and C. Reisinger, *Tankred von Lecce*, Köln 1992, 41–65, 77–130.

[6] *Breve chronicon de rebus Siculis*, ed. J.L.A. Huillard-Breholles, *Historia Diplomatica Friderici secundi*, I/2, Paris 1852, 891.

[7] A. Dante, *Divina Comedia*, Paradiso, Canto 3, lines 96–123.

[8] T. Kölzer, *Urkunden und Kanzlei der Kaiserin Konstanze, Königin von Sizilien (1195–1198)* (Studien zu den normannisch-staufischen Herrscherurkunden Siziliens. Beihefte zum *Coex diplomaticus regni Siciliae*) 2, Cologne 1983, 8.

[9] *Anonymi Vaticani Historia Sicula, Rer. Ital. SS* VIII, 778.

[10] A. Heskel, *Die Historia Sicula des Anonymus Vaticanus und des Gaufredus Malaterra. Ein Beitrag zur Quellenkunde für die Geschichte Unteritaliens und Siziliens im 11. Jahrhundert*, Diss. Kiel 1891.

[11] F. Chalandon, *Histoire de la domination normande en Italie et en Sicilie*, II, Paris 1907, 305ff; J.J. Norwich, *The Kingdom in the Sun*, 227ff.

securing the marriage of his daughter Maria with William II. His attempt failed.[12]
In early 1171 two years of negotiations with King Henry II of England for the
marriage of his daughter Joan to William II came to a sudden end after the murder
of Thomas Becket.[13] A second attempt in 1172 at arranging a marriage with the
Byzantine princess and sole heiress Maria was blessed with only a brief period of
hopeful success. Although negotiations had been successfully completed and the
envoys on both sides had sworn to carry out the contract faithfully the emperor
Manuel Komnenos changed his mind. As Romuald of Salerno states:

> Imperator iuramenti sui et promissionis oblitus, filiam suam regi statuto
> loco et termino non transmisit.[14]

William II spent some weeks at Taranto, Monte Gargano and Bari waiting for the
promised arrival of his bride, but princess Maria never arrived in the Kingdom of
Sicily. Romuald of Salerno gives no reason for the emperor's change of mind. In
anger and dismay William II returned to Palermo via Salerno. In 1173 the
emperor of the west, Frederick Barbarossa, sought to support his political plan of
breaking up the inimical alliance of the Lombard cities, Pope Alexander III and
Sicily by drawing the young king of Sicily into the Hohenstauffen camp. This aim
was to be achieved by the marriage of the emperor's daughter Beatrix to William
II, then about twenty years of age. According to Romuald of Salerno William II
declined such a marriage because of his loyalty to the pope and the curia.[15] While
these marriage negotiations for William II were being pursued there is never any
mention that Constance was ever the object of similar negotiations.

Yet in 1168 a critical situation made it apparent that marriage to Constance
might open the path to a legitimate hold on the Norman throne of Sicily. During a
revolt against the chancellor Stephen of Perche and his French fellow-
countrymen at Messina rumour was spread that King William II had been mur-
dered and the chancellor's younger brother was to marry Constance in order to
camouflage the usurpation by an appearance of legitimacy.[16] It was then that it
became obvious that through Constance it would be possible to claim the Norman
throne despite the existence of King William II's younger brother, Henry of
Capua. When even he died in summer 1172 Constance became the first in line of
succession after William II.

In spite of this precarious situation – with only two legitimate descendants of
the Hauteville dynasty alive to guarantee the stability and peace of the Norman

---

[12] Romualdi Salernitani, *Chronicon*, ed C.A. Garufi, *Rer. Ital. SS* VII/1, 254–255; D.J.A. Matthew, 'The chronicle of Romuald of Salerno': *The Writing of History in the Middle Ages, Essays
presented to R.W. Southern*, ed. R.H.C. Davis and J.M. Wallace-Hadrill, Oxford 1981, 239–274. F.
Dölger, *Regesten der Kaiserurkunden des oströmischen Reiches von 565–1453* (Corpus der griechischen Urkunden des Mittelalters und der neuerern Zeit, ed. Akademien der Wissenschaften in
München und Wien, Reihe A: Regesten, Abt. I) II, München/Berlin 1925, nrr. 1470; J. Parker,
'The attempted Byzantine alliance with the Sicilian Norman kingdom (1166/67)', *Papers of the
British school at Rome* 24 new ser. 11 (Studies in Italian medieval history presented to E.M.
Jamison, London 1956) 86 ff.
[13] A.L. Poole, *From Domesday Book to Magna Carta 1087–1216*, Oxford 1951, 331–332.
[14] *Romualdi Saleritani Chronicon*, 261–262.
[15] *Romualdi Saleritani Chronicon*, 265–266
[16] Hugo Falcandus, *Liber de regno Sicilie* c.55, ed. G.B. Siragusa, Fonti per la storia d'Italia 22
(1897) 150; T. Kölzer, *Urkunden und Kanzlei der Kaiserin Konstanze*, 8f.

kingdom of Sicily – King William II delayed any steps leading to marriage. The young king, in his early twenties, took no steps to ensure that legitimate children would guarantee continuity for his kingdom. William could have resumed negotiations with Westminster soon after the reconciliation between King Henry II and Pope Alexander III in 1172. His long delay and the papal initiative seems to suggest that William might still have preferred marriage with a Hohenstaufsen princess, a daughter of Frederick Barbarossa, although, according to Romuald of Salerno, he had declined an offer of this kind by the emperor in 1173 out of respect for pope and curia.

However, in winter 1175/76 it was Pope Alexander III who took the initiative by encouraging William II to resume negotiations with King Henry II of England with a view to marriage with his daughter Joan.[17] William II, then about twenty-three, eventually sent his envoys to London in spring 1176. After the necessary negotiations they returned to Palermo with the young Joan Plantagenet, his bride of twelve years and six months. On 13 February 1177 Joan was solemnly anointed and crowned Queen of Sicily.

The Pope's initiative in this matter was most likely determined by the fear of a Sicilian-Hohenstaufen alliance which would have robbed the papacy of its most important and powerful ally in southern Italy, and, even more threatening, the *patrimonium Petri* would have become enclosed by two inimical powers. Due to the permanent threat to the Norman kingdom in Sicily by Emperor Manuel Komnenos's plan of restoring the Byzantine empire to its old size and might, William II may have – in the long run – preferred a Hohenstaufen alliance.[18]

Thus it seems that the marriage of William II and Joan of England in 1176/77 was engineered by papal diplomacy and pressure. Did William II, because of this marriage, give up all plans for a family alliance with the Hohenstaufen? He still had one card in his hand – his aunt Constance who could be married to one of the sons of Frederick Barbarossa: Frederick, Henry or Konrad.

During the papal schism from 1159 to 1177 a plan for a Hohenstaufen – Hauteville marriage could not be realized: the papacy, the Lombard cities and the kingdom of Sicily had formed a firm alliance opposing the Latin emperor Frederick Barbarossa. The peace of Venice in autumn 1177 changed the political scene. It brought an end to the period of imperially nominated anti-popes opposing the rightful Pope Alexander III, it brought reconciliation and peace to the Lombard cities and a pledge of fifteen years of peace between the emperor Frederick and his son Henry and the king of Sicily.[19]

Why was the plan of a Hohenstaufen-Hauteville marriage not carried out after this peace of Venice in 1177? The minority of Barbarossa's son Henry – he was twelve years old – was no serious obstacle since betrothal of infants and minors occurred quite frequently among the aristocracy. By his marriage to Joan Plantagenet William II felt committed to the politics of his father-in-law who was in opposition to the emperor because of the serious Hohenstaufen-Welfen conflict which had broken out between Frederick Barbarossa and Henry the Lion, Duke of

[17] *Romualdi Saleritani Chronicon*, 268.
[18] W. Ohnsorge, *Abendland und Byzanz. Gesammelte Aufsätze zur Geschichte der byzantinisch-abendländischen Beziehungen und des Kaisertums*, Darmstadt 1958, 400f; G. Ostrogorsky, *Geschichte des byzantinischen Staates*, München 1965, 570ff.
[19] *MGH LL Constitutiones* I, nr. 260, 362ff; *GiQ* II, 428–431.

Bavaria and Saxony. Henry the Lion was King Henry II's son-in-law and King William II's brother-in-law. Siding with the emperor by forming a marriage alliance between the Hohenstaufen and Hautevilles of Sicily would have put a great strain on relations between Westminster and Palermo.[20]

Despite these international aspects the unique situation of the Hauteville dynasty must be remembered as well. Did William II prefer to delay the marriage of his aunt Constance until his own marriage was blessed with children, thus securing for himself the succession in the Norman kingdom of Sicily? But as long as the king had no children of his own it was quite obvious that Constance or a child of hers would legitimately succeed to the royal throne of Sicily. This prospect of Constance succeeding William, possibly married to a Hohenstaufen prince, must have caused considerable concern to the curia in the late seventies and early eighties of the twelfth century. It had been alerted to act in 1173 when the Hohenstaufen-Hauteville marriage plan first became known. William's allegiance to pope and curia prevented the project in 1173; this allegiance of the Norman king of Sicily to his papal liege lord seems to have continued beyond 1177. The precarious situation within the Hauteville dynasty and William's political aims and alliances meant that a marriage for Constance was long put off. The laws of biology naturally set limits to the prospects of delaying such a marriage indefinitely.

Why did the betrothal eventually come about in October 1184, since the fact that King William II's marriage had been childless had been known for some years? Why did he seemingly act against the interests of his brother-in-law, Henry the Lion? Why did William change his policy of loyalty to pope and curia? What were his reasons in 1184?

There was a new pope: Lucius III had succeeded Alexander III in September 1181. He was an old man who sought peace rather than confrontation and who, while still cardinal bishop of Ostia, had developed a mutual friendship with the Emperor Frederick Barbarossa during the negotiations at Venice in 1177. Despite his pro-Hohenstaufen feelings and his desire for peace a Hohenstaufen-Hauteville marriage was not in the pope's interest and certainly not initiated by him as Johannes Haller has suggested.[21] However, William probably felt less resistance from Lucius III than from Alexander III and the cardinals of the curia to his plan for Constance's marriage.

Was William II so greatly in need of imperial support that he gave up his loyal relations with the pope, his feudal lord? There was no threat from the Byzantine emperor any longer. He had suffered a devastating defeat at Myriokephalon in 1176 and had eventually died in 1180.[22] Since then Byzantine power had gradually declined due to the weak regency of the dowager empress Maria of

---

[20] A.L. Poole, *From Domesday Book to Magna Carta*, 326–328, 339, 362–363.

[21] J. Haller, 'Heinrich VI und die römische Kurie', *Mitteilungen des Instituts für österreichische Geschichte (MIÖG)* 35, 1914, 414ff; criticism by A. Hofmeister, review in *Historische Zeitschrift* 115, 1926, 205; K. Hampe, *Deutsche Kaisergeschichte in der Zeit der Salier und Staufer*, 12th reprint, Heidelberg 1968, 211; G. Baaken, 'Unio regni ad imperium. Die Verhandlungen von Verona 1184 und die Eheabredung zwischen König Heinrich VI und Konstanze von Sizilien', *Quellen und Forschungen aus Italienischen Archiven und Bibliotheken (QFIAB)* 52, 1972, 247f.

[22] G. Ostrogorsky, *Geschichte des byzantinischen Staates*, 332f.

Antioch and the terror regime of Andronikos Komnenos. Bad government, opposition within the state and the defeat of Byzantine troops at the hands of Hungarian and Serbian armies in the Balkans had removed the former threat of the mighty Byzantine empire to the Norman kingdom of Sicily. Moreover, growing Byzantine weakness invited Sicilian expansion into the eastern Mediterranean.[23] Some modern historians consider that William gave permission for his aunt's betrothal to Barbarossa's son Henry in order to safeguard by this marriage alliance with the western empire the Norman invasion of the eastern empire planned for 1185.[24] Since Emperor Frederick Barbarossa and his son Henry VI had sworn a solemn oath on 14 August 1177, under the umbrella of the Venice peace negotiations, to wage no war of any kind against the Sicilian kingdom for the next fifteen years, that is to say until 1192, it would seem that such an alliance was unnecessary.

Thus it appears that there were no outside threats to the kingdom of Sicily which might have induced William II to give his consent to his aunt's betrothal to the Hohenstaufen Henry VI in October 1184. Therefore, reasons within the Norman kingdom must be sought and carefully investigated. Perhaps William II, about thirty years old, and his Queen, about twenty years old, had delayed the betrothal of his aunt in order to wait for a successor to the throne to be born to them. By 1184, despite his prayers that God would avert the infertility of his marriage and despite copious gifts and grants to the abbey of the holy Virgin at Monreale William II may have realised that his mariage to Joan Plantagenet would remain childless.[25] Thus, under the pontificate of the mellow pope Lucius III, he decided to put forward once more his old plan of bringing about a Hohenstaufen-Hauteville marriage. For this reason he ordered the magnates of his realm to convene at the episcopal city of Troia in Apulia in 1184/85 on the occasion of the betrothal of Constance to Henry. He demanded that they promise by oath to loyally and faithfully support Constance and her Hohenstaufen husband if he, William II, should die without offspring.[26]

This bleak possibility was not merely the concern of the court at Palermo, but also of the European powers. During William's reign it led to the gradual decline in authority of the Norman kingdom of Sicily. Barons and ecclesiastics were increasingly emancipating themselves in their actions from royal control and rule. About 1179 Pope Alexander warned William II to maintain firm order in his realm and to protect the churches of his kingdom from the attacks of his counts, barons and knights. Little is known about the following years but there is no reason to think that William II managed to subject the nobles of his realm.[27]

The story of Tancred of Lecce may be indicative of the fall and rise of

23 F. Chalandon, *Histoire de la domination Normande*, 401ff.
24 K. Jordan, 'Investiturstreit und frühe Stauferzeit (1056–1197)', in. B. Gebhard and H. Grundmann, *Handbuch der Deutschen Geschichte*, I, Stuttgart 1957, 326.
25 *Ryccardi de Santo Germano Chronica*, ed. C.A. Garufi, Rer. Ital. SS VII/2, 4; L.T. White, *Latin monasticism in Norman Sicily*, Cambridge/Massachusetts 1938, 132–145.
26 G. Baaken, 'Unio regni ad imperium', 277ff.
27 F. Chalandon, *Histoire de la domination Normande*, 417f; J. Deer, *Papstum und Normannen. Untersuchungen zu ihren lehensrechtlichen und kirchenpolitischen Beziehungen. Studien und Quellen zur Welt Kaiser Friedrichs II*, I, Wien/Köln 1972, 259f; Alexander III's letter in W. Holtzmann, 'Zur Kirchenpolitik König Wilhelms II', *Studi medievali in onore di Antonio di Stefano*, Palermo 1956, 294.

members of the aristocracy and consequently the strength and weakness of the royal power in the Sicilian kingdom in the second half of the twelfth century. Barely three weeks after the death of William II, Tancred was made king on 8 December 1189 with the powerful assistance of Matthew of Ajello, the vice-chancellor. It was common knowledge that he and some other magnates of the *curia regis* strongly opposed Constance's marriage to the Hohenstaufen Henry VI.[28]

Tancred was the illegitimate son of Roger, duke of Apulia, and Emma, daughter of Archad, count of Lecce.[29] Duke Roger, who died in 1148, was the eldest son of King Roger II. Tancred was therefore a cousin of William II. After his father's death, anxious to prevent any trouble for the future, his grandfather Roger II kept Tancred and his younger brother William in close custody in Palermo. From 1156 to 1161 he was involved in various revolts against his uncle William I and was subsequently banished from Sicily. During the mild regency of the dowager queen Margareta Tancred was pardoned and returned as count to Lecce. Through military brilliance he rose to fame and won great esteem. Francesco Giunta points to the demonstrative inscription above the main door of the abbey of SS Nicolò e Cataldo.[30] It celebrates Tancred as *magnus comito* and seems to express Tancred's self esteem and ambition. His swift seizure of the throne on 8 December 1189, within three weeks of William II's death, was probably the result of ambitions of this kind which he appears to have fostered for a long time.

Bearing in mind all these arguments it becomes quite clear that the lack of an heir for William II steadily increased Tancred's chances of a claim to the throne. To prevent him achieving this aim William II agreed to the betrothal of his aunt in October 1184. Gilbert of Mons's statement seems to confirm this conclusion when he says that William II gave his aunt in matrimony to Henry VI hoping that his kingdom would thus pass into her hands.[31]

How then did the betrothal come about? Whose initiative was it? Johannes Haller's theory that the pope himself brought about the Hohenstaufen-Hauteville marriage is not convincing and has been rejected by modern historians.[32] Nor does initiative from the imperial side seem likely since it cannot be supported by any sources. Although Otto of St Blasien states that after the dispatch of an embassy to William II the emperor had his son betrothed to Constance, the dispatch of this embassy was probably not the initial step in negotiations leading to the betrothal.[33] It seems more likely that the initiative for the planned betrothal

[28] T. Toeche, *Jahrbücher der deutschen Geschichte*, Darmstadt 1965, 142f; H. Ottendorff, *Die Regierung der beiden letzten Normannenkönige, Tancred und Wilhelm III, von Sizilien und ihre Kämpfe gegen Kaiser Heinrich VI*, Diss. Bonn 1899, 12f; D.R. Clementi, 'Some unnoticed Aspects of the Emperor Henry VI's Conquest of the Norman Kingdom of Sicily', *Bulletin of the John Rylands Library*, 36, 1953/54, 328–359; D.R. Clementi, 'The Circumstances of Count Tancred's Accession to the kingdom of Sicily, Duchy of Apulia and the Principality of Capua', *Mélanges Antonio Marongiu*, Bruxelles 1968, 57–80.
[29] J. Deer, *Papstum und Normannen*, 260; P.F. Palumbo, *Gli atti di Trancredi e Guiglelmo III di Sicilia, Atti del convegno internazionale di studi Ruggeriano* II, Palermo 1955, 475.
[30] F. Giunta, *Magnus comito Tancredus, Storiografia e storia. Studi in onore di Eugenio Dupré Theseider II*, Roma 1976, 648.
[31] *Gisleberti chronicon Hanoniense* c. 33, ed. L. Vanderkindere, Bruxelles 1904, 66.
[32] See above note 21.
[33] See above note 3.

came from the Sicilian court at Palermo. The brief accounts by the Hohenstaufen biased writers can be ignored in favour of the reports by Gilbert of Mons and Richard of San Germano who confirm that William II was the originator of the plan for the betrothal of Constance to Henry VI.[34]

How were the negotiations conducted? It is unlikely that William II directly approached the emperor with his proposal for the betrothal. The peace of Venice in 1177 had put an end to open enmity between the empire and the Sicilian kingdom, yet the two powers did not entertain any close relations to deal with such delicate matters. Furthermore, William II himself had snubbed the emperor in 1173 by rejecting the offer of marriage with the imperial princess Beatrix. Finally, William's close relations with England and the continuing exile of his brother-in-law, Henry the Lion, forbade the opening of direct negotiations with the Hohenstaufen court with the goal of a political marriage union. This close link between the Sicilian king and his English father-in-law however makes it likely that the opening of negotiations about the Hohenstaufen marriage was furthered via the English court.[35] According to Richard of San Germano William II discussed the marriage plan with Archbishop Walter of Palermo who was on good terms with the court of Henry II through Peter of Blois.[36] Possibly, as suggested by Walter's correspondence with Peter of Blois, the archbishop advised William II to involve his father-in-law in the negotiations with the imperial court.[37] In fact, Henry II sent his son-in-law, Henry the Lion, then living in exile in England, to the famous Whitsun diet of Mainz in May 1184.[38] Henry the Lion, the Welf, was to offer the emperor an English-Hohenstaufen alliance against France. Since, in the context of this offer, Henry the Lion also requested the lifting of the sentence of banishment from the emperor, it can be concluded that Barbarossa's reprieve of Henry the Lion was to be in return for the Sicilian betrothal plan which was most attractive to the Hohenstaufen emperor. Albert of Stade writes *ad annum 1184* in his *Annales Stadenses*:

> imperator celeberrimam habuit curiam Moguntiae . . . ibi confirmatum est matrimonium Constantiae cum filio imperatoris.[39]

Although the emperor welcomed both the English offer of an anti-France alliance and the offer from Sicily he made no quick decision at Mainz with regard to the pardon of Henry the Lion. He did not grant the Welf's request by a spontaneous act of grace at that meeting. Yet not long after the splendid Whitsun diet, celebrated as the grand culmination of medieval chivalry, in July 1184, the emperor must have dispatched his envoys to Palermo, as mentioned by Otto of St

[34] *Gisleberti chronicon Hanoniense*, 66; *Ryccardi de Sancto Germano Chronica*, 6; G. Fasoli, *Scritti di storia medievali*, Bologna 1974, 359ff.

[35] A.L. Poole, *From Domesday Book to Magna Carta*, Oxford 1951, 331; O. Engels, *Zur Entmachtung Heinrichs des Löwen, Festschrift für A. Kraus*, Münchner Historische Studien, Bd. 10, Kallmünz 1982, 54.

[36] *Ryccardo de Sancto Germano Chronica*, 6; J.A.L. Loewenthal, For the biography of Walter Ophamil, *EHR* 87 (1972) 75ff.

[37] Migne, *PL* 207, 195ff.

[38] O. Engels, *Zur Entmachtung Heinrichs des Löwen*, 50ff; O. Engels, *Der Niederrhein und das Reich im 12. Jahrhundert, Königtum und Reichsgewalt am Niederrhein*, Klever Archiv 4, Kleve 1983, 93ff.

[39] *Annales Stadenses, MGH SS* XVI, 350.

Blasien. The envoys were to travel to the court of Palermo to negotiate the details of the marriage contract, to be confirmed by oath by the nobles of the respective realms at Augsburg, Bavaria, and at Troia, Apulia in 1184/85.[40]

Towards the end of August 1184, shortly before the emperor set out for his long-planned meeting with Pope Lucius III at Verona, he sent Philip of Heinsberg, Archbishop of Cologne, to the English court to confirm the Plantagenet-Hohenstaufen alliance which had been agreed in Mainz, a marriage proposal for one of the imperial princesses with Richard Lionheart.[41] The archbishop, surely at the emperor's suggestion, advised Henry II to seek the pope's mediation in the case of Henry the Lion. Henry II immediately dispatched his envoys to Verona. On their way they met the emperor at Milan in the second half of September 1184 and then continued their journey to meet Pope Lucius III. The English envoys to the pope seem to have had a dual task: to implore the pope to intercede with the emperor on behalf of Henry the Lion and to secure the Hohenstaufen-Hauteville betrothal plan in return for this reprieve.

Barbarossa needed the pope's consent for the marriage plan in order to ensure the imperial coronation of his son Henry which Pope Lucius had already conceded before the Verona meeting.[42] The emperor had seized the initiative in this deal by refusing to spontaneously pardon Henry the Lion at Mainz and by the offers made at the court of Westminster through the archbishop of Cologne. Gervase of Tilbury comments that by an excellent plan the emperor succeeded in bringing about the marriage of Constance to his son:

> Tandem exquisito Fredericus concilio amitam regis Guillermi . . . Henrico . . . filio suo, copulat Constantiam, spe concepta, quod deficiente prole legitima ex rege Guillermo, amita tamquam propinquior succedens iura imperii redintegret.[43]

In the matter of the Hohenstaufen-Hauteville marriage plan Frederick Barbarossa could expect effective promotion of his plans with Lucius III by Henry II of England whose interests in this case were congruous with those of the emperor. Henry sought the reprieve of his son-in-law, Henry the Lion, and stability of the dynasty for his daughter Joan, wife of William II of Sicily. Besides the Sicilian royal couple Henry was certainly the most qualified promotor of the betrothal plan to support the survival of the Hauteville dynasty, and he had no fear of uniting Sicily with the empire.

Moreover Pope Lucius had always been prepared to negotiate and there were ample possibilities for compromise within the points on the agenda for the Verona conference. The emperor had good reason to hope, with the support of the English king, for the pope's consent to the betrothal of Constance to Henry VI and his assent to the imperial coronation of his son.[44]

The conference at Verona was only partly the success it had promised to be. No single incident can be made responsible for the failure of negotiations. The pope seems to have been informed only at Verona about the planned betrothal of

---

[40] G. Baaken, 'Unio regni ad imperium', 272ff.
[41] R. Knipping, *Die Regesten der Erzbischöfe von Köln im Mittelalter* II, Bonn 1901, nr 1232.
[42] G. Baaken, 'Unio regni ad imperium', 226f.
[43] *Gervasii Tillberiensis Otia imperialia, MGH SS* XXVII, 381.
[44] F.X. Seppelt, *Geschichte der Päpste*, III, München 1956, 291ff.

Constance to the emperor's son. Yet during the early part of the negotiations the emperor appears to have felt that the pope was prepared to accept the plan. He consented to pardon Henry the Lion by 19 October 1184 and about two weeks later, on 29 October, a period of time a messenger would take for the journey from Verona to Augsburg, the betrothal of Henry VI to Constance was made public in Augsburg.[45]

Lucius III was conciliatory towards the Hohenstaufen-Hauteville marriage, as shown in the *Chronicon Slavorum* of Arnold of Lübeck and the *Gesta Treverorum*.[46] Both emphasise however that the cardinals of the *curia* finally caused the pope to change his mind and to refuse Henry VI imperial coronation. This fact is confirmed by the *Chronica Regia Colonensis* and by Albert of Stade.[47] The marriage of Constance and Henry was fixed for January 1186; the imperial coronation delayed till Easter 1191.

Otto of St Blasien writes about the marriage of Henry and Constance:

> The citizens of Milan besought Emperor Frederick I, as a demonstration of their having regained imperial grace, to celebrate the wedding of his son Henry with Constance in their city. The emperor complied with their wish in order to bind them firmly to the empire through which they had suffered so much, and he invited all the barons of Italy to a general diet in Milan. Together with the assembled nobles and princes from north of the Alps and the nobles and princes from Lombardy, Tuscany, Campania, Apulia and Sicily the emperor and his son, King Henry, the bridegroom, left the city to meet and welcome the bride with the most magnificent splendour and royal pageantry and led her into the city. There the wedding was celebrated on 27 January 1186. It was a day of honour for the empire. At these splendid festivities the Lombards completely won the emperor's grace and favour, and after having reconfirmed the peace a general pardon was granted, that is to say all the former evils were not to be remembered for ever; the emperor basked in the sunshine of bliss at the Lombards' manifold proofs of subjection and obedience.[48]

What was the prelude to this epoch-making union of the dynasties of Hohenstaufen and Hauteville? It brought about a fundamental change of the balance of power between the European realms. The alliances of the papacy with the Norman kingdom of Sicily, the Lombard cities and the kingdom of England against the *rex Teutonicorum et imperator Romanorum* were terminated. It brought to an end the enmity of the Latin empire towards the Norman kingdom of Sicily which had lasted for more than a century.

The prelude to this marriage between Henry VI and Constance of Sicily was marked by hostilities. Ever since the papacy under Leo IX had adopted the

---

[45] O. Engels, *Zur Entmachtung Heinrichs des Löwen*, 54.

[46] *Arnoldi Chronica Slavorum MGH SS* XXI, 195; *Gesta Treverorum cont.* III 6, *MGH SS* XXIV, 384.

[47] *Chronica regia Coloniensis MGH SS in usum scholarum*, 134; *Annales Stadenses MGH SS* XVI, 350.

[48] *Chronica Ottonis de Sancto Blasio MGH SS in usum scholarum*, 39–40; *GiQ* II 467.

Normans of the south as their vassals against the emperor there was ample cause for conflict.[49] The advance of Norman power in southern Italy and more particularly the inauguration in 1130 of the new Norman kingdom of the south – although performed by the anti-pope Anaclet II – offered a special challenge to the *rex Teutonicorum et imperator Romanorum semper augustus*. For in creating his new kingdom Roger II had acquired territories and rights which had formerly been vested not only in Byzantium but more immediately in the Western empire. St Bernard of Clairvaux stressed this point when he wrote to Emperor Lothair III in about 1135 denouncing King Roger II as *invasor imperii* – a usurper of imperial rights:

> It is not any of my business to incite to battle, but I do say, without hesitation, that it is the concern of a friend of the Church to save her from the mad fury of the schismatics; that it is the duty of Caesar to uphold his own crown against the machinations of that Sicilian usurper. Just as it is to the injury of Christ that a man of the Jewish race (the father of Peter Leonis = Anaclet II was a converted Jew) has seized for himself the See of Peter, so it is against the interests of Caesar that anyone should make himself the King of Sicily.[50]

In 1137, in alliance with the legitimate pope Innocent II the emperor waged a terrible war in Italy against the tyrant of Sicily. Since Roger II withdrew to the island part of his kingdom the emperor did not achieve his aim, a decisive victory in battle. On the contrary, the war turned out to be Roger's triumph which severely damaged the empire. When Lothair III died in Tyrol on his way back from Italy on 4 December 1137 he was a defeated ruler. The continuing enmity between Emperor Conrad III and Roger II is also one of the themes in John of Salisbury's *Historia Pontificalis*.[51] Because of his suppression of the Church John censures Roger:

> Rex enim aliorum more tyrannorum ecclesiam terrae suae redegerat in servitutem.[52]

Roger's modern Norman state was not only a danger for the imperial power and territories in Italy. He sided with the Welf party in its feud against the Hohenstaufen emperors Konrad III and Frederick I by giving financial support to Welf VI, cousin of Konrad III and uncle of Frederick I.[53]

The great medieval historian Otto of Freising, related to both the Hohenstaufen and the Welf dynasty, described at great length the emperors' wars against Roger whom he, like John of Salisbury, called tyrant *ad antiquorum Siculorum formam*

---

[49] *Romualdi Saleritani Chronicon*, 182; J. Deer, *Das Papstum und die süditalienischen Normannenstaaten 1053–1212*, Göttingen 1969, 11–15; see also note 2.
[50] *Letters of St Bernard of Clairvaux*, ed. B.S. James, London 1953, ep. 142; H. Wieruszowski, 'Roger II of Sicily, *rex tyrannus*, in twelfth-century political thought', *Speculum* 38, 1963, 46–78.
[51] *Historia Pontificalis* of John of Salisbury, ed. M. Chibnall, Edinburgh 1956, 58.
[52] *Historia Pontificalis* of John of Salisbury, 65.
[53] Genealogical tables of Hohenstaufen and Welfs: C.W. Previté-Orton, *The Shorter Cambridge Medieval History*, I, Cambridge 1953, 556–557; *Propyläen Weltgeschichte*, ed. G. Mann und A. Nitschke, V, Berlin-Frankfurt/Main 1991, 430–431.

tyrannorum.[54] Rahewin, Otto's continuator, never used the name of Roger or William in his *Gesta Friderici;* he only speaks of *that Sicilian* in the most derogatory way.[55] The emperors of the east and the west formed alliances against Roger II who had stolen territories and rights from their empires in order to create his new Sicilian kingdom. None of these alliances was ever powerful and determined enough to effectively attack or conquer the new Norman kingdom of the south, and indeed the threat grew less as time progressed. In the 1170s the Byzantine peril weakened and eventually vanished due to interior revolts and defeats. The danger from the western emperor was suspended for fifteen years by the agreement of Venice in summer 1177.

Henry VI's marriage to Constance on 27 January 1186 had far-reaching consequences. It made him the closest legitimate male relative to King William II of Sicily. King William II's death on 18 November 1189 made him the legitimate heir to the Norman kingdom of Sicily through his wife Constance. The impending threat of the Hohenstaufen take-over of the Norman kingdom of the south created formidable opposition among members of the *magnates curiae* and other members of the aristocracy who feared the loss of their estates and influence.[56] They rallied around Tancred of Lecce and supported his claim to the royal throne in November 1189. Yet Tancred's kingship and the support for it by the opposing members of the *magnates curiae* was short-lived and collapsed with his death on 20 February 1194. During the summer and autumn of that year Henry VI and Constance moved south to rightfully take possession of the kingdom of Sicily. On 20 November 1194 Henry entered Palermo and on Christmas Day Tancred's seven-year-old son, recently crowned King William III, mounted the altar steps of the cathedral of Palermo, expressed his will to relinquish his claim to the throne and handed over the royal crown.[57] Then Henry was crowned King of Sicily with the *corona regni Siciliae et Calabriae et Apuliae* which Anaclet II, the anti-pope, had sent Roger II as a papal gift with the order that all his legitimate successors were to be crowned with it. Henry was robed in the royal robes of his predecessors including Roger's magnificent coronation cloak adorned with lions hunting camels.[58] This cloak, the dalmatic, and the other coronation vestments became part of the imperial coronation robes in the centuries to come. They are still preserved in the treasury in Vienna.[59]

Emperor Henry VI, now king of Sicily, was crowned in the presence of all the nobles of the kingdom. They were relying on the general amnesty assured to them for their support of Tancred.[60] A few days after the coronation some monk is said

---

[54] *Otto von Freising Chronik*, ed. W. Lammers, Freiherr vom Stein-Gedächtnisausgabe XVI, Darmstadt 1990, 540 and 532, 542, 548.

[55] Otto von Freising und Rahewin. *Die Taten Friedrich*, ed. F.J. Schmale, Freiherr vom Stein-Gedächtnisausgabe XVII, Darmstadt 1986, 170, 184, 186, 198, 278, 294.

[56] D.R. Clementi, 'Some unnoticed Aspects of the Emperor Henry VI's Conquest of the Norman kingdom of Sicily', *Bulletin of the John Rylands Library* 36, 1953/54, 328–359; D.R. Clementi, 'The Circumstances of Count Tancred's Accession to the Kingdom of Sicily, Duchy of Apulia and the Principality of Capua', *Mélanges Antonio Marongiu*, Bruxelles 1968, 57–80.

[57] *Ryccardi de Sancto Germano Chronica*, 16–17.

[58] J. Deer, *Der Kaiserornat Friedrichs II*, Bern 1952, 56–60.

[59] *Weltliche und Geistliche Schatzkammer (der Wiener Burg)*, ed. Kunsthistorisches Museum, Wien 1987, 134–148.

[60] *Ryccardi de Sancto Germano Chronica*, 17–20.

to have intercepted some letters pointing to a treacherous revolt by some members of the aristocracy. Forgetting all assurances and promises Henry retaliated most violently. He acted brutally against William III, his mother and brother; he had leading members of the magnates captured and tortured, and some put to death; he had the royal treasury plundered. Gold, jewels, royal insignia and robes were carried across the Alps by 160 horses. Henry did not stop there. He did not respect the independence and integrity of his new realm. By reorganising the administration he reduced the kingdom of Sicily to an imperial province like Tuscany or Ancona-Romagna. Thus Henry took back into imperial governance those lands which, since the 1050s, under papal suzerainty, Norman activities had taken from the empire, and engulfed the *patrimonium Petri* on all sides so that the worst fears of the papacy came true.[61]

Emperor Henry VI was at the peak of his power. From 1189 he had suppressed various revolts in the lower Rhine area and in Saxony, had acquired large fiefs in the upper Rhine valley and in the valley of the river Elbe, had reaped a gigantic ransom for Richard Lionheart and made him his vassal, was planning to do likewise with the kingdom of Aragon, had succeeded his father as presumptive emperor after Barbarossa's death in the river Saleph on 10 June 1190 and was crowned *imperator Romanorum semper augustus* together with his wife by Pope Celestine III at Easter 1191. Adopting King Roger II's policy towards the eastern Mediterranean Empire, Henry VI used Sicily as his base and pursued his father-in-law's ambitious plans. At the request of embassies from Armenia, Cyprus, Syria and Tripoli he accepted the kings of these realms as vassals of the Roman emperor. He even planned to conquer the Byzantine empire and in order to legalise this attack had his brother Phillip married to Irene, the heiress presumptive of the Byzantine empire.[62]

Having accumulated this power and wealth Henry VI decided to change the constitutional law of the German kingdom. Since the time of the Saxon kings it had been the privilege of the members of the high aristocracy to elect the new king. Henry planned to substitute this election by the right of hereditary succession, and this right was to be vested in the Hohenstaufen dynasty. The *Annales Marbacenses* state:

> In the year 1196 the emperor convened a diet at Würzburg at mid-Lent. There the emperor wanted to establish with the princes a new law, never heard of in the Roman empire: 'In the Roman empire the kings should succeed according to the law of inheritance as they do in France and in other realms.' The princes present assented to this new law and confirmed their assent by their seal.[63]

By this enormous expansion of the power of his rule and by involving himself in all the international tensions and conflicts the Roman empire became more vulnerable than ever so that the slightest drawback would have had detrimental effects. Henry's unexpected death at the age of thirty-two on 28 November 1197

---

[61] D. Abulafia, *Frederick II*, London 1988, 79–86.
[62] K. Jordan, *Investiturstreit und frühe Stauferzeit (1056–1197)*, B. Gebhardt and H. Grundmann, *Handbuch der Deutschen Geschichte*, I, Stuttgart 1957, 333–337.
[63] *Annales Marbacenses*, 1194, *MGH SS* XVII, 167; *GiQ* II, 470.

created a sudden power vacuum which caused the catastrophe of 1197/98. Two kings were elected in 1198, the Welf Otto IV and Henry's brother Phillip. This double election brought about another round in the Hohenstaufen-Welfen feud and ten years of civil war.

But let us return to 1194. During the summer and autumn of 1194 the emperor and the empress were moving south to take possession of the kingdom of Sicily. The imperial couple separated because the empress was pregnant. Her age of forty and the conditions of the roads in Lombardy and the Marken required a rather slow progress south. About mid-December 1194 she reached the region of Ancona. When she arrived at the small town of Jesi not far from Ancona she felt that her baby was due.

Right from the beginning of her pregnancy Constance was concerned about one thing. She knew her enemies and those of Henry on both sides of the Alps would question the birth of her child. They would point to her age and her long infertility and state categorically that the child was not hers. For this reason she was determined to do anything to secure utmost certainty in this matter. In the middle of the market square of Jesi she had a huge tent put up to which any lady of the town was to have free entry if she wished to be present at the birth. On St Stephen's day, 26 December 1194, a day after her husband had been crowned King of Sicily in the cathedral of Palermo, the empress gave birth to her only son. A day or two later she returned into the market square and proudly breast-fed her baby. This demonstration of the Hauteville spirit overcame any possible scepticism about the rightful heir in Europe and displayed that the Norman spirit was not yet completely dead.

The Hauteville spirit reappeared during the following century in a new, even more brilliant shape when Constance's son, originally named Constantine but later baptised Frederick Roger after his grandfathers, grew up. These names stand for a political programme: Roman imperial domination of the world, Hohenstaufen greatness of the empire and Norman statecraft.[64]

Frederick, the *puer Apuliae*, was orphaned early by the death of his father Henry on 28 September 1197 and his mother Constance on 27 November 1198. Shocked by her husband's ferocity and brutality towards the kingdom of Sicily Constance first tried to mitigate her late husband's oppressive policy by getting rid of his chief administrators and the Hohenstaufen occupational forces. She then severed the link between the Hauteville dynasty and the Hohenstaufen empire. On behalf of her three-year-old son she renounced his claims to *rex Teutonicorum* and *imperator Romanorum semper augustus* and had him crowned king of Sicily, thus securing for him the kingdom of Sicily by acknowledging in his name the overlordship of the pope and by placing him under the tutelage of Pope Innocent III against Markward of Anweiler's claim of guardianship for young Frederick. When the Welf Emperor Otto IV, son of Henry the Lion and grandson of Henry II of England, attacked Italy and Sicily in 1209/10 Pope Innocent decided to encourage Frederick to win back the crown of the *rex Teutonicorum*. Thanks to the

---

[64] E. Kantorowicz, *Kaiser Friedrich der Zweite*, 1927; reprint Stuttgart 1991; D. Abulafia, *Frederick II*, London 1988.

charm of his personality and the assistance of the French king he achieved this goal, of being elected and receiving royal coronation in 1212.

The pope perceived that German kingship was a necessary step towards the *imperator Romanorum* assenting to the union of Sicily and the empire. Frederick granted assurances to the Church and *patrimonium Petri* in 1213 and on the occasion of his imperial coronation in 1220 he consented to treaties which were to mitigate the dangers of an accumulation of power and the engulfing of Rome on either side. It was to no avail – the union of empire and Sicily caused the same insurmountable problems as in his father's times. Frederick quickly organised German affairs by granting privileges to spiritual lords (*Confoederatio cum principibus ecclesiasticis* of 1220) and temporal princes (*Statutum in favorum principum* of 1232) in order to secure the election of his son as *rex Teutonicorum*, but laying the foundations for the future territorial states as competition to the central power of the king. He himself, however, concentrated on imperial Italy which he tried to organise administratively by assimilating Sicily and by reshaping its administration at the assizes of Capua in 1220 and the *constitutiones* of Melfi in 1231. Feudalism, administration, judiciary, military and economy were subordinated to the law of rational absolutism. All life was directed to the ruler and originated from him. The ensuing rivalry between emperor and pope developed into bitter enmity despite the successful crusade of 1228/29 which opened the Holy Land to peaceful pilgrims for ten years. This was achieved by negotiation rather than by war. Yet the bitter conflict between empire and papacy, interspersed by periods of peace, continued and survived Frederick II's lifetime. It only came to an end when the last Hohenstaufen Konradin was executed by the papal auxiliaries of Anjou at Lucera in 1266 thus finally freeing the Church from the Hohenstaufen threat.

Although Frederick II is best remembered as emperor of the west, he never forgot that he was also king of Sicily, not only grandson of Frederick Barbarossa but also grandson of Roger II. He displayed this by the splendour of his court, by his exotic animals such as lions, leopards and peacocks, by his love for Italian and Arabic as well as *volgare* Sicilian poetry and literature, his passion for classical architecture like the gate of Capua and his hunting palaces like Castel del Monte in Apulia. He demonstrated his Norman roots by his boundless desire for knowledge in the fields of art and science, philosophy and religion. He enjoyed philosophical disputation and religious dialogues and dictated six volumes of *De arte venandi cum avibus,* a masterpiece in scientific observation and methodolgy. These activities and interests earned him the title of *Stupor Mundi* and made him the first Renaissance prince two hundred years before that period.

The betrothal of Constance to Henry VI was initiated by the royal court at Palermo. For a considerable period of time there had been a plan for a union of the Hohenstaufen and the Hauteville dynasties. Considerations with regard to the curia and the English king were dropped when William II's illegitimate cousin, Tancred, uttered claims for the Sicilian royal throne. Due to English mediation, encouraged by the pardon for Henry the Lion, the emperor managed to obtain the pope's consent despite the cardinals' radical resistance to the plan. The marriage brought an end to a century of hostilities between the empire and the Norman rulers of the south and determined the course of history for more than two generations. William II followed a well-used pattern of improving the prestige of the Hauteville dynasty by arranging a marriage with a member of a superior dynasty, the powerful Hohenstaufen.[65] Yet did not his attempt to save his ailing dynasty through an advantageous marriage eventually lead to the ruin of the Norman kingdom of Sicily?

---

[65] V. D'Alessandro, 'Nobilità e parentela'. See above, pp. 91–7.

THE COINAGES OF NORMAN APULIA AND SICILY IN THEIR INTERNATIONAL SETTING[1]

Philip Grierson

The coinages of Norman Apulia and Sicily are without question the most remarkable of late eleventh- and twelfth-century Europe. Western Christendom had a coinage limited to two denominations of small silver coins, a penny or denier and a much more rarely issued halfpenny or obol, with a marginal minting of gold on Islamic models in northern Spain and at Salerno and Amalfi. The Norman states of the south had coinages predominantly of gold and copper, with silver coins only of consequence from the mid-twelfth century onwards and always subordinate to the gold and copper. We seem in a different world.

The contrast is particularly striking if one looks specifically at the coinage of the Norman homeland, for the deniers of the dukes were among the most deplorable in Europe.[2] The deniers – there were no obols – were ill-struck and badly designed, having for types a cross and a type derived from the 'temple' of one of the main coin issues of Louis the Pious but blundered and corrupted almost beyond belief. The legends had become no more than a series of strokes, going back to the names of Duke Richard and of the mint (ROTHOMAGVS) and not attempting to reproduce the name of the reigning duke; they were ultimately to disappear altogether. In contrast, when the Normans conquered England they found in operation an admirably organized and efficient minting system,[3] with some sixty mints striking at any given moment the same type of coin and placing on each the names of ruler and mint and of the moneyer responsible for their issue, so that he could be brought to book if his coins were later found to be defective. This system the conquerors took over with a minimum of change, but it

Acknowledgments. I am most grateful to Lucia Travaini for having read and greatly improved this paper, though since there are some points on which we do not see eye to eye she is not to be held responsible for its assertions. The original text was also modified in a few places to take account of information provided by other papers at the conference.

[1]   The following abbreviations are used: *AIIN* = *Annali del Istituto Italiano di Numismatica*; *BCNN* = *Bollettino del Circolo Napoletano di Numismatica*; *BdN* = *Bollettino di Numismatica*; *NC* = *Numismatic Chronicle*; *RIN* = *Rivista italiana di numismatica*; *RN* = *Revue numismatique*; *RSS* = *Rassegna storica salernitana*. The most comprehensive survey of the coinage, in tabular form, is in Giulio Sambon, *Repertorio generale delle monete coniate in Italia e da Italiani all'estero dal secolo V° al XX°*. I. *Periodo dal 476 al 1266*, Paris 1912.

[2]   The standard studies are F. Dumas, 'Les monnaies normandes (Xe–XIIe siècles), avec un répertoire des trouvailles', *RN*[6] 21, 1979, 84–140, and F. Dumas and J. Pilet-Lemière, 'La monnaie normande – Xe–XIIe siècle. Le point de la recherche en 1987', in *Actes du deuxième congrès international d'archéologie médiévale (Caen, 2–4 octobre 1987)*, ed. H. Galinié, Caen 1989, 125–31.

[3]   Concise and clear summary in M. Blackburn, 'Coinage and currency under Henry I: a review', *ante* 13, 1991, 49–81.

did not cause them to undertake any monetary reforms in Normandy itself. Only a brief experiment in the late eleventh century of using personal names on the coins, presumably those of moneyers though viscounts have been suggested, indicates Anglo-Saxon influence, but it was quickly abandoned and led to nothing.

But while in England the Normans could take over and continue to operate a uniform if complex minting system, in south Italy and Sicily a different situation obtained. There was no uniformity. Their mainland conquests consisted partly of Byzantine and partly of Lombard territory, the latter made up of several principalities, and each of these had its own coinage system. Sicily, with the most mixed cultural background of any Mediterranean land, had been in Muslim hands for the previous two centuries, and even here the Normans did not take over a unified Muslim state. The authority of the Kalbite governors, who had themselves virtually displaced the nominal Fatimid sovereigns, had crumbled in the 1040s and 1050s, and the Normans had to eliminate, one after the other, a series of local rulers comparable to the Reyes de Taifas in Spain.

The main monetary system on the mainland was that of the Byzantines.[4] This used the traditional three metals of antiquity, gold, silver and copper, with a gold coin (solidus or nomisma; fig. 1), a silver coin (miliaresion) worth a twelfth of this, and a heavy copper coin (follis, or follaro in Italian; figs 2, 3) worth 1/24th of the miliaresion. But while in most of the Empire the miliaresion was a coin actually in circulation, in Italy it seems to have been mainly if not exclusively a money of account, possibly because such miliaresia as reached Italy tended to be exported to the silver-using areas of north Italy and the West. In the second half of the eleventh century, however, the Byzantine coinage system was falling into confusion, for the gold coins, after seven amazing centuries of stability, were being seriously debased. This followed on their curious division into what were effectively two denominations, a coin of the traditional weight which came to be termed an histamenon and was made concave – the technical term was trachy – instead of flat, and a slightly lighter coin known as a tetarteron. This debasement of the gold had in due course serious consequences for both the silver and the copper, and required a major currency reform, effected by Alexius I Comnenus in 1092, to put things right.

The new coinage,[5] which was to last in its main elements for the whole of the Norman period, broke with tradition in that all save the lowest denominations of copper (initially the lowest was of lead) were of various alloys, not of pure metals, and all save these lowest denominations were made concave, like the debased histamena in the mid eleventh century. There were normally four denominations in the new system. At the top was a gold nomisma (fig. 4), slightly alloyed with silver but known as a hyperpyron ('super-pure'), of the traditional weight (4.55g) but only 20 1/2 carats fine (854/1000). Its fractions were a one-third hyperpyron of the same weight but only a third of its fineness, a coin of black billon (silver-copper alloy) worth 1/48th of a hyperpyron, and a small copper coin known as a tetarteron (fig. 5), worth 1/18th of this or 1/864th of a hyperpyron. Occasionally

---

4 For what follows see Philip Grierson, *Byzantine Coins*, London 1982, 191ff., and Michael F. Hendy, *Studies in the Byzantine Monetary Economy c.300–1450*, Cambridge 1985, 504–12.
5 Grierson, 215ff.; Hendy, 513ff. It was Hendy who in 1969 first identified Alexius's reform of 1092 and worked out its denominational pattern, which had mystified all earlier scholars.

half-tetartera were struck also. The old silver and heavy copper coins worth respectively 1/12th and 1/288th of a nomisma had in fact been replaced by three levels of base coins worth respectively 1/3rd, 1/48th and 1/864th of a hyperpyron, providing a lower unit at the base of the system and different values for its intervening levels. Byzantium supplied Norman-Italian coinage with a number of coin types, with the use of copper, and occasionally with the concave fabric.

The coinages of the non-Byzantine states of southern Italy, essentially the principality of Salerno and the smaller duchies of Naples, Gaeta, Sorrento, Capua and Amalfi, can be more briefly dealt with. They seem largely to have relied on Byzantine coinage for their needs save in gold, for which they drew on Sicilian taris, and in silver, for which they could make some use of north Italian *pavenses* and *luccenses*, Imperial denari struck at Pavia or Lucca. They struck no silver coins at all, and only two of them, Salerno and Amalfi, struck gold. The gold coins, however, had only a quarter the value of the Byzantine nomisma, so that the absence of silver coins was of less consequence. They[6] were copied from the tenth-century gold coins of the Fatimids in Sicily, and are not full dinars but their quarters (*rub'ai*). They were called locally *taris* or *tareni* – the word *tari* was a descriptive term, from an Arabic word meaning 'newly struck', but misunderstood by the Latins as the name of the denomination[7] – and the copies had pseudo-Arabic inscriptions and were of much baser gold (about 12 carats). The type, both at Salerno and Amalfi (fig. 6), had a central pellet and one or two outer circles of legend, being copied from the coins of the tenth-century Fatimid caliphs Al-Mu'izz (935–75) or Al-'Aziz (975–96), while the Sicilian taris encountered by the Normans had in contrast a later type with several lines of legend in the field instead of a central pellet. The other denomination struck locally, mainly at Salerno, was a large copper follaro (fig. 7) very variable in weight (about 4–8g) with a great variety of types, some Byzantine in inspiration but others more or less original (busts of saints, buildings, texts such as DEO GRATIAS or AMOR POPVLI, and so on).[8] Their issue started under Gisulf II of Salerno (1052–77) in the mid eleventh century,[9] and their visual attractiveness is marred by their being normally overstruck on Byzantine folles or on each other, with resulting mixing

---

[6]   P. Grierson, 'La monetazione amalfitana nei secoli XI e XII', in *Amalfi nel Medioevo: Convegno internazionale 14–16 giugno 1973*, Salerno 1977, 215–43, reprinted in his *Later Medieval Numismatics (11th–16th Centuries)*, Variorum Reprints, London 1978, no. IV; L. Travaini, 'I tarì di Salerno e di Amalfi', *Rassegna del Centro di cultura e storia amalfitana* 10, 1990, 7–71.

[7]   S.M. Stern, 'Tari', *Studi medievali*[3] 2, 1970, 177–207. The explanation, for long a mystery, was given independently by S.A. Goitein.

[8]   *Corpus Nummorum Italicorum*, XVIII, Milan 1939, 307ff. Remo Cappelli, *Studio sulle monete della zecca di Salerno*, Rome 1972, is more convenient, but does not completely supersede either the *Corpus* or Memmo Cagiati, *I tipi monetali della zecca di Salerno*, Caserta c.1923. The coin attributions in all three require extensive revision. See next note.

[9]   The dating of the Salernitan follaro to the reign of Gisulf II, and not a century earlier, was argued in P. Grierson, 'The Salernitan coinage of Gisulf II (1052–1077) and Robert Guiscard (1077–1085)', *Papers of the British School at Rome*, 24, 1956, 37–59 (Italian transl. in *BCNN* 42, 1957, 9–44) and 'La cronologia della monetazione salernitana nel secolo XI', *RIN* 74, 1972, 153–65 (both reprinted in his *Later Medieval Numismatics* (above, note 6), nos. II, III). It is now generally accepted, despite the objections of Cappelli. See G.L. Mangieri, 'I follari di Gisulfo II e Roberto il Guiscard', *RIN* 88, 1986, 105–21, and the account of the controversy in his bibliographical article, 'La monetazione medievale di Salerno: Rassegna bibliografica', *RSS* 11, 1989, 345–86. The minting of Salernitan taris, however, dates from the early years of the century.

of designs. This unsightly practice, saving the mint labour and money, was borrowed from Byzantium, and it can always be taken as a sign of minting under strain. It is useful to the numismatist, however, for in some series it is his only guide to the relative chronology of the coins.

Finally there is the coinage of Sicily[10] on the eve of the Norman conquest of the island between the invasion of 1071 and the fall of Butera, the last Muslim stronghold, in 1091. Its coinage has till recently been assumed to have been one limited to gold quarter-taris minted at Palermo. The apparent absence of any form of small change was hard to understand, and recent studies have shown that it was only apparent. There was indeed no coinage of copper coins like those of the mainland, though copper *felous* – this itself is an Arabic loan-word from the Latin follis – were struck in other parts of the Muslim world. But there was a substantial coinage of tiny silver coins, *kharrubas* or 1/16th dirhams, which cannot have had values greatly superior to those of the follari of the mainland.[11] They had escaped detection because of their minute size, and are hard to date with any precision, for because of their size – they are about 9mm in diameter and weigh about 0.2g – only fragments of the rulers' names are ever visible. It is also possible that silver weights or tokens, which were minted in Sicily as elsewhere under the Fatimids in great profusion, were used as small change, but the balance of probability is against it.[12]

These then were the three, largely distinct coinage systems which the Normans found in existence in the lands they conquered. They naturally brought with them their own picture of what a monetary system should involve – notional *livres* and *sous* of 240 and 12 *deniers* respectively, and real silver deniers. At least some of them brought stocks of such deniers and continued to receive them from their homeland. Documents[13] and occasional coin finds of *rothomagenses*[14] showed

---

[10] P. Balog, 'La monetazione della Sicilia araba e le sue imitazioni nell'Italia meridionale', in *Gli Arabi in Italia: cultura, contatti e tradizioni*, ed. Francesco Gabrieli and Umberto Scerrato, Milan 1979, 611–28; 'Contributions to the Arabic metrology and coinage. III. On the Arabic coinage of Norman Sicily', *AIIN* 27–8, 1980–1, 137–54. The best collection of material is in Bartolomeo Lagumina, *Catalogo delle monete arabe esistenti nella Biblioteca Communale di Palermo*, Palermo 1892, and an important hoard of 386 coins, buried in about 1076, is described by N. Lowick, 'Un ripostiglio di monete d'oro islamiche e normanne da Agrigento', *BdN* 6–7 (1986), 145–66. The coinage is included in Sambon's *Repertorio* (above, note 1), and in Rodolfo Spahr, *Le monete siciliane dai Bizantini a Carlo d'Angiò (582–1282)*, Zürich/Graz 1976.

[11] P. Balog, 'The silver coinage of Arabic Sicily', *Atti della Seconda Settimana di Studi italo-arabi, Spoleto, 9–12 ottobre 1977*, Rome 1979, 1–21; P. Balog and F. D'Angelo, 'More on the Arabic silver kharruba of Sicily', *AIIN* 30, 1933, 123–8.

[12] In favour, P. Balog, 'Note sur quelques monnaies et jetons fatimites de Sicile', *Bulletin de l'Institut d'Egypte* 37, 1956, 65–70; 'Fatimid and Post-Fatimid glass jetons from Sicily', *Studi Maghrebini* (Centro di Studi Maghrebini, Naples) 7, 1975, 125–48; 'Fatimid glass jetons: token currency or coin-weights?', *Journal of the Economic and Social History of the Orient* 24, 1981, 93–109; against, M.L. Bates, 'The function of Fatimid and Ayyubid glass weights', *ibid.*, 63–92, and a paper given at Milan in May 1992 at the centennial celebrations of the Società italiana di numismatica.

[13] V. von Falkenhausen, 'La circolazione monetaria nell'Italia meridionale e nella Sicilia in epoca normanna secondo la documentazione d'archivio', *BdN* 5, 1986, 55–80.

[14] A. Sambon, 'Les deniers rouennais, monnaie courante du comté d'Aversa près de Naples aux XIe et XIIe siècles', *Gazette numismatique française* 2, 1898, 325–30; G. Libero Mangieri, 'Gruzzoli di monete medievali e moderne rinvenute nel castello di Salerno', *BdN* 4, 1986, 205–30, esp. 210–13.

that these continued to arrive, if only in small quantities, down to the time when Henry II became count of Anjou in 1151 and Norman coins were abandoned in favour of the more highly esteemed deniers of Le Mans, Angers and Tours; *angevini* in fact occasionally appear in north Apulian documents of the last decades of the twelfth century.[15] But such Norman coins as reached the south contributed nothing to the designs of those struck by the newcomers, and there seems to have been no idea of introducing a denarial coinage like that of Normandy, and as indeed existed in northern Italy. The system of livre/sou/denier was in consequence replaced by new ones based on the new coinages which the newcomers struck.

These new coinages can be considered under three headings: those of Robert Guiscard and his successors in the duchy of Apulia down to 1127, the coinage of Sicily down to 1140, and the coinages of Apulia and Sicily down to the end of the Norman dynasty in 1194. The date 1140 is that of the synod of Ariano at which major coinage changes were introduced by Roger II, and one can make a further division in c.1180/5 when other substantial changes, not documented in the written sources of the Regno but identifiable from the coins, were made by William II. The coinages in question have been the subject of much work in recent years, and for the mainland I have largely had to rely on the publications of my friend, Giuseppe Libero Mangieri, and, for Sicily, on those of the late Paul Balog and of Lucia Travaini, who has recently come to Cambridge to work as my research associate on the multi-volume *Medieval European Coinage* in course of publication. For the earlier literature I may venture to refer to a brochure of my own describing the study of medieval numismatics in the Mezzogiorno during the past four centuries,[16] though for Salerno it is less detailed and bibliographically less useful than an article of Libero Mangieri already referred to in note 9.

First, the coinage of the mainland down to 1127. Actually I propose to simplify my task by speaking on the coinage of the duchy of Apulia, which occupied almost the whole of southern Italy. There had in Lombard times been separate coinages in copper elsewhere, notably at Capua and Gaeta, and these were continued under more or less independent Norman rulers, at Gaeta to 1136 and Capua to 1154, and even subsequently after the annexation of both places by Roger II. But the coins circulated only locally and their history, although interesting because of their varied coin types, is less well understood, for we lack any modern studies. They were limited to copper, with no gold.

Robert Guiscard, however, was able to take over in 1078 the mint of the princes of Salerno at Salerno itself, and he and his two successors Roger Borsa (1085–1111) and William (1111–27) continued to strike gold taris and copper follari as his predecessor had done, with none of the three attempting to introduce a coinage in silver. Robert's pseudo-Arabic taris of Salerno continued those of Gisulf without change, and cannot be satisfactorily distinguished from those of the Lombard period. His follari are also anonymous, as many of Gisulf's had been, and their attribution to him depends on their dating by overstrikes. The types that are certainly his are often remarkable, notably one (fig. 8) apparently

15 Von Falkenhausen, 74.
16 Philip Grierson, *Tarì, Follari e Denari. La numismatica medievale nell'Italia meridionale*, Salerno 1991.

minted to celebrate his capture of Salerno and its great fortress. Its obverse is Byzantine in inspiration, the dukes's facing bust being copied from that of a gold nomisma of Nicephorus III, or possibly one of Constantine IX; the pellets on the cloak and the cross in the ruler's right hand show that the model was not a follis of Romanus I, as might have been expected in view of the commonness of these coins in the region. The reverse shows a striking representation of the fortifications and cupolas of Salerno with the proud legend VICTORIA. Others are religious in character, with busts of St Peter or St Matthew, or such an invocation as XC/RE/XC/IMPE (*Christus regnat, Christus imperat*) ostentatiously completing in a Latin form the IC/XC/NI/KA (*Iesous Khristos Nika*) on a slightly earlier Byzantine follis. Roger's and William's follari, unlike those of Robert Guiscard, usually bear the ducal name and title in large letters across the field: ROGE/RIVS, GVI/DVX or VV/DVX. A notable coin of Roger (fig. 9) has his name in Greek: PωΓE/PIOC/ΔOVΞ. It has consequently been sometimes supposed that it was minted at Bari or Brindisi, i.e. in Byzantine Italy where Greek would be a natural language in a mint, but in its fabric and general appearance it does not differ from his Salernitan coins, and mints should not be multiplied *praeter necessitatem*.

Amalfi, like Salerno, had been a mint in Lombard times and continued to be one under the Normans, for to it can be assigned a series of follari struck by a certain Manso with the title of *vicedux* (fig. 10), unknown in Lombard times, as well as gold taris continuing the issues of the preceding period.[17] Manso's name shows him to have been a Lombard and to have probably belonged to the earlier ducal family who also frequently bore it, and presumably he minted by ducal permission. The same must also have been the case with Fulco de Basacers, a Norman knight known to us from written sources between 1083 and 1119 and whose coins are dated by overstrikes to the last quarter of the eleventh century.[18]

These coins in any case represent exceptional issues struck in the years immediately following the conquest, and they did not last. The dukes of Apulia were not prepared to accept baronial minting. Robert's successor Roger Borsa and Richard continued to mint gold at Salerno and Amalfi, and copper at Salerno. At Amalfi there were interesting changes in the designs, for instead of being purely Muslim they now sometimes have on one side a cross in the field and on the other a face, or the letter R (fig. 11), though whether this stands for *Rogerius* or *Ricardus*, in the latter case making the coin one of Guiscard, is uncertain. A stranger feature is that the gold coins of these two mints, less than 20km apart, differ in fineness, the Salernitan ones being slightly superior to the Amalfitan ones, and that this difference was perpetuated in the future, right down to the opening decades of the Hohenstaufen period. Why they were not made uniform, and indeed why the separate gold coinage of Amalfi was not simply suppressed, is hard to explain. But Amalfi was the more important city commercially, and its wide overseas connexions ensured that its coins had a well-established place in mercantile transactions.

[17] G. Libero Mangieri, 'I follari amalfitani di Mansone V', *RSS* 13, 1990, 49–79, and 'La monetazione di Salerno alla luce del tesoretto del S. Salvatore *de Fondaco*', *RSS* (in the press), the latter refuting the arguments of P. Peduto, 'Il gruzzolo del S. Salvatore *de Fondaco* a Salerno: follari, tarì, denari del secolo XI', *RSS* 16, 1991, 33–71, who wished to make them earlier.
[18] G. Libero Mangieri, 'I follari salernitani de Fulco de Basacers', *Actes du 11e Congrès international de numismatique, Bruxelles, 1991* (in the press).

It was in the reign of Roger Borsa that Alexius I carried out his monetary reform at Constantinople, but its only obvious effect on the coinage of south Italy was eventually to bring about a reduction in the size of the Apulian follis. The Byzantine reform involved the replacement of the follis, which in the second half of the eleventh century had fallen in weight to about 6g, by an appreciably smaller coin, a tetarteron weighing about 4g, a quarter the weight of the old follis before the decline in weight began. Similarly in the 1120s the weight of the Salernitan follis was reduced to about 3g, determining what was to be the weight of the Salernitan copper coins under Roger II. Exactly when the change was made, and how the new coin was related in value to its predecessor, we do not know. Numismatists tend to describe the lighter coins as 'follis fractions' (*frazioni di follaro*), but it seems that contemporaries called them *ramesini* ('copper', from *rame*), a word attested in written records from the mid 1120s.[19] Salernitan coinage in the twelfth century has still to be made the object of serious study.

I pass to the coinage of Norman Sicily, which is much more remarkable than that of the mainland. The Arabs had had a coinage of gold taris and tiny silver coins, with possibly some use of glass tokens as small change, but had not minted in copper. The Normans continued the gold and initially the silver coins, but added heavy follari of the mainland pattern and ultimately large silver coins as well. The coinage struck by the Normans in Sicily is also much more ostentatiously multi-cultural in its mixing of languages and types.

The continuation of the gold raised a difficulty that did not exist on the mainland. The gold coins of Salerno and Amalfi, which the Normans in any case only began to strike a few years after their earliest Sicilian ones, bore only pseudo-Arabic legends and were presumably minted by Christian workmen. Their continuation thus faced the Normans with no very acute problems of a religious nature. But in Sicily they inherited a mint at Palermo and set up a new one at Messina, both staffed by Arabic workmen, striking coins giving the name of the mint and the name and style of the ruler in correct Arabic, dated in the Muslim fashion by the years of the Hijra, and having the kalima, the Muslim profession of faith, in the field. A too abrupt Christianization of the coins would produce ones lacking an essential condition of acceptability and would offend the religious susceptibilities of most of the island's inhabitants.

What took place, over the next half-century, was a process of gradual adaptation. Palermo was captured by Robert Guiscard and Roger of Calabria in January 1072, and in the very year of the conquest coins were struck which made no change other than styling Robert 'the most great duke (*duqah*) sovereign of Sicily (*malik Siqilliyah*)'.[20] But Robert returned at once to the mainland and Roger's subsequent coins are more likely to style him *qummus* (i.e. *comes*) or *sultan*.[21] Subsequent changes, best followed on Spahr's plates, were gradual.[22] Dating by

[19] L. Travaini, 'La riforma monetaria di Ruggiero II e la circolazione minuta in Italia meridionale tra X e XII secolo', *RIN* 83, 1981, 133–53.

[20] Lagumina, *Catalogo* (above, note 10), 226–34, reprinting the article in which he first published this newly discovered and important coin.

[21] J. Johns, 'I titoli arabi dei sovrani normanni di Sicilia', *BdN* 6–7, 1986, 16–17, 36–7.

[22] In addition to the material set out in Spahr, many points are usefully discussed in L. Travaini, 'Two hoards of Sicilian Norman tarì', *NC* 145, 1985, 177–208, and 'Il ripostiglio di Montecassino e la monetazione aurea dei Normanni in Sicilia', *BdN* 6–7, 1986, 167–98.

the Hijra, fortunately for numismatists concerned with chronology, remained a feature of the Muslim types in most metals down to the mid twelfth century, and continued on some issues even later. Unfortunately the dies for the gold were normally larger than the flans, so that the date, or part of it, is apt to be off flan and illegible. But the profession of faith was replaced by the Greek letter *tau*, the latter filling the field (fig. 12). Christians could accept this as a cross, for such a form, without an upright above the cross-beam, was sometimes used in art. Others could place any interpretation upon it they pleased, for it was not the symbol of the Christian faith in its normal form. Only in the 1130s, after the Norman government had long been in power and Roger II was king, was the *tau* replaced by a normal cross, its Christian character emphasised by the letters IC XC NI KA (for *Iesous Khristos Nika*) that surrounded it (fig. 13). It has been suggested[23] that the *tau* was inspired by the Greek T of ancient coins of Taranto of the fourth and third centuries B.C., and iconographically this is possible, but the motive is most likely to have been a desire to avoid the customary form of a cross.

Otherwise the coins of Roger I, apart from a probably brief issue of small silver *kharrubas* (fig. 14),[24] are copper follari. (A large silver coin is probably a modern forgery.) He deviated from the Salernitan tradition of frequently changing types and struck only two, very different in design and fabric and presumably of different mints and different dates. One (fig. 15) has for types an ornate cross having in its quarters RO/GE/CO/ME and a Greek *tau* with the marginal legend CALABRIE ET SICILIE. It is frequently overstruck on other coins in the mainland fashion and is commonly attributed to Mileto, Roger's chief residence in his duchy of Calabria. Despite the use of the *tau*, linking it with the Sicilian taris, this is probably correct. The other coin (fig. 16), much more striking in appearance, has on one face a knight on horseback holding lance and banner, and on the other the representation of a seated Virgin and Child in profile. The designs are Western and to all intents and purposes original. That of the knight was presumably taken from a seal, on which such a type, easier to show on the broad flan of a seal than on the much smaller flan of a coin, was already common. A facing Virgin and Child was to become a common coin-type in Byzantium in the twelfth century, but one with the Virgin seated sideways does not otherwise occur and was perhaps suggested by some venerated local statue. The coin is also commonly ascribed to Mileto, but the fact that it is never found overstruck on or by other copper coins makes a mainland mint unlikely. On the other hand, one hesitates to ascribe so conspicuously Christian a coin type to a Sicilian mint at so early a date, but I believe Messina is possible. Hoard evidence may eventually decide the matter.

A feature of the subsequent coinage is its multi-cultural character. The languages of the inscriptions are indifferently Latin, Greek, or Arabic, with sometimes more than one on the same coin. A small copper coin of William (fig. 17) may read in Latin *Operata in urbe Messane* and *Rex W Scds*, in Arabic *Struck by order of the great king who glories in God – The King William the Second.*

---

[23] Travaini, 'Le prime monete argentee' (next note) 171, 186–90. There is a study of the ornamentation of the *tau* by R. Ciferri, 'Tentativo di seriazione dei "Tari" normanni e svevi d'Italia', *Italia Numismatica* 11, 1960, 13–16.

[24] L. Travaini, 'Le prime monete argentee dei Normanni in Sicilia: un ripostiglio di kharruba e i modelli antichi delle monete normanne', *RIN* 92, 1990, 171–98.

Thematic contents are varied, especially after Roger's acquisition of the royal title in 1130, but are predominantly either Byzantine (figs 18, 19) in their use of the figures of the king and of Christ or some saint, or Muslim (fig. 20), with a Cufic inscription variously arranged in the field. As with the inscriptions, no attempt is made to keep the elements distinct; a coin may have an image of the Virgin on one side, a Cufic legend on the other. Both Roger II and William II sometimes number themselves 'the Second' in Latin numerals or Arabic words, and it is interesting to note that Roger calls himself this only in his period as count; after his coronation he becomes *malik* or *rex* or *anax* ('ruler') without a numeral. The last title, which occurs only once, is a curiosity, for it is the sole known use in numismatics of this ancient Greek word. Greek coins of the classical period were not struck in the names of kings, and a Hellenistic ruler will style himself *basileus* instead of using the archaic *anax*, with its echoes of Homer and the great trage-dians. There is also what appears to be an isolated use of Italian, the first appearance of the language on any coin. It is one thick, concave follaro (fig. 21) of the period c.1115/c.1125, for the bust of Christ, normally accompanied by the letters IC XC, has instead GE S/SV. Whether the S is simply displaced and this is to be read as *Gesus*, or it is separate and one should read *Senhor Gesu* ('Lord Jesus'), is hard to say, but the initial G is clear and would be impossible in either Latin or Greek.

A striking feature is the absence of any figured gold coinage comparable to that of Byzantium, though Roger had no objection to appearing on his copper coins in the full panoply of a Byzantine emperor, clothed in chlamys or loros and having on his head a stemma with pendilia, just as he is shown in the great mosaic in the Martorana. How much difference Roger's acquisition of the duchy of Apulia in 1127 made to the coinage of Sicily is not clear, for while his Arabic coins are dated his others are not. Worth emphasising, however, is the fact that after 1127 the coinage of the mainland remained distinct from that of Sicily. Salerno and Amalfi continued to strike their own taris, though now with inscriptions in correct Arabic and, where required, Christian in content. An Amalfitan tari of Roger (fig. 22) has on one side a Roman capital R with, in Arabic above and below, 'Roger the King', and on the other side a monogram of RX (for *rex*) and, again in Arabic, 'Protector of Christianity'. There is also some interchange of types in the copper, with Salernitan follari borrowing typical Sicilian types like a lion's mask or a palm-tree. But the coins remain small (fig. 23) and the types were constantly changed, exactly with what object we do not know. Equally such places as Capua and Gaeta continued to strike their own copper coins, and when Roger estab-lished a footing in north Africa at Mahdia that lasted for about ten years, he struck there gold dinars,[25] i.e. coins of the same denomination and high gold content that were customary in the region, instead of trying to impose the quarter-dinar taris of his Sicilian and mainland mints. One usually thinks of Norman administration as strongly centralizing in character, but in coinage this was not the case.

[25] H.H. Abdul-Wahab, 'Deux dinars normands de Mahdia', *Revue tunisienne*[2] 1, 1930, 215–18. For the background, D. Abulafia, 'The Norman kingdom of Africa and the Norman expeditions to Majorca and the Muslim Mediterranean', *ante* 7, 1984, 26–49.

[26] A. Sambon, 'Monetazione di Ruggiero II, re di Sicilia (1130–1154)', *RIN* 24, 1911, 437–75, esp. 457–64, but requiring correction on a number of points; L. Travaini, 'Entre Byzance et

In 1140, ten years after Roger had acquired the royal title, he put into effect a major change in the coinage.[26] It cannot reasonably be termed a monetary reform, for there is no reason to believe that the state of the coinage was particularly unsatisfactory or that reform was necessary, though it did simplify the coinage system. What took place was the replacement of the copper *ramesini* by new and lighter coins, the introduction of two new denominations of base silver to bridge the gap between the gold and the copper, a change in the tari type in Sicily – the Latin cross was replaced by a Greek one and the royal name and title moved from the field to the circumference (fig. 24) – and a certain tying together of the monetary systems of the duchy and the island. The changes are described and bitterly condemned by the contemporary historian Fulco of Benevento, but the forced exchange of old coins for new is rarely popular and Fulco's attitude is coloured by his general distaste for all Roger's activities.

The two new coins were the ducalis and its third, both supposed to be of 50 per cent silver but probably in practice rather less. The ducalis (fig. 25) – it took its name from the duchy of Apulia, where it was expected to circulate – was Byzantine in inspiration,[27] though it did not correspond in metallic content or value to any specific Byzantine denomination and could not have been confused with any of them. The obverse has a common Byzantine type, a facing bust of Christ Pantocrator, but with a mixed Greek-Latin legend (IC XC RG IN AETRN, *Iesous Khristos regnat in aeternum*). The reverse shows two standing figures, as on many Byzantine coins, but while on Comnenian coins these are customarily the emperor and some heavenly personage, Christ or the Virgin or some saint, Roger's coin has the emperor and his son Roger, recently created duke of Apulia. Roger is in formal Byzantine imperial costume and each is identified by his title (R RX SCLS or R DX AP), and the coin, unusually for a non-Arabic coin, is dated but by the king's regnal year, AN(no) R(egni) X, reckoned from his coronation in December 1130.

The Arabic counterpart of the ducalis, its one-third (*tercia ducalis*), has much simpler types, an ornate cross and a legend in the field (fig. 26). The legends are the date (A.H.) and mint name ('the city of Sicily', i.e. Palermo) in Arabic and the name of the coin (TERCIA DVCALIS) in Latin. The Latin incomprehension of the function of dating on coins is shown by the way in which, while the one-thirds bear a succession of A.H. dates corresponding to the 1140s, the AN X was treated as a fixed part of the design and left unaltered. It did, however, have the advantage of calling users' attention to the importance Roger attached to his coronation in 1130.

The reform of 1140 established the basic pattern of the coinage for the next few decades. The same denominations were struck under William I and William II, William I's ducales being of the same two-figure type and William II's (fig. 27) having W RX and a date palm as types and his 'ducalis' being formally called an

---

l'Islam: le système monétaire du royaume normand de Sicile en 1140', *Bulletin de la Société française de numismatique* 46, 1991, 200–4.

[27] The type was apparently suggested by a contemporary electrum trachy of John II showing the emperor and St George (Grierson, *Byzantine Coins*, nos. 1067–8). Many of the details, however, appear to have been copied from a Thessalonican coin of Alexius I (*ibid.*, no. 1025), presumably because the mint had retained, as possible future models, a selection of coins in circulation at the time of the conquest.

apuliense and accompanied by 1/6th and 1/12th fractions as well as one-thirds (figs 28, 29). Different types of copper coin continued to be struck in the duchy and the island, and the precise values accorded to the Salernitan and Amalfitan taris in the new system are unknown. A few changes of greater note took place in the 1180s.

One of these was a reduction in the fineness of the gold coins that has only recently come to light. It has always been known from the written sources that Sicilian taris were 16 1/3 carats fine, and any suspicions that such a figure might only be true of the Hohenstaufen and early Angevin periods were laid to rest some years ago, when Andrew Oddy of the British Museum showed by the specific gravity analysis of 130 specimens in my collection and that of the British Museum that it held good over the whole two centuries 1071–1278.[28] But a more refined analysis by proton activation of the metals used in the alloy shows that while up to the 1180s this consisted mainly of silver, after that it was mainly copper.[29] Since copper is less valuable than silver the total value of the coins was reduced, though not by much. Written sources from outside Sicily show that this change was known to at least some contemporaries and that they took account of it in their monetary transactions, for it would affect the exchange rates between taris and other coins of the day.

The other change is that the striking of Sicilian taris to something approaching a uniform weight of 1.06g, i.e. a quarter of a notional dinar of 4.25g, was abandoned. This weight had never been very closely followed. Individual coins of the early Norman rulers often fell to about 0.8g and occasionally rose to 1.3g or 1.4g, something that would have been impossible if the coins had been struck *al pezzo*, i.e. with the weight of each specimen checked before it left the mint. But from the 1180s onwards the coins cease to weigh even approximately 1g, the variations becoming greater with the passage of time and taris of the Hohenstaufen period varying from 0.2g to about 10g, though with the highest and lowest figures rather rare. Although this sounds to us unsatisfactory it must have saved the mint money, and by providing smaller and larger coins may well have been welcome to users. Individual coins, because of their irregularity, had probably passed by weight anyway – this has been the case with gold coins in substantial transactions at all periods in history – and the existence of much heavier and lighter coins would often have been found useful to merchants. The same was done, it is worth noting, with other coinages in the Near East, though usually in the direction of providing either fractions or multiples but not both. The gold coins of western fabric struck in the kingdom of Jerusalem in the late twelfth century exist only as cut-up fragments,[30] and since no complete specimens have yet come to light we do not know whether the full coins were regular or irregular in weight. The Mamluqs in Egypt in the thirteenth century, however, did not strike their gold coins to the traditional weight of the dinar (4.25g) but quite

[28] P. Grierson and W.A. Oddy, 'Le titre du tari sicilien du milieu du XIe siècle à 1278', *RN*[6] 16, 1974, 123–34; also P. Balog, C. Mancini, P. Petrillo Serafin and L. Travaini, 'Nuovi contributi sul contenuto aureo e la tipologia del tarì', *AIIN* 27–8, 1980–1, 155–84, and Oddy's analyses of a further 70 taris in Travaini, 'Two hoards . . .' (above, note 22), 205–8.

[29] Study by L. Beck, L. Travaini and J.-N. Barrandon now in the press.

[30] J.D. Brady, 'A firm attribution of Latin gold coinage to twelfth-century Jerusalem', *American Numismatic Society: Museum Notes* 23, 1978, 133–47.

irregularly, with individual specimens going up to 6g or 7g,[31] and the fourteenth-century merchant Pegolotti,[32] writing about conditions in the 1280s, notes that at Alexandria the Egyptian 'besants' only passed by weight: *perchè non sono iguali de peso, e quale pesa poco e quale assai, donde però si se ne fae pagamento a peso di bilance.* The same, he says also (p. 71), was true of the silver coins.

William II also made another change of significance in his coins, for he reintroduced a heavy denomination of copper and a fraction, its third. The heavy coin, a follaro (fig. 30) weighing about 10.5g and having for types a lion's mask (inspired by a classical coin of Messana) and a palm tree (copied from ones of Palermo), is one of the most striking in the Norman series. Its fraction (fig. 31) has the same obverse but on the reverse a Cufic legend, 'The King William the Second'. I argued some years ago[33] that the two coins were unrelated to each other, despite their identity of obverse type, and that the follaro, which is anonymous, was a coin of Roger II's of the 1120s. It could indeed be regarded as evidence that Roger, before the acquisition of Apulia had brought him many Greek-speaking subjects and closer contacts with Byzantium, was concerned with finding classical precedents for his authority in the form of a supposed 'kingdom' of Sicily, for which such coin types might appear highly appropriate. Lucia Travaini had convinced me that I was wrong, and my suppositions fanciful.[34] William II did indeed revive a heavy copper coinage, apparently as part of a reform of which his multiplication of silver fractions also formed a part, though it is not mentioned in our written sources and cannot be very precisely dated.

With this confession of error it is perhaps time for me to conclude. I began by saying that the coinage of the Normans in the South was in my judgment the most remarkable of twelfth-century Europe. This was due to its diversity rather than to any other quality; it notably lacked the stability of the Anglo-Norman coinage contemporary with it. This diversity is of course only one aspect of the Norman-Sicilian cultural achievement as a whole, the ability to bring together a wide range of elements, Latin, Greek – classical as well as Byzantine if one is concerned with coin types – and Arabic, and blend them into a system that worked. Visually, at the least, I hope I will have left you with the conviction that the coinage of Norman Italy and Sicily is well worthy of study, and that it is one that is far from having delivered up all its secrets.

---

[31] Stanley Lane-Poole, *Catalogue of Oriental Coins in the British Museum*, IV, London, 1879, nos. 473–7, 495, etc., with weights of 5.95g, 7.45g, 5.64g, etc.

[32] Francesco Balducci Pegolotti, *La Pratica della Mercatura*, ed. Allan Evans, Cambridge, Mass, 1936, 71.

[33] P. Grierson, 'Guglielmo II o Ruggiero II? Una attribuzione errata', *RIN* 91, 1989, 195–204.

[34] L. Travaini, 'Aspects of the Sicilian Norman copper coinage in the twelfth century', *NC* 151, 1991, 159–74, esp. 166–74. She points out that the lion's mask is not an exact copy of that on the coins of Messana, and prefers to relate it to the lion's head extensively used in the sculptures, textiles, and other decorative artefacts of the Norman period. But it is hard to believe that the finding of ancient coins of Messana in Sicily did not suggest its use on William's coins.

ILLUSTRATIONS

The coins are in the Fitzwilliam Museum, Cambridge, with the exception of no. 7, which is in the Museo Nazionale, Rome.

Plate I

1. Nomisma (histamenon) of Constantine IX (1042–55). 4.37g.
2. Follis of Romanus I (920–44). 6.60g.
3. Anonymous follis, Class G (c.1070). 9.02g.
4. Nomisma (hyperpyron) of Alexius I (1082–1118). 4.30g.
5. Tetarteron of Alexius I (1082–1118). 3.89g.
6. Amalfitan tari, 11th century. 0.92g.
7. Follaro of Gisulf II of Salerno (1052–77). 3.63g.
8. Salernitan follaro of Robert Guiscard (1059–85), probably minted in 1078. 6.97g.

Plate II

9. Follaro of Roger Borsa (1085–1111) with name and title in Greek. 2.70g.
10. Amalfitan follaro of Manso *vicedux*. 2.50g.
11. Amalfitan tari of Roger II as duke of Apulia (1127–30). 0.87g.
12. Sicilian tari of Roger I (1072–1101) or Roger II as count (1105–30). 0.95g.
13. Sicilian tari of Roger II, c.1030. 0.90g.
14. Silver *kharruba* of Roger II. 0.22g.
15. Follaro of Roger I (1072–1101). 3.81g.
16. Follaro of Roger I. 10.36g.
17. Small follaro of William II (1166–89). 1.06g.
18. Follaro of Roger II as count (1105–30). 3.99g.
19. Follaro of Roger II as count. 4.76g.
20. Small follaro of Roger II as king (1130–54). 1.24g.

Plate III

21. Follaro of Roger II as count (1105–30). 7.19g.
22. Amalfitan tari of Roger II as king (1130–54). 0.67g.
23. Salernitan follaro of Roger II as king. 1.52g.
24. Sicilian tari of Roger II, struck after 1140. 1.34g.
25. Ducalis of Roger II, struck after 1140. 2.41g.
26. One-third ducalis of Roger, dated A.H.538 = A.D.1143/4. 0.75g.
27. Apuliense of William II (1166–89). 1.73g.
28. One-third apuliense of William II. 0.86g.
29. One-sixth apuliense of William II. 0.41g.
30. Restored follaro of William II. 10.39g.
31. One-sixth follaro of William II. 1.94g.

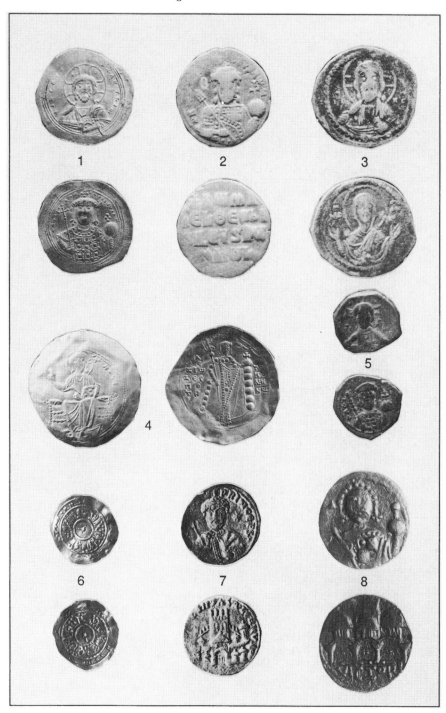

Plate 1

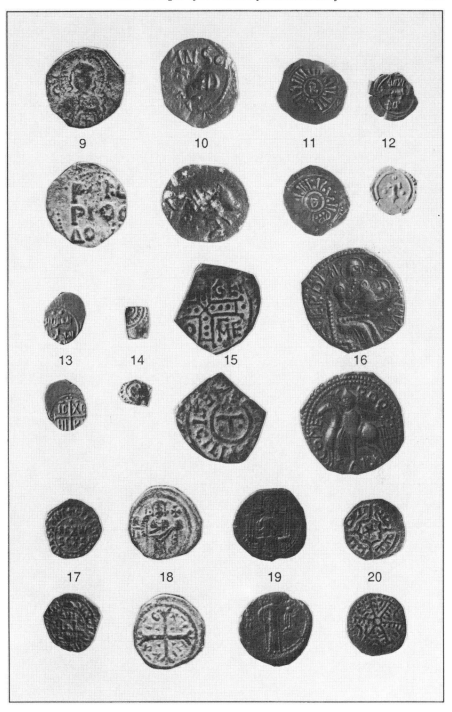

Plate 2

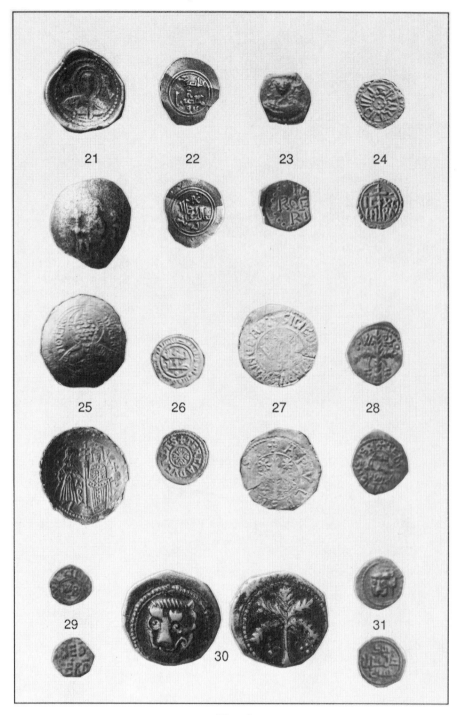

Plate 3

THE NORMAN KINGS OF SICILY AND
THE FATIMID CALIPHATE

Jeremy Johns

The de Hauteville rulers of Sicily were parvenus. Tancred, lord of Hauteville-la-Guichard near Coutances, had owed only ten knights' service to Duke Robert.[1] It was Tancred's inability to provide for his twelve sons that drove eleven of them south to seek their fortunes.[2] None of these eleven vaunted his patrimony, and it was left to their sons to adopt the style *de Altavilla*.[3] The de Hautevilles hastened to add nobler blood to the line. The first emigrant generation tended to marry into the families of their leading allies in Italy.[4] Only in the second generation did they begin to ally themselves with the royal houses of Europe.[5] Thus, when Roger II had himself crowned king of Sicily on Christmas Day 1130, he had inherited from

---

[1] Geoffrey of Malaterra, *De rebus gestis Rogerii Calabriae et Siciliae comitis et Robertis Guiscardi ducis fratris eius*, ed. E. Pontieri, *RIS²*, V.i, Bologna 1927–28, I.xl, 25.

[2] Malaterra, I.v, 9.

[3] William, son of Geoffrey the fourth or fifth son of Tancred and Muriel, and a familiar and baron of Roger I, witnessed documents in 1091–1101 as *Guilielmus de Altavilla*: L.-R. Ménager, 'Inventaire des familles normandes et franques emigrées en Italie méridionale et en Sicile (XIe–XIIe siècles)', in *Roberto il Guiscardo e il suo tempo. Relazioni e comunicazioni nelle Prime Giornate normanno-sveve (Bari, maggio 1973)*, Fonti e Studi del *Corpus membranarum italicarum*, XI (Centro di Studi normanno-svevi, Università degli Studi di Bari), Rome 1975, 318–319. (Reprinted with additions in L.-R. Ménager, *Hommes et institutions de l'Italie normande*, London 1981.)

[4] Robert Guiscard married first Alberarda, daughter of the powerful Apulian baron Giraldo of Buonalbergo ('Ceste choze fut lo commencement de accrestre de tout bien à Robert Viscart': Amatus, III.xi, 126), and then, in 1058, Sichelgaita, sister to the Lombard prince Gisulf of Salerno (Malaterra, I.xxx, 22; Amatus, IV.xxiii, 197; cf. F. Chalandon, *Histoire de la domination normande en Italie et en Sicile,* 2 vols, Paris 1907, I.154, n.2). Robert's brothers had already forged strong ties with Gisulf's family: Humphrey was married to the sister of Duke Guy of Sorrento, Gisulf's uncle, and William of the Principate had married Guy's daughter. Count Roger's third and most important marriage (1089) was to Adelaide, niece of Boniface del Vasto of Savona, 'famosissimi Italorum marchionis' (Malaterra, IV.xiv, 93; cf. E. Pontieri, 'La madre di re Ruggero: Adelaide del Vasto contessa di Sicilia, regina di Gerusalemme (?–1118)', in *Atti del Convegno Internazionale di Studi Ruggeriani (21–25 aprile 1954)*, 2 vols, Palermo 1955, II.328–330, and H. Houben, 'Adelaide "del Vasto" nella storia del regno di Sicilia', *Itinerari di Ricerca Storica* IV, 1990, 10–22).

[5] Bohemond, prince of Antioch, married Constance, daughter of Philip I of France (Orderic, XI.12, vol. VI.70; cf. R.B. Yewdale, *Bohemond the First*, New York 1917, 110–111); Count Roger married one daughter, Constance, to Conrad, the son of the Emperor Henry IV (Malaterra, IV.xxiii, 101), and another, Busilla, to Coloman king of Hungary (Malaterra, IV, xxv, 102); and Roger II married Elvira, the daughter of Alfonso VI of Castile (Romuald of Salerno, *Chronicon*, ed. C.A. Garufi, *RIS²*, VII.i, Città di Castello – Bologna 1934–35, 222; cf. Chalandon, II.105). In the next generation, of course, Constance married the Emperor Henry VI, and William II wed Margaret, the daughter of Garcia IV Ramirez of Navarre; in the next again, William II married Joanna of England. (For a recent discussion of the marriage-politics of the de Hautevilles, see D'Alessandro, *supra* 91–97.)

his ancestors no trapping of monarchy in which to robe himself. Nor, in Sicily, had he conquered an ancient kingdom which he could assume intact merely by ascending to the vacant throne. The Sicilian monarchy, its constitutions, laws, ceremonies, and regalia, had all to be built *ex novo*, and, once the foundations had been laid in 1130, King Roger and his ministers exercised an eclectic taste in furnishing the new royal structure. Monarchies past, including the tyrants of Magna Graecia, and present, including the Capetian kings of France and the emperors of Byzantium, all contributed elements to the new monarchy.[6]

The Arabic facet of the de Hauteville monarchy was systematically described by Michele Amari and by his diligent editor Carlo Alfonso Nallino.[7] It was Amari who first listed its components: Arabic fiscal administration and chancery, palace architecture and decoration, ceremonial and regalia, and the patronage of Arab scholars and poets.[8] Amari seems to have had little doubt as to the origins of the Arabic facet of Norman kingship: the de Hautevilles simply modelled themselves

---

[6] Magna Graecia: H. Wieruszowski, 'Roger II of Sicily "Rex-Tyrannus"', in twelfth-century political thought', *Speculum* xxviii, 1963, 46–78 (reprinted in H. Wieruszowski, *Politics and culture in medieval Spain and Italy*, Storia e Letteratura, Raccolta di Studi e Testi 21, Rome 1971, 51–97); S. Turkheim, 'Un exemple d'imitation dans le monnayage de Guillaume II, roi de Sicile (1166–1189)', *Proceedings of the International Numismatic Symposium on contemporary coin imitations and forgeries*, ed. I Gedai and K. Birò-Say, Budapest 1980, 217–221; L. Travaini, 'Le prime monete argentee dei normanni in Sicilia: un ripostiglio di kharrube e i modelli antichi delle monete normanne', *Rivista italiana di numismatica e scienze affini* XCII, 1990, 186–192. Capetians: E. Kitzinger, 'The mosaics of the Cappella Palatina in Palermo: an essay on the choice and arrangement of the subjects', *Art Bulletin* 31, 1949, 269–292. Byzantium: E. Kitzinger, 'On the portrait of Roger II in the Martorana in Palermo', *Proporzioni* 2, 1950, 30–40; E. Kitzinger, *The mosaics of St Mary's of the Admiral in Palermo*, Dumbarton Oaks Studies 27, Washington 1990. There is a large bibliography upon the sources of the Norman monarchy of Sicily, e.g. L.-R. Ménager, 'L'institution monarchique dans les états normands d'Italie. Contribution à l'étude du pouvoir royal dans les principautés occidentales, aux XIe–XIIe siècles', *Cahiers des civilisations médiévales* 2, 1959 303–331, 445–468 (reprinted in *Hommes et institutions*); R. Elze, 'Zum Königtum Rogers II von Sizilien', *Festschrift Ernst Schramm*, 2 vols, Wiesbaden 1964, I.102–116; P. Delogu, 'L'evoluzione politica dei Normanni d'Italia fra poteri locali e podestà universali', *Atti del congresso internazionale di studi sulla Sicilia normanna (Palermo 1972)*, Palermo 1973, 51–104; W. Ullman, 'Roman public law and medieval monarchy: Norman rulership in Sicily', in W. de Vos *et al.* eds, *Acta Iuridica: essays in honour of Ben Beinart*, Cape Town 1979, 157–84; C.D. Fonseca, 'Ruggero II e la storiografia del potere', in *Società, potere e popolo nell'età di Ruggero II. Atti delle terze giornate normanno-sveve, Bari, 23–25 maggio 1977*, Centro di studi normanno-svevi, Università degli Studi di Bari, Bari 1979, 9–26; G.M. Cantarella, *La Sicilia e i Normanni. Le fonti del mito*, Il mondo medievale 19, Bologna 1988: all with useful further bibliography.

[7] Amari's *Storia dei Musulmani di Sicilia* was first published in 3 vols in Florence in 1854–1872. Amari died in 1889 before he himself could complete a much needed revised version. A much amplified and thoroughly revised edition was seen through the press by Nallino in 3 vols, Catania 1933–1939.

[8] Arabic administration: Amari, *Storia*, III.450–460; M. Amari, 'Su la data degli sponsali di Arrigo VI con la Costanza erede del trono di Sicilia e su i divani dell'azienda normanna in Palermo', *Atti della Reale Accademia dei Lincei, Memorie della Classe di Scienze morali, storiche e filologiche*, 3rd ser., 2, 1878, 409–438 (reprinted in M. Amari, *Studi medievistici*, ed. F. Giunta, Palermo 1970). Art and architecture: Amari, *Storia*, III.840–890; M. Amari, *Le epigrafi arabiche di Sicilia trascritte, tradotte e illustrate*, 3 vols, Palermo 1875–1885 (reprinted Palermo 1971, ed. F. Gabrieli). Ceremonial and regalia: Amari, *Storia*, III.453–457. Arab Scholars and poets: Amari, *Storia*, III.460–471, 671–790.

upon the Kalbid emirs of Sicily, who, in turn, had imitated the Fāṭimid caliphs of Egypt.[9]

There are, however, considerable difficulties with this initially persuasive hypothesis. First, the Kalbids lost their hold upon Sicily in the mid 1040s, twenty years before the Norman invasion, and ninety before the foundation of the monarchy. From 1044 until 1062, Sicily was divided between several petty rival lordships.[10] Thus, there was a long interregnum between the fall of the Kalbids and the foundation of the Norman kingdom. Second, although the Normans did inherit certain institutions from the Muslim rulers of the island, such as the mint and the *dīwān* or fiscal administration, none of the most characteristic components of the Arabic facet of the Norman monarchy appears until after 1130. And, third, where the evolution of Arabic components can be traced from the period of conquest until after the foundation of the monarchy, it is evident that they were reformed radically in c.1130, and thereafter more closely resemble the equivalent institutions in the contemporary Muslim world than the Arabic institutions inherited by the early Norman rulers of Sicily.

It is necessary, therefore, to make the distinction between those components of the Arabic facet of the Norman monarchy which were inherited from the Muslim rulers of Sicily, and those which were imported from the contemporary Muslim world after c.1130. This will be best demonstrated by considering briefly three examples: the architecture and decoration of the Norman palaces; the structure and practices of the Norman *dīwān*; and the Arabic titles of the Norman kings.

The Arabic titles of the Normans in Sicily developed in three stages.[11] In the first, Robert Guiscard and Roger I had their feudal titles transliterated from Latin or Greek into Arabic. Thus Duke Robert appears on his coins as *Abārt al-dūqa*, 'Robert the duke', and Count Roger as *al-qummus akh al-dūqat Ajjār*, 'Count Roger, brother of the duke'.[12] In the second stage, Roger I, the young Roger II, and the regent Adelaide, have their scribes and mint officials experiment with various Arabic terms which translate as precisely as possible their feudal titles. Roger I now appears as *sulṭān Ṣiqilliyya*, 'lord of Sicily'; Adelaide and Roger are *mawlātu-nā al-sayyida wa-mawlā-nā al-qummus Rujjār*, 'our lady regent and our lord Count Roger'; and Roger II is just that, *Rujjār al-thānī . . . sulṭān*, 'lord Roger II'.[13] The third stage, which opens with Roger's coronation in 1130, marks a clear break with the past: new titles and formulae are employed which have nothing in common with the Greek and Latin royal titles.[14] King Roger is styled 'the royal, sublime, Rogerian, supreme majesty, may God make his days eternal and give strength to his banners',[15] while William II introduces one of his decrees

[9] Amari, *Storia*, III.875: 'Se i principi normanni seguirono gli usi dei Kalbiti, questi a lor volta aveano imitati i califi del Cairo'.
[10] Amari, *Storia*, II.482–488, 613–620; U. Rizzitano, 'Ibn al-Ḥawwās', *Encyclopaedia of Islam*, 2nd edn, III.788; U. Rizzitano, 'Ibn al-Thumna', *Encyclopaedia of Islam*, 2nd edn, III.956.
[11] There follows a brief summary based on J. Johns, 'I titoli arabi dei signori normanni di Sicilia', *Bollettino di Numismatica* 6–7, 1986, 11–54; J. Johns, 'Malik Ifrīqiyya: the Norman Kingdom of Africa and the Fāṭimids', *Libyan Studies* 18, 1987, 89–101; and a section of J. Johns, *Duana Regis. Arabic Administration and Norman Kingship in Sicily*, forthcoming.
[12] Johns, 'Titoli arabi', 36, cat. 1–7.
[13] Johns, 'Titoli arabi', 37–39, cat. 9–10, 13–17.
[14] Johns, 'Titoli arabi', 39–49, cat. 18–63.
[15] Johns, 'Titoli arabi', 43, cat. 43.

as 'the high, to-be-obeyed order, may God increase it in prestige and in efficacy . . . of the sublime, royal, ruling, Williamian majesty, magnificent, desirous of power through God, aided by His omnipotence, victorious through His strength, king of Italy, Lombardy, Calabria, and Sicily, defender of the pope of Rome, protector of the Christian faith, may God perpetuate his reign and his days, make eternal his times and his years, carry his armies and his banners to victory, and give strength to his swords and to his pens'.[16]

Comparing this third stage with the two that precede it, it is apparent that this is no longer a Latin, feudal tradition of titulature, transliterated or translated into Arabic, but rather an almost completely independent tradition which belongs to the Islamic world and which, moreover, has no traceable ancestor in Sicily.[17]

The second example to illustrate the distinction between the inherited and the newly imported components of the Arabic facet of the Sicilian monarchy concerns the practices and structure of the Norman *dīwān* or Arabic fiscal administration. During the conquest of Sicily, Count Roger had his men seize the records of the fiscal administration of the island, and, from 1093, these formed the basis for the distribution of lands amongst his supporters. These records were polyptychs, lists of the names of the heads of tax-paying households, called *jarā'id* (sing. *jarīda*) in Arabic. New *jarā'id* were issued to feudatories by Roger I and by the regent Adelaide and Roger II until 1111, but thereafter no new Arabic documents were issued until after 1130. Over the next decade, the *dīwān* was reformed and a range of new bureaucratic practices were introduced, culminating in c.1145 with the reform of the landholding regime founded by Roger I in the 1090s. Feudatories were compelled to submit their original privileges to the royal *dīwān* for scrutiny: only if they proved satisfactory, were they reissued, at a price. During this reform, the *dīwān* was restructured, and new administrative offices were introduced.[18]

The royal *dīwān* had essentially the same duties after 1130 as the Arabic administration had had since c.1093, namely the administration of the royal demesne. In this task, it made use of the *jarā'id*, which had evolved only a little way from their origins in the fiscal administration of Muslim Sicily. But if these elements demonstrate continuity with the pre-conquest past, others attest to the importation of a new bureaucratic structure and new bureaucratic practices.

The most conspicuous of the latter is the new, elegant, and highly professional *dīwānī* script, employed in all royal documents from c.1130 onwards. The surviving Arabic documents from the comital period are all written in different scripts, none of which can be considered the ancestor of the royal *dīwānī*.[19] Nor do the very rare surviving examples of pre-conquest Arabic script from South

---

[16] Johns, 'Titoli arabi, 47, cat. 53.

[17] Johns, 'Titoli arabi', 20–29.

[18] This is a much simplified summary of long and complicated argument: Johns, *Duana Regis*.

[19] The 4 documents are: (1) Palermo, Archivio capitolare, no. 5, photo in J. Johns, 'The Muslims of Norman Sicily, c.1060–c.1194', D.Phil. thesis, University of Oxford 1983, pl. 1; (2) Catania, Archivio capitolare, arabo-greco no. 1, photo in Johns, 'Muslims', pl. 2; (3) Palermo, Archivio di Stato, Tabulario di S. Filippo di Fragalà, no. 9, photo in G. La Mantia, *Il primo documento in carta (Contessa Adelaide, 1109) esistente in Sicilia e rimasto sinora sconosciuto*, Palermo 1908; (4) Paris, Bibliothèque nationale, Suppl. Gr. no. 1315,1, photo in A. Guillou, *Les actes grecs de S. Maria di Messina*, Istituto siciliano di studi bizantini e neoellenici, Testi no. 8, Palermo 1963, pls IIa/b.

Italy and Sicily bear any relationship to the royal script.[20] In Norman Sicily, the royal *dīwānī* is encountered only in the royal palace and the court, and the private documents of the island display a variety of scripts none of which is morphologically related to royal *dīwānī*.[21] On the other hand, the royal *dīwānī* does closely resemble *dīwānī* scripts from contemporary Egypt and the Levant.[22] The strong probability is that the royal *dīwānī* script was imported into Sicily from an east Mediterranean chancery.

A second new chancery practice concerns the royal signature. The early de Hautevilles either did not sign their Arabic documents, or used their Greek signature. The Norman kings, too, often used their Greek signature, but occasionally employed an Arabic personal cypher or *ᶜalāma*. Roger and William II used the same *ᶜalāma*, *al-ḥamdu li-' llāh wa-shukran li-anᶜumi-hi*, 'Praise be to God, and thanks for his blessings', while that of William I was *al-ḥamdu li-' llāh ḥaqq ḥamida-hu*, 'Praise be to God, it is fitting to praise him'.[23]

The use of the *ᶜalāma*, in place of the ruler's personal name, has been called 'the classical Islamic method of signature'.[24] It was the Fāṭimid caliphs who first made use of the *ḥamdala* (an *ᶜalāma* beginning with the phrase *al-ḥamdu li-' llāh*) as the ruler's signature, and all Fāṭimid caliphs employed the formula *al-ḥamdu*

---

[20] See, for example, the bilingual gospel of St Luke of 1043 from Calabria: Paris, Bibliothèque nationale, Suppl. Gr. no. 911, photo in K. and S. Lake, *Dated Greek Miniscule Manuscripts to the year 1200*, *Monumenta Palaeografica Vetera*, Boston, Mass., American Academy of Arts and Sciences, 1st ser., 1934– , fasc. V, pls 265 and 283; and in H. Omont, *Facsimilés des manuscrits grecs datés de la Bibliothèque nationale du IXe au XIVe siècles*, Paris 1891, pls XVIII and XVIII/i. The script of the Palermo Qur'ān of 982–83 is still further from Norman *dīwānī*: Istanbul, Nuruosmaniye Library, MS. 23, and London, Nasser D. Khalili Collection, QUR261 and QUR368 (F. Déroche, *The Abbasid tradition. Qur' ans of the 8th to the 10th centuries*, vol. I of J. Raby, ed., *The Nasser D. Khalili Collection of Islamic Art*, Oxford 1992, I.146, no. 81).

[21] See, for example, S. Cusa, *I diplomi greci ed arabi di Sicilia pubblicati nel testo originale, tradotti ed illustrati*, 2 vols, vol. 1 in 2 pts, vol. 2 never published, Palermo 1868 (*sic*, corr. 1874)–1882 (reprinted, Köln/Wien 1982), pl. IA: an act of sale from Palermo, 1161. Albrecht Noth has tentatively identified a few Maghribī features in the royal script (A. Noth, 'I documenti arabi di Ruggero II', in C. Brühl, *Diplomi e cancelleria di Ruggero II*, Accademia di Scienze Lettere e Arti di Palermo, Palermo 1983, 205–206), but these occur neither frequently nor with any regularity. It is likely, therefore, that they indicate not the ancestry of the script itself, but rather the geographical origins (Ifrīqiyya or Sicily) of some of the scribes who used it. John Wansbrough ('Diplomatica Siciliana', *Bulletin of the School of Oriental and African Studies* 47, 1984, 14, n.12) also makes this point.

[22] Compare, for example, the Fāṭimid documents illustrated by: G. Khan, 'A copy of a decree from the archives of the Fāṭimid chancery in Egypt', *Bulletin of the School of Oriental and African Studies* 49, 1986, 439–453; D.S. Richards, 'A Fāṭimid petition and a "small decree" from Sinai', *Israel Oriental Studies* 3, 1973, 140–158; S.M. Stern, *Fāṭimid decrees. Original documents from the Fāṭimid chancery*, London 1964; S.M. Stern, 'Three petitions of the Fāṭimid period', *Oriens* 15, 1971, 172–209; and S.M. Stern, 'An original document of the Fāṭimid chancery concerning Italian merchants', in *Festschrift G. Levi della Vida*, I.529–538.

[23] Ibn Jubayr, *Riḥlat al-Kinānī*, ed. M.J. de Goeje and W. Wright, Oxford 1907, 325. Roger attached his *ᶜalāma* to the endowment charter of George of Antioch's foundation, S. Maria dell'Ammiraglio: Cusa, no. 70, 68–70. William II's *ᶜalāma* is close to that used by Roger II and William I upon issues from the mint of al-Mahdiyya, *al-ḥamdu li-' llāh ḥaqq ḥamida-hu wa-ka-mā huwa ahl-hu wa-mustaḥiqq-hu*, 'Praise be to God, it is fitting to praise Him, for He deserves praise and is worthy of it': H.H. Abdul-Wahhab, 'Deux dinars normands de Mahdia', *Revue Tunisienne* ns 1, 1930, 215–218; Johns, 'Malik Ifrīqiyya', 92–3.

[24] Stern, *Fāṭimid decrees*, 123–124.

li-'llāh rabb al-ᶜalam, 'Praise be to God, the Lord of the Universe'.[25] Similarly, the de Hauteville kings all used *ḥamdala*s for their *ᶜalama*s, although the formulae they employed were those appropriate to the leading officers of the Fāṭimid court, not to the caliph himself.[26]

Not just *dīwānī* practices but also the structural organization of the *dīwān* itself underwent change after the foundation of the kingdom. Before 1130, there survives no Arabic term for the office which administered the affairs of the de Hauteville demesne, and it is only during the reforms of 1145 that it is first named as *al-dīwān al-maᶜmūr*, literally 'the populous' or 'busy *dīwān*'.[27] Soon afterwards, in 1149, another office appears, called *dīwān al-taḥqīq al-maᶜmūr*, literally 'the busy *dīwān* of verification'. While *al-dīwān al-maᶜmūr* was responsible for the administration of all royal rights and possessions in Sicily and Calabria, the *dīwān al-taḥqīq al-maᶜmūr* was responsible for compiling and preserving the registers of the boundaries of all lands, upon which the fiscal administration of the island was ultimately dependent. The *dīwān al-taḥqīq al-maᶜmūr* was also responsible for controlling donations of lands and men out of the royal demesne and, to this extent, it supervised the activities of *al-dīwān al-maᶜmūr*.[28]

Before it appears in Sicily, the *dīwān al-taḥqīq* is known only in Fāṭimid Egypt.[29] The circumstances surrounding the creation of this office by the vizier al-Afḍal in 1107–1108 are strikingly similar to those associated with its

[25] Stern, *Fāṭimid decrees*, 127–128; Khan, 450.
[26] King Roger's *ᶜalama* is very close to a vizieral form: *Al-ḥamdu li-'llāh shukran li-niᶜmati-hi*, see D. Sourdel, 'al-Djardjarā'ī (4)', *Encyclopaedia of Islam*, 2nd edn, II.462. It may be significant that, from 1137, all Fāṭimid viziers bore the title *malik*, the Arabic designation of the Norman kings: D. Ayalon, 'Malik', *Encyclopaedia of Islam*, 2nd edn, VI.261–262.
[27] *Al-maᶜmūr* is an epithet traditionally applied to royal institutions within Islam: it simply expresses the pious wish that the institution will be always 'populous' or 'busy' (Amari, *Storia*, III.237; Noth, 217). The term is in no way descriptive of the functions or activities of the *dīwān* (*pace* C.A. Garufi, 'Sull'ordinamento amministrativo normanno in Sicilia: Exhiquier o diwan? Studi storici diplomatici', *Archivio storico italiano*, 5th ser., 27, 1901, 229, 236–238). In Norman Sicily, the term is used of other royal institutions such as the royal palace (Cusa, 44), and the royal *ṭirāz* (F. Bock, *Die Kleinodien des Heil-Römischen Reiches Deutscher Nation nebst den Kroninsignien Böhmens, Ungarns under der Lombardei*, 2 vols, Vienna 1864, I.27–31, II.6/8).
[28] This is a brief summary of the conclusions of Johns, *Duana Regis*, where the following rather different interpretations are discussed in detail: Amari, 'Su la data', 431; Amari, *Storia*, III.327–328, n.2; M. Caravale, 'Gli uffici finanziari nel Regno di Sicilia durante il periodo normanno', *Annali di storia del diritto* 8, 1964, 178–185 (reprinted in M. Caravale, *Il regno normanno di Sicilia*, Milan 1966, 206–209); E. Caspar, *Roger II (1101–1154) und die Gründung der normannisch-sicilischen Monarchie*, Innsbruck 1904, 314–317; Chalandon, II.647–653; Garufi, 229, 236–238; L. Genuardi, 'I defetari normanni', in *Centenario della nascita di Michele Amari. Scritti di filologia e storia araba*, 2 vols, Palermo 1910, I.217–218; E. Mayer, *Italienische Verfassungsgeschichte von der Gothenzeit bis zur Zunftherrschaft*, 2 vols, Leipzig 1909, II.384–388; E. Mazzarese Fardella, *Aspetti dell'organizzazione amministrativa nello stato normanno e svevo*, Milan 1966, 29; Noth, 217–18; H. Takayama, 'The financial and administrative organization of the Norman kingdom of Sicily', *Viator* 16, 1985, 150–51 *et pass*.
[29] The main sources for the Fāṭimid *dīwān al-taḥqīq* are the fifteenth-century writers al-Qalqashandī (*Ṣubḥ al-aᶜshā fī ṣināᶜat al-inshā'*, 14 vols, ed. Muḥammad ᶜAbd al-Rasūl Ibrāhīm, Cairo 1913–1920, and Index, Cairo 1972, III.493–94) and al-Maqrīzī (*Al-Mawāᶜiẓ wa-'l-iᶜtibār fī dhikr al-khitat wa-'l-āthār*, ed. Būlāq, 2 vols, Cairo 1853 [reprinted Beirut c.1970], I.401; *Ittiᶜaz al-hunafā'*, ed. Jamāl al-Dīn al-Shayyāl, 3 vols, Cairo 1967–73, III.69, 338, 340–41), whose reports seem to be largely based upon the *Nuzhat al-muqlataynfī akhbār al-dawlatayn*, a lost work by Ibn al-Tuwayr (d.1220): cf. W.J. Björkman, *Beiträge zur Geschichte der Staatskanzlei im islamischen Ägypten*, Hamburg 1928, 83; A.R. Guest, 'A list of writers, books, and other

introduction to Sicily. Al-Afḍal founded the office at the time of a major reorganisation of land-holding in Egypt, and its main duty was to supervise and to control this process and the subsequent reallocation of estates.[30] There is, at the very least, a strong *prima facie* case that the *dīwān al-taḥqīq* was imported to Sicily from Egypt to serve exactly the purpose for which it had originally been created.[31]

The third and last example concerns the architecture and decoration of the Norman palaces. There survive the substantial remains of six principal royal palaces in and around Palermo from the period after c.1130: the Palazzo Reale, l'Uscibene or al-Mannānī near Altarello di Baida, il Maredolce or la Favara near Brancaccio, and il Parco at Altofonte, all founded by Roger II; la Zisa, begun by William I and completed by William II; and la Cuba, with la Cubula and la Cuba Soprana, built by William II.[32] But two major obstacles impede discussion of the evidence. First, nothing survives of the palaces of Sicily before the Norman conquest, and almost nothing from the period before 1130.[33] And, second, only scattered fragments survive of the Fāṭimid palaces of Cairo, so that the best comparanda available are the Ifrīqiyyan palaces of the Fāṭimids and of their Zīrīd and Ḥammādid clients, which all date from the tenth to early eleventh century, and thus predate the Norman palaces by more than a century.[34]

authorities mentioned by El Maqrīzī in his Kitat', *Journal of the Royal Asiatic Society* 34, 1902, 117; and C. Cahen, 'Quelques chroniques anciennes relatives aux derniers Fatimides', *Bulletin de l'Institut Français d'Archéologie Orientale du Caire* XXXVIII, 1937, 10–14 and 16, n.1.

[30] Ibn Muyassar, *Akhbār Miṣr*, ed. H. Massé, Cairo 1919, 42; al-Qalqashandī, III.494; al-Maqrīzī, *Itticāz*, III.338, 340–41.

[31] For a full discussion of this subject, see Johns, *Duana Regis*.

[32] Palazzo Reale: F. Valenti, 'Il palazzo reale di Palermo', *Bollettino d'Arte* 4, 1924–1925, 512–528; M. Guiotto, *Palazzo ex-reale di Palermo. Recenti restauri e ritrovamenti*, Palermo 1947; R. Delogu and V. Scuderi, *La reggia dei normanni e la Cappella Palatina*, Florence 1969. Uscibene: A. Goldschmidt, 'Die normannischen Königspaläste in Palermo', *Zeitschrift für Bauwesen* 48, 1898, 542–590; Amari, *Storia*, III.842–844; S. Braida Santamaura, 'Il "Sollazzo" dell'Uscibene', *Architetti di Sicilia*, 1.i, 1965, 31–42. Maredolce: Goldschmidt; S. Braida Santamaura, 'Il castello di Favara. Studi di Restauro', *Architetti di Sicilia*, 1.v–vi, 1965, 21–34. Altofonte: L. Anastasi, *L'arte nel parco reale normanno di Palermo*, Palermo 1935; S. Braida Santamaura, 'Il palazzo ruggeriano di Altofonte', *Palladio* 23, 1973, 185–197. Zisa: G. Bellafiore, *La Zisa di Palermo*, Palermo 1978; G. Caronia, *La Zisa di Palermo. Storia e restauro*, Palermo 1987; U. Staacke, *Un palazzo normanno a Palermo. La Zisa. La cultura musulmana negli edifici dei Re*, Palermo 1991. Cuba: S. Bellafiore, *La Cuba di Palermo*, Palermo 1984; G. Caronia and V. Noto, *La Cuba di Palermo*, Palermo 1988; P. Lojacono, 'L'organismo costruttivo della Cuba alla luce degli ultimi scavi', *Palladio* ns 3.v–vi, 1953, 1–6.

[33] Amari (*Storia*, II.407, 515–516, III.121, 844) identified King Roger's suburban palace of Maredolce or La Favara with the Qaṣr Jacfar mentioned by Ibn Jubayr (329–330), and argued that the latter had originally been built by the Kalbid emir Jacfar (997–1019). There is no evidence for or against this hypothesis.

[34] For the Fāṭimid palaces in Cairo, see the still largely reliable reconstruction of R. Ravaisse, 'Essai sur la topographie du Caire d'après Maqrizi', *Mémoires . . . de la Mission Archéologique Française au Caire*, I/iii, 1887, 407–80 and III/iv, 1890, 33–114; also, K.A.C. Creswell, *The Muslim architecture of Egypt*, 2 vols, Oxford 1952, I.33–35, 128–30, pls 38–39. For the surviving fragments of the ceiling of the Fāṭimid palace: M. Herz, 'Boiseries fatimites aux scultures figurales, *Orientalisches Archiv*, III/4, 1913, 169–74, pls XXVII–XXIX, esp. XXIX/18–19 which shows scenes not in Pauty's catalogue; E. Pauty, *Les bois sculptés jusqu'à l'époque Ayyoubide (Catalogue général du Musée Arabe du Caire)*, Cairo 1931, 48–50, pls XLVI–LVIII; G. Marçais, 'Les figures d'hommes et de bêtes dans les bois sculptés d'époque fāṭimite conservés au Musée Arabe du Caire', *Mémoires . . . de la Mission Archéologique Française au Caire (Mélanges*

There can be no doubt that the Norman palaces belong to the same family as the earlier Ifrīqiyyan structures. The solid geometry of the ground-plan of the Zisa or of the Cuba reveals their parentage with the Zīrīd palace at Ashīr (figs 1 and 2). Again, the symmetrical arrangement of rooms on either side of a central axis links the two groups of palaces, as does the canonical employment of the inverted-'T' plan on the central axis, a feature which suggests that the space was intended for ceremonial use (figs 1 and 2). Similarly, the solid, four-square plan of the Torre Pisana in the Palazzo Reale, with its central chamber placed within a surrounding ambulatory, finds a close parallel in the Qaṣr al-Manār at the Qalᶜa of the Banī Ḥammād (figs 3(A) and 4).

The architectural decoration of the two groups of palaces is also clearly connected. The exteriors present a severely sober and restrained aspect, characterized by tall blind arches, for example on the Qasr al-Manār at the Qalᶜa of the Banī Ḥammād in Ifrīqiyya and on the Cuba in Palermo.[35] The interiors share many decorative features in common, such as the use of *muqarnas* or stalactite vaulting, which first appears in the Maghrib from Fāṭimid Egypt in the Qalᶜa of the Banī Ḥammād.[36] *Muqarnas* vaulting in stucco and wood is found in the Palazzo Reale and l'Uscibene, and in la Zisa and la Cuba. Other decorative features in the Norman palaces proclaim their Islamic origins, such as the fountain in the Zisa: water flows from a lion-head spout or *sabīl*, over an inclined marble slab or *shadirwān*, and into a series of rectangular basins linked by channels. This arrangement seems to hark back to Persian antecedents, but can be seen in the tenth-century houses of Fusṭāṭ, whence it was presumably passed to Sicily.[37]

Finally, the magnificent painted wooden ceiling of the Cappella Palatina, and the less well-known painted ceilings of Palermo cathedral, Cefalù, and la

Maspero III) 68, 1940, 241–257. For a further fragment, probably from the western palace, now in the Louvre: E. Anglade, *Catalogue des boiseries de la section islamique (Musée du Louvre)*, Paris 1988, 59–63, no. 32. See also: V. Meinecke-Berg, 'Materialen zu fāṭimidischen Holzdekorationen in Kairo I: Holzdecken aus dem fāṭimidischen Westpalast in Kairo', *Mitteilungen des Deutschen archäologischen Instituts abteilung Kairo* 47, 1991, 227–233; and Sabiha Khemir, 'The palace of Sitt al-Mulk and Fāṭimid imagery', Ph.D. thesis, School of Oriental and African Studies, University of London 1990, which contains important new evidence. For the Ifrīqiyyan comparanda: L. Golvin, 'Note sur le décor des façades en Bérbérie Oriental à la période sanhâgienne', in *Études d'Orientalisme dédiées à la mémoire de Lévi-Provençal*, 2 vols, Paris 1962, II.581–589; L. Golvin, *Recherches archéologiques à la Qalᶜa des Banu Hammad, Algérie*, Paris 1965; L. Golvin, 'Le palais de Ziri à Achir (dixième siècle J.C.)', *Ars Orientalis* 6, 1966, 47–76; A. Lézine, *Architecture de l'Ifriqiya. Recherches sur les monuments aghlabides*, Paris 1965; A. Lézine, *Mahdiya. Recherches d'archéologie islamique*, Paris 1965; A. Lézine, 'La salle d'audience du palais d'Achir', *Revue des Études Islamiques* 37, 1969, 203–218; G. Marçais, *L'architecture musulmane d'Occident. Tunisie, Algérie, Maroc, Espagne et Sicile*, Paris 1954. For discussion, see especially U. Scerrato, 'L'architettura', in F. Gabrieli and U. Scerrato, *Gli Arabi in Italia*, Milan 1979, 307–342.
[35] For the Qalᶜa: Golvin, 'Note sur le décor des façades', 584–85; Golvin, *Recherches archéologiques*, 67–71, 96–100. For the Cuba: the works cited in n.32, above.
[36] For *muqarnas* in general: D. Behrens-Abouseif, 'Mukarnas', *Encyclopaedia of Islam*, 2nd edn, VII.501–506; and F. Fernandez-Puertas, 'Mukarbas', *Encyclopaedia of Islam*, 2nd edn, VII.500–501. For *muqarnas* at the Qalᶜa: L. Golvin, 'Les plafonds à muqarnas de la Qalᶜa des Banū Ḥammād et leur influence possible sur l'art de la Sicile à la période normande', *Revue de l'Occident Musulman et de la Mediterranée* xvii, 1974, 63–69.
[37] G. Marçais, 'Salsabil and sadirwan', in *Études d'Orientalisme dédiées à la mémoire de Lévi-Provençal*, 2 vols, Paris 1962, II.639–648. For the Zisa: Caronia, figs 71–73; compare with the panel from the Cappella Palatina, Gabrieli and Scerrato, fig. 56. For the Fusṭāṭ houses: A. Bahgat and A. Gabriel, *Fouilles d'al-Foustat*, Paris 1921.

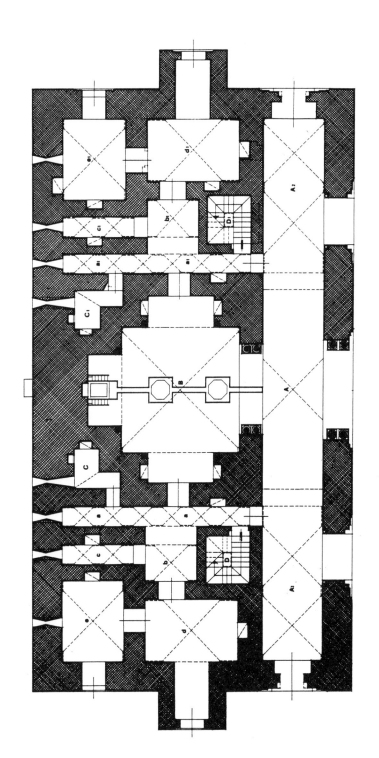

Fig. 1. Palermo, the Zisa: ground plan (after Bellafiore)

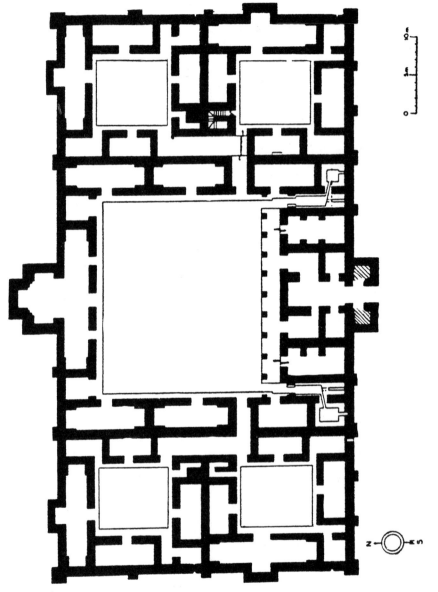

Fig. 2. Ashīr, Algeria, Zīrīd palace: ground plan (after Golvin)

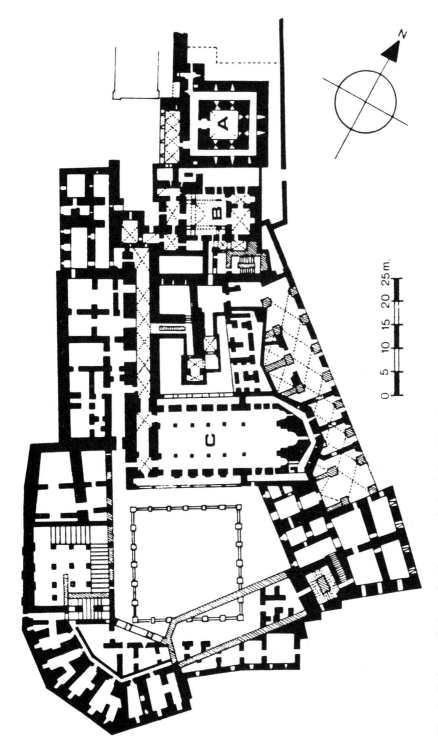

Fig. 3. Palermo, Palazzo Reale: ground plan (after Valenti)

Fig. 4.
Qalᶜa Banī Ḥammād, Algeria: reconstruction section and plan (after Marçais)

Magione, clearly belong to the world of Islam.[38] The dominant iconographic theme in the ceiling of the Cappella Palatina, the pleasures of the court cycle, finds exact parallels in surviving beams from the ceiling of the Fāṭimid western palace in Cairo (1058): seated drinkers, musicians, dancing girls, and hunting

---

[38] Cappella Palatina: U. Monneret de Villard, *Le pitture musulmane al soffitto della Cappella Palatina in Palermo*, Rome 1950. Palermo cathedral: G. Bellafiore, *La cattedrale di Palermo*, Palermo 1976, figs 146–47. Cefalù: M. Gelfer-Jorgensen, *Medieval Islamic symbolism and the paintings in the Cefalù cathedral*, Leiden 1986. La Magione: Amari, *Storia*, III.881, n.2. For alternative views to that advanced here upon the origins of the Sicilian ceilings: D. Jones, 'The Cappella Palatina in Palermo: problems of attribution', *Art and Archaeology Research Papers*, 2, 1972, 41–57; Monneret de Villard, *passim*; J. Sourdel-Thomine, 'Le style des inscriptions arabo-siciliènnes à l'époque des rois normands', in *Études d'Orientalisme dédiées à la mémoire de Lévi-Provençal*, 2 vols, Paris 1962, I.307–315.

scenes.[39] The Islamic orientation of the ceiling is also revealed by the Arabic inscriptions which run around the borders of the main panels, reciting a litany of royal power, repeating over and over thirty royal epithets or *alqāb mamlakāt*: 'victory and perfection and perfection and ability and power and reputation and lasting good and wealth and acquisition and victory and power . . . '.[40]

It should be stressed that the Sicilian palaces do not casually or accidentally resemble those of Islam, nor are they slavish copies which ignore the spirit of the originals. On the contrary, it is manifest that the architects, masons, plasterers, carpenters and painters employed in the royal palaces of Palermo all worked within a living and evolving tradition of design and craftsmanship. That nothing survives of palace architecture in Sicily before c.1130 does not prove, of course, that this tradition had died out in Sicily and had to be imported by the Normans after the foundation of the kingdom. But it is extremely difficult to imagine how ateliers of specialized craftsmen could have kept alive their arts and skills over the century of war and insecurity which separated the fall of the Kalbids from the foundation of the Norman monarchy.

Having made the distinction between those components of the Arabic facet of the Norman monarchy which were inherited from the Muslim rulers of Sicily, and those which were imported from the contemporary Muslim world after c.1130, and having seen that there is a strong case to be made that a source of these imports was the Fāṭimid court of Egypt, it is now necessary to discuss the evidence for relations between Palermo and Cairo.

By far and away the most informative piece of evidence for relations between the two courts is a letter from the caliph al-Ḥāfiẓ (1130–1149) to King Roger, dated to the winter of 1137–1138. The letter is quoted in full by al-Qalqashandī (1355–1418), the greatest of all Mamlūk writers upon the secretarial art, and has been the subject of a study by Maurice Canard.[41] Space does not permit a thorough discussion of the letter here, and only five points will be stressed.

First, the Egyptian chronicler Ibn Muyassar reports that Norman military activity in Ifrīqiyya in 1123 and 1143 had prompted the exchange of ambassadors between Cairo and Palermo.[42] It is thus intriguing to find in this letter the two rulers apparently collaborating in the Norman annexation of what were technically Fāṭimid lands. In a previous letter, Roger must have given an account of the

---

[39] (Abbreviations used in this note: MdV = Monneret de Villard, *Le pitture*; P = Pauty, *Les bois*.) Seated drinkers: MdV, figs 178–188, 193–199; P, pl. LIV. Musicians: MdV, figs 200–217; P, pls LII–LIV. Dancing girls: MdV, figs 219–220; P, pls XLIX, L, LIII, LVII. Hunting scenes: (birds of prey on prey) MdV, figs 157–62, 164, 166, 199, 246; P, pls L, LII–LIV; (mounted falconers) MdV figs 247–248; P, pl. LVI; (lion hunting from horseback) MdV, figs 233–34; P, pl. LVI.

[40] Amari, *Epigrafi*, II.32–42, no.6, pl. 3–4; Monneret de Villard, 31–33, 65–66, and plates. Compare, for example, with the inscriptions from the twelfth-century epigraphic wooden frieze reused in the mosque of al-Mu'ayyad in Cairo (1415–20) and now in the Museum of Islamic Art: J.D. Weill, *Les bois à épigraphes jusqu' à l'époque mamlouke (Catalogue général du Musée Arabe du Caire)*, Cairo 1931, 22–3, no. 646, and 24–5, no. 649.

[41] Al-Qalqashandī, VI.458–463; M. Canard, 'Une lettre du caliphe fāṭimite al-Ḥāfiẓ (524–544/1130–1149) à Roger II', *Studi Ruggeriani*, I.125–146 (reprinted in M. Canard, *Miscellanea Orientalia*, London 1973). For the man and his work, see C.E. Bosworth, 'al-Ḳalḳashandī', *Encyclopaedia of Islam*, 2nd edn, IV.509–511. For the sources of the *Ṣubḥ*, see Björkman, 75–86. The Arabic text of the letter with an English translation and commentary are given as an appendix in Johns, *Duana Regis*.

[42] Ibn Muyassar, 63, 85.

capture of the island of Jarba by a Sicilian fleet in 1135–1136. In his reply, al-Ḥafiẓ not only accepts Roger's explanation of his actions – the need to destroy a lawless nest of pirates – but even warmly commends them.

Second, al-Ḥafiẓ's letter reveals that commercial relations were uppermost in the minds of the two rulers. Before 1126, Roger had sent one of his leading administrators, George of Antioch, who was later to become his vizier, as ambassador to Cairo. The embassy, which may be linked to the Fāṭimid embassy of 1123, was a great success, and George is said to have secured considerable financial advantage for his master.[44] In his letter, the caliph thanks Roger for the favourable treatment which a ship, trading in al-Ḥafiẓ's personal interests, had received from Roger's officers. As a mark of his gratitude, the caliph promised to waive the customs at Alexandria and Cairo upon cargoes belonging to Roger himself, to his vizier George of Antioch, and to 'the two ambassadors who are yet to arrive'.[45]

Third, the letter demonstrates that, upon at least one occasion, the Fāṭimid *dīwān* instructed the Norman chancery, probably in the correct form of Arabic regnal titulature. Towards the end of the letter, al-Ḥafiẓ refers to a gaffe committed by Roger's secretary in an earlier letter, and to the excuses which he had made in mitigation: 'As to [your] secretary's explanation', he writes, 'in answer to the accusation made against him – to wit, that, in translating from one language to another, the meaning may become confused and the sense altered, specially if a word is used which does not have the same meaning in both languages . . . his explanation has been accepted.' As Canard remarks, the term in question seems to have been a title.[46]

Fourth, the passage just discussed demonstrates that al-Ḥafiẓ's letter must have been at least the fourth in a regular correspondence between the two rulers. First was the letter in which Roger's secretary caused offence; next came the caliph's reply, correcting the error; then, the letter in which the secretary made his excuses; and finally came the surviving letter.

Fifth, and finally, in his concluding paragraph, the caliph refers to the exchange of gifts between the two rulers.[47] He acknowledges the safe arrival of Roger's gifts, and announces that his ambassador had been entrusted with gifts for the king. The gifts were listed in a separate inventory which has not survived, but they were undoubtedly rich and costly items befitting the status of donor and recipient, and they may have included regalia. The Berber historian Ibn Ḥamādu, writing in c.1220, described the ceremonial parasol (*al-miẓalla*) used by the Fāṭimids, and added: 'No dynasty other than the Fāṭimids is known to have used this parasol,

[43] Al-Qalqashandī, VI.459, lines 3–11; Canard, 'Une lettre', 129–131.

[44] Al-Tijānī, *Riḥla*, ed. H.H. ᶜAbd al-Wahhāb, Tunis 1958, 333.

[45] Al-Qalqashandī, VI.460, lines 5–6; cf. Canard, 'Une lettre', 133–134. The ambassadors may have been from the Norman city of Salerno: F. Ughelli, *Italia sacra*, 2nd edn N. Coleti, 10 vols, Venice 1717–22, VII.399; Romuald, 233.

[46] Al-Qalqashandī, VI.463, lines 4–7; Canard, 'Une lettre', 144. Canard believed this passage to indicate that Roger's chancery used Greek, not Arabic, for correspondence with the Fāṭimids, but the secretary is undoubtedly excusing himself for an unhappy rendition of a western term, whether Greek or Latin, into Arabic (cf. Noth, 216).

[47] Al-Qalqashandī, VI.463, lines 8–19.

except for the King of the Europeans in Sicily . . . the latter received it amongst the other gifts which [the Fāṭimids] were accustomed to send them'.[48]

In short, from as early as 1123 until at least 1143, relations between the courts of Palermo and Cairo were close and cordial. The two rulers regularly exchanged ambassadors, letters, and gifts. At least one item of Fāṭimid regalia was imported from the Fāṭimid to the Norman court, and upon at least one occasion the Fāṭimid *dīwān* sought to correct the usage of its Sicilian counterpart. This is exactly the sort of international climate in which Norman rulers and their officers could have modelled the Arabic facet of the Sicilian monarchy upon the Fāṭimid caliphate. After 1153, relations between Cairo and Palermo deteriorated rapidly, but, by then, the Islamic facet of the Norman monarchy had already developed an independent dynamic.[49]

What of relations between the Normans of Sicily and other Muslim powers in the Mediterranean? The nearest Muslim neighbours to Sicily were the Zīrīds of al-Mahdiyya. Although the Zīrīds had made some attempt to reinforce Sicily at the time of the conquest, they had withdrawn from the struggle in 1075, and by 1086 had a pact of non-aggression with Roger I.[50] There is some evidence, too, of close and cordial relations between the Normans and the Ḥammādids.[51] But this harmony, which seems to have had its roots in commerce, broke down in 1117, when the Roger II intervened on behalf of the rebellious lord of Qābis. The Zīrīds sought help from the Almoravids, and Roger retaliated harrying the Ifrīqiyyan coast, and by allying with Raymond-Berengar II, count of Barcelona: the quarrel rumbled on until at least 1128.[53] Soon thereafter good relations were restored, for it was a 'dishonourable' peace between the Zīrīds and the Normans that provided the pretext for the Ḥammādid attack upon al-Mahdiyya in 1135, which a Norman fleet helped to repel.[54] Thereafter, until the conquest of the Ifrīqiyyan littoral was begun in 1143, the Zīrīds were Norman puppets. In 1147, a Norman fleet occupied al-Mahdiyya, and brought an end to Zīrīd rule.[55]

The preceding summary of relations between the Normans and their western Muslim neighbours reveals that this relationship was of a very different nature from that between the Normans and the Fāṭimids. Although contacts between Sicily and the Zīrīds were particularly frequent in the period leading up to and

---

[48] Ibn Ḥamādu, *Akhbār mulūk Banī ʿUbayd (Histoire des rois ʿObaïdites)*, ed. and Fr. trans. M. Vonderheyden, Paris 1927, 15, 28; cf. Canard, 'Une lettre', 126. For the *mizalla* at the Fāṭimid court, see: al-Musabbiḥī, *Akhbār Miṣr*, ed. A.F. Sayyid and T. Bianquis, Cairo 1978, 61, 66, 70, 86, 99; M. Espéronnier, 'Les fêtes civiles et les cérémonies d'origine antique sous les Fatimides d'Egypte. Extrais du tome III de *Ṣubḥ al-aʿshā* d'al-Qalqashandī', *Der Islam* 65, 1988, 49.
[49] Canard, 'Une lettre', 127.
[50] Malaterra, III.viii–ix, 61; Amari, *Storia*, III, 152–153. The non-aggression pact may have existed as early as 1078. In 1086 Roger was invited by the Pisans and Genoese to join them in a raid against al-Mahdiyya but declined on the grounds that he had a pact with the Zīrīds. Amari, *Storia*, III.160; Malaterra IV.iii, 86–87.
[51] *Chronica Monasterii Casinensis*, ed. H. Hoffmann, MGH, XXXIV, Hannover 1980, IV.50, 516 (Peter the Deacon); Amari, *Storia*, III.375–376; H.R. Idris, *La Berbérie orientale sous les Zīrīdes, X–XII siècles*, 2 vols, Paris 1962, I.308–9.
[52] Amari, *Storia*, III.376–379; Idris, I.318–24.
[53] Amari, *Storia*, III.379–398; Idris, I.319–24; D. Abulafia, 'The Norman kingdom of Africa and the Norman expeditions to Majorca and the Muslim Mediterranean', *ante* VII, 1985, 30–32.
[54] Amari, *Storia*, III.406–407; Idris, I.342–45.
[55] Amari, *Storia*, III.422–424; Idris, I.355–58.

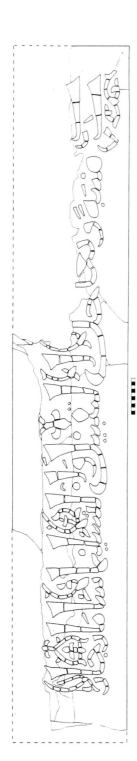

Fig. 5. Inscription No. 1

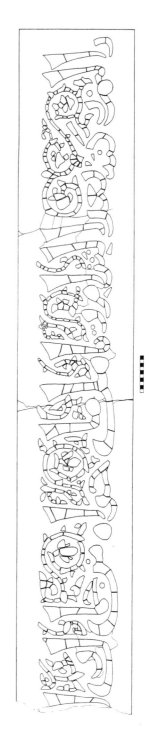

Fig. 6. Inscription No. 2

immediately following the foundation of the Sicilian monarchy, these were not exchanges between two equals, as between Roger and al-Ḥāfiẓ. Sicily was always the dominant partner, now openly hostile and aggressive, now merely domineering. By or soon after 1130, the Zīrīds had been reduced to the rôle of helpless stooges, clinging desperately to the last shreds of independent power while the Normans prepared leisurely to do away with them altogether. It is difficult to believe that Roger and his ministers would have chosen to model the Arabic facet of the Norman monarchy upon these pathetic creatures.

It has now been shown that certain significant elements of the Arabic facet of the Norman monarchy were imported from the contemporary Muslim world after c.1130, and it has been argued that the most likely source of these imports was the Fāṭimid court of Cairo. In conclusion, I shall discuss one further piece of evidence which demonstrates beyond all doubt that the Normans modelled the Arabic facet of their monarchy upon the Fāṭimid caliphate of Egypt.

In the courtyard of the Galleria regionale della Sicilia in Palazzo Abatellis are fragments of two splendid Arabic inscriptions consisting of blocks of grey cipollino marble inlaid with characters in green porphyry and stylised floral decoration in red. The inscriptions are now set in concrete cases, and so are difficult to inspect and measure satisfactorily.

No. 1 (inventory no. 5105) measures 1.91m long, 0.32m wide and 0.065m thick (fig. 5).[56] The characters are approximately 0.20m high. The two long sides of the marble block are polished, while the short sides are rough, which suggests that the block was the jamb of a frame, so that the words *dār a[l-]* . . . would have been upon the architrave. The vertical line begins with what appears to be the word *minnatan*, 'graciously', but the word has been crudely repaired and the reading is uncertain.[57] Whatever the case, this line of the inscription obviously begins in the middle of a phrase, which presumably was carried on from the preceding frame, perhaps that on the right.

The vertical line may be read:

منة' ويعجل التقبيل وَالتسليما سامًا رجار

. . . *minnatan (?). Wa yuʿājilu 'l-taqbīla wa 'l-taslīma. Sāmā Rujjāru* . . .

'. . . graciously (?). And he will hurry to the kiss and to the greeting. Roger vied with . . .'[58]

---

[56] B. Lagumina, 'Iscrizione araba del re Ruggero scoperta alla Cappella Palatina in Palermo', *Rendiconti della Reale Accademia dei Lincei, classe di scienze morali, storiche e filologiche*, 5th ser., 2, 1893, 231–234. I am most grateful to Prof. A.F.L. Beeston, St John's College, Oxford, for his invaluable advice upon both inscriptions.

[57] Lagumina tentatively reads the first word as *miṣṣatan* (from the root *maṣṣa*, 'to suck' ?), and translates '. . . il meglio [dei beni] (?)'. This is perplexing. He suggests that the word was originally written with a *mīm* instead of a *ṣād*, but then altered.

[58] Lagumina translates: '. . . il meglio [dei beni] (?); e si affretta a dare il bacio e il saluto. Ha conteso [nella gloria] Ruggiero . . .'.

The line is written in the metre *kāmil*, and contains part of an adulatory verse, which appears to refer to an act of homage paid to a ruler. There can be no doubt that the ruler was King Roger. In the first place, Roger is mentioned by name, and this can scarcely be a reference to Count Roger. In the second, the inscription was found *ex situ* in the south aisle of the Cappella Palatina, and so is associated with Roger's palace.[59] And, in the third, it is executed in the same technique as the surviving fragments of inscriptions from King Roger's palace in Messina, now in the Museo regionale di Messina.[60] These, too, seem to have come from a rectangular frame; they have characters of green porphyry inlaid into marble, and are composed in *kāmil*. The vertical fragment of the Cappella Palatina inscription reads *dār a[l]* . . . , 'the home of . . .', and this too recalls the Messina inscription where the royal palace is called *dār al-khulūd*, 'the home of eternity', a term for paradise.[61] This inscription is not in itself particularly significant here, and its main purpose is to support the conclusion that the second inscription now in the Palazzo Abatellis also came from Roger's palace.

No. 2 (inventory no. unknown) measures 1.845m long, 0.327 wide, and 0.048 thick (fig. 6).[62] The characters are approximately 0.020m high. The inscription was once kept in a cellar of the Cappella Palatina, and was given to the Royal Museum in Palermo by Vittorio Emanuele in 1863. There is good reason to assume that the two inscriptions were part of a single decorative scheme. They are both made in the same manner, and the scale of the two inscriptions is identical. The metre of the verse of No. 2, however, is *ramal* not *kāmil*, and so the two fragments are not part of the same inscription, although they obviously belonged to a single scheme of decoration. No. 2 seems to have been set horizontally, as part of a continuous band of inscription: perhaps, as we shall see below, the architrave of a rectangular frame. The bottom edge of the block has been smoothed, and four deep holes have been drilled into it, presumably for the pins which secured the block in its original setting. This, and the other two intact sides bear traces of what is presumably the original mortar. The left-hand side is broken.

[59] Lagumina describes the discovery of the inscription. In 1892, a new organ was installed by the architect Giuseppe Patricolo in the south aisle of the Cappella Palatina beneath the ambo. Several fragments of the inscription were found behind the marble dado, where they formed part of the blocking of an entrance to a stair leading down to the crypt. (This stair was reopened during restoration work in 1927.)

[60] M. Amari, 'Su le iscrizioni arabiche del palazzo regio di Messina', *Atti della Reale Accademia dei Lincei, classe di scienze morali, storiche e filologiche*, 3rd ser., 7, 1881, 103–112 (reprinted in Amari, *Epigrafi arabiche*, ed. F. Gabrieli, Palermo 1971, 123–136).

[61] There are other echoes of the text of the Messina inscription in the two fragments from Palermo. In No. 1, the phrase *sāmā Rujjāru* recalls the following line from Messina (admittedly, a rather dubious reading by Amari): *sāmā al-kawākib bī Rujjāru l-malik*, literally, 'for me, King Roger strove to excel the stars'. Similarly, the reference in the Messina inscription to the 'beauty' (*jamāl*) in Roger's palace, recalls the exhoration in Palermo inscription No. 2 to 'contemplate the beauty that it contains' (*ta'mmal mā ḥawā-hū min jamālī*).

[62] Amari, *Epigrafi*, I.31–2, no. V, tav. II, fig. 3.

It may be read:

... ر الثم ركنَهُ بعد الِتِزَامِ وتامل ما حواه من جمال وا ...

'. . .r (?) iltham rukna-hū baᶜda 'ltizāmī wa ta'mmal mā ḥawā-hū min jamālī
wa . . .'

'. . . kiss its corner after clinging [to it], and contemplate the beauty that it
contains, and . . .'[63]

The verse apparently urges the visitor to perform an act of adoration by kissing the
corner of a structure and by embracing it, and to wonder at the treasures therein.

What was this structure? The architect Giuseppe Patricolo, who discovered
inscription No. 1, claimed that it 'must have been part of the ancient chancel
screen' of the Cappella Palatina.[64] This is most unlikely. Although nothing is
known about the form of the original chancel screen, it is surely most improbable
that it would have incorporated profane Arabic verses written on this monumental
scale. Another, more satisfactory provenance must be sought.

A first clue comes from the text of fragment No. 2 which suggests that it was
originally placed close to the external corner of a structure. A second clue lies in
the similarities between the fragmentary inscriptions from Palermo and the fragments of the much more substantially preserved inscription from Messina. As has
already been mentioned, both inscriptions were executed in the same technique,
one which is not found elsewhere in Sicily, and belonged to rectangular frames.
The text of the Messina inscription leaves no doubt that it once adorned Roger's
palace: it refers to 'this lofty palace' (dhā al-qasr al-mushayyad), to 'the
palace of the sultans' (qasr al-salāṭīn), and to the legendary pre-Islamic palace of
al-Khawarnaq. Moreover, the exhortation 'Enter, o peers of the realm' (yā
maᶜshar al-mulk udkhulū) suggests that the inscription belonged to a door to the
palace. On this basis, Amari, calculating the total length of the Messina inscription
at 30m, concluded that it must have framed two doors of the palace.[65] The echoes
of the Messina inscription in the Palermo fragments suggest that they too adorned
the palace, and the fact that the fragment No. 1 comes from a rectangular frame
1.91m high may indicate that it too belonged to the surround of a door. We are
thus looking for a door, near a corner, in the palace.

The third clue is provided by where both fragments were found: admittedly out
of their original settings but, nonetheless, both in the Cappella Palatina. This
makes it likely (although far from certain) that they originally came from the
palace chapel. Recent research upon the Cappella Palatina suggests that under
Roger II the nave and side aisles did not function as part of the chapel but rather
constituted a palace hall or aula, occidented upon the royal dias. If this interpretation is accepted, it follows that the palatine hall would have been the setting most
appropriate to the inscription. The principal entrance has always been through the

---

[63] Amari translates: '[T'appressa?] e bacia il canto di questo [edifizio] dopo averlo abbracciato e
contempla le belle cose ch'e' racchiude. E . . .'
[64] Lagumina, 231.
[65] Each frame would have consisted of a lintel 4m long, and two jambs each 5.5m tall.

present main door in the west end of the south wall, but the two smaller doors pierced through the west wall, on either side of the royal dias, and the door (now blocked) in the west end of the north wall are also original. All of these are located near to corners of the building, and thus fit the criteria for the original location of the inscription. Moreover, the exteriors of them all have been extensively remodelled at various times, so that virtually nothing remains of the original twelfth-century decoration. Thus, one or more of these doors is most likely to have been the original of the inscription.[66]

Turning from the possible location of the inscription to its content; as Amari realised, fragment No. 2 contains an explicit and unmistakable reference to an essential part of the rite of the *ḥajj* or pilgrimage to Mecca. At the beginning and end of the *ḥajj*, pilgrims perform the *ṭawāf* or circumambulation of the KaᶜBa, seven circuits, pausing each time to kiss the black stone embedded in the east corner (*al-rukn al-aswad*), and to press their breasts against the wall between the black stone and the door to the KaᶜBa (*al-multazam*). The precise allusions to this rite contained in the language of the verse, and particularly in the use of the words *rukn* and *iltazam*, make its meaning utterly explicit.

Amari remarked that Muslim visitors to the Norman court would have been horrified by this invitation to adore the palace of a Christian king with the very rites reserved for the adoration of the KaᶜBa (and this horror would have been all the stronger had the inscription adorned the palace chapel).[67] Amari was absolutely right, but he missed a crucial point. The Muslims of Sicily were Sunnī and professed allegiance to the ᶜAbbāsid caliph.[68] Certainly, they would have been shocked and incensed by such sacrilege, but not so loyal adherents of the Fāṭimid regime. The Fāṭimids were a branch of the Ismāᶜīlīs, a Shīᶜī sect, and they, alone amongst the dynasties of medieval Islam, encouraged their followers to adore them as manifestations of the divine.[69] Examples of panegyric survive which explicitly compare the Fāṭimid palace with *al-ḥarām*, the Meccan sanctuary, and suggest that it was considered appropriate to adore the palace with rites otherwise reserved to the *ḥajj*. An anonymous tenth-century north African poet unequivocally compared the Fāṭimid palace at al-Mahdiyya with the *ḥarām* at Mecca, and

---

[66] The palatine aspect of the west end of the chapel under Roger II was first suggested by Ernst Kitzinger in a paper to the 1981 Dumbarton Oaks Symposium upon Art in Norman Sicily. See also: S. Ćurčić, 'Some palatine aspects of the Cappella Palatina in Palermo', *Dumbarton Oaks Papers* 41, 1987, 125–144; E. Borsook, *Messages in mosaic. The royal programmes of Norman Sicily 1130–1187*, Oxford 1990, 20–22; and W. Tronzo's forthcoming article in *Image and Word*. For the development of the west end of the chapel, see B. Brenk, 'La parte occidentale della Cappella Palatina a Palermo', *Arte medievale* 2nd ser., 4/2, 1990, 135–150.

[67] 'Ma qui l'adulazione arrivava all empietà. I Musulmani avvezzi a girare intorno la Casa di Dio, la Caaba, a baciar la pietra nera incastrata in un canto di quella, doveano inorridire all'invito di *adorare* nello stesso modo la casa del re.'

[68] Ibn Jubayr, 332.

[69] W. Madelung, 'Ismāᶜīliyya', *Encyclopaedia of Islam*, 2nd edn, IV.198–206; M. Canard, 'Fāṭimids', *Encyclopaedia of Islam*, 2nd edn, II.850–862. On Fāṭimid ceremonial and propaganda: M. Canard, 'L'imperialisme des fatimides et leur propagande', *Annales de l'Institut d'Études Orientales de la Faculté des Lettres d'Alger* VI, 1942–1947, 200–229 (reprinted in M. Canard, *Miscellanea Orientalia*, London 1973); M. Canard, 'Le cérémonial fatimite et le cérémonial byzantin. Essai de comparison', *Byzantion* XXI, 1951, 355–420 (reprinted in M. Canard, *Byzance et les musulmans du Proche Orient*, London 1973); P.A. Sanders, 'The court ceremonial of the Fāṭimid caliphate in Egypt', Ph.D. thesis, Princeton University, New Jersey 1984. (It is to the latter work that I owe my knowledge of the passages of Fāṭimid panegyric cited below.)

added that 'Just as the pilgrim kissed the corner (*rukn*) [of the Ka^cba], so have we kissed the walls of your palace'.[70] And the Spanish panegyricist Ibn Hāni' (d.973?) described a visit to the Fāṭimid palace in Cairo in these words: 'We are carried by noble camels, across vast expanses of desert, on pilgrimage to the *ḥarām* of the *imām*. Our dust covered locks are blessed by our coming to kiss the corner of his palace'.[71]

Here, the primary significance of the inscription from Roger's palace in Palermo, which urges the visitor to adore it in a manner which orthodox Islam reserved for the Ka^cba, is that it can have been borrowed only from the Fāṭimids, because no other Muslim dynasty encouraged such heterodox practices. Added to the evidence for close and cordial contacts between the two courts throughout the second quarter of the twelfth century, this incontrovertible borrowing demonstrates that King Roger and his ministers did model the Arabic facet of the newly founded Sicilian monarchy upon the Fāṭimid caliphate of Cairo. They may, perhaps, have also imitated other models, although there is no proof positive evidence that they did, but they most certainly imitated the Fāṭimid caliphate.

But exactly how far did King Roger and his successors carry their imitation of the Fāṭimids? Did they, for example, actually appear before their subjects in Fāṭimid garb? Seven panels on the ceiling of the Cappella Palatina show representations of a seated ruler, flanked by a pair of attendants. He wears a three-peaked and jewelled bonnet, and a seamless robe of patterned or figured fabric heavily adorned with gold, with inscription bands on the neck, arms, cuff and hem. The ruler is bearded and has what appear to be European features. In his right hand he holds a wine-cup, and in his left a stylised flower or leaf (fig. 7). These Sicilian panels closely resemble representations of seated rulers in a pose traditional in the world of Islam since at least the tenth century.[72] They are particularly close, for example, to a marble relief from al-Mahdiyya which

---

[70] Ibn ^cIdhārī, *al-Bayān al-Mughrib*, ed. G.S. Colin and E. Levi-Provençal, 2 vols, Leiden 1948–1951, 184; trans., 261–262: 'Les poètes . . . firent des éloges qui frisaient l'infidélité, comparant Mehdiyya à la Mekke et disant d'autres choses indignes d'être citées . . . Les poètes d'Ifrikiyya firent . . . des poésies dont nous citerons quelques vers pour montrer ce que ce prince [^cUbayd Allâh] jugeait permis et laissait dire en poésie: . . . 'Tu t'installes sur un noble sol qu'ont préparé pour toi tes glorieux messagers. Si le temple et ses entours, si les tombeaux qui s'y trouvent ont une haute importance, il est au Maghreb une noble demeure vers laquelle se tournent les faces des ceux qui prient et qui jeûnent: c'est la sacrée et respectable Mehdiyya, de même que l'on trouve au Tehāma la ville sacrée. Le *Mak'àm Ibràhim* peut n'y être pas, tes pieds en foulant le sol de cette cité font comme s'il y était; et si le pèlerin va à la Mekke donner un baiser au coin sacré (*rokn*), nous donnons le nôtre aux parois de ton palais!'
[71] Ibn Hāni', *Dīwān*, ed. Zāhid ^cAlī, Cairo 1933, IX.12–13, 147–48. For Ibn Hāni': M. Yalaoui, *Un poète chiite d'Occident au IVème/Xème siècle: Ibn Hāni' al-'Andalusi*, Tunis 1976.
[72] For example: the medallion of the ^cAbbāsid caliph al-Muqtadir (908–32) in Berlin, Staatliche Museen, Münzkabinett (H. Nützel, 'Eine Porträtmedaille des Chalifen el-Muktadir billah', *Zeitschrift für Numismatik* 22, 1900, 259–265; J. Sourdel-Thomine and B. Spuler, *Die Kunst des Islam*, Berlin 1973 [= *Propyläen Kunstgeschichte* 4], 240, pl. 155/a–b; the medallion of the ^cAbbāsid caliph al-Ṭā'i^c and the Būyid emir ^cIzz al-Dawla (975) in Istanbul, Arkeoloji Müze (M. Bahrami. 'A gold medal in the Freer Gallery of Art', in G.C. Miles, ed., *Archaeologica Orientalia in Memoriam Ernst Herzfeld*, Locust Valley, N.Y., 1952, 18–19; J. Walker, 'A unique medal of the Seljuk Tughrilbeg', in H. Ingholt, ed., *Centennial publication of the American Numismatic Society*, New York 1958, 691–95; Sourdel-Thomine and Spuler, 267, pl. 204/c–d). See also Sourdel-Thomine and Spuler, 311, pl. 268/c.

Fig. 7.
Palermo, Capella Palatina ceiling, painted panel (photo R. Hillenbrand)

Fig. 8.
Al-Mahdiyya, Tunisia: carved marble relief (after Marçais)

probably portrays the Fāṭimid caliph (fig. 8).[73] Did the Sicilian king actually look like the seated rulers in these images, so that they are literally portraits of the king?

Before answering this question, it will be helpful to discuss what is un-doubtedly the most familiar image of King Roger. This is the mosaic panel in S. Maria dell'Ammiraglio which shows Roger, dressed in the costume of the Byzantine emperor, receiving his crown from Christ.[74] In his magisterial study of the mosaics of S. Maria, Ernst Kitzinger points out the remarkable resemblance between the mosaic panel and a Byzantine ivory relief in the Pushkin Museum in Moscow which shows the emperor Constantine VII (913–959) receiving his crown from Christ.[75] As Kitzinger observes, the close resemblance of the mosaic to this relief can only be explained if it is assumed that an authentic Byzantine design served as a model for the mosaic panel. 'What degree of "realism" ', Kitzinger asks, 'may be attached to it [Roger's portrait] as a portrayal of the Norman king? Can it at one and the same time conform with an established prototype and be a recognizable portrait?' And, after listing and accepting the evidence that Roger did actually appear before his subjects in the attire of the Byzantine emperor, Kitzinger persists: 'Yet the question remains to be asked

[73] Tunis, Musée National du Bardo: Marçais, *L'architecture*, 117, fig. 76; M. Brett, *The Moors. Islam in the West*, London 1980, 65.
[74] Kitzinger, *The mosaics of St Mary's*, 189–197, 313–316, pls XXIII, XXV, 121–122, 165, 166–67, 171.
[75] Kitzinger, *The mosaics of St Mary's*, 190, n.344, pl. 190.

whether, or to what extent, the figure in the mosaic corresponds to that which contemporaries attending the King on a ceremonial occasion actually saw'.[76]

Kitzinger answers these questions by way of a discussion of Roger's costume and insignia. He argues, on the one hand, that the material and written evidence for what Roger actually wore does not include the regalia depicted in the mosaic panel, and, on the other, that these regalia, and in particular the jewelled loros and open diadem, had long fallen out of fashion in the Byzantine court. He concludes that the mosaic panel is not a realistic portrait of King Roger, but, on the contrary, is based upon a much earlier pictorial model. The mosaic panel, he argues, should be considered to be what Ernst Schramm has called a 'pictorial mold', by which is meant 'a stereotyped form passed on regardless of whether it corresponds to reality because it was still felt to be suitable in terms of its content'.[77] In short, although it seems clear from independent evidence that Roger did appear before his subjects in the guise of the Byzantine emperor, the mosaic panel of the king in S. Maria is not a realistic portrait of the king, but an image of his authority, a symbol of his power.

Returning, now, to the representations of seated rulers from the ceiling of the Cappella Palatina, we have already seen that they correspond to an established prototype. There is, however, an important difference between the Islamic prototype of the panels from the chapel ceiling and the Byzantine model for the mosaic of King Roger. Byzantine artists representing the ruler could draw upon a wide repertoire of images, of which the ruler crowned by Christ was only one.[79] Thus, as Kitzinger stresses, the choice of that particular model was highly significant.[80] In complete contrast, the canon of Islamic representational art, from the ninth century until the fourteenth, contained virtually a single pose appropriate to the monarch, that of the seated ruler.[81] Thus, the artists of the Cappella Palatina had only one prototype at their disposal, whether they were to paint a generic representation of royalty personified or the realistic portrait of a specific king. It follows that we cannot safely assume the panels from the royal chapel to be realistic portraits of the Sicilian king, and that we cannot take them to be evidence that he wore the costume of an Islamic ruler.

There is little independent evidence, written or material, upon this subject. Certainly, none of the surviving vestments of the Norman kings are derived from the Fāṭimid wardrobe, but this does not mean, of course, that other pieces of

---

[76] Kitzinger, *The mosaics of St Mary's*, 190–91.

[77] Kitzinger, *The mosaics of St Mary's*, 195. Cf. P.E. Schramm, *Herrschaftzeichen und Staatssymbolik*, 3 vols (Schriften der MGH, Deutsches Institut für Erforschung des Mittelalters, 13/i–iii), Stuttgart 1954, I.18: ' "Bildmodel": so möchte ich jene festen Formen bezeichnen, die – ohne Rücksicht darauf, ob sie der Wirklichkeit entsprachen – weitergegeben werden, weil sie dem Inhalt nach noch immer als passend empfunden wurden'.

[78] For the evidence that Roger appeared as the Byzantine emperor: K.A. Kehr, *Die Urkunden der normannisch-sicilischen Könige*, Innsbruck 1902 (reprinted Aalen 1962), 247, 265; Brühl, 67; Kitzinger, 'On the portrait of Roger II', n.3; D. Déer, *Der Kaiserornat Friedrichs II*, Bern 1952, 13–7; H. Enzensberger, *Beiträge zum Kanzlei- und Urkundenwesen der normannischen Herrscher Unteritaliens und Siziliens,* Kallmünz 1971, 89–92.

[79] A. Grabar, *L'empéreur dans l'art byzantin*, Paris 1936.

[80] Kitzinger, 'On the portrait of Roger II'; Kitzinger, *The mosaics of St Mary's*, 195–96.

[81] I know of no comprehensive study of this subject. E. Esin, '*Oldruğ-Tugruğ*, the hierarchy of sedent postures in Turkish iconography', *Kunst des Orients*, 7/i, 1970–71, 1–29, illustrates the complexity and range of the theme. See also the works cited in n.72 above, and their bibliography.

Sicilian royal costume, now lost, were not in the Fāṭimid style.[82] That this was indeed the case is suggested by the written sources. Ibn Jubayr, who visited the outer precincts of William II's palaces at Messina and Palermo in 1184–85, reports that the Sicilian king resembled Muslim rulers in many aspects of his rule, and, specifically, that 'the display of his finery is like the rulers of the Muslims' (*izhār zīnati-hi bi-mulūk al-muslimīn*).[83] Here, the word *zīna*, translated as 'finery', could well refer to costume. Similarly, the great historian Ibn al-Athīr, who is probably reporting the testimony of the Zīrīd prince Ibn Shaddād who visited Sicily in c.1156, records that the Sicilian court resembled that of Muslim rulers.[84] Ibn Jubayr seems to imply that the fashion for wearing Muslim dress had spread outside the court amongst the citizens of Palermo when he records that the Christian women 'dress in the costume of Muslim women . . . covered up and veiled'.[85] These sparse references do not amount to much, perhaps, but they are sufficient to suggest that, in all probability, the Norman kings did wear Islamic costume. The written sources do not, however, furnish details as to the precise nature of that costume, and, as we have seen, the representations of seated rulers from the ceiling of the Cappella Palatina cannot safely be used as evidence for what the Norman king actually wore. In short, the question whether the Sicilian ruler carried his imitation of the Fāṭimid caliph so far as to wear Fāṭimid vestments cannot be satisfactorily answered.

Did Roger's courtiers really embrace the walls and actually kiss the corner of his palace, as they were urged to do by the inscriptions from the Cappella Palatina? Again, the surviving evidence does not allow an unequivocal answer. Nonetheless, it seems to me clear that Roger's imitation of the Fāṭimid caliphate cannot have gone this far. The implicit meaning of the Fāṭimid rite was that the caliph, as the spiritual and biological descendant of the prophet Muḥammad, conveyed a holiness to his palace so that it became like the sanctuary of the Kaᶜba at Mecca. Roger, for all his adoption and adaptation of the trappings of Islamic monarchy, was a Christian ruler, and he would never have knowingly permitted his courtiers to revere him in a rite which acknowledged by implication the authenticity of Muḥammad's mission and the sanctity of the Meccan sanctuary. Nor is it likely that Roger's courtiers would have done so. His Muslim subjects, as Amari remarked, would certainly have recognised the allusion to the Islamic pilgrimage. As Sunnī Muslims, they would have been horrified by the heretical blasphemy of the Fāṭimid rite had they recognised it as such. In any case, they would have been utterly repelled by its adaptation to a Christian ruler and his palace chapel.[86] His Christian subjects would not for the most part have been able to read the Arabic verses, still less to understand their meaning, and neither his Latin barons nor his Greek ministers are likely to have taken with enthusiasm to

[82] For Sicilian royal costume: Bock, *Die Kleinodien*; H. Fillitz, *Die Insignien und Kleinodien des Heiligen Römischen Reiches*, Vienna and Munich 1954; A. Lipinski, 'Le insegne regali dei sovrani di Sicilia e la scuola orafa palermitana', in *Atti del Congresso internazionale si studi sulla Sicilia normanna, Palermo, 4–8 dicembre 1972*, Istituto di storia medievale, Università di Palermo, Palermo 1973, 162–194; Kitzinger, *The mosaics of St Mary's*, 192–93 and notes.
[83] Ibn Jubayr, 325.
[84] Ibn al-Athīr, *Al-Kāmil fī 'l-ta'rīkh*, ed. C.J. Tornberg, 14 vols in 8, Leiden 1867–74, X.133.
[85] Ibn Jubayr, 333.
[86] The *saraceni palatii*, themselves confined to the court, participated as far as they were able in the pilgrimage to Mecca and Medina: Ibn Jubayr, 326; Romuald, 234–36.

such an outlandish ritual. We may, I think, be confident that the rite was never performed in the Norman palace.

If this is correct, then it would seem to follow that the original meaning of the verses cannot have been understood by Roger and his ministers, and that those Muslims who did understand preserved a prudent silence. Therefore, the model copied in Sicily was not the rite itself, but rather the verse inscriptions which described it. Here we are on dangerous ground, for, as we have seen, almost nothing survives of the Fāṭimid palaces of Cairo, but it does seem to follow that they must have been adorned with inscriptions which included verses similar to those reproduced in Palermo. Reports of these would have been carried to Sicily, either by ambassadors to the Fāṭimid court or by artisans imported from Egypt, in such a way that it came to be believed at Palermo that verses urging courtiers to embrace the royal palace and kiss its corner were a characteristic symbol of Islamic royal authority, wholly appropriate to the Sicilian king.

This hypothesis incidentally helps to explain a puzzle. So far as I am aware, there exists no reference to the rite later than the caliphate of al-Muᶜizz (953–75). Indeed, there seems to be no evidence, independent of the panegyric verses exemplified above, that these rites were ever actually performed at the Fāṭimid court.[87] It is thus difficult to imagine how information about the rite could have reached Palermo as late as the twelfth century. But if the model imitated at the Norman court was not the rite itself but rather the inscriptions containing the Arabic verses which described it, then this difficulty disappears.[88]

It is ironic that, while it is the rite described in these verses that demonstrates incontrovertibly that the Norman kings modelled themselves upon the Fāṭimid caliphate, they did not imitate the rite itself, but merely the verse inscriptions which described it. There is a sense in which this characterises the whole imitation of the Fāṭimids by the kings of Sicily: they took as their model the external symbols of the caliphate, but ignored or remained ignorant of their intrinsic significance. This contrasts strongly with the Norman kings' imitation of Byzantium. As Kitzinger has shown, the model for the mosaic representation of King Roger in S. Maria was carefully chosen: it embodies Roger's ideal of absolute monarchic power, rejects the claims of the papacy over his kingdom, and constitutes an explicit challenge to the Byzantine emperor. It is 'an extraordinarily pregnant and concise statement in visual terms of Roger's concept of his own power and authority'.[89] In complete contrast, Roger's adoption and adaptation of Fāṭimid royal symbols had no ideological basis. Roger and his ministers may or – more probably – may not have been aware of the ideological foundations of Fāṭimid authority, but the king certainly laid no claim to them. Fāṭimid prototypes were chosen primarily because the caliphate was the most accessible and splendid exemplar of Islamic royal authority, not for the particular nature of the Fāṭimid monarchy. As the correspondence with al-Ḥafiz shows, Roger and his ministers were fully aware that the caliph himself was little more than a puppet, and that the caliphate was a hollow institution, long dominated by a succession of virtually

---

[87] I owe this perceptive observation to Ms Jane Jakeman, a D.Phil. student of St John's College at the Oriental Institute, Oxford.

[88] If this is so, then it suggests that the inscriptions adorned the eastern palace first built for al-Muᶜizz, and not the western palace which was completely rebuilt in 1058.

[89] Kitzinger, *The mosaics of St Mary's*, 191–97.

independent viziers.[90] The Fāṭimid caliphate was bankrupt, the Fāṭimid caliph was a powerless manikin, but the Fāṭimid palace was still a rich mine from which symbols of royal power could be extracted for the Norman court. Roger's model was neither the person of al-Ḥāfiẓ, nor the institution of the caliphate, but the gorgeous symbols of Islamic monarchy accumulated within the Fāṭimid palace. Roger stood outside it, and contemplated the beauty that it contained. He appropriated whatever symbol enhanced his own monarchy, but was attracted only by its external form, and cared nothing for its intrinsic meaning.

[90] Canard, 'Fāṭimids', 857–58 and bibliography.

THE *ORATIO DE UTENSILIBUS AD DOMUM REGENDAM PERTINENTIBUS* BY ADAM OF BALSHAM

Patrizia Lendinara

Adam of Balsham owes his fame to the *Ars Disserendi* or *Ars Dialectica*[1] which he wrote in 1132; but he is also the author of an *Oratio de utensilibus ad domum regendam pertinentibus*,[2] which takes the form of a letter addressed by Adam to a certain Anselm. The addressee of the *Oratio* has not been identified yet, and this is only the first of an interesting chain of interconnected problems presented by the fictitious letter written by Adam, which offers valuable insights on the contemporary society on both sides of the Channel. Most importantly the *Oratio* is an intriguing and little-known example of contextualized lexicography, which deserves to be studied for what it can tell about the level of the knowledge of Latin in the twelfth century.[3]

The work purports to describe a visit paid by Adam of Balsham to his home estate and has been taken, by Manitius[4] and the editors of the work,[5] as apparent evidence of a trip back to England, after a number of years spent in France. The

---

[1] The treatise has been published by L. Minio-Paluello, *Adam Balsamiensis Parvipontani Ars Disserendi* (*Dialectica Alexandri*) (Twelfth Century Logic. Texts and Studies, 1), Rome 1956. See also his important essay 'The "Ars Disserendi" of Adam of Balsham "Parvipontanus" ', *Mediaeval and Renaissance Studies* 3, 1954, 116–69.

[2] This is the title which occurs in the *accessus* of Paris, Bibliothèque Nationale MS lat. 14877. In other MSS (either in the *accessus* or the rubrics) the work is called *Epistola* (or *Oratio*) *magistri Ade Parvipontani* (or *de Parvo Ponte*); Adam's letter is also known as *Phale tolum* (from the two first words).

[3] The *Oratio* has been recently taken into examination by T. Hunt, *Teaching and Learning Latin in 13th-Century England*, 3 vols, Cambridge 1991, I, 165–77 and II, 37–62. Hunt is more interested in the use to which the *Oratio* was put and the accompanying commentaries and glosses, than in the work itself.

[4] M. Manitius, *Geschichte der lateinischen Literatur des Mittelalters*, 3 vols, Munich 1911–1931, III, 202–204.

[5] There are four complete editions of the *Oratio*, besides that by Hunt I, 172–76. Each one is based on a different MS: A.H. Hoffman von Fallersleben, *Epistola Adami Balsamiensis ad Anselmum*, Neuwied 1853, used a MS in the collection of Ferdinand Franz Wallrafs (now Köln, Historisches Archiv MS W*76). I am grateful to Dr Deeters of the Historisches Archiv of Köln for supplying me with this information which completes and corrects the data in Minio-Paluello, 'The "Ars Disserendi" ', 118; M. Haupt, for the text printed in his communication in *Berichte über die Verhandlungen der Königlich Sächsischen Gesellschaft der Wissenschaften zu Leipzig*, Phil.-hist. Kl. 1, 1849, 276–85, made use of Leipzig, Universitätsbibliothek MS 172; A. Scheler, 'Trois traités de lexicographie latine du XIIe et du XIIIe siècle. III', *Jahrbuch für romanische und englische Literatur* 8, 1867, 75–93, repr. in a separate vol., Leipzig 1867, 119–37, based his text on Brügge, Stadsbibliotheek MS 536; B. Hauréau, 'Notice sur le numéro 14877 des manuscrits latins de la Bibliothèque Nationale', *Notices et extraits des manuscrits de la Bibliothèque Nationale et autres bibliothèques* 34, 1, 1891, 44–54, repr. in his *Notices et extraits de quelques manuscrits latins de la Bibliothèque Nationale*, III, Paris 1891, 203–16, used Paris, BN MS lat. 14877 (which

letter, far from being the faithful report of a journey, is just the means for a clever scholar such as Adam to reply to Anselm's criticism, mocking, in his turn, contemporary personages and vogues. The single descriptions of the castle and its surroundings are made up by long strings of uncommon Latin words, building up lengthy sentences, which are correct from a grammatical point of view, but redundant and at times meaningless. Contrived in this way the letter is a shrewd reply to a remark made against Adam: as can be gathered from his prefatory remarks, Anselm had reproached him for using too plain language. Adam retorts with a display of unusual terms, such as *phala* 'tower' or *tholus* 'dome', to mention just the first two words of the *Oratio* ('Phalae tolum cillentibus radiis ...').[6] To be properly understood the charge raised against Adam should be set in the context of the many quarrels which sprang up between the masters of Paris (and other French towns) in the first part of the twelfth century, as some remarks in the letter show.[7] We are now unable to recover all the elements of the contest, which saw Adam pay back his adversaries with such a shrewd and caustic reply, but we are left with an interesting piece of lexical bravura which can still be unravelled and expounded.

Adam of Balsham[8] is also called Adam of Petit Pont (Adamus de Parvo Ponte or Parvipontanus): he is one of the English scholars who made a name for himself by going to teach in Paris in the twelfth century.[9] Arriving there in 1132, he set up

he collated in part with Paris, Arsenal MS 3807 and Cambridge, Gonville and Caius College MS 136) (see also notes 3, 28, 46 and 71).
[6] All reference will be to Hunt, I, 172–76, with the sole exception of the first sentence – 'Falle tholum scillentibus radiis' (172, 1) – which is quite corrupt in the version of the *Oratio* in London, BL MS Add. 8092, printed by Hunt. None of the available texts can be regarded as a critical edition. The fifteen known MSS of *Oratio* present several difficulties for the spelling and corruption of the hard words which occur in the work and owing to the glosses and commentaries which accompany the text and their (respective) lay-out.
[7] See, *inter alia*, F. Bertini, 'Riflessi di polemiche fra letterati nel prologo della "Lidia" di Arnolfo di Orléans', *Sandalion* 1, 1978, 193–209; B.M. Marti, 'Hugh Primas and Arnulf of Orléans', *Speculum* 30, 1955, 233–38; S. Pittaluga, 'Asini e Filosofastri (Da Aviano a Vitale di Blois)', *Sandalion* 8–9, 1985–86, 307–14 and B. Roy and H. Shooner, 'Querelles de maîtres au XIIe siècle: Arnoul d'Orléans et son milieu', *Sandalion* 8–9, 1985–86, 315–39. An interesting remark about Adam, unknown to Minio-Paluello, is quoted in the last article. In his commentary on Ovid's *Metamorphoses* Arnoul explains 'ex merito' by saying: '*Ex merito* secundum hoc quod meruit. Verbi gratia, multi librum magistri ADAM ipso uiuente "Culum artis" uocabant, qui modo eundem "Oculum artis" uocant' (at 330–31).
[8] He was born about 1105 at Balsham (Cambridgeshire) and belonged to a family of French origin (possibly coming from Beauvais). In 1147 he was appointed canon of Paris and in the same year he witnessed against Gilbert de la Porrée at the Parisian consistory (see J. Leclercq, 'Textes sur Saint Bernard et Gilbert de la Porrée', *Mediaeval Studies* 14, 1952, 107–28 at 107–109); in 1148 he attended the Council of Reims; Adam died on 6 August of an unknown year, according to the necrology of Le Val, diocese of Bayeux (A. Molinier, *Obituaires de la province de Sens* I, I (Recueil des historiens de la France. Obituaires, 1), Paris 1902, 630). What is known about his life has been inferred from the remarks contained in the *Oratio* and the frequent references to Adam in contemporary and later works (see note 14). Adam has been identified with the canon ('Adam canonicus Parisiensis') who was appointed bishop of Saint-Asaph in Wales in 1175 and died in 1187. Such an identification is rejected by Minio-Paluello, 'The "Ars Disserendi" ', 165–66, Huygens, 828 (see note 14) and Häring, 321 (see note 15) but it is still maintained by Gabriel, 10 (see note 13).
[9] The pattern of Adam's career is similar to that of John of Salisbury, Alexander Nequam and John of Garland. R.W. Southern, 'England's First Entry into Europe', in his *Medieval Humanism*

a school near the Petit-Pont,[10] whence his surname. The doctrine and methods of Adam persisted among some Paris masters, and his pupils were also given the sobriquet of Parvipontani,[11] from the place were they resided or taught. Adam was an expert in the technique of argumentation and a fine textual critic.[12] The novelty of his methods and the value of his treatise *Ars Disserendi* is now widely recognized.[13] His contemporaries left us with contrasting appraisals on his work and personality.[14]

Some of the references to Adam contained in the works of scholars who belonged to the same milieu[15] might help to explain the reasons why he composed, besides his treatise on logic, a piece such as the *Oratio de utensilibus*, so different in aim, content and language. John of Salisbury reports a remark that he attributes to Adam himself: 'dicebatque se aut nullum aut auditores paucissimos habiturum,

and other Studies, Oxford 1970, 135–57 at 140 remarks that: 'English scholars moved freely among the schools of Europe (. . .), England was a colony of the intellectual Empire of France (. . .), nearly every English scholar of distinction went to France to study and after did not return'.

[10] A. Berty and L.M. Tisserand, *Histoire générale de Paris. Topographie historique du Vieux Paris. Région centrale de l'Université*, Paris 1897, 357–63 (Rue du Petit-Pont). See also the illustrations in V.W. Ecgbert, *On the Bridges of Mediaeval Paris*, Princeton (N.J.) 1974. The school at the Petit-Pont is described in a letter (no. 4) by Guy de Bazoche (W. Wattenbach, 'Aus den Briefen des Guido von Bazoches', *Neues Archiv der Gesellschaft für ältere deutsche Geschichtskunde* 16, 1, 1891, 67–113 at 73: 'Pons autem parvus aut pretereuntibus aut spatiantibus aut disputantibus logicis dedicatus est').

[11] R.W. Hunt, 'Studies on Priscian in the Twelfth Century. II', *Mediaeval and Renaissance Studies* 2, 1950, 1–56 at 54–5. Hunt quotes a passage from a still unprinted portion of the *Ars Versificatoria* of Gervase of Melkley. Other groups of scholars were called after their master (e.g. Albericani, Porretani). At least twenty-five schools could be counted within a hundred miles of Paris in the twelfth century, according to R.W. Southern, 'The Schools of Paris and the School of Chartres', in *Renaissance and Renewal in the Twelfth Century*, ed. R.L. Benson and G. Constable, Cambridge, Mass. 1982, 113–37 at 119.

[12] See the remark by Alexander Nequam in his *Corrogationes Promethei*: 'Ubi Terricus deceptus legit "plunulas", antequam iste uenisset in manus magistri Ade Parui Pontis' (P. Meyer, 'Notice sur les "Corrogationes Promethei" d'Alexandre Neckam', *Notices et extraits des manuscrits de la Bibliothèque nationale et autres bibliothèques* 35, 2, 1897, 641–82 at 677); Terricus is Thierry of Chartres.

[13] See Minio Paluello, *Adam Balsamiensis*, xxi; 'The "Ars Disserendi" ', 135–40; A.L. Gabriel, 'English Masters and Students in Paris during the Twelfth Century', in his *Garlandia. Studies in the History of the Mediaeval University*, Notre Dame/Frankfurt a.M. 1969, 1–37 at 10; E. Tacchella, 'Giovanni di Salisbury e i Cornificiani', *Sandalion* 3, 1980, 273–313 at 302–305; P.V. Spade, 'Five Early Theories in the Mediaeval *Insolubilia*-Literature', *Vivarium* 25, 1987, 24–46 at 24–5.

[14] This evidence has been for a large part collected by Minio-Paluello, 'The "Ars Disserendi" ' at 159–68. Famous, besides the accounts of John of Salisbury, are the allusions contained in the *Metamorphosis Goliae Episcopi* vv. 193–196 (ed. T. Wright, *Latin Poems commonly attributed to Walter Mapes*, London 1841, 21–30 at 28 and R.B.C. Huygens, 'Mitteilungen aus Handschriften', *Studi Medievali* 3rd ser. 3, 1962, 747–72, at 771) and in chapt. XIX of the *Historia Ierosolymitana* by William of Tyre (ed. R.B.C. Huygens, 'Guillaume de Tyr étudiant. Un chapitre (XIX, 12) de son "Histoire" retrouvé', *Latomus* 21, 1962, 809–29 at 823 and 827–28).

[15] On Adam and the other masters who taught in Paris in the first part of the twelfth century see R.L. Poole, 'The Masters of the Schools at Paris and Chartres in John of Salisbury's Time', *The English Historical Review* 35, 1920, 322–42 repr. in his *Studies in Chronology and History*, Oxford 1934, 223–47 (at 335, 339 and 342); Gabriel, 7–10; N. Häring, 'Chartres and Paris Revisited', in *Essays in Honour of Anton Charles Pegis*, ed. J.R. O'Donnell, Toronto 1974, 268–329 (at 321–22); P. Riché, 'Jean de Salisbury et le monde scolaire du XIIe siècle', in *The World of John of Salisbury*, ed. M. Wilks. Oxford 1984, 39–61 (at 46).

si ea simplicitate sermonum et facilitate sententiarum dialecticam traderet, qua ipsam doceri expediret'.[16] This means that Adam did not explain dialectic with the clarity that was its due, according to John of Salisbury.[17] It was the difficulty of Adam's treatise which was criticized by his adversaries and certainly not its plainness. According to Minio-Paluello the treatise was written in 'a very artificial style, revealing Adam's passion for complicated patterns of sentences, for symmetry and parallelism, a vocabulary rich in new technical meanings, a systematic exclusion of most traditional terms of the art'.[18] In the light of these remarks, the main motivation given by Adam for writing the *Oratio* seems quite naive: 'Sed quoniam illum planum modum loquendi, quo uti consuevi, flumini visum usquequaque in ima admittenti comparabas, nobiliorem autem tibi videri dicebas orationem fluvio tenebrosa profunditate stagnanti comparandam, ad arbitrium geram tibi morem' (172, 14–17). Anselm's complaint might be addressed not against the style, but against Adam's vocabulary. He was apparently reluctant to use words which come from Greek, at least in teaching, as he remarks explicitly in the *Ars Disserendi*: 'docendo enim verbis grecissare nec placet nec convenit, quare non ex his que de arte docendi sunt sciendum' (Bk II, lvi).[19] This might have been the reason for Anselm's complaint, but the *Oratio* is not that full of Grecisms. There might be a more subtle reason for Adam's parade of words. As a matter of fact, in the letter there are not only unusual words, but a variety of common words; *ollae* and *patellae* are listed alongside *chrysendeta* and *anaglypha* (*vasa*). Adam, in my opinion, was rather replying to those who disliked his – extremely modern – use of an abstract terminology. In criticizing the emptiness of verbosity, he was himself, for once, being verbose. Another remark by John of Salisbury might give us the necessary clue: 'Solam "convenientiam" sive "rationem" loquebantur, argumentum sonabat in ore omnium, et asinum nominare uel hominem aut aliquid operum nature instar criminis erat aut ineptum nimis aut rude et a philosopho alienum'.[20] The remark is directed against the school of Cornificius, but there were some connections between Adam's teaching and that of the Cornificians.[21] It was the novelty of his language, the dearth of concrete terms, the new technical meaning given to old words[22] which were criticized by his adversaries and Adam chose to reply with this – apparently innocent – letter.

The initial description of the castle towering among thickets of thorn and bramble-bushes is interrupted by Adam's address to Anselm ('Pape! autem inquies, o mi Anselme, ut iam video, quorsum [h]oc tam scabrosum orationis respicit initium?' (172, 3–4)), who explains the reasons for writing his letter. The

---

[16] *Metalogicon* III, iii (ed. C.C.J. Webb, *Ioannis Saresberiensis episcopi Carnotensis Metalogicon Libri IIII*, Oxford 1929, 134).
[17] John of Salisbury, who appreciated the content of the *Ars*, did not like its style: 'Et utinam bene dixisset bona que dixit' (*Metalogicon*, IV, iii, ed. Webb, 167).
[18] 'The "Ars Disserendi" ', 117.
[19] Ed. Minio-Paluello, 41, 14–16; see also his remark: 'Latinis grecissare libet' (Bk II, xcvii at 67, 9). Many Grecisms were introduced in the second recension of the *Ars*: e.g. *aporiati* (Bk II, cii at 68, 19) or *pronoea* (Bk III, cxxxiii at 86, 16).
[20] *Metalogicon* I, iii ed. Webb, 12.
[21] Minio-Paluello, 'The "Ars Disserendi" ', 142–43 and 145–46; Tacchella, 302–305.
[22] For Adam's technical words of logic see Minio-Paluello, *Adam Balsamiensis*, xx; some of these features were modified in the second recension of the *Ars* where new examples were also added, see *idem*, xx-xxi, 'The "Ars Disserendi" ', 145–46 and Tacchella 304.

humble tone of the preface – 'Quoniam etiam, sed hoc rationabilius, latine orationis copiam in dies minui querebaris et rerum usitatissimarum nomina igno-
tissima esse vere dicebas, [i]deoque iam pene absoleta aput eruditos celebrari
oportere aserebas, in hoc autem quoque ex arbitrio tibi morem geram' (172,
19–22) – does not square with the tone of the concluding remarks 'Quod quidam
a ph[i]lologis, qui sola verba iactant, sicut numquam credi et sicut numquam
intelligi, et sicut inutile putari, sic illis inutile esse a me sepe accepisti(s).' (176,
27–29).

Adam adds a further reason for writing the letter, saying that he wanted to
instruct Anselm on how to run an estate. At the same time he wants to warn him
against too strong an attachment to material property, which would divert Anselm
from pursuing the true good. This adds a justification for the lists which follow
and gives Adam the opportunity to take further revenge on Anselm, who is
portrayed as a recent landowner, in contrast to Adam who prefers the modest
salary of a master to his paternal domain. Adam is reminded of his lineage and
name by a relative that he meets in the palace:

> 'Quid ergo', inquit consobrinorum qui aderant unus, 'cum sis nascione
> Anglicus, patria Balsamiensis et genere Bellvacensis, mansione, iam
> diutiore quam voluisse[m], Parisiensis, nu[m]cquid alicubi rurale edificium
> huic simile vidisti? Nonne tibi, si fieri posset, honestius iudicares rure
> paterno frui quam salarii lucello addictum fuisse?' (175, 13–17)

Unfortunately the identity of Anselm is unknown and it is remarkable that a scribe
who copied the *Oratio* at the end of the thirteenth century (in Cambridge, Gonville
and Caius College MS 136) identified him with Anselm of Canterbury (who died
in 1109), in an unlikely but intriguing guess. The name of a Magister Anselmus is
included, among other witnesses, in a charter by Peter Lombard, bishop of Paris
(1159–1160);[23] but such a coincidence of name, place and time does not have any
stronger support and the identification has been discarded by Minio-Paluello.[24]

The letter begins with describing the family estate where Adam is back after a
certain number of years spent in France. The castle is surrounded by fields and
pastures: there are horses of different breeds and a party of huntsmen passes by.
Once in the castle, which is protected by a rampart and a ditch, the visitor is
greeted by a multitude of relatives. In the great hall he also meets some hangers
on, whose appearance is sketched minutely. Supper is ready, so that food and drink
can be listed in detail. There are persons in attendance and several musicians
entertain the guest. The visit of the castle is resumed after the refreshment, to
begin with the tower where the armoury is lodged. The tour includes the library,
the chapel, the storehouse, the granary, the yard and the stables. The visitors do not
disdain to have a look at the wine-cellar and the kitchen. Then Adam turns back

---

[23] R. de Lasteyrie, *Cartulaire général de Paris ou recueil de documents relatifs à l'histoire et à la
topographie de Paris*, I, Paris 1887, 362 no. 415: 'astantibus (. . .) magistro Manerio (. . .) magistro
Anselmo'. Manerius might be the student of Peter Abelard mentioned in the *Metamorphosis
Goliae Episcopi* (v. 205) in the passage where Adam also is remembered (v. 194). See E. Lesne,
Les écoles de la fin du VIIIe siècle à la fin du XIIe (Histoire de la propriété ecclésiastique en
France, 5), Lille 1940, 232 note 10.
[24] 'The "Ars Disserrendi" ', 118.

to the hall where, after inspecting weaving implements, clothes and ornaments, he is finally free to retire to his apartment and fall asleep, not before listing the furniture of his chamber.

The *Oratio* opens with a quite bombastic description in which Adam carefully selects his words:

> Phalae tolum cillentibus radiis cum jam perspicuum prospicerem, ecce accellerantem morabantur tesqua cum scabriis, dumeta cum quisquiliis, confraga rubetis circumvallata.[25]

The first sentence has an involuted construction; the assonances (to begin with *l-l-l* in the first three words) and the other word-plays (e.g. 'perspicuum prospicerem'[26]) are carefully contrived and the thorns and bushes hint metaphorically at the difficulty of the language that Adam will employ in his letter.[27] Moreover, the first word, that is *phala*, is richly suggestive and, in my opinion, it points to the following use of a *phaleratus sermo* 'ornamented style'.[28] *Phala* 'wooden tower', *phalera* 'horse-trappings' and *phalanx* 'phalanx' were associated in medieval etymology,[29] as the commentary on the *Oratio* in Paris, BN MS lat. 14877 shows: '*Phala, tor de fust*, a phalon, quod est lignum; vel dicitur phala a phalando, et est summitas cæli. Inde phalanx, gis, est caterva cælestis. Item, a phala, quod est lignum, dicitur phalanga, gæ, *tinel*. Item a phalan, græce, quod est ornare latine, dicuntur phaleræ, arum, *harnas*. Inde phaleratus, ta, tum . . .'.[30]

The following descriptive sections are less affected, as far as the vocabulary and style are concerned, and Adam borrows freely from his sources, adding only a few fillers.[31] The various descriptions do not follow a set scheme and Adam

---

25 Ed. Hauréau, 43.

26 The Brügge MS has 'prospicuum prospicerem' see Scheler, 76.

27 The passage reminds of the use of *dumetum* in Cicero, *Acad. Quaest.* II, 35: 'cum sit enim campus in quo exultare possit oratio, cur eam tantas in angustias et Stoicorum dumeta compellimus?' ed. O. Plasberg, *M. Tullius Cicero, Academicorum Reliquiae cum Lucullo*, Stuttgart 1922, repr. 1961, 82; also *quisquilia* is used metaphorically by Cicero; for Adam's use of this author, see below.

28 This feature is pointed out in the *accessus* to the *Oratio* in Berlin, Staatsbibliothek Preussischer Kulturbesitz MS lat. fol. 607: 'Quamvis Moyses perceperat quo[modo] in carminibus verba falerata .i. ornata et exotica . . . eantur, tamen magister Adam de Parvo Ponte per verba alicuantulum inusitata proponit se scribere' (Hunt II, 58 note 168). For a similar *accessus* to the *Merarium* see Hunt I, 350.

29 Lat. *phala* is a word for which an Indo-Mediterranean origin has been put forward (from a base **fala*, whence also *falarica*); *phalera* is a loanword from Gk. φάλαρα (neutr. pl.) (from φάλος); *phalanx* is a loanword from Gk. φάλαγξ 'phalanx' (the primary sense of the Greek word is 'round piece of wood, log').

30 Hauréau, 41. See also the gloss (in fol. 154 of the same MS) quoted by Hauréau, 56: '*Phalæ tolum* et cet. Versus: Græce phalando lignum notat, ut phala monstrat./ Inde phalanx venit, inde phalanga, phalangæ./ Inde phalarica sit, pharo phalerasque phaloque.' In the first line of the *Distigium* by John of Garland there occurs the word *phalerae* – 'Cespitat in phaleris ippus blattaque supinus' (Hunt, I, 328) – and the initial verse of the *Exoticon* of Alexander of Hales – 'Chere theoren quem gignos crucis andro phalando' – contains *phalando*, which is glossed with *ligno* (Hunt, I, 304). A commentary on the *Exoticon* (Hunt I, 305) quotes the *Oratio* as regard to this word: '*Phalando* . . . phala -le turra lignea unde in Phale tolo dicitur "Phale tolum etc" [. . .] et inde dicitur hec phalanx -gis .i. societas [. . .] Similiter phalere -arum dicitur, que sunt ornamenta equina'.

31 Consider, for example, 'Inde usque ad portam et apothecam (*Etym.* XV, v, 8) et horrea (*ibidem*), hentheca (*ibidem*) multiplici referta, videbamus' (174, 28–29).

achieves the goal of listing a very high number of words without being tedious. The words employed by Adam are for the most part drawn from the *Etymologiae* of Isidore of Seville.[32] The words are borrowed mainly from Books XV–XX of the encyclopaedia. In several instances Adam borrows the words listed by Isidore as well as his remarks, e.g.: 'cervinos, qui olim gauran(t)es a vulgo vocabantur' (173, 2–3).[33] Isidore is referred to by name once ('secundum Isodori distinctionem' (173, 1)), in connection with the list of horse breeds, which draws on *Etym.* XII, i, 48. In some instances the order in which the words are listed in the sentences of the *Oratio* follows the order of the occurrence of the terms in the relevant section of the *Etymologiae*:

> Parte altera poculorum genera, fialas, pateras, crateres, ciatos, calatos, cimbias, calices, scalas, ampulas; parte tertia enofora, flaceis, lagenas, situlas, cantoros, ydrias, catinas, orcas, urceos, urceolos, sina, cereolos, dolia, cuppas, olearia et semicadia, scorticas, lenticulas. (175, 5–8)[34]

In other instances words drawn from different parts of the *Etymologiae* are wittily combined. The description of the armoury draws on *Etym.* VIII, v (*De armis*), vi (*De gladiis*) and ix (*De faretris*):

> Quibus inspectis, phalam licebat ascendimus, in qua armorum genera diversa speculari licebat. Stabant autem inter hastilia falarice torno facte, caice quas et cateias et teutonos nominant, pila, venabula, lancee amentate, ferrateque trudes vel sudes et acute cuspidis conti. In te(u)cis autem latentia intuebamur spicula et scorpiones in pharetris, arcus in coritis, mucrones in vaginis, pugiones in dolonibus. (174, 8–13)[35]

Adam is particularly skilful in employing the tools offered by his main source, that is the *Etymologiae*. An amusing example is offered by the manipulation of the section on the family relations (Bk IX). The ludicrous effect of the passage is

---

[32] According to Manitius, III, 204 a series of variant readings points to the use of a MS belonging to the T family, see *Isidori Hispalensis Episcopi Etymologiarum sive Originum libri XX*, ed. W.M. Lindsay (Oxford Classical Texts), Oxford 1911, but, in the absence of a critical edition of the *Oratio*, it is impossible to draw any conclusion concerning the branch of the tradition of the *Etymologiae* on which Adam drew.

[33] Drawn from *Etym.* XII, i, 53: 'Cervinus est quem vulgo guaranen dicunt'. For a multiple borrowing from Isidore, compare 'anologium, pulpito scene quod orcestra dicitur simile' (174, 26) with *analogium* (*in eo lector vel psalmista positus*) (*Etym.* XV, iv, 17), *pulpitum* (*in eo lector vel psalmista positus*) (XV, iv, 15) and *orchestra autem pulpitum erat scenae* (XVIII, xliv). All reference is to Lindsay edition.

[34] See respectively *Etym.* XX, v, vi and vii: *phiala* (v, 1–2), *patera* (v, 2), *crater* (v, 3), *cyathus* (v, 4), *calathus* (v, 5), *cymbium* (v, 4), *calix, scala, ampulla* (v, 5), *oenophorus* (vi, 1), *flasca* (vi, 2), *lagena* (vi, 3), *situla* (vi, 4), *cantharus* (vi, 3), *hydria* (vi, 4), *catinus, orca, urceus, urceolus* (vi, 5), *seriola* (vi, 6), *dolium, cuppa* (vi, 7), *olearium* (*vas*), *hemicadium, scortia* (vii, 1), *lenticula* (vii, 4); for *sinum* 'large round drinking vessel' see Varro, *De lingua Latina* V, 123 and Nonius Marcellus, *De compendiosa doctrina* 547 M.

[35] See *Etym.* XVIII, vi–ix: *hastile* (vii, 6), *falarica* (*est telum ingens torno factum*) (vii, 8), *caia, cateia* (*Huic meminit Vergilius dicens: 'Teutonico ritu soliti torquere cateias'*) (vii, 7), *pilum* (vii, 9), *venabulum* (vii, 4), *lancea* (*est hasta amentum habens in medio*) (vii, 5), *trudis* (*cum ferro lunato*) (vii, 3), *contus* (*acuta rotunditas*) (vii, 2), ? *theca* (ix, 3), *spicula* (viii, 1), *scorpio* (vii, 3), *faretra* (ix, 1), *arcus* (ix, 5), *corytus* (ix, 2), *mucro* (vi, 2), *vagina* (ix, 2), *pugio* (vi, 6), *dolo* (ix, 4).

produced by the clever utilization of the source and can be fully appreciated only by a reader who is able to spot it and recognize to which use (or rather misuse) it is put:

> Introeunti occurrunt qui me puerum vide[r]ant anno iam duodecimo reventem vis(it)entes: primo fratres (*Etym.* IX, vi, 5) germani (vi, 6) et nothi (v, 24) – nam uterinos (vi, 7) et spurios (v, 24) et favonios (v, 25) habere matris monogamia (vii, 14) pro[h]ibuerat; deinde consobrini (vi, 14) – patrueles (vi, 13) enim ibi reliqueram unde veneram, fratrueles (vi, 15) autem matertere (vi, 15) castitas non contulerat; (173, 14–18)

A different and more focused kind of satire is seen in another passage of the *Oratio*. Once again it is from a book of the *Etymologiae* (Bk X) that Adam draws the words which go to make up the description of a personage that the visitor sees during dinner in the castle:

> Inter cenandum autem quesivi a quodam colaterali mihi quisnam ille esset quem colomen, apparatorem, calamistratum, cesium, atratum, tiphatum[36] ibi cernebam. Et ille respondit 'Hunc plagiatorem, scevium, intentorem, biliosum, multatorem, ganeonem, oblact[at]orem, femellarium, buccum, balburrum, susoronem, lanistam, abigium nolo [ut] cognoscas'. Tunc ego subridens 'si verum', inquam, 'dicis, satis hominem notificas, (173, 43–48)[37]

The subtle juxtaposition of the anatomic terms listed by Isidore (*Etym.* Bk XI) allows Adam to sketch the most hideous portrait of a personage who was certainly not one of his friends:

> set ille quis est qui malis inequalibus, toxillis dissimilibus, oblongo ocello, columpna narium obliquata, pirula obtusa, penulis retractis, interfinio extante se uno aspectu notabilem prebet? (173, 48–50)[38]

This personage, according to the letter, lives in the castle, but more likely he was someone familiar both to Anselm and Adam and possibly belonged to the Paris circle of scholars.

Adam betrays a good knowledge of classic authors: one of the first sentences: 'Ego vero, si forte cotidiani cibi satietatem sapore acide te relevare dellectat' (172, 4–5) is modelled on a passage of Cicero's *De inventione*: 'Ut cibi satietas et fastidum aut subamara aliqua re relevatur aut dulci mitigatur'.[39] The next sentence

---

[36] Possibly 'haughty'; the neologism (a derivative of *typhus* 'arrogance') is not recorded elsewhere; other editions of the *Oratio* have *gypsatum* 'covered with gypsum', which does not match with the preceding adjective, *atratum*.

[37] Drawn from the *Etymologiae* are *apparitor* (X, 18), *calamistratus* (X, 57), *atratus* (X, 15), *plagiator* (X, 220), ? *scaevus* (X, 253), *biliosus* (X, 30), ? *mulcator* (X, 178), *ganeo* (X, 114), *oblectator* (X, 144), *femellarius* (X, 107), *bucco* (X, 30), ? *balbus* (X, 29) and *baburrus* (X, 31), *susurro* (X, 249), *lanista* (X, 159), *abigeius* (X, 14). *Calo* (here with a negative meaning 'drudge', as in Cicero and Horace) is a common glossary word (which mainly occurs in the plural *calones*); for *caesius* 'having grey or blue eyes' see Varro, *De lingua Latina* (VIII, 76); *intem(p)tator* 'trier' (here possibly 'tempter') occurs for the first time in the Vulgate (*Iac* 1, 13).

[38] See *mala* (XI, i, 44); *tonsilla* (i, 57) (I would suggest that the original reading was *maxillae* 'jaws'(i, 44–45)), *narium columna, pirula, pinnula, interfinium* (i, 48).

[39] *M. Tullius Cicero, Rhetorici libri duo qui vocantur de inventione*, ed. E. Stroebel, Stuttgart 1915, repr. 1965, 23 (I, 17).

'scriptiuncule materiam causam modum paucis verbis, adverte, pandam' (172, 5–6) echoes Virgil ('nunc qua ratione quod instat / confieri possit, paucis (adverte) docebo.' *Aen.* IV, 115–116). An entire line of Virgil ('ferratasque trudes et acuta cuspide contos' *Aen.* V, 208) is embodied in the list of arms: 'ferrateque trudes vel sudes et acute cuspidis conti' (174, 11–12).[40] It is interesting to remark that Adam interpolated the variant reading *sudes*[41] in his quotation. The reference 'secundum Maronis distinctionem' (172, 27) should be emended, as it is Varro, and not Virgil, who is referred to in the relevant passage of the *Etymologiae* ('ut Varro docet' XV, xiii, 6).

Adam made use of other sources. The quotations from Aulus Gellius are quite large and easily recognizable,[42] as they involve the borrowing of a series of words or long passages of the original. The *Noctes Atticae* were studied in the Middle Ages not only for their content, but also for their unusual vocabulary. Adam too does not seem interested in the stories told by Gellius, but rather in the technical vocabulary of some chapters of his work.[43] Gellius (*Noct. Att.* X, xxiii, 2) is echoed in the list of drinks: 'et potus item tria genera – celia, mulsum, [vinum] succinatum, nam lorea, passum, murina deerant' (173, 36–37). The first of the larger borrowings occurs at the end of the description of the dinner. Gellius's quotations from other Latin writers (Caesellius Vindex and Ateius Capito) are borrowed as well:

Post autem cenam luricines et tibicines audire iocundabamur. Deerant autem liticines, quos lituo cantare dicit Vindex[44] Cesellius in lectionum antiquarum conmentariis. Set et si[ti]cines deerant, quos aput sitos, id est supultos canere dicit Acteus Capito in coniectaneis. (174, 3–6)[45]

The same reworking of the original is evident in the description of the arms which are not to be found in the armoury of the castle: once again the quotation from Gellius is introduced by the verb *deero* 'lack', chosen by Adam to highlight these further borrowings, which are not drawn from his main source, but contribute to his word parade:

Deerant tela, iacula, gladii, quorum nomina in istoriis veteribus reperiuntur, hec 'soliferea, gesa, sparri, rumi, gestri, mesacule, rumpie, simbones,

---

40 Virgil's line was quoted in *Etym.* XVIII, vii, 2 as such: 'Eferatasque trudes et acuto cuspide contos' (*ferratasque* MS C).

41 Such a reading occurs in the so-called Mediceus MS of the *Aeneid* (Firenze, BML MS lat. xxxix, 1).

42 All reference is to *A. Gellii Noctes Atticae*, ed. P.K. Marshall, 2 vols (Oxford Classical Texts), Oxford 1968.

43 Adam's use of Gellius was pointed out by M. Hertz, *A. Gellii Noctium Atticarum libri XX*, Berlin 1883–1885, 2 vols, II, xxxiv–xxxvi. Gellius is quoted in the *Ars Disserendi*: e.g. at III, cxxxiii ed. Minio-Paluello, 86, 3–4 (from *Noct. Att.* V, xv).

44 The reference is to the grammarian Caesellius L. Vindex, whose work *Stromateus sive lectiones antiquae*, is known through later authors such as Gellius. Hunt emends the MS, which has *Judex*, at this place; several MSS of the *Oratio* share the reading *Judex Tessellius*.

45 Adam draws on: ' "Siticines" (. . .) "liticines et tubicines". Sed Caesellius Uindex in *conmentariis lectionum antiquarum* scire quidem se ait liticines lituo cantare et tubicines tuba; quid istuc autem sit, quo siticines cantant (. . .) Nos autem in Capitonis Atei *coniectaneis* invenimus "siticines" appellatos, qui apud sitos canere soliti essent, hoc est uita functos et sepultos' (*Noct. Att.* XX, ii, 2).

verutenses, clunacula, lingule', de quo genere Nevius in tragedeia Hesiona dixit 'sine mi gerere morem videar lingua verum lingula'. (174, 18–22)[46]

It is remarkable that the quotations are drawn both from Bk X and XX of the *Noctes Atticae* a choice which points to the use of a florilegium, although the coupling of these two books of Gellius's work is rather unusual.[47]

One further source was identified by the fourteenth century scribe of Leipzig, UB MS 172 and listed, besides Isidore and other more vague references, in the colophon 'Explicit expositio super faletholum magistri ade a petro preposito suo laboriose conquisita et excerpta a libris jeronimi gregorii. augustini. ysidori. pauli. ad karolum regem magistro gerhardo scripta'.[48] Paul the Deacon dedicated his compendium of the epitome of *De verborum significatu* by Festus to Charles the Great, 'Domno Regi Karolo Regum sublimissimo'.[49] His work was drawn upon by glossaries; it also became a sourcebook for several authors. A few words of the *Oratio* go back to this compilation, e.g. *condictum*, other terms explained by Paul the Deacon also occur in other lexicographers such as Nonius Marcellus (*murrina*)[50] and in Isidore's *Etymologiae* (*cardo, decumanus, investes, squalidus,* etc.).[51]

Some of the words ascribed to Isidore or the other sources might be known to Adam through all-Latin glossaries. The *Oratio* contains a small number of words which were likely drawn from glossaries, e.g. *magalia, obgannire, parasitaster*.[52]

---

[46] Hunt, in line with his quite disputable editorial procedures, emends the words of the *Oratio* on Gellius: 'semiphalarica, soliferrea, gaesa, lancea, spari, rumices, trifaces, tragulae, framea, mesanculae, cateiae, rumpiae, scorpii, sibones, siciles, ueruta, enses, sicae, machaerae, spathae, linguale, pugiones, clunacula. De "lingula" (. . .) cuius meminit Naevius in tragoedia *Hesiona*. Versum Naevi apposui: sine me gerere morem uidear lingua, uerum lingula.' (*Noct. Att.* X, XXV, 2–3). This passage and its variant readings in Oxford, Bodleian Library MS Rawlinson G 99 are taken into examination by R. Ellis, 'A Contribution to the History of Transmission of Classical Literature in the Middle Ages, from Oxford MSS', *The American Journal of Philology* 10, 1889, 159–64.

[47] For the transmission of Gellius see M. Manitius, 'Beiträge zur Geschichte der römischen Prosaiker im Mittelalter. V. Gellius', *Philologus* 48, 1889, 564–66 and P.K. Marshall, J. Martin and R.H. Rouse, 'Clare College MS 26 and the Circulation of Aulus Gellius 1–7 in Medieval England and France', *Mediaeval Studies* 42, 1980, 353–94. The work was used, *inter alia*, by John of Salisbury, see J. Martin, 'John of Salisbury and the Classics', *Harvard Studies in Classical Philology* 73, 1969, 319–21 (abstract of her Harvard Diss.); 'John of Salisbury's Manuscripts of Frontinus and Gellius', *Journal of the Warburg and Courtauld Institutes* 40, 1977, 1–26; 'Uses of Tradition: Gellius, Petronius, and John of Salisbury', *Viator* 10, 1979, 57–76 and R.M. Thomson, 'William of Malmesbury, John of Salisbury and the *Noctes Atticarum* [sic]', in *Hommages à André Boutemy*, ed. G. Cambier (Collection Latomus, 145), Brussels 1976, 367–89.

[48] Haupt, 276.

[49] *Sextus Pompeius Festus, De verborum significatu quae supersunt cum Pauli epitome*, ed. W.M. Lindsay, Leipzig 1913, repr. Hildesheim 1965, 1.

[50] 551 M.: *Nonius Marcellus. De compendiosa doctrina*, ed. W.M. Lindsay, 3 vols, Leipzig 1903, repr. Hildesheim 1964, 884. A use of Nonius might be surmised for *conluvio* 82 M., *investes* 45 M. and *sinum* (see note 34). On the other hand, *murrina* also occurs in other works known to Adam and in glossaries.

[51] See respectively 34, 21 (*condictum*) and 131, 1 (*murrina*); 62, 26; 62, 25; 506, 1–2; 441, 8.

[52] G. Goetz, *Corpus Glossariorum Latinorum a Gustavo Loewe incohatum*, 7 vols, Leipzig 1888–1923, repr. Amsterdam 1965 (hereafter *CGL*). In the first instance ('magalibus sive mappalibus' (Hauréau, 46; Scheler, 78; Hunt, 172, 28–29 has only 'mappalibus') Adam borrows both the lemma and *interpretamentum*: 'Magalia mappalia id est tabernaculum' (*CGL* IV, 112, 41); 'Obgannit subtiliter murmurat' (*CGL* V, 469, 54; 573, 41; 574, 8) 'Parasitaster diminutiuum nomen est a parasito' (*CGL* V, 585, 16).

Adam did not make use of class-glossaries:[53] he did not resort to this sort of compilations (which were made up by several sections, each one grouping terms related to a specific topic) and to compose the *Oratio*, whose sections usually contain words belonging to the same lexical field (e.g. the description of the kitchen), he drew rather on the *Etymologiae*.[54]

There are a few sentences (in the descriptive sections) which cannot be derived from the above-mentioned sources, and it is possible that they describe something which had a counterpart in English (or French) reality. There were necessarily some descriptions of the estate for which Adam could not find a model either in the Spanish encyclopaedia of the seventh century or in his other sources. The structure of the main building, several features of its architecture (reflecting the contemporary way of life and military technique), the neighbourhood of the manor and even the landscape are contemporary. Adam might have had some familiar estate in mind when he sketched this accurate description:

> Et iam circuitu pergirato, ab occidentali domus fronte, qua prius in meniana exieramus, ad orientalem partem nunc a promtuariis venimus. Egredimur deinde ex latere septemtrionali, ubi hostium patebat, meridiano, quo primo introieramus, oppositum . . . (175, 20–23)

In this respect the *Oratio* can be regarded as a small but precious source, yielding interesting details such as:

> Ecce vallum aspicio mole terre intrinsecus regecta, circumluvio extrinsecus velud ad ripam alludente, vallos innumerabiles sudibus vi lentatis intextos, inter[vallis] angustis distantes, velud munitionem sustinentes. (173, 11–13)

The *Oratio* has many forerunners in literary (or rather utilitarian) compositions of the late Latin period and the Middle Ages. It shares some of their features and, at the same time, has some individual traits. To insert words drawn from glossaries and encyclopaedic compilations into a lexical continuum had been a teaching tool employed by masters since the Late Roman period. One of the elements of the *Hermeneumata Pseudo-Dositheana*, a schoolbook used to teach Latin to Greeks (or possibly Greek to Latins) is the colloquium.[55] In these colloquies, which are entirely fictitious too, the pupil is questioned about his daily activities. 'Hodie quid fecisti?' asks the master, and the boy replies: 'Surrexi mane expergefactus et uocaui puerum. Iussi aperire fenestram. . .',[56] giving details about his

---

[53] For a general introduction on the different types of glossaries see G. Stein, *The English Dictionary before Cawdrey* (Lexicographica, Series Maior, 9), Tübingen 1985; class-glossaries are taken into examination at 32–43.

[54] It must be remarked that the *Etymologiae* had been one of the main sources of Anglo-Saxon class-glossaries such as the Glossary of Antwerp and London, see R.T. Meyer, 'Isidorian "Glossae Collectae" in Aelfric's Vocabulary', *Traditio* 12, 1956, 398–405.

[55] For the use to which the *Hermeneumata* were put in the Middle Ages see A.C. Dionisotti, 'From Ausonius' Schooldays? A Schoolbook and its Relatives', *Journal of the Roman Studies* 72, 1982, 83–125; 'From Stephanus to Du Cange: Glossary Stories. Part I', *Revue d'histoire des textes* 14–15, 1984–85, 303–36 and 'Greek Grammars and Dictionaries in Carolingian Europe', in *The sacred nectar of the Greeks: the Study of Greek in the West*, ed. M.W. Herren (King's College London Medieval Studies, 2), London 1988, 1–56.

[56] *CGL* III, 379.

morning washing and dressing, the visit to the baths, his school lesson, etc. The questions are a mere fictional device to allow the pupil to practise with the words he had already memorized and which are listed in other sections of the *Hermeneumata*. The *Hermeneumata* had a large circulation in the Middle Ages, especially in the British Isles, where they were introduced very early.[57] Whereas the original colloquies were written in Greek and Latin, those composed in the British Isles were written in Latin and furnished with occasional glosses in Latin, Celtic or Old English.[58] The most famous of these colloquies is that written by Ælfric, abbot of Eynsham.[59] In this piece, which is accompanied by a continuous interlinear gloss in Old English, various personages (a hunter, a fisherman, a cook, etc.) debate about the value of their respective occupations. The fictitious dialogue allows the pupil who plays the part of the hunter to list all the animal names he has learned. In his turn, the oblate who impersonates the fisherman displays his knowledge of fish names and so on. The ability of Ælfric bestows a natural allure on the conversation and also his *Colloquy* has been taken for evidence of Anglo-Saxon life.[60] One of the pupils of Ælfric, a certain Ælfric Bata is the author of an enlarged version of the *Colloquy* and of other colloquies, which are called 'difficiliora' in the MS which contains them.[61] In these 'harder' colloquies the lexicographic intent is much more evident. The lists of the trees which are supposed to grow in the orchard of the monastery amount to some hundred different species and among the hunter's quarry there are animals which never belonged to the English fauna: 'Capio utique ceruos et ceruas et uulpes et uulpiculos et muricipes et lupos et ursos et simias et fibros et lutrios et feruncos. . .'.[62] The abovementioned scholastic colloquies offered Adam a model for building up long sentences with words drawn from glossaries,[63] but they are devoid of the polemic intent which gives life to the *Oratio*.

We have rather to look to France to find models for this feature of his letter. At the end of the ninth century Abbo of Saint-Germain-des-Prés wrote a long poem in three books: the *Bella Parisiacae urbis*.[64] The third book of the poem is not concerned with the siege of Paris, but is aimed to instruct a young cleric (addressed as 'cleronomus'), through a series of maxims such as: 'Basileus constes,

[57] According to G. Baesecke, *Der Vocabularius Sti. Galli in der Angelsächsische Mission*. Halle a. d. S. 1933, 81 and 109, a copy of the *Hermeneumata* was taken along by Theodore of Tarsus, the archbishop of Canterbury (669–691). On the role of Theodore as a teacher see M. Lapidge, 'The School of Theodore and Hadrian', *Anglo-Saxon England* 15, 1986, 45–72.

[58] See G.N. Garmonsway, 'The Development of the Colloquy', in *The Anglo-Saxons. Studies in some Aspects of their History and Culture presented to Bruce Dickins*, ed. P. Clemoes, London 1959, 248–61.

[59] G.N. Garmonsway, *Ælfric's Colloquy*, London 1939, repr. Exeter 1978.

[60] *Ibidem*, 14–5.

[61] W.H. Stevenson and W.M. Lindsay, *Early Scholastic Colloquies* (Anectoda Oxoniensia, Mediaeval and Modern Series, 15), Oxford 1929, 67; Ælfric Bata's colloquies are printed at 27–66, 67–74, 75–102.

[62] Stevenson and Lindsay, 80. A similar artificiality characterises the other colloquies printed by Stevenson and Lindsay, 1–11, 12–20 and 21–26.

[63] On the relationship between colloquies and glossaries see P. Lendinara, 'Il *Colloquio* di Ælfric e il colloquio di Ælfric Bata', in *'feor ond neah'. Scritti di Filologia Germanica in memoria di Augusto Scaffidi Abbate*, Palermo 1983, 173–249.

[64] See P. Lendinara, 'The Third Book of the *Bella Parisiacae Urbis* by Abbo of Saint-Germain-des-Prés and its Old English Gloss', *Anglo-Saxon England* 15, 1986, 73–89.

abstemius antigraphusque' (III, v. 26).[65] It is evident that the hexameter is made up by a series of words drawn from glossaries.[66] Abbo's verses intended to mock the penchant for rare words (in particular words of Greek origin) which characterized the works of many contemporary scholars.[67]

The descriptive sections of the *Oratio* might also be compared to certain portions of a poem known as the *Quid suum virtutis*, which was once attributed to Hildebert of Lavardin. The poet, who is a virtuoso of enumeration, describes the effect of the music played by Orpheus on the different elements of the creation, whose names are skilfully strung in his verses:

> En pisces muti vocis dulcedine capti
> Extantes summis conspiciuntur aquis.
> Non gurgustia, non hamus, non retia terrent,
> Quin caput emersi dulce melos capiant.
> Lucius et mullus, lupus, allec, tructa, timallus,
> Hamio cum squilla, scorpio cum clepea,
> Congrus, esox, unguis, lolligo, locusta, peloris,[68]

These are, in my opinion, the two models followed by Adam. The scholastic colloquies provided the model for stringing together long lists of words belonging to the same semantic field. This is evident in several lists of the *Oratio*, e.g.: 'Continebat autem archa quam aperuerat apisces, infulas, pillea, galliaria, ciclare, feminarum diademata, capitula, nimbos, mitras cum redimiculis, reculas, vittas cum tenuis, reticula, discriminalia, acus, ancias, inaures et hec omnia capitis ornamenta erant.' (175, 45–48).[69] Poems such as the *Bella Parisiacae urbis* or the *Quid suum virtutis* share lexicographic concern with the scholastic colloquies and draw consequently on the same sources, but they aim rather to show the learning of the author and to parade his lexical virtuosity. They are similar to the *Oratio* in their covert satire. Abbo mocked his adversaries, by showing what he was capable of doing with 'hard' words and Adam showed Anselm what a large extent of

---

[65] *Abbonis Bella Parisiacae urbis*, ed. P. von Winterfeld, *MGH, Poetae Latini Aevi Carolini* IV, 1, Berlin 1899, 72–121.

[66] All the difficult words of the third book of the poem were glossed by Abbo himself. Both *basileus* and its gloss *rex* and *antigraphus* and its gloss *cancellarius* occur in the *Scholica graecarum glossarum* (B 1 and A 30). *Abstemius* and its gloss *sobrius* have a counterpart in the *Liber glossarum* (A 403) and other glossaries, e.g. *CGL* V, 6, 19, etc.

[67] A mocking vein animates a contemporary poem by Ucbald of Saint-Amand, the *Ecloga de calvis* (ed. P. von Winterfeld, *MGH, Poetae Latini Aevi Carolini* IV, 1, Berlin 1899, 265–71), made up of 146 lines which contain only words beginning with the letter C. This poem, which can be rightly considered a lexical bravura, makes use of a different stock of words. There are several medieval works, both in verses and prose, written in a vein similar to Adam's: a survey of such compositions has yet to be written. Among the works which put glossary words to a (possible) jocular use is the *Praefatio* to the so-called Salmasian sylloge (Paris BN MS lat. 10318) ed. D.R. Shackleton Bailey, *Anthologia Latina*, I. Stuttgart 1982, 28–31.

[68] A. Paravicini, *Quid suum virtutis. Eine Lehrdichtung des XI. Jahrhunderts* (Editiones Heidelbergenses, 21), Heidelberg 1980, vv. 677–683. For this and other features of the poem see P. Lendinara, 'Una nuova versione del *Quid suum virtutis*', *Schede Medievali* 14, 1988, 15–28.

[69] The words are drawn from *Etym.* XIX; xxx and xxxi: *apex* (xxx, 4), corona (xxx, 1–2), *infula* (xxx, 4), *pilleum* (xxx, 5), *galearium* (xxx, 5), ? *cidarim* (xxx, 6), *diadema* (xxxi, 1), *capitulum* (xxxi, 1; 3), *nimbus* (xxxi, 2), *mitra* (xxxi, 4; 5), *redimicula* (xxxi, 5), *discriminalia* (xxxi, 8), *acus* (xxxi, 9), ? *antiae* (xxxi, 8), *inaures* (xxxi, 10).

vocabulary he could master. The maxims for the cleric, as well as the descriptions of the English estate, are a mere pretext, a frame into which to insert lines or sentences full of common and uncommon words.

Such words, at least in the intention of the authors, were not meant to be taught or learned, but this was the use to which Abbo's poem and Adam's letter were put by the following generations of scholars, who used both works as school exercises.[70] It is interesting to note the difference between the original destination of the *Oratio* and the use it was put to. The polemic aspect was disregarded and the letter was valued as a repository of 'exotic' vocabulary, as the remark which prefaces its version in Cambridge, Gonville and Caius College MS 136 shows: 'Materia hujus opuscoli sunt nomina diversa et exoticaque, in redeundo a Gallia in Angliam, vidit, in notando res diversas'.[71] The words selected by Adam and strung together in jest had the unexpected result of making his letter so popular: the *Oratio* was copied over and over and supplied with glosses and commentaries, which prove that Adam's work remained popular for more than two centuries.[72]

The *Oratio de utensilibus* does not occupy an isolated place in the context of the lexicographic production of the twelfth century and the following period. It has been considered the model of the *De nominibus utensilium* by Alexander Nequam.[73] This work is not animated by any polemic intent: it begins with the statement: 'Qui bene vult disponere familie sue et rebus suis, primo provideat sibi in utensilibus et in suppellectilibus'[74] and its only concern is to enumerate a share of Latin words which are grouped according to their semantic fields. Nequam does not provide any sort of frame and the words are monotonously listed in sentences such as this: 'In quoquina sit mensula, super quam olus apte minuatur et lecticula et pise et pultes et fabe frece et fabe silique et fabe ex[s]ilique et milium et cepe et huiusmodi legumina, que resecari possunt.'[75]

Nequam had attended the school of the Petit Pont[76] and was an admirer of

---

[70] See respectively Lendinara, 'The Third Book', 83–85 and Hunt, I, 170.

[71] P. Meyer, 'Les manuscrits français de Cambridge IV. Gonville et Caius College', *Romania* 36, 1907, 481–542. Meyer printed a few excerpts of the *Oratio* and the accompanying glosses (at 485–88). V. Rose, *Egidii Corboliensis Viaticus*, Leipzig 1907, xvii–xix, included extracts from Wolfenbüttel, Herzog August Bibliothek MS Guelf. 13. 10 Aug. 4°; J.K. Floyer and S.G. Hamilton, *Catalogue of MSS preserved in the Chapter Library of Worcester Cathedral*, Oxford 1906, 186–88, printed the fragment of the *Oratio* in Worcester Cathedral MS Q. 50.

[72] Further witness for the success of the *Oratio* is provided by the catalogues of medieval libraries, see Manitius, III, 204 and Hunt, I, 166.

[73] See Häring, 321; Gabriel, 19–20 and Hunt, I, 177.

[74] Hunt, I, 181, 1–2. The work is published at 181–90 from London, Wellcome Historical Medical Library MS 801^A; it had been previously printed by T. Wright, *A Volume of Vocabularies illustrating the Conditions and Manners of our Forefathers, as well as the History of the Forms of Elementary Education and the Languages spoken in this Island*, Priv. print. 1857, 96–119 (from London, BL MS Cotton Titus D. xx, with excerpts from Paris MSS supplied by M. Delisle) and by A. Scheler, 'Trois traités de lexicographie latine du XIIe et du XIIIe siècle. II', *Jahrbuch für romanische und englische Literatur* 7, 1866, 58–74 and 155–173, repr. in a separate vol., Leipzig 1867, 84–114.

[75] Hunt, I, 181, 3–5. The work has several connections with *Sacerdos ad altare* (which contains a list of writing tools), see Hunt, I, 250–73; on *De nom. utens.* see Hunt, I, 177–90 and II, 63–122.

[76] 'Qua Modici Pontis parva columna fui' (*De laudibus divinae sapientiae* X, v. 334 ed. T. Wright, *A. Neckam, De Naturis Rerum with the Poem of the same Author De Laudibus Divinae Sapientiae* (RS), London 1863, 503); see Gabriel, 19. On the links between the second recension of the *Ars Disserendi* and Nequam see Minio-Paluello, *Adam Balsamiensis*, xxii.

Adam of Balsham;[77] it is possible that he drew the inspiration for his *De nominibus utensilium* from the *Oratio de utensilibus* but, at a closer inspection, the two works reveal a number of considerable differences. First of all, they differ in the subject-matter and, as a consequence, in the topics (and with them the class of words employed). Also the sources of the two works are different and Nequam does not borrow either from Isidore or the literary sources to which Adam had recourse. The *Oratio* merely provided the model for the lay-out of the lexical description. Nequam's treatise, as well as the following works of the same kind did away with its elaborate frame. A new presentation of Latin vocabulary, combined into a sort of continuous discourse was inaugurated by Nequam and Adam's influence might not be that relevant.

In my opinion, the *De nominibus utensilium* is rather the descendant of the class-glossaries which were in use in England since the Anglo-Saxon period (also Ælfric's *Glossary* belongs to this kind of glossary) and continued to be popular in the Anglo-Norman age. The language taught at school was still Latin, but instead of listing a group of terms under a heading or rubric, Nequam put them together in a series of sentences with a repetitive structure. Several portions of the *De nominibus utensilium* have a parallel in the sections of Anglo-Norman glossaries. There is a close relationship between the *De nominibus utensilium* and an Anglo-Norman *Nominale*.[78] Several sections of this glossary (which contains eighteen different classes of words) have a counterpart in Nequam's treatise, to begin with the house (sect. II), the arms (III) and the other buildings (IV). There are also parallels with the names listed in the *Nominale* for different tools and house implements (VI), articles of food (VII), fish (VIII), bed furnishing (IX), domestic animals (XIII), domestic birds (XIV) and wild birds (XVI).

The evolution of society produced a change in the content of class-glossaries and brought along an increase in the number of the subject fields – which were only eight in Ælfric's *Glossary*. Life was no more confined to the monastery, the pupils were lay schoolboys and the schools were now located in towns full of life. The new glossaries came to include sections of words connected with the new and manifold activities: trades and tradesmen and the various articles made and sold. The lists of words became more mundane, the sections on the house furniture, clothes and ornaments became larger and the object of everyday life came to include implements peculiar to women, spinning and weaving tools, etc. This is in part true of the *De nominibus utensilium* and will become particularly evident in other lexicographic works[79] such as the *Dictionarius* of John of Garland.[80] The *Oratio*, owing to its main source, is not that 'modern'; to be faithful to the frame

---

[77] Nequam calls Adam: 'nostro fulgens tempore sidus' (*Suppletio defectuum operis* II, 1578 quoted from Minio-Paluello, 'The "Ars Disserendi" ', 161).

[78] J. Priebsch, 'Ein anglonormannisches Glossar', in *Bausteine zur romanischen Philologie. Festgabe für Adolfo Mussafia zum 15. Februar 1905*, Halle 1905, 534–56. Only half of the entries of the glossary are printed.

[79] An interesting work, with large lists of tradesmen and their goods, apparently unknown to Hunt, was published by G. Waitz, 'Handschriften in englischen Bibliotheken', *Neues Archiv der Gesellschaft für ältere deutsche Geschichtskunde* 4, 2, 1878, 323–93 at 339–43 (from London, BL MS Add. 8167).

[80] For the *Dictionarius* see Hunt, I, 191–203, with edition of the text from Dublin, Trinity College MS 270 at 196–203 and II, 123–56. The work had been taken into examination and printed by A. Scheler, 'Trois traités de lexicographie latine du XIIe et du XIIIe siècle. I', *Jahrbuch für romani-*

of his letter, Adam is compelled to exclude also 'traditional' lexical fields such as the animal names (with the exception of the horses) and to introduce the names of the human body and its parts on the pretext of portraying the mysterious inhabitant of the castle. Moreover, he never loses control over his material and therefore the lexical selection of the *Oratio* is characterized by a great restraint. Adam would never include a hippopotamus among the fish courses as Nequam does in his description of the kitchen.[81]

Notwithstanding the presence of common situations – the kitchen and its implements, the house furniture, the bed furnishing, the clothes and the personal ornaments, the food, the building and equipment of castles and the arms (I follow the order in which the groups of words occur in the *De nominibus utensilium*) – there is no overlapping between the two works, and the same result is obtained when the *Oratio* is compared to the *Dictionarius* of John of Garland. The three works share a few words: the names of a couple of arms: *iaculum* and *gaesum* (*Oratio* and *Dict.*), which both occur in the above-mentioned *Nominale*;[82] shared is also the well known pair of horse caparisons: *antela* and *postela* (*Oratio* and *De nom. utens.*). A number of implements of the kitchen and the table – *caccabus*, *manutergium*, *olla* and *patella* – occur in all the works under examination (the first two are also included in the *Nominale*),[83] *urceus* is found both in the *Oratio* and the *Dictionarius*, while *urceolus* is shared by the *Oratio* and the *De nom. utens.*; Adam of Balsham and John of Garland include the *hydria* and the *pelvis* in their lists, while Adam and Nequam have *parapsis*, *mantile* and *gausape* in common.

There were several different glossaries in circulation, whence vocabulary could be drawn and only a small portion of such texts is now available in print. On the other hand, the twelfth- and thirteenth-century works where vocabulary was collected in continuous discourse are far from being a homogeneous corpus. They were not written with the same audience in mind and their authors were moved by different aims. The *Oratio* by Adam of Balsham holds a prominent position among the works of this kind: its structure is well balanced and the content enlivened by witty remarks; this 'false' letter lends itself to different readings and deserves to be read anew.[84]

---

sche und englische Literatur 6, 1865, 43–59, 142–62, 287–321, and 370–79, repr. in a separate vol., Leipzig 1867, 1–83 and by T. Wright, 120–38.

[81] 'Item salsamentum omnibus pissibus non dicitur competere, nam sunt diversi, utpote mugiles, amphivia, congrus, murena, musculus, ep[h]imera, gobio, melanurus, capito, ypotamus. . .' (Hunt, I, 181–17–19).

[82] Sect. III at 537: 'hec gesa, *gisarme*'; 'hoc iaculum vel telum, *dart*'.

[83] Sect. VI at 538: 'hoc manitergium, *touvalle*', 'hic cacabus vel lebes, *cauderon*'. The same words occur in other Middle English glossaries printed by T. Wright, *Anglo-Saxon and Old English Vocabularies*, 2 vols, 2nd edn, edited and collated by R.P. Wülcker, London 1884, repr. Darmstadt 1968 (= WW). These compilations offer a counterpart for words of the *Oratio* (which do not occur in the *Etymologiae*) such as *cenovectorium* WW 571, 48; 572, 4 or *epiraedium* WW 628, 30.

[84] I am most grateful to Marjorie Chibnall who wanted the fifteenth Battle Conference to be held in Palermo and kindly invited me to give a paper.

THE GENESIS AND CONTEXT OF
THE CHRONICLE OF FALCO OF BENEVENTO

G.A. Loud

The creation of the unified kingdom of Sicily and its crucial first decade, when its founder King Roger (1130–54) struggled to repress the forces of rebellion and separatism on the mainland, are known to us primarily from two contrasting contemporary chronicles, one by a supporter and admirer of the king, the other by a dogged opponent. The former, Abbot Alexander of Telese, wrote expressly about the king and justified his 'Deeds of King Roger of Sicily' (c.1136) by saying that, 'I ought not to be blamed if I, a monk, have brought to the notice of posterity by my pen warlike deeds which have happened in modern times, since even in old and holy histories many similar stories are told of Saul and David and other kings', and he continued that his purpose was to describe 'the extent to which his [Roger's] power was outstanding in the days of our own century, and with how much terror he controlled the provinces as far as Rome'.[1]

It is easy to assume that it was the spectacular career of King Roger and the campaigns which he fought that was the sole inspiration for a renewal of chronicle writing in southern Italy in the years after 1130 (after a period when historical work was largely confined to a very few, and very brief, sets of annals and a handful of monastic chartularies). It is also easy, perhaps too easy, to contrast the flattering, indeed propagandist, picture of the first King of Sicily in the pages of Alexander of Telese with the very hostile view shown by Falco, a notary, and later judge, of Benevento. To Alexander Roger's conquest and unification of southern Italy was divinely ordained and his perjured opponents reaped the due reward of their treason and perfidy, while Roger fulfilled his God-given mission to bring peace to the south. 'Therefore it is no wonder that he was able with the aid of God to bring all these lands under his power, since everywhere he

Research for this article was made possible by grants from the Wolfson Foundation and the British Academy, and by tenure of a Balsdon Senior Research Fellowship at the British School at Rome. I am also greatly indebted to the facilities provided by Professore Elio Galasso, Direttore of the Museo del Sannio at Benevento.

[1] *Gesta Rogerii Regis Siciliae*, proem, ed. G. Del Re, *Cronisti e scrittori sincroni napoletani* I, Naples 1845, 88. On Alexander see especially D.R. Clementi, 'Alexandrini Telesini "Ystoria Serenissimi Rogerii Primi Regis Siciliae", Lib.IV.6–10. (Twelfth Century Political Propaganda)', *Bullettino del istituto storico italiano per il medio evo* lxxvii, 1965, 105–26; and also N. Cilento, 'La "coscienza del regno" nei cronisti meridionali', *Potere, società e popolo tra età normanna ed età sveva. Atti delle quinte giornate normanno-sveve 1981*, Bari 1983, 165–184 and P. Delogu, 'Idee sulla regalità: l'eredità normanna' in the same volume, especially 186–192. There is too a brief discussion in G.A. Loud, *Church and Society in the Norman Principality of Capua 1058–1197*, Oxford 1985, 170–2. A new edition of Alexander's history by Ludovica De Nava for the 'Fonti per la storia d'Italia' has just been completed.

ruled he promulgated such mighty and thorough justice that continuous peace
was seen to endure. As the Psalmist says, "his place is made in peace" '.[2] To
Falco however Roger was a tyrant, worse even than Nero, and those who fought
against him fought for freedom and the protection of their homes against a greedy
and savage invader.[3] Indeed he has been described by one modern commentator
as 'the mouthpiece of the impoverished and oppressed people of Campania and
Apulia', and another has suggested that it was his own unfortunate experience
during the Rogerian conquest, namely his exile in Naples in 1134–7, which led
him to turn to historical writing.[4]

But while one would not deny that Falco of Benevento was extremely hostile to
King Roger, the *rex nefandus* as he saw him, this comparison does beg two
important questions. First of all Falco's chronicle as it now survives covers the
years 1102 to 1140. The chronological coverage is as we shall see very uneven,
but it is only a third of the way through that Roger of Sicily makes his first
appearance, after the death of Duke William of Apulia in July 1127 and with his
claim to be the duke's legitimate successor.[5] The focus before 1127 is on events
within Benevento and the area immediately surrounding the city, with excursus
on the history of the papacy (the city's overlord since the 1070s). Thereafter,
though the campaigns in both Apulia and Capua are covered in detail, there is still
a strongly Beneventan and civic focus. Falco's chronicle needs therefore to be
considered far more than it has been hitherto in its local and specifically urban
context. Secondly close examination of the chronicle must be made to ascertain
exactly when and how it was written, because it is not at all clear that it was
produced at one go, or that the attitudes within it are entirely consistent. Can we,
in fact, assume that it was the career of King Roger which led Falco of Benevento
to write his chronicle?

There are very real problems here. The earliest surviving manuscript of the
chronicle dates only from the sixteenth century, and the exemplar which the
writer of that manuscript copied was already incomplete.[6] As it now survives
the chronicle opens in mid-sentence discussing disputes as to who was to rule
as the Pope's representative in Benevento in 1102, and it concludes, also in

---

[2] *Al. Tel.* I.21, pp. 99–100. The quotation is from Psalm 76.2.

[3] *Falconis Beneventani Chronicon*, ed. Del Re, *Cronisti* I, 221, 'Regem vero testamur aeternum,
Judicemque communem, Neronem crudelissimum Imperatorem paganorum in Christianos stra-
gem talem non legimus exercuisse', and 220–1, 'Clamabant quidem prius morti velle succumbere,
quam sub nefandi Regis imperio colla submittere'. Cf. among many other examples, 208, 219
'Quod numquam a saeculo est auditum, Rex ipse in Christianos operatus est', 223–4, 228, 247–8.
Delogu, 'Idee sulla regalità', 189.

[4] H. Wieruszowski, 'Roger II of Sicily. *Rex Tyrannus* in twelfth-century political thought',
Speculum xxxviii, 1963, 75. E. Gervasio, 'Falcone Beneventano e la sua cronaca', *Bullettino del
istituto storico italiano per il medio evo* liv, 1939, 59. For a recent attempt at a rather different
viewpoint, M. Oldoni, 'Realismo e dissidenza nella storiografia su Ruggero II: Falcone di Benevento e Alessandro di Telese', *Società, potere e popolo nell'età di Ruggero II. Atti della terza
giornata normanna-sveve 1977*, Bari 1980, 259–83. Unfortunately this is not a very penetrating
study.

[5] *Falco*, 192–3. The printed edition in Del Re (above, n. 1) comprises pp. 161–252. All the
references which follow are to this edition. The chronicle can also be found in L.A. Muratori,
Rerum Italicarum Scriptores V, Milan 1724, cols. 82–133. A new edition by Edoardo D'Angelo is
in preparation.

[6] For the manuscript tradition, Gervasio, 'Falcone Beneventano e la sua cronaca', 76–102.

mid- sentence, with a denunciation of the evils created by Roger II's new coinage in 1140. Furthermore, in an autobiographical aside in his account of the year 1133 we are told that the papal rector of the city, Cardinal Gerard of S. Croce, 'took the advice of Rolpoto the constable and other wise men from the city and appointed the notary Falco, scribe of the Sacred Palace and the writer of this little work, as one can read at its beginning, to be a city judge'.[7] Needless to say this attribution at the beginning of the history no longer survives.

The incomplete transmission of Falco's chronicle is thus very similar to that of the biography of William the Conqueror by William of Poitiers, which similarly lacks both beginning and end. And just as the full version of William's work was used by Orderic Vitalis, from whom some clues as to its lost later stages can be derived, so too with Falco.[8] It has long been recognised that his history was later used by the author of the chronicle of S. Maria di Ferraria. This brief, but itself rather interesting work, which drew on a wide variety of earlier south Italian sources, was written at the Cistercian monastery of Ferraria in the diocese of Teano in the first half of the thirteenth century, being begun probably before 1220.[9] The author of the Ferraria chronicle may have had access to Falco's work, and to the earlier *Annales Beneventani*, either at or through the monastery of S. Maria in Gualdo, just north of Benevento, which was reformed from Ferraria in 1220.[10] The importance of the Ferraria chronicler's use of Falco lies in the fact that the former used a fuller, and probably the complete, version of the Beneventan chronicle. The entries in the Ferraria Chronicle for the years 1140–4 would seem both from content (including considerable attention to Benevento) and style to be largely derived from Falco's work, and the likelihood is therefore that his chronicle actually concluded in 1144 and not 1140.[11] Furthermore the Ferraria chronicle's account of the capture of Benevento by Pope Paschal II and Duke Roger of Apulia in the late autumn of 1101 would also appear to have been derived from Falco's work. This entry uses the word *apostolicus* to describe the Pope, as Falco does, and continues that the citizens 'cum honore debito apostolicum susceperunt', a phrase very characteristic of his chronicle.[12]

The capture of Benevento in December 1101, which ushered in a period when,

---

[7]   *Falco*, 218. 'Cumque praedictus Girardus Cardinalis Rector praesset civitati, consilio cum praedicto Rolpoto Comestabulo accepto, et aliis civitatis sapientibus, Falconem notarium, scribam sacri Palatii, istius opusculi factorem, sicut in principio legitur, iudicem civitatis ordinavit.'

[8]   See *The Ecclesiastical History of Orderic Vitalis*, ed. M. Chibnall, 6 vols, Oxford 1969–81, II, xviii–xxi. R.H.C. Davis, 'William of Poitiers and his History of William the Conqueror', *The Writing of History in the Middle Ages. Essays Presented to Richard William Southern*, ed. R.H.C. Davis and J.M. Wallace-Hadrill, Oxford 1981, 98–100.

[9]   B. Schmeidler, 'Ueber die Quellen und die Entstehungszeit der Chronicon S.Mariae de Ferraria', *Neues Archiv für altere Deutsches Geschichtskunde* xxxi, 1905–6, 13–57, esp. 53–7. O. Bertolini, 'Gli Annales Beneventani', *Bullettino del istituto storico italiano per il medio evo* xlii, 1923, 74–81.

[10]   *Chronicon Ignoti Monachi Cisterciensis S. Mariae de Ferraria*, ed. A. Gaudenzi, Naples 1888, 37. Schmeidler, 'Ueber die Quellen', 47–8. S. Maria in Gualdo was itself founded in 1156–61, cf. *Chron. Ferraria*, 30 and *Le Cartulaire de S. Matteo di Sculgola en Capitanate (1177–1239)*, ed. J.M. Martin (Codice Diplomatico Pugliese XXX), Bari 1987, pp. xxv–xxvi.

[11]   *Chron. Ferraria*, 27–8. Gervasio, 'Falcone Beneventano', 70–6. Schmeidler's examination, 'Ueber die Quellen', 43–6 is not quite as satisfactory.

[12]   *Chron. Ferraria*, 15. Schmeidler, 'Ueber die Quellen', 44. Cf. *Falco*, 175, 217, 228 and (without the exact parallels) 251. The suggestion by Bertolini, 'Annales' 78–9, that this passage depends on the lost early recension of the *Annales Beneventani* is much less convincing.

under Paschal II, the city was under much tighter papal control than it had been hitherto, would mark a logical place for Falco's chronicle to have commenced, though it could be, as one scholar has suggested, that our author started with the death of Urban II in 1099.[13] The exact starting point must remain conjectural, but it seems certain that it was not long before 1101 and that the chronicle as it was written did include an account of the siege.

When did Falco write his chronicle? This question is in turn bound up with another one, of how he wrote the work, in one go, or perhaps in several stages. Most scholars who have examined or used the chronicle have assumed the former answer, but as will be shown this is by no means a foregone conclusion. To solve the problem one must however rely largely on the text itself, for the entirely post-medieval manuscript tradition cannot, *ipso facto*, provide any assistance.

The most obvious and significant feature of Falco's work is that, while it relies on an annalistic framework, with each year beginning with the year of the incarnation, the number in the indiction and (generally) the pontifical year of the then pope, the coverage from year to year varied considerably. (It should be noted in passing that Falco began each year on 1 March, a practice largely confined to Benevento and Venice.)[14] The surviving text begins with a relatively detailed narrative of the year 1102, then up to 1112 there are very brief annalistic entries, indeed for 1103, 1104 and 1111 only the year itself and the indiction number is recorded, while for 1106 we are simply told 'In the following year Henry, King of the Romans, died'.[15] The 1112 entry is larger, though still only a paragraph; that for 1113, the first entry to carry a pontifical year, while still relatively short, is several times longer than that for 1112. The years 1114 and 1115 are treated as one continuous entry with a long account of the internal disputes at Benevento between those seeking all-out war with the city's Norman neighbours, and the party headed by Archbishop Landulf II which favoured an accommodation with them, and of Landulf's increasingly stormy relations with Paschal II which culminated in the archbishop's deposition.[16] For 1116 there is no more than a long paragraph, devoted to Pope Paschal's problems with the Roman nobility, while for 1117 there is only a three sentence annalistic entry. From 1118 onwards the coverage is generally more even with usually at least a thousand words per year and on occasion more. But there are still inconsistencies. The entry for 1125 is much shorter than usual (only about three hundred words) and devoted entirely to a description of an earthquake at Benevento, and for 1126 there is only a one sentence notice of the death of the Emperor Henry V.[17] Then, after Roger II's first campaigns on the mainland are treated at reasonable, if hardly excessive, length,

---

13 Gervasio, 'Falcone Beneventano', 72. For the historical context to the capture of the city and for Paschal's policy towards Benevento, O. Vehse, 'Benevent als Territorium des Kirchenstaates bis zum Beginn der Avignonesischen Epoche, I Bis zum Ausgang der Normannischen Dynastie', *Quellen und Forschungen aus Italienischen Archiven und Bibliotheken* xxii, 1930–1, 108–124.
14 R.L. Poole, 'The beginning of the year in the Middle Ages', in his *Studies in Chronology and History*, Oxford 1934, 6–7. The practice was not however confined at Benevento to Falco, as Poole suggested. The entries in the *Annales Beneventani* from 1110 onwards also used it, Bertolini, 'Annales', 89, as did at least some Beneventan charters. Was it in fact Beneventan notarial practice?
15 *Falco*, 161–2.
16 *Falco*, 165–172.
17 *Falco*, 192.

the entry for 1129 is fairly short, no more than a paragraph. Once the civil war commenced in earnest in 1132 the narrative becomes more detailed, both for that year, with a splendid account of the Battle of Nocera in July, and for King Roger's Apulian campaign of 1133, with Falco lamenting at length about the barbarity of the King and his troops,[18] and then describing the factional quarrels once again wracking his native city. 1134 is then treated more cursorily, and 1135 and 1136 passed over with a paragraph apiece which are largely concerned with events at Naples, though the explanation for this becomes apparent a little later when the author writes that 'the above said Falco the judge' along with various other persons 'who had been exiled for three years, returned to their homeland with the Pope [Innocent II]'s permission . . . praising the greatness of the Celestial King who had brought them rejoicing after tribulation and lamentation'.[19] Though this passage is studiously cast in the third person, there can be no doubt that the Falco the judge was the chronicler himself, and the presumption must be that he had spent his exile in Naples, which had been during this period the chief and most secure base for the rebels against King Roger.[20]

By contrast with what immediately precedes it Falco's account of the year 1137 is the longest in his whole chronicle, describing the Emperor Lothar's invasion, the investiture of Count Rainulf of Alife as Duke of Apulia, Benevento's surrender to Innocent II and his own return from exile, King Roger's campaign on the mainland after the German army had withdrawn, his defeat by Duke Rainulf at Rignano in October, his great privilege to the city of Benevento in November, and the inconclusive discussions held soon afterwards at Salerno to seek an end to the papal schism. There then followed sections on the three following years, of reasonable but not excessive length, breaking off in October or November 1140 (the last date to be mentioned was the King's departure from Salerno on 4 October 1140). The Ferraria Chronicler's entries for the subsequent years, taken in part from Falco, are relatively brief, but how far he may have contracted his original is not at all clear.

The uneven nature of the coverage suggests that whatever else Falco was doing he was not, as was his contemporary the Genoese chronicler Caffaro, working from notes which he was compiling every year contemporaneously with events.[21] It might of course reflect the nature of the sources which Falco was using. The sketchy annals up to 1112 have been shown to be dependent on a recension of the *Annales Beneventani*, written at the abbey of St Sophia in the city, although this particular recension was not quite the same as either of the surviving versions of these annals, and was probably rather earlier in composition than them. But after the notice at the start of 1112 of the building of the chapel of St Bartholomew

---

[18] Especially notable in his account of the execution of the rebel Roger of Plenco at Montepeloso, *Falco*, 219, 'Mirabatur omnis exercitus, et facta Regis horrebat, coelorum Regum deposcens, ut tanto Tyranno et crudeli viro resistere dignaretur'.

[19] *Falco*, 231.

[20] The King's difficulties in besieging Naples were graphically described by *Al. Tel.* III.20, pp. 138–9.

[21] *Annali Genovesi di Caffaro e de'suoi continuatori* I, ed. L.T. Belgrano, Rome, Fonti per la storia d'Italia, 1890, 59. Caffaro here wrote that he had begun to write down the names of the consuls of the city and what had happened every year in Genoa from when he was twenty, had done so up to the present time (he was then, 1160, eighty) and would continue to do so as long as he lived.

Falco's account proceeds independently.[22] Thereafter there are occasional references to written sources, though generally to ones which the chronicler himself
does not propose to use. Falco, for example, gave only a brief notice of the First
Lateran Council of 1123 but added that many other things were enacted there in
addition to those that he had mentioned; he would omit these because 'I think
that people would consider me tiresome if I tried to include everything in this little
book. You will find everything noted and written down elsewhere'.[23] Under the
year 1130 Falco wrote that 'it has indeed very frequently (*saepissime*) been
related how the commune [of Benevento] had been created'. Unless he was
casting back to his own very brief account of the creation of the commune in
1128, which seems unlikely, Falco was here referring to other (now lost) written
accounts.[24] If so then this is itself significant, suggesting that there may have been
more historical record made at Benevento than is now apparent.

As befitted a notary Falco also showed considerable interest in charter evidence, even though only one document was quoted verbatim in the chronicle,
namely King Roger's privilege to the city of Benevento in November 1137.[25] In
his description of the dispute between the Beneventan nunneries of St Peter and
S. Maria di Porta Somma in 1121 he noted that both sides produced charters, the
Abbess of St Peter's including one of Duke Luitprand (from the 750s therefore)
which described S. Maria as being subordinate to St Peter's, while the privileges
of S. Maria showed that in more recent times the house had been independent. He
noted too that the details of the 1132 agreement between Count Rainulf and his
fellow rebels and the city of Benevento were recorded in a sealed charter, copies
of which were fixed to every gate of the city 'for the memory of posterity'.[26] Yet
despite this interest, and his obvious concern with chronology evinced by his
careful concern with the dating of events (a welcome contrast to Alexander of
Telese) – testimony once again to his notarial background[27] – Falco did not
primarily rest his chronicle on written material. Rather he relied on what he
himself had seen or on the eyewitness testimony of others. Indeed early in the
chronicle he wrote that, 'for God is my witness that I have written down nothing
except what I have seen or heard'. Later he wrote that if he were to describe
everything that he had seen then he would grow weary under the strain of such
work.[28] But he also acknowledged the testimony of others. Describing the inauguration of Prince Robert II of Capua at New Year 1128 he said 'we have heard

---

[22] Bertolini, 'Annales', 39–42, 74–6. The recensions of the *Annales Beneventani* date c.1113/4
and to the early months of 1119 respectively. The latter were to be extended by a continuator into
the 1130s, ibid., 30–2.

[23] *Falco*, 188.

[24] *Falco*, 202, cf. 200.

[25] *Falco*, 237–8.

[26] *Falco*, 184–6, 211.

[27] Cf. C.J. Wickham, 'Lawyers' time. History and memory in tenth- and eleventh-century Italy',
Studies in Medieval History Presented to R.H.C. Davis, ed. H. Mayr-Harting and R.I. Moore,
London 1985, 66–7. The different attitude to dating might also be seen to reflect the contrasting
genres of 'history' (Alexander) and 'chronicle' (Falco), on which see B. Gueneé, 'Histoires,
annales, chroniques. Essai sur les genres historiques au Moyen Age', *Annales. Economies,
Sociétés et Civilisations* xxviii, 1973, 997–1016. But as Gueneé himself admits, *ibid.*, 1004–8, the
distinction between the two types was often blurred and only became firmly established in the
later Middle Ages.

[28] *Falco*, 169, 206.

from those that were there that by their testimony some five thousand men had gathered for the anointing of this great prince'. And in his description of the battle of Nocera he wrote that he had heard of the fierce resistence of the King's forces in the early stages of the fighting 'from the mouths of those who were there'.[29]

When Falco wrote is however quite another matter. Certainly it was not just the earliest section, the source for which has been identified, that was written later than the events described. Writing of the King's coronation at Palermo in December 1130 Falco said that, 'Prince Robert of Capua placed the crown on his head, for which he did not receive a proper recompense'.[30] Clearly that was written in the consciousness of at least some of the Prince's later tribulations. A little later he wrote that Prince Robert was then (*tunc*) in 1131 a *fidelis* of Pope Anacletus; this was surely written at least a year later when Robert had rebelled against the King and thus gone over to the side of the rival Pope Innocent, and quite possibly only after the Prince and Count Rainulf had actually gone to meet Innocent in the Lateran in the spring of 1133.[31] It could of course have been written a lot later still. And indeed under the year 1130 Falco wrote how a man called John the Joker (*Jocularius*) was seriously wounded by Anacletus's partisans in Benevento, but despite his injuries recovered and lived on for many years (*plures postea advixit annos*).[32] This section of the chronicle would seem to have been written considerably later than the events it described.

Later on, in describing what happened in 1133, Falco denounced Cardinal Crescentius, the Anacletan Rector of Benevento, for attempting to submit Benevento 'to the cruelty of this King Roger of, so I say, execrable memory' (*execrandae, ut ita dicam, memoriae*). This has been taken to suggest that the passage was written after King Roger's death in 1154.[33] One might argue that this one reference was due to a copyist rather than to Falco himself; in the absence of any manuscript evidence this is a moot point, though such an argument might be considered a rather feeble way to dispose of a difficulty. One might also suggest that *memoria* could be translated as 'reputation' just as well as 'memory', indeed it would surely have to be taken in this sense if the passage was written in King Roger's lifetime. In this context however it is worth pausing to review what we know of Falco himself.

Apart from his promotion to be a judge in 1133 and his exile in 1134–7, Falco himself revealed his presence in the chronicle by several quite graphic autobio-

---

[29] *Falco*, 195, 203. The exact date of Robert II's inauguration is not clear. Falco said that Honorius II arrived at Capua on 30 December, and that 'without delay' he summoned the prelates of the area for the ceremony.

[30] *Falco*, 202.

[31] *Falco*, 204, and cf. 217 for the Lateran meeting. However, that the rebellion implied *ipso facto* rejection of Anacletus and recognition of Innocent is suggested by a letter from Bishop Henry of S. Agata dei Goti (in the Principality of Capua) to Pope Innocent describing with great relish the King's defeat at Nocera and the plundering of his baggage, *Monumenta Bambergensia*, ed. P. Jaffé (Bibliotheca Rerum Germanicarum V), Berlin 1868, 442–4, no. 259. Cf. Loud, *Church and Society in the Norman Principality of Capua*, 148–9, 157. H. Hoffmann, 'Hugo Falcandus und Romuald von Salerno', *Deutsches Archiv für Erforschung des Mittelalters* xxiii, 1967, 130–4 devotes great learning and ingenuity to showing that *tunc* could often mean 'now' as opposed to 'then' in medieval Latin. Nonetheless the passage in *Falco*, 204 clearly refers to events in the past.

[32] *Falco*, 203.

[33] *Falco*, 223. F. Chalandon, *La Domination Normande en Italie et en Sicile* (2 vols, Paris 1907) I.xlii, but cf. Gervasio, 'Falcone Beneventano', 24.

graphical references. Discussing the *inventio* and translation of the relics of various local saints initiated by Archbishop Landulf in 1119, he wrote that he himself, though unworthy, had kissed their bones. He had also been present at the consecration of Abbess Bethlem of S. Maria di Porta Somma in 1121, and he was present too at the translation of the relics of St Barbatus, the great early missionary bishop of the Beneventans, in 1124, and once again reverently kissed the bones.[34] All this suggests that he was already an adult and indeed quite an important figure in Benevento by this period (as indeed one might expect from his later promotion to be one of the half-a-dozen city judges).

But we are not by any means dependent on the testimony of the chronicle alone. Fifty years ago some important and pioneering paleographical work (aided by the practice at Benevento as elsewhere in Italy of notaries appending their private sign manual to documents) identified a series of charters written by Falco as notary or witnessed by him as judge. The dating of some of the documents cited in that study should be slightly modified, and five more charters written by Falco and unknown to its author have now come to light. But the fundamental importance of this essay and the conclusions derived from it remain unchanged. Falco can now be identified as the scribe of ten charters written between 1107 and 1128, and as the judge who witnessed a further six between 1137 and September 1143.[35] These dates fit perfectly with what we know of his career from the chronicle, including his exile in Naples. Whether he was also the notary Falco who wrote a charter for St Sophia in 1092 is impossible to say, for this survives only in the copy in the abbey chartulary, the so-called *Chronicon Sanctae Sophiae*, where the sign manual was not reproduced.[36]

Furthermore, in September 1161 a notary called Trasemundus, son of the late (*quondam*) judge Falco, and his wife made two separate donations to the infirmary of St Sophia, Benevento.[37] It seems very probable that he was the son of the chronicler. If so then Falco was undoubtedly dead by 1161, though for the purpose of dating the composition of the chronicle this does not really much advance our argument. But we can go further than this. The notary Trasemundus had been active in Benevento for nearly a quarter of a century before his gifts to St Sophia; indeed, significantly, he wrote all six of the surviving charters authenticated by Falco as judge, that of 1137 being Trasemundus's earliest appearance as a notary.[38]

---

[34] *Falco*, 178, 183, 189.

[35] Gervasio, 'Falcone Beneventano', 18–31. For a revised list see below appendix I.

[36] Cod. Vat. Lat. 4939 fol. 162v. The appalling transcription of F. Ughelli, *Italia Sacra*, 2nd edn by N. Colletti, Venice 1717–21, X.504–5 has the notary's name as *Talco*, cf. Gervasio, 'Falcone Beneventano' 27. Ughelli's edition of this chartulary is so bad as to be best avoided. Prof. J.M. Martin is now preparing a new edition for the 'Fonti per la storia d'Italia' series.

[37] Benevento, Museo del Sannio, Fondo S. Sofia, vol. 13 nos. 12–13. For an edition of the latter, below, appendix II no. 2.

[38] There was another Falco the judge active at Benevento in this period, but Trasemundus was clearly not his son, for he was the judge who authenticated both the 1161 documents, which make clear that Trasemundus's father was by this stage dead. The importance of the notarial sign in identification is manifest; the other Falco *iudex* had a sign manual markedly different from that of the presumed chronicler. He first appeared witnessing a lease by the *custos* of S. Maria de Grausone of Benevento in December 1145, Benevento, Biblioteca Capitolare, Cartella 409 no. 1. Trasemundus had an active career of more than fifty years and is last found as late as August 1188, Benevento, Museo del Sannio, Fondo S. Sofia, vol. 13 no. 22. A large selection of Beneventan notarial signs (though not unfortunately any relevant here) can be found in *Le più antiche*

Given that Falco was already active as a notary in 1107, and possibly a good deal earlier still, that his judicial activity ceased after 1143, and that the man who was very probably his son was old enough to act as a civic notary in 1137, this all strongly suggests that he was dead by 1154, and that his work on the chronicle was completed soon after its coverage apparently ceased in 1144. Indeed it seems likely that he died soon after that date.

However a close examination of the chronicle text with its inconsistent coverage already discussed at some length suggests a much more complicated process of composition. To begin with, Falco's attitude to some of the leading actors in his story was not entirely consistent. For example, Count Rainulf of Alife played a prominent, indeed quite heroic, role in the second half of the chronicle from the outbreak of the south Italian civil war proper in 1132. Falco described how in that year King Roger had received Rainulf's estranged wife, the King's own sister, and had sent her to Sicily. While admitting that Rainulf's conduct towards her had not been entirely admirable – 'Count Rainulf had inflicted many insults and injuries (*convicia multa et afflictiones*) on his wife' – nonetheless he depicted the Count as the injured party, particularly since his son too had been detained by the King. 'Every day the Count tearfully begged and advised his men that, having trust in God alone, they should cast away fear and lay down their terror; it would be recounted triumphantly to the whole world [he said] how, trusting in justice, we defended our homes and chose rather to perish by the sword than to allow foreign hands to invade our property.' And it was his courage which was responsible for the victory at Nocera when the battle had seemed to be lost.[39] Throughout the succeeding narrative Rainulf was portrayed as a gallant and impressive figure, and when he died in 1139, two years after his investiture by Innocent II and the Emperor Lothar as Duke of Apulia, Falco accorded him a glowing, if hardly very convincing, obituary notice. The people, he claimed, 'lamented a most pious Duke and father of all, who laying aside vindictiveness had ruled over his duchy with sweetness and humanity'. He went on to describe Rainulf as 'that most warlike and magnanimous of men'.[40] On the other hand when, twenty years earlier, Count Rainulf first appeared in Falco's account, the chronicler's attitude towards him was much more ambiguous. Falco described in some detail the *guerra* between Rainulf and Count Jordan of Ariano, in which his sympathies seemed to be very much with the latter who was at that stage (1119) on good terms with the Beneventans. Rainulf's military operations were portrayed as ineffective and his conduct was at least implied to be bombastic. 'Despite what he had so often said, he did not dare to attack the *castellum* or to prepare for the sound of battle . . . Count Jordan, who was careful and of great wisdom, knew the impudence (*protervia*) of Count Rainulf and that audacity of this sort did not come from the treasures of prudence.' However by the time his account had reached 1137 Falco was telling the reader that 'the Pope chose Count Rainulf, a man both prudent and discreet' to be Duke of Apulia.[41] It seems unlikely that Falco was writing these two sections of the chronicle as part of the same process, or indeed that this earlier section was written after 1132 or 1133 when Falco's loyalty to Benevento's independence and to Innocent II had committed him to oppose the King and hence to support Count Rainulf as leader of the anti-Rogerian forces.

Neither does it seem likely that the discussion of Honorius II's attempt to create a south-Italian coalition opposing Roger of Sicily in 1127/8 was written at the same time as the last part of the chronicle. The picture presented of Count Rainulf in 1127/8 was once again less than flattering. Both he and his nominal overlord Prince Robert II of Capua were lukewarm in their support of the Pope. Rainulf failed adequately to assist the people of Benevento in their attack on the *castrum* of Hugh 'the Infant', a Rogerian supporter and old enemy of the city. 'Seeing that neither the Count nor the Prince was exerting any energy to bring them help, as they had promised to the Pope that they would, the Beneventans were amazed at such delays and became fearful and demoralised . . . Count Rainulf started to make excuses to justify abandoning the expedition.' Falco went on to report that 'the Prince and the Count made excuses to Pope Honorius for their deceitful tricks' (*dolosas suas machinationes*).[42] Obviously there is a problem here in assessing how far Falco might have allowed his wish to report what really happened, however unpalatable, to overcome any partiality for Count Rainulf. Nonetheless the dissonance between the picture of the Count in 1127/8, which hardly portrayed him in a creditable light, and the later and very flattering depiction strongly suggests that they were written at two different periods.

A similar, if perhaps a little less dramatic, change can be detected in the chronicler's attitude to Robert II of Capua. In the summer of 1128 'the Prince, who was delicate of body and unable to sustain hard work, began to waver in his loyalty to the Pope'. The latter, we are told, realised the 'deceitfulness' (*fraudem*) of the Prince and the other barons, whereas it was Roger of Sicily's partisan Alexander of Telese who pointed out that the Prince's army was beginning to disintegrate because its wages were in arrears (*deficientibus sumptuum stipendiis*).[43] Yet Falco's attitude to the Prince in the 1130s was rather different and much less dismissive. Robert was portrayed as answering the King's envoys who demanded his obedience in 1132 with dignified restraint. 'Let your revered King know that we shall never accept justice from him, as you say we should, until he restores to Count Rainulf his wife and child, and furthermore also restores to his power the city of Avellino and its citadel which he has taken for himself.' The Prince was then shown encouraging his own vassals 'wisely and carefully' (*discreta et diligenti cura*). While his role in the civil war was less obviously heroic than Rainulf's, being largely taken up with the search for outside support, from Innocent II, the Pisans and the Emperor Lothar, Falco portrayed him as energetic and determined. Towards the end of his account of the year 1133 he wrote that 'it should be remembered that Pope Innocent and Prince Robert were labouring with great effort and much danger to free us all'.[44] Can this passage have been written at the same time as the entry for 1128?

One might also suggest that the attitude to the King in the chronicle was not entirely consistent. Certainly Falco's view of Roger of Sicily was never very warm for Roger was, after all, a threat to the cherished independence of

---

42 *Falco*, 198.
43 *Falco*, 199. *Al. Tel.* I.14, pp. 95–6.
44 *Falco*, 208, 224.

Benevento. He wrote that in 1127 'pride turned his mind towards the seizure of the ducal honour'.[45] Nonetheless at this stage Falco's view of him was still relatively dispassionate. Even in his description of the events of 1132, while Falco was clear that the King's opponents had right on their side, his attitude to Roger was not wholly negative, or at least not couched in the terms which were to become the norm in the last part of the chronicle. The only real denunciation of the King at this stage was that put into the mouth of Robert of Capua in his speech to his vassals, and that purported to (and probably did) give the substance of a speech that had actually been made. It is noticeable that according to Falco the King made valiant efforts to rally his fleeing troops at the battle of Nocera. (By contrast Falco later gleefully recorded that at the defeat at Rignano in October 1137 Roger was the first to turn and run.)[46]

But from 1133 onwards Falco's attitude towards the King hardened. Roger became the tyrant incarnate, perpetrator of acts of frightful savagery and possessing no redeeming feature whatsoever. It was from this point onwards that he was regularly characterised as 'the wicked King' or as the *rex tyrannus*, 'the enemy of the Christian religion'.[47] This reflected a change in the nature of the military campaigns in southern Italy, for from 1133 onwards the King forsook his hitherto relatively lenient treatment of those in rebellion against him and deliberately made examples of the Apulian towns which opposed him, clearly hoping that these exhibitions of 'frightfulness' would coerce others into surrendering. But given that Falco's own attitude seems to have changed, can we be so certain that his account of the years 1127–32 was written at the same time as that of 1133 and subsequent years?

Corroboration for this thesis comes in his attitude to Cardinal Crescentius, the Anacletan Rector of Benevento. Falco's view of Anacletus himself was always pretty unsympathetic, although it should be noted that his account of the double papal election of 1130 could have been a lot more partisan than in fact it was. As he made clear, Anacletus was determined to destroy the commune which had emerged at Benevento, and it was hardly likely therefore that Falco would regard him with favour. But in his account of events at Benevento in 1131 he displayed a certain sympathy for the dilemma which faced Crescentius who, anxious for his own safety and mindful of the murder of his predecessor William in 1129, wanted to appease the leaders of the communal movement, but was under strict orders from Anacletus not to do so.[48] However, describing what happened two years later Falco denounced Crescentius, 'the so-called Cardinal', and his associates, whose wicked plans were frustrated by the Divine intervention of God 'who maketh the devices of the people to no effect' (incidentally the only direct biblical quotation in the chronicle). The source of Falco's animosity was made very clear; 'in the alleged name of the Roman See they planned to make the city of Benevento, which had for a long time flourished in freedom and in fealty to St Peter, submit to the cruelty of this King Roger of execrable reputation' [*memoria*, see above p. 183].[49] By this stage in the narrative Falco had been promoted by Innocent and his

[45] *Falco*, 194.
[46] *Falco*, 213, 236.
[47] *Falco*, 219–21.
[48] *Falco*, 201, 204–6.
[49] *Falco*, 222–4. The quotation on p. 223 is from Psalm 33.10, though Falco conflated two

Rector, Cardinal Gerard, to be a judge and was thus firmly and publically committed to the side opposing Anacletus and King Roger. His animus at this point against Crescentius is easily explicable, but the contrast between this and his much more neutral, and even mildly sympathetic, earlier tone is marked.

These changes in attitude as well as the great variety in the scale of the coverage from year to year suggest that different parts of the chronicle were written at different stages, and that it was not the product of a single, sustained period of composition in, perhaps, the mid-1140s when the full and now lost version of the chronicle ceased. There is in addition one further piece of evidence which supports the same conclusion. In November 1137 King Roger sought to win over the citizens of Benevento by granting a privilege exempting them from the various exactions hitherto levied by the local nobility on their property outside the city. Here he was only granting them what the Emperor Lothar, and the local nobles under Lothar's pressure, had already conceded to the citizens earlier in the same year, although not surprisingly Roger's privilege made no reference to this earlier imperial generosity. But Falco discussed both sets of concessions at some length, and quoted the full text of Roger's privilege, or at least what purported to be the text, the only document to be accorded such treatment in the chronicle [see above p. 182 and n. 25]. Immediately afterwards the narrative passed on to the inconclusive negotiations convened by the King at Salerno in November or early December 1137 with the representatives of the two rival popes. The chronicler's attitude to the King in this section was much more neutral than it had been hitherto, omitting the usual hostile epithets, and indeed Roger was shown making a very full and careful examination of the cases of both parties. Incredibly Falco here described the King as 'sagacious in mind and far-seeing in counsel', a far cry from the ritual denunciation which had studded the narrative from 1133 onwards.[50]

This revised opinion of King Roger is explicable in the context of the good opinion brought about in the city by the privilege, and indeed Falco recounted that, much though they admired the steadfastness of Duke Rainulf in the face of the King's counter-attack in the autumn of 1137, the people of Benevento stayed loyal to the King and Anacletus.[51] This would suggest that this passage was written either very soon after the events in question or after the peace between the King and Innocent II in the summer of 1139, when Falco might have been expected to modify his attitude towards the King, but certainly not at the same time as the earlier passages so hostile to Roger II. The latter is the more likely answer, for to complicate matters further the text of the privilege, though not necessarily the substance, has on diplomatic grounds been identified as a forgery. Why Falco wished to alter the text is unknown. It seems highly unlikely that he was inventing the whole thing. It may be that the King's concession was rather less generous than Falco claimed, but if that was the case why did his attitude to Roger change, and how would underbidding the Emperor serve the King in

---

different phrases of the same verse which actually reads 'Dominus dissipat consilia gentium . . . et reprobat consilia principum', not as he rendered it 'reprobat consilia gentium'.

[50] *Falco*, 234–5, 237–8 (for Roger's privilege), 238–9 (the Salerno conference).

[51] *Falco*, 238; cf. also the reference here to 'the lord Archbishop Rossemannus', to whom Falco seems to imply at this point a certain legitimacy. He was an Anacletan appointment. Later Falco refers to him as 'the archbishop appointed by Peter Leone', who was expelled from the city by Innocent, *ibid.*, 247.

securing the support of Benevento at a period when his fortunes were still very much in the balance? The obvious explanation might seem to be that Falco did not have the genuine text of the privilege to hand and therefore created his own version, on the basis of a good knowledge of the diplomatic of the royal scriptorium and quite possibly using as a model an earlier royal privilege for St Sophia.[52] Now the Ferraria chronicle, in a passage almost certainly derived from the lost ending to Falco's work, recorded that in 1143 the King abrogated the exemption he had previously granted and sent his chancellor Robert of Selby to the city, who confiscated the privilege itself. Soon afterwards the Archbishop of Benevento was arrested on his way to the pope by a royal baron Thomas (some sources call him Thomasius) de Feniculo.[53] But before we conclude that the text of Roger's privilege in the chronicle must therefore have been written after 1143, when the genuine document was no longer available to be consulted, another point is worth considering. Had the 1137 passage been written in the light of hindsight after 1143 it would surely have been inconceivable that Falco would not have devoted some of his choicest invective to denouncing the fraudulence and untrustworthiness of the King. Professor Brühl concludes that the false text was composed c.1141/2, and this supposition seems quite feasible.

The chronicle of Falco of Benevento was thus written in stages, and not as a continuous whole. Neither, however, was it simply written year by year, as for example were Caffaro's Genoese annals, for we have already seen that the 1130/1 section must have been written some time after he events in question, and in any case composition on a strictly annalistic basis year by year would not explain the gaps and the differences in the scale and scope of the coverage for particular years.

What therefore were the stages by which the chronicle was written? A tentative reconstruction might be along the following lines. Falco probably began to write his history round about the year 1122. He based it partly on what he himself had seen at Benevento, and partly on information derived from a Roman or Curial source (for he was well-informed about events in Rome and concerning the papacy, including Gelasius II's journey to France and death at Cluny).[54] He combined this with an earlier set of annals, or quite possibly more than one set. Up to 1112 he used a variant, probably an earlier recension, of the surviving St Sophia annals. Since the earliest of the two extant versions of these has been dated to 1113 or very soon afterwards then a first recension can have been written only very slightly earlier, in 1112/13.[55] That Falco had access to such a manuscript comes as no surprise. The monastery of St Sophia was right next to the Sacred Beneventan Palace, the old princely palace and still the governmental centre of the city, where Falco worked. He wrote charters for donors to the abbey, including one recording a transaction at which he had been present in the chapter house in August 1127,

---

[52] *Rogerii II Regis Diplomata Latina*, ed. C.-R. Brühl (Codex Diplomaticus Regni Siciliae, Ser. I, vol. II(i)), Cologne 1987, 131–3, no. 47.
[53] *Chron. Ferraria*, 27; note the 'Quid multa?' so characteristic of Falco. For Thomasius de Feniculo, a royal justiciar who was active between 1144 and 1182, see E. Cuozzo, *Catalogus Baronum. Commentario* (Rome, Fonti per la storia d'Italia), 1984, 278–9, and G.A. Loud, 'Monarchy and monastery in the Mezzogiorno: the abbey of St. Sophia, Benevento and the Staufen', *Papers of the British School at Rome* lix, 1991, 287–8. He was the son (or possibly grandson) of the Hugh *Infans* who had been harassing the city in 1127–8, for which *Falco*, 194–6.
[54] *Falco*, 175–6.
[55] cf. n.22 above.

and in January 1115 had written a *memoratorium* charter for Abbot Bernard. The election and deaths of the abbots were noted in his chronicle, and he went into considerable detail about the dispute there which followed the death of Abbot Bernard in 1120.[56] But Falco did not just use annalistic sources up to 1112. There are indications that one was used in the following pages also. Why otherwise, after the long, detailed and graphic account of the tribulations of the Constable Landulf de Graeca and the deposition of Archbishop Landulf II at the Council of Ceprano, should the section for 1114/15 conclude with a quite separate entry?

> In this year the cathedral church of St. Mary was enlarged on the advice of Landulf de Graeca. In this year Archbishop Landulf of Benevento was arrested, and Landulf de Graeca, who had been expelled from the city of Benevento, returned and received the constableship.[57]

Whoever wrote this did not write the account of the Council of Ceprano. Then, after the 1115 section was concluded with a brief notice of the promulgation of the Truce of God at Troia, the 1116 section was devoted entirely to events at Rome concerning the Pierleone family, with just one sentence on the restoration of Archbishop Landulf. The brief 1117 entry is entirely annalistic, and was surely derived from the same set of annals as the entry cited above, though whether they were a continuation of the ones up to 1112 used earlier or another set entirely is impossible to determine. Cetainly the extant *Annales Beneventani* contain no entries at all for these years.

Round about 1122 Falco combined what he himself had seen, or just possibly recorded earlier c.1115, with this other annalistic and Roman material. The 1123–5 section was probably then written soon after the earthquake of October 1125. If this was the case, and our author did not then take up his pen again for some time, it would explain why the year 1126 was left blank. The subject matter of the 1123–5 section seems however to be slightly different from what precedes it, with the 1123 entry being devoted to the Lateran Council, in no great detail, that of 1124 to the *inventio*, translation and miracles of St Barbatus, and the 1125 entry to the earthquake. For these three years there is no reference either to internal disputes in the city or to its relations with its Norman neighbours. Hence one might suggest that this section was not composed at the same time as the account up to 1122.

One would not wish to be dogmatic about the details. It might be, although on balance this is less probable, that the whole lot up to this point was written c.1125/6, incorporating the earlier annalistic material. Alternatively it may be that the 1113/15 section was written separately, soon after the events in question, and later padded out with the annalistic material on either side and continued from 1118 to 1122. This is a somewhat more plausible hypothesis, and if true then the 1122 work would mark the second rather than the first stage of writing.[58] What-

---

[56] Pergamene Aldobrandini [formerly (until 1990) on deposit at the Biblioteca Apostolica Vaticana, now at Frascati], Cartolario I nos. 57 (edited below appendix II no. 1) and 45 (see appendix I no. 3). *Falco*, 181–3.

[57] *Falco*, 172.

[58] It is notable that in 1115 Falco mentioned the promulgation of the Truce of God at Troia, whereas he did not refer to another promulgation of the Truce by Calixtus II, also at Troia, in November 1120, even though one of those present on this second occasion was Abbot John of St

ever the case, it seems clear that the early stages of the chronicle were in fact a compilation which was organised on the present basis in the 1120s.

The 1127–9 sections describing Count Roger's seizure of the Duchy of Apulia were probably written together, and not too long afterwards, certainly before 1132, since the attitude shown in this section towards Rainulf of Alife remained decidedly ambiguous. The 1130/1 sections were written rather later, though probably only at the end of 1132 or in the very first months of 1133. At the end of the 1131 entry Falco wrote that, 'if life be granted to us we shall describe in the subsequent narrative how it happened that Crescentius, the afore-mentioned judges, their friends and nearly forty others came to be exiled from the city'. Crescentius and his followers were driven from Benevento in the summer of 1132 and before the battle of Nocera (25 July 1132), so Falco was writing after this.[59] But despite the reference to the injured John *Jocularius* living 'for many years' after being wounded in January 1131,[60] it would seem from the still relatively restrained attitude to the King that this section was written before the summer campaign of 1133, describing which Falco really launched into his denunciations and atrocity propaganda about King Roger. Might the reference to John *Jocularius* possibly be a later interpolation?

The 1133/4 sections were probably written contemporaneously or very soon afterwards. They concluded with the return of the Anacletan partisans to Benevento, and although he does not mention it at this point it was then that Falco was exiled.[61] It was only after his return to his native city, or just possibly immediately before that in the summer of 1137, that he started once again to write. The 1135/36 entries are brief and have nothing concerning Benevento in them. They were probably written during 1137 itself. The tone towards King Roger was still very hostile. Most of the long 1137 section was probably written during the autumn of that year, though it seems that the last part, dealing with the royal privilege to Benevento and the negotiations at Salerno, was written separately and rather later. The attitude to the King here represented a distinct modification to that which came before.[62] When this last part of the 1137 section was written must depend on when the forged text of the royal charter was compiled, but at the latest this was before 1143, and might have been some time earlier. Depending on when it was produced, the last sections of the chronicle may have been written either contemporaneously with events or in one continuous operation in the early 1140s. To judge by the Ferraria chronicle Falco continued his work up to 1144, but the 1137 passage must have been written earlier, even if the section from 1138 onwards might have been written at one go. With no original to work from after 1140 any hypothesis must be highly speculative.

Sophia, *Les Chartes de Troia (1024–1266)*, ed. J.M. Martin (Codice Diplomatico Pugliese XXI), Bari 1976, 168–71, no. 43. This might suggest that the 1115 and 1120 sections of the chronicle were written at different times.

[59] *Falco*, 206, 210.

[60] *Falco*, 203.

[61] *Falco*, 227 said that Anacletus ordered the houses of some of the Beneventans to be destroyed. Was his one of them?

[62] By contrast earlier in the 1137 account Falco said that after the capture of the citadel at Bari by the imperial army, 'the whole of Italy, Calabria and Sicily resounded with this great victory, giving thanks to the Heavenly King and rejoicing at being rescued from the jaws of so great a tyrant', *Falco*, 232.

Other scholars may in future modify and improve on this scenario for the writing of Falco's chronicle. But it seems undoubted that, whenever he began writing, it was before 1127, and thus before the entry into mainland affairs of Roger of Sicily. It cannot therefore have been his conquest which impelled Falco to write. What in fact the Beneventan notary started to write was a civic chronicle about his own native town, incorporating within it certain events concerning the papacy, the overlord of Benevento. It was the peculiar circumstances of the Rogerian conquest which led him, perhaps c.1130, perhaps rather later, to extend the scope of his work to include a wider parameter of south Italian affairs.[63]

The great value of Falco's work lies not merely in the careful detail with which he described the campaigns of King Roger and his enemies, but also in his account as an eye-witness of, and participant in, affairs in Benevento. His tiresomely repetitive refrain of 'O reader, if you had been there'[64] was more than just a rhetorical device. His account of the murder of the papal Rector, William, in 1128 takes on new resonance when one realises that Falco himself had acted as the Rector's notary.[65] He was almost an exact contemporary of Caffaro, and these two were the first lay civic chroniclers of medieval Italy. For all the occasional infelicities of style his work compares very favourably with Caffaro's for detail and vividness, and quite eclipses Maragone's rather later Pisan annals. Falco's preoccupations, and the scenes of civic life and factional struggle he depicted at Benevento, were very similar to those of the urban chroniclers of northern Italy. Like them he was concerned with civic peace, and, even though involved himself in factional dispute, lamented its existence. The great religious ceremonies which he reported in the earlier part of his chronicle did something to heal such divisions. He wrote that in 1119, 'you would have seen a most unusual procession and something unheard of for many years, the city of Benevento moved only by honour and love for the Saints'.[66] The combination of civic and religious patriotism which Falco revealed was that of urban, communal Italy, and had its exact parallels in the cities of the north.[67] The factional quarrels within the city, with the expulsion of the losing party and the destruction of their homes, also followed the same pattern as in Lombard or Tuscan cities, and there too a deep desire for domestic peace was engendered by such disputes.[68] And in the presentation of civic tradition and civic memory, it was members of the profession which was above all used to the written word and most familiar with the importance of

---

[63] The role of civic patriotism in Falco's chronicle is stressed by Cilento, 'La "Coscienza del regno" ' [above note 1], 189–90, without exploring the full implications.

[64] E.g. *Falco*, 181–2, 213, 215, 219, 221, 230, 234, 242, 251.

[65] *Falco*, 200. *Codice Diplomatico Verginiano*, ed. P.M. Tropeano, 10 vols, Montevirgine 1977–86, ii.296–9, no. 169.

[66] *Falco*, 178.

[67] Cf. with the *inventiones* of saints described by Falco and the civic rituals which resulted in the *inventio* of SS. Castor and Pollimus at Milan in 1105, as recounted by Landulf of St Paul, *Historia Mediolanensium*, ed. C. Castiglioni, RIS², Bologna 1934, 20–1.

[68] For the destruction of the houses of a losing faction, J. Larner, *Italy in the Age of Dante and Petrarch*, London 1980, 107–8, 115, and Ottobono Scriba, *Annales* ad. an. 1187, in *Annali Genovesi di Caffaro e de' suoi continuatori* II, ed. L.T. Belgrano and C. Imperiale di Sant'Angelo, Genoa, Fonti per la storia d'Italia, 1902, 22–3. In 1161 the consuls of Genoa had had the houses of those who breached the peace destroyed, *Annali Genovesi* I.61. For the longing for peace, Landulf, *Historia Mediolanensium*, 14, and G. Martini, 'Lo spirito cittadino e le origini della storiografia comunale lombarda', *Nuova rivista storica* liv, 1970, 16.

memory who played an increasingly important role – the notaries. They were the natural chroniclers of the city in the age of the commune.[69]

If we are looking for parallels to the historical work of the notary and later judge at Benevento, then our gaze should be directed, not so much at the other chroniclers of Norman Italy, Alexander of Telese, or (earlier) Malaterra, Leo Marsicanus or Amatus, but rather at the contemporary or later urban chroniclers of the north.[70] That in turn should lead us to think about the nature of society at Benevento in the twelfth century, and as to whether Benevento was a-typical of the towns of southern Italy at this period. Benevento had a commune in existence earlier than did Florence. But if we look for southern parallels one may note that Bari too had, as Benevento did up to the siege of 1101, an apparently elective patrician principate, which was savagely brought to an end by King Roger in 1139. Other south Italian towns tried and failed to vindicate their independence after 1127.[71] Had they succeeded in doing so, rather than being incorporated into a unitary south Italian kingdom whose rulers sternly repressed communal independence and subordinated the commercial prosperity of its towns to royal monopolies and the exigencies of their foreign policy, the history of Italy might well have been very different.

[69] Martini, 'Lo spirito cittadino', 21–2, and for a much fuller discussion, G. Arnaldi, *Studi sui cronisti della marca trevigiana nell'età di Ezzalino da Romano*, Rome 1963, 111–31. Landulf of St Paul, though a cleric, and as Martini rightly points out, 'Lo spirito cittadino' 14–5, very much in the ecclesiastical tradition of history writing, still made a career for himself as a scribe and 'consulum epistolarum dictator', in other words as a notary, *Historia Mediolanensium*, 15.

[70] One might however see the late tenth-century *Chronicon Salernitanum*, [ed. U. Westerburgh, Stockholm 1956], as a precursor, in at least some respects. There is a most valuable discussion of this work by P. Delogu, *Mito di una città meridionale*, Naples 1977, chapter 3. Delogu stresses, 70–1, that while it was not as such 'una cronaca cittadina' but a history of the Princes of Salerno and their principality, the author's viewpoint was still essentially civic.

[71] *Falco*, 249. Vehse, 'Benevento als Territorium des Kirchenstaates I', 108–115. For an important discussion of this issue, J.M. Martin, 'Les communautés d'habitants de la Pouille et leur rapports avec Roger II', *Società, potere e popolo nell'età di Ruggero II* [above n.4], 73–98, especially 88–96.

APPENDIX I

The Charters Written by Falco of Benevento or
Authenticated by Him as Judge

This list supersedes that derived from Gervasio, 'Falcone' pp. 18–32.

[A]   *Charters Written by Falco as Notary*

(1) Benevento, Museo del Sannio, Fondo S. Sofia, vol. 12 no. 36 (November 1107). Deathbed donation by a priest, John, to the church of St Peter, Benevento, of his half-share in a house.

(2) Pergamene Aldobrandini, [formerly in the Biblioteca Apostolica Vaticana, now at Frascati] Cartolario I no. 40 (August 1109). Donation to St Sophia by Guidelmus, grandson of Prince Pandulf [V?] of Capua of his share of the churches of St Benedict and St Paul at Benevento.

(3) Pergamene Aldobrandini, Cartolario I no. 45 (January 1115). *Memoratorium* made by Abbot Bernard of St Sophia of an agreement with Richard *filius Ricardi*, lord of the *castrum* of S. Amando, concerning a mill belonging to St Sophia's dependency of S. Angelo, Ariano.

(4) Museo del Sannio, Fondo S. Sofia, vol. 28 no. 7 (November 1118). *Memoratorium* made on behalf of St Sophia by Maynardus its *prepositus*, of an agreement with various men to cultivate the lands of the abbey at Monte S. Vitalis.

(5) Museo del Sannio, Fondo S. Sofia, vol. 12 no. 38 (March 1118). Donation to St Sophia of a vineyard by Hugh 'the Infant' son of q. Hugh.

(6) Museo del Sannio, Fondo S. Sofia, vol. 34 no. 3 (1122). Exchange between St Sophia and the *custodes* of the church of St John. Gervasio, 'Falcone Beneventano' 21 dates this to 1119, and the catalogue at the Museo del Sannio to 1109. However, though damaged and difficult to read, the dating clause can be deciphered to reveal that it comes from the third year of Calixtus II, and the abbot's name is John, elected 1120, not Bernard, as it would have been with either of the other two dates.

(7) Pergamene Aldobrandini, Cartolario I no. 57 (August 1127). Donation to St Sophia of the *castellum* of Archipresbitero and the church of St Peter there by Raleri son of Aimeric. (Edited below, appendix II no. 1.)

(8) Archivio Segreto Vaticano, A.A. Arm. LXVIII.4999 no. 4 (November 1127), edited by D. Girgensohn, 'Documenti beneventani inediti del secolo XII', *Samnium* xl, 1967, 296–8 no. 6. Sale by Ibo the cleric and his brother Poto to the apostolic chamberlain John, on behalf of the Beneventan Curia, of land next to the River Calore.

(9) Archivio Segreto Vaticano, A.A. Arm. LXVIII.4999 no. 6 (c.1127). Sale to the apostolic chamberlain John, on behalf of the Beneventan Curia, of a third share of a property. (Only part of this document survives, the early clauses are missing)

(10) *Codice Diplomatico Verginiano* II.296–9 no. 169 (January 1128), Gervasio wrongly dates this to 1126. The Rector William of Benevento compensates Richard Paccone for damage suffered by his property outside the city by granting him a house belonging to a vassal of Hugh 'the Infant'.

[B]   Charters Authenticated by Falco as Judge

(11) Museo del Sannio, Fondo S. Sofia, vol. 13 no. 4 (July 1137). Donation to St Sophia by Romuald son of q. John of a house, vineyard, and a part share in the church of St John at Porta Somma.

(12) *Codice Diplomatico Verginiano* III.252 no. 259 ter (September 1140, not 1139 as Gervasio, 'Falcone Beneventano' 21). The cleric Everard, *custos* of the church of the Saviour, Benevento, takes possession of two houses that have been placed as surety for a loan.

(13) Museo del Sannio, Fondo S. Sofia, vol. 13 no. 7 (August 1142). Donation to St Sophia of a stretch of the River Calore by the brothers Riso and John, sons of q. Roffred.

(14) Museo del Sannio, Fondo S. Sofia, vol. 10 no. 3 (1142). Double charter recording agreements between Abbot John of St Sophia and, respectively, Samnitus Punianellus and Cioffus Punianellus about the church of St Columba near the River Calore.

(15) Museo del Sannio, Fondo S. Sofia, vol. 2 no. 7 (July 1143, not 1142 as alleged by Gervasio, 'Falcone Beneventano' 22). Abbot John of St Sophia confirms the election of Absalon as prior of the monastery of St Onufrius 'de Gualdo Mazzoca' and concedes to the brothers of that house the right of free election of the prior in future.

(16) Museo del Sannio, Fondo S. Sofia, vol. 13 no. 6 (September 1143, not 1140, as alleged by Gervasio, 'Falcone Beneventano' 22). Donation to St Sophia by Dionisius son of q. Peter Bernardus of lands and vineyards outside Benevento and the church of St Angelo Mosclone.

APPENDIX II

(1)   (August 1127) Raleri son of Aimeric donates the *castellum* of Archipresbitero and the church of St Peter to the monastery of St Sophia, Benevento, in the chapter house of which the transaction takes place. He reserves half the income from the *castellum* during his own and his father's lifetime. Pergamene Aldobrandini, Cartolario I no. 57. Beneventan script, faded on left hand side. This is edited here as an example of the type of document written by Falco and other Beneventan notaries in the early twelfth century.

In nomine domini anno millesimo centesimo vicesimo septimo dominice incarnationis et tertio anno pontificatus domini Honorii secundo summi ponti/ficis et universalis papae mense augusto quinta indictionis. Ego Raleri filius aimerici declaro me in meo dominio habere / castellum quod vocatur Archipresbiteri et ecclesiam vocatam sancti petri. Ad quam predictum castellum pertinentem una cum hominibus / et hereditatibus pertinentiis predicte ecclesie et prefati castelli. Nunc autem statum humane fragilitatis percogitavi / in mea sanitate consilio habito et licentia ipsius mei genitoris et domini Girardi avunculi mei a quo castellum illud teneo et predictam ecclesiam. cupio eandem ecclesiam et castellum ipsum cum omnibus hominibus et pertinentiis eorum in inte/grum sicut illa possideo per salute animarum predicti genitoris mei et mea et parentum meorum et predicti Girardi offerre deo et in monasterio sancte sophie de benevento de quo dominus Iohannes venerabilis abbas preest. / Quapropter bona mea voluntate in capituli ipsius monasterii in presentia confratrum et Benedicti iudicis et Transonis clerici et notarii et advocati et Falconis notarii atque scribe et Alferii filii quondam . . . per librum quem / manu accepi obtuli deo in predicto monasterio predictam ecclesiam et castellum illud cum omnibus hominibus et hereditatibus et pertinentiis ipsius ecclesie sicut illa integra possideo. Et ex inde nec mihi vel cuique alicui / nil (re)servavo habendo. sed totam ipsam ecclesiam et castellum illud cum omnibus hominibus et hereditatibus et per/tinentiis suis cum inferius et superius cum viis et aquis et anditis suis et omnibus suis pertinentiis / deo et in predicto monasterio per salute anime mee et predicti mei genitoris et parentum meorum et predicti Girardi optuli. Ea itaque ratione ut amodo et semper tu predictus dominus Iohannes abbas et tui successores / et quibus a vobis datum paruerit et illorum heredum totum ipsam meam oblationem habeatis et possideatis faciendo / quodcumque volueritis sine contradictione mea et meorum heredum et sine qualibet contrarietate et per meam et meorum / heredum defensionem ab omnibus hominibus omnibusque partibus. Quod si taliter illam vobis non defenderimus aut si aliquo / tempore per quamlibet rationem causari vel contendere vobiscum vel cum vestris successoribus aut cum quibus a vobis datum / paruerit vel illorum heredum presumpserimus querendo illud vel ex inde vobis tollere aut contrare seu minuere / vel si hoc removere quesierimus quingentos solidos constantinos penam nos vobis componere obligavi. et in antea / omni tempori inviti taciti et contempti maneamus. atque inviti illud vobis defendamus sicut dic(tum?) est per / eandem obligatam penam. Tantum eidem genitori meo et mihi nobis viventibus reservo medietatem / reddituum eiusdem tantum castelli. Reliquam medietatem et integram ecclesiam cum possessione sua et / fidelitatem hominum a presenti die ad proprietatem ipsius monasterii dedi et tradidi tibi prefato domino / abbati Iohanni. Ad hobitum predicti mei genitoris et mei qui super vixerit integra medietas reddituum / quam mihi reservo statim post meum hobitum ad proprietatem ipsius monasterii deveniat. et te prenomi/natum Falconem notarium atque scribam Sacri beneventani palatii taliter scribere rogavi et precepi / qua [*sic*] interfuisti. Actum in capitulo ipsius monasterii. Feliciter.

    + Signum crucis proprie manus Raeli.

    + Signum crucis proprie manus Rogerii . . . eresco.

    + Ego Transo clericus et notarius me subscripsi.

    + Ego qui supra Benedictus iudex.

(2)   (September 1161) The notary Trasemundus, son of the late Falco the judge, and his wife Truda make a donation of property at Cupuli outside Benevento to the infirmary of the monastery of St Sophia. Benevento, Museo del Sannio, Fondo S. Sofia, vol. 13 no. 13. Beneventan script. Four sections from the right hand side of the parchment have been torn away.

In nomine domini. Anno dominice incarnationis millesimo centesimo sexagesimo primo. Et tertio anno pontificatus domini Alexandri / tertii summi pontificis et universalis papae. Mense Septembro. decimo indictionis. Nos Trasemundus notarius filius quondam Falconis iud(icis) . . . / ego mulier nomine Truda filia quondam Landulfi. et que sum uxor eiusdem trasemundi notarii. Declaramus nos per. . . / in dotem ex parte ipsius Landulfi olim soceri meique trasemundi notarii et genitoris me(i)que trude rem que est v(inea) . . . / asprum foris in loco cupuli de qua quadem re mihi ipsi trasemundo notario pertinet medietas. mihique predicte Trude . . . / velud in omnibus una nostra continet carta traditionis a parte ipsius Landulfi quam scripsit Petrus notarius. In qua sub. . . / dauferius iudex. Sed qua dominus Albertus decanus bone memorie monasterii sancte sophie unde deo tuen(do) dominus Iohannes / venerabilis quartus abbas pr(ae)esse dinoscitur nuper construxit quandam ecclesiam vocabulo domini Salvatoris propinquo infirmarium / prefati monasterii. ut ibi gra(tia?) infirmorum divina officia celebretur. Ideo nos compuncti divina inspiratione intuentes / omnia que videntur fore caduca et transitoria. providimus pro anime nostre et parentum nostrorum redemptione totam ipsam / rem vineam terram et asprum et salicetum offerre deo in eodem ecclesia ad curam et substentationem et refectionem infirmorum / ipsius infirmarii. Qua propter dum nobis congruum est et salutiferum omnibus modis. bona nostra voluntate. / ambo unanimiter parique consensu mihique mulieri consentiendo idem vir meus et mundoaldus coram falcone / iudice. per hanc cartam obtulimus deo in eadem ecclesia ad curam et substentationem et refectionem infirmorum eiusdem infirmarii prefati cenobii totam et integram ipsam rem vineam terram asprum et salicetum que predix(i) . . . / habere foris in loco cupuli. Et de ipsa nostra oblatione nec nobis nec cuique alteri rese(rvavimus) . . . / habendo. Sed totam et integram ipsam rem cum inferius et superius cum viis et anditis suis . . . / predic(te) car(te) et omnium aliorum munimi(num) inde pertinen(tium) et continentium ab omnibus suis pertinentiis et continentiis . . . /ve deo in eadem ecclesia ad curam et substentationem et refectionem infirmorum ipsius infirmarii predicti cenobii / ut supra obtulimus pro anime nostre et parentum nostrorum redemptione. Ea rationi. ut amodo et semper pars eiusdem / ecclesie et predicti infirmarii integram eandem nostram oblationem sicut prelegitur habere et possidere valeant securiter / inde faciendo omnia quecumque voluerint. sine contradictione nostra et nostrorum heredum. et sine cuiuscumque requisitione. / et per nostram defensionem ab omnibus illis hominibus et part(ibus) quibus vel vobis illud vel exinde a nobis datum paruerit vel oblig(atum). / reservato nobis usufructu de tota ipsa re cunctis diebus vite nostre. Et si forte contingit me eandem mulier(em) / ad necessitatem venire. Si pars eiusdem infirmarii noluerit mihi subvenire potest(atem) habem de ipsa re tantum alienandi unde / me abiliter regere possim. sive si monachari voluero debeat dare quindecim romana(tos) in monasterio in quo monachabor. Si qua vero ecclesiastica secularis(que) persona hanc nostram oblationem a proprietate predicte ecclesie et eiusdem infirmarii alien(are) / seu aliquo modo subtrahere temptaverit. a salvatore mundi qui proprio ore dignatus est promere infirmus (et) / visitastis me[72] et cetera se sentiat excomunicari et in Iude traditoris nosca se agnoscat . . . / numerandum. et sicut nathan et abiron eos t(erra) absorbeat. et quod superius deletum est legitur . . . / quod aut supra legitur reservato nobis usufructu de tota ipsa re sicut intelligatur. quod si ego ipsa / Truda superadvixero post obitum predicti viri mei potest(atem) habeam vita mea totam ipsam rem tenere / dominari et frui et de frugio ipso facere quodcumque voluero. Idem si heredes nostri hanc nostram oblationem infringere temptaverint vel si hoc removere quesierent du-plum id unde agitur penam eos conponere oblig(amus). hac nostra oblatio in/viol-ata permaneat. quod aut supra legitur quod ego ipsa truda habeam potestatem de ipsa re tantum alienandi unde me abiliter regere possim. ita intelligatur quod solum modo medietatem de ipsa re habeam potestatem alienandi. Et notand(um) / quod si ego idem trasemundus notarius post obitum ipsius mee uxoris superad-vixero. potestatem habeam totam ipsam rem tenere / dominari et frui vita mea. Hanc cartam scripsi Ego qui supra Trasemundus notarius qui predictam obl(ationem) feci ut supra legitur cum eadem uxore mea.

+ Ego qui supra Falco iudex.[73]

---

[72] *Matthew* 25.36.
[73] For him, see above n. 38.

THE SWORD ON THE STONE: SOME RESONANCES OF A MEDIEVAL SYMBOL OF POWER

(THE TOMB OF KING JOHN IN WORCESTER CATHEDRAL)[1]

Jane Martindale

The intrepretation of signs, once the field of soothsayers or astrologers, now needs to be included in the repertoire of medieval historians. Traditional historical techniques will not always reveal 'the way forms, symbols and words become charged with what might be called cultural meanings', or enable us to determine the meaning of signs employed in those 'non-linguistic methods of communication' which have an important part to play in every society.[2]

Few signs can have been charged with a wider range of cultural meanings during medieval centuries than the sword, but this study takes its inspiration from one particular sword and from the specific context in which it is still to be found today. This is the drawn sword carried by the Angevin King John on the sculpted marble effigy which surmounts his tomb in Worcester cathedral. A naked sword held in a royal grasp in this funerary setting is unique in western Europe. However, since in the past little importance seems to have been attributed to this image, it became clear that 'King John's sword' required further investigation, even though the entwined themes of warlike symbol and religious setting have often seemed during the course of this investigation to raise a number of apparently insoluble problems.[3] Not the least of these is that, as was observed at an earlier

[1] This paper could not have been completed without the assistance and goodwill of those who have been caught up in my interest in 'King John's sword' and the many problems raised by this rather esoteric topic. I am grateful to the members of the Battle Conference in 1991 who encouraged me to continue with what was then only the germ of an idea – and especially to the Director, Dr Marjorie Chibnall; and also to colleagues in the Schoool of Art History and Music at the University of East Anglia who responded to an earlier version of this paper, as well as to those present at Palermo/Carini in 1992. My thanks especially to the following who at various stages generously provided me with information, suggested new approaches and interpretations, or saved me from error, Dr M. Clanchy, the Rev. H.E.J. Cowdrey, Dr D. Crouch, Dr W. Fröhlich, Dr L. Grant, Professor P. Grierson, Mr T.A. Heslop, Professor R. Hill, Professor C. Holdsworth, Dr G. Loud, Dr J. Nelson; and the paper would never have been begun or completed without the advice and generous help of my husband Andrew Martindale.

[2] E.H. Gombrich, *In Search of Cultural History*, Oxford 1969, 44; G. Mounin, *Introduction à la sémiologie*, Paris 1970, 19; cf. *On the Medieval Theory of Signs*, ed. U. Eco and C. Marmo, Amsterdam/Philadelphia 1989, 3–41.

[3] John's tomb is categorised as one of a sequence of monuments 'of fitting dignity' made for English kings between the years 1066–1485, R.A. Brown, H.M. Colvin and A.J. Taylor, *The History of the King's Works*, i, *The Middle Ages*, London 1963, 478. For an important account in which the rituals of death and burial are considered in conjunction with royal monuments, E. Hallam, 'Royal burial and the cult of kingship in France and England, 1060–1330', *Journ. Med. Hist.* viii, 1982, 359–79; and cf. the still indispensable account by W. St John Hope, 'On the

'Battle conference', the images on such elaborate tombs as those of King John tended to be invested 'with multiple and often contradictory significance'.[4]

'Chance plays little part in the way in which a sovereign is represented', observed Alain Erlande-Brandenbourg in his influential study of the 'funerals, burials and tombs of the French kings before the thirteenth century'; he went on to assert that the monuments devised for the Angevin rulers of the English kingdom were also 'heavy with meaning' and with 'political significance'.[5] The sculpted memorial to King John is a recumbent effigy of black purbeck marble, still visible and remarkably well-preserved in the choir of Worcester cathedral; but because of its place in the history of English sculpture, this effigy has frequently been discussed primarily as a work of art, or historically as one of a continuous series of memorials to kings of the English [Plate 1]. However, it was also a monument to the last ruler of the Angevin dynasty who governed – however briefly – the great continental empire which had been brought into being by John's father, King Henry II. The 'Angevin empire' and the Anglo-Norman state in the widest sense of the term provide the context for King John's extraordinary monument; and no further justification will be given for the view that a wider European world provided the cultural setting, as well as contributing to what might be called the 'iconographic vocabulary', of the sculpture in Worcester cathedral. After all even in the last decade of the thirteenth century the heart of John's son, the English king King Henry III, was sent for burial to the convent of Fontevraud on the Loire; and there can be little doubt that members of

funeral effigies of the Kings and Queens of England with special reference to those in the abbey church of Westminster', *Archaeologia* lx, 1906, 517–70 (for John's tomb, 525–6). John's effigy is treated chiefly as a notable work of sculpture by E.S. Prior and A. Gardner, *An Account of Medieval Figure Sculpture in England*, Cambridge 1902, 577–81 (pl. 580); F.H. Crossley, *English Church Monuments, AD. 1150–1550*, London n.d., 225; and in the influential account by L. Stone, *Sculpture in Britain: The Middle Ages*, London 1953, 104–5, 116, 251 (pl. 87). The burial and monuments of the Angevins are discussed against the background of a longer timescale and developments within the Capetian kingdom by A. Erlande-Brandenburg, *Le roi est mort, étude sur les funérailles, les sépultures et les tombeaux des rois de France jusqu'à la fin du XIIIe siècle*, Paris 1975, especially 15–17, 121–3; and as part of a broader series of European developments by K. Bauch, *Das Mittelalterliche Grabbild, Figürliche Grabmäler des 11 bis 15 Jahrhunderts in Europa*, Berlin/New York 1976, 54 (for John), 87 (fig. 125); see also next n.

[4] M. Bur, 'Les comtes de Champagne et la *Normannitas*: sémiologie d'un tombeau', *ante* iii, 1980, 22–32 (citation, 32); this discussion of the vanished monument to Count Theobald III of Champagne (died 1201) to a considerable extent provided the inspiration for the present study. The value of funerary monuments as sources for '*Bedeutungsforschung*' and '*une histoire des mentalités*' has been emphasised together with the reservation that 'iconographic' and 'formal' analyses will not on their own bring out the 'meaning' of these tombs, G. Schmidt, 'Die gotische "gisants" und ihr Umfeld– Überlegungen zum Wirklichkeitsbezug spätmittelaterlicher Grabmäler', *Kunsthistoriker* iv, 1987, 65; cf. the same author's 'Typen und Bildmotiv des Spätmittelalterlichen Monumentalgrabes', in *Skulptur und Grabmal des Spätmittelalters in Rom und Italien*, ed. J. Garms and A. Romani, Vienna 1990, 13–19. An incomparably wide-ranging study was provided by E. Panofsky, *Tomb Sculpture, its Changing Aspects from Ancient Egypt to Bernini*, London 1964, 39–55 (for medieval developments).

[5] 'Retenons . . . l'idée que la figuration d'un souverain n'obéissait pas aux lois d'hasard', Erlande-Brandenburg, *Le roi est mort*, 122; but elsewhere he expressed the view that on the monuments to English rulers 'le caractère royal de la personne royale est à peine indiqué'; but cf. below, 240.

Plate 1.
Effigy of King John (detail), Worcester cathedral, choir

this dynasty continued to be attached to their ancestral county with its royal burial-place.[6]

The recumbent effigy on King John's tomb provides the point of departure for this paper, but the naked blade grasped in the king's left hand supplies its central theme. Although the sword was so widely employed as a symbol of authority and power throughout the whole medieval period, details connected with how or when a weapon was ceremonially carried seem rarely to have been discussed; although it has been remarked that on (say) the *Bayeux Tapestry* 'the princely presence is usually signalled by armed men around the seat of state'. Separate scenes on that largely non-linguistic source show that princes were not only surrounded by armed men on ceremonial occasions, but – even if not engaged in warfare or combat – frequently themselves carried a sword.[7] The message communicated by the appearance of this weapon in such scenes may not be wholly understood today, or may convey confusing or contradictory signals, but it should not be ignored. In similar fashion the meaning of the drawn sword on King John's tomb has never attracted particular attention, although a naked sword is represented on only a handful of other aristocratic tomb-effigies in western Europe. No other king is commemorated with a drawn sword at his side.[8] One of the main aims of this paper is to consider what meanings might have been attached to King John's drawn sword in the Anglo-Norman and Angevin world of the late twelfth and earlier thirteenth centuries.

At the end of the twelfth century widely differing conventions were employed

---

[6]   Richard I's heart was buried in Rouen cathedral, while John's was taken to the Premonstraten-sian house at Croxton in Leicestershire by its abbot, Hallam, 'Royal burial and the cult of kingship', 364–5 (fig. 1, the effigy created for Richard's heart); and for John, A.L. Poole, *From Domesday Book to Magna Carta*, 2nd edn Oxford 1955, 485 n.41. The royal writ authorising the despatch of Henry III's heart to Fontevraud in the year 1291 is printed by Hope, 'Funeral effigies', 527–8. In general on the practices of dismemberment and preservation of the corpses of the great, Erlande-Brandenburg, *Le roi est mort*, 27–31, 118–19; see the same author's detailed discussion of the Angevin monuments, 'Le "cimitière des rois" à Fontevrault', *Congrès archéologique (Anjou)* lxiv, 1964, 482–92; and M. Desfayes, 'Les tombeaux de coeur et d'entrailles en France au moyen âge', *Bulletin des musées de France* xii, 1947, 18–20. For the evolution of ecclesiastical attitudes towards the practices of evisceration and dismemberment, E.A.R. Brown, 'Death and the human body in the later Middle Ages: the legislation of Boniface VIII on the division of the corpse', in *The Monarchy of Capetian France and Royal Ceremonial, Variorum Collected Study Series*, London 1991, 221–70. For a more detailed account of John's monument, below, nn. 15, 17.
[7]   K. Leyser, 'Some reflections on twelfth-century kings and kingship', in *Medieval Germany and its Neighbours, 900–1250*, London 1982, 250 and n.28 – a contrast is made with the rather more 'civilian' kingship of the twelfth century. The designer of the *Bayeux Tapestry* portrayed both Count Guy of Ponthieu and Duke William seated bearing swords when 'receiving visitors', or engaged in some solemn transaction, *The Bayeux Tapestry*, ed. Sir F. Stenton *et al.*, London 1957, plates 11, 14, 18, 29 (Harold's oath before Duke William); cf. pl. 34 – a representation of a standing figure handing King Harold a sword as he 'resides' during his coronation; see also *The Bayeux Tapestry, the Complete Tapestry in Colour*, ed. Sir D. Wilson, London 1985, pls 10, 13, 16, 25, 31. The 'semiology' of the sword in the *BT* would presumably have varied according to the occasion and circumstances when it was being employed, although naturally its character as artefact and weapon (together with other arms) has attracted more attention, Sir James Mann in ed. Stenton, 55–58, 65–6; Wilson, 224; and see above, J. Alexander, 4; below, Ian Peirce, 267–74.
[8]   Below, 210–21. However, for a thought-provoking examination of the uses to which the possession of swords might be put during the later twelfth century, E. Mason, 'The Hero's invincible weapon: an aspect of Angevin propaganda', in *The Ideals and Practice of Medieval Knighthood*, ed. C. Harper-Bill and R. Harvey iii, 1990, 121–37.

for monuments to kings, ranging from the visual austerity of the Salian and Staufen burials within the German kingdom to the strictly non-figurative magnificence of the Norman-Sicilian tombs which were concentrated in Palermo and the region surrounding the city [see Plate 7, below, 222]. The effigies created as memorials to the Angevin rulers of England take on an additional historical significance when they are placed in this setting; while the realisation that the character of royal power could at this time be communicated through a great variety of 'signs' is in any case also intrinsically important. An essential preliminary to any analysis of the range of possible meanings associated with the sword on King John's monument seems therefore to involve a broad discussion of contemporary royal monuments and tomb sculpture. At the same time, if the study of tomb-sculpture is entirely divorced from a consideration of the liturgy and ceremonial of death, many features of these monuments will be incomprehensible. By the late twelfth century, indeed, it has been supposed that funerary monuments were directly influenced by the character of the ceremonies which preceded interment; furthermore, the great value attached to rituals of death and commemoration have increasingly come to pre-occupy historians as well as scholars from other disciplines. And the tombs of the Angevin kings of England certainly demonstrate the great value attached by contemporaries to monastic prayer and the intercession of saints. John, in particular chose to be buried in a monastic cathedral church, whose last Old English bishop had been recently canonised.[9] Before attempting to determine whether the weapon placed in the king's hand by the sculptor of King John's effigy would have been an image or symbol which the king's contemporaries could have 'decoded' simply and rapidly, it also seems desirable to consider some of the general linguistic and non-linguistic associations of the sword as symbol and sign of authority and power. In particular, this type of examination may help to explain why a drawn sword is so rarely found on funerary monuments, despite being a widely used symbol in many other contexts, both visual and verbal. The broader cultural significance of the sword will take up the second part of this paper. Initially, the historical circumstances of King John's death and burial must be briefly outlined.

When King John died at Newark in October 1216, Henry his eldest son and heir, was only nine years old. England was divided by civil war, while an army led by the future Capetian ruler Louis VIII dominated the eastern half of the kingdom. The men who had remained loyal to the king prepared to take John's corpse westwards because, in the words of his own testament, '. . . I desire my

---

[9] The laity's desire for both monastic prayer and burial is illuminatingly examined and explained by C. Holdsworth, 'The piper and the tune: medieval patrons and monks' (The Stenton Lecture, 1990), University of Reading 1991, esp. 7–9, 17–21. For an overview bringing together all aspects of death and its memorials during nearly two thousand years, P. Ariès, *The Hour of Our Death* (transl. H. Weaver), London 1981, 140–201 (for the 'tame death and 'guarantees of eternity'), 202–93 (on tombs and memorials visible to all). The development of the practice of remembering and praying for the dead within the liturgy is traced from earliest Christian times in the great work by J. Jungmann, *The Mass of the Roman Rite: its Origins and Development* (transl. F. Brunner), 2 vols New York 1955, esp. i 55–8, 129–31, 204–7; ii 121, (but esp. on the *memento* of the dead) 237–48; cf. in general J. Bossy, 'The Mass as a social institution, 1200–1700', *Past and Present* c, 1983, 36–46. A review of the early sources and enormous literature now devoted to the practices of commemoration is provided by J. Gerchow, '*Societas et fraternitas*: a report on a Research-Project based at the Universities of Freiburg and Münster', *Nomina* xii, 1988–89, 153–71.

body to be buried in the church of Saint Mary and Saint Wulfstan of Worcester'. The king's decision can probably be traced back to a pilgrimage he made to Wulfstan's tomb about ten years before his death.[10] The author of the vernacular verse biography of William Marshal certainly laid great emphasis on the exact siting of John's burial '. . . *il gist entre se[i]nt Volstan/ E un autre corseint molt prés . . .*'; but this author's chief object seems to have been to show that the last rites took place with the reverence and public ceremony due to John's office. The papal legate, Cardinal Guala, received the body and 'enough clergy and *cheva-liers* surrounded the bier . . . [and] a great service was performed for him, as was fitting for a king, according to God and according to law'.[11] These sentiments seem to have embodied conventional ideals which were regarded as widely ap-plicable during the late twelfth and early thirteenth centuries, since this author attributed a very similar outlook to Richard on his arrival at Fontevraud for King Henry II's funeral – 'Bury [him] richly, the king my father has this right, as is owed to so high a man'.[12]

At this time during the first decades of the thirteenth century the early con-struction of a commemorative monument immediately after an individual's death does not normally appear to have been a matter of especial urgency. The author of William Marshal's life, for instance, showed no interest whatever in such visible and permanent memorials, although he undoubtedly had an eye for the external trappings surrounding the rituals of death. Certainly there is no record of the precise date when John's effigy was carved, and no information about the patron(s) who commissioned it, or designed its unusual iconography.[13] On stylistic

---

[10] *Imprimis igitur volo quod corpus meum sepeliatur in ecclesia sancte Marie et sancti Wulstani de Wigorn'*, T. Rymer *et al.*, *Foedera* (new edn), London 1816–19, i, 144. For an account of the king's death and a translation of his testament, W.L. Warren, *King John*, London 1961, 275–7; cf. Poole, *Domesday Book to Magna Carta*, 485–6. For John's devotion to St Wulfstan, and his desire to be buried in Worcester (together with the suggestion that the king probably also had an ulterior motive related to the method of Wulfstan's episcopal appointment), Emma Mason, *Saint Wulfstan*, Oxford 1990, 113–14, 281–83; cf. also P. Draper, 'King John and St Wulfstan', *Journ. Med. Hist.* x, 1984, 41–50.

[11] *Histoire de Guillaume le Maréchal*, 3 vols ed. P. Meyer, Paris 1891–1901, lines 15205–15228; cf. the extremely lengthy account of the Marshal's own burial and almsgiving for his soul, lines 18999–19094 (lines 18203–18968 are devoted to the Marshal's actions immediately before death). This verse-life, which is of especial significance in the present context because of William Marshal's lifelong service to members of the Angevin dynasty, seems unlikely to have been written earlier than c.1225, M.D. Legge, *Anglo-Norman Literature and its Background*, Oxford 1963, 306–8; cf. D. Crouch, *William Marshal, Court, Career and Chivalry in the Angevin Empire, 1147–1219*, London 1990, 1–8 and throughout for this biography's value as a source of informa-tion for contemporary secular actions and attitudes.

[12] *Histoire*, ed. Meyer, lines 9358–60; cf. below, 219–20.

[13] *None* of the descriptions of royal or 'noble' funerals in the *Vie de Guillaume le Maréchal* is followed by any reference to the creation of a permanent memorial, cf. lines 9104–9244 for King Henry II's funeral. The early departure of Queen Isabella, John's widow, from the English kingdom indicates that she could scarcely have been responsible for commissioning the monu-ment to her dead husband (her return to Angoulême has been dated to the year 1218), F.M. Powicke, *Henry III and the Lord Edward. The Community of the Realm in the Thirteenth Century*, Oxford 1947, 172; D.A. Carpenter, *The Minority of King Henry III*, London 1990, 153. (I am grateful to Dr Carpenter for confirming that during his work on King Henry III's reign he has found no further record traces relating to the planning or cost of John's tomb.) It appears that the tombs of Henry III's children who died young supply the earliest accounts in English records of payment for royal funerary monuments, *King's Works*, 478.

grounds the effigy has been dated as late as c.1240, but that never seemed compatible with another view advanced, that the sculpted figure on the tomb must have been carved at a time when the details of John's funeral in Worcester cathedral were still vivid in men's minds.[14] Annals written at the nearby abbey of Tewkesbury contain a statement that King John's remains were ceremonially placed in 'a new sarcophagus' during the year 1232: if that entry is accepted literally then it seems improbable that any tomb sculpture would have been completed before that year. [15] Significantly, too, before 1219 King John's tomb was covered with a silken cloth, suggesting that his burial-place was marked with no more than a slab.[16]

But, whatever the precise date attributed to King John's sculptured effigy, it undoubtedly belongs to the category of 'status-specific' monuments which proliferated in subsequent centuries. In the twentieth century the royal attributes of crown and sceptre are still immediately identifiable; but originally the royal magnificence of the king's figure would have been conveyed through the rich colouring of the robes, and the many 'jewels' which once glittered on clothes and *regalia* alike. Every feature is carved with considerable realism, notably the detail of the sword with its deeply gouged fuller and lozenge-shaped pommel [Plate 2].[17]

---

[14] Stone, *Sculpture in Britain*, 116; Prior and Gardner, *Medieval Figure Sculpture*, 580–81 – without discussion this effigy is dated c.1240 (see fig. 655), but these authors regarded the dating-problem as being chiefly important for solving problems of stylistic development and artistic change within the kingdom; cf. Crossley, *English Church Monuments*, 225 (also dated 1240). That dating has been followed by Bauch, *Grabbild*, 87; but cf. next note.

[15] The categorical dating of 1232 given by the authors of the *King's Works*, 478 and n. 5, rests on the Tewkesbury entry: *Johannes rex Angliae ponitur in novo sarcofago, die Sancti Dunstani, praesente domino rege Henrico filio, Huberto de Burgo justiciario, Radulfo de Nova Villa cancellario, priore de Wigorniae, Roberto electo Theokesberiae, filia eiusdem Johannis quondam uxore juvenis Mariscalli, et multis aliis*, in *Annales Monastici* i, ed. H. Luard, *RS* 1864, 84. Cf. Mason, *Saint Wulfstan*, 238, n. 89. The tomb is now sited in the middle of the choir just below five steps (two further ascend to the high altar and the reredos designed by Sir G.G. Scott). In its present form the effigy of black purbeck is placed on an 'altar tomb' of paler marble (the whole over 3ft 6in tall) which is of sixteenth century confection, and described as recently renovated when the antiquary Leland visited the city and cathedral, *The Itinerary of John Leland in or about the years 1535–43*, 5 vols., ed. L. Toulmin Smith, new edn Carbondale 1964, v, 230: *In presbyterio. Johannes rex, cujus sepulchrum Alchirch sacrista nuper renovavit.* There follows a reference to the *sacellum* in which *Arturius princeps* (d.1502) *sepultus est.*

[16] The accounts of the elder Marshal presented after his death in 1219 included an entry '*ad cóóperiendam tumbam R. [i.e. regis] j samitum et j pannum sericum per Johannem mariscallum*, *Roll of Divers Accounts for the Early Years of the Reign of Henry III*, ed. F.A. Cazel Jnr, *Pipe Roll Soc.* new series, xliv, 1982, introd. v and 36. My thanks to Michael Clanchy for this fascinating reference. It bears a striking resemblance to a description of a great tomb being covered with brocade, surrounded by candles and incense '*pur grant honur*' which occurs in Marie de France's Lai, *Yonec*, lines 498–506, see below nn. 73–4.

[17] The whole length of the sword on the effigy is 40¼in., the width of the blade tapers from 2¾in just below the hilt to 1⅝in at the base (1m 15mm, 72mm, 40mm respectively). There is undoubtedly room for a technical study of the sword, too. The king's figure in effigy is approximately 5ft 4in. In the past there was considerable debate (which cannot be entered into here) over whether the effigy was coloured naturalistically, or gilded; however, even today a careful examination of the monument on the spot shows how realistically the effigy would have been decorated with 'jewels' – e.g. on the king's overtunic (dalmatic) the banded collar had indented spaces for five jewels, each sleeveband space for four; the royal belt was jewelled at the waist and on the tip of the end falling straight to the king's feet (three altogether); each glove had a large space for one jewel, and a small jewelled ring was worn on the right hand. The pommel of the sword has a large

In its own time there would have been few comparable secular effigies visible in any of the great churches in the English kingdom, and the monument would have been in every respect remarkable.[18] If the innovative character of the effigy had been more generally acknowledged, its unusual iconography would probably have attracted greater attention than has been the case. Almost the only details which have attracted comment have been the bishops on either side of the king's head; however some improbable identifications have been attached to these little figures which occupy a place more usually taken by censing angels.[19] The unusual character of the king's drawn sword seems to have been ignored, and so has the the lion gnawing the king's swordblade.[20] Why should John have been portrayed in this way, when his father's and brother's swords lie sheathed by their sides on their monuments? Given the importance attached to their swords by all warriors of high status, such distinctions would surely have held meaning when these monuments were constructed in the late twelfth and early thirteenth centuries.

There are further grounds for speculating on the meaning which King John's drawn sword might have conveyed at the time when his monument was designed. Today it perhaps seems strange that this ruler should have been portrayed in a more aggressive manner than Henry II or his brother Richard. John after all was

oval indentation (for enamel, or to hold a relic ?). The number of spaces for jewels on the crown is more difficult to determine, because of its rather battered state (nine or ten?). Equally the little censing bishops were provided with spaces for jewels on their mitres, gloves and collars.

[18] Down to the time of the religious changes in the sixteenth century monuments commemorating Kings Henry I (d.1135 – formerly in the church of Reading Abbey) and Stephen (d.1154 – in the abbey church at Faversham) also existed, but unfortunately no detailed descriptions have survived. In the sixteenth century the abbot of Faversham referred only to Stephen's 'honourable sepulture', *King's Works*, 478; and, although in the late fourteenth century King Richard II refused to confirm Reading's privileges unless repairs were done for the 'tumbam et ymaginem Henrici quondam regis Anglie progenitoris nostri et fundatoris abbatie predicte', that does not prove what form the 'image' took – or even whether it was contemporaneous with the king's death in 1135, see *Reading Abbey Cartularies*, ed. B.R. Kemp, Camden Fourth series xxxi 1986, 107 (no. 116), 25 May 1398. There is therefore no means of deciding whether John's monument was based on those of earlier kings buried in the English kingdom; moreover, by the time of John's death none of the marble or stone effigies of 'knights' would have as yet been set up, Prior and Gardner, *Medieval Figure Sculpture*, 588–602 and 605–7; Stone, *Sculpture in Britain*, 114–15 (who comments on the dating-problems associated with the majority of these thirteenth-century effigies).

[19] The bishops (identifiable as such by their mitres) are described as 'Saints Oswald and [incorrectly] Dunstan, between whose shrines the tomb was originally placed', Stone, *Sculpture in Britain*, 116 (with reference to the angels), 251. That error may well have led to the bishops' identification as 'St Oswald et l'évêque de Dunster'(?), Erlande-Brandenburg, *Le Roi est mort*, 116 n. 57; although scepticism has been registered, Bauch, *Grabbild*, 87. *Dunstan* was not of course buried at Worcester: as has already been seen it was devotion to *Wulfstan* which prompted John to request burial in that monastic cathedral, above nn. 9–10.

[20] Comparison should be made with the *motif* found on a number of near-contemporary ecclesiastical monuments in England on which winged longtailed beasts bite the croziers held by a series of abbots of Peterborough. They, in their turn, rest their feet on the beasts' backs, Stone, *Sculpture in Britain*, 116; Prior and Gardner, *Medieval Figure Sculpture*, figs 650–51 (and cf. 648, 652 for episcopal examples dating from c.1180). The allusion in those cases is probably to Ps. 90.xiii (Vulg.): *Super aspidem et basiliscum ambulabis, et conculcabis leonem et draconem*. Perhaps the iconography of John's effigy implies that he was 'trampling' the lion rather than any more mythical beast? For similar devices on the London Temple secular effigies, below, PL. 13. On the other hand it has also been argued that lions on tomb-sculpture symbolised 'subterranean forces, of death the grave and hell-fire . . . expressed in Psalm 21: 22, *Salva me ex ore leonis . . .*', J. Deér, *The Dynastic Porphyry Tombs of the Norman Period in Sicily*, Cambridge Mass. 1959, 66.

Plate 2.
Effigy of King John

responsible for the loss of much of the Angevins' dynastic patrimony within the Capetian kingdom, and he has been almost universally condemned by modern historians for inertia or incompetence in military affairs. John, as an Occitan poet wrote, 'has a soft and cowardly heart, no man can trust in him'; and by some of his subjects at least he was also scornfully described as 'softsword'.[21] It was Richard, not John, who was mourned by another Occitan poet as the most valiant man to have lived for a thousand years (*'Mortz es lo reis, e son passat mil an c'anc tant pros hom non fo . . .'*): and it was Richard who was compared with the victorious rulers, Alexander, Charlemagne, and Arthur.[22]

When King John died it was still relatively uncommon for royal or aristocratic tombs to be surmounted with the image of an individual whose identity would be conveyed through symbols denoting office, or understood by means of the representation of clear signs of position and status. That background to later developments emerges with particular clarity from the comprehensive survey of the medieval *'Grabbild'* made by Kurt Bauch, in which material from the English kingdom is placed alongside funerary sculpture surviving from the rest of western Europe. The rarity of recumbent secular effigies is also confirmed by post-medieval drawings or written descriptions – for it is impossible to study surviving medieval tombs in their historical context without making some attempt to compare survivors with monuments which have been lost – whether destroyed as the result of religious reaction, political revolution, or simple neglect.[23] Even a rapid survey of existing monuments (or of those which once existed) will show that royal and aristocratic commemorative monuments took many forms: in particular, it is a mistake to assume that men and women of the highest status were necessarily provided with the most elaborate monuments, or that an 'individualised' image of

[21] *'Johannem mollegladium'*, Gervase of Canterbury, *Gesta Regum*, ed. Wm Stubbs, *Gervasii Cantuariensis opera*, ii RS, 92–3; for the occitan condemnation *'E puois a cor flac, recrezen,/ Ja mais nus hom en el no ponh'* (composition dated to around the time of the loss of Poitou), H.J. Chaytor, *Savaric de Mauléon, Baron and Troubadour*, Cambridge 1939, 16–17; J.C. Holt, 'King John', in *Magna Carta and Medieval Government*, London 1985, 99 and 103; and 'The Origins of Magna Carta' in the same collection, 139. For a vigorous condemnation of John's defects as general and politician, J. Gillingham, *The Angevin Empire*, London 1984, 81; and cf. *idem*, 'Conquering kings: some twelfth-century reflections on Henry II and Richard I', in *Warriors and Churchmen in the High Middle Ages, Essays Presented to Karl Leyser*, ed. T. Reuter, London 1992, 173–4.

[22] *Les poèmes de Gaucelm Faidit, troubadour du XIIe siècle*, ed. J. Mouzat, Paris 1975, no. 50: *Fortz chausa es que tot lo major dan*, lines 10–18 (interestingly a version *'francisée'* provides evidence for the interest in, and wider circulation of, this *planh* on Richard's death); cf. below, 233 for further evidence for the Angevins' links with 'legendary heroes'.

[23] Bauch's survey and analysis are concerned to establish a 'typology' of tomb-effigies as well as to trace developments in different regions of Europe, *Grabbild*, 3–44 (for the 'beginnings'), 81–8 (for earlier English examples); cf. for the 'fünf Haupttypen des Totenbildes', Schmidt, 'Die gotische "gisants" und ihr Umfeld', 66. The most comprehensive collection of drawings of funerary monuments within the French kingdom was made for Roger Gaignières (1642–1715): see for their publication, J. Adhémar and G. Dordor, *Les tombeaux de la collection Gaignières, dessins d'archéologie du XVIIe siècle*, 4 vols. *Gazette des Beaux-Arts*, 1974, 1976–7; while for the removal of an important number of these drawings from the French royal collection, E.A.R. Brown, 'The Oxford collection of the drawings of Roger de Gaignières and the royal tombs of Saint-Denis', *Transactions of the American Philosophical Society* lxxviii, 1988, 1–74.

a ruler was regarded as the most suitable – or the sole – means of representing a dead king.

Memorials to the Norman kings of England, for instance, had differed considerably in their character and type. William Rufus (d.1100) was covered by a simple stone slab when his body was interred under the crossing tower of Winchester cathedral.[24] And, although William the Conqueror's tomb in St-Étienne de Caen had been embellished with gold and gems given for that purpose by Rufus himself, it was still strictly non-figurative: that first Norman king of the English had received as his memorial a stone structure raised above the floor on small pillars. According to Orderic Vitalis, its chief decoration was provided by an epitaph composed by Archbishop Thomas of York and inscribed in gold on one of its sloping-sides.[25] Admittedly, even in the eleventh century a tomb might be criticised for being too plain: Helgaud (the biographer of the Capetian King Robert who died in 1031) deplored that at the time he was writing the king's body had not even been covered with a stone recording his name – let alone one with an inscription (*sine titulo ornati lapidis, sine nomine, sine litteris iacet cuius in toto terrarum orbe gloria et memoria in benedictione est . . .*).[26]

Throughout the eleventh century (and perhaps also during the twelfth) monuments do not seem to have been planned or carefully designed before an individual's death. Kings and members of the secular aristocracy were more pre-occupied with their place of burial than with the form which a permanent memorial might take. Political and secular considerations possibly influenced the choice of burial-site, but so also did deeply felt religious sentiment; and even if more than one ecclesiastical community claimed the right to bury a king, the individual's decision seems still to have been respected. John's desire that his body should be placed near Wulfstan's tomb in Worcester cathedral, for instance, bears a strong resemblance to the Capetian King Philippe Ier's wish to be buried near the site of St Benedict's shrine in the abbey church at Fleury-sur-Loire. Both kings wished to lie close to saints for whom they had a special personal devotion, but in making his decision each gave offence to another religious community. The Capetian king's choice (he died in 1108) offended the monks of the ancient and wealthy royal monastery of St-Denis; while John apparently countermanded an earlier wish to be buried in a Cistercian church (probably his own recently founded

---

[24] Hope, 'Funeral effigies', 521; *King's Works*, 477; Hallam, 'Royal burial', 360. The rumours that the tower fell in 1107 as the result of the unshriven king's burial in so sacred a place are disposed of by F. Barlow, *William Rufus*, London 1983, 429–31 (with discussion of whether a tomb opened in 1868 could still have contained the remains of Rufus).

[25] Unusually for this period the name of the craftsman was noted by Orderic, iv, 110–13. Before the Wars of Religion the tomb was 'soutenus sur trois petits pilastres de pierre blanc', see E.A. Freeman, *The History of the Norman Conquest of England*, 6 vols, London 1870–79, iv, 721–3; D.C. Douglas, *William the Conqueror*, London 1964, 362–3. This original tomb was desecrated in 1562, the next (put up in the seventeenth-century) was destroyed in 1793.

[26] This author may have been writing as early as 1033, but at any rate before the year 1041, *Helgaud de Fleury, Vie de Robert le Pieux*, ed. R.-H. Bautier and G. Labory, *Sources d'histoire médiévale*, Paris 1965, 136 and introd. 36–7. King Robert seems only to have got an effigy over two hundred years later 'placé avec le gisant de sa femme Constance d'Arles en 1263 dans le bras nord de Saint-Denis', Erlande-Brandenburg, *Le roi est mort*, no. 74 and figs 136, 151; and Brown comments on the simplicity of the St-Denis tombs before the late twelfth century, 'Burying and unburying the Kings of France' in *The Monarchy of Capetian France*, ix, 244.

house at Beaulieu in Hampshire).[27] On the other hand the Empress Matilda's wish to be buried in the Norman monastery of Le Bec at first incurred her father's displeasure, since King Henry considered that this monastic house did not sufficiently reflect his daughter's dignity and position; but eventually this remarkable woman – who never quite made good her claim to be the rightful Queen of the English – was buried in the religious house which she had originally chosen.[28]

The importance attached to place of burial can be illustrated in a number of different ways, as can the more general concern with funerary ceremonies and burial. Sometimes a tomb might be moved to a more honorific place, or sited in a position to which an especial meaning would be attached. During the second half of the twelfth century, for instance, the Angevin King Henry II (Mathilda's son by her second husband) was present in the abbey-church of Fécamp at a ceremony when the tombs of two of the early Norman dukes were 'translated' to places near the altar of the Trinity; he also ensured that his eldest son William (who died young) was buried in the church of Reading Abbey at the feet of his great-grandfather, King Henry I. Both those actions could be interpreted as having a political and dynastic significance, but the character and form of the monument seem to have been a secondary consideration in these cases – at least no monument was described by the contemporaries who noted the events.[29]

Royal monuments constructed to commemorate rulers buried within the French kingdom have an obvious relevance to any discussion of Anglo-Norman and Angevin royal tombs, whether or not the latter as rulers of England chose to be buried in their island kingdom or somewhere in the continental parts of their 'empire'. Unfortunately direct comparisons are not always easy, since both the Capetian 'reconstructions' of the thirteenth century and the mutilations and

---

[27] At St-Benoît the Capetian king was buried in the choir before the high altar and his tomb was greatly honoured there, Erlande-Brandenburg, catal. nos. 80 and 86–7, and A. Fliche, *Le règne de Philippe Ier, roi de France (1060–1108)*, Paris 1912, 559–63 (but also 77 for Abbot Suger of St-Denis's interpretation of that royal decision as implying that the king regarded himself as unworthy to be buried near the shrine of St Denis). John's promise 'abbatiam se ordinis Cisterciensis facturum . . . seque ibidem sepeliendum' seems to have been very general and was made in the first year of his reign, according to the Margam annalist, *Annales monastici* i, 25; cf. Hallam, 'Royal burial', 377 n. 5. According to the local Worcester annalist John's pilgrimage was made in Sept. 1207 (*circa festum nativitatis beatae Mariae*), *Annales de Wigornia*, ed. H. Luard, *Ann. monastici* iv, 395 (391–2 for miracles at Wulfstan's tomb and the canonisation); cf. E. Kemp, *Canonization and Authority in the Western Church*, Oxford 1948, 104–6, 176; Mason, *Saint Wulfstan*, 281. On John's foundation of Beaulieu, and the rather doubtful reputation of its contemporary abbot, D. Knowles, *The Monastic Order in England*, (2nd edn), Cambridge 1963, 346, 367–8, 657–8.
[28] Hallam, 'Royal burial', 360–1. The chronicler Robert of Torigny attributed especial importance to her consecration in Rome, M. Chibnall, *The World of Orderic Vitalis*, Oxford 1984, 53–4; and cf. *idem, The Empress Matilda, Queen Consort, Queen Mother and Lady of the English*, Oxford 1991, 61, 190–2. Because the chief focus of this paper is on the sword's place on tomb-effigies, monuments to royal or aristocratic women have mostly been excluded from this discussion.
[29] The two first cases are cited as support for Henry II's 'strong interest in genealogy' by Hallam, 'Royal burial', 361–2 (it seems likely that the child William's burial may have been intended to make a political point, too, by emphasising the Angevin King Henry II's descent from the Anglo-Norman line); but for Henry II's own early wish to be buried in the church of Grandmont in the Limousin, Hallam, 'Henry II as a founder of monasteries', *Journal of Ecclesiastical History*, 1977, 120–21. Cf. also below, 219–21; and for the impact of the re-organisation of the royal tombs in St-Denis on attitudes towards the Capetian monarchy, Brown, 'Burying and unburying', ix 246.

destruction of the post-medieval era need constantly to be borne in mind when considering any royal commemorative monument within France. It is nevertheless fairly clear that, between the death of Clovis in 511 and the beginning of the thirteenth century, only *one* of the kings who ruled 'France' was commemorated soon after his death by a recumbent effigy or *gisant*. Throughout that period of over six hundred years the burial-places of fifty-six kings are known.[30] Not surprisingly the first contemporary effigy was made for the most recent of the Capetian kings, Louis VII (who succeeded his father in 1137 and died in 1180): he chose his own Cistercian foundation of Barbeau as his last resting-place. In the church of Barbeau the king was commemorated with a magnificent monument – undoubtedly completed before the death of his last wife Queen Adela in 1206, but more probably undertaken soon after 1180; and his widow made lavish grants of gems and precious metals to decorate the *sepulcrum* which was to cover his burial-place. King Louis was represented crowned and carrying a sceptre on his effigy [Plate 3] in a fashion which seems to have influenced the iconography devised for his descendants' monuments in the abbey-church of St-Denis during the course of the thirteenth century.[31] Some royal effigies had admittedly already begun to appear in churches of the Capetians' kingdom slightly earlier in the twelfth century, but they all had a strongly retrospective character. The earliest of the series of *gisants*, for instance, commemorated the Merovingian King Childebert who had died in the year 558; but it appears to have been executed only a little before Easter of the year 1163, and was to be found in the Parisian church of St-Germain-des-Prés. At about this time the monks of St-Rémi at Reims were experimenting with a rather different iconography, for they put up two seated statues as monuments to their benefactors of the Carolingian dynasty, Kings Louis IV and Lothair (d.954 and 986).[32] As late as the mid-twelfth century, therefore, in the Capetian kingdom no uniform conventions governed the construction of a memorial to a dead ruler, while hesitation and some doubt must have surrounded the way in which a king was to be portrayed.

Although Louis VII was commemorated with a recumbent effigy soon after his own death, it was not until the thirteenth century that the Capetian dynasty came to adopt the *gisant* as the standard image for the way in which kings were to be represented after death. It has has even been argued that, until that time, the

---

[30] My calculations are based on the comprehensive entries for royal burial-sites and monuments established in calendar form by Erlande-Brandenburg, *Le Roi est Mort*, 134–82 – but unlike Erlande-Brandenbourg I have not included the entries made for royal women.

[31] This important monument is now only known from drawings made before the Revolution, Erlande-Brandenburg, *Le roi est mort*, 76, no. 86 and figs 37–8; Hallam, 'Royal burial', 369; and it has been argued that Louis VII's elaborate memorial prompted the monks of St-Denis to transform the organisation of the royal tombs in their care, Brown, 'Burying and unburying', ix 244–6. On official Cistercian reluctance to permit members of the laity to be buried within their churches, Holdsworth, 'The Piper and the Tune', 20–1.

[32] The date assigned to the (still-extant) Childebert effigy is linked to the dedication of the church by Pope Alexander III (the king was represented recumbent as a donor carrying a building in his right hand and a sceptre in his left). The general disposition of the Reims figures of the Carolingian rulers is known only from drawings of pre-Revolutionary date, although some fragments of impressive carving have been found during the course of excavations on this site. (Dating of between 1135–40 has been suggested, associated with a contemporary refurbishment of the choir of St-Rémi), Erlande-Brandenburg, *Le roi est mort*, catalogue no. 7 and figs 43–6; nos. 64, 66 and figs 59, 60–2; Bauch, *Grabbild*, 40–1 (figs 45–51).

Plate 3.
Effigy of King Louis VII (Gaignières Collection, Bodleian Library, Gough MSS)

monks of the abbey of St-Denis – where after all many kings and their consorts had been buried – remained more 'conservative' than communities which were influenced by contemporary practices in England or the territories ruled by members of the Angevin dynasty.[33] Only after the commissioning of new monuments and the re-arrangement of the *nécropole des rois* in St-Denis, would effigies of virtually identical character convey the majestic impression of dynastic continuity and royal legitimacy which the rulers of France were so eager to promote and to preserve at a later date.[34] The iconography evolved on behalf of the Capetians was remarkably uniform. None of these kings was ever portrayed girded with a sword or any other weapon, or clothed in any fashion which openly drew attention to the warlike character of his royal office. On all these effigies of the later twelfth and thirteenth centuries the consecrated kings are represented crowned and carrying sceptres; and these symbols must have been deliberately chosen.[35] The pacific iconography of Capetian monuments seems also to be supported by anecdotes which circulated in the late twelfth century about Louis VII's way of life; furthermore, the absence of any militaristic signs on these royal effigies seems similar to the way in which kings were represented in early Gothic sculpture in the Ile-de-France. Little by little (in the words of Erlande-Brandenburg) this dynasty's concept of kingship came to be 'crystallised in stone'.[36]

The German kings of the eleventh and twelfth centuries received only the plainest funerary monuments. The bodies of the five Salian rulers buried in the cathedral of Speyer between the years 1039 and 1208 were covered with simple slabs of stone. The tombs in that 'necropolis' were so little individualised that at first only an inscribed plaque or funerary crown accompanying the body to the grave allowed each man or woman to be identified; other grave-goods and symbols of royalty, also deposited at the time of burial, were rarely of great intrinsic value.[37] However, in view of the treasure expended on the building-programme of

---

[33] Brown, 'Burying and unburying', ix 242–3.

[34] For the stages by which this 'grandiose conception' was evolved during the latter part of the reign of St Louis, Erlande-Brandenburg, *Le roi est mort*, 78–83; Hallam, 'Royal burials', 372, 377 and fig. 5; Brown, 'Burying and unburying', IX 246–7 – but note that figs 3–4 show a diagram of changes effected in the choir by order of Philip IV, after an earlier re-organisation of the thirteenth century.

[35] *Le roi est mort*, 121–2, with plates XXXV–XLII for the monuments – or drawings of monuments – of the so-called 'commande de Saint Louis' which included rulers of the Merovingian, Carolingian and Capetian dynasties. Even an individual who had not been king, like the Carolingian Charles Martel, was represented crowned on his monument in the church of St-Denis. For the additional item of the *main de justice* found on some later royal effigies, Brown, '*Persona et gesta*: the image and deeds of the thirteenth-century Capetians, the case of Philip the Fair', and 'The ceremonial of royal succession in Capetian France: the double funeral of Louis X', both in *The Monarchy of Capetian France*, v 226, and vii 229.

[36] The N. portal of St-Denis has a series of sculpted kings on the archivolt: these, together with three kings from the jamb of the same portal, are all crowned and carry sceptres but no weapons (despite heavy restoration in the nineteenth century, the restorations appear to preserve the original iconography). Cf. also the kingly figure on Senlis cathedral, the Solomon represented on the N. transept of Chartres, and the rather earlier O.T. king (dated 1145–50) from the destroyed portal of N-D. de Corbeil, W. Sauerländer, *Gothic Sculpture in France, 1140–1270* (transl. J. Sondheimer), London 1972, 397, 400 and pls 30, 48–9, 42, 92 (dated to c.1170–1220). Note too the suggestive remarks on the cultivation of a 'civilian' image by Capetian kings of this date, K. Leyser, 'Twelfth-century kings and kingship', 248–51 and above n.2.

[37] Conrad II (d.1039) was the first ruler to be buried in this church near the steps leading to the

this church (together with the lands lavished on the canons of Speyer) this simplicity cannot have been dictated by economic necessity: the choice of plain monuments was surely a matter of preference. The church of Speyer, built and endowed by Conrad II and his descendants, would have been a more lasting and magnificent memorial than the mere 'configuration' of an individual king or emperor on a tomb.[38]

The tombs of the Norman and Staufen rulers of Sicily provide further evidence for the wide variety of form and appearance assumed by royal memorials during the twelfth and early thirteenth centuries; but in the Sicilian kingdom the 'signal' of royalty was transmitted through the use of a rare and costly marble – porphyry. Porphyry was a material which had immediate imperial associations, although grandeur and power seem also to have been conveyed by the way in which sarcophagi were originally intended to be sited as memorials to these rulers (who were of course interred in Monreale and Cefalù as well as in the cathedral of Palermo). Moreover, virtually no 'figurative' signs were employed on these monuments: discreet symbols signifying royalty were combined with costly materials in a way never found in contemporary memorials from north of the Alps.[39] Individually, some of the characteristics of those late twelfth-century tombs may have been anticipated at an earlier date, for rulers from both the Carolingian and Ottonian dynasties had been interred in classical sarcophagi; but the elements which are integrated in the Staufen monuments of the twelfth and thirteenth centuries are of very different character. Altogether, the Norman-Sicilian tombs evoke a rather different kind of restraint from the tomb-slabs of northern Europe; and in any case there could scarcely be a more pronounced contrast between these extraordinary monuments and the recumbent effigies made for northern kings, great laymen and ecclesiastics, from about the later twelfth century.[40]

---

crypt in the eastern choir. Subsequently his tomb, and those of his successors who had been placed close to him, were moved on more than one occasion before the so-called *Kaisergruft* was constructed in the early twentieth century. For a survey of the archaeological problems and earlier bibliography, see the record of the 1992 exhibition held in Speyer, *Das Reich der Salier, 1024–1125, Katalog zur Ausstellung des Landes Rheinland-Pfalz*, Sigmaringen 1992, 286–9. Conrad was interred with a funerary crown, as were Henry III (d.1056 – also with orb) and Henry IV (d.1106 – with crucifix and reliquary crosses as well as a sapphire ring). The tomb of Henry V (d.1125) was broken into during the sack of the city by the French in 1689, and in 1900 only a small cross and two spurs remained, *Das Reich der Salier*, 289–95 (with plates); cf. P. Schramm and F. Mütterich, *Denkmale der deutschen Könige und Kaiser*, *Veröffentlichungen des Zentralinstituts für Kunstgeschichte in München*, ii. 1962, nos 149, 158, 166; Hallam, 'Royal burial', 360.

[38] However, the scale and magnificence of the church is no longer regarded as proof that it was built in a spirit of conscious rivalry with the great Burgundian church of Cluny, W. Sauerländer, 'Cluny und Speyer', in *Investiturstreit und Reichsverfassung, Vorträge und Forschungen* xvii, 1973, 9–31 (esp. 30–1); see also *Der Dom zu Speyer*, ed. H. Kubach and W. Haas, in *Die Kunstdenkmäler von Rheinland-Pfalz*, Munich 1972, 19–45, containing documentary and chronicle references to royal endowment and building of the church, together with details of the royal burials within the church and their subsequent fates.

[39] The fundamental discussion is by J. Déer, *The Dynastic Porphyry Tombs of the Norman Period in Sicily*, Cambridge Mass. 1959, 70–90, 126–65 (these monuments as a group have been interpreted as directly proclaiming Norman-Sicilian 'imperial pretensions'); cf. Hallam, 'Royal burial', 370; however, now see below, Livia Varga, 307–15.

[40] The tomb of Otto III at Aachen needed to be made of red sandstone (for lack of porphyry?), Déer, *Dynastic Porphyry Tombs*, 149; but Otto II had been buried in Rome in a magnificent porphyry sarcophagus, later broken up in the destruction of Old St Peter's, Schramm and

One reason for this elaborate detour is to show that around the year 1200 there were as yet few precedents for the creation of representational royal effigies. But there is still one more detour to be made. It is to the tomb of Rudolf of Swabia, the anti-king buried in the cathedral of Merseburg and commemorated soon after his death in 1080 with a monumental bronze effigy placed over his grave. Rudolf's monument was described in a twelfth-century source as an *imago ex ere fusa atque deaurata* (an 'image moulded and gilded out of bronze'): the king is represented as a living man with opened eyes, although the bronze effigy is no longer gilded. He is crowned and carries the symbols of royal office – including the orb topped with a cross; while on the raised rim of the effigy a laudatory inscription praises the anti-king's achievements and emphasises his warlike qualities [Plate 4]. It has been remarked that this unique artefact cannot have emerged 'from nothing'; but historically and culturally what seems equally extraordinary is that throughout the German kingdom it didn't apparently lead anywhere either in the immediate future.[41] In its detail the iconography of this monument is quite close to that of the royal *gisants* of the later twelfth and early thirteenth centuries, so in almost every way Rudolf's effigy is an exception to the chronological sequence just considered. As has often been emphasised, too, it is the earliest medieval tomb-effigy of a layman to have survived; but in Rudolf's own Germany over two hundred years were to pass before another king was commemorated figuratively in this fashion. The carved effigy on the grave-slab of Rudolf of Hapsburg (d.1291) – significantly the first ruler to be so commemorated in the cathedral of Speyer – seems to have broken the mould of established convention as far as royal monuments in the German kingdom were concerned.[42] To historians of the twentieth century it may seem ironical that an anti-king was

Mütterich, *Denkmale*, 145–6, 292–3, no. 78. The antique marble (*not* porphyry) sarcophagus in which the remains of the Emperor Louis the Pious (d.840) were placed in the church of St Arnulf at Metz was carved with a representation of the Israelites crossing the Red Sea, and was only much later surmounted with an effigy, Erlande-Brandenburg, *Le roi est mort*, 38–9, 60–1, 151–2; but it is now questioned whether the Emperor's remains were first interred in the chapter-house (as used to be supposed) before being moved to the church c.1049, R. Melzak, 'Antiquarianism in the time of Louis the Pious and its influence on the art of Metz', in *Charlemagne's Heir, New Perspectives on the Reign of Louis the Pious (814–840)*, ed. P. Godman and R. Collins, Oxford 1990, 629–32. For problems surrounding the antique 'Proserpine' sarcophagus in which the remains of Charles the Great were probably interred, Erlande-Brandenburg, 36, 39, 63, 109, 150.
[41] 'Ein Werk dieses Ranges entsteht nicht aus dem Nichts' Bauch, *Grabbild*, 11–14 and figs 3–4, 6; 305 for the description of the effigy from the twelfth-century *Casus monasterii Petrishusensis*; Bauch considers that the artistic affinities of this effigy are with the bronze figure of the crucified Christ from Helmstedt, and with royal warrior figures on the scabbard of the *Reichschwert* (now respectively in Werden and Vienna), figs 5, 7–8; P. Lasko, *Ars Sacra: 800–1200*, London 1972, 137, 166 (stresses the late Ottonian qualities of the metalwork). Cf. also H. Sciurie, 'Die Merseburger Grabplatte König Rudolfs von Schwaben und die Bewertung des Herrschers im 11 Jahrhundert', *Jahrbuch für Geschichte des Feudalismus* vi, 1982, 173–83. For the political and ideological context of this tomb-slab, J. Vogel, *Gregor VII und Heinrich IV nach Canossa, Zeugnis ihres Selbstverständnisses, Arbeiten zur Frühmittelalterforschung*, ix, 1983, 239–53.
[42] 'Es handelt sich um das älteste figürliche Grabmal eines Laien aus dem Hochmittelalter', *Das Reich der Salier*, 427; cf. Schramm and Mütterlich, *Denkmale*, no. 162. The contrast with the powerful rulers of the early *Kaiserzeit* whose tombs were not surmounted with an effigy is made by Bauch, *Grabbild*, 96–7 and figs 146–7 (for the thirteenth-century Hapsburg effigy. Rudolf lies crowned with his feet on a lion, but the other symbols of kingship – orb and sceptre? – are now broken).

Plate 4.
Effigy of 'Anti-King' Rudolf of Swabia, cathedral of Merseburg

commemorated with the earliest medieval 'royal effigy' while his chief antagonist – the legitimate ruler Henry IV – was eventually interred under a plain slab in Speyer cathedral. Such a comparison is probably anachronistic, but the apparent reluctance within the German kingdom to use a figurative model for royal memorials throughout the twelfth and earlier thirteenth centuries still needs investigation and discussion.

Rudolf of Swabia's effigy in Merseburg cathedral certainly raises a number of interesting questions about the emergence of the tomb-effigy as the model for future royal monuments. Because this did not provide a pattern for Salian monuments it might be supposed that it was not widely known in German aristocratic or royal circles. Far from it, since Otto of Freising records an anecdote about this costly memorial which must have been circulating orally for about a century. It concerns a visit allegedly paid by the Emperor Henry IV himself to Merseburg, and recalls the emperor's reaction to the monument. In the church Henry saw the anti-king's tomb, which prompted some unnamed courtier to ask him, ' "Why should he permit a man who had not been [truly] king to lie buried as if in royal honour?" And, the King replied: "If only all my enemies lay [dead] in such honour!" '[43]

Some of the overtones of that instructive anecdote seem likely to be lost on a modern reader, but it nevertheless conveys the message that the legitimate ruler of the German kingdom was neither impressed by the ecclesiastical heaping of posthumous honour on his rival, nor by the *regalia* with which the 'usurper' had been adorned on his tomb. In general, too, an educated layman might have taken exception to the inscription which surrounded the effigy with its praise heaped on the anti-king, for – even if Rudolf were compared to Charles the Great – its dominant message was that he had been a 'holy sacrifice of battle, death was life for him, he fell for the Church' (*Qua vicere sui ruit hic sacra victima belli:/ Mors sibi vita fuit ecclesiae cecidit*).[44] For papal and ecclesiastical apologists that might be the highest praise but it seems unlikely that a secular ruler would have thought the 'semiotic' of Rudolf's tomb propitious. How far would any king have wished to be remembered principally as a '*sacra victima belli*'? Of interest also is the fact that no sword is actually represented on the effigy, although Rudolf's skill in

---

[43] Otto (close relative, as well as the biographer, of the Emperor Frederick Barbarossa) retails this anecdote in the context of his account of Pope Gregory VII's incitement of the German princes to rebel against Henry IV, *Ottonis et Rahewini Gesta Friderici imperatoris*, ed. G. Waitz, *MGH in usu scholarum*, Hanover 1912, 23; '. . . et in aecclesia Merseburch cultu regio sepelitur. Fertur de imperatore . . . [a phrase implying that this story is unlikely to have been transmitted *via* any earlier written source, as John Cowdrey kindly pointed out to me] . . . quod, cum pacatis paulisper his seditionem motibus ad predictam aecclesiam Merseburch venisset ibique prefatum Rudolfum velut regem humatum vidisset, cuidam dicenti, cur eum, qui rex non fuerat, velut regali honore sepultum iacere permitteret, dixerit: "Utinam omnes inimici mei tam honorifice iacerent" .' John Cowdrey first drew my attention to Otto's anecdote at Cluny in 1988, and I should like to thank him for this and for all his subsequent help. Cf. the translation in *The Deeds of Frederick Barbarossa, Otto of Freising and his Continuator, Rahewin*, ed. C. Mierow, *Records of Civilization*, Columbia 1953, 40–1; Sciurie, 'Die Merseburge Grabplatte', 182.

[44] Bauch, 305 n. 33 prints the whole inscription; but for a different reading of the earlier lines, Vogel, 239 n. 270; and for the use of language emphasising Rudolf's death as a 'martyr', Sciurie, 'Die Merseburge Grabplatte', 182 (fig. 4 for the anti-king's mummified hand preserved in the cathedral).

Plate 5. Effigy of King Richard I, Fontevraud

counsel and with the sword (*consilio, gladio*) are mentioned in the inscription.[45] Altogether with hindsight it is worth speculating that Rudolf of Swabia's monument might actually have set back the 'cause' of royal tomb-effigies in Germany for a number of generations.

When the memorials made for the first three Angevin kings of England are considered against this wider European background the novelty of the monuments created for them is all the more remarkable. Although (as has just been seen) recumbent effigies had begun to mark the burial-places of some kings by the late twelfth century, monuments of this type were far from numerous at the time of King Henry II's death in 1189; while even during the decades before King John's death a high proportion of royal monuments were still non-figurative in character. And, where a monument did incorporate a tomb-effigy, there appears to have been some confusion over the conventions to be employed in representing the human figure. Should an individual be envisaged as a living human being, or alternatively was a recumbent pose meant, automatically as it were, to signal that the person represented was no longer alive?[46] There was probably also some doubt over the meaning to be conveyed by particular material objects. A consecrated ruler could of course be identified by the appearance of crown and sceptre, for these symbols were regarded as exclusively royal, but there were other 'royal ornaments' too; while one of the earliest in the series of retrospective effigies of 'French' rulers also portrayed the king as a donor-figure carrying the model of a church. No royal funerary monument before those of the three Angevins (Henry II, Richard, and John himself), ever seems actually to have portrayed a king with a sword as well as with the other items of *regalia* (crown, sceptre) already mentioned. So the naked sword on King John's tomb turned out to have far greater interest as a sign than when it first aroused my interest in the choir of Worcester cathedral. It seems also to acquire a wider cultural and historical importance.

In their own day all the Angevin royal effigies were modelled on what seems to have been a relatively new type of monument. Not only are these effigies 'status-specific', but (as has been widely recognised) they also recall the funerary ceremonies which preceded burial. In particular, the effigy of King Henry II bears a striking resemblance to the written description of the procession taking the dead king's body from the great castle of Chinon on the River Vienne to his place of burial in the abbey of Fontevraud. He was 'dressed in royal array, with a golden crown on his head, having gloves on his hands and a golden ring on his finger, a sceptre in his hand . . . [He had] boots woven of gold cloth, and spurs on his feet . . . *girded with a sword* [my italics] . . . he was lying with his face uncovered.' In

---

[45] An interesting association between this memorial inscription and references to 'sacrificial kings' in the polemical writings produced during the investiture struggle was made by I.S. Robinson, *Authority and Resistance in the Investiture Contest*, Manchester 1978, 119–20. Moreover, it is surely significant that Henry IV and his advisers were prepared to argue that Rudolf's death occurred '*non nostra, sed Dei virtute*', Vogel, 239.

[46] The problems relate crudely to whether a figure is represented with open or closed eyes (contrast the closed eyes of the Fontevraud effigies with John's open ones), and whether the feet seem to rest in a lying position or are represented as though the figure were really standing, see Schmidt for a discussion of whether any of these characteristics could be interpreted eschatologically or idealistically, 'Die gotischen "gisants" und ihr Umfeld', 65–8. More usually, these features have been described by English art-historians stylistically in terms of a growth of realism or naturalism, Stone, *Sculpture in Britain*, 115–17.

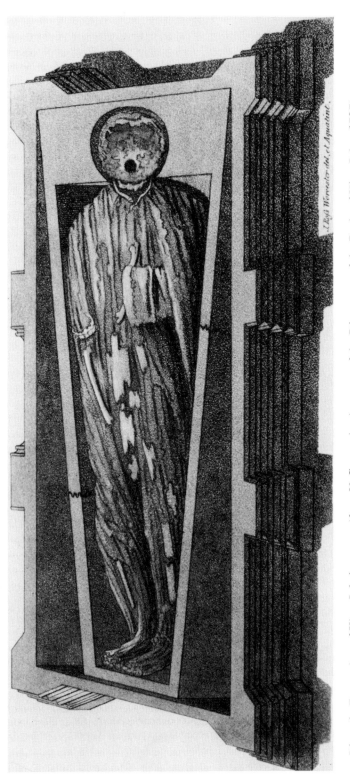

Plate 6. Engraving of King John's corpse (from V. Green, An Account of the Discovery of the Body of King John, 1797)

most respects that written account is borne out by the appearance of the surviving effigy; but on his monument the king's sword is no longer girded round his waist, for the sword-belt is unbuckled and the weapon lies in its scabbard by Henry's side. That is also the way in which the sword was portrayed on Richard's effigy [Plate 5].[47] Those who saw these figures must have been faced with images – in idealised form certainly – evoking individuals in a liminal state between the funeral ceremony and their bodies' committal to the earth. In the terms suggested by Panofsky such effigies appear to have had both a retrospective and a prospective purpose: they certainly recall the worldly position of the individuals commemorated but, placed in the choir of a monastic church, they would also provide an ever-present reminder of the individuals for whom spiritual commemoration and intercession were requested. In the case of a royal monument a 'magic provision for the future' and the recollection of past magnificence could be combined in the portrayal of the human figure.[48]

John's effigy in Worcester cathedral, like that of his father, also appears to have been modelled on the way in which the king's body was brought to burial, even if there are some important differences of detail – for instance the king's open eyes. In this case, however, there is no detailed medieval description of the ceremony with which John was brought from Newark to Worcester; nevertheless, a record made when the tomb was opened in July 1797 points to some remarkable similarities between the effigy and the way in which the king was arrayed for interment. In Stone's words – based on the eighteenth century account – 'the effigy closely follows the clothing and attitude of the body within the tomb, *including the sword in the left hand*'. But Stone did not draw attention to one of the most significant discrepancies: whereas the effigy of the king forever grasps a bared (and extremely realistic) sword, the rusted weapon found by the body in the coffin was covered with tattered leather and wooden fragments. It had not been drawn from its scabbard.[49] A comparison can surely be made with the corpse of the Emperor Frederick II who was arrayed for burial with all his *regalia*, including a sword on the left side girded over his dalmatic. The magnificent state in

---

[47] *Gesta regis Henrici secundi*, ed. W. Stubbs RS, ii 71, cf. 344. The difference between the textual reference to the sword and its position on the effigy was remarked by Hope, 'Funeral effigies', 523, but not by Erlande-Brandenburg, *Le roi est mort*, 16–7; cf. 'Le cimitière des rois', 482–5; see also Bauch, 317 nn. 141–2, (figs 78–9); and, on 'Liegefiguren in standessspezifischer Haltung', Schmidt, 'Die gotischen "gisants" und ihr Umfeld', 67. (Many photographs of these well-known monuments are taken from the opposite side, so that the sword is not seen). The equally remarkable effigy of Eleanor of Aquitaine is not relevant to the present discussion, although taken together all three monuments draw attention to the innovatory character of the effigies designed for these members of the Angevin dynasty.

[48] Panofsky, *Tomb Sculpture*, 16 (relates to Egyptian memorials, however). By the mid-twelfth century a tomb and its monument could already be the focus for 'individualised' liturgical celebration, as is shown by King Henry II's foundation for his father at Le Mans, below n. 53; cf. Holdsworth, 'The piper and the tune', 19–21.

[49] Stone, *Sculpture in Britain*, 115–16; Hope, 'Funeral effigies', 526; cf. Poole, *From Domesday Book to Magna Carta*, 486 n. 1. (the sword is not mentioned). For the engraving (in which the sword is unfortunately not visible), V. Green, *An Account of the Discovery of the Body of King John in the Cathedral Church of Worcester, July 17th 1797*, London/Worcester 1797 (opposite title page).

*Plate 7.
Engraving of
corpse of Emperor
Frederick II,
Palermo cathedra
(from F. Daniele, 1
Regali Sepolcri de
Duomo di Palerm
Naples 1784)*

which the emperor had been clothed after death was revealed when the royal tombs in Palermo cathedral were opened in the eighteenth century. [Plate 7].[50]

The two masculine effigies at Fontevraud appear to embody a new type of royal monument in which the dominant theme is a reminder of the rites of death. However, in their detail these Angevin tombs have certain features in common with a number of non-royal monuments preserved (or recorded) in the Loire region and further south. The draped bed or bier on which Henry II and Richard lie can be compared with the base of a clerical tomb at Asnières not far from Fontevraud, as well as with some rather battered tombs formerly within Queen Eleanor's duchy of Aquitaine in the abbey-church of Maillezais. That was echoed in the (now destroyed) monument which commemorated Bishop Peter of Poitiers, friend of Robert of Arbrissel, the ecclesiastical founder of the convent of Fontevraud [Plate 8].[51] The Maillezais monuments have an additional importance because they apparently provide a number of early examples of retrospective dynastic monuments from a house founded five generations previously by ancestors of Queen Eleanor. Those battered warrior-effigies really are girded with swords but – without positive identification of the men whom these figures commemorate – it is impossible to say whether their weapons have a symbolic significance in addition to the more obvious message that the effigies covered the graves of warriors.[52]

Anyone searching for the image of a drawn sword on a monumental effigy before the early thirteenth century is obliged to venture outside the charmed circle of royal tombs. Indeed, the only surviving example which is undoubtedly earlier

---

[50] F. Daniele, *I regali sepolcri del duomo di Palermo*, Naples 1784, 100–07 and plates O–Q. Unfortunately it is impossible to say whether by that time in the mid-thirteenth century rulers (or for that matter members of the military aristocracy) were normally buried with weapons, although in previous centuries swords had frequently been deposited in such tombs – e.g. for Merovingian royal burials, Erlande-Brandenburg, *Le roi est mort*, 32–6. Sufficient examples survive to suggest that the practice may have continued to be more widespread than now appears, e.g. when the tomb of Lothar III (d.1132) in Brunswick was opened in 1620 a sword was found, Schramm and Mütterich, *Denkmale*, nos. 170, 215. Possibly the Emperor Henry V (whose grave in Speyer was violated in 1689) had also been buried with a sword, since he was certainly provided with spurs, *Das Reich der Salier*, 295. For several burials with swords from Spanish royal tombs of the later thirteenth century, E. Oakeshott, *Records of the Medieval Sword*, Woodbridge 1991, 70, 72.

[51] For the draped beds from Asnières and Maillezais, Bauch, 56–7 (figs 83, 81–2 respectively – together with comparisons with Spanish monuments); Sauerländer, *Gothic Sculpture*, 448–9; Adhémar, *Tombeaux de la collection Gaignières*, i, 12 no. 8 (but the bishop's death-date is wrongly noted). A scene from a capital in the church of Cunault-sur-Loire portraying the funeral of St Philibert (which does not seem to have been previously noticed) is equally interesting because it shows a funeral procession in which the draped bier is almost identical with the ones on which the royal figures at Fontevraud rest. Considerations of space make it impossible to illustrate these here.

[52] Considerable problems of dating and attribution surround these effigies. The figures are clothed in chain-mail with swords girded over their armour; the heads are so battered that it is impossible to tell whether they were represented with eyes opened or closed, although the outlines of a cushion or pillow on which the heads rested can still be seen. These effigies were probably from tombs commemorating dukes of Aquitaine, but the evidence is far from clear and the effigies were removed from a religious house which suffered terrible damage both during the Wars of Religion and the Revolution. However, it is known that at least three eleventh-century dukes of Aquitaine were buried at Maillezais (c.1030, 1036, 1039), before Montierneuf at Poitiers became a ducal burial-church, *Chronique de St-Maixent*, ed. J. Verdon, *Classiques de l'histoire de France au moyen âge*, Paris 1979, 116, 118. These are problems which will be discussed in greater detail elsewhere.

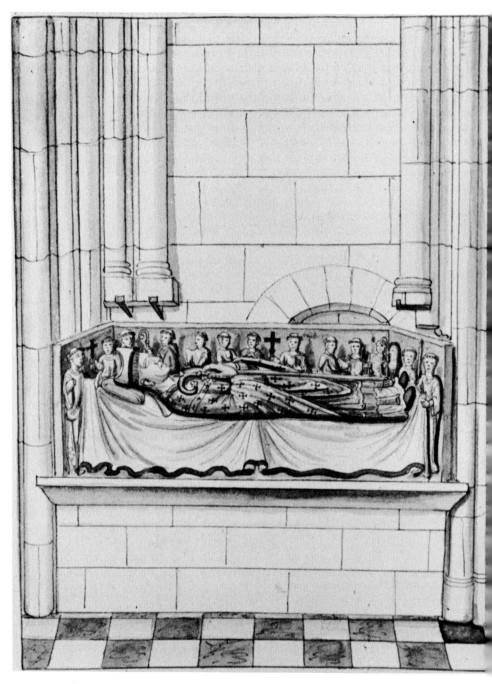

Plate 8.
Tomb of Bishop Peter of Poitiers, formerly Fontevraud (Gaignières collection, Bodleian Library, Gough MSS)

in date than John's effigy is depicted on a memorial which is rarely cited on account of this peculiarity, even though its importance has otherwise been much discussed. This is an enamel plaque portraying King Henry II's own father, Count Geoffrey *'le Bel'* of Anjou (d.1151) [Plate 9]. Before the Revolution of 1789 that formed part of a more elaborate commemorative monument to this count in the cathedral church of Le Mans; and, although by the eighteenth century it was placed in a vertical position on a pillar in the nave, it was originally designed to be attached to Geoffrey's tomb (possibly at a sloping angle).[53] Like the effigy of Rudolf of Swabia, Geoffrey's memorial provoked written comment, for the author of the late twelfth-century *Historia Gaufredi ducis* described it as an 'image worthily decorated with gold and gems'. Although Geoffrey was not of course a king, his status and identity are conveyed on the brightly coloured panel by means of the heraldic signs which cover his long shield and his pointed cap. He is a 'prince', not recumbent but upright, alive, and actively brandishing his sword. Moreover, a verse inscription surrounding the figure informs the reader that his weapon was to be used to put plunderers of the Church to flight.[54] Panofsky singled out this unique object as being a 'memorial portrait' not to be compared with the 'funerary effigies' of the twelfth century; however that assertion seems a trifle anachronistic – given the absence of memorial portraits in Western Europe in the mid-twelfth century. The general 'stiff' appearance of the image has been attributed to the 'taste and Germanic memories', of the Empress Mathilda, Geoffrey's widow, but Madame Gauthier also commented that the Count 'wields his sword like a sceptre'. Here the sword is more than a weapon: it signifies Geoffrey's power and authority as a 'prince'.[55]

The sword as a symbol of royal power most visibly united Church and ruler in a medieval kingdom through the employment of this weapon in the sacring of a king. During the course of the eleventh century a reformer and polemicist like Peter Damian reminded the Emperor Henry IV of that association when he wrote,

---

[53] This is now in the Musée Tessé in Le Mans. The vicissitudes of this, the largest 'plaque de parement jamais produite par les émailleurs médiévaux', are described in detail by M.-M. Gauthier, *Emaux du moyen âge occidental*, 2nd edn, Fribourg 1972, 81–2, and plate 4; catal. no. 40, 327. It seems probable that the plaque was completed before the year 1161 when Henry II made a foundation for two priests to serve daily at the altar *quod est ante sepulchrum patris mei*, but it could have been made at any time during the previous ten years. A drawing made for Gaignières shows that little damage has occurred, Adhémar, *Les tombeaux de la collection Gaignières*, i, no. 21; no. 20 of that edn provides a comparison with a similar enamel plaque formerly attached to an episcopal tomb in the cathedral of Angers.

[54] The expanded text reads: ENSE TUO PRINCEPS PREDONUM TURBA FUGATUR/ ECCLESIISQUE QUIES PACE VIGENTE DATUR, *Emaux*, 82 (this is compared by Mme Gauthier with the tomb of Rudolf of Swabia for the sentiments expressed). From the description of the 'reverenda imago, ex auro et lapidibus decenter impressa', and the reference to the Count's figure as though 'superbis ruinam, humilibus gratiam distribuere videtur', it seems likely that the author of the *Historia* must also have read the inscription, *Chroniques des comtes d'Anjou et des seigneurs d'Amboise*, ed. L. Halphen and R. Poupardin, *Collection de textes pour servir à l'étude et à l'enseignement de l'histoire*, Paris 1912, 224 – however the author of the *Historia* attributes the disposition of the tomb to Bishop William of Passavant (d.1187) rather than to any member of the count's family.

[55] Gauthier, *Emaux*, 82; Panofsky, *Tomb Sculpture*, 50–1 – a contrast is made between the figure of Geoffrey and the rather battered mosaic commemorating a Count of Flanders (formerly in the church of St-Bertin). That representation was flush with the floor, and the head of the count rested with closed eyes on a cushion.

Plate 9.
Funerary plaque of Count Geoffrey 'Le Bel' formerly in the cathedral of Le Mans

'the king is girded with a sword so that he may go armed against the enemies of the Church'. Peter Damian was here probably drawing on assertions found in the consecration *ordines* of the western church, for those *ordines* make a direct association between the king's girding with the sword and his duty to pursue wrongdoers and enemies of the Christian religion. And, according to the rubric found in the coronation *ordo* of one English pontifical, girding with the sword had an almost constitutive importance because 'with the sword, . . . he [the king] shall know that the whole kingdom is committed to him'.[56] The swords placed by the side of the effigies of the Angevin kings Henry II and Richard were perhaps included on their biers because this weapon formed part of the 'royal ornaments' of a consecrated king – in Erlande-Brandenburg's terms these weapons were 'heavy with meaning' indeed. These swords also formed part of an 'iconographic vocabulary' which, in such terms, should have been entirely acceptable to the Church. John's sword too could be interpreted as a reminder of this ruler's consecrated status; although, since the figure on the effigy carried a drawn sword and was portrayed with open eyes, a rather different meaning may well have been conveyed (or been intended) to those who visited or passed by this ruler's tomb.[57]

One hypothesis which seemed worth examining was that the unusual iconography of John's monument could be explained through reference to some specific moment in the ritual of sacring. Unfortunately the rubrics of consecration *ordines* rarely provide sufficient detail to show whether or not a king was expected to withdraw his 'coronation' sword from its scabbard during the course of the ceremony; interestingly however, there is some evidence to show that outside the immediate sphere of English ceremonial such a gesture might be required. An imperial *ordo* of the late twelfth century, for instance, reveals a significant variation on the usually brief rubric: the emperor-elect ascends the steps to the altar of St Peter, where 'the Roman high priest [i.e. the Pope] 'gives him a naked sword (*dat ei nudum ensem*), saying: "Receive the imperial sword, for vengeance on evildoers and reward of the righteous . . ." And he kisses him'. The rite continues: 'And the Emperor having taken the sword from the hand of the Pope first brandishes it and then immediately replaces it in its scabbard'.[58] The elaboration

---

[56] For Damian's assertion (made in the year 1065) and its possible ambiguities, I. Robinson, *Authority and Resistance in the Investiture Contest,* 120–3; cf. *The Pontifical of Magdalen College,* ed. H.A. Wilson, Henry Bradshaw Society xxxix, 1910, 92: *Et cum ense totum regnum sibi fideliter ad gerendum secundum supradicta verba sciat esse commendatum, dicente metropolitano . . .* The consecrator was to stress that the king's function was to strive for equity, but also to avenge unjust deeds and to defend the weak. The king must remember that he is the type of the world's Saviour, with whom he should desire to reign. On the formulae of this *Ordo* (the 'Third English Ordo'), J. Nelson, 'The Rites of the Conqueror', *ante* iv, 1982, reprinted in *Politics and Ritual in Early Medieval Europe,* London 1986 (cited from the latter), 378–9 and 382–4.

[57] A dead ruler could no longer wield a sword; and, when it is remembered that at Fontevraud both Kings Henry II and Richard are portrayed with their eyes closed and the swords placed by their sides on a bier, it seems possible that attention was being drawn to this fact. However that interpretation is hypothetical.

[58] R. Elze, *Die Ordines für Weihe und Krönung des Kaisers und der Kaiserin, MGH, Font. iur. germ.,* Hanover 1960, XV *Der Ordo von Apamea,* 47–50. Similar gestures characterised the (later) medieval Polish consecration *ordo* which contained the additional detail that the sword was to be transferred to the king's left hand – i.e. the hand in which John holds the sword on the Worcester effigy – A. Gieysztor, 'Gesture in the coronation ceremonies of medieval Poland' in *Coronations, Medieval and Early Modern Monarchic Ritual,* ed. János Bak, Berkeley, California 1990, 158. My

Plate 10.
Seal of King Richard I

of this imperial rite is suggestive, but it seems too remote from the Anglo-Norman or Angevin rulers of England either to account for the way in which John's sword is represented on his effigy, or to provide any explanation of how this weapon came to be so startlingly distinguished from those of his father and brother. In more general terms swords and their bearers undoubtedly played an important part in royal coronations – as can be seen from the elaborate description of the ceremonial of King Richard's magnificent consecration service in 1189.[59]

The crown remained the most unambiguous and magnificent of the *regalia*; but under Anglo-Norman and Angevin rulers the sword is also frequently employed

thanks to Janet Nelson for supplying me with this reference, and for helpful discussions on all aspects of the association between consecration and *regalia*.

[59] The brother of the King of Scots, the Earl of Leicester, and John himself, bore 'tres gladios regios sumptos de thesauro regis, quorum vaginae desuper per totum auro contectae erant' in the procession which preceded the king; while the archbishop's grant of the sword to Richard is described as the 'gladium regni ad malefactores ecclesiae comprimendos', *Chronica Rogeri de Hoveden*, RS iii, 9–10; cf. *Gesta regum*, ii, 80–1; Gillingham, *Richard the Lionheart*, 2nd edn, London 1989, 129. The Magdalen College Pontifical's rubric for the girding is that the king 'shall receive the sword from the bishops' with the postscript 'accinctus autem ense' (see previous note); but this does not provide any enlightenment as to whether the sword was ritually taken from its scabbard. On the *BT* the sword given to Harold at his consecration seems to be represented as though unsheathed but, since there is considerable variation in the way in which these weapons are portrayed, it is difficult to be categorical on this point, see Wilson's edn pl. 31, cf. 9–11, 13 (swords represented by filled-in stitching with a heavy outline, mostly sheathed). But on pl. 25 – Harold's oath to William – the Duke's sword in its scabbard is represented only by a stitched outline.

Plate 11.
Seal of King John

in the iconography of kingship in England. Although William the Conqueror's repeated crown-wearings were undoubtedly intended to emphasise the magnificence of the new régime as well as its legitimacy, the character of Norman power might well have been conveyed more directly through the drawn sword portrayed on some coin-types of the Conqueror and his successor. The sword had apparently never appeared as a sign of royal power on coins of pre-Conquest date.[60] But as a symbol of royal authority displayed during the king's lifetime the importance of the drawn sword is revealed with greatest force in the iconography of English royal seals. From the time of the Conquest to the mid-thirteenth century the 'majesty' side of the great seal *always* shows the king seated, crowned, and carrying a drawn sword (generally held at an oblique angle to his

[60] M. Biddle, 'Seasonal festivals and residence: Winchester, Westminster and Gloucester in the tenth to twelfth centuries', *ante* viii, 1985, 51–72; and for the liturgical acclamations associated with these occasions, H.E.J. Cowdrey, 'The Anglo-Norman *Laudes Regiae*' in *Popes, Monks and Crusaders*, London 1984, VIII, 48–58. For examples of the ruler bearing a sword on coins, *English Romanesque Art, 1066–1200*, Exhibition Catalogue, London 1984, nos 394 (King William I, moneyer Godric, Thetford – 'the first English coin-type to present the king holding a sword'), 400–2 and 405 (King William II, coins struck respectively at Maldon, Tamworth, Colchester and Bristol). Although not a frequent sign on royal coin-types, there are other infrequent examples – e.g. a coin of the Emperor Henry V struck at Dortmund shows that ruler with sceptre and a drawn sword carried in the right hand, *Das Reich der Salier*, 239–40 (no date attributed to the specimen). The drawn sword was also occasionally used at a later date on the coinage of the English kings as ducs de Guyennne, as Professor Philip Grierson kindly informed me.

body); while, by the late twelfth century at the latest, the great seal is held to symbolise the authority of the king himself [Plates 10 and 11]. As Richard FitzNigel wrote in his description of the power wielded by the officers and barons at the Exchequer: 'it is so potent . . . that no man may break its laws or be bold enough to resist them . . . its records and judgments may not be impugned. [The Exchequer] has this signal authority . . . on account of the excellence of the royal image (*regie ymaginis* – i.e. the royal seal) which is . . . preserved in the treasury'.[61] The portrayal of the majestic king as a militant figure would serve as a reminder of his authority and power even during repeated or lengthy absences.[62] By contrast no French royal seal of this period represents the king armed [Plate 12].[63]

The 'royal images' of Anglo-Norman and Angevin rulers included weapons among the signs which denoted their power. Unlike their Capetian counterparts, they seem to have had little desire to exclude warlike symbols from the iconography or symbolism of kingship; moreover, the government and political control of the English had depended on military victory and superiority, so the sword would inevitably have signified more than the mere threat or sanction of force, as might be implied in the prayers pronounced at the time of the king's consecration. In the context of the present argument it is important that the iconography of the Angevin royal funerary monuments appears to have drawn on the same stock of signs and symbols as was employed to convey the power of a *living* king. The weapons on the Fontevraud effigies commemorating Henry II and Richard may therefore have been designed both to include the full range of royal ornaments bestowed on a king at the time of his conscration, and to draw attention to the most important secular symbol of royal office with which he was girded on that occasion. Another possibility is that John's drawn 'sword on the stone' on his effigy in Worcester might even be intended to make a visual reference to the king's drawn sword on his seal of 'majesty'. The possibility that there was a correlation between the way in which a king was portrayed in life and in death seems to be confirmed by the (admittedly very different) French royal iconography. The effigies of Capetian rulers – where those exist for the years before the beginning of the thirteenth century – and their seals both convey a message which is far more pacific than the iconography employed on behalf of their greatest subjects and rivals, the Angevin kings of the English.

---

[61] *The Course of the Exchequer by Richard Son of Nigel*, ed. C. Johnson, *Medieval Classics*, London 1950, 14 (my translation has slightly modified the editor's words); cf. pp. 19, 21, and especially 61–2 – where the importance of the seal as an instrument of government can be judged by the statement that the royal seal and Domesday Book are kept in the Treasury.

[62] *English Romanesque Art*, 301–5 includes examples of great seals of all the English kings between Edward the Confessor and John; and see for Henry I, P. Chaplais, 'The seals and original charters of Henry I', in *Essays in Medieval Diplomacy and Administration*, London 1981, XVII 260–76; for Richard I, L. Landon, *The Itinerary of King Richard I*, Pipe Roll Soc. new series xiii, 1935, Appendix A, 173–80 and plates. I should like to thank my colleague Sandy Heslop for his expert help on this aspect of my paper.

[63] G. Tessier, *Diplomatique royale française*, Paris 1962, 192–7 (pls V, VII), and especially 194: 'La juxtaposition de ces deux insignes du pouvoir, sceptre (*sceptrum*) et le bâton (*baculus, virga*), est, on le sait, une des caractéristiques de la symbolique royale française'. An exception is provided by the earlier years of Louis VII's reign when, before his divorce from Eleanor of Aquitaine (1152), he employed a two-sided seal on which the king in (pacific) majesty was combined with the equestrian 'sword-wielding' image appropriate to his position as DUX AQUITA-NORUM, 196.

Plate 12. *Seal of King Louis VII as* Rex Francorum *and* Dux Aquitanorum *(after A. Luchaire,*
Etudes sur les actes de Louis VII, *Paris 1885)*

Even as a symbol of power the sword did not have exclusively royal associations. Before the late eleventh century a drawn sword was also used to signify comital or ducal power, as is obvious from the reverse of the English royal seals which portray the ruler as *dux Normannorum*; and on such 'images' the sword is normally wielded in a far more aggressive and belligerent manner than on the majesty face of the royal seal. The sword was also employed as the principal symbol of ducal authority in the inauguration rites composed for the dukes of Normandy; while in the early thirteenth century the author of the *Life* of William the Marshal also wrote as though he considered that the duke was actually 'made' by investiture with the sword.[64] A sword in this context might be understood as the sign of a 'sub-royal' power, brandished by a 'prince' like Count Geoffrey of Anjou, or employed by the designer of the Bayeux Tapestry to convey the authority exercised by men like the Duke of the Normans and the Count of Ponthieu.[65]

A sword could be used as a sign of power legitimately licensed by the Church, and indeed often exercised on its behalf – but it was still primarily a weapon. Consequently a visual representation of a sword would be unlikely to convey a meaning which was 'stable' or 'constant', since as a visual image a sword would convey multiple – and possibly conflicting or contradictory – meanings. Ecclesiastical theorists could refer to it as a symbol intended to guarantee the maintenance of peace or justice, but for many beholders it would as readily evoke associations of conflict and death. Sometimes there is a hint that this ambiguity was even consciously exploited, but normally the message communicated by means of visual signs is far less easily understood than written references to the use of the sword as symbol. The scene depicted on the 'Pierpoint Morgan leaf' related to the great Winchester Bible provides an excellent illustration of the ambivalence of the sword as a visual symbol, for on the same register of this folio King Saul is shown standing with naked sword held upright, followed immediately by David's execution of Goliath with a sword almost the boy's equal in size. There could scarcely be a better illustration of the image of a sword employed by a king (even an Old Testament king) as the sign of his exercise of justice, and then quite openly as a death-dealing weapon.[66] It is on such multiple and conflicting meanings that it is now necessary to pause.

Legend clustered around swords even of historical figures during the twelfth century, but sometimes there was a complete confusion between historical reality and 'fiction'. It was widely reported, for instance, that the Norman King Roger II's victories led him to commemorate the conquest of Sicily and his control of

---

[64] After the death of King Henry II, Richard travelled north and 'A Roem fu dus ceint d'espée . . . Li dus passa en Engleterre . . .', ed. Meyer, i, lines 9555ff.; Gillingham, *Richard the Lionheart*, 127–8. In the Norman ducal *ordo*, the girding of the sword followed the granting of a ring to the duke by the archbishop. At this point the latter prays 'ut omnis hostium suorum fortitudo. virtute gladii spiritualis frangatur', *Ordo ad ducem constituendum, The Benedictional of Archbishop Robert of Rouen*, ed. H.A. Wilson, HBS xxiv, 1903, 159; and in general H.Hoffman, 'Französische Fürstenweihen des Hochmittelalters', *Deutsches Archiv* xviii, 1962, esp. 98–102 (for Normandy).

[65] The apparent reluctance of the Capetians to employ the sword as a sign of royal authority lends some support to this hypothesis. Moreover, developments in the fourteenth century show that the Capetians and their successors had need of a 'symbol' to signify their judicial authority (the *main de justice*) instead of the sword which had served the Norman and Angevin English kings, see Tessier, *Diplomatique royale*, 195.

[66] *English Romanesque Art*, 121–2, no. 65 (with bibliography), illustrated, 57 – the scenes in question occupy the top third of the registers of this folio; cf. below, Peirce, Pl. 2, p. 253.

Apulia, Calabria – even Africa – with an elaborately inscribed sword (APULUS ET CALABER, SICULUS MIHI SERVIT ET AFER); and, although there seems to be no factual support for that anecdote, it still provides a glimpse of the value attached to the sword as a symbol of power and military might.[67] But the value attached by the secular aristocracy to the sword as weapon and artefact emerges even more vividly from contemporary vernacular literature. In the *Chanson de Roland* the named swords of Charlemagne, and of the heroes Roland and Oliver – *Joieuse, Durendal, Halteclere* – assume an extraordinary prominence. Apart from the fact that even his Saracen opponents seem to know the name of Roland's sword, Durendal is *'bele e clere e blanche/ Cuntre soleill si luises e reflambes'* – only a naked blade could be so described –; while in his dying monologues Roland also addresses his sword, reciting an epic catalogue of all the countries which Durendal has helped him to conquer. The historical King Roger of Sicily would have understood at least some of the sentiments underlying these last actions of the dying hero.[68]

A curious testimony to the blurring between 'history' and 'legend' is the circulation in the 'real world' of the actual swords supposedly held and possessed by fictional heroic warriors. Indeed, as has recently been shown by Dr Emma Mason, during the later twelfth century members of the Angevin dynasty were involved in theft, gift, and probably also fabrication, to provide themselves with these secular relics of men whose exploits had become merged with those of genuine historical figures. The young king – Henry II's son and namesake – took what he thought was Durendal itself as loot from its custodians when he visited the Virgin's shrine at Rocamadour; but otherwise the swords obtained by members of this Angevin house were chiefly associated with the 'matter of Britain', and English royal records prove that in December 1207 John himself thought that he had obtained the sword of Tristan, hero and lover of Iseut.[69] A legendary sword could also serve political and diplomatic ends when, as a crusader during his stay in Sicily, King Richard even obtained considerable naval supplies from King Tancred in return for the gift of 'the excellent sword of Arthur, formerly the noble King of the British, which the Britons call *Caliburn'*.[70] The wide diffusion and appeal of the cycles of legend attached to the heroes of both *chansons de geste* and romance are also demonstrated by their visual representation in places where these heroes (and recollections of their deeds) would have been seen by a far wider circle of people than could ever have aspired to the possession of a hero's sword. On the West portal of Verona cathedral (c.1139), for instance, the named

---

[67] One version of the anecdote which circulated in Anglo-Angevin circles asserted (erroneously it appears) that this same inscription formed the legend placed on Roger's *seal*, D. Abulafia, 'The Norman kingdom of Africa and the Norman expeditions to Majorca and the Muslim Mediterranean', *ante* vii, 1984 (Appendix: King Roger's sword), 48–9. Given Anglo-Norman and Angevin use of a sword on the royal seal, that confusion between sword and seal seems highly significant.

[68] *La Chanson de Roland*, ed. F. Whitehead, Oxford 1942, 68, lines 2316–17, 2320–2335 – 'Pur ceste espee ai dulor e pesance'.

[69] Mason, 'The Hero's invincible weapon', 126, 131.

[70] Landon, *Itinerary*, 47: Richard made the gift at Catania on 6 March 1191; Gillingham, *Richard the Lionheart*, 159; Mason, ' The hero's invincible weapon', 129–30. It is interesting that Henry II had apparently been involved in the search for Arthur's tomb at Glastonbury, *Giraldus Cambrensis, Opera Historica*, ed. G.F. Warner, RS viii, *De principis instructione*, 127–8.

sword Durendal (actually inscribed DURINDARDA) is represented in Roland's hand; while Arthurian scenes of combat are to be found carved on Modena cathedral.[71] For the laity the sword was at the centre of a range of associations which frequently can have had little to do with religious ritual of the Church or with any carefully constructed intellectual programme. Even the religious rituals of knighthood of the twelfth century appear to have been superimposed on gestures and ceremonial of earlier date which laid far greater weight on the secular elements of this 'rite of passage'.[72] Furthermore, incidents in twelfth-century romance occasionally remind historians how difficult it might have been for ecclesiastical authorities to limit, or to 'tame' the range of the sword's associations. An episode from the works of 'Marie de France' illustrates this point. Although the *lai* known as *Yonec* recalls 'sorrow and grief . . . suffered for love', the final incident revolves around the use of an ancestral sword. In this complicated account of aristocratic passion and betrayal, a son kills his stepfather because the latter had been responsible for his true father's death: the instrument of revenge was the sword which had been handed by his dying father to the mother of their as yet unborn child. She was to confide it to their son and – years later after the lady eventually fulfilled the bequest – the youth 'struck off his stepfather's head, and thus with his father's sword avenged his mother's grief.'[73] The sword was surely the weapon with which to wreak a noble revenge; and Marie de France wrote as though she thought it particularly fitting that Yonec was both told of his mother's tragic history and killed his stepfather within a monastery – beside his own father's tomb. It seems unlikely that 'in real life' this view would have found favour with ecclesiastical authorities for whom the drawing of weapons and the shedding of blood in a sacred place were sacrilegious.[74]

The sword was primarily a weapon whose associations were with violence and

---

[71] R. Lejeune and J. Stiennon, *The Legend of Roland in the Middle Ages* (transl. C. Trollope) 2 vols., London 1971, i 61–8 (for critical discussion of the identification and extensive bibliography), ii pls 35–44; cf. also the inscribed incidents from the Roland cycle from a lost mosaic in Brindisi cathedral (dated c.1178), ii figs. 64–78. For Modena, R.S. Loomis, 'The oral diffusion of the Arthurian Legend', in *Arthurian Literature in the Middle Ages, a Collaborative History*, ed. Loomis, Oxford 1959, 60–2; Mason, 'The hero's invincible weapon', 130.

[72] For the distinctions made between a sword employed ritually within a church as a symbol marking the transmission of 'public office', and its use in 'knighting' ceremonies which were only gradually influenced by the liturgical *expertise* of churchmen, see J. Flori, *L'Idéologie du glaive, préhistoire de la chevalerie*, Geneva 1983, 168–73; and *idem*, 'Les origines de l'adoubement chevaleresque: étude des remises d'armes et du vocabulaire qui les exprime dans les sources historiques latines jusqu'au début du XIIIe siècle', *Traditio* xxxv, 1979, 209–72 (esp. 209–14, 221–4). For these developments within the Anglo-Norman world, cf. Chibnall, *The World of Orderic*, 142–5.

[73] *Sun parastre ad le chief tolu;/ De l'espie que fu sun pere/ Ad dunc vengié le doel sa mere, Lais, Marie de France*, ed. A. Ewert, Oxford (revised edn) 1960, 95–6 *Yonec*, lines 542–4; for the translation, *The Lais of Marie de France*, ed. G. Burgess and K. Busby, London 1986, 93. (Note that the story depended on the birth of a son.) Despite the controversy which surrounds the identity of Marie de France, these *lais* were likely to have been widely known in the circle of the Angevin court, since they were dedicated to 'nobles reis' (probably Henry II and his son the young king), see Ewert's edn, introd. viii–ix.

[74] Yonec's father's tomb was sited in the chapterhouse of an abbey within a 'castle' where Yonec, his mother and his stepfather, found themselves receiving hospitality on their way to *Karlion*, *Marie de France*, lines 481–506; *The Lais of Marie de France*, 93. The author does not condemn either the act of revenge or the place in which it was committed; and within some unspecified time Yonec was accepted by the population as his true father's successor.

bloodshed. In general that had been acknowledged for centuries by ecclesiastical authorities: church councils had laid down that no members of the clerical order should personally bear arms of any kind, but ought to be defended by members of the laity who had been trained to fight.[75] But, even so, there could still be ambiguity and doubts over the boundaries between the sacred and the secular. Laymen's weapons might gain a spiritual (or perhaps magical) force through the relics preserved within the hilt of a sword – although few could have equalled Roland's Durendal which, according to the poet, preserved in its hilt 'a tooth of St Peter and the blood of St Basil, hairs of 'monseigneur St Denis and clothing of St Mary'.[76]

Whether it was a king's consecration, or the funerary rites performed for him after his death, a church provided the setting for ceremonies which were not solely religious in their action or associations but which included 'pageantry, spectacle and splendour [which were] an integral part of the political process and the structure of power' throughout the whole medieval world.[77] The sword was one of the most potent symbols of royal power in that 'political process'; and during the course of the consecration ceremony it moved from a secular to a higher religious plane when it became the sign that the king's right to wield his sword was acknowledged and even licensed by ecclesiastical authority. As consecrated ruler, too, a king had the right to bear this weapon within the consecrated space of a church.[78]

In most circumstances, however, ecclesiastical authorities showed a deep aversion to the carrying of weapons within the church's 'material temple'; and it seems likely that this aversion in some some way helps to explain the apparent reluctance to represent a drawn sword within a church, even on the tombs of men who had been personally girded with a sword during the course of a royal consecration. Fears that a sacred place would be desecrated and polluted undoubtedly lay at the root of this aversion, whose strength can be sensed from the elaborate liturgy developed for 'the reconciliation of a sacred place'.[79] Throughout Europe

---

[75] Subsequent legislation tended to be based on the prohibitions of the Council of Chalcedon of 451 forbidding clerks to engage in *militia*, see F. Prinz, *Klerus und Krieg im früheren Mittelalter*, Monographien zur Geschichte des Mittelalters, Stuttgart 1971, 1–12 (5 n.11); J. Cowdrey, 'The peace and truce of God in the eleventh century', *P and P* xlvi, 1970, 42–67; older works were reviewed by H. Hoffmann, *Gottesfriede und Treuga Dei, Schriften der MGH*, Stuttgart 1964, see 260–1 for an extended text condemning the use of the sword by clerics.

[76] *Roland*, ed. Whitehead, 68, lines 2346–8; Mason, 'The Hero's Invincible Weapon', 127 n. 31. It ought to be remembered also that invocations to God or the Virgin, as well as religious sentiments of a more general kind, might be engraved on a sword's blade, hilt and/or pommel. For a variety of surviving examples, Oakeshott, *Records*, 38, 56 (the imperial sword, additionally bearing the arms of Otto IV, nephew of the Angevin Kings Richard and John), 59, 82, 84 (?c.1200).

[77] D. Cannadine, 'Introduction: divine rites of kings', in *Rituals of Royalty, Power and Ceremonial in Traditional Societies*, ed. D. Cannadine and S. Price, Cambridge 1987, 1, 12.

[78] Above 227–8. One twelfth-century consecration *ordo*, however, omits any kind of girding ritual within the church and lays down that the elect should already be wearing this weapon: *Precingatur ense optimo aureo et circumcinctus balteo . . .*, R. Elze, 'Königskrönung und Ritterweihe. Der Burgundische Ordo für die Weihe und Krönung des Königs und der Königin', in *Institutionen, Kultur und Gesellschaft im Mittelalter, Festschrift für Josef Fleckenstein*, Sigmaringen 1984, 326–42 (333).

[79] For an example, *De reconciliatione loci sacri, Pontifical of Magdalen College*, 127. For an exhaustive discussion of this topic by Bishop Durandus of Mende (d.1296), *Rationale Divinorum*

during the eleventh and twelfth centuries violence or bloodshed occurring within a church were especially condemned: within the English kingdom, for instance, homicide committed in a church was treated as unemendable unless the king extended his mercy to the perpetrator of the deed.[80] In Germany it was regarded as sacrilege even to draw a sword within the precincts of a church. To do so, it was explained, offended God because a church and its surroundings were reserved by God for Himself.[81] By the eleventh century that prohibition was extended: 'nobody shall carry a sword in church, unless it be the royal [sword]. (. . . *nemo gladium in ecclesiam portet, regali tantum excepto . . .*)'; but the royal (or imperial) sword was permitted because it had been conferred ceremonially on a layman within a church by an ecclesiastic.[82]

In the context of these religious prohibitions and regulations, it seems possible that the the representation of a drawn sword within a church was as likely to give rise to associations of conflict and violence as to thoughtful or subtle reflection on whether a specific weapon had spiritual rather than secular and material connotations. Nevertheless, it seems significant that John's own confessor condemned those 'detestable' *ingrati* who, once they had been crowned by the clergy, showed no compunction in attacking the church with the sword with which they had been girded for the church's defence (. . . *gladium,quo ab ecclesia ad ipsius accinti sunt defensionem . . . repente nudant, acuunt et vibrant dilecerationem*).[83] It obviously needs to be recognised that the representation of a drawn sword on John's effigy could have had a far wider range of connotations and associations for highly educated clergy than would have been available to the majority of the laity (or for that matter to many clergy). For such men John's 'sword on the stone' might have been a reminder of the extraordinary political *volte-face* of the king's last years, when he subjected his kingdom to Pope Innocent III – an action by which ecclesiastical authority was undoubtedly exalted. But, if this drawn sword were

---

Officiorum, 2 vols., Lyon 1584, i, 29–31 (lib. I, cap. vi, 38–46); cf. Ariès, *The Hour of Our Death*, 11–13, and cf. 29–31, 41–46.

[80] *Leges Henrici Primi*, ed. L.J. Downer, Oxford 1972, 114–15, 110–11, 125, 214, 247: cl. 12,1a (cl. 11,1a describes the procedure if the king permits compensation); cf. 21,1; 68,2; 79,5. These regulations and the attitudes which they embody were taken from the pre-Conquest *Laws* of Cnut, see Commentary, 326–7. The penalty for slaying a '*ministrum altaris*' was outlawry with forfeiture of all goods, 208–9: cl. 66,1.

[81] *Si quis temerarius atrium ecclesiae evaginato gladio praesumptuoso intraverit, sacrilegium facit* . . . And a New Testament passage is quoted which leaves no room for doubt: 'Omnes enim qui acceperint gladium, gladio peribunt' (adaptation of Matt. 26), *Acta conciliorum et epistolae decretales . . .*, ed. P. Labbe and P. Cossart, 12 vols, Paris 1715–, vi, cols. 440–1 (*Concil. Tribur*. a. 895, cl. 6). Cf. the practical problems implied in some eleventh-century Italian regulations forbidding any priest to say mass with 'daggers hanging about him' or wearing spurs (*Nullus cum cultellis foris pendentibus, nullus cum calcaribus*), *Acta conciliorum*, vi, col. 790 (*synodalia* of Bishop Ratherius of Verona, c.1009).

[82] *Acta conciliorum*, vi col. 829 (*Concil. Seligenstadt* a.1022, cl. 8). For the ecclesiastical theory that the sword as 'a gift from God' was conferred at his consecration on the emperor who was thus permitted 'to enter the church "*cinctus cum gladio*" ', W. Ullmann, *The Growth of Papal Government* (2nd edn), London 1965, 159 n. 1.

[83] This occurs in a sermon of the Cistercian Abbot John of Ford (and must therefore have been written before his death in 1214), *Johanni de Forda, Super extremam partem Cantici Canticorum, Sermo CXX*, ed. E. Mikkers and H. Costello, *Corpus Christianorum Continuatio Medievalis* xvii, Turnholt 1970, i, 472. My thanks to Christopher Holdsworth for directing me to this important passage, and for information about its author.

indeed commissioned to exemplify in marble some aspect of the 'two sword' theory, there seems to be no surviving trace of any contemporary exegesis suggesting that on his effigy King John was actually wielding his sword for the Church – unlike his grandfather Count Geoffrey le Bel. Perhaps, in view of John's personal reputation, such an interpretation would have been met with scepticism or incredulity. It might even have provoked the retort '*mollegladium*', 'softsword'.[84]

The monument to King John has been recognised by art historians as a work of exceptional quality and interest which has been assigned an influential place in the development of English sculpture. Why then did the detailed iconography of the effigy apparently have so little subsequent influence on the portrayal of dead rulers, and why was the drawn sword as an image so rarely used on funerary monuments at a time when most members of the lay aristocracy were warriors and 'knights'?[85] For, apart from the commemorative plaque to Geoffrey le Bel, there are remarkably few monuments in which this sign was employed. Within the English kingdom there is of course a remarkable series of effigies of 'active knights' who lie forever in arrested movement, but only one surviving monument of thirteenth century date commemorates a man who has actually drawn his sword from its scabbard.[86] This [Plate 13] comes from a group of military effigies arranged in the church of the Temple in London, and it has often been regarded as a memorial to William Marshal – a man perhaps better qualified than any of his contemporaries to lie in death with his sword drawn.[87]

---

[84] Cf. n. 21 above. This is not the place to discuss the 'two sword theory', although it is necessary to note how widely eminent churchmen differed in their views. E.g. for St Bernard's view that the pope held *both* swords, although he should confer the 'material sword' on the king, Ullmann, *Growth of Papal Government*, 430–3; contrast the view, 'Aecclesia non habet gladium', based on Christ's admonition to St Peter (Matt. 26): 'Converte gladium in vaginam . . .', *The Letters of Peter the Venerable*, 2 vols., ed. G. Constable, Cambridge Mass. 1967, i, 446; ii, 228.

[85] Two of the three Beaumont founders of the Norman monastery of Préaux (buried *in capitulo Pratellensi*) were portrayed on a lost 'group monument' recumbent but bearing drawn swords; unfortunately that is now apparently only known from an engraving of poor quality, J. Mabillon, *Annales Ordinis Sancti Benedicti*, Paris 1713, v, 328 – my thanks to Sandy Heslop for drawing my attention to this important monument. Unfortunately it is difficult to date this openly 'dynastic' series of effigies (the men commemorated apparently died during the years between c.1050 and 1166); but on the political position of the Beaumonts, Chibnall, *Anglo-Norman England*, 76–7, 93–4; Crouch, *The Beaumont Twins*, Cambridge 1986, 3–4.

[86] Generically such figures are classified under the heading 'Die aktive Liegefigur' with the comment that they are especially to be found in England, Schmidt, 'Die gotischen "gisants" und ihr Umfeld', 68–9. For illustrations of these knightly monuments, Prior and Gardner, *Medieval Figure Sculpture*, 588–96, 602, 609, 623 (examples go down to the early fourteenth century); Stone, *Sculpture in Britain*, 116–17; Bauch, *Grabbild*, 121–40 (*Die Krieger*), although cf. 187–8 for one memorial in Florence to a rider-figure (died 1289) wielding a drawn sword. Cf. the later monument to Sir Otto of Grandison (d.1359) in the church of Ottery St Mary, Devon, J. Dalton, *The Collegiate Church of Ottery St Mary*, Cambridge 1917, 39–45 and pl. XII.

[87] Crouch, *William Marshal*, 51–2, and 187, 192–4; and for a cautious acceptance of the Temple effigy as the Marshal's monument, 132, 179. These effigies were restored in the nineteenth century, E. Richardson, *The Monumental Effigies of the Temple with an Account of their Restoration in the year 1842*, 2 vols., London 1843, i, plates 1–10 and commentary – the figure generally identified with the Marshal is plate 6 (from which the fig. in the text of this paper is taken). The antiquary Camden noted an inscription *comes Pembrochiae* on this tomb, but there is no guarantee that the identification would have been contemporary with the Marshal's death, Richardson, 22; cf. Bauch, *Grabbild*, pl. 200 (but the drawn sword is not visible in this photograph); Stone, *Sculpture in Britain*, 251 for the virtual destruction of these monuments in bombing raids during 1941.

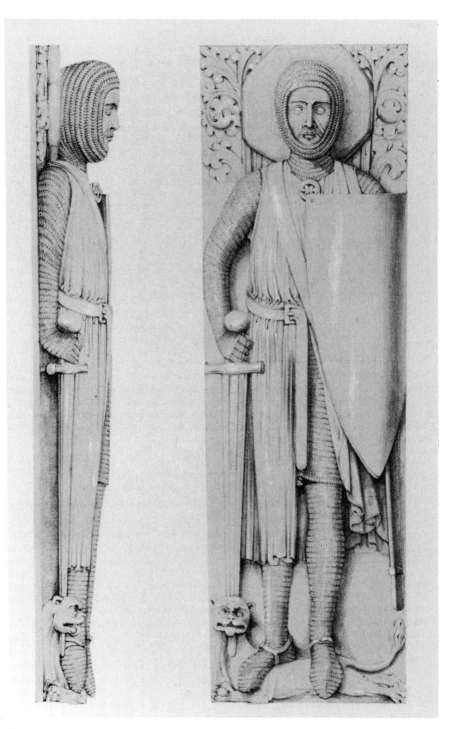

Plate 13.
Effigy of 'William Marshal', Temple Church, London (E. Richardson,
The Monumental Effigies of the Temple Church, *London 1843)*

The 'multiple' but often 'contradictory' signs which could be conveyed by the sword as an image have often been touched on during the course of this study, and it is time finally to return to the question of whether the 'cultural meanings' associated with that image prevented the portrayal of a drawn sword in a sacred space. There are, for instance, a number of indications that in practice ecclesiastical prohibitions against the carrying of arms within a church were obeyed, and that violent crimes committed in such a setting might be punished with especial severity. The notorious killing of Count Charles 'the Good' of Flanders which took place in the church of St Donatian in Bruges during Lent 1127 is of particular significance in this context, for all accounts emphasise that the count was at prayer, while his murderers concealed their 'drawn swords' beneath their cloaks before attacking him at the altar. In Galbert of Bruges's narrative great emphasis is laid on the pollution of the church, for references to the killers' 'drawn' and 'bloody' swords are repeated again and again; afterwards the purification and re-consecration of the building are described alongside the horrific punishments meted out to the count's killers.[88] A dramatic incident from Monte Cassino in the mid-eleventh century displays some of the same features as the episode just cited, although possibly its 'cultural and social overtones' are more difficult to perceive.[89] On the one hand the chronicler stresses that a party of Norman *milites* who paid a visit to the abbey 'left their arms outside the church' (*foris ecclesiam armis depositis*) – 'according to custom' (*iuxta consuetudinem armis depositis . . .*) comments the later recension; but, unlike the later Flemish writer, he did not apparently condemn the members of the local population who through a series of misunderstandings killed some of the party after they had entered the church to pray. Fifteen of the company were slaughtered.[90]

A vernacular work which probably had a wider circulation than the Latin narratives just cited also provides an interesting insight into twelfth-century attitudes and standards of behaviour in this respect. Tristan, accused of adultery with Queen Iseut and now on his way to execution, seemingly makes the best of a last opportunity for private prayer. He spies a chapel on a rock so precipitous that 'even a squirrel' would die in leaping from it. The interest in this context lies in the way in which the hero convinces his guards (*ses meneors*) that it is safe to allow him to enter alone to pray: ' "Lords, there is only this one entrance: *each of you holds a sword* [my italics]. You know very well that I can't get out without coming back past you," . . . One of them said to his companion: "We can surely

---

[88] One of Galbert's descriptions states that the principal plotter, his *milites* and *servientes* entered the church 'simul acceptis gladiis nudis sub palliis', *Histoire du meurtre de Charles le Bon comte de Flandre (1127–8) par Galbert de Bruges*, ed. H. Pirenne, Collection de textes 1891, 20–21, cf. 25; for the purification, 26–38 throughout. See also Suger, *Vie de Louis VI le Gros*, ed. H. Waquet *CHFMA* (2nd edn) 1964, 242. The socio-economic significance of this incident cannot be pursued here.

[89] Problems relating to the pursuit of such topics are discussed by Gombrich, *In Search of Cultural History*, 44.

[90] *Chronica Monasterii Cassinensis*, ed. H. Hoffmann, *MGH*, *Scriptores* xxxiv 1980, 309–10 (*A* is the original version of Leo of Ostia of c.1100, the addition is contained in recensions of slightly later date, printed as *CDMS*). My thanks to Graham Loud who drew my attention to this interesting incident and for supplying me with the reference. There are obvious difficulties in the interpretation of this tantalising passage, which would repay more detailed study.

let him go in" . . .'[91] What were the assumptions which the poet's contemporaries would have taken for granted? Would they have recognised that even guards put in charge of a brave and wily man did not take swords into a church, any more than a criminal condemned to die would have been permitted to wear his sword under escort? Does this episode prove that by the late twelfth century the regulations of the church had been 'internalised' and were normally observed? Or should the whole incident be regarded as fantasy, like the legendary ending associated with 'Tristan's leap'? For Tristan was a hero: unarmed he went straight through the chapel, and leapt through the east window: 'He would rather jump than have his body burned in public . . .'[92]

As long as King John's drawn sword could be regarded as no more than an uninteresting feature of a 'dingy relic' its neglect was understandable, but it seems surprising that this neglect should have persisted in more recent years.[93] The drawn sword clasped in King John's left hand contributes an entirely novel iconographical feature to the way in which a king was represented after death, even though that can only be appreciated after detailed comparisons with other European royal monuments. At one level such comparisons make King John's effigy not merely interesting, but unique; although viewed from another standpoint it can also be claimed that the conventions employed for the tombs of King John's father and brother at Fontevraud were developed and adapted in an ingenious way for the monument in Worcester cathedral. It has also been widely recognised that the funeral effigies of Henry II and Richard I portrayed those kings adorned with the *regalia* with which they had been consecrated; an image of a king crowned and armed reflects the ceremonial of royal consecration more closely than the selective choice of symbols with which the Capetian kings came to be associated. John's drawn sword, in particular, may have been intended to draw attention – not only to the material object which signified possession of the English kindom – but also to a sign which emphasised the forceful character of Angevin kingship during each ruler's lifetime, and which was strikingly displayed on his great seal of majesty.

Nevertheless, King John's naked sword remains an enigma. It has been suggested in this paper that the 'resonances' of the sword as an instrument of violence and bloodshed were too strong to enable a drawn sword to be universally accepted as a symbol of royal power after death within the material temple of the Church. The sanctions of religion might all too easily clash with the rather different attitudes and assumptions of a secular aristocracy. In order to support that argument – even tentatively – it has been necessary to range widely over both space and time, and to explore a number of ways in which 'forms, symbols and

---

[91] ' "Seignors, n'i a que ceste entree;/ A chacun voi tenir s'espee./ Vos savez bien ne pus issir,/ Par vos m'en estuet revertir"/ . . . Or l'a l'un d'eus dit a son per:/ "Bien le poon laisier aler." ', Béroul, *Le roman de Tristan, Tristan et Iseut, Les poèmes français, la saga norroise*, ed. D. Lacroix and P. Walter, Paris 1989, 64, lines 934–9, 939–40.

[92] Beroul, 66, lines 944–64 (the site of this feat has already been identified by the poet as a real rock, according to the inhabitants of Cornwall, 'Cornevalan'). Moreover – however artificial the timing seems – when Tristan's 'maistre' Gouvernal comes to the rescue, he brings *two* swords with him, his own and Tristan's, *Avoc le suen l'en aportoit*, lines 974–6.

[93] See the report made by an official of the Office of Works during the nineteenth-century, cited by Canon J. Wilson, 'Was the effigy of King John in Worcester cathedral originally coloured, or gilt?', *Associated Architectural Societies' Reports and Papers* xxii, 1913–14, 488.

words' could interact and 'become charged with what might be called cultural meanings'. That investigation could not have been undertaken without making some assumptions about 'non-linguistic methods of communication' and their value in relation to more traditional types of historical evidence. By their very nature the connotations and medieval meanings of some of these signs and symbols remain elusive; while the pursuit of their 'interactions' sometimes proves inconclusive. It would surely be impossible to prove any case relating to King John's sword – up to the hilt.

THE NORMANS THROUGH THEIR LANGUAGES

Lucio Melazzo

It is now a matter of common knowledge that every language organizes its classification of experience by forming sense groups and associating them with specific sound sequences. The criterion by which this classification is made is arbitrary in that there is no reason why a language should arrange meanings in groups in one way rather than another. If every language made up of perfectly discrete signs corresponded to a reality made up of perfectly discrete units and if such a biunivocal correspondence were so precise that one and only one notion corresponded to each sign and one and only one sign related to each notion, one would not speak of the arbitrary character of meaning. This is not the case, however. So, while the question of whether language or reality is prior in determining the structural organization of a multiplicity that is not perfectly differentiated is still under discussion, the consequence of the non-existence of a direct connexion between the referent and the corresponding signifier must not be underestimated. An intermediary between the referent and the signifier is supplied by the meaning, the determination of which is variously influenced: on the one hand by the situation and on the other hand, from a formal point of view, by the linguistic context. The existence and the conditions of this mediation give semantics, in addition to its linguistic aspect, both a psychological and a logico-philosophical aspect. The former pertains to the motivation and the attitude of the individual in the act of communicating linguistically, while the latter concerns the problems of both the symbolical function of linguistic signs and the acquisition and conveyance of knowledge. That being stated, diverse possibilities for semantic investigation arise. On the one hand, the different meanings of one signifier can be carefully examined in order that the corresponding notional field may be precisely defined. On the other hand, the different meanings through which a particular concept is indicated can be chosen as an object of research.

In this paper I shall bear in mind the latter form of investigation in putting forward a hypothesis which could prove useful in the field of history.

I shall start by referring to events that occurred in the south of Italy and in Sicily about the middle of the eleventh century. The facts we are interested in are related to events in the life of George Maniaces. As is well-known, between 1038 and 1040 this famous Byzantine commander attacked the Muslims and reconquered the city of Syracuse together with a great part of eastern Sicily. At that point, however, George Maniaces fell out of favour with Emperor Michael IV the Paphlagonian. Being an epilectic, Michael had left the affairs of government largely to his brother, the eunuch John, who suspected Maniaces of cherishing ambitious designs and thereupon recalled him to Constantinople. On his arrival in 1040 the commander was sent to prison, but a short time later he was released by Emperor Michael V Calaphates, who had succeeded his uncle Michael IV in

December 1041. The new emperor entrusted Maniaces with the command of a military expedition to the south of Italy where the Normans had invaded Apulia and the governor Argyros had rebelled against the central government. In April 1042 Maniaces landed at Taranto and advanced to Matera, but on the news of the accession to the throne of Constantine IX Monomachos he revolted against the new ruler, proclaimed himself emperor and moved to Durrës, whence he marched at the head of his army towards Constantinople. He engaged the imperial forces in the neighbourhood of Salonika and died in battle in 1043.

While relating the facts which had occurred in the south of Italy since Maniaces was summoned back to Constantinople, Michael Attaleiates gives us an interesting piece of information.[1] According to this chronicler, the return to Constantinople of the man who had been the real victor in the struggle against the Arabs had as its necessary consequence the loss of Sicily. As well as the island, the Greeks also lost most of their army. The following is a short account of the circumstances leading up to this disaster. The Ἀλβανοί and the Λατῖνοι were people who lived south of western Rome near the Italian territories of the Eastern Empire and had, up to a short time before, been allied to the Byzantines, sharing the right of citizenship with them and professing the same religious faith. Quite unexpectedly, they turned into enemies, when Duke Michael Docianos, who had then taken over command, outraged their leader while under the influence of drink: σὺν αὐτῇ (i.e. τῇ Σικελίᾳ) καὶ τὸ πλεῖστον τοῦ στρατεύματος ἀπολώλει Ῥωμαίοις. οὐ μὴν δὲ ἀλλὰ καὶ οἵ ποτε σύμμαχοι καὶ τῆς ἰσοπολιτείας ἡμῖν συμμετέχοντες, ὡς καὶ αὐτῆς τῆς θρησκείας, Ἀλβανοὶ καὶ Λατῖνοι ὅσοι μετὰ τὴν ἑσπερίαν Ῥώμην τοῖς Ἰταλικοῖς πλησιάζουσι μέρεσι, πολέμιοι παραλογώτατοι ἐχρημάτισαν ἐμπεπαρωνηκότος εἰς τὸν ἄρχοντα τούτων τοῦ τότε τὴν στρατηγίαν ἰθύνοντος Μιχαὴλ δουκὸς τοῦ Δοκειανοῦ.[2]

Some Ἀλβανοί and Λατῖνοι, whose identification did not cause historians any problems for a long time, are mentioned in the passage quoted above. These Ἀλβανοί and Λατῖνοι were regarded by scholars as Albanian and Latin contingents of the Byzantine army or as auxiliary troops of the Byzantines, until Era L. Vranoussi argued that both interpretations were untenable.[3] As she has acutely observed, Michael Attaleiates does not speak of mutinous soldiers, but alludes to two groups of people who resided in the regions south of Rome, between Rome and the Byzantine territories. These people were not soldiers fighting in the ranks of the Byzantine army but allies of Byzantium, enjoying the privileges of ἰσοπολιτεία; they professed themselves Christians (not Muslims) like the Byzantines and they did not treat their archon as a mere commander. Moreover, in referring to an episode which has been handed down by other sources he emphasizes the reason for both those people's taking up a hostile attitude towards

---

[1] Being a lawyer and a teacher of law in Constantinople, this author was named Attaleiates after the town of Attaleia in Asia Minor, which was his birthplace. As is known, he wrote a chronicle of events that he had witnessed between 1034 and 1079.

[2] *Corpus Scriptorum Historiae Byzantinae*, henceforth *CSHB*, Bonn 1853, 9.

[3] Ἔρας Λ.Βρανούση, 'Οἱ ὅροι Ἀλβανοί καὶ Ἀρβανῖται καὶ ἡ πρώτη μνεία τοῦ ὁμωνύμου λαοῦ τῆς βαλκανικῆς εἰς τὰς πηγὰς τοῦ ια´ αἰῶνος', Σύμμεικτα ii, 1970, 207–254. Most of the first part of my paper puts forward the argument propounded in this work. More or less twenty years ago it gave me much pleasure to hear this Greek lady explain her theory in a seminar in the University of Palermo. Her talk made so strong an impression on me that it was natural for me to think of it in tackling the varangian question from a linguistic point of view.

the Byzantines, namely Michael Docianos' insolent behaviour towards their archon.

We can now compare what Michael Attaleiates says with what is found in John Scylitzes' Chronicle.[4] As we read there, between 1038 and 1040 George Maniaces happened to have as his companions in arms, as well as his regular troops, five hundred Frankish soldiers. These had been sent from Transalpine Gaul under the command of a leader named Arduin, a lord who held land and was not subject to anyone else's command. With the help of these soldiers, he succeeded in getting war trophies from the Saracens: ἔτυχε προσεταιρισάμενος (Γεώργιος ὁ Μανιάκης) καὶ Φράγγους πεντακοσίους ἀπὸ τῶν πέραν τῶν Ἄλπεων Γαλλιῶν μεταπεμφθέντας καὶ ἀρχηγὸν ἔχοντας Ἀρδουῖνον τὴν κλῆσιν, χώρας τινὸς ἄρχοντα καὶ ὑπὸ μηδενὸς ἀγόμενον, μεθ᾽ ὧν τὰ τῶν Σαρακηνῶν εἰργάσατο τρόπαια.[5] When George Maniaces was recalled to Constantinople, his place was taken by Michael Docianos. The new commander refused to give the Franks the pay they usually drew from month to month and, as was said, went so far as to offend their leader, who had come to ask him to treat the soldiers fairly and not deprive them of the due reward for their labours by ordering him to be whipped with ignominy. As a result, the Franks rebelled: μὴ παρέχων γὰρ (Μιχαὴλ ὁ Δοκειανός) κατὰ καιρὸν τοῖς Φράγγοις τὸ παρεχόμενον αὐτοῖς ἐφ᾽ ἕκαστον μῆνα σιτηρέσιον, μᾶλλον δέ, ὥς φασι, καὶ τὸν ἡγεμόνα τούτων, ἀφιγμένον ὡς αὐτὸν ἐφ᾽ ᾧ παρακαλέσαι ἠπίως χρῆσθαι τοῖς στρατιώταις καὶ μὴ ἀποστερεῖν τούτους τοῦ τῶν πόνων μισθοῦ, ὑβρίσας καὶ μαστιγώσας ἀτίμως ἠνάγκασε τοὺς ἀνθρώπους ἀποστατῆσαι.[6] When the duke realized that the Franks were rising up in arms against the Byzantines, he underestimated the danger and did not gather all the available forces before moving to the attack against the insurgents. He was therefore defeated, lost most of his troops and was able to save his own skin with dishonour only by fleeing and taking refuge in Cannae. Subsequently, eager to wreak revenge on his adversaries, he launched a new attack in great strength but once more he suffered defeat, since another army, not slight in number and composed of those Italians who resided by the River Po and in the regions on this side of the Alps, had joined the Frankish soldiers: προσεταιρισαμένων τῶν Φράγγων καὶ ἄλλο πλῆθος οὐκ ὀλίγον ἀπὸ τῶν Ἰταλῶν τῶν περὶ τὸν Πάδον τὸν ποταμὸν καὶ τὰς ὑπωρείας οἰκούντων τῶν Ἄλπεων.[7]

As we learn from Scylitzes' narrative, the name of the outraged leader was Arduin and he was at the head of five hundred Frankish soldiers from France, that is from the country where the Normans lived. These people rose up in a body, after their leader had been whipped by order of Docianos. At first the Byzantine duke had to settle accounts with the Franks alone but then he found himself facing an army made up of both Franks and Italians who came respectively from beyond the Alps and from northern Italy. Consequently, according to Scylitzes, about the year 1040 two peoples, who had settled in southern Italy, crossed

---

4 The chronicle of events written by this Byzantine author of the second half of the eleventh century begins from the year 811 and goes as far as the year 1079. As we know, most of it was incorporated by George Cedrenos into his universal history.

5 *Corpus Fontium Historiae Byzantinae*, henceforth *CFHB*, v, 425.

6 *CFHB*, v, 426.

7 *CFHB*, v, 426.

swords with the Byzantines. They were the Φράγγοι, that is Normans, descendants of the mixed Scandinavian and Frankish race that had settled in Normandy in the ninth century, and the Ἰταλοί, namely Lombards or Longobards, who had been living in Italy for centuries. These events have been passed on to us in detail and with some variations by several contemporary Latin sources[8] and especially by William of Apulia.[9] This author has left us in his verses a vivid account of the role played by Arduin in inciting the Normans to attack the Byzantines. Changed by the epic into the legendary hero who rose against Byzantine oppression in southern Italy, Arduin, whom the continuator of Scylitzes' work wrongly believed to be Robert Guiscard's uncle,[10] belonged to the military nobility of Milan. He had been appointed τοποτηρητής of Melfi and honoured with the title of 'candidatus' obtaining both a function and a rank the Byzantines awarded as a rule to those of their allies who enjoyed ἰσοπολιτεία.[11]

Thus, the Λατῖνοι of whom Michael Attaleiates speaks are the old inhabitants of Italy whom Scylitzes calls Ἰταλοί, namely the Lombards or Longobards. The Normans, the Φράγγοι of Scylitzes, are named Ἀλβανοί by Michael Attaleiates. This term, which is not an ethnic but just a common noun, should be written with a small ἀ- and corresponds to the well-known word of mediaeval Latin *albani*, meaning "aliens" and denoting those who, as foreigners, were not subjects of the country in which they had settled.

The English definition of *albanus* which is to be found in J.F. Niermeyer's dictionary states that the term is a conjectural Frankish word meaning 'a man belonging to a different jurisdiction'.[12] It may hence be inferred that having at a certain time been taken into mediaeval Latin the term under discussion derives from a hypothetical Frankish form *aliban*, which may be supposed to derive in turn from the Latin adverb *alibi* 'elsewhere'. As the use of *albanus* in the numerous sources collected under the respective entries in both J.F. Niermeyer's and C. Du Cange's dictionaries clearly shows, there can be no question but that the noun had a legal connotation in as much as it referred to people living in a foreign country who were not naturalized and were therefore subject to special rules of law.[13]

---

8 Amatus, ii, 17–18, 31. *MGH*, v, 55; v, 58; vii, 675–676. *RIS*, v, 1–8. *PL*, cxlix, 1083.
9 Guillaume de Pouille, *La geste de Robert Guiscard*, ed. M. Mathieu, Palermo 1961, 109–111.
10 *CSHB*, Bonn 1839, 720.
11 Βρανούση, 224.
12 See the entry *albanus* in J.F. Niermeyer's *Mediae Latinitatis Lexicon Minus*, 2 vols, Leiden 1954–76. The word *albani* listed in C. Du Cange's *Glossarium Mediae et Infimae Latinitatis*, 10 vols, Niort 1883–88, is defined as 'Advenae, Alienigenae, Adventitii'. The term is retained in the Modern French substantive *aubain* which refers to an individual who has not the right of citizenship in the foreign country where he lives. This substantive has its most direct predecessor in the Latin variant *aubenus*, which is found among other forms of the word *albanus* in both the above-mentioned dictionaries. This variant occurs in Latin documents of the French area and shows velarization of pre-consonantal *l* and palatalization of stressed *a*, i.e. two phonetic phenomena which occurred in the passage from Latin to Old French.
13 Derivatives of *albanus* which have a clear, juridical value are *albanagium* and *albania*. The former indicates either the power of a lord to seize the movables left by an alien who has died without any heir living within the lord's jurisdiction or a payment by the heirs dwelling elsewhere for the release of an inheritance. The latter refers to a mortuary from the goods of an alien. A verb *albanare* 'to enrol in the class of *albani* or to regard as *albani*' is to be found in C. Du Cange's dictionary where an etymological explanation by Walafrid Strabo is also quoted. According to this author, the Scots were the first to be called *albani*, because of their almost innate habit of

It is highly probable that the Normans, who began to appear in the south of Italy from 1017 and obtained their first permanent possession in 1030[14] were considered aliens. From the facts under discussion, however, we can draw inferences of considerable interest. To begin with, the noun ’Αλβανοί, being a word of Latin origin, must have arrived in Byzantium from Southern Italy, where it undoubtedly applied to the foreigners from Normandy; otherwise Michael Attaleiates could not have applied it as a correct denomination for the Normans either in the passage mentioned above or in another where, saying that George Maniaces rose against the Emperor Constantine IX Monomachos with his Byzantine and Norman soldiers, he calls the former 'Ρωμαῖοι and the latter ’Αλβανοί: Γεώργιος, ᾧ Μανιάκης ἐπώνυμον, ἐκ τῆς ’Ιταλικῆς ἀρχῆς ἐπαναστὰς μετὰ τῶν ἐκεῖσε συνόντων στρατιωτῶν 'Ρωμαίων καὶ ’Αλβανῶν.[15] Secondly, the denomination ’Αλβανοί must have come into use initially among government officials of the Byzantine Empire, hierarchs of the Orthodox Church or local archons, who held their office in the dominion of Southern Italy and were therefore compelled to resort to the Latin of that time in their writings. It follows from this assumption that the official statements and records which were sent in all likelihood from the Italian domains to Byzantium were very frequently written by men with a good knowledge of both Latin and Greek and contained, therefore, the term *albani* or ἀλβανοί, referring to those people who had arrived there from the north and for whom the name of Normans would come to the fore much later. If these suggestions are correct, then it is inconceivable that those northern people, who had dealings with the Byzantines while they were in the pay of the Eastern Empire, should have been unaware that the denomination *albani* or ἀλβανοί was applied to them. If this is so, then those people who were driven to emigrate from overpopulated, strife-ridden Normandy and drawn to the south of Italy by talk of fertile lands and news of local conflicts which it appeared easy to take advantage of must have consented to be called by the name of *albani* or ἀλβανοί at least until their leaders succeeded in gratifying their burning wish to get a piece of land and thus become part of the complicated play of forces. Furthermore, there are good grounds for supposing that when the Normans settled in southern Italy they used the name *albani* for a certain time to refer to themselves, if we consider that the Greek form ἀλβανοί has its stress on the last syllable and not, as one would expect, on the penultimate, that is on the same syllable as the Latin word *albáni* pronounced in a manner consistent with the normal rules of the Latin system of accentuation.[16] The Greek form ἀλβανοί instead of *ἀλβᾱνοι can have come only from a Latin *albaní* stressed on the last syllable. Such a form uttered with a particular foreign accent can have flowed only from the mouths of people who had spoken Old French from birth and

wandering. This is obviously an explanation based on a false etymology which connects *albanus* with the Old Irish name for a Scot *Albanach*, a derivative of *Albu* 'Scotland'.

[14] This is the date when Duke Sergius IV of Naples gave the fee of Aversa to Rainulf Drengot.

[15] *CSHB*, Bonn 1853, 18.

[16] Even though vowel quantity had not been distinctive in Latin any longer since about the end of the third century A.D., the substantive *albanus* must have been stressed on the penultimate syllable like all other older terms ending in *-ānus*, to which it undoubtedly conformed. This must have been the case, since the accent generally did not shift throughout the evolution of Latin.

transferred the habit of stressing the last syllable of all words from their native language to any other language they had to speak.[17]

I shall now make a leap in time and space and examine the name *Varangians*. This is the name by which the Vikings of Scandinavia were known to the Slavs and Byzantines. There are many indications that in the ninth and tenth centuries Scandinavians were active along the Volhov and the upper reaches of the Dnieper, the Volga and their tributaries.[18] Descending the Volga to the Black Sea in the tenth century bands of these people raided the coasts of the Byzantine Empire and probably penetrated as far east as the Caspian Sea. Once they had come into contact with Byzantium, they began to move to the Eastern Empire not only as merchants and warriors but also as mercenaries. So, from the end of the tenth century the term *Varangians* is applied to the Northmen, including also Saxons and Anglo-Saxons, who made up the personal guard of the Byzantine Emperors; they were noted for their courage and fidelity, but also took a decisive part at times in making and unmaking emperors.[19]

The name *Varangians* has been interpreted in various ways, which are well-known and need not be mentioned here.[20] There is now a general agreement that the derivation is from a Germanic form *$w\bar{a}ragangja$- composed of $w\bar{a}ra$- 'vow, confidence (in), faith (in), agreement' and a form *gangja*- based on the Indo-European root *$ghengh$- 'to go'.[21] This type of formation is present in other Germanic languages and is particularly well attested in Old Norse.[22] For example,

---

[17] This habit of stressing the last syllable of any word had resulted from the loss of all final and median post-tonic vowels. As is well-known, these vowels dropped out in the passage from Latin to Old French.

[18] The problem of the *Varangians* has far too often been connected with that of the origins of the first Russian state and this has given rise to much controversy among scholars. The paper that A. Riasanovsky read in April 1968 in Spoleto during the sixteenth Week of Study organized by the Italian Centre for Studies on the Late Middle Ages and the ensuing discussion are indicative on this subject. Both can be found in *I Normanni e la loro espansione in Europa nell' alto medioevo*, Spoleto 1969, 171–204, 553–569.

[19] The history of the section of the Byzantine armed forces which went in its heyday under the name of *Varangians* and also an outline of both the origins of those people and the historical and geographical conditions which led to their appearance in the east Roman army can be found in S. Blöndal, *The Varangians of Byzantium*, Cambridge 1978.

[20] The various interpretations of the name Varangians are discussed in Blöndal, 4–14.

[21] This is the etymology accepted by J. De Vries in his *Altnordisches Etymologisches Wörterbuch*, Leiden 1962. Of course, as well as *wæringi* which is found in Old Icelandic, *wæringr* is the form in which the substantive appears in the nominative singular in Old Norwegian. Moreover, as a result of a well-known phenomenon in Old Norse, the velar *g*- of the descendant of *$gangja$*- disappeared because in the compound word it was preceded by a consonant. The independent Old Norse word *gengi* 'accompanying, escort, help' is believed to come from an original noun *ga-gangja*, on which are also based the forms of both Old Saxon *gigengi* 'series' and Old English *(ge)genge* 'troop'. Well-known phenomena, in the history of Greek and Russian, clearly prove the connection of *wæringi* with βάραγγος and *varjagŭ*. The Byzantine-Greek form shows a stem, βάραγγ- where α of -ραγ- is assimilated to that of βα-, which reproduces æ. The stem *varjag*- of the Old Russian substantive certainly derives from a form *$var\varrho g$-. On the origin of the Arabic term *Varank* see Blöndal, 6.

[22] The idea of 'going' is always present in these formations, the first part of which may be a prefix, an adjective or a noun. Thus, for example, the three Old Norse substantives *foringi* 'leader', *armingi* 'beggar' and *heiðingi* 'wolf' indicate respectively the man who goes ahead of others, the man who goes round as a poor man and the animal which goes round tablelands or heaths. The prefix *for* 'ahead (of)' is easily identified in *foringi*, while the adjective *armr* 'poor'

erfingi and *bandingi* in Old Norse indicated, respectively, someone who went round with an inheritance and someone who went round in chains. Consequently *wæringi* could refer in a satisfactory manner to someone who went round with pacts. In every day usage, however, *erfingi* and *bandingi* meant, respectively, 'heir' and 'prisoner', while in all likelihood *wæringi* signified 'foreigner'. This was in fact the meaning of the Old English noun *wærgenga*, of the Longobardic noun *uuaregang* and of the Latinized forms *wareguangus* or *waregnangus*, *garagangus* and *wargengus*, which are found in Latin documents of the Germanic area.[23] If several nouns belonging to different Germanic languages and formally connected with the Old Norse term here under discussion clearly meant 'foreigner', it is more than plausible that in the beginning *wæringi* too had the same meaning and only in the course of time became a name applied to the Northmen by the Slavs and the Byzantines. If this hypothesis is well-grounded, it must be recognized that for a period of several centuries Northmen were called foreigners by the Slavs and the Byzantines. The term for foreigner being of Old Norse origin, these two peoples must have learnt this denomination from the Northmen themselves. This implies that the Northmen applied the name of foreigners to themselves.

As we have seen, other Northmen were initially called foreigners in the south of Italy. This is unlikely to have been fortuitous. But why should the concept of foreigner be expressed by a term in fact meaning 'someone who went round with pacts'? The answer, in my opinion, is to be found in this passage from the Edict of Rothari: 'Omnes uuaregang, qui de exteras fines in regni nostri finibus aduenerint

---

and the noun *heiðr* 'tableland, heath' can be separately recognized in *armingi* and in *heiðingi*. Although they have slightly different meanings, the Gothic substantive *fauragangia* 'steward' and the Old English substantive *foregenga* 'forerunner' correspond exactly in form to *foringi*, while *heiðingi* can be compared to an analogous Old English compound *hæðstapa* 'heath-stalker, wolf, stag', the second part of which is related to the Old English verb *stæppan* 'to step, go, advance'. It is also interesting to observe that in addition to *lausingi* 'freed, without a homeland', where one can recognize the adjective *lauss*, another substantive is attested with the same meaning: *leysingi*, which in its first part may have been influenced by comparison with the verb *leysa* 'to loosen, untie, free'. It is from *leysingi*, taken over as a loan-word, that the Old English forms *leising*, *līesing*, *līsing*, and *lȳsing*, which all mean 'freedman', are thought to derive.

[23] To these forms, which are found under the entry *warengangi* in C. Du Cange's dictionary, I have not added *waringus* and *warganeus*. Both of these forms are to be found in J.E. Niermeyer's dictionary. The former term is correctly regarded as a separate entry because of its meaning, which is exclusively that of 'soldier adventurer'. The latter term is listed under the entry *wargengus*, but derives, in my opinion, from the substantive *wargus*, meaning 'homeless, robber, vagabond'. Furthermore, accepting a reading of L.A. Muratori, Niermeyer lists the form *waregnangus*, while Du Cange prefers a reading which leads him to recognize the existence of a form *wareguangus*. This is not the time to deal with the problem, which would require the direct consultation of the document. I shall only say that both forms could be justified: whereas *waregnangus* could be compared to *warengangus* on the basis of the almost identical pronunciation of the clusters *-gn-* and *-ng-*, *warenguangus* would derive from the transference of the labial feature of *w-* to the first *g* (> *gu*) in the second part of the compound. In *garagangus*, on the contrary, *w-* (> *g-*) has lost its labial feature and has been assimilated to the first *g* or both the subsequent *g*'s. Finally, it may be that the spelling of *warengangus* derives from a process which began with the intrusion of an *n* before the first *g* in the second part of the compound and originated from the desire to produce two identical *-ng-* clusters in sequence.

seque sub scuto potestatis nostrae subdederint, legibus nostris langobardorum uiuere debeant, nisi si in aliam legem ad pietatem nostram meruerint'.[24]

As we know, this edict officially formulated juridical matter taken from Germanic oral tradition based on the memory of both the king and the elders: 'Praesentem uero dispositionis nostrae edictum, quem deo propitio cum summo studio et summis uigiliis a celestem faborem praestitis inquirentes et rememorantes antiquas legis patrum nostrorum, quae scriptae non erant, condedimus, et quod pro commune omnium gentis nostrae utilitatibus expediunt, pari consilio parique consensum cum primatos iudices cunctosque felicissimum exercitum nostrum augentes constituimus in hoc membranum scribere iussimus'.[25] We can therefore imagine that in Germanic juridical use the possibility existed for all those who left their place of origin to be granted pacts by the leaders of the territories to which they had moved. The foreigner was thence one who might enter into such pacts. This use which was customary among Germanic peoples probably caused those Northmen who, after the stage of raids and armed attacks, decided to settle in territories inhabited by people of different stocks, to adopt a certain bold habit of negotiating their juridical position with those who were in power there. It is precisely as a result of this juridical tradition that we find the Northmen in the Slav and Byzantine territories called *Varangians*. The Francisized Northmen of Normandy, too, cannot have forgotten this custom if they continued to accept the appellation *Albani*, which, like *Væringiar*, equally meant foreigners.

---

[24] *Leges Langobardorum*, ed. F. Beyerle, Witzenhausen 1962, 89.
[25] *Leges Langobardorum*, 93.

THE KNIGHT, HIS ARMS AND ARMOUR
c.1150–1250

Ian Peirce

The main intention of this paper is to investigate in some detail the armour and weapons of the well-armed warrior over a period of a century, commencing around 1150, and to follow up any developments which occur. Needless to say, this is one area of research which is sorely in need of attention. Where possible, I shall illustrate knightly equipment over this period, with surviving artefacts. Finally, I intend to inspect the splendid mounted knights of Monreale Cathedral cloisters and compare them with other images of knights of the same period in France, Spain and England.[1]

Before I begin however, let us remind ourselves of the appearance of the well-armed warrior of c.1100–1150.[2] He wears a mail shirt or hauberk as his main body armour, usually stretching to the knees and split fore and aft to facilitate mounting. The sleeves may be elbow length or stretch to the wrists. He wears a mail coif under the helmet which may or may not be an integral part of the main garment. In some cases, his lower legs are protected by mail chausses, which even well into the twelfth century were still generally worn only by the affluent. His head is protected by a conical shaped helmet with the skull made in one piece, with a reinforcing brow-band and nasel separately applied by riveting, similar in construction to the surviving helmet of St Wenceslas. Conversely, the helmet could be formed in the spangenhelm construction, namely consisting of triangular curved plates riveted inside a framework of bands. His shield is kite-shaped and may be carried by grasping leather straps of various configurations. In addition, it could be suspended from the neck by a broad leather strap. He carries a broadsword of a type specifically suitable for hacking and slashing, which when not in use was placed in a simple undecorated scabbard. The knight's other offensive weapon is the ash or apple-wood lance of some nine to eleven feet in length.

Changes in style of any item of clothing, or indeed any object, may occur as a result of the consumers' personal tastes or the manufacturer's ability literally to come up with a bright idea, to improve sales. One would assume that the already well-armed warrior, he who regularly engaged in combat, was aware of developments in arms such as the crossbow and therefore knew of the steps to be taken to improve his armour and the chances of survival. There again it is probable that

---

[1] I am indebted to Dr David Nicolle for his interest and tremendous help during the development of this paper, not least in providing me with numerous slides and photographs, but also for his keen support at all stages.

[2] See also Ian Peirce, 'The Knight, his Arms and Armour in the Eleventh and Twelfth Centuries', *The Ideals and Practice of Medieval Knighthood: Papers from the First and Second Strawberry Hill Conferences*, ed. C. Harper-Bill and Ruth Harvey, 1986, 157.

Plate 1.
Joshua initial from the Winchester Bible (reproduced by permission of the Dean and Chapter of Winchester)

the skilled smiths, those engaged in the manufacture of war equipment, could quite simply conceive a revolutionary modification while casually beating away at a sword blade or riveting the brow-band to a conical helmet. Clearly, both warrior and smith fed each other with information and thus changes in the appearance of the fighting man took place. By c.1170 some modifications to the body armour had taken place and are clearly recorded in the Winchester Bible[3] and a leaf related to the same Bible,[4] both of c.1160–80.

During the last quarter of the twelfth century, it became increasingly popular to have the long sleeves of the hauberks terminating in mail mittens, or mufflers, as they were also called. Thus, the ingenuity of the armourer had not been idle, for he had overcome the difficulties of encasing the hand in a flexible and

---

[3]   Cathedral Library, f.209, Winchester.
[4]   Pierpont Morgan Library, MS 619, New York.

Plate 2.
The important leaf related to the Winchester Bible (reproduced by permission of the Pierpont Morgan Library, New York)

impenetrable barrier. Claude Blaire points out that the illuminated initial letter in the Book of Joshua, in the Winchester Bible, shows the first stage in this development, whereby the knights wear hauberks with sleeves which extend over the backs of the hands but leave the fingers and thumb bare. (Plate 1).

Usually, however, the muffler is depicted as a bag-like extension to the sleeve with a separate stall for the thumb. The mail did not extend over the palm of the hand, as this would lessen the ability to grip. Instead, the palm was covered with a layer of fabric or thin pliable leather and most conveniently split to allow easy disengagement of the hand as and when required. Many illustrations of mufflers show a leather thong or cord interwoven through the mail and round the wrist, which surely must be a simple but effective precautionary measure to minimise the problem of the mail sleeve dragging at the hand.[5]

A single scene from the remarkably detailed mid-thirteenth century French manuscript, the Maciejowski Bible, shows not only the mufflers described above but another not so popular form, where the separate fingers are mailed. Yet another variant clearly shown on a wall painting in Santi Giovanni e Paulo, Spoleto, shows mittens only on the sword hand. (Plate 3).

It is after 1150 that illustrations of mail chausses become common, up to which point this essential refinement had been worn solely by the affluent.[6] Two main styles existed, both suspended from the girdle of the breech and under the hauberk. The first is admirably illustrated in the leaf related to the Winchester Bible and consists of a close fitting stocking of mail, often with a garter-like support threaded through the mail below the knee and often covering the foot as well. For a lifelike representation of this item, that on the statue of Roland on the west front of Verona Cathedral is possibly the best. This unusually detailed carving dates from c.1139 and the fact that the warrior clearly has a mail chausse on the left leg only shows him to represent a man who would fight on foot, in disciplined ranks, probably kneeling on the right leg and forming a shield wall with his comrades.[7] The second consisted of a weight-reducing web of mail covering the front of the leg, laced together at the back and again under the sole of the foot. This feature is beautifully portrayed on the well-known and early representation of the death of Becket, c.1190–1200.[8] Yet another death of Becket, this time the fresco from the church of Santi Giovanni e Paulo at Spoleto, shows a similar feature which may be even earlier, say about the late 1170s and therefore, I believe, the earliest illustration of this important development. (Plate 3). A studded variety also emerged in the first half of the thirteenth century and is clearly illustrated in the Westminster Psalter.[9]

The mail coif was generally attached to the mail shirt, but there is some good evidence on the Bayeux Tapestry that it could also be a separate item. Claude Blair states that there is no other illustration of a separate coif earlier than the third quarter of the thirteenth century, but I disagree with this statement, for there

---

5 Claude Blair, *European Armour*, London 1958, 29.
6 Blair, 28.
7 D. Nicolle, *Arms and Armour of the Crusading Era 1050–1350*, New York 1988, 476.
8 For this illustration see Ian Peirce, 'The Development of the Medieval Sword, c.850–1300', *The Ideals and Practice of Medieval Knighthood: Papers from the Third Strawberry Hill Conference*, ed. C. Harper-Bill and Ruth Harvey, 1988. 152.
9 BL MS Royal 2A, XXII f.220.

Plate 3.
Fresco depicting the death of Becket. Santi Giovanni e Paulo, Spoleto

is some evidence that the dismounted knights on the wall paintings at Copford Church indeed have separate coifs.[10] These date from c.1150. Again the figure of Gideon in the Bible d'Averbode from Liège, Belgium, dated c.1170 almost certainly wears a separate coif.[11] In the various scenes illustrated on the façade of the Cathedral of San Donnino, Fidenza, Italy, at least one well-armed warrior wears a separate mail coif. These date from c.1200.[12] No hauberk with the coif attached, that is, integral with the garment itself, has survived. Many thirteenth-century manuscripts show that the coif was fitted with a ventail, that is, a specially shaped flap of mail, which could be drawn across the mouth for added protection before action and was attached to the right side of the coif by a strap or lace.[13] Ventails are mentioned in literary sources before the end of the eleventh century and appear to be intended in several eleventh-century manuscript illustrations including the Bible of Roda and the Farfa Bible.[14] Fortunately they are very clearly shown as a well-established feature on a carved relief *in situ*, in the cloisters of the monastery of Santo Domingo de Silo, Spain, c.1135–40.[15]

Somewhere around the mid-twelfth century knights are often shown wearing a long, often very long, flowing, sometimes sleeveless, fabric garment over their hauberks. Its true name is coat armour, but modern students of arms and armour prefer the term surcoat. There is still much discussion over the reason for its introduction and the sheer matter of its popularity points to it possessing some form of benefit for the wearer. Several reasons have been put forward for its introduction but none is based on any definite evidence. It has been suggested that it was a kind of waterproof and indeed my own thoughts go along these lines.[16] Perhaps it had been impregnated with goose or duck fat, or animal fat for that matter, which would certainly repel the effects of a hard shower or sudden downpour. To reinforce my own opinion, I must quote the words of Allen Brown who suggested that the thought of a hauberk in the rain would make any batman blanch.

An equally good suggestion, although not generally accepted in modern times, is that the surcoat was first adopted by the Crusaders as a protection against the Palestine sun. Certainly a light-coloured garment would reflect an enormous amount of incident radiation, while a loose-fitting voluminous garment, probably an imitation of those worn by the Saracens, would allow the passage of cooling currents of air between it and the hauberk. Fortunately, I may comment as one who has experienced extremes of weather while wearing a hauberk and all other knightly equipment, sometimes mounted, other times not. I recall a day near Southampton, in 1986, when the shade temperature reached 90°F. I wore no surcoat and well remember the discomfort I experienced. I also remember the need to retire to the local inn, almost twice an hour, for refreshment.

According to Claude Blair, the earliest known illustration of a surcoat is that worn by Waleran de Beaumont, count of Melun and earl of Worcester, on his seal

10 Blair, 27. See also Nicolle, 352.
11 Bibliothèque de l'Université, Liège, Belgium, MS 363 B, f.16v. See also Nicolle, 434.
12 Nicolle, 475.
13 Blair, 27.
14 Paris, BN MS lat. 6, f.145r and Rome, Vatican Library, Cod. Lat. 5729, f.94v.
15 Nicolle, 256.
16 Blair, 28.

Plate 4.
Illustration from the Eneid of Heinrich von Veldeke. Note the highly detailed helmets and surcoats (reproduced by permission of the Deutsche Staatsbibliotek, Berlin)

appended to a charter dateable to before 1150. This is an interesting, as well as early, illustration of a surcoat for it possesses wrist-length sleeves, a style which did not appear again until after 1250. This example hugs the body fairly closely as far as the hips, after which it flairs out into a flowing ankle-length skirt, split, as one would expect, to facilitate riding. The sleeves fit closely to the wrists, where they then widen suddenly to form long streamer-like tippets.[17] Very similar surcoats, but without the sleeves, are also shown on the illuminated initial letter from the Winchester Bible c.1160–70 (Plate 1) and in the work of Heinrich von Veldeke c.1200, although the German manuscript shows the garment to be slightly shorter and in one instance the wearer boasts his own personal heraldry upon his chest.[18] (Plate 4). This latter illustration depicts the style which remained popular until c.1320. Similar examples are also shown upon the wall paintings of Claverley, Shropshire. (Plate 5).

The defensive armour of the well-armed mounted warrior was completed by the kite-shaped shield which protected his front and left side, including a large portion of the left leg. This was the standard shield of the knight, although manuscript illustrations show it to have been popular among infantry also. Its shape allowed it to fit conveniently into the space between the rider and the horse's neck, without actually pressing upon the animal. These shields were generally constructed of wood, perhaps lime wood, well known for its toughness, and were covered in leather with a reinforcing strip, probably of steel, around the rim. This latter feature prevented the deep bite of a sword slash. They also carried a central, sometimes prominent, boss, again of metal. It was actually curved along its major axis, effectively wrapping around the rider and thus maximising protection. It could be carried by a variety of strap arrangements and could be hung about the neck or shoulder, thus freeing the left hand for controlling the horse with the reins. This type of shield remained popular until c.1200, but the evidence of sculpture and manuscript illustrations, suggests that from the middle of the twelfth century, the curved top became less prominent.[19] Indeed by the early years of the thirteenth century it had become quite flat.[20] This modification resulted in a triangular-shaped shield, which remained in use until c.1250, but before this date a smaller model had already come into general use.[21]

Manuscript illustrations rarely depict shields with accuracy to detail, but sculpture and metalwork artefacts invariably give the information we need, even down to individual rivet heads and delicately executed decoration. The carved capitals in the cloister of Monreale Cathedral are widely recognised as superb examples of south European Romanesque art. They are the last in a series of three important Italo-Norman collections of carvings showing military scenes. The others are those above the north door of San Nicola at Bari, which are generally thought to

---

[17] Blair, 28–9. Edmund King has shown that this second seal of count Waleran was in fact used from 1139–41 (Edmund King, 'Waleran, count of Meulan, earl of Worcester (1104–1166)', *Tradition and Change*, ed. Diana Greenway *et al.*, Cambridge 1985, 165–80 and pl.4.

[18] Deutsche Staatsbibliotek, Berlin, MS Germ. 20282. This important manuscript is replete with highly detailed illustrations of mounted and dismounted warriors.

[19] For good examples of these shields see Ian Peirce, 'The Knight, his Arms and his Armour', 161.

[20] A fine example may be found in La Charité Psalter: BL MS Harley 2895, f.51b. This is also illustrated in Janet Backhouse, *The Illustrated Manuscript*, Oxford 1979, 31 (see Plate 12).

[21] Several of these smaller models are portrayed in the wall paintings at All Saints, Claverley, Shropshire.

Plate 5.
A portion of the equestrian frieze, Claverley, Shropshire (c.1200)

date from 1099 to 1106, and the portal above the north door of the church of La Martorana in Palermo, from c.1140 to 1143. These last two are clearly too early for my needs. Those at Monreale are dated from c.1170 to 1180 and the vast number and quality of the military scenes can bring tears of joy to the eyes of a student of warfare. Many types of shield abound, some borne by mail-clad knights, others by lightly armoured infantry. Some have flat tops, some still retain their curved and earlier feature, but in most cases the detail is exquisite (see Plate 12).

The conical shaped helmet, so popular in the previous century, remained in general use until the latter part of the thirteenth century. Some short time after 1150, however, a round-topped model, often without a nasel became increasingly popular. This type is well illustrated in the leaf from the Winchester Bible where it is shown with and without a nasel extention over the nose and clearly forged in one piece. (Plate 2). Around 1180 another variant emerged, basically cylindrical in cross section, sometimes with a slight taper from brow-band to its flat or slightly domed crown.[22] Two of these styles are shown in a single French manuscript from the late twelfth century and all remained in use beyond 1250.[23]

By the 1170s we often see these styles of helmet fitted with a face-guard, very similar in shape and design to a modern welding mask, often pierced with holes for ventilation and bearing two slits for the eyes.[24] Some were fitted as an accessory to the head defence, while others, as we shall see later, were an integral part of the helmet. This addition had a two-fold benefit, in as much as it gave far

[22] Blair, 29. See also The Guthlac Roll, BL, MS Harley Roll Y. 6.
[23] General M. Weygand, *Histoire de L'Armée Française*, 1961, 43.
[24] Blair, 30.

more effective protection to the wearer, especially to the front or sides of the face. Lastly, it gave the wearer a most terrifying and menacing appearance.

One of the most detailed, and best, illustrations of such a face-guard may be seen on a wall painting depicting the murder of Becket, to be found *in situ*, in the church of Santi Giovanni e Paolo at Spoleto in Italy. (Plate 3). Here the face-guard is fitted to a helmet with a forward-angled crown and gives the impression of being worn in addition to a mail coif. David Nicolle is of the opinion that, although this painting was executed just north of the Norman kingdom of southern Italy and Sicily, it may be taken as showing some typical aspects of southern military equipment.[25] It is possible that this important painting dates from the consecration of the church in 1174, the year after Becket's canonisation, and along with another splendid fellow from the cloisters of Monreale Cathedral, dating from 1174 to 1182,[26] according to one authority, and from 1176 to 1189[27] to another, may represent two early and detailed depictions of this important and far-reaching addition to the essential equipment of the well-armed warrior. Indeed, they may well be the earliest representations for their part of the world.

Probably the earliest illustration of a face-guard is that contained in the Spanish Beatus Commentaries on the Apocalypse in the Archaeological Museum of Madrid. In this early twelfth century manuscript, a well-armed warrior wears a hauberk and carries a kite-shaped shield and broadsword. His helmet has a low dome to it, not unlike that of St Wenceslas and bears a large face-guard or visor, which, apart form the eye slits, protects all of the front of the face.[28] (Plate 6). Again from Spain, warriors on the Arch of Triumph of Christianity Catalonia, *in situ* at the Monastery of Santa Maria Ripoll, wear interesting helmets, one of which looks uncommonly like a face-guard or visor built around a broad robust nasel. This dates from c.1150.[29] Yet again from Spain, and to be found on the south door of Santa Maria la Real Sanguesa, Navarre, we have a simply carved, tiny figure featuring one of the clearest representations of a helmet with a fixed visor, that is a face-guard built in one piece with the conical low-domed helmet. This remarkable and important set of carvings is generally dated to c.1155.[30] (Plate 7). Another group of carvings incorporated on a doorway from the church of San Vincente Martyr Frias, in Castile, from 1170 and now in the Metropolitan Museum of Art, New York, shows combat between Spaniards and Moors. Two dismounted figures, both well armoured, have helmets bearing face-guards which clearly appear to be integral with the dome of the helmet.[31] It is remarkable and of considerable significance that the latter four sources all come from the same quarter of Spain – the north east – clearly pointing to that region being apparently much associated with the development and refinement of the face-guard.[32] It must

---

[25] Nicolle, 522.

[26] J. Jacquiot and E. King, *Larousse Encyclopedia of Byzantine and Medieval Art*, London 1963, 298.

[27] G.H. Crichton, *Romanesque Sculpture in Italy*, London 1954, 147. For the Monreale face-guard see Nicolle, 513.

[28] See also Nicolle, 258.

[29] Nicolle, 274.

[30] This model is not unlike that illustrated in Spanish Beatus Commentaries on the Apocalypse MS mentioned above.

[31] Nicolle, 560.

[32] It is not possible to do justice to these important developments in Spain, within the confines of

be noted that other well-preserved and highly detailed carvings at Rebolledo de la Torre, Provence Burgos (Plate 15) and c.1186 at Ribos de Campo Par Palensia and Santillana del Mar, Prov. Santander, both late twelfth century, add much more weight to this postulation.

Even in the eleventh century, and commonly in the twelfth, many helmets are illustrated with somewhat broader nasel extensions, which indicate a concerted attempt to give the warrior better head protection in battle. This modification, as one would expect, easily progressed towards the face-guard which, in turn, prompted by fervent negotiation between armourer and professional warrior, developed little by little into the great helm.[33] The face-guard appears to be well established by the end of the twelfth century and shortly after, this basic design had a rigid short neck-guard added, a further step towards the birth of the great helm. Around 1220, plates had extended round the sides to join the face-guard, thus creating an almost cylindrical all-enclosing head-piece of steel.[34] Until c.1300 they were almost always flat-topped.[35]

This rapid development from the use of a face-guard to an early form of great helm as we know it, is not easy to follow chronologically, utilising illustrations from manuscripts and other pictorial sources. Two German manuscripts fortunately fill a gap in our knowledge. The first, the Enied of Heinrich von Veldeke, probably of the late twelfth century, has a variety of interesting styles, including flat or relatively flat-topped types with or without nasels. Other models include prototypes of great helms consisting of flat-topped helmets with face-guards and yet others which can only be described as early forms of great helm, that is, those incorporating protection for the sides and back of the neck.[36] (Plate 4). Other warriors have flat-topped great helms with the face-guard replaced by a mail coif, covering all but the eyes. This one manuscript does much to direct attention to the tremendous breadth of styles available at this early period.

The second manuscript, the Jungfrauenspiegel of Trier, of c.1200, also contains many highly detailed early forms of the great helm.[37] For the style of the great helm at c.1230–1240 one need look no further than one splendid knight on the façade of Wells cathedral. The broad eye-slit is reinforced at the edges with an additional piece of metal, which also runs down the front of the helmet. Ventilation holes cover both sides of the front. Just by chance, the figure on the right of the one above wears no helm, but he does wear the means to support one. This item, the arming cap, was fashioned of cloth with large padded squabs to support the helm and reduce unwanted movement.[38]

The Maciejowski Bible of c.1250 is one of the most remarkable manuscripts to have come down to us and may be regarded as the finest source for all things

---

this paper. They are, however, to be the subject of a forthcoming paper. It does appear as if the face-guard was in use in north-east Spain some decades before it was in the more northern parts of Europe. Similarly, so were early forms of great helms. (See Plate 15).

[33] For a broad nasel see the eleventh-century ivory reliquary from San Millan de la Cogolla, Spain. See also the Beatus of Liebana, Spain c.1220. Pierpont Morgan Library, New York, MS 429.

[34] Blair, 30.

[35] Blair, 30.

[36] Nicolle, 433.

[37] To be found at the Kestner Museum, Hannover, West Germany. Illustrated in Blair, 21.

[38] For illustrations of the helm and arming cap see Blair, 30 and 34.

Plate 6.
Early illustration of a face-guard (early twelfth century).
Archaeological Museum of Madrid

military. One particular scene contains three fully developed great helms, all worn over the mail coif and all almost identical to the Wells cathedral example.[39] Even taking into consideration the dates given above, there is good evidence of a few isolated examples of their use before the turn of the century. The engraved

[39] Pierpont Morgan Library, New York, MS 638, f.10. Part of this particular scene is illustrated in *The Ideals and Practice of Medieval Knighthood III*, 154.

Plate 7.
A clear and early representation of a face-guard fashioned in
one piece with the conical helmet. Santa Maria la Real
Sanguesa, Navarre (c.1155)

stone funerary slab of Nicola III de Rumigny of c.1175, now lost, shows a fully mailed warrior wearing what can only be described as a fully developed great helm.[40] If the slab was indeed manufactured in or soon after the year of his death, then it represents one of the earliest images of this important development.

[40] Nicolle, 431.

Plate 8.
A well preserved conical helmet bearing a broad-based nasel and decoration.
Private collection

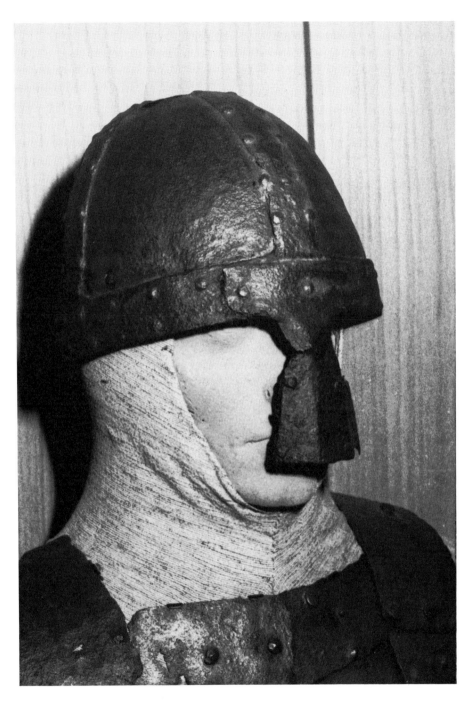

Plate 9.
Conical helmet of spangenhelm construction bearing a great broad nasel.
Private collection

One of the most popular helmets was the small hemispherical cervellière or bascinet, which from the middle of the thirteenth century was frequently worn under the mail coif.[41] When worn in this manner, it gave a slightly bulbous look to the head. Many manuscripts and effigies dating from the first half of the century bear coifs which, to judge by their outlines, would seem to conceal cervellières.

It is noteworthy and to some degree disturbing that the visually striking wall paintings at Claverley, Shropshire, have not received more attention, especially by those who have studied the armour of this period and ought to know better. Nowhere are more face-guards shown in a single scene. All the helmets bear this feature, some attached to flat-topped helmets and others to conical helmets with lavish domes. Two face-guards appear to be simply attached to the nasel while two others have a reinforcing strip fastened to the lower portion of the latter, imparting greater rigidity to the face-guard, combined with strength.[42] (Plate 5).

Typically, they consist of a curved plate riveted to the brow-band of the helmet, covering the front and sides of the face and pierced with eye-slits. The lower portion is also pierced with numerous holes to improve ventilation. These paintings are usually dated to the late twelfth or early thirteenth century. Certainly tiny flat-topped shields predominate and point to an early thirteenth century date, but the various styles of face-guards hint strongly at the 1180s. One possible answer to this dilemma, may lie in the following notion. Claverley may have been something of a backwater and the paintings executed by local artists with poor access to current styles of knightly dress. In all probability, the paintings were executed in about 1200 and therefore some time after the advent of this new appendage to the helmet.

It is always exciting to break new ground, especially in a field where newly discovered artefacts are either few, or in such a tatty state, as to require a good deal of imagination to call up a clear visual image of their original form. Recently, I was asked to give my opinion on a number of medieval helmets in a private collection. They are in an excellent state of preservation. The first is well preserved with a skull which appears to have been forged in one piece. The nasel is separate and gives the impression of being riveted to the skull. This specimen is of particular importance, not only for its fine condition, but also because of the attempt at decoration above the brow. This criss-cross pattern also carries over onto the top of the nasel. The broad base of the nasel is clearly an attempt to improve the protection enjoyed by the wearer. (Plate 8). The second has an almost identical skull-shape and may be classified as high-domed. Here the nasel is cruciform in shape and firmly attached to the skull by five robust-looking rivets. Four rivets on the nasel extensions may indicate the presence of a face-guard at some time. Likewise, rivet holes round the brow may well point to this specimen carrying a reinforcing band or padded lining, or even both, in its original form. (Not illustrated). The last is of a type which fills the gap in our knowledge between the standard conical helmet and that fitted with a face-guard. (Plate 9). It is of a robust spangenhelm construction and highly popular from late Roman times to the fourteenth century, but the startling feature is the great broad nasel, extending to well below the mouth and fully three inches wide at its lower end.

---

[41] See in particular, the Pierpont Morgan Library, MS 638, f.10v, f29v, f10r, f11r, which show a cervellière worn under a mail coif.
[42] Nicolle, 352.

Incorporated in the nasel is a wide flange, which covers and is firmly riveted to the brow-band. In this specimen, we have an early attempt to achieve greater protection for the face using a technique commonly paralleled in the twelfth century manuscripts and especially the later ones. All three of these helmets could date from the twelfth or first half of the thirteenth century.[43]

The main offensive weapons of the well-armed warrior were the lance, which we will see later, and the most noble of weapons, the sword. Up to c.1150, the sword was straight and double-edged and, except for some hilt variations, similar to those used by the Vikings. Almost all had a shallow valley down each side of the blade to reduce weight and a straight, or occasionally curved, cross which protected the hand. The pommel, often of a circular disc or even 'D' or walnut shape, counteracted the mass of the blade and improved wieldability. Many bore iron inlaid inscriptions and others more elaborate decoration and inscriptions picked out in gold, silver or latten. They usually weighed two to three pounds and could be wielded with great ease by the strong arm of a battle-proven warrior. Thrusting was possible but they were better suited to hacking and slashing. Very few significant changes occurred in the overall form of the broad sword between 1150 and 1250. As one would expect there were some slight differences from the basic form, but only those which took into consideration the personal preferences the warrior might have with regard to pommel and cross style and elements of decoration.[44] Consider also that many of these weapons had been handed down and gratefully received by sons, especially when a particular weapon had gained a track record of some note in previous decades. Yet again one would expect variation if an old, but still serviceable, blade was rehilted or a fine hilt received a new blade. During our period hilts tended to be more decorated and the manner by which the scabbard was suspended from the sword belt changed decade by decade. Many manuscripts confirm the current styles. The Winchester Bible illustrates swords both in and out of their scabbard. (Plate 2). All three swords in this one scene have pommels and crosses of gold and this is significant, for some surviving examples have traces of gold and other decorative metals applied to the elements of the hilt. In fact it is extremely rare in medieval art for the cross of the sword to be shown gilded, whereas pommels are often so shown. Most curiously, it has been observed in surviving examples that when a pommel is silvered, and they often were, so was the cross.[45]

One quite outstanding sword, which in actuality dated from c.1100, but as a type could also fit into the late twelfth century, is almost identical to one shown on the Winchester Bible. We know little of its medieval story, except that it was a fine looking and beautifully balanced weapon and so it still remains. It carries two inscriptions upon its blade, INNOMINEDOMINI on one side and GICELINMEFECIT upon the other, and this is not all, for the delicately turned ends of the cross have been fashioned into tiny panther heads. I have handled this magnificent weapon on two occasions and have noted that traces of gold still linger on the pommel,

---

[43] I am most grateful to Ewart Oakeshott for drawing my attention to these remarkable helmets and for allowing me to use the photographs in his possession. Also I extend my sincere thanks to the owner of these three remarkable pieces.

[44] See Peirce 'Medieval Sword', 150–56.

[45] My thanks to Ewart Oakeshott for this important observation.

indicating that at one time it was gilded. There is no trace of gold upon the cross.[46]

Another sword, recently dated to c.1150–1200, is on permanent exhibition at the Wallace Collection, London. It is of a type widely illustrated in manuscripts and although the blade is heavily corroded, the whole sword still emits powerful hints of its knightly past. Quite recently I asked for it to be photographed and the pommel and cross inspected for traces of silver. The blade was also examined and the remains of a silver inlaid inscription found, including the letters H T.[47]

My next example is from a private collection and survives in an excellent state of preservation.[48] The pommel and cross are of copper and may have been gilded at one time. The circular disc pommel has a cross engraved upon both sides and the splayed end of the cross-guard is incised with a tiny grotesque figure, of a style which may point to an English origin for the hilt. The blade, however, is older and may date from the early part of the twelfth century; it had evidently been approved by a swordsmith as still serviceable when he rehilted it c.1250. There is evidence of this hilt style being used in the first half of the twelfth century as may be seen on the seal of Richard Bassett c.1122–1129 or 1134.[49]

Yet another sword from our period, is that magnificent specimen in the Burrell Collection, Glasgow. Its excellent condition suggests it to be a river find and its dark red-brown patination colour led Sir James Mann to believe it had been recovered from the Danube. Due to the preservative qualities of the river mud, even the leather-covered wooden grip survives in an excellent condition. The cross is octagonal in cross-section and the recessed pommel is of a similar shape. The fullered blade carries the letters A C L I engraved and inlaid with latten. This is a large weapon with a blade length of 36 inches and is unusually heavy, weighing 3¾ pounds.[50] I am assured by Ewart Oakeshott that, if used correctly, it handles well. (Plate 10).

Few swords can be successfully traced back to their origins. One such sword does exist and was briefly discussed by me in a previous paper. I make no excuses for including it again, as at one time it resided here in Palermo and is clearly of local interest. Well attested legend has it, that it was given by San Olegario to one Raymon Berengar, count of Barcelona, by order of Calixtus III, 1168–1183. The count, upon his death, duly presented his horse and arms to the Order of the Knights of St John of Jerusalem and the sword was deposited in the treasury of the cathedral at Palermo. This remarkably well preserved weapon is complete with its scabbard and is typical of swords of the twelfth century. Some two centuries later, it was taken from Palermo and sent to Saragossa for the coronation of Marti I of Aragon, which took place on 13 April 1399.[51] Sir James Mann cast doubt on the dating of the sword, on the sole ground that 'the form of the hilt was of the thirteenth century rather than the twelfth century'. However, two swords

---

[46] This sword is illustrated in Peirce, 'Medieval Sword', 148.

[47] My thanks are due to David Edge of the Wallace Collection for the details of these findings. More details of this sword are to be found in the Wallace Collection catalogues, vol. 2, cat. no. A458.

[48] See Ewart Oakeshott, *Records of the Medieval Sword*, Woodbridge 1991, 33.

[49] Illustrated in *Sir Christopher Hatton's Book of Seals*, ed. L.C. Loyd and D.M. Stenton, Oxford, 1950, no. 407.

[50] See Oakeshott, 104.

[51] Oakeshott, 68–9, who first drew my attention to this unique weapon.

Plate 10.
Sword of c.1200–1250
with a blade of fine
quality and with its
original leather grip
surviving. Burrell
Collection, Glasgow

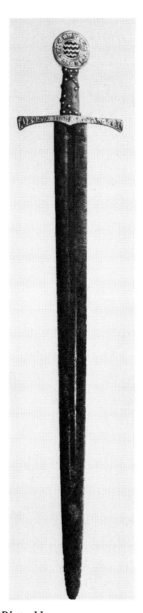

Plate 11.
The Santa Casilda
Sword (first half of the
thirteenth century)
(reproduced by
permission of the Board
of Trustees of the Royal
Armouries)

with almost identical hilts were unearthed by Jormo Leppaaho while clearing Viking graves in 1950, proving that these hilt types were actually in use in the twelfth and late eleventh centuries.[52] It was kept at Saragossa cathedral until 1888 and eventually arrived at the Musée de l'Armée, Paris where it remains.

Few weapons survive in such pristine condition as the so-called 'Sword of Santa Casilda', now in the Instituto del Conde de Valencia de Don Juan, Madrid. It is one of those rare examples in which the hilt is regally enriched with both decoration and inscription, but we would be wise not to assume automatically that its scarceness today is an indication that few swords were bedecked in this lavish manner; it is merely that others have not survived or as yet been discovered.

This style of hilt was in use even as early as c.1130 although (Plate 11) an acceptable date for the weapon under discussion would be c.1200–1250. The blade is of a type which remained popular from c.950 to well into the fourteenth century and is of an identical pattern to the sword of Ramon Berenger. The pommel and cross are of gilded iron and gilded bronze respectively, the former bearing a central circular, but unidentified, coat of arms, surrounded by the inscription in Gothic letters: AVE MARIA PLENE GRATIA. The cross is handsomely executed and bears a Spanish inscription on both sides: the translation is GOD IS THE VANQUISHER OF DEATH. The wooden grip is bound with red leather and retains sufficient remnants of criss-cross leather thongs, delicately emplaced with tiny gilt pins, to give an accurate impression of its original appearance. I am assured by Ewart Oakeshott, who has closely inspected and handled this weapon, that it is a supreme specimen of a knightly medieval sword and is as sweet and well-balanced in the hand as it is beautifully proportioned.

There can have been few more spectacular sights than that of a mounted knight with lance couched, bearing down upon the foe, and some of the very best images of the knight of c.1250 are to be found in the Maciejowski Bible. In the introduction to *The Ideals and Practice of Medieval Knighthood* 1, 1986, Christopher Harper-Bill defined the knight as 'a superbly efficient fighting machine'. In all our dealings with, and investigations into, all aspects of knighthood, we should remind ourselves of this important definition.

Many aspects of the cost of this professionalism have been dealt with elsewhere, but we must not pass by without acknowledging the years of dedication that were necessary to achieve the high standard of horsemanship expected of the successful knight.[53] We know, or we think we know, all the aspects of his role in battle. Yes, he used his sword and yes again, he was expected, at the drop of a hat, to deliver the shock-tactic of the charge: but do we ever give due consideration to the conditions under which he operated? Set aside the geographical hazards embodied in that role, expertly guiding a spirited destrier over unfamiliar, hostile country and contemplate the strength and skill required to deliver a series of accurate sword blows or a well-directed lance thrust, while simultaneously controlling the pace and direction of his horse. Furthermore, battles were noisy events, made so by a blend of clashing weapons, by terrified and wounded horses and by wounded and dying foe and friends.

Images of mounted knights are many and varied and I now intend to illustrate

[52] Peirce, 'Medieval Sword', 142–3.
[53] R.A. Brown, 'The Status of the Norman Knight', in *War and Government in the Middle Ages: Essays in Honour of J.O. Prestwich*, ed. J.B. Gillingham and J.C. Holt, Woodbridge 1984, 28–9.

Plate 12.
*The better preserved of the two mounted knights in the cloisters of Monreale
Cathedral, Sicily*

Plate 13.
A finely preserved knight. Former chapel of the Templars at Cressac

some of the known, and perhaps not so well known, examples of c.1170–1180; a period when they are particularly prolific, especially in sculpture. There is not time available here to investigate thoroughly the influences present in the carved capitals of Monreale cloisters, except to say that different art historians have differing views. Some feel French influences predominate, others those of Componian. As far as weaponry is concerned, western European, Byzantine and Islamic elements are clearly present.

There are only two mounted knights, both on the same capital and both wearing hauberks. (Plate 12). One is clearly short-sleeved. The treatment used to indicate mail is interesting and comprises an array of closely placed holes, a technique employed at San Nicola, Bari and La Martorana at Palermo. Both figures couch their lances and to some degree are hunched behind their kite-shaped shields, in order to present a smaller target. This attitude is reminiscent of the warriors of Modena Cathedral. They both wear conical helmets, which include what can only be described as mailed ear-flaps, which may be specifically a Sicilian feature. The warrior with the undecorated shield wears a fine example of a forward-angled crown type helmet. The saddles are of necessity deep and are quite unusually secured by two girths rather than one, a feature which appears on all the other horses at Monreale. These two exquisite figures mostly demonstrate clear western European influence.[54]

The finely preserved wall paintings in the former chapel of the Templars at Cressac are generally thought to date from c.1170–1180. (Plate 13). They survive in two registers, one of which is in a much more detailed hand and includes this typical knight of the second half of the twelfth century. He has a long-sleeved hauberk, with a coif worn over a long tunic. He has no mittens. His helmet is of a very tall-domed variety, with an extremely wide nasel. He is sitting firmly astride his destrier in a deep saddle and his decorated shield is flat-topped for better vision and acutely curved to achieve maximum protection. He demonstrates the couched lance to perfection and his weapon carries a gonfanon at the business end to assist in identification when in action. He is employing the 'nearside to nearside' method of attack, where the lance is placed diagonally across the horse's neck, to seek a target on the left.[55] This technique was common practice in the late twelfth century.

Sadly, the tiny but highly important mounted knights in the chapter house of the Abbey of Saint-Georges-de-Boscherville have received some damage, but sufficient remains to suggest much of their former glory. They are part of a capital illustrating the capture of Jericho and date from c.1170. (Plate 14). The more complete figure wears a long hauberk with a split skirt, long sleeves and a mail coif. Here the treatment used to indicate mail consists of a mesh of incised irregular scales, not unlike the skin of a snake. He carries a broad sword, but that of his companion is far better preserved. He wears a high-domed conical helmet without a nasel extension. Neither warrior apparently holds a shield. In overall

[54] See especially David Nicolle *The Monreale Capitals and the Military Equipment of Later Norman Sicily*, Instituto De Estudios Sobre Armas Antiguas Consejo Superior De Investigiones Cientificas, 1980.

[55] See Peirce, *ante* x, 245–6.

[56] Wilson, *The Bayeux Tapestry*, London 1985, pls 67–68.

Plate 14.
Mounted knights. Chapter House, St Georges-de-Boscheville

Plate 15.
The splendid knights of Rebolledo de la Torre. Prov. Burgos (c.1186)

form, these two are not unlike that group of Norman knights on the Bayeux Tapestry, swords aloft, bearing down upon the enemy.[56]

The knights from Rebolledo de la Torre are also slightly damaged, but the portions which remain are as fresh as the day they were carved. Both wear long hauberks with split skirts and long sleeves such as we would expect to see at this period. Here the mail has been reproduced most realistically, even to the degree of accurately representing the manner in which the mail hangs about the body of the warrior. Both are to some extent couching their lances, especially the one on the right, who has successfully pierced the defence and the helmet of his opponent. He carries a well-defined kite-shaped shield which is creased along its major axis, rather than curved, and he bears it high and close to his body. His adversary carries a circular decorated shield. Both socketed lance heads are well-defined, although they do not appear to have a cross-bar to prevent over-penetration. (Plate 15). The most striking and interesting items of their apparel, are their helmets worn over the mail coif. Both are identical and clearly of a type forged in one piece. This model gives superb protection for the sides and back of the head and neck and even extends down below the chin and the nape of the neck. The front is pierced with eye holes. Clearly we have here an early and effective form of great helm, a helmet which completely encases the whole head. Viewing these examples, it is easy to visualise the natural progression which took place from the simple conical helmet with nasel to one fitted with a face-guard, finally culminating in the elegant model worn by the knights of Rebolledo de la Torre.

The knights of Barfreston near Dover are badly worn, but not so one of their dismounted colleagues. In consequence, it is possible to formulate a fairly accurate picture of their original form. The figure on the right is the better of the two; he is bedecked with a flat-topped shield and a conical helmet without the nasel, and wears a hauberk.[57] In essence, he is not much different from the other knights we have viewed, a fact which is confirmed by the well-preserved figure above him.

The successful knight depended totally upon an experienced team of supporters, supplying the essential skills for the exercise of specialist military functions. Within that select body, the armourer and the weaponsmith held the highest of positions. Their days were spent repairing, adjusting, modifying and innovating, all to keep their knight in a state of readiness for war. Their part in moulding the image of the knight was considerable, and all was done with the skill of their hands and the sweat of their brow.

[57] Nicolle, 350.

THE USES OF THE FRANKS IN ELEVENTH-CENTURY BYZANTIUM

Jonathan Shepard

'Mercenaries' have often been associated by historians with the decline which they discern in eleventh-century Byzantium. The hirelings have been viewed as the opposite of the 'soldier peasants' who were supposedly one of the empire's pillars in its heyday. For example, P. Charanis wrote: 'The enrolled soldiers [from among the "free peasantry"], neglected and reduced to poverty, had neither the will nor the equipment to fight. The mercenaries who replaced them helped to complete the disintegration of the state'.[1] A similarly negative view was taken by R. Jenkins: to replace the 'peasant-soldiers', 'the expensive and otherwise unsatisfactory system of importing foreign mercenaries was widely resorted to'.[2] Such blanket condemnations are rarer in recent historical writing, but we may note, without prejudice, J.J. Norwich's verdict that 'mercenaries were by their very nature unreliable, being loyal to their paymasters only for as long as they received their pay, or until someone else offered them more'.[3] Among these mercenaries, according to Charanis, 'the most turbulent and intractable were the Normans'.[4] He cites Hervé, Robert Crispin and Roussel of Bailleul, all three of whom did indeed desert from or rebel against the emperor. Roussel's treachery in the early to mid-1070s has often been narrated or summarised: he tried to create lordships for himself in Asia minor and his adventures only came to an end when he was brought into custody by a young Byzantine commander.[5] We hear rather less about Roussel's subsequent career – how, after a spell in prison, he was released and sent to fight under the orders of that same young commander against other rebels or how subsequently he himself led another operation on behalf of his

---

[1] P. Charanis, 'The Byzantine Empire in the Eleventh Century', *A History of the Crusades*, i, ed. K.M. Setton and M.W. Baldwin, Madison, Milwaukee, 1969, 204.

[2] R. Jenkins, *Byzantium: the Imperial Centuries* A.D. 610–1071, London 1966, 365; cf. S. Vryonis, *The Decline of Medieval Hellenism in Asia Minor and the Process of Islamization from the Eleventh through the Fifteenth Century*, Berkeley 1971, 4,76.

[3] J.J. Norwich, *Byzantium*, ii, *The Apogee*, London 1991, 339.

[4] Charanis, 200.

[5] e.g. L. Bréhier, 'Les aventures d'un chef normand en Orient', *Revue des cours et conférences de la Faculté des Lettres de Paris* xx, 1911, 172–88; K.M. Mekios, *Der Fränkische Krieger Ursel de Bailleul*, Athens 1939, 14–32; D.I. Polemis, 'Notes on Eleventh-Century Chronology: 6, the Revolt of Roussel', *Byzantinische Zeitschrift* lviii, 1965, 66–8; J. Hoffmann, *Rudimente von Territorialstaaten im byzantinischen Reich (1071–1204)*, Munich 1974, 13–20; Vryonis, 106–08; M.J. Angold, *The Byzantine Empire, 1025–1204. A Political History*, London 1984, 93–4; J.-C. Cheynet, *Pouvoir et contestations à Byzance (963–1210)*, Paris 1990, 78; *Oxford History of Byzantium*, iii, ed. A.P. Kazhdan *et al.*, New York/Oxford 1991, 1814–15.

imperial employer, carrying it out effectively.[6] We also hear less of the simple fact that foreign mercenaries continued to be employed by the emperor in the closing decades of the eleventh century and during the twelfth, a period of political stability in comparison with the middle years of the eleventh century and, even, of imperial revival.

The employment of mercenaries was not, then, necessarily disastrous in itself and the presence in the army of mercenaries from the Latin west was not utterly incompatible with strong and enduring emperors. In fact, Alexius Comnenus, the emperor generally credited with the Byzantine recovery and a noted employer of western mercenaries, had been the young commander who had brought Roussel back to Constantinople in chains in the mid-1070s. Alexius, of all people, might have been expected to know better than to recruit such men, if western mercenaries were so inherently unreliable.

It would be facile to try and turn the argument inside out, claiming that 'Frankish' mercenaries were invariably loyal or an unqualified benefit to the Byzantine state. For patently they did sometimes rebel, and there were doubts about their employment on the part of some Byzantines. It seems preferable to start from what is reasonably certain: that there is no evidence of the employment of 'Franks' in significant or substantial numbers by Byzantine provincial or expeditionary force commanders before c.1038 or by the central government before c.1047. We shall ask why they began to be employed more extensively then, but not earlier, and note the impact which they seem swiftly to have made on Byzantine observers. And it is worth glancing at such evidence as exists about the nature and conditions of their service and the careers of individual commanders. Those careers about which we know something mostly involve revolts and at first sight confirm the darkest prognostications about western mercenaries. It must, however, be remembered that it was the colourful risings of rebels that excited the curiosity or moralising tendencies of the chroniclers, and there may well have been many 'Frankish' commanders whose service in Byzantium was almost as illustrious as Crispin's or Roussel's, but who never behaved in such a way as to attract attention in the chronicles; that is, they never revolted. And underlying our enquiry will be the question of whether the 'Franks' were of positive military value, and if so, in what way – did they possess some martial skill or equipment which other peoples lacked? Perhaps we shall find that the 'Franks' were, on the whole, as neutral as their weapons and their mounts, being amenable enough, if attentively handled by an employer acquainted with their customs, foibles and needs.

First, though, two more basic questions must be raised: what did the Byzantines mean by the name 'Frank' and did they utilise any term precisely corresponding to the English word 'mercenary'; and, as a rider to the second question, does a term specifically meaning 'mercenary' appear in Byzantine sources in the eleventh century, or earlier? The first question brings us to the

---

[6]   Michael Attaleiates, *Historia*, ed. I. Bekker, Bonn 1853, 252–4, 257; Scylitzes Continuatus, *E synecheia tēs chronographias tou Ioannou Skylitzē*, ed. E.T. Tsolakes, Thessalonica 1968, 175–6; John Zonaras, *Epitome Historiarum*, iii, ed. T. Büttner-Wobst, Bonn 1897, 717; Nicephorus Bryennius, whose lengthy account of Roussel's insurrection in the mid–1070s forms the basis of most secondary works' accounts, is laconic about the final episodes in his career before his sudden death: *Histoire*, ed. and French tr. P. Gautier, Brussels 1975, 148–9, 166–95, 254–5.

problem of whether the persons under discussion can be described as 'Normans' at all, and raises the issue of what constituted a 'Norman' identity, or warranted appellation as 'Norman'. Suffice it to say here that the name 'Frank' had been in Byzantine use since Late Antiquity and could denote western Christian peoples in general, inhabitants of the *regnum Teutonicum* as well as of Gaul. It commonly denoted those living in, or hailing from, north of the Alps, but of course any Norman in the south could still fit that description reasonably comfortably in the eleventh century. No term specific to the Normans (whether of the north or the south) became current in Byzantine high-style literary works. There, they could be termed 'Frank', 'Italian', 'Celt' or 'Latin'. The lack of precision is not entirely the fault of Byzantine writers' archaising tendencies or ignorance. The origins and allegiances of those Romance-speakers arriving in Byzantium by way of southern Italy from further afield were not homogeneous and the labels which these newcomers applied to themselves – or had applied to them by local record-keepers – were variegated.[7] At any rate, 'Franks' could designate persons owing some form of allegiance, direct, indirect or ancestral, to the duke of Normandy. Robert Guiscard is called Robert 'the Frank' in a work of the 1070s and I believe that most of those 'Franks' first mentioned *en masse* in Byzantine sources for the mid-eleventh century would have answered that description;[8] so would many of their successors in the later eleventh century, although men from other parts of the west, such as Flanders and Germany were now in the imperial service, too. It is impossible to substantiate this belief with a full body of evidence, but it is significant that on two of those rare occasions when we have scraps of prosopo-graphical evidence on 'Frankish' commanders, they have Norman connections: a twelfth-century family history of the Crispins lays claim to Robert Crispin; and the valour and zest for battle of Roussel de Bailleul is recorded by Geoffrey Malaterra in his account of Count Roger's victory on the river Cerami, in Sicily in 1063.[9] And when Anna Comnena wishes to bestow unambiguous – and high –

---

[7] William of Apulia writes of *Franci* and *Francigenae* in relating the newcomers' exploits in southern Italy: *La geste de Robert Guiscard*, ed. M. Mathieu, Palermo 1961, 118, 120, 122, 138. His protagonists feature as *Normanni* and *Galli* throughout the work. See also Geoffrey Malaterra, *De rebus gestis Rogerii Calabriae et Siciliae Comitis et Roberti Guiscardi Ducis, RIS²*, v.1, ed. E. Pontieri, *praefazione*, xxxiii; Orderic, iv, 34, n. 5.

[8] Cecaumenus, *Strategikon*, ed. and Russian tr. G.G. Litavrin, Moscow 1972, 186, 254. A Greek charter issued by the *katepano* Eustathius in 1045 mentions the disturbances caused by *tōn Frankōn*, i.e. the Normans under William Iron-Arm: *Codice diplomatico barese*, iv, *Le pergamene di S. Nicola di Bari*, ed. F.N. di Vito, Bari 1900, 67. For discussion of the usage of *Frangos* ('Frank') in Byzantine sources, see Litavrin, n. 460 on p. 441; *Oxford Dictionary of Byzantium*, i, 803.

[9] Robert Crispin is described as *Northmannia egressus* in *De nobili genere Crispinorum*, Migne, *Patrologia latina*, cl, col. 737; J. Armitage Robinson, *Gilbert Crispin, Abbot of Westminster*, Cambridge 1911, 14. Roussel is designated by Malaterra (ed. Pontieri, 43) as *de Ballione*, a toponym which is not peculiar to Normandy: see Du Cange's disquisition on Norman families which are possible candidates for kinship with Roussel, reprinted in Nicephorus Bryennius, *Commentarii*, ed. A. Meineke, Bonn 1836, 221–6. Roussel's origins remain undetermined, but his movements are not dissimilar in pattern to Crispin's or, most probably, those of other Norman fortune-seekers – from the Normanno-Italian south to Byzantium. Crispin, after seeing action against the Moslems in Spain, was in southern Italy in June 1066 and within a couple of years he had crossed to Byzantium: G.A. Loud, 'A Calendar of the Diplomas of the Norman Princes of Capua', *Papers of the British School at Rome* xlix, 1981, 121–2; cf. E.M.C. van Houts, 'Normandy and Byzantium in the eleventh Century', *Byzantion* lv, 1985, 555–6. The dates of Roussel's

praise on her brother-in-law, Nicephorus Euphorbenus, for his equestrian skills, she says that 'if one were to see him on horseback, one would not have supposed that he was a Roman, but that he had come from Normandy (*Normanothen*)'. She singles out his skill in wielding his long lance and protecting himself with his shield.[10] Anna was, of course, writing in the 1130s and 1140s, but in a way this makes her usage the more remarkable; for by that time many *non*-Norman knights and grandees from the west were serving with the imperial forces, and it may be that Anna was using a kind of figure of speech which had been coined at a time when Normans were, to Byzantine eyes, *the* model of superb military horsemanship. But perhaps the strongest reason for supposing that many of the mercenaries described as 'Franks' in Byzantine sources had some sort of Norman associations is what is at least a coincidence: mention of 'Frankish' mercenaries begins for about the same period that we first hear in western sources of Normans and their associates in southern Italy serving the *basileus*.

The other question, of what was the Byzantine term for 'mercenary' and whether it was a novelty in eleventh-century Byzantine sources, opens up a huge and oddly uncharted subject. Only a few preliminary observations can be offered here. Foreigners – non-Greek-speaking outsiders – had been in the armed service of the empire from the fourth century A.D., but not all of them were full-time, professional warriors, arriving as armed individuals and serving, or intending to serve, only for a limited period. Many arrived in groups, or as the arms-bearing members of entire peoples, and not always by invitation of the government.[11] These were not so much soldiers of fortune as invaders or immigrants in quest of lands, but constituting a pool of military manpower. It was always possible for individuals to join the ruling élite of Byzantium, earning through martial prowess senior military commands and court titles. These entailed annual payments to them in gold by the emperor personally, access to the Great Palace's banquets and other ceremonies, and entry into the Byzantine 'establishment'.[12]

It must, however, be emphasised that the precise role and the numbers of 'aliens' in imperial service varied greatly over the centuries, according to the types of warfare which the armed forces were undertaking. So long as their stance

---

departure from Count Roger's service and arrival at Byzantium are not known; but seeing that he was a member of Crispin's 'company' (*hetaireia*), he could well have arrived as such: Bryennius, 146–7.

[10] Anna Comnena, *Alexiad*, ii, ed. B. Leib, Paris 1943, 197. The context of the remark is a campaign of the mid-1090s.

[11] On the recruitment of non-'Romans' in the fourth century, see J.H.W.G. Liebeschuetz, *Barbarians and Bishops*, Oxford 1990, 11–25, 40–7. The imperial authorities sometimes retained and equipped groups of professional warriors even beyond the frontier: M. Kazanski, 'Contribution à l'histoire de la défense de la frontière pontique au Bas-Empire', *Travaux et Mémoires* xi, 1991, 506–08. It should be noted that the degree of the government's reliance on foreign-born troops varied markedly during the first half of the sixth century: J.L. Teall, 'The Barbarians in Justinian's Armies', *Speculum* xl, 1965, 299–300, 309–12, 321–2. I owe the latter reference to Douglas Lee, Trinity College, Cambridge.

[12] See, for example, P. Charanis, *Armenians in the Byzantine Empire*, Lisbon 1963, 29–30, 33–4; H. Ditten, 'Prominente Slawen und Bulgaren in Byzantinischen Diensten (Ende des 7. bis Anfang des 10. Jahrhunderts)', *Studien zum 8. und 9. Jahrhundert in Byzanz*, ed. H. Köpstein and F. Winkelmann, Berlin 1983, 115, 117; G. Dédéyan, 'La contribution des arméniens à l'effort de guerre de Byzance (IV–XI siècles)', *Colloque international d'histoire militaire (Histoire militaire comparée* I), Montpellier 1981, 37–9.

was essentially defensive, there was only an occasional need for large quantities of extra military manpower. The one prominent role for non-Greek warriors was that of guarding the Great Palace and the emperor's person. The imperial *hetaireia* ('bodyguard') was made up mainly of foreigners (probably of noble stock): c.900 it contained enough western Europeans – 'Franks' – for them to be mentioned by name alongside Saracens and Khazars.[13] But their numbers were modest, and they probably served essentially as exotica, adding mystique to the court ceremonial. A change came when Byzantine strategy shifted to one of large-scale offensives in the mid-tenth century; substantial tracts of land were annexed, and these needed to be garrisoned and defended. This expansionism became a declared policy of Basil II (976–1018), and what could be called a 'habit of expansionism' continued to prevail up to the mid-eleventh century.[14] Byzantium's armed forces had previously consisted to a large extent of part-time soldiers, trained for guerilla warfare and the defence of their localities.[15] So it is not surprising that we find the government trying to introduce new tactics for sustained offensives, or that one of the sources of soldiers trained or seasoned in the attack lay abroad – among the Armenians, above all, but also the Hungarians, the Rus, the Khazars and the Bulgarians. Already in the 950s, the Byzantine expeditionary force to Syria consisted of several different peoples, inspiring an Arabic poet to write that 'people of all languages and all nations were assembled there, and only their interpreters could understand what they were saying'; the poet claimed that their successive ranks 'covered the east and the west'.[16]

In order to raise sizable enough units of foreign warriors of quality, Byzantium needed not only the permission but also the active cooperation of their respective lords or overlords; for a ruler or ruling élite could not be indifferent to the exodus of a significant proportion of his (or its) military manpower. Thus the invasion force of 958 seems to have been raised to a considerable extent through agreements with the rulers of such peoples as the Bulgarians and the Rus.[17] In 974, a force was sent by Ashot III, 'king of kings' of Armenia, to assist Emperor John Tzimisces in campaigning against the Arabs. Tzimisces had apparently requested that Ashot should also send 'food and provisions' for them. The figure given by Matthew of Edessa for this contingent – 10,000 men – may not be unduly inflated.[18] It is comparable with the figures we have for other foreign armies sent by established rulers to aid Basil II in the later tenth century: 12,000 cavalrymen are said to have been sent in 979 by the ruler of Tao (Tayk), a principality in the western borderlands of Georgia and Armenia;[19] and a decade or so later 6,000 Rus warriors were sent by Prince Vladimir of Kiev to rescue Basil, who was

---

[13] N. Oikonomides, *Les listes de préséance byzantines des IX et X siècles*, Paris 1972, 176–7.

[14] J. Shepard, 'Byzantium Expanding', *New Cambridge Medieval History*, iii, ed. T. Reuter (forthcoming).

[15] G. Dagron and H. Mihăescu, *Le traité sur la guérilla de l'empereur Nicéphore Phocas*, Paris 1986, 184–6, 190–3, 276.

[16] A.A. Vasiliev, *Byzance et les Arabes*, 2.ii, Brussels 1950, 333 (Mutanabbi).

[17] Vasiliev, 2.ii, p.368 (Abu Firas).

[18] Matthew of Edessa, *Chronicle*, tr. A.E. Dostourian (unpublished Ph.D. thesis, University Microfilms, Ann Arbor, Michigan 1972), 20; P.E. Walker, 'The "Crusade" of John Tzimisces in the Light of New Arabic Evidence', *Byzantion* xlvii, 1977, 313; Dédéyan, 43.

[19] P. Peeters, *Histoires monastiques géorgiennes*, *Analecta Bollandiana* xxxvi–xxxvii, 1917–19, 22.

facing a massive military revolt in which most of his eastern army had joined.[20] None of these figures is utterly certain, but it seems most likely that units numbering several thousand apiece were in play; and the repeated mention of Armenian and Rus warriors in chronicles and military manuals for the period suggests that their numbers were kept up.[21] This was presumably achieved partly through the cooperation of the various princes of Armenia and of the ruler of the Rus. Almost certainly, the king of Hungary provided soldiers to liaise with Basil's army during the closing stages of his war against the Bulgarians.[22]

So while there was a substantial increase in the number of foreign-born warriors in Byzantium from the later tenth century, this probably owed much to the intervention of their lords, ordering or urging them to serve with the Byzantines. Undoubtedly, some individuals or small groups did turn up, for example those who had long been manning the imperial bodyguard; and we occasionally hear of larger war-bands arriving in quest of employment: for example, a band of eight hundred Rus sailed down to Constantinople in the mid-1020s 'in the hope of becoming mercenaries'.[23] However, this episode was recorded because it was so singular, ending with the massacre of the war-band by the Byzantine authorities. And in any case, it seems to me probable that the Russo-Scandinavians, with the mobility which their boats gave them, and with their well-armed warrior élite, formed something of a special case.[24] Few other peoples possessed the means to travel to Byzantium reasonably rapidly and cheaply, bearing military skills and weaponry that were of keen interest to the empire. Even in the case of the Armeno-Georgians, neighbours of the empire, the cooperation of the princes or the 'king of kings' seems to have been needed to transfer really large units, thousands rather than hundreds to serve the emperor.

This, in turn, could help to explain why a term having the specific sense of 'mercenary' is slow to emerge in Byzantine sources covering the period. Foreign warriors or units are generally referred to as 'allies' or 'auxiliaries' (*symmachoi, symmachikon*), or simply as 'foreigners' (*ethnikoi*).[25] I suggest that the term 'allies' was not just a euphemism to obscure the extent to which the expanding

---

[20] Stephen of Taron (Asoƚik), *Histoire universelle*, tr. F. Macler, Paris 1917, 164.

[21] Armenians: Leo the Deacon, *Historia*, ed. C.B. Hase, Bonn 1828, 14, 28, 64–5; John Scylitzes, *Synopsis Historion*, ed. H. Thurn, New York/Berlin 1973, 268, 275, 316, 321; *Praecepta militaria*, ed. J. Kulakovsky, *Zapiski Imperatorskoi Akademii Nauk, Istoriko-Filologicheskoe Otdelenie*, viii, no. 9, St Petersburg 1908, p.1. Rus: *Praecepta*, ed. Kulakovsky, 2; *Campaign Organization* (*De re militari*) in G. Dennis, *Three Byzantine Military Treatises*, Washington, D.C., 1985, 280–1, 294–5, 312–13.

[22] G. Györffy, 'Zur Geschichte der Eroberung Ochrids durch Basileios II.', *Actes du XII Congrès international des Etudes byzantines*, ii, Belgrade 1964, 149–52.

[23] Scylitzes, 367.

[24] S. Blöndal, *The Varangians of Byzantium*, tr. and revised by B.S. Benedikz, Cambridge 1978, 49–50, 56–60; J. Shepard, 'Yngvarr's Expedition to the East and a Russian Inscribed Stone Cross', *Saga-Book of the Viking Society* xxi, pts 3–4, 1984–85, 230, 275.

[25] *symmachoi/symmachikon*: e.g. Leo VI, *Tactica*, Migne *Patrologia graeca*, cvii, cols 956, 1037; *Campaign Organization* ed. Dennis, 292–3; H. Ahrweiler, 'Un discours inédit de Constantin VII Porphyrogénète', *Travaux et Mémoires* ii, 1967, 399; J.-A. de Foucault, 'Douze chapitres inédits de la *Tactique* de Nicéphore Ouranos', *Travaux et Mémoires* v, 1973, 308–09. *ethnikoi*: Oikonomides, 176–7, 208–09; *Praecepta*, ed. Kulakovsky, 2; R. Vári, 'Zum historischen Exzerptenwerke des Konstantinos Porphyrogennetos', *Byzantinische Zeitschrift* xvii, 1908, 82; Constantine VII Porphyrogenitus, *Three Treatises on Imperial Military Expeditions*, ed. and tr. J.F. Haldon, Vienna 1990, 118–19. I am grateful to the *Thesaurus Linguae Graecae* (University of California, Irvine)

empire relied on foreign soldiers: it was accurate, in that many of the Armenians and Russo-Scandinavians and others were serving as, in effect, allied forces, led or despatched by their overlords; they had not ventured to Byzantium on their own account, as soldiers of fortune. Thus it is not solely Byzantine literary conservatism that accounts for the lack of currency of a term having the specific sense of 'foreign warrior serving in return for pay'. Such a term does appear with reference to the later tenth century in the chronicle of John Scylitzes: *misthophoroi*, or *misthophorikon*, meaning, literally, 'wage-receivers, salary-earners' or a force composed of such persons. But Scylitzes was writing a century later;[26] by then, *misthophoroi/misthophorikon* was in vogue as a term, being treated as interchangeable with the older terms *symmachoi* and *ethnikoi*,[27] We cannot be sure which term was in the source upon which Scylitzes drew, and in any case the episodes to which he applies it are set in, or on the borderlands with, the Abbasid caliphate, and the term is not used of employees of the Byzantine state.[28]

If a term having the specific sense of 'mercenary, soldier for hire' (*misthophoros*) became common in Byzantine sources only from the eleventh century onwards, this could support the proposition that most of the foreign-born warriors at Byzantium before that time were serving essentially at the behest of their rulers. Of course, they must have been paid something, and if the pay or other rewards had seemed to them unsatisfactory, they would not have stayed long. But if the only people besides the Armenians providing substantial quantities of volunteers were the Russo-Scandinavians, it may be no coincidence that their homeland was not endowed by nature with precious metals or luxury goods other than amber, furs and walrus-ivory. In other words, they may have been relatively easily satisfied with their pay, whatever precise form it may have taken – perhaps a mixture of coins, gold and silver vessels, silks and precious cloth. Harald Hardraada is indeed said to have returned to the north with a mass of gold which 'twelve young men could scarcely lift'; but his was an extraordinary haul, exciting comment from both Adam of Bremen and Snorri Sturluson, and leaving an unparalleled mark on mid-eleventh-century Scandinavian coin designs.[29]

for conducting a word search for *symmachikon, ethnikoi, misthophoroi, misthophorikon* in the works of Procopius, Nicephorus, Theophanes Confessor, Theophanes Continuatus, George Monachus Continuatus, Constantine VII and John Scylitzes. The searches of some of these writers are not yet in final, 'corrected', form, but the general pattern of terms for denoting foreign warriors before the eleventh century is clear.

[26] W. Seibt, 'Ioannes Skylitzes. Zur Person des Chronisten', *Jahrbuch der Österreichischen Byzantinistik* xxv, 1976, 83–5.

[27] *symmachoi* continued to be used in, e.g. Bryennius, ed. Gautier, 91, 259, 265, 271; likewise with *ethnikoi*, e.g. in late eleventh-century exemption charters: *Actes de Lavra* i, ed. P. Lemerle *et al.*, Paris 1970, 198, 243; cf. H. Ahrweiler, *Recherches sur l'administration de l'empire byzantin aux IX–XI siècles, Bulletin de Correspondance hellénique* lxxxiv, 1960, 34 and nn.8 and 9, repr. in Ahrweiler's *Etudes sur les structures administratives et sociales de Byzance*, London 1971, no.8.

[28] Scylitzes, 318, 319, 333. *misthophorikos* had been used by classical historians and is to be found in several of the works which were excerpted for the encyclopedic compilations of Constantine VII, e.g. *Excerpta de legationibus*, ed. C. de Boor, Berlin 1903, 10, 68, 70, 71, 159, 412, 548. Constantine did not, however, find use for the term in his own writings. Already in Late Antiquity the term seems to have been fairly rare, and to have been used primarily of compliant barbarian rulers or individuals retained by a fee, e.g. Agathias, *Historiarum Libri Quinque*, ed. R. Keydell, Berlin 1967, 195; Procopius, *Anecdota (Secret History)*, ed. and tr. H.B. Dewing, London 1935, 250, 292. For the former reference I am grateful to Douglas Lee.

[29] Adam of Bremen, *Gesta Hammaburgensis Ecclesiae Pontificum*, ed. B. Schmeidler,

It is tempting to contrast diametrically these Russo-Scandinavians and the 'allies' drafted to Byzantium by their rulers with, on the other hand, the 'Franks' who appear quite abruptly in Greek and Latin sources on mid-eleventh-century Byzantium – self-serving, materialistic volunteers, to whom pay was of overriding concern, and who were swift to mutiny if left unsatisfied. Surviving literature of Norman inspiration about the Normans' early contacts with the 'Greeks' encourages this kind of black-and-white comparison. Writers such as William of Jumièges, Amatus of Monte Cassino or William of Apulia play up the Norman rulers' or leaders' competitiveness towards the emperor, and the readiness of Norman warriors to rebel against him.[30] Scandinavian saga-writers and scalds, in contrast, tend to highlight the northerners' loyalty and devoted service for the emperor: even the fame-seeking Hardraada competes with and outwits a rival commander, 'Gyrgir' (i.e. George Maniaces), rather than the emperor himself. However, these self-images should not be taken entirely at face-value, and some nuancing is in order. For in fact the first substantial unit of Franks was recruited into Byzantine service by traditional, diplomatic, means. The Normans – a term which will henceforth be used interchangeably with Frank – are said to have been despatched to the expeditionary force bound for Sicily by Prince Guaimar V of Salerno, at the request of the expedition's commander, George Maniaces.[31] Such recruiting of local 'allies', whether by the central government or the commander on the spot, was not uncommon on the eve of major offensives intended to bring about the annexation of land.[32] The invasion force of 1038 also contained Rus, Scandinavians, so-called 'Lombards' from northern Italy, and men from Apulia and Calabria who had presumably been enlisted directly by the Byzantine authorities. In fact, the Normans were not particularly significant in terms of numbers. There were three hundred of them, according to Amatus of Monte Cassino, serving under their own commander, a son of Tancred de Hauteville, William Iron-Arm, newly arrived from Normandy together with his brother Drogo.[33]

Hanover/Leipzig 1917, 196, *schol.* 83 (84); cf. 154; Snorri Sturluson, *Heimskringla*, tr. S. Laing, rev. by P. Foote, London 1961, 165, 172, 178; P. Grierson, 'Harold Hardraada and Byzantine Coin Types in Denmark', *Byzantinische Forschungen* i, 1966, 132–8. On the paucity of finds of Byzantine gold coins in Scandinavia, see C. Morrisson, 'Le rôle des Varanges dans la transmission de la monnaie byzantine en Scandinavie', *Les pays du nord et Byzance (Scandinavie et Byzance), Actes du colloque nordique et international de byzantinologie*, Uppsala 1981, 134, 136.

[30] Jumiéges, 112–13 relays motifs purporting to illustrate Duke Robert's dignified bearing, self-restraint and lack of greed and resourcefulness vis-à-vis the Greeks. Their origin – before being incorporated into the 'B-redaction' of Jumièges' text – is unknown. They also appear in some sagas' versions of the visits of Harald Hardraada and King Sigurd of Norway to Byzantium: van Houts, 545–7. On the self-image of courage and greed for material gain propounded in writings from Norman milieux, see J. Bliese, 'The Courage of the Normans', *Nottingham Medieval Studies* xxxv, 1991, 10–11, 15–16.

[31] Amatus, 66–7; Malaterra, ed. Pontieri, 10; Leo Marsicanus, *Chronica Monasterii Casinensis*, ed. H. Hoffmann, *MGH SS*, xxxiv, Hanover 1980, 298; W. Felix, *Byzanz und die islamische Welt im früheren 11. Jahrhundert*, Vienna 1981, 208.

[32] For example, in 1045 Constantine IX obtained the assistance of Abul-Aswar, emir of Dvin, for the final campaign against the Armenian royal capital, Ani; Scylitzes, 436; V. Minorsky, *Studies in Caucasian History*, London 1953, 52–3.

[33] Amatus, 67; Leo Marsicanus, 298. Scylitzes' claim (p. 425) that five hundred 'Franks' had been recruited by Maniaces directly 'from Transalpine Gaul' is questionable, although not utterly inconceivable. It could reflect the recruiting efforts of his successors in Italy, for example John Raphael, a few years later. See below, 289.

We shall not attempt a collation of the Greek accounts of the Sicilian expedition with the Norman ones: Geoffrey Malaterra focuses on the Normans' role, and depicts them as reconquering eastern Sicily virtually single-handed. One may, however, note two features of the campaign. Firstly, the Normans appear to have fought as cavalry, since they took part in the battle of Troina at which the imperial mounted forces charged the enemy position in three battle-lines (*tres acies*). The horses' legs were protected with coverings of iron platelets against the caltrops (*tribuli*) which the Arabs had laid around their camp.[34] Thus from the first, the Normans seem to have been serving in the capacity for which they were to become famous; at this early stage, though, they would have been far outnumbered by the Byzantines' own cavalry. The second, and more celebrated, feature of the campaign is the Normans' quarrel with the Byzantine military authorities, apparently over their pay as well as over the division of spoils after the battle of Troina. It should however, be noted that there is no specific evidence of overt trouble between the Normans and the Byzantines before the battle of Troina early in 1040, almost two years after the landing on Sicily. And the aggression seems to have come from the Byzantine general, Maniaces, not from the Normans. Maniaces is said to have had beaten around the camp Arduin, a man of north Italian stock but conversant with Greek (in contrast to the newcomers from Normandy). In his capacity as spokesman for, and a commander of, the Normans, he had presumed to complain about their lack of prizes after Troina.[35] There is ample evidence that Maniaces' behaviour was violent and intemperate towards fellow-Byzantines as well as towards foreign troops. He inflicted a beating on his fleet-comander, Stephen, publicly insulting him, and even the Scandinavians seem to have been uncharacteristically restive. Harald Hardraada, who commanded a five-hundred-man strong Scandinavian unit, is represented in the *Heimskringla* as being continually at odds with Maniaces.[36] Moreover, not all the Normans withdrew from the expeditionary force in the company of Arduin, Drogo and William Iron-Arm, and it may be that Norman writers and one of Scylitzes' sources exaggerate the seriousness of the quarrel over booty and the scale of the Normans' withdrawal.[37] For it seems that enough warriors stayed

---

[34] Nilus, *Vita S. Philareti, Acta Sanctorum*, April, i, col. 608; Felix, 210. The Normans' role in the battle is underscored by Malaterra, 11. His claim should not be dismissed out of hand, for according to the disinterested Nilus (col. 608), the Arabs proved unable to endure even the first impact of the imperial forces' assault; this description, general as it is, may perhaps foreshadow the later, more celebrated, accounts of the Normans' charge. See also Anonymus Vaticanus, *Historia Sicula, RIS*, viii, col. 749.

[35] Amatus, 72–3; Malaterra, 11–12; William of Apulia, 110–11; Scylitzes, 426. For Arduin, see *Dizionario biographico degli Italiani*, iv, Rome 1962, 60–1 (R. Manselli); Felix, 210–11; W. Jahn, *Untersuchungen zur normannischen Herrschaft in Süditalien (1040–1100)*, Frankfurt am Main 1989, 25–9.

[36] Scylitzes, 406; *Heimskringla*, tr. Laing and Foote, 163–4. The *Heimskringla's* credibility at this point is reinforced by its mention of the departure of the 'Latin men' (p.164). The figure for the size of Harald's contingent is given by Cecaumenus, 282. On the harshness of Maniaces' treatment of the Apulians in 1042, see V. von Falkenhausen, *Untersuchungen über die byzantinische Herrschaft in Süditalien vom 9. bis ins 11. Jahrhundert*, Wiesbaden 1967, 59, 91.

[37] Hervé is said to have campaigned with Maniaces in Sicily and to have stayed in 'Roman' service thereafter: Scylitzes, 484; cf. J. Shepard, 'Byzantium's Last Sicilian Expedition: Scylitzes' testimony', *Rivista di studi bizantini e neoellenici*, ns 14–16 (xxiv–xxvi), 1977–79, 152, n.1.

behind to form the core of a unit which was still called the 'Maniakatoi' (after Maniaces) forty years later.[38]

These considerations do not drain the Normans' self-image of all validity. They had already proved to be self-willed as warriors in the service of the princes of Salerno, and Prince Guaimar is said by Malaterra to have been delighted to send off the three hundred in response to Maniaces' request for aid.[39] And in being prepared formally to protest about booty and pay, the Normans were behaving differently from almost all the other allied forces in Byzantine service known to us. It must, however, be remembered that the Normans were approaching Byzantium by a different direction from that of most other foreign soldiers of the *basileus*. For although supplied by a satellite ruler at the Byzantines' request, the Normans were not his native subjects and they had been employed by him primarily as mercenaries.[40] Money and material rewards might be expected to have weighed heavily with them, and thus they were soldiers of fortune, of a cast which the Byzantines had seldom encountered before. Unlike the Russo-Scandinavians, they hailed from, or had hired themselves out in, regions where coin was a not insignificant means of remuneration for goods and services.[41] And they presumably expected to be paid thus by their Byzantine employers. We have no precise evidence of the form or extent which Maniaces' payments to them took, but according to Scylitzes they were paid a monthly 'wage' (*sitēresion*), and it was upon their failure to receive this 'pay for their labours' that they

[38] The 'Maniakatoi' are attested as a unit consisting of 'Franks from Italy', recruited by George Maniaces and still operational in the 1070s. However, our earliest – late eleventh-century – source about them is inaccurate in several respects, for example, representing the dispute as one between the Franks and Maniaces' successor, thereby exonerating Maniaces from responsibility for it: Scylitzes Continuatus, ed. Tsolakes, 167; Shepard, 'Sicilian Expedition', 151–2. It is very probable that some of the Franks recruited by Maniaces stayed in the Byzantines' service indefinitely, but there is no explicit evidence that they or other Normans took part in the rebellion which he mounted upon returning to Italy in 1042. He is depicted by William of Apulia (pp. 126–7) as trying unsuccessfully to recruit Argyrus and the Normans to his cause at that time. The tenuous or non-existent nature of some of the unit's soldiers' links with the famed general may have become blurred over time; after a substantial influx of Franks into imperial service in 1047, the prestigious label may have been extended to distinguish all those Franks already in the imperial service. The warriors of the 1070s may have been their sons, nephews or other kinsmen. See also Bryennius, 268–9; Anna Comnena, ii, 117; Ahrweiler, *Recherches*, 34, n.10.

[39] Malaterra, 10.

[40] While William and Drogo had only arrived at Guaimar's court shortly beforehand (Amatus, 67; Leo Marsicanus, 298), other Norman warriors had been in the employ of the princes of Salerno and other southern Italian potentates since the 1020s, if not earlier: F. Chalandon, *Histoire de la domination normande en Italie et en Sicile*, i, Paris 1907, 57–8, 67; E. Pontieri, *I normanni nell' Italia meridionale*, Naples n.d., 93; S. Tramontana, *I normanni in Italia*, Messina 1970, 125–31; H. Hoffmann, 'Die Anfänge der Normannen in Süditalien', *QF* xlix, 1969, 130–1, 143; R. Bunemann, 'Roberto il Guiscardo, *terror mundi*', *Archivio Storico Siciliano*, Serie iv, 12–13, 1986–87, 9–10; Jahn, 22–3; J. France, 'The Occasion of the Coming of the Normans to Southern Italy', *Journal of Medieval History* xvii, 1991, 201–02. For the last-mentioned reference I am grateful to Matthew Bennett.

[41] D. Bates, *Normandy before 1066*, London 1982, 96–7; P. Grierson, 'The Salernitan Coinage of Gisulf II (1052–1077) and Robert Guiscard (1077–1085)', *Papers of the British School at Rome* xxiv, 1956, 37–8, 59; idem, 'Monete bizantine in Italia dal VII all' XI secolo', *Settimane di studio del centro italiano di studi sull' alto medioevo* viii, 1961, 42, 54–5; A. Guillou et al., *Il mezzogiorno dai bizantini a Federico II* (*Storia d'Italia*, iii), Turin 1983, 66–7; J.M. Martin, 'Economia naturale ed economia monetaria . . .', *Storia d'Italia. Annali*, vi, *Economia naturale, economia monetaria*, Turin 1983, 197–202.

complained.[42] If (as is likely) they were serving as heavy cavalry, and if they had to meet out of their own pockets some of the running expenses of their horses and equipment – for example, the iron platelets for the horses' legs at Troina – then matters of payment or rights to some plunder would, understandably, have been of quite pressing concern to them. Conversely, Maniaces, after nearly two years' slow advance through siege warfare in a theatre remote from the central government, may well have been unable to provide payment in a form customary to the Normans, such as money.

This, the first appearance of the Normans in imperial Byzantine service, seems to have been quite fortuitous and, in the literal, geographical sense, peripheral. But if William de Hauteville and his companions happened to form a small component in one of the last of Byzantium's expansionist expeditions, other Franks soon became embroiled in the internal strife of the empire. For the overriding fear of mid-eleventh-century emperors was of *coups d'état* by their own generals. In fact, George Maniaces, the commander who recruited the first discernible intake of Normans into Byzantine service, rebelled in 1042–3. And it is during another military revolt, that of Leo Tornicius in 1047, that we first hear of Franks operating in the capital, Constantinople. The earliest firmly datable instances of the term *misthophoroi/-phorikon* ('wage-receivers/-ing') occur, so far as I know, only from this time onwards.[43] The arrival of the Franks in Byzantine service may well have contributed to the coining of the term, or rather, to its re-striking, in that *misthophoros* means 'mercenary' in classical writers such as Thucydides and Polybius, who were known to educated eleventh- and twelfth-century Byzantines.[44]

What seems to be the earliest Byzantine reference to a sizable contingent of Franks recruited from the west directly to serve the emperor expressly associates them with money. John Mauropous celebrated in an oration the suppression by Constantine IX Monomachus of Tornicius' rebellion. The rebellion finally collapsed with the capture of Tornicius shortly before Christmas, 1047, and the oration itself was delivered on 30 December of the same year. The emperor is said to have sent for 'barbarian armies from the west and the north'; upon the arrival of the western army, which is described as having been 'abroad' (*hyperorion*), 'the emperor added strength to the hands of them all [i.e. all those in the western army] with great gifts and splendours of titles and all sorts of other kindnesses,

---

[42] There may well have been discontent over both pay and the distribution of booty; the Latin sources focus only upon the latter issue: Scylitzes, 426. *siteresion* is a term used by Cecaumenus, 276, meaning a regular monthly stipend, distinct from *khortasmata*, 'feed', and *roga*, probably an annual lump sum. Cecaumenus, however, is referring to foreign-born and Byzantine bodyguards of the emperor, rather than to field-troops on campaign, and his usage may not be identical to Scylitzes'. See also Ahrweiler, *Recherches*, 8, n. 2; 12, n. 3.

[43] The earliest instance of all known to me comes in the oration of John Mauropous discussed below and delivered on 30 December 1047: *Quae in Codice Vaticano Graeco 676 supersunt*, ed. P. de Lagarde, *Abhandlungen der historisch-philologischen Classe der königlichen Gesellschaft der Wissenschaften zu Göttingen* xxviii, 1882, repr. Amsterdam 1979, 188. See also Attaleiates, 122, 127, 146, 148, 156 (denoting, *inter alios*, Germans and steppe-nomads). As these examples indicate, the Franks were by no means the only foreign warriors to be hired by the government in the mid-eleventh century. They do, however, seem to have been the most prominent.

[44] See above, n. 28. See also G. Buckler, *Anna Comnena*, Oxford 1929, 205–06, 488: A.P. Kazhdan and A.W. Epstein, *Change in Byzantine Culture in the Eleventh and Twelfth Centuries*, Berkeley/London 1985, 138.

but above all else he filled [their hands] up with gold; for this people is outstand-ingly fond of money (*philochrēmaton*)! Thus he sends them off most quickly, eager to the combat, having given them excellent instructions on what must be done, and provided them with the best of his generals as their commanders'.[45] This combat-ready host from the west is not identified by an ethnic name, but its obvious provenance is from somewhere in southern or south-central Italy and it most probably consisted mainly of Normans or other scions of Francia.[46] It appears to have been won over with lavish promises of money.[47] The men making up this force seem to have been fairly numerous, in that they comprise a whole unit in the emperor's strategy of encircling the rebel general's army, and several Byzantine generals need to be placed in command of them. There were probably already some Normans at Constantinople, veterans of Maniaces' campaign or associates of the Italian-born magnate, Argyrus, who had been summoned from Bari to Constantinople a year or two earlier. Argyrus is said by a chronicle composed in his native Bari to have led out 'some Franks and Greeks' from the city-walls during Tornicius' siege in late September/early October, 1047.[48] But

[45] Mauropous, ed. de Lagarde, 192. See divergent views in J. Shepard, 'John Mauropous, Leo Tornicius and an alleged Russian army . . .', *Jahrbuch der Österreichischen Byzantinistik* xxiv, 1975, 62–3, 89; A.P. Kazhdan, 'Once more about the "alleged" Russo-Byzantine Treaty and the Pecheneg Crossing of the Danube', *Jahrbuch der Österreichischen Byzantinistik* xxvi, 1977, 66–70.

[46] The very small proportion of non-Norman knights from southern Italy or, indeed, of knights from elsewhere in Italy known to have gone on the First Crusade and the *arrière-croisade*, suggests that the native Italian component would have been modest in mid-eleventh-century expeditionary forces, too: B. Figliuolo, 'Ancora sui normanni d'Italia alla prima crociata', *Archi-vio Storico per le Province Napoletane* civ, 1986, 9–11, 13; cf. A.V. Murray, 'The Origins of the Frankish Nobility of the Kingdom of Jerusalem, 1100–1118', *Mediterranean Historical Review* iv, 1989, 293. The role of a Bulgarian force 'sent for from the west' is prominent in Attaleiates, 29; but they scarcely constituted an army living 'over the border, abroad (*hyperorion*)'; nor did they have a notorious appetite for money. And, as Byzantine subjects, the emperor's furnishing of them with 'instructions' and 'the best of his generals' would scarcely have been worthy of mention in Mauropous' oration. Moreover, they engaged the rebels from the west, whereas Mauropous' western army seems to have been sent forth from the capital by Constantine IX.

[47] The 'greed' of northern and western 'barbarians' in general had been decried by Byzantine writers since the sixth century and the 'love of money' of the 'Franks', in particular, was noted by Emperor Maurice at the end of that century: *Strategikon*, ed. G.T. Dennis and German tr. E. Gamillscheg, Vienna 1981, 370–1. The 'Franks'' susceptibility to pecuniary offers on account of their greed is averred by Leo VI, who adds that he himself had observed the phenomenon in those who spent time in Italy and became 'barbarised': *Tactica*, cols 965, 968. The westerners' alleged preoccupation with money could reflect the fact that a monetary economy persisted in a more robust condition in Italy and parts of Francia than in most other areas; payments in coin were therefore more immediately useful to Italians and Franks than they were to 'barbarians' from lands lacking any regular circulation of money. See above, n.41.

[48] Anonymous of Bari, *Chronicon, RIS*, v. 151. Argyrus is credited with a conspicuous, if less heroic, role in the defence of the capital by Scylitzes, 440. The context for the incident mentioned in these two sources is the very beginning of Tornicius' overt revolt and thus before the arrival of armies 'from the west and the north'. Argyrus had employed Normans in his efforts to counter Maniaces' rebellion in southern Italy in 1042–43: William of Apulia, 124–9. Although he is said subsequently to have released these Normans from the imperial service (pp. 132–3), he probably retained contacts with leading Normans even after his move to Constantinople, and he could well have been instrumental in the summons of a force from the west in 1047. See also von Falken-hausen, 59–60, 94.

this incident is quite distinct from the arrival of 'the barbarian army' fresh from the west, later that autumn.

From this time onwards we encounter a series of mentions of western mercenaries in Byzantine and Armenian sources, together with some seals of leading individuals named in these sources. Taken together, they form quite a solid, coherent, bloc of evidence, and stand in contrast with the sources' silence about 'Franks' in the central government's forces before the later 1040s. At about the same time, the government re-armed 15,000 Pecheneg prisoners-of-war, sending them off to fight the Turks in the east; it also began to retain the services of Turkish chieftains and their war-bands.[49] The emperor, uncertain of his own generals' fidelity and facing an unexpected bout of turbulence on his eastern borders, was looking for seasoned and manipulable military manpower.

The evidence for the mid-eleventh century becomes ample enough to permit a sketch of the Normans' role during the first phase of their service at Byzantium. They seem to have been posted almost immediately to the eastern front, where as late as 1048–49 major offensive expeditions were being launched, in an attempt to pre-empt the Turks' raids. They were also deployed for purposes of defence, manning towns such as Manzikert against the raiders. But they do not seem to have constituted permanent garrison forces in towns in the eastern borderlands. The Franks, like the Scandinavians, are said to have been 'dispersed' in wintertime, presumably to live off the land.[50] This in turn suggests that, at least at first, they may not have required a constant heavy outlay from the central treasury.[51] More probably, they were a burden upon the hapless local population, and we may note that the exemption from the 'billetting' (*mitaton*) of foreign warriors was a privilege sought after by wealthy landowners such as large monasteries. Revenues could also be raised in cash on the spot for the benefit of the foreign troops, judging by a charter of 1060.[52] The places where we hear of the Normans being quartered in winter are in Asia minor, in the Armeniakon theme (i.e. province). Certain of their leaders were granted landed estates, and even castles,

---

[49] Scylitzes, 460. For the employment of units of Turks and individual Turks from the mid-eleventh century onwards, see C.M. Brand, 'The Turkish Element in Byzantium, Eleventh/Twelfth Centuries', *Dumbarton Oaks Papers* xliii, 1989, 2–3.

[50] Scylitzes, 485, 394.

[51] Cecaumenus, writing in the mid-1070s with reference to the 1040s and earlier, maintains that foreign warriors were then content with fairly humble titles and served in exchange for basic necessities: *Strategikon*, ed. Litavrin, 280. He was polemicising and cannot be regarded as an unimpeachable authority (cf. Litavrin, n. 1138 on 579). However, it should be noted that his criticism is directed at the (in his view) excessively senior titles bestowed on certain non-royal foreign employees of the emperor, rather than at the inherently high expense of foreign-born warriors. He assures the emperor, 'if you like, I can bring you as many of these mercenaries (*ethnikoi*) as you wish for a bit of bread and some clothing' (ed. Litavrin, 278); these items, and the expectation of 'a few *nomismata* (*solidi*)' will ensure their faithful service (p. 278). Cecaumenus does raise the spectre of disloyalty, but as the consequence of over-promotion rather than under-payment. He is exercised by the promotion of non-royal foreigners to top commands. He may have been unduly confident of his ability to manage foreign mercenaries on minimal remuneration, but he does seem to have been drawing on empirical experience of the middle years of the century. See also below, 298.

[52] *Actes de Lavra*, i. ed. Lemerle *et al.*, 198. This seems to be the earliest extant charter to name 'Franks' among those *ethnikoi* who are not to be billetted, or to have revenues assigned to them. Charters of 1044 and 1049 for the Nea Mone on Chios mention only the Rus by name: K.N. Kanellakes, *Chiaka Analekta*, Athens 1890, 548, 551.

there.[53] It was presumably the government's intention that they should obtain a stake in the empire's well-being, and an interest in eventually settling down to a life of domesticity on their estates. The Armeniakon theme was over 1,500 kilometres from southern Italy, where other Normans were, in the 1050s, harrying the Byzantine authorities and beginning to threaten their key bases. The imperial government presumably felt confident of its ability to maintain control of the Frankish recipients of lands and castles. Various Armenian princes and their entourages received extensive landholdings and senior administrative posts in Cappadocia and also, in the mid-eleventh century, in the selfsame Armeniakon theme.[54] But there is no evidence that all the Frankish rank-and-file received land-grants to support them and the fact that they needed to be assigned winter-quarters suggests otherwise.

From the first, the Franks served primarily as cavalry, and their horses presumably remained with them in their winter-quarters through the period when pasturing was impossible. We can infer their mounted role from operations in which they engaged in 1049. They were included among 'the eastern regiments' which were transferred to the west to deal with hordes of Pechenegs who were on the rampage in the Balkans.[55] And they now had their own commander, whereas two years earlier they had been put under the command of Byzantine generals, according to John Mauropous. Hervé, or 'Erbebios ho Frangopolos' (as he is termed on his Greek-language seal),[56] commanded the left wing of what is described as 'the Roman phalanx';[57] in reality, it probably consisted mainly of Hervé's fellow-Franks. The Byzantines were routed and a Byzantine chronicle relays the allegation that the commanders were the first to flee, being unable to bear the thundering of the horses' hooves. This is an implausible allegation, but it could convey an eye-witness' impression of the unusually loud noise created by a cavalry charge of a type hitherto unfamiliar even to Byzantine military men.[58] At any rate, the Franks' numbers would have been quite substantial, if they made up the left wing of the 'Roman' battle-line. The likelihood of this is enhanced by the

---

[53] Scylitzes, 485, 490 (Hervé); Attaleiates, 125 (Crispin); Attaleiates, 199 (Roussel). It would not be surprising if these properties had some link with the imperial stud farms, on which see Constantine VII, *Three Treatises*, ed. Haldon, 184 (commentary). For Crispin's fortress, see below, 297.

[54] G. Dédéyan, 'L'immigration arménienne en Cappadoce au XI siècle', *Byzantion* xlv, 1975, 78–85.

[55] Scylitzes, 467. They belonged to, if they did not themselves exclusively constitute, a unit or units called 'the fellow-countrymen' (*ta homoethnē*): 467. See also Ahrweiler, *Recherches*, 28, n. 7.

[56] Hervé's seal was published by G. Schlumberger, 'Deux chefs normands des armées byzantines au XI siècle', *Revue historique* xvi, 1881, 295; *idem*, *Sigillographie de l'empire byzantin*, Paris 1884, 659–60. See below, 297.

[57] Scylitzes, 468.

[58] Scylitzes (468–9) claims that the only general to stand his ground was Catacalon Cecaumenus, implying that Hervé was among those who fled. The source of this section of the chronicle is a laudatory biography or memoirs of none other than Cecaumenus; so its allegations were distinctly subjective: J. Shepard, 'A Suspected Source of Scylitzes' Chronicle', *Byzantine and Modern Greek Studies* xvi, 1992, 171–81. Even so, Cecaumenus could have been slanting to his own credit a generally observed incident from this battle. The Franks' charge which, according to Anna Comnena, 'could punch a hole through the walls of Babylon' (*Alexiad*, iii, ed. Leib, 115) was already regarded as remarkable by Psellus, writing of Crispin's showing in 1072: *Chronographia*, ii, ed. E. Renauld, Paris 1928, 170.

fact that there were, in 1057, two Frankish *tagmata* stationed at Coloneia, to the east of the Armeniakon theme.[59] At that same time, there were also Franks stationed in Constantinople, and assuming that a *tagma* contained at least five hundred men, one may suppose a minimum of, say, 1,500 Frankish fighting men in the Byzantine forces.[60]

Numbers such as these, which do not seem to strain the sources' testimony, could not be maintained for long without an intake of new blood. And in fact we find evidence of Byzantine recruiting efforts in the west in the wake of the arrival of 'the barbarian army' from there in 1047. Argyrus, the Italian-born official who had demonstrated his commitment to Constantine IX during Tornicius' siege of the capital, was sent back to southern Italy in 1051, at least partly in order to recruit Norman mercenaries. According to William of Apulia, Argyrus offered the Normans 'quantities of money, much silver, precious garments and gold', if they would cross over to the Byzantines, who were 'engaged in grave struggle against the Persians [i.e. the Turks]'.[61] The same invocation of warfare against the Moslems to the east was made by a Byzantine embassy to Duke William of Normandy not very long afterwards and, as we have seen, the Normans were principally employed on the eastern front during the first phase of their service in Byzantium.[62] The Byzantine embassy to William was trying to raise troops, and thus we see Byzantium continuing to use traditional, 'diplomatic' channels to recruit what could have been termed an 'allied' force. William of Apulia claims that Argyrus' recruiting efforts were a total failure: the Normans were well-aware that his ulterior purpose was to induce them to give up the imperial territories which they had seized in southern Italy. But it is questionable whether all the 'counts' whom Argyrus approached with promises of money were as unresponsive as William claims: for it was probably to a large extent from southern Italy that the numbers of the Franks at Byzantium were replenished. It is anyway noteworthy that the target of these two relatively well-attested attempts at recruiting was Normans. There is indirect evidence suggesting that in the 1040s a military commander in southern Italy, John Raphael, was attempting, with apparent success, to gain recruits for his 'Varangian' contingent through the good offices of Edward the Confessor in Winchester.[63] And by the late 1060s, if not

---

[59] Scylitzes, 490.

[60] Ahrweiler (*Recherches*, 26) stresses that *tagmata* varied between one another in size and that the numbers of a given *tagma* may have fluctuated over time; moreover, figures for the sizes of *tagmata* are few, and not necessarily reliable. Nonetheless, the tenth-century works on strategy seem to assume a complement of at least five hundred men in a *tagma*, and the three hundred Franks whom Hervé roused to revolt formed only part of the contingent quartered in the district (Scylitzes, 485). So an estimate of at least five hundred men *per* unit does not seem overblown.

[61] William of Apulia, 134–5.

[62] *Gesta Guillelmi*, 144–5.

[63] It seems more likely that the seal of John Raphael excavated in Winchester arrived while he was commanding 'Varangians' in Italy, rather than at some later date. The seal was struck while he was *prōtospatharios epi tou theophylaktou koitōnos kai ek prosōpou tou pantheou*, before he took up the post of '*katepano* of Italia' in autumn, 1046: Anonymous of Bari, 151; V. Laurent, 'Byzance et l'Angleterre au lendemain de la conquête normande', *The Numismatic Circular* lxxi, 1963, no. 5, pp. 93–6. von Falkenhausen (92–3) suggests that the seal validated a document brought back by a returning veteran. This is very possible, but the location of the find – in an important royal administrative centre – suggests that the document had been despatched for some specific purpose. That Edward the Confessor may have received an enamelled cross-encolpion

earlier, significant quantities of Germans (known to the Byzantines by their Slavic name, Nemitzoi) were serving in Asia minor, presumably with the approval of the royal authorities in Germany.[64]

It is, however, probably not an accident of source-survival or merely a reflection of the Normans' penchant for magnifying their self-importance and their duke's international standing, that our clearest-cut evidence of mid-eleventh Byzantine recruiting efforts in the west concerns these warriors. For William of Apulia was, paradoxically, doing less than justice to the positive qualities of the Normans which attracted the Byzantines' attention. Undoubtedly, there was the calculation that the more Normans syphoned out of Italy, the fewer would remain to pare away at the empire's outposts there; this was a variant of the 'divide-and-rule' diplomacy which Byzantium had long been practising. And the sheer need for serviceable warriors of any stripe is suggested by the sudden re-armament of the 15,000 Pechenegs who had been settled as farmers in the Balkans. Nonetheless, there are indications that the Normans' martial qualities – of leadership and ingenuity, as well as courage – made an immediate impact upon their Levantine hosts, to the point of becoming almost proverbial. Soon, they were serving as a prop in ceremonial displays of majesty. One may glance at four illustrations of this, none of them particularly obscure, but seldom considered in light of the fact that they are all set within the first ten years or so of the Normans' arrival at Byzantium in force.

In 1054, a 'Frank' – a bachelor and apparently an ordinary rank-and-file soldier – volunteered to slip out of the town of Manzikert and to destroy a Turkish ballista which had been bombarding the walls with huge rocks. It was the man's resourcefulness and initiative that excited the admiration of Matthew of Edessa. The Frank is said to have asked for a strong and fearless horse, 'put on his coat of mail and placed his helmet on his head. Taking a letter, he attached it to the end of his spear . . . [as if] he were a courier'. He rode towards the Turkish camp, halted by the ballista, pretending to admire it, and then suddenly pulled out three bottles full of naphtha ('Greek Fire'), one by one, and threw them against the machine from three different sides. He rode '[quick] as an eagle' around the ballista, according to the Armenian chronicler, and the machine was reduced to ashes. The Frank was summoned to Constantinople where the emperor rewarded him with gifts and a senior title.[65]

A few years later, a Frankish commander named Randolph distinguished himself fighting with the forces loyal to Michael VI against a major, and successful, military rising. He alone stood his ground when the imperial troops turned to flee. He wandered into the thick of the fray, looking for a man of note with whom to do

---

from the *basileus* was proposed, on the basis of suggestive antiquarian evidence, by K. Ciggaar, 'England and Byzantium on the Eve of the Norman Conquest', *ante* v, 1982, 91–5.

[64] Germans, including noble or illustrious ones, were serving on Romanus IV's campaign in 1069 (Attaleiates, 125), and they could act as cavalry (Attaleiates, 146–7). See also A. Hohlweg, *Beiträge zur Verwaltungsgeschichte des oströmischen Reiches unter den Komnenen*, Munich 1965, 51.

[65] Matthew of Edessa, tr. Dostourian (as in n.18), 140–2. A similar account is provided by Attaleiates (46–7). The two versions probably draw independently upon a widely circulating tale of 'derring do'; the tale equally probably recorded an actual event, observed from the walls of Manzikert by a medley of witnesses. See also R. Janin, 'Les "Francs" au service des byzantins', *Echos d'Orient* xxix, 1930, 64.

battle. 'And when he learnt that Nicephorus Botaneiates [a senior rebel comman-der] was roaming about . . . he went in quest of him, crying out from afar and enjoining him to wait and declaring his name, who he might be and for what purpose he was summoning him'. Botaneiates obliged and they fought in single combat with swords. Randolph's shield was cut in half, while his sword failed to damage Botaneiates' helmet. He was taken prisoner and brought before the leader of the rebellion. It appears that, at least at this dying stage of the battle, he was fighting on foot.[66] Randolph, who held the court title of *patrikios*, thus excited the admiration of the military man who is the ultimate source of this story.[67] Another, rather less anecdotal, instance of admiration for individual Normans comes from the historian Michael Attaleiates. We are told that after repeated defeats at the hands of the Pechenegs in pitched battles, Constantine IX, 'despairing of the unmanliness of his generals' and of their 'folly' in matters of strategy and tactics, posted troops to various forts and put in command of them a 'Latin', 'a splendid man in moments of crisis and second to none in realising what must be done'.[68] The commander, who may well be identifiable as Hervé,[69] would together with his men observe the nomads' movements, only sallying forth from the towns to surprise them when the nomads were scattered and pillaging the surrounding countryside. In this way, they recovered much of the booty, killing or capturing many of the nomads, and they are said to have put an end to the continual raiding. Thus a westerner was, after probably no more than a dozen years' service at most, put in charge of Byzantine troops for a major operation. In part, the appointment may reflect Constantine's distrust of his own generals rather than their 'unmanli-ness', and Attaleiates may be simplifying matters in order to hold up an ideal foreign-born general to his Byzantine readers.[70] But the command is also a tribute to the positive qualities of initiative and adaptability which such men as this 'Latin' and Randolph really did display. The track-and-destroy tactics against the Pechenegs were quite different from the pitched battles in which the Normans had shown their mettle hitherto. It is partly due to such leadership qualities that we are far better-informed about the Norman commanders than we are about the names and circumstances of virtually any other foreign-born commanders since the early Byzantine empire.

A final example of the Normans' instant celebrity at Byzantium brings us into the sphere of literary topoi and imperial, or rather, mock-imperial, ceremonial. Michael Psellus offers an eye-witness account of the reception which the rebel general Isaac Comnenus accorded him and his fellow-emissaries from Emperor

---

[66] Scylitzes, 495–6. The witness of Codex Ambrosianus C279 inf. at p.496. 68 is preferable to that of all the other manuscripts; for it alone is consistent with what has been stated earlier in the text: that Botaneiates was serving on the rebels' side, *against* the emperor Michael VI (488–9).

[67] Above, n. 58.

[68] Attaleiates, 35.

[69] Hervé was then the leading Frank in Byzantium, and he was a commander during operations against the Pechenegs in 1049: Scylitzes, 468–9. However, that there were other Franks in senior positions is indicated by the seals of 'Ounpertos': see below, n. 127.

[70] The 'Latin' was not put in supreme command, a post given to Bryennius the *patrikios* who also, under his title of 'ethnarch', took charge of all the Frankish and Russo-Scandinavian contingents: Scylitzes, 471. The 'Latin' seems thus to have been temporarily detached from his compatriots. Bryennius' loyalty proved to be less than total: immediately after Constantine IX's death, he tried to seize the throne for himself, Scylitzes, 479; Cheynet, 66.

Michael VI in 1057. The reception in the rebel camp was intended to impress upon them the legitimacy of the rebel cause. Around Isaac were arrayed guards of honour fit for an emperor: the outer ring of guards consisted of 'Italians' (who can, in the context, hardly be other than Normans[71]) and 'Tauroscyths', i.e. Russians or Russo-Scandinavians. Psellus' description may not be particularly familiar to western medievalists and so it seems worth recalling the details. They correspond in most respects with other Byzantine allusions to Frankish warriors and to the representations in sagas and other sources of Russo-Scandinavian warriors' deportment during the Viking Age. According to Psellus, the Normans and the Russians were fearsome-looking: 'both glaring fiercely, but the one people [i.e. the Normans] painting themselves and plucking their eyelashes while the others [i.e. the Russians] retained their natural looks; the former impulsive in their charges (*tais hormais*), mercurial and impetuous, the latter manic and full of bile; those [i.e. the Normans] irresistible in the first shock of their charge, but soon losing their momentum, the others [i.e. the Russians] less violent in rushing forwards but unsparing of their blood and having no regard at all for their wounds'.[72] These warriors are said to have 'supported' their one-edged battle-axes on their shoulders and to have held out the shafts of their 'lengthy lances (*epimēkē dorata*)' in such a way as to form a kind of 'roof' over the spaces between them. This description forms part of an elaborate literary set-piece which draws on various stereotypes of an emperor holding court and is devised with considerable artifice.[73] While it cannot be regarded as a photographic recollection of an event, the most wilful distortions are those involving Psellus' own role in the proceedings.

Three brief remarks must do duty for the fuller discussion which Psellus' description warrants. Firstly, although his wording could be taken to mean that each warrior brandished both lance and battle-axe, he seems to indicate that the axe was merely rested on the shoulder rather than being borne in a holster or with straps in such a way as to leave both hands free. A warrior holding a battle-axe would scarcely have been able to hold out a 'lengthy' lance in a dignified fashion, even if he were able to grasp his battle-axe with just one hand. In other words, each warrior was wielding only one of these weapons. Battle-axes were the most characteristic weapon of the Russo-Scandinavian, and later of the Anglo-Saxon warriors at Byzantium, and axe-bearers are pictured, albeit anachronistically, as guarding the palace in an illustrated chronicle.[74] So it is most probable that the

---

[71] J. Hermans, 'The Byzantine View of the Normans – another Norman Myth?', *ante* ii, 1979, 85.

[72] Psellus, i, ed. Renauld, 97.

[73] R. Beaton, ' "*De vulgari eloquentia*" in Twelfth-century Byzantium', *Byzantium and the West, c.850–1200*, ed. J.D. Howard-Johnston, Amsterdam 1988, 261–2.

[74] They are depicted in an early ninth-century scene by the twelfth-century Norman Sicilian manuscript of Scylitzes' chronicle: A. Grabar and E. Manousaka, *L'illustration du manuscrit de Scylitzès de la Bibliothèque Nationale de Madrid*, Venice 1979, fig. 10 (fol. 26va); p. 31. Cf. Blöndal and Benedikz, 183; P. Schreiner, 'Zur Ausrüstung des Kriegers in Byzanz, dem Kiever Russland und Nordeuropa nach bildlichen und literarischen Quellen', *Les pays du nord et Byzance (Scandinavie et Byzance), Actes du colloque nordique et international de byzantinologie*, Uppsala 1981, 235–6. According to Psellus (ii, 90–1) 'not more than four' Russians ('Tauroscyths') penned Isaac Comnenus in with their spears, holding him to his seat in the cavalry battle at Petroe in 1057. But it is very unlikely that they could have managed this if they, too, were mounted, *pace* Blöndal and Benedikz, 108, 183. Russians had been using spears while on horseback since at least the tenth century: *Russian Primary Chronicle*, tr. S.H. Cross and O.P. Sherbowitz-Wetzor, Cambridge,

'Tauroscyths' – probably, in this context, mainly Russians – carried the axes, while overhead arched lances were held by the Normans. Presumably the lances were, in 1057, regarded as the Normans' most distinctive weapon.[75]

Secondly, the characterisation of westerners as irresistible in their first onrush but lacking in staying-power is also to be found in Anna Comnena.[76] The impact of 'the Franks" charge, on horseback or on foot, and their limited stamina, are themes of Byzantine military manuals from the sixth century onwards, but they should not for that reason be discounted.[77] After all, no Late Antique stereotype for the Russians was available to Psellus and it could well be that he was representing, albeit in caricature, the tactics actually practised by western warriors at Byzantium in the mid-eleventh century. He shows awareness of the impact of their charge in relating Crispin's destruction of his opponents' battle-line.[78] It is not impossible that Psellus' description conveys a layman's impression of the halts and *volte-faces* which use of the couched lance involved. There is reason to suppose that this technique was being practised by the Franks in Byzantium before the early 1070s; for at that time a systematic attempt to introduce – or re-introduce – Byzantine cavalrymen to it seems to have been undertaken, presumably under Frankish inspiration.[79] Both Psellus' experience of his reception in Isaac Comnenus' giant tent and his pen-portrait of the incident some years later belong to a time when attempts to convert the lance into a kind of mobile battering-ram were still, in all probability, experimental and variegated.[80]

Mass., 1953, 80. But it was as 'axe-bearers' that they, the Scandinavians and, later, the Anglo-Saxons were best known to the Byzantines, e.g. Psellus, i, ed. E. Renauld, Paris 1926, 118; cf. T.G. Kolias, *Byzantinische Waffen. Ein Beitrag zur byzantinischen Waffenkunde von den Anfängen bis zur lateinischen Eroberung*, Vienna 1988, 165–6; line-drawing, 169: 4.

[75] The lance of the Normans has been estimated as 'between nine and eleven feet in length': I. Peirce, 'Arms, Armour and Warfare in the Eleventh Century', *ante* x, 1988, 244. It should be noted that Byzantine heavy cavalry were, in the tenth and presumably the eleventh century/ies, equipped with lances 3.75 metres in length, apparently for purposes of throwing: Kolias, 192.

[76] Anna Comnena, iii, ed. Leib, 28. See also above, n.58. Anna's theme that the westerners' charge, although formidable, could be broken up by Byzantine ingenuity and resolve is illustrated by, for example, her tale of the repulse of Crusaders marauding outside the walls of Constantinople: Anna Comnena, ii, ed. Leib, 223–4, 226. The eventual fatigue of the Franks' horses (albeit after allegedly 'climbing and descending many mountain ridges') is an important element in an anecdote of Attaleiates, 190–1.

[77] Maurice, *Strategikon*, 368–71; Leo VI, *Tactica*, cols 965–8.

[78] Psellus, ii, 170. Only Crispin is singled out by name, but 'those around him' whom he led in the charge seem most likely to have been Franks under his command.

[79] According to Bryennius (264–7), Nicephoritzes, logothete of the Drome in the aftermath of Manzikert, set about trying to form a new élite regiment. After learning how to maintain a firm seat on their horses, the men were trained to charge full-tilt at one another in opposing 'squadrons' and to hit one another as hard as possible with untipped lances. Those who consistently showed courage in this were chosen to form the 'phalanx of the Immortals'. This exercise, in which a premium was placed on the impetus of the charge, and hence maximum impact of the lance, is most comprehensible if the lance was in a firmly fixed position. By the 1090s, Nicephorus Euphorbenus was 'taking in his arm' (*enagkalisamenos*) his lance and wielding it as expertly as a Norman. Anna's phraseology (ii, 197) suggests that Nicephorus' lance was fixed beneath his arm: Kolias, 207–08 and n. 128; above, 278. Bryennius and Anna were writing in the second quarter of the twelfth century, but they were not necessarily ignorant or anachronistic about the circumstances of late-eleventh-century warfare. Bryennius had been put in charge of Constantinople's walls at the time of the First Crusade, while Anna heard many stories from her father, and was keenly interested in tactics and weaponry.

[80] The two main ways of holding the couched lance are illustrated by D. Nicolle, 'The Impact of

Thirdly, and finally, Isaac Comnenus' reception for Psellus and his fellow emissaries was not merely a show of force involving fierce-looking aliens and their sometimes exotic equipment. It was also a show of legitimacy, in which a rebel general was trying to demonstrate possession of the hallmarks of an established imperial court.[81] The Russo-Scandinavians had regularly formed tbe bodyguard of emperors since the late tenth century whereas the Normans, if the foregoing arguments hold true, had only been serving in substantial quantities for ten years in 1057. Their presence in a quasi-imperial bodyguard is another indication that they rapidly gained a reputation for martial prowess and, even, trustworthiness in Byzantium.

'Trustworthiness' was not a quality of the Normans which received especial prominence from their propagandists and apologists, and in fact Byzantine writers do sometimes refer to the Franks as 'treacherous by nature'.[82] But Byzantine political life was itself riddled with distrust, not only the emperors' fear of rebellions by Byzantine-born commanders but also those commanders' misgivings about one another. The number of well-planned and partly or wholly executed bids for the throne by army officers was quite limited during the first two-thirds of the eleventh century.[83] But suspicion was rife and it was here that the *political* use of the Franks was considerable, from their role in the suppression of Tornicius' rebellion onwards. The rank-and-file did not have particular loyalties towards ambitious Byzantine generals and from an early stage they were allotted commanders of their own stock, such as Hervé. Thus they had little occasion to forge close personal ties with Byzantine officers.[84] The obstacle which this posed to disgruntled Byzantine generals is shown clearly in the biography or memoirs of one such general, Catacalon Cecaumenus, a key conspirator in the coup of 1057 – and not to be confused with the author of the *Strategikon*, whose surname was also Cecaumenus. He is said to have been particularly worried by the proximity to his country estate of two Frankish and one Russian regiment, in case they should learn of the plot, seize him and send him to the emperor in Constantinople.[85] His solution was to fabricate imperial letters instructing him to mobilise the regiments of the region. First, he suborned two native Byzantine regiments, taking the commanders aside individually and offering them a choice of participation in the rebellion or decapitation. He then applied the same

the European Couched Lance on Muslim Military Tradition', *Journal of the Arms and Armour Society* x, 1980, plate III: E, F, p.19. See also *eundem, Arms and Armour of the Crusading Era 1050–1350*, i, New York 1988, 297; D.J.A. Ross, 'L'originalité de "Turoldus": le maniement de la lance', *Cahiers de civilisation médiévale* vi, 1963, 131–5 and figs 5–9; Peirce, 244–5; Kolias, 204–05, 208. It is worth noting an (undated) seal of a certain Tancred, whose reverse depicts him 'galloping to right and stomping with his horse a fallen enemy'; his right hand holds a long spear, *not* in the couched position, while his left holds an oval shield: G. Zacos and J.W. Nesbitt, *Byzantine Lead Seals*, ii, Berne 1984, 341 (no. 718); *Plates*, Berne 1985, plate 70.

[81] D. Smythe, 'Why do Barbarians stand round the Emperors at Diplomatic Receptions?', *Byzantine Diplomacy*, ed. J. Shepard and S. Franklin, Aldershot 1992, 306–07, 312.

[82] Attaleiates, 125. The 'inconstancy' of the westerners, especially from the First Crusade onwards, is a leitmotif of Anna's *Alexiad*, e.g. ii, 206, 233; iii, 11, 16, 29.

[83] Cheynet, 36, 38, 40, 42–3, 48–9, 51, 54, 57–8, 59–61, 66, 68–70, 74.

[84] Hervé is termed 'commander of the *homoethnē*' by Scylitzes (467), referring to events in 1049. See above, n. 55.

[85] Scylitzes, 490. For Scylitzes' heavy reliance on the work relating Cecaumenus' feats, see Shepard, 'Suspected Source', 172–6.

approach to 'those from the barbarians'.[86] We are told that by this ploy he 'easily' terrified them into cooperating with him. It must have been men from these same regiments that provided the guard-of-honour of 'Italians' and 'Tauroscyths' in Isaac Comnenus' tent a few months later.

We should not suppose that the Normans' presumed loyalty towards the reigning emperor was wholly born of sentiment and gratitude for gifts and favours. Money had a good deal to do with it and, to that extent, the judgement of Lord Norwich and earlier historians has some merit.[87] The emperor was the Normans' paymaster, and while their monthly salary was disbursed by expeditionary force commanders on occasion, the more lucrative rewards came directly from the emperor, for example, the stipends and other gifts bestowed on senior court title-holders at Easter. The country estates of Norman commanders were presumably either granted to them directly by the emperor, or bought with money received from him.[88] We do not have much detailed information about the finances of Byzantine regiments, but it is clear that control of reserves of money or other valuables was essential for any rebellion starting out from the provinces. The dilemma of Leo Tornicius in 1047 was that he and his accomplices 'had to raise an army and had no money ready to hand, nor anything else to induce army commanders to join forces with them'. Other rebels, such as Bardas Sclerus, sought to alleviate their initial shortage of cash by seizing tax-collectors and their monies and then, in effect, attempting to raise taxes of their own.[89] And the personal liquid assets of Byzantine aristocrats and generals seem to have been quite limited.[90] It was, therefore, to the government that one looked for 'serious money'. And here, the Normans' very expectation of regular pay in coin – partly dictated by the cost of maintaining their armour, weapons and distinctive riding gear – was an advantage to the emperor. For provided he was able to pay them thus, they were unlikely to join in a military revolt: their commanders had virtually no prospect of mounting the throne themselves, whether by force of arms or invitation from the civilian 'establishment' inside Constantinople.[91] Neither were their pay disputes with the emperor likely to evoke widespread sympathy from Byzantine-born soldiers or from the local population in the provinces where they were quartered.[92] So even if they did take up arms from a sense

---

[86] Scylitzes, 491.

[87] Norwich, 339; above, 275.

[88] The 'abundant wealth' with which Roussel's wife ransomed him from the Turks may well have been earned as pay or prize money: Attaleiates, 192–3; Scylitzes Continuatus, 160. The possibility that she was rich in her own right cannot, however, be totally excluded.

[89] Psellus, ii, 17; Scylitzes, 316; Cheynet, 164–5.

[90] A few great families do seem to have disposed of sizeable quantities of coin, sufficient to maintain an army: J.-C. Cheynet, 'Fortune et puissance de l'aristocratie (X–XII siècle)', *Hommes et richesses dans l'Empire byzantin*, ii, *VIII–XV siècle*, ed. V. Kravari, J. Lefort and C. Morrisson, Paris 1991, 204–05. However, even for them the logistical problems of linking up their sometimes secluded hoards of coins or bullion with the soldiers were formidable.

[91] Roussel of Bailleul very probably did come to harbour imperial ambitions, but he was aware of the need to field a Byzantine-born candidate for the throne, Caesar John Ducas: only then could *Byzantine* troops be expected to rally to his cause: Attaleiates, 189–90; below, 300.

[92] The Normans who, under Arduin and other veterans of the Sicilian expedition, took to attacking the imperial authorities and to pillaging in Apulia in 1041–2 do not seem to have enjoyed much active support from the rural population: William of Apulia, 118–19; Cheynet, *Contestations*, 387 and nn. 34, 36.

of grievance over pay, this had more the character of a mutiny than a military rebellion, in that it had little chance of spreading throughout the army.

These were, I suggest, the considerations underlying the emperors' employment of western mercenaries in the mid-eleventh century and, so long as the money was to hand, the policy worked.[93] Yet we hear of three insurrections on the part of prominent Frankish commanders, Hervé, Crispin and Roussel: are not these an indictment of a policy formed by calculations of short-term political survival? A glance at each may suggest that while these outbursts showed up the risks of employing Franks as right-hand men, only the third of them posed a really serious threat to the government, and this in highly exceptional political and military circumstances.

The defection of Hervé, the talented commander of Frankish mercenaries in 1057, seems to have been a matter of offended dignity as well as greed. He was apparently indignant at the derisive way in which Michael VI turned down his request for a more senior title, at the same Eastertime rewards ceremonies at which Isaac Comnenus and Catacalon Cecaumenus failed to gain satisfaction for their demands and decided on rebellion. Hervé withdrew to his country estate, but induced only three hundred of the Frankish cavalrymen quartered there or nearby to join him. No less significantly, he is said to have been unaware of the conspiracy then being hatched by other Byzantine generals, including his neighbour in the Armeniakon theme, Catacalon Cecaumenus.[94] Presumably there was little trust, or social contact, between them and Hervé. The Frankish outsider turned instead to a Turcoman chieftain, Samuch, and they agreed to launch raids together on Byzantine territory from across the border. However, mutual suspicion between Franks and Turks ran high and while they were encamped near Khliat, by Lake Van, Samuch made a surprise attack on Hervé and his three hundred. The Franks defeated the Turks in battle, but were easy prey to treachery at the hands of the emir of Khliat, who was in league with his correligionist, Samuch. Hervé was captured and became the emir's prisoner, but subsequently he re-entered the

---

[93] This proposition touches on the fundamental questions of whether western mercenaries gave value for money to the Byzantine state and of how much money – and other valuables – was spent on them. A systematic examination of them, while vitiated by lack of precise or reliable figures, might be inclined towards a positive evaluation by the following considerations: (1) mercenaries such as those who 'sailed through together with (*syndiapleusantōn*)' Crispin, apparently all the way to Constantinople, would have been able to bring heavy gear such as armour, lances, firm saddles and, perhaps, horses with them: Attaleiates, 122. They would thus have spared the imperial treasury the expense of supplying these and, perhaps, of raising and training the horses. (See, however, M. Bennett, *supra*, 49–51 on the difficulty of transporting horses by sea.) (2) The number of Frankish mercenaries may well have fluctuated markedly over time, rising from initially modest proportions to perhaps well over 3,000 in the reign of Romanus IV and then falling sharply during the reign of Nicephorus III Botaneiates (1078–81) and the earlier years of Alexius' reign. See below, 303. Seeing that quite small units of western cavalry often proved more than a match for much larger hosts of Turkish or Pecheneg light cavalry, they may well have been regarded as 'cost-effective', even if the monthly pay and the other cash benefits of each warrior were substantial. (3) There are clear indications of growth in the population and the economy of the empire through the eleventh century. If, as is quite possible, the central treasury was able to tap the expansion of the monetary economy, its controllers may well have regarded Normans 'outstandingly fond of money' as highly appropriate tools for the implementation of imperial policy. See A. Harvey, *Economic Expansion in the Byzantine Empire 900–1200*, Cambridge 1989, 264; above, 286; above, n. 51.
[94] Scylitzes, 484–5.

service of the empire and received a top military command. His lead seal seeks, in a standard Byzantine invocational formula, the Lord's help for 'thy servant Hervé Frangopōlos *magistros*, *vestēs* and *stratelatēs* of the east'.[95] It had been the title of *magistros* that he had earlier sought unsuccessfully from Michael VI. The command of *stratelatēs* of the east put him in charge of Byzantine as well as Norman troops, for it seems to have involved supervision of all the eastern regiments. A recent predecessor had been Catacalon Cecaumenus.[96] Thus Hervé's secession seems to have been regarded by the imperial authorities as an impulsive act of vengeance, caused by frustration over rewards and recognition, rather than anything more premeditated. His seal signals his devotion to St Peter, who is shown *en buste* on the face of the seal. Such portrayals of St Peter are rare on Byzantine seals and this is an indication that Hervé retained the attachment of his fellow-Normans in the west to the saint. But Hervé was obviously no less intent on displaying the two successive court titles, *vestēs* and *magistros*, which he had received from the emperor, listing the most illustrious one first.[97]

A not dissimilar career pattern was followed by another commander, Robert Crispin. He had, according to Amatus of Monte Cassino, gone to Constantinople 'pour faire chevalerie souz lo pooir de lo Impereor'.[98] Within a few years – far more quickly than had been the case with Hervé – Crispin rebelled, apparently out of dissatisfaction with the titles and gifts he had received from Romanus IV Diogenes. He set upon tax-collectors whom he encountered and divested them of their monies, and began to plunder from other persons.[99] He was able to beat off successive attacks by Byzantine troops stationed nearby, and one of his assets was possession of a fortress standing 'on a lofty crest, hard to reduce', in the Armeniakon theme.[100] He and his men subsequently sought shelter there. This situation may seem to have ominous overtones of southern Italy, where the Normans had already shown their capacity to switch from being mercenaries to being predators and appropriators of strong points. But Crispin's rising, for all its vigour, did not last more than a few months, and it was isolated. Upon the mobilisation of a large army, led by Romanus IV himself, Crispin asked for an amnesty. The emperor granted it, reportedly 'on account of the nobility of the man and his renown for feats and deployments (*diataxeis*) in war'.[101] Romanus soon changed his mind, apparently because of allegations that Crispin's penitence was tactical, dictated by the absence of most of his comrades, whom he had left behind in his castle; he would, once the opportunity arose, 'make an attempt' upon the emperor. On these grounds, he was dismissed from the army. However,

---

[95] Schlumberger, 'Chefs normands', 295; *idem*, *Sigillographie*, 659–60.
[96] Scylitzes, 467; cf. R. Guilland, *Recherches sur les institutions byzantines*, i, Berlin-Amsterdam 1967, 389.
[97] Hervé's title guaranteed him a stipend of, apparently, sixteen pounds of gold a year, and a pre-eminent position in the ceremonial life of the imperial court: Oikonomides, 294; J.-C. Cheynet, 'Dévaluation des dignités et dévaluation monétaire dans la seconde moitié du XI siècle', *Byzantion* liii, 1983, 469, 474.
[98] Amatus, 15.
[99] Attaleiates, 123.
[100] Attaleiates, 125. The fortress is most likely to have been granted to Crispin by the government; for he would not have had the siege-equipment to capture it, or the time prerequisite for a blockade.
[101] Attaleiates, 124.

Attaleiates emphasises that Crispin's own case for his defence had not been clearly refuted, and the prosecution rested on suspicion and the vehement denunciation of a German noble.[102]

Attaleiates may have been predisposed in Crispin's favour, holding his soldierly virtues up as a model for 'Romans' to emulate. But Attaleiates was not alone in his appreciation. Within three years Crispin had been rehabilitated and restored to his former command. His fighting zeal was kindled with hopes of vengeance upon Romanus, who had now been declared deposed by his co-emperor at Constantinople, Michael VII Ducas. Michael had, after bringing him back from exile at Abydos, earned his good will by lavishing upon him the gifts and honours which Romanus had begrudged him.[103] Clearly material gain and self- esteem counted for much with Crispin, as with Hervé, but the episode also suggests that Crispin's animus was in many ways a personal one, aimed at an emperor who had been covetous and ungrateful – an unjust lord – and that it could readily be assuaged. Furthermore, Crispin seems to have been well-aware of his utility and value to his employers, and was adept at demonstrating it. He and a small band of companions dealt with 'a great host' of Turks shortly before his encounter and temporary reconciliation with Romanus. And he is said to have greatly raised the fighting spirit of 'the soldiers' – seemingly, Byzantine ones – upon joining them on the eve of battle.[104] This could well have made even a massive outlay on gifts and pay for Crispin appear 'cost-effective' to the imperial government, much as it may have annoyed Byzantine generals. Cecaumenus' warning of the resentment of 'Roman' officers at the appointment of foreigners to top commands may well have been inspired by the career of Crispin, which had been played out only a few years earlier.[105] Such resentment would not necessarily have been unwelcome to the emperor, since it reduced the likelihood of joint action between Byzantine rebels and foreign-born generals. And the latter, if aggrieved with their employer, could not count on support from Byzantine generals: Crispin's stand at his fortress, 'Black Castle' (Maurokastron), in 1069 had been a lonely one. Thus out of the Normans' material aspirations and desire for honours and the jealousy of some Byzantine generals a kind of political equilibrium could be struck. Michael Psellus could write of Crispin on the day of his death that, 'changing his ways, he subsequently showed himself as well-disposed as initially he had been inimical' towards the Byzantines.[106] Crispin presumably died in or near the Great Palace, for news of his death to reach Psellus so swiftly.

The aforementioned equilibrium was, however, already upset by the time Psellus wrote his brief obit note on Crispin in, probably, 1073. The defeat and capture of Romanus IV at Manzikert and his subsequent release by the Seljuk sultan, Alp Arslan, inaugurated a period of civil war, financial crisis and incursions by foreign marauders. Both Romanus IV and Michael VII could lay claim to be legitimate emperors, and neither was of long-established imperial lineage. In

---

[102] Attaleiates, 125.
[103] Attaleiates, 170–1. According to Bryennius (134–5), Crispin's long-nurtured anger with Romanus spurred him into his precipitate charge against Romanus' battle-line in 1072.
[104] Attaleiates, 124–5, 171.
[105] Cecaumenus, 278. See above, n. 51.
[106] Psellus, ii, 170.

the aftermath of Manzikert Romanus was able to raise substantial quantities of additional troops quartered in provinces as far north and north-west as the Pontus, Paphlagonia and Bithynia.[107] And even after the defeat and blinding of Romanus in the summer of 1072, military units hostile to Michael VII's government remained operational, especially in Cilicia and Cappodocia.[108] Meanwhile, bands of Turcomans were on the rampage in Asia minor. In these turbulent conditions, Michael VII regarded the Normans as potential instruments of recovery. He tried repeatedly, and eventually successfully, to forge a marriage-tie with Robert Guiscard, who had captured Bari, Byzantium's last major base in Italy, in 1071. Michael's aim was, as a Byzantine chronicler put it, 'through them or with them [the Normans] to ward off their [the Turks'] extraordinary assault against Romania'.[109] Thus the individual fortune-seekers were, in Michael's plan, to be supplemented by 'allies' – soldiers sent or led by a cooperative ruler – in the traditional sense. However, now that Byzantium's eastern provinces lacked a modicum of political cohesion, the opportunities for a sustained rebellion by talented individuals and, even, the formation of self-sustaining principalities, were ripe. They were taken by Philaretus, Romanus IV's military governor in Marash. Being himself of Armenian stock, he used his affinities with the numerous Armenian immigrants in Cilicia to gain control of several other Cilician cities and later took over Edessa and Antioch.[110] The conditions of anarchy were not lost on another foreign-born commander, Roussel of Bailleul, and in 1073 – when negotiations for a marriage-tie between Michael VII's house and Guiscard's were under way – he abandoned the army sent out by Michael against the Turks and led off four hundred Frankish soldiers of the company which he had taken over from Crispin. It is alleged by one chronicler that he had long been planning his secession;[111] but even if this was the case, it is significant that he acted only when the Byzantine state's apparatus was in glaring disarray, and when even the ruling family of the Ducases was divided. The emperor's uncle, Caesar John

---

[107] Attaleiates relates that Diogenes' troops compelled the soldiers dispersed by Michael VII's government in these provinces 'to become under him' (*genesthai hyph' heauton*): Attaleiates, 172–3.

[108] Among them were the Armenian duke of Antioch, Katachour and, most probably, Cappodocian units having longstanding affinities with Diogenes and his family: Cheynet, *Contestations*, 398, 407–08.

[109] Scylitzes Continuatus, ed. Tsolakes, 170. See H. Bibicou, 'Une page d'histoire diplomatique de Byzance au XI siècle: Michel VII Doukas, Robert Guiscard et la pension des dignitaires', *Byzantion* xxix–xxx, 1959–60, 44–9, 52–4; W.B. McQueen, 'Relations between the Normans and Byzantium 1071–1112', *Byzantion* lvi, 1986, 429–32.

[110] C.J. Yarnley, 'Philaretos – Armenian Bandit or Byzantine General?', *Revue des études arméniennes*, ns ix, 1972, 336–9, 342–9; Hoffmann, *Rudimente*, 5–10.

[111] Bryennius, 148–9. Roussel was accused of having chosen to disregard Romanus IV's orders to lead his Franks forward to join the advance-guard and attack the fortress of Khliat: Attaleiates, 148–9. This is one of a number of allegations levelled by Byzantine writers at senior commanders implicated in the débacle, and it should be treated with caution. Zonaras (ed. Büttner-Wobst, 699) states that Roussel was 'persuaded' to withdraw by a Byzantine commander, Tarchaneiotes. The incident may well have sprung from a tactical decision made by Roussel on the spur of the moment. He had shown similar independence of mind during the battle on the Cerami in 1063. He threatened never again to give 'aid' (*auxilium*) to Count Roger unless he agreed to a further assault on the numerically far superior Saracens: Malaterra, 43. Such a self-willed demeanour was not tantamount to premeditated rebellion.

Ducas, was debarred from government or a military command, upon suspicion that he might seize the throne for himself.

Roussel's rising, which has long attracted scholarly notice, would repay further study.[112] He, like Hervé, issued seals which give his family name as 'Frangopōlos', a newly-coined term meaning, literally, 'son of a Frank'. Roussel's seal cites a single court-title, *vestēs*; this was a dignity which had earlier been conferred on Hervé. The seal's face depicted the Mother of God, in a design common on contemporary Byzantine seals, and this could suggest some familiarity with, and public espousal of, Byzantine religious ways. Hervé's seal, in contrast, had depicted St Peter.[113] A systematic study would assess the significance of the fact that Roussel initially tried to impose himself upon Lykaonia and Galatia, well-populated and well-watered regions containing some extensive plains suitable for heavy cavalry yet far from Roussel's own properties in the Armeniakon theme.[114] His ambitions were clearly sweeping, in territorial terms, from the outset; but whether from the first he had designs on the imperial throne is uncertain. His capture in battle of Caesar John Ducas, who had been rehabilitated in order to lead an army against him, was fortuitous and his subsequent proclamation of John as emperor suggests skilful opportunism, exacerbating the rivalries and distrust within the Ducas family. It may only have been at this stage that he raised his own sights to the level of the throne.[115]

The imbroglio involving Caesar John cannot, however, be examined here, and discussion must be confined to one proposition: for capable but numerically restricted foreigners such as the companies of Normans in Byzantine service, support from the local population was a *sine qua non* of any lasting rebellion. Roussel, unlike the previous Norman malcontents, managed to obtain it in the region of the Armeniakon theme, to which he eventually withdrew, and apparently also earlier in Lykaonia and Galatia. The local inhabitants had been left largely unprotected by the central government. They may well have been willing to cooperate with, and offer goods and services to, anyone who could protect them against the Turks' wide-ranging incursions. Roussel is said to have levied tax from the towns in the vicinity of Amaseia, a strategically important and prosperous town on the main east-west road in northern Asia minor. The district had briefly served as Romanus IV's base in autumn, 1071, during his campaigning to regain his throne. The inhabitants are said to have paid up to Roussel out of a mixture of 'fear or good-will'.[116] Their payments are expressly said to have been in 'money' (*chrēmata*) and it appears that part of the proceeds went to the Frankish soldiers, who were stationed in Roussel's 'former castles'. From these

---

[112] See above, n. 5.

[113] Schlumberger (*Sigillographie*, 660, 663–4) corrected to *vestēs* a reading of the seal's legend which he had earlier taken as *vestiaritēs*: 'Chefs normands', 296. See above, 297. Roussel's seal belongs to the earlier part of his Byzantine career, since *vestēs* was a fairly modest title. Midway through his rebellion, after his capture of Caesar John and proclamation of him as emperor, he declined Michael VII's offer of the very senior title of *curopalatēs*: Attaleiates, 187.

[114] K. Belke and M. Restle, *Galatien und Lykaonien (Tabula Imperii Byzantini iv)*, Vienna 1984, 46, 70, 76–7, 88–9.

[115] Attaleiates, 188; Bryennius, 176–7; above, n. 91.

[116] 'phobō ē eunoiā', Bryennius, 187 and *apparatus criticus*. Gautier's proposed insertion of *mallon* after *phobō*, i.e. 'fear *rather than* good-will', is not necessary. Cf. Meineke's edition (as in n. 9 above), 85.

strongpoints, the warriors were able to deter Turks from seriously molesting their localities, while they provided a market for agricultural producers who regularly brought their goods to them.[117]

It seems, then, that Roussel managed to establish a fairly high degree of order within his lordship, yoking together the interests of peasant farmers, townsfolk and his own soldiery, who appear to have been receiving wages in money. The collection and subsequent disbursement of coin could have been undertaken by the local Byzantine officials. At the same time, the fiscal demands made on the population may well have been lighter than those which the Byzantine state had made of them. Roussel's forces were sufficiently numerous to provide garrisons over an area which encompassed the city of Neocaesarea, some one hundred kilometres east of Amaseia. Their total may not have fallen far short of the 2,700 warriors who are said to have comprised Roussel's army at a slightly earlier stage of his insurrection.[118] Even so, their numbers are likely to have been far inferior to those of the rival Byzantine armies which had been raising revenues and requisitioning goods from the Armeniakon theme's inhabitants in the recent past. For the fodder and basic maintenance of his cavalry horses, Roussel could to some extent rely on the properties which must have been attached to his 'former castles'. Thus his costs in fending off the Turks need not have weighed heavily upon the local population and, judging by their reluctance to cooperate with the central government's emissary in bringing him to book, they did not.

The ingenuity of that emissary, Alexius Comnenus, in ensnaring Roussel is celebrated at length by his daughter and son-in-law, respectively Anna Comnena and Nicephorus Bryennius. Their inclination to exaggerate the odds pitted against the hero and to magnify his resourcefulness in adversity is palpable, but the direct and indirect evidence which they yield points consistently to the abiding popularity of Roussel and his fellow-Franks with the local population. The citizens of Amaseia are said to have rioted and some even tried to set Roussel free, after Alexius incarcerated him there. Their cry was that 'they had suffered nothing terrible from him'; and Alexius is said to have been so fearful that 'the powerful' would persist in stirring up the mob to liberate Roussel that he pretended to blind him; then Roussel was presented, blind-folded, to the populace, so as to dash all hopes that he might lead them again.[119] Alexius was also convinced that if the other Franks were left in their fortresses a new 'tyrant' (i.e. usurper of governmental authority) would emerge from among them and regain control of the area. He therefore stayed on himself, blockading individual fortresses and eventually forcing the garrisons to surrender or withdraw. Alexius' precautions strongly imply that the local peasants were disposed to do business with the Franks: his troops had to patrol access-routes to the forts in order to intercept supplies, and

---

[117] Attaleiates, 199; Bryennius, 184–5; Scylitzes Continuatus, 161. See also Hoffmann, *Rudimente*, 19, 119.

[118] Attaleiates, 189; cf. Bryennius, 179, n.6. Attaleiates' incidental indication (p.199) of the limitations of Roussel's forces in terms of numbers is preferable to Anna's claim that a large, heterogeneous force was confronting her heroic father: *Alexiad*, i, 10, 11.

[119] Bryennius, 190–3; Anna Comnena, i, 15. These two works offer a version of Alexius' feats and schemes which probably owed much to Alexius' telling of them. While Roussel apparently won the sympathies of 'the powerful' of the town and district of Amaseia, Philaretus seems to have alienated the wealthy in Antioch and Edessa: Yarnley, 351–2.

the garrisons' lack of stocks of provisions suggests that they may have taken for granted that a steady stream of essentials would be forthcoming from local producers.[120]

Roussel's had been a well-organised and fairly protracted insurrection, enjoying support from persons of substance – 'the powerful' – in Amaseia;[121] presumably they believed that their property would be secure, and not over-taxed, under Roussel's regime. Even so, Roussel's experiment was unequal to the resources, or rather, the reputation for resources, of the Byzantine state. Alexius Comnenus gained custody of Roussel through promising vast rewards and bribes to a Turkish war-band; Roussel for his part could not convincingly hold out the prospect of similar riches to them. Alexius did not, in fact, have the ready money to hand, and he had to turn to the citizens of Amaseia in order to raise funds with which to reward the Turks for handing over their Frankish captive. Here, too, the reputation of state power was still formidable. Alexius' warning to the populace of the 'wrath of the emperor' in the event of their persistent refusal to cooperate with him and unrest seems to have found its mark.[122] Thus ended 'the greatest rebellion of all',[123] part-intervention in the rivalry for the imperial throne, part-bid opportunistically to create a dominion comparable to the lordships which had recently been imposed in southern Italy.

Finally – and at the price of ignoring Norman involvement in the rebellions and civil wars of the later 1070s – one may glance at the position of Alexius Comnenus.[124] He himself became emperor through a *coup d'état* in 1081. There can be no doubt that he respected the fighting qualities of western warriors, and they played a part in his armies even when the enemy was Robert Guiscard's Normans, in the early 1080s.[125] Alexius is not recorded as having suffered any rising or serious mutiny from the units of westerners under his command; sometimes, in fact, he seems to have been more suspicious of his own, Byzantine-born

---

[120] Bryennius, 192–3.

[121] Alexius' tactics against Roussel and his fellows amounted to attrition, and the entire operation must have lasted well over a year. See Bryennius, 183, n. 5; 193, n. 2; 194, n. 1; Polemis, 67–8, 76; Cheynet, *Contestations*, 78 and n. 2.

[122] Bryennius, 190–1; Anna Comnena, i, 14.

[123] Bryennius, 208–09.

[124] Normans certainly participated in the civil wars, serving in the armies of both Nicephorus III Botaneiates and the rebel Nicephorus Bryennius in 1078: Bryennius, 268–71. 'Franks . . . from Italy' were summoned to the Balkans to take part in the revolt of Nicephorus Basilaces soon afterwards: Attaleiates, 297; Scylitzes Continuatus, 182. Occasionally, a Frankish contingent is recorded as having been persuaded by fellow-Franks on the opposing side to join them. Such an act of desertion, and the subsequent rite whereby the deserters placed their right hands between the hands of their new employer, Nicephorus Bryennius, were observed by Alexius Comnenus during a battle in 1078: Bryennius, 274–5; Anna Comnena, i, 24. But there is no reason to suppose that the turning of coats was more prevalent among the Franks than among the Byzantines. One *condottiere* of possible Norman-Italian extraction, Longibardopoulos, was taken prisoner together with several Byzantine generals by the Slav prince of Zeta, Constantine Bodinos, in 1072. He was subsequently married to a sister of Constantine, and put in command of an army consisting mainly of 'Lombards and Serbs'; but he reverted forthwith to the emperor's side: Scylitzes Continuatus, 163, 165; Cheynet, *Contestations*, 79, 389.

[125] Anna Comnena, i, 152; F. Chalandon, *Essai sur le règne d'Alexis I Comnène*, Paris 1900, 76–7, 90–1; Hohlweg, 64.

troops. In 1085, after the collapse of Guiscard's final offensive against him, he is said to have recruited the majority of Guiscard's men into his own service.[126]

There seem to me to be three main reasons for Alexius' confidence that he could cope with western employees, and for his apparent success. Firstly, once a modicum of order had been restored to the Byzantine polity, the chances that a Frankish rising would be able to hold out for long against the state's resources were slighter than ever. In other words, even Roussel's lordship in northern Asia minor was possible only in the conditions of military paralysis and administrative collapse of the 1070s. Secondly, Alexius had learnt the lessons of the *mode d'emploi* of western mercenaries from personal experience. It is notable that although he allowed some of them their own commander, Constantine Humberto-poulos, this man had been living in Byzantium for some time; he was not a newcomer who had raised his own company in the west. In fact, judging by his Christian name, he had been brought up in an eastern orthodox milieu.[127] Equally, Alexius does not seem to have allowed the 'Franks' to congregate in a particular theme, as they had done in Armeniakon before Roussel's rising. Moreover, their numbers in the 1080s and earlier 1090s seem to have been quite modest, and the unit of five hundred or so cavalrymen despatched by Robert of Flanders seems to have been regarded as of capital significance by Alexius: presumably, they represented a major addition to his existing reserves of western warriors.[128] In contrast, the aggregates of Frankish warriors at Byzantium around the time of the battle of Manzikert were substantial: the 2,700 commanded by Roussel at one stage of his insurrection did not represent the grand total of Frankish veterans still at large on

---

[126] Anna Comnena, ii, 60; William of Apulia, 256–7; Orderic, iv, 38–9 and n.1. The entry of one Norman commander, a certain Roger, into Byzantine service at about this time is recorded in his epitaph: Nicholas Callicles, *Carmi*, ed. R. Romano, Naples 1980, 94. Roger's precise origins in 'the Frankish land' – presumably Normandy – remain uncertain: Callicles, 175–6 (commentary); D.M. Nicol, 'Symbiosis and Integration. Some Greco-Latin Families in Byzantium in the Eleventh to Thirteenth Centuries', *Byzantinische Forschungen* vii, 1979, 123–4.

[127] Constantine may have been the son of a certain 'Ounpertos', *patrikios, strategos* and Dom-estic of the regiment of the Noumeroi, whose seal awaits full publication: J. Jouroukova, 'Sceaux de Constantin Humberto', *Actes du XIV Congrès international des Etudes byzantines*, iii, Bucharest 1976, 237; cf. J.-C. Cheynet, 'Du prénom au patronyme: les étrangers à Byzance (X–XII siècles)', *Studies in Byzantine Sigillography*, ed. N. Oikonomides, Washington, D.C., 1987, 59. But it is very unlikely that 'Ounpertos' *patrikios* is identifiable with the 'Hubertus' who features as the fifth son of Tancred de Hauteville's second marriage in Malaterra, 9 ('Humbertus' in Muratori's ed., *RIS*, v, 550). For the death of 'Humbertus', brother of Robert Guiscard, is recorded in the *Chronicon Breve Northmannicum* s.a. 1071 (*RIS*, v, 278[vi]) without any indication that he died in, or had ever visited, Byzantium. In any case, Constantine Humbertopoulos was, very probably, of mature years by 1081 when, as a senior army commander, he swung his support from Nicephorus III to Alexius Comnenus, thereby greatly enhancing Alexius' chances of seizing the throne. His seals indicate a protracted series of promotions at Alexius' hands: Jouroukova, 235–6. Cf. McQueen, 437.

[128] The five hundred were posted from key point to key point: Alexiad, ii, 109–10, 135; F.L. Ganshof, 'Robert le Frison et Alexis Comnène', *Byzantion* xxxi, 1961, 72–3. At about the same time, another unit of westerners, perhaps numbering two hundred cavalrymen or less, was serving under the command of Taticius: Anna Comnena, ii, 67–8. The abduction of just fifty horses from Bohemond's host in 1108 was treated as a major achievement, and their abductor, William Claret, was rewarded with the senior title of *nobelissimos*: Anna Comnena, iii, 116; Hohlweg, 37, 71. The euphoria perhaps reflects on the limited supply of mounts – and skilled riders – at Byzantium as well as the blow which had been dealt to Bohemond.

imperial soil.[129] And, as witness the recruitment of cavalrymen through the count of Flanders, the provenance of the westerners was more diverse than it had been a generation earlier. These changes were in part forced upon Alexius by the loss of most of Asia minor and by his lack of sufficient money to pay for a large army. But he used such money as he had effectively, and we hear of no disputes specifically to do with pay during his reign.[130]

A third asset of Alexius was his appreciation of the importance of personal bonds and military fellowship to his western soldiers. He had ample opportunity to observe this while a commander of western mercenaries during the 1070s, as well as during operations against Roussel and his companions. Alexius took some westerners into his inner circle of counsellors, and was accessible to many more. He was prepared to socialise with them and his easy familiarity with the leading Crusaders was the despair of his historian-daughter. She recorded that he would even allow them into his private quarters in the palace.[131] But it was through tolerance and accessibility such as this that he gained a reputation for generosity and special indulgence towards warriors, a reputation which found its way, side by side with the celebrated defamatory assessments, into the works of Orderic Vitalis and William of Tyre. To Orderic – or rather, most probably, to one of his sources – Alexius appeared 'affable to warriors and a most generous giver of gifts'.[132] Alexius seems, in particular, to have noted the respect which western knights generally showed for the oath of fealty. I think it quite probable that all western commanders, if not all new recruits from the west, had been required to

---

[129] Cheynet, *Contestations*, 398, n. 96.

[130] Conversely, Alexius egged on Bohemond's 'counts' to demand of him their outstanding 'salaries' (*misthous*); he promised that those who entered his own service would receive salaries 'sufficient . . . according to their wishes', Anna Comnena, ii, 32. Alexius' political testament to John II, his son and heir, enjoins him to maintain treasuries full of gold to dispense on any future Crusaders and opines that officials should display graciousness when bestowing gifts and prizes: P. Maas, 'Die Musen des Kaisers Alexios I.', *Byzantinische Zeitschrift* xxii, 1913, 357, 358. Cheynet (*Contestations*, 368) suggests that Humbertopoulos' involvement in a plot in 1091 was precipitated by discontent with his rewards. But it could well be that he was by then sufficiently attuned to the ways of the Byzantine ruling élite to engage in their intrigues against the emperor. He was quite rapidly rehabilitated and restored to a senior command: Anna Comnena, ii, 146–7, 193; Cheynet, *Contestations*, 96 and n.3.

[131] Anna Comnena, iii, 162. Stephen of Blois boasted to his wife that Alexius had 'kept me with him most respectfully' for ten days, and he was probably not Alexius' only satisfied Crusading guest in 1097: H. Hagenmeyer, *Die Kreuzzugsbriefe aus den Jahren 1088–1100*, Innsbruck 1901, 139. The forementioned Roger (n.126) is made to exclaim in his epitaph: 'Alexius Comnenus, lord of the Ausonians, opened his heart to me, and what beyond? I found a sea of gold, and came to glory': Callicles, ed. Romano, 94.

[132] Orderic, iv, 14–15; cf. ii, 202–03; iv, 16–17, v, 276–7; 278–9 (*positive*); Orderic, v, 42–7; 56–9. 334–9 (*negative*); William of Tyre, *Chronicon*, i, ed. R.B.C. Huygens, Turnhout 1986, 262, 320–2, 436–7 (*sympathetic or positive*); William of Tyre, i, 167, 178–9, 186–90, 193, 211–12, 368–9, 466–7 (*negative*). P.W. Edbury and J.G. Rowe reasonably suggest that William's 'two voices' echo his different sources about the First Crusade: *William of Tyre, Historian of the Latin East*, Cambridge 1988, 134–6. Alexius' bounty evoked mixed reactions at the time of the First Crusade, as Anselm of Ribemont's contemporary letter shows: after receiving priceless gifts at their final audience with him, the Crusading leaders withdrew, 'some with good will and others otherwise': Hagenmeyer, 144–5, 258. But Stephen of Blois was probably not the only leader to have been entranced (Hagenmeyer, 138–9, 219–20), and even those who fared worst at Alexius' hands in 1097 could still subsequently look to him for aid, for example, Raymond of Toulouse (William of Tyre, i, 437, 466).

take an oath to him personally and to perform homage, from the opening stages of his reign onwards. Thus a bond of honour and mutual fidelity was superimposed on the contract between pay-master and 'wage-receivers' (*misthophoroi*).[133] It was on the strength of his long experience as a largely successful commander of mercenaries that Alexius insisted so stubbornly on the rendering of homage and fealty by all the leading members of the First Crusade. If he was then disappointed, this was because the Crusaders were for the most part pursuing goals which lay, in every sense, beyond him. And his disappointment, although hymned so eloquently by Anna Comnena, was not absolute or such as to induce a change of course. For Alexius continued, during and after the Crusade, to recruit western warriors into his service.[134]

---

[133] Alexius is the likeliest eye-witness source of the story of how the Frankish troops under his command deserted to Bryennius and proffered him their right hands in 1078: Bryennius, 274–5; Anna Comnena, i, 24; above, n. 124. Alexius, whether or not an oath had earlier been given to him by the Franks, seems to have judged that it was taken seriously by them, rather than that Frankish mercenaries were incorrigibly fickle or treacherous. Anna mentions 'the oath customary with the Latins' which Robert of Flanders is depicted as swearing at the time of his pledge to send five hundred cavalrymen to Alexius from Flanders: Anna Comnena, ii, 105. Robert's was presumably an oath of very general good faith, since he was not about to perform service in person to Alexius, but the episode suggests that Alexius was already then, in 1089, exacting oaths of *fides* from leading westerners. See J. Shepard, ' "Father" or "Scorpion"? Style and Substance in Alexius' diplomacy', *Colloquium on the Reign of Alexius Comnenus*, ed. M.E. Mullett (forthcoming).

[134] Anna Comnena, iii, 17–18; Orderic, v, 276–7; vi, 102–03; Shepard, ' "Scorpion" ' (forthcoming).

A NEW ASPECT OF THE PORPHYRY TOMBS OF ROGER II, FIRST KING OF SICILY, IN CEFALÙ

Livia Varga

The material, shape and early date of the two royal tombs originally located in the cathedral of Cefalù place them among the most exceptional monuments of twelfth-century Europe. As a consequence they attracted regular attention from as early as the thirteenth century.[1]

From the art historical point of view, Joseph Deér, the recent monographer of the *Dynastic porphyry tombs of the Norman period in Sicily*,[2] has resolved many of the problems which have challenged scholarly minds since Vasari.[3] Among the few hypotheses which remain unresolved, there is one which occupies the central theme of this study: what was the original placement of the two porphyry sarcophagi, donated in 1145 to the cathedral of Cefalù by Roger II, first king of Sicily,[4] and what could be their function or role, other than that they were made to contain the earthly remains of the king.[5]

To answer these questions, it is first necessary to review the architectural history of the cathedral of Cefalù in the twelfth century.

It is well known, that the cathedral of Cefalù, dedicated to the Saviour and to Saints Peter and Paul, was a favourite foundation of Roger II, one which he had chosen as his burial church. The foundation charter was issued by him in 1130/31.[6] Cefalù was colonized by Augustinian canons from Bagnara and was

---

I wish to express my gratitude to Dr Ernö Marosi, director of the Art Historical Institute of the Hungarian Academy of Sciences in Budapest, whose comments on an earlier draft of this paper were much appreciated. Particular thanks are due to Mrs Jane Lynch of the Inter-Library Loan Service of the University of Toronto, whose generous assistance facilitated my work.

[1] G. Wolf, 'Ein unveröffentliches Testament Kaiser Friedrichs II', *Zeitschrift für die Geschichte des Oberrheins* 104, 1956, 1–51; J. Deér, *Dynastic Porphyry Tombs of the Norman Period in Sicily*, Cambridge, Mass., 1959.

[2] As above.

[3] G. Vasari, *Le Vite . . .*, ed. G. Milanesi, I, Florence 1906, 283; F. Daniele, *I regali sepolcri del Duomo di Palermo*, Naples 1784; R. di Gregorio, *Discorsi intorno alla Sicilia*, Palermo 1821; G.B. Tarallo, *Memoria sopra i regali sepolcri del Duomo di Monreale*, Palermo 1826; G. di Marzo, *Delle Belle Arti in Sicilia*, I–V, Palermo 1858–64; S. Bottari, 'La tomba di Frederico II.', *Commentari* II, 1951, 162–168; A. Zanca, *La cattedrale di Palermo*, Palermo 1952.

[4] 'Sarcophagos vero duos porphyriticos ad decessus mei signum perpetuum conspicuos in praefata ecclesia stabilimus fore permansuros, in quorum altero iuxta canonicorum psallentium chorum post diei mei obitum conditus requiescam, alterum vero tam ad insignem memoriam mei nominis, quam ad ipsius ecclesiae gloriam stabilimus', R. Pirri, *Sicilia Sacra*, Palermo 1772 (3rd edn.), 800; Deér, 3; O. Demus, 'Rezension', *Kunstchronik* 13, 1960, 11–19.

[5] An investigation of the possible role of the tombs in the liturgy is planned by the author.

[6] 'Ego Rogerius rex . . . feci aedificare templum (episcopatus ab initio fundationis suae in loco qui dicitur Cephaludum . . .)', Pirri, 799.

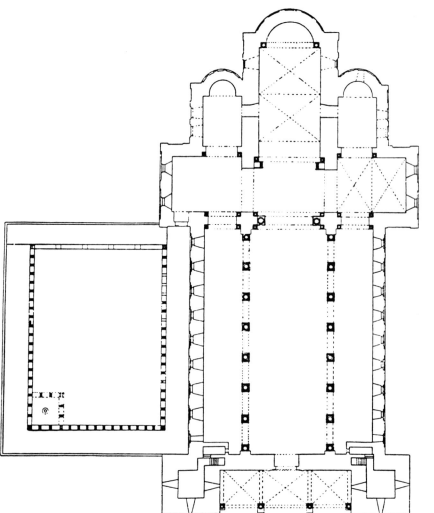

Fig. 1. *Ground plan of the cathedral of Cefalù, from Krönig*

made a bishopric by the Antipope Anacletus II in 1131. Between 1139 and 1166 its bishop was titled as *electus*; thereafter, the episcopal rank was reestablished.[7]

The present cathedral is essentially a western-style Romanesque basilica, containing three parallel apses in the east, a large transept, a three aisled nave and two towers at the west end of the building.[8] The church has two particular features: Otto Demus pointed out, that the crossing is not, as usual, a square, and that it was not intended to be the centre of the building. The other characteristic is to be found in the presbytery, where the three parallel apses are separated from each other by two walls. These walls are pierced by an arcade on each side of the main apse in the second bay of the presbytery from the east, and as a consequence, the apses communicate with each other.[9] This specific solution is well known in Sicily and was used in Mazara dell Vallo, in the Cathedral of Palermo, at Catania, Monreale and later at Agrigento.[10] Although examples of the use of such communicating apses are known in the West,[11] this solution is by no means western in character. From the late fourth century A.D. on, there were many churches built in this way in the East, some of them in Constantinople itself.[12] There can be little doubt, therefore, that the idea of communicating apses is Eastern in origin (Fig. 1).

The cathedral of Cefalù is not a homogeneous building. The relative chronology of its different parts has led to much debate.[13] Because we do not know the original way of covering the presbytery, the core of the debate is mostly about the date of the present early cross-ribbed vaults and the relation of the crossing and the transept to the presbytery and to the nave, which similarly takes us to the same problem of the vaults. It is generally accepted that the twelfth-century building activity started in 1131 or shortly after. Views differ over what was accomplished during the first building period (c.1131–1145/50).[14] It is very probable that originally a flat roofed basilica was planned, and that the eastern part of the church was built to a certain height, as also were the surrounding walls. The execution of the nave belongs to a later period. The first change of plan occurred as early as the 1140s, when the transept was already under way, and it was decided to vault the presbytery and possibly even the entire building. The two bays of the main apse are covered with cross-ribbed vaults, as is the south wing of the transept. The other parts of the cathedral were never vaulted. The change in plan occurred through strong French- and Anglo-Norman influence. Indeed, from

7   L.T. White, *Latin Monasticism in Norman Sicily*, Cambridge, Mass., 1938, 194–201.
8   O. Demus, *The Mosaics of Norman Sicily*, New York 1950, 6–9.
9   'communicating apses' is an expression of R. Krautheimer, used in his *Early Christian and Byzantine Architecture*, Harmondsworth 1966, 261.
10 G. di Stephano, *Monumenti della Sicilia Normanna*, Palermo 1965, about Mazara del Vallo, 10–13, Monreale, 65–69, Palermo, 74–81, Agrigento, 118–19.
11 P. Héliot, 'La Cathédrale de Cefalù, sa chronologie, sa filiation et les galeries murales dans les églises romanes du midi', *Arte Lombarda* X, 1965, 21, n. 8.
12 A. Grabar, *Martyrium*, Paris 1946, I, figs 46, 49, 86, 93; Krautheimer, 193, 205, 208, 244, 260, 261, 262, 299; C. Mango, *Byzantine Architecture*, New York 1976, 165, 167, 172, 178, 206, 285 etc.
13 di Stephano, 44–6, with full bibliography.
14 H.M. Schwarz, 'Die Baukunst Kalabriens und Siziliens im Zeitalter der Normannem. I. Die lateinischen Kirchengrundungen des 11. Jahrhunderts und der Dom in Cefalù', *Römisches Jahrbuch für Kunstgeschichte* 6, 1942–44, 1946, 1–112; Demus, *Mosaics*, 6–7; W. Krönig, *Cefalù, der sizilische Normannendom*, Kassel 1963, 10–12; Héliot, 31–4; di Stephano, 49–55.

the first decade of the twelfth century, many French- and Anglo-Norman churches received cross-ribbed vaults. The end of the first building period in Cefalù, after the original plan was changed, can be relatively safely dated. A mosaic inscription in the apse contains the date 1148, and states that not only the mosaic decoration, but the 'building' itself was finished by this time.[15] The term 'building' obviously refers to the presbytery, and perhaps the eastern part of the transept. We remember that in 1145, Roger II donated the two porphyry sarcophagi to the church of Cefalù. They were to be placed 'iuxta canonicorum psallentium chorum'.[16] It is difficult to imagine, that the royal sarcophagi were placed in an unfinished part of the building. This is the main reason, why one may suppose that the vaults in the main apse must have been completed by the time of the donation and placement of the tombs, that is by 1145. In 1154, when the great king died, his remains were buried in the cathedral of Palermo, instead of being carried to Cefalù. This very fact indicates, that the church of the Saviour was neither completed nor consecrated by this time.[17] It also means, that in practical terms it lost the potential of becoming the funerary church of the Hauteville dynasty.

The next building campaign, which fell somewhere between 1148 and 1154 or even between 1154 and 1166, can be characterized by the diminishing enthusiasm and financial generosity of the royal patron.[18] Apparently only the transept was finished during this period, including the inside arcades under the vaults in the south wing. Neither the crossing nor the north transept-arm was, however, vaulted. The successors of Roger II needed another ten to fifteen years to finish the church. During the third campaign, the facade was finished, the towers and the side aisles covered, and the nave constructed and covered. The cloister was probably built in the 1170s.

A petition of the canons of Cefalù c.1170 also helps indirectly to determine the end of the last building period.[19] The canons requested again the remains of Roger II and William I, and the document was sent to king William II. The church of Cefalù must have been nearly, if not entirely finished by 1170, otherwise the canons would not have been in a position to send such a strongly formulated request to the king, reminding him of their right, which had been refused four years earlier. By 1166, the church had certainly still not been consecrated. From the same petition we learn that William I on his deathbed ('in obitu patris tui') begged the canons of Cefalù to be patient with their request concerning the transfer of the remains of his father, 'donec ecclesia . . . consecraretur'.

The donation charter of Roger II does not describe the tombs. We only know, that they were 'sarcophagos vero duos porhyriticos', and that the king used the word 'conspicuos' to characterize them. One of the tombs was intended to contain his mortal remains, and the 'alterum vero tam ad insignem memoriam mei

[15] 'Rogerius Rex egregius plenis (plenus) pietatis/ hoc statuit templum motus zelo deitatis/ hoc opibus ditat variis varioque decore/ ornant magnificat in salvatoris honore/ ergo structori tanto salvator adesto/ ut sibi submissos conservet corde modesto/ anno ab incarnatione D(omini) millesimo/ centesimo XLVIII indictione XI anno v(ero)/ regni eius XVIII hoc opus musei factum est'.
[16] Pirri, col. 800.
[17] White, 196–201.
[18] Explained by the rising importance of the cathedral of Palermo. Deér, 3–14.
[19] K.A. Kehr, *Die Urkunden der normannisch-sizilischen Könige*, Innsbruck 1902, suppl. no. 21, 439f.; Deér, 5.

nominis, quam ad ipsius ecclesiae gloriam stabilimus', that is, the other to main-tain the 'august memory of my name and the glory of the church itself'.[20] We learn furthermore from the petition of the canons of Cefalù, that the king 'duo lapidea monumenta cum summa diligentia fabricari fecit'.[21] In other words, the two tombs were not reworked antic sarcophagi, but had been expressly built for the Church of Cefalù, just before 1145. In making the donation and choosing the placement of the sarcophagi, the king had consciously selected the church of the Saviour as his burial place. This choice was his 'principalis causa, quando civita-tem Cephaludi reedificavit et ecclesiam ibi fundavit'.[22] It was William I who promised the translation of his father's remains, initially in 1154, shortly after Roger's death, and for the second time from his own deathbed in 1166. His wishes notwithstanding, the sarcophagi in the Cathedral of Cefalù remained empty. In 1215, the Hohenstaufer emperor, Frederick II ordered that they be taken to Palermo, where eventually one of them would become 'pro sua et patris sui sepultura'.[23] The two sarcophagi have resided in the Cathedral of Palermo ever since. From 1215, they became part of the so-called 'Cimeterio Regale', located in the southern transept-wing of the cathedral.[24] Between 1781 and 1801 as a result of Ferdinando Fuga's rebuilding of the interior of the old cathedral, the tombs were removed to their present cramped position in the last two western chapels of the south aisle.

According to the investigation and identification of Joseph Deér, Roger II's two sarcophagi presently contains the remains of Frederick II (+1250), Rex Romanorum, and that of Henry VI (+1197), King of Sicily.[25]

The two sarcophagi are almost of the same length, but that of Frederick II stands a little lower and is much narrower than the other. Its trough is held by two pairs of supports, representing lions, while that of Henry rests on fluted pillars, flanked by curving legs, also fluted, terminating in lion's claws. The lid of the sarcophagus of Frederick II is embellished with three medallions or clipei on each side, representing on the left a winged lion, the symbol of St Mark, the Pantocra-tor in the middle, and on the right an eagle, the symbol of St John. On the other side, is a representation of the Virgin with the Child in the middle, flanked by an angel, the symbol of St Matthew and a winged ox, the symbol of St Luke. The most important emblematic representations are on the short sides of both of the sarcophagi. Frederick II's tomb depicts a crown in the gable, while the trough is decorated with a lion's head, holding a ring in his mouth. The lion is both a heraldic beast and the symbol of the guardian of the tomb.[26] On the other short side of the same sarcophagus, is a purely decorative rosette on the gable and a composite Greek cross, a religious symbol on the trough. Both symbols are known from contemporaneous coins and from the decoration of the Cappella Palatina.

The south end of Henry's sarcophagus is decorated with a large, ornamental

[20] Pirri, col. 800; Deér, 1–2.
[21] Kehr, suppl. no. 21, 439f.; Deér, 6–8.
[22] Kehr, as above.
[23] Pirri, 805; Deér, 16–25.
[24] G. di Marzo, II, 251; G. di Bartolo, *Monographia sulla Cattedrale di Palermo*, Palermo 1903, 35; Deér, 89–90.
[25] Deér, 46–77; Demus, 'Rezension' 12.
[26] Deér, 68.

disk, and with a crown on the gable, symbols of the monarchy. On the north side of the trough a human hand holds a ring. The fingers are represented on the inside, holding an ivy leaf. The lid is decorated with a rosette.

Joseph Deér remarked, that the ring-shaped handle with the ivy leaf is an antique motif, much used for the decoration of luxury tubs.[27] Later on, when those tubs were used as sarcophagi for various saints and martyrs, the hand was interpreted as the hand of God, and the ring shaped handle became a *corona vitae*.[28] The emblematic crown, symbol of the monarchy on the gable of Frederick II's sarcophagus lid, is a camelaucum, the imperial male crown, while on the short side of Henry VI's tomb, is a representation of a Byzantine type female crown. While the appearance of the camelaucum supports Deér's opinion, that this is the tomb which was originally intended to contain Roger II's remains, the representation of the Byzantine type female crown on the other sarcophagus, raises the question of, whether it was originally to have been given for the glory of the church and town of Cefalù. The opinion expressed by Otto Demus offers a much more logical solution. Although Roger II was a widower at the time of the donation of the sarcophagi, he intended to remarry and did so after 1145. It may therefore be supposed that the second tomb was intended for the remains of his future wife.[29]

Looking at the tombs in their present position, standing under their canopies with fastigia, and recognizing the placement of the emblematic representations, it is evident that both were designed to be seen from their most important side, that is by the north short side in the case of Frederick II's tomb and by the south short side in that of Henry VI's, with the representation of the crowns clearly indicating the rank of the person for whom each was made. This solution seems to be a highly unusual one, because neither the antique, nor the medieval sarcophagi's main sides were the short ones. Their most important decorations or inscriptions were invariably placed on their long sides. To my knowledge, there is only one exception to this rule, the sarcophagus of St Stephen of Hungary, made in 1038, shortly after the death of the king.[30]

It is certainly not unimportant to determine what the tombs represented and where they might have been located in the church of Cefalù, in such a way, that only their short sides were visible.

We have no direct documentary evidence concerning the original placement of the tombs, other than Roger's great charter of 1145, in which he indicated that the location of the tombs was to be 'iuxta canonicorum psallentium chorum'.[31] Contrary to the generally accepted opinion, according to which the tombs were placed somewhere in the choir, Deér, interpreting the latin text, argued, that the two sarcophagi were situated 'iuxta', near, or adjoining the presbytery but not in it.[32] In his opinion, there was simply not enough available space in the main apse for the almost one and a half metre long tombs to be placed on opposite sides of the altar. For some undisclosed reason, he also rejected the side apses as possible

---

[27] Deér, 75.
[28] Deér, 76.
[29] Demus, 'Rezension' 13.
[30] Dr E. Marosi's kind information.
[31] Pirri, col. 800.
[32] Deér, 8.

resting places for the tombs. According to him, the 'iuxta . . . chorum' meant the right and left wings of the transept respectively.

The above-mentioned chronology of the choir and transept of the church of Cefalù does not support Deér's hypothesis. The work on the south side of the transept and its vaults could not have commenced before the apse vaults were completed, which, in my opinion, occurred by 1145, to be followed by the mosaic decoration by 1148. The type of arcades used just below the vaults of the south transept wing points to terminus post quem date for the construction of those vaults by 1154. There is absolutely no reason to suppose, that the church canons placed the precious tombs of the founder of their church in an unfinished part of the building. This act would also have been in total contradiction to the medieval tradition.[33] The sarcophagi must have been placed in the presbytery, the only finished and decorated part of the building, near the altar, the only dignified location for the founder's tombs.

The sarcophagi could, indeed, have stood with their short sides facing west, on both sides of the main altar. The main apse was wide enough to allow it. But the petition of the canons in c.1170 contains a sentence which indirectly can help to determine the possible location of the tombs. William I went to Cefalù shortly after the death of his father, and the above-mentioned petition contains a valuable reference to their layout inside the church, as stipulated by the king: 'omnis populus civitatis cum ad altare causa offerendi accederet, in dextra parte ante sepulcrum patris sui omnes transirent ut orarent pro anima eius, in redeundo vero ab altari in sinistra parte iuxta alterum sepulcrum redirent ut similiter orarent pro eius anima, qui in eo sepeliendus erat',[34] that is: 'When all the people of the city approach the altar with the purpose of making an offering, they should go by the right hand side, in front of the sarcophagus of his father, so that they might pray for his soul, and, returning from the altar, they should go by on the left, next to the other tomb, so that, they might pray for the soul, of whomsoever is to be buried in that tomb'. This vague direction given by the king somehow indicates, that there was some distance between the altar and each tomb. Considering the ground plan of the church of Cefalù once again, there is only one possible location which would be in accordance with this description, namely under the two arcades, cut in the two western bays of the presbytery walls. If the tombs were situated in this manner, under the arcades, only the short side of each tomb bearing the emblematic representation and the canopy with the fastigium could be seen from the main apse, while the other short side would have been visible from the corresponding side apse. Imagining the tombs in such a location, the association with the reliquary sarcophagi is unavoidable.

The reliquary sarcophagus was a substitute for the tomb. Its main function was to house the remains, often the whole body of the deceased. Therefore, its size had to be big enough, sometimes well over two metres, imitating the shape of the tomb, or 'cercueil'. They were almost invariably made of the most precious materials, of gold and silver, of enamel and precious stones. Consequently their size often reflected the importance and wealth of the church which housed them. The presence of the relics in these reliquary tombs enchanted the faithful and gave consolation. The number of the large reliquary sarcophagi rose from the

---

[33] Grabar, I, 521f.
[34] Kehr, no. 21, 439f.; Deér, 9.

middle of the twelfth century, especially in the Rhine and Meuse valleys, at Visé, Stavelot, Maastricht, Cologne and Aachen, but at the end of the twelfth and in the thirteenth century the use of this kind of reliquary was usual in France, Switzerland and Italy as well. During the Middle Ages, the remains of saints and martyrs were more and more often taken out from their loculi of the crypts and were placed in the church. First, they were placed in the altar, which allowed the priest to celebrate the Eucharist literally 'on the blood of the martyrs', later on, behind the altar, in a tomb. The reliquary sarcophagi are the substitute of such tombs.[35]

In Cefalù, the two tombs under their canopies certainly gave the impression of being placed in a niche or loculus near the altar, in such manner as precious reliquary-sarcophagi were not uncommonly kept in the churches which housed them. A surviving example of an original loculus is to be found in the western crypt wall of the collegiate church of Celles, where the 139cm long reliquary-tomb of St Hadelin was supposedly kept from 1046 until its translation to the church of St Martin at Visé in 1338. Only the main, in this case short side, of the reliquary was visible from this loculus, where it would have remained except when taken out for designated religious festivities.[36]

The reliquary of St Remacle in a somewhat similar location was also viewed from the short side in Stavelot. The famous altar, which contained the twelfth-century reliquary, was commissioned by Abbot Wibald (1130–1158) of Stavelot. The altar has not survived, but it is known from a drawing of 1661.[37] The main short side of the reliquary is easily recognizable in a porch-like niche, in the middle of the altar.[38] The location of the two sarcophagi in Cefalù reminds one also of the later western medieval practice of placing the sarcophagi or other types of 'monumenta' around the apse, under the arcades, separating the apse from the ambulatory, as can still be seen in a great number of churches.

Since the last quarter of the fourth century A.D. nothing had been more popular among Western Christians than the veneration of relics. Not only could the bodies and belongings of saints and martyrs be relics, but the bodies of kings and emperors as well, because they were considered both divine and human at the same time.[39] It is known from Roger II's charter of 1145 that the two porphyry tombs were expressly made for the king, whose sacred body was to be placed in one of them. Automatically, therefore, the tombs themselves became sacred objects, as much reliquaries as sarcophagi. The petition of c.1170 of the canons of Cefalù is very instructive about this matter too. It records that 'in dextra parte ante sepulchrum patris sui omnes transirent ut ORARENT pro anima eius . . .'. We know that this event occurred while the tombs were still empty. That the faithful and the

---

[35] Grabar, 12–43; J. Braun, *Die Reliquiare des christlichen Kultes und ihre Entwicklung*, Freiburg i/Br. 1940, 177–181; A. Frolow, *Les reliquaires de la vraie croix*, Paris 1965, 22–25; M.M. Gauthier, *Emaux du moyen âge occidentale*, Fribourg 1972, 146–149; *Rhin-Meuse. Art et Civilisation 800–1400*, exhibition catalogue, Cologne/ Bruxelles 1973, 134–143; F. Niehoff, 'Umbilicus Mundi – Der Nabel der Welt', *Ornamenta Ecclesiae. Kunst und Künstler der Romanik*, exhibition catalogue, Köln 1985, III, 53–72.
[36] R. Didier and A. Lemeunier, 'La châsse de Saint Hadelin de Celles-Visé', *Trésors d'art religieux au pay de Visé et Saint Hadelin*, exhibition catalogue, Visé 1988, 99, n. 65.
[37] Liège, Archives de l'Etat.
[38] P. Lasko, *Ars Sacra: 800–1200*, Harmondsworth 1972, 185ff.; Rhin-Meuse, 249.
[39] Grabar, 12–13.

king himself venerated them in this manner clearly suggests that they were treated as reliquaries. They were the 'microcosmos inside the church, buildings inside the building', like other reliquary-sarcophagi.[40]

It is not surprising, that the canons of Cefalù continued to request the return of the sacred royal remains, and that they opposed the removal of the reliquary-sarcophagi from Cefalù. The bishop and the canons were fully aware of their high spiritual value, whose very presence in the presbytery implied holiness and an elevation of status for the church itself. This is the main reason why the canons insisted in the petition of c.1170 that if the 'monumenta', that is the two tombs, were removed from their church, one might just as well raze the entire building to the ground.[41]

[40] Niehoff, 53–72.
[41] Kehr, suppl. no. 21, 439f.; Deér, 5.